Deviant Behavior

THIRD EDITION

Deviant Behavior

Erich Goode
State University of New York at Stony Brook

PRENTICE HALL, *Englewood Cliffs, New Jersey 07632*

Library of Congress Cataloging-in-Publication Data

Goode, Erich.
    Deviant behavior / Erich Goode. -- 3rd ed.
       p.   cm.
    Includes bibliographical references.
    ISBN 0-13-204041-7
    1. Deviant behavior. 2. Criminal behavior.   I. Title.
HM291.G646 1990
 364.1--dc20
                                                89-38272
                                                CIP

Editorial/production supervision: Cece Munson
Cover design: 20/20 Services, Inc.
Manufacturing buyer: Carol Bystrom

Acknowledgments for use of copyrighted material
appear on pp. vii–viii, which constitute a
continuation of the copyright page.

Printed in the United States of America

10 9 8 7 6 5 4 3 2 1

ISBN 0-13-204041-7

Prentice-Hall International (UK) Limited, *London*
Prentice-Hall of Australia Pty. Limited, *Sydney*
Prentice-Hall Canada Inc., *Toronto*
Prentice-Hall Hispanoamericana, S.A., *Mexico*
Prentice-Hall of India Private Limited, *New Delhi*
Prentice-Hall of Japan, Inc., *Tokyo*
Simon & Schuster Asia Pte. Ltd., *Singapore*
Editora Prentice-Hall do Brasil, Ltda., *Rio de Janeiro*

To My Mother

Credits

Contents

4

CONTEMPORARY SOCIOLOGICAL THEORIES OF DEVIANCE   57

5

DRUG USE AS DEVIANT BEHAVIOR   88

6

ALCOHOL USE AND ALCOHOLISM   119

7

HETEROSEXUAL DEVIANCE *142*

8

MALE AND FEMALE HOMOSEXUALITY *173*

9

VIOLENT BEHAVIOR *212*

10

FORCIBLE RAPE *247*

11

PROPERTY CRIMES *269*

12

WHITE-COLLAR CRIME *289*

13

MENTAL DISORDER *314*

EPILOGUE *336*

REFERENCES *341*

INDEX *373*

Preface

The study of deviant behavior is intrinsically fascinating. Nearly all of us love to look at "knavery, skulduggery, cheating, unfairness, crime, sneakiness, malingering, cutting corners, immorality, dishonesty, betrayal, graft, corruption, wickedness, and sin—in short, deviance" (Cohen, 1966: 1). Part of that sense of fascination is voyeuristic: We want to see things that are forbidden, excluded, hidden from our everyday gaze. Some of it stems from our sense of righteousness: We have been virtuous, yet other people have broken the rules. Are we missing out on something? Are these others gaining an unfair advantage over us? Why aren't they being punished? In addition, many of us have the feeling that deviance and crime may be, by their very nature, thrilling, seductive; there may be "moral and sensual attractions in doing evil," to quote the subtitle of a recent essay on the subject (Katz, 1988).

Whatever the reason, deviance is a perennial favorite among topics of interest to most of us—and that includes undergraduates. What student would fail to find robbery, murder, rape, white-collar and corporate crime, pornography, prostitution, homosexuality, alcoholism, and drug use and abuse fascinating? At the same time, instructors struggle to make a fundamental point in the study of deviance: The sociologist's attraction to the field is guided mainly by theoretical, not thrill-seeking, motives. We are interested in *rule-making, rule-breaking,* and *reactions* to rule-breaking. What ties together the topics generally treated in studies on deviance is social control and punishment. If we find such investigations titillating, so much the better; but that is not their main function. The goal of any student of deviance is the investigation of social structure and process—why and how society and social relations work, and why and what happens when they don't.

In spite of recurrent complaints that sociologists of deviance too often focus on the scandalous, the dramatic, the sensationalistic (Gouldner, 1968; Liazos, 1972; Piven, 1981), recent developments have demonstrated that behavior traditionally studied by sociologists of deviance does have momentous consequences and does reveal crucial sociological processes. In 1987, a front-running presidential candidate is caught in an extramarital affair, and his campaign is abruptly short-circuited; and views concerning the "new morality," as well as current relations between public figures and the press, are widely discussed. Also in 1987, again, the sexual liaison of an extremely popular televangelist is revealed, and his multimillion-dollar financial empire is wrested from his control.

In 1989, a woman jogger is gang-raped in New York City's Central Park; since the victim is white and her alleged attackers are Black, subsequent discussions of the incident reveal painful racial fissures in the supposedly liberal city. Indeed, the incident itself is said to touch off even more intolerant attitudes toward Blacks by many of the city's whites (Klein, 1989). Moreover, media attention to the incident and its virtual blackout on news about similar attacks on poor and minority women reveal racial and class biases in the press's coverage of deviant behavior.

Throughout the 1980s, the scourge of AIDS has focused attention on, indeed, has exacerbated the heterosexual majority's negative attitudes toward, the homosexual minority—another representative on that list of categories to which sociologists of deviance are said to have paid altogether too much attention (Liazos, 1972: 106, 107). If anything, the AIDS crisis reveals basic sociological processes by emphasizing that homosexuals are a despised minority to begin with, and their medical problems of interest to the heterosexual majority only when they begin to threaten the latter's very existence (Shilts, 1987).

In 1984, a white man riding a New York City subway shoots four Black teenagers who approach him and ask him for money; the ensuing public uproar reveals deeply held attitudes toward crime and race on all sides

of the controversy—fear among whites of crime; their feeling that Blacks are likely perpetrators and whites, their likely targets; and the suspicion among Blacks that whites overreact to this fear out of racist attitudes.

In fact, deviance, including the behavior of "nuts, sluts, and deviated preverts," *is* central to sociological structures and processes (Ben-Yehuda, 1985: 3). The subject matter of the investigation is less important than how one goes about that investigation. (True, some behaviors are more pivotal and tell us more about how society works than others, but that must be examined in each case and cannot be assumed in the first place.) Unless one studies behavior on the level of mere description, social structures and processes can be revealed by examining some of the traditional topics in the sociology of deviance. The point is not to study "nuts and sluts" to the exclusion of more uplifting topics (racism, sexism, and the oppression of the working class, for instance), but to examine whatever reveals how wrongdoing and denunciation work. By all means, bring on the studies of corporate and white-collar crime! (In fact, in the past decade in the study of deviance and crime, studies of white-collar crime have blossomed.) To the extent that one can be sanctioned for engaging in it, it is deviant. And to the extent that "damaging, unethical" behavior (to quote Liazos) is neither condemned nor formally punished, well, it just isn't deviant, is it?—an interesting contradiction worthy of study!

Too often, approaches, perspectives, and theories in the study of deviance have been taken as competitive and mutually exclusive. "If X approach is right, Y must be wrong," commentators seem to be saying. In fact, in deviance research, different aspects of almost any phenomenon are highlighted by different approaches; few perspectives seem to be directly competitive in the logical sense. In the sociology of deviance, there is no single, grand, overarching theory that can guide our observations through the many aspects and phases of deviant behavior. The many perspectives simply address and illuminate pieces of the puzzle, but none puts them all together into a coherent picture (Davis, 1980: 13; Wright, 1984: v–vi). At the same time, observers too often treat deviance theories as if they were competing or mutually exclusive; as if they focused on the same questions, their differences being resolvable by examining a clear-cut data set. Although this is true of a small number of limited theoretical approaches, much of what passes for deviance theory is incommensurable. Any thorough examination of the subject of deviant behavior, then, must be thoroughly eclectic and broadly focused theoretically. This edition carries on the more eclectic tradition that was begun with the book's second edition.

The third edition of *Deviant Behavior* represents a substantial revision. The introductory discussion, entitled "Looking at Deviance" in the previous edition, has been expanded into two chapters. A great deal of material has been added to the chapters on deviance theory, including a discussion of Cohen's and Cloward and Ohlin's additions to the Mertonian anomie scheme, a summary of control theory, and a delineation of various brands of Marxist theory, including vulgar utopian Marxism. The second edition's chapter on behavior, labeling, and identities was eliminated as too specialized and addressed more or less exclusively to interactionist sociologists. The two chapters on drug use were consolidated into one. In the chapter on heterosexual deviance, the sections on premarital, marital, extramarital, and postmarital sex were eliminated; and the section on pornography was considerably expanded. Forcible rape, a section in the previous edition, was expanded into a whole chapter. White-collar crime, originally a section in the chapter on property crime, is now an entire chapter; the chapter on property crime has been expanded and is now devoted entirely to property crime as such. Almost as much material has been added (or deleted) as was carried over into the new edition. In short, the third edition of *Deviant Behavior* is a new book, very different from its predecessor.

I owe a debt of gratitude to a number of friends and colleagues who have helped me by supplying information and otherwise assisting me in the preparation of this edition. They include Nachman Ben-Yehuda, William McAuliffe, Lester Grinspoon, Henry Pontell, Rick Troiden (whose death just a few weeks ago causes me unspeakable grief), Michael Kimmel, Gilbert Herdt, Ronald Hinch, Joseph Jones, Gina Bisagni, Stanley Cohen, Martin Levine, and my wife, Barbara Weinstein. In addition, I would like to thank the many students who have enrolled in my deviance courses over the years. Their questions, comments, and suggestions have been extremely valuable to me in improving this book. Last, I would like to thank the men and women who have contributed the accounts published in this volume. I admire their bravery and their candor, and I am deeply grateful to them for sharing their experiences and their feelings with me and with the readers of this book.

Erich Goode

CHAPTER
1

Deviance:
An Introduction

Humans are evaluative creatures. We continually make judgments about the behavior of others—and ourselves—and those individuals who engage in that behavior. In societies everywhere, there are rules governing the behavior of members; throughout human history rules that dictate correct and incorrect behavior have been laid down, and enforced. Sociologists call behavior that is regarded as wrongdoing, that generates negative reactions in individuals who witness or hear about it, *deviance* or *deviant behavior*.

What exactly is deviance? How may we define deviant behavior? What comes to mind when you encounter these words? To many students, and to the man and woman on the street, the terms "deviance" and "deviant" sound distinctly nefarious and vile. They conjure up images of evil deeds, degenerate practices, activities of an abysmally corrupt nature. "Deviants," the popular image would hold, are perverts, junkies, murderers, child

molesters, skid row alcoholics, pimps, drag queens, perhaps inmates of an insane asylum—in short, sick, twisted, violent, dangerous, corrupt, decadent people.

The first and most fundamental axiom that anyone observing, thinking about, or describing a social scene or aspect of social reality must accept is: "Things are often not what they seem" (Berger, 1963: 23). The public image of deviance may bear a very loose relationship to what we would discover if we were to take a closer look at it. It is the sociologist's job to take as close a look at deviants and deviance as possible. By doing this, we can assemble a more accurate, richer, more meaningful picture of our subject matter if we were to adopt a *subterranean* view of it. In other words, we cannot rely on popular notions of deviance—ideas we might hold before learning very much about it. Though popular myths about deviance may influence the phenomenon, they are not the phenomenon itself. We want to look behind publicly approved versions of reality, to see through official smoke screens portraying the way things are supposed to be, to understand why and how popular myths and misconceptions arise and are sustained. We need, in other words, to examine deviant behavior itself.

Although most people are able to supply concrete examples of the phenomenon of deviance, a general definition would be more difficult for most of us to come up with; although most of us recognize deviance when we come across it, we may not be able to spell out exactly what it is in general. Let's begin our exploration of deviance by looking at several examples, concrete instances of what some people might see as wrongdoing.

In March 1987, a popular televangelist

What Is Deviant Behavior?

On the first day of class, I asked the undergraduates enrolled in a recent course on deviant behavior to write examples of what they regarded as deviant behavior. I received almost 800 replies from the 230 students in the course. Some replies were completely idiosyncratic, that is, were offered by only one student. In all, there were 80 examples given by only one student, including pretending you are a bird, laughing at a funeral, spitting in the professor's face when you receive a poor grade, walking on your knees for 12 hours a day, wearing shorts when it snows, driving on the left side of the road, putting your clothes on backward, sky diving, having sex with an animal, breaking wind when others are around, being a member of the KKK, asking for a single slice of turkey in a deli, being an artist, showing up late for a meeting, and begging for money when you're rich.

At the same time, we would suspect that examples that were thought of by more than a very few students would, in turn, be more widely regarded as deviant by the general public. Clearly, if students spontaneously think of a given example of behavior as deviant, they regard it as such; however, if they do not offer it as an example, they do not necessarily not regard it as deviant. Also, the more students that think of a certain behavior as deviant, the more widely it will be so regarded. A number of examples of deviant behavior were not idiosyncratic and were offered by many students. Murder was, by far, the most common response, with exactly half of the class saying it a good

example of deviance. Rape was second, with a bit over one third of the students (37 percent) offering it as an example. Tied for third place, offered by nearly a quarter of the class (23 percent), were homosexuality and robbery. Stealing was in sixth (17 percent), and prostitution and drug abuse (13 percent each) tied for seventh place. Table 1–1 presents the behaviors that were cited by more than 10 students as examples of deviance.

Would you regard these forms of behavior as instances of deviance? What other—or better—examples could you come up with? And what is it that *makes* these good examples of deviance—or examples of deviance at all? These and similar questions will be explored in the first two chapters of this book, and, indeed, throughout the book.

TABLE 1.1 What Is Deviant Behavior?

Form of Behavior	Percent Offering as Example
Murder	50
Rape	37
Homosexuality	23
Robbery	23
Stealing	17
Illegal drug use	13
Prostitution	13
Incest	10
Walking naked in the street	8
Drug dealing	6
Suicide	6
Child abuse	6

---

named Jim Bakker resigned his ministry in scandal. Bakker had been the chairman of the PTL (Praise the Lord) club, a financial and spiritual empire that included a satellite television station, a television program (*The Jim and Tammy Show*), which Bakker co-hosted with his wife, Tammy Faye, and a religious theme park, Heritage USA, the third-most-popular theme park in the nation, after Disney World and Disneyland. These enterprises grossed substantially in excess of $100 million annually in recent years, and yet there was deep trouble in the Rev. Bakker's financial and spiritual empire, which is why he was forced to resign.

Bakker's ministry was assumed by the Rev. Jerry Falwell, a fundamentalist Baptist preacher who also has a popular religious television program and runs a preaching empire. Falwell accused Bakker of numerous serious spiritual and financial improprieties, including

- A sexual liaison with a church secretary and subsequent financial bribes totaling more than $250,000 in hush money to keep the episode a secret
- Vaguely specified homosexual liaisons
- Approval and encouragement of "mate swapping" by PTL members
- Financial extravagances, including the purchase of an air-conditioned doghouse, the installation of $60,000 worth of gold-plated bathroom fixtures in the Bakker's house, and the purchase of a Rolls-Royce to adorn a hotel roof
- Fiscal irresponsibility, leaving the PTL some $70 million in debt and the Internal Revenue Service searching for an unaccounted-for sum of over $12 million

Bakker denied Falwell's accusations concerning his alleged homosexual practices and tolerance of mate-swapping, but admitted to foolishness and poor judgment in the other areas (King, 1987; Freedman, 1987; Watson, 1987).

Bernhard Goetz, a slender, white, 37-year-old electrical engineer living in New York's Greenwich Village, sat in a subway car opposite four Black teenagers, Darell Cabey, 19, Troy Canty, 19, Barry Allen, 18, and James Ramseur, 19. Two of them, Canty and Allen, stood over Goetz, and Canty said, "Give me $5." The young men were unarmed, although two had screwdrivers in their pockets. (It was revealed later that they carried the screwdrivers not as weapons, but to pry open machines in video parlors to steal quarters.) Hearing the request, Goetz stood up, unzipped his jacket, and asked Canty what he had said; Canty repeated his demand. Goetz then drew an unregistered nickelplated .38 caliber revolver from his jacket and, assuming a combat stance, gripped the gun with two hands and began firing at the youths, wounding all of them. Seeing Cabey sprawled on the seat, apparently unharmed and playing possum, Goetz said, "You seem to be doing all right. Here's another," and shot him in the back, severing his spinal column and leaving him paralyzed for life from the waist down.

When the train came to a halt, Goetz slipped out, ran through the tunnel along the tracts to the next station and out into the street to his apartment, changed clothes, packed a bag, rented a car, and drove to Vermont. In a motel room, he took the revolver apart and dumped the pieces, along with his jacket, in some woods nearby.

The four young men Goetz shot, it turns out, were not strangers to crime. All had been arrested before—and at least two would be arrested again—on charges as serious as armed robbery and rape. Still, the central issue in the explosion of debate that followed the news stories covering the case was whether Goetz's armed attack on the four youths was justified. Was he threatened by them in any way? Did Canty's demand for $5 constitute a threat, or was it a simple innocuous request? Did Goetz have the right to gun down four unarmed teenagers because they approached him and asked for money? Goetz insisted the quartet was about to make him a victim, that it was their intention to rob him. He claimed he responded much as a cornered rat about to be "butchered" would have. "I just snapped," he said. On his way to Vermont, Goetz phoned a neighbor and said, "Those guys, I'm almost sure, are vicious, savage people" (Friedman, 1985: 38).

Two weeks after the shooting, Goetz walked into a police station in Concord, New Hampshire, and turned himself in, explaining he was the fugitive wanted in the subway shooting. He talked to the police about the incident for about four hours, two of which were videotaped. The Concord police transferred Goetz to New York City police jurisdiction to stand trial. In June 1987, Goetz was acquitted of all charges, including attempted murder and assault with a deadly weapon, except the possession of a licensed handgun. Members of the jury—2 Blacks, 10 whites—insisted that Goetz's acquittal had nothing to do with the fact that he was white and his victims were Black.

In a poll taken slightly more than a week after Goetz turned himself in to the police, residents of New York City and Long Island were asked the following question: "Recently, a man named Bernhard Goetz was arrested for having shot four young men he believed were going to rob him. . . . Do you think that it was right or wrong for him to shoot the four young men? Over half the sample (54 percent) said it was right; only 29 percent said it was wrong; 17 percent weren't sure. Interestingly, when confronted with a more general formulation, the answers were quite different. Only 25 percent of the respondents answered yes to the question: "Is it justifiable to shoot a person you think is going to rob you, even if you have not been threatened with a weapon?"—the circumstances of the case in a nutshell. Given the racial background of attacker and victims, it is entirely possible a racial interpretation could be read into the incident. Blacks, however, were only slightly less likely to say Goetz was right (47 percent) than whites were, indicating that the racial angle was only one of several aspects embedded in the case. Still, just under half of the respondents (45 percent) said public reaction would have been different had the shooter

been Black and his victims been white; 49 percent disagreed (Bookbinder, 1985; Stengel et al., 1985; Johnson, 1987).

Dr. Joseph Cort was a research scientist at the Mount Sinai School of Medicine. His work on synthetic hormones was regarded as so valuable that the Vega Corporation supported him and his research in the hope that he would develop a drug that could be used in the treatment of hemophilia. Such a drug, if patented and successfully marketed, could yield millions of dollars in profits to a drug company, making Vega's interest in Dr. Cort's work understandable. Cort submitted data on a series of experiments he had conducted to the patent office that indicated his synthetic hormones would cure hemophilia. Based on the data, Vega was granted a patent on the drug. Dreams of unlimited profits danced in the heads of Vega executives.

One day, disheveled and distraught, Dr. Cort walked into the office of Vega's president and admitted he had fabricated the data on which the drug patent was based. "I knew immediately it was disastrous," Vega's president said. The head of the Mount Sinai School of Medicine stated: "The value of that patent . . . is now something less than zero." A colleague who recommended Cort for the Vega research summed up the implication of the fabrication: "What Cort did was professional suicide. He would have been better off robbing a bank." Said Cort, now unemployed: "It's so important to get a patent before someone else does. . . . Nobody told me to fake it. It was a stupid thing to do. But I was under a lot of pressure and things got a bit confused. I had to earn the money for research, or die." Executives at Vega and colleagues at Mount Sinai agreed that the pressure to which Cort was exposed was no different from that felt by any other research scientist (Farber, 1982).

In September 1978, Charles Daniels was arrested and charged with sexual assault and attempted murder. A 10-year-old boy said that he had seen Daniels throw a 2-year-old boy from the roof of a three-story building. Daniels claimed the detective who arrested him threatened to castrate him unless he talked. The detective said he had a dozen witnesses to the crime. Daniels replied he knew nothing about the sexual assault. Unable to make bail, he awaited trial in the Queens House of Detention. When asked by other inmates what he had been arrested for, Daniels naively told the truth. A day later, several inmates set his clothes on fire. Soon after, he was beaten unconscious. He was transferred to a segregated unit. One night while he was asleep, someone hurled boiling water through his cell bars. At his trial, the jury delivered a guilty verdict; Daniels was sentenced to a maximum of 18 years.

Not long after his incarceration at Sing Sing, prison officials learned through an informer of a contract among inmates to kill Daniels. He was put in isolation to protect his life. Over the next three years, he was transferred to three other prisons, each time because his identity became known to the other inmates.

In August 1982, nearly four years after his arrest, a state appeals court reversed Daniels' guilty verdict and ordered a new trial. It turns out that the police had withheld key evidence from the defense and prosecution lawyers—specifically, that, at the time of his testimony, the 10-year-old boy who was the only witness against Daniels was under psychiatric treatment as emotionally disturbed, and that the boy had identified someone else on the roof prior to identifying Daniels. In addition, newly discovered evidence indicated that the 2-year-old victim was not thrown from a roof and was probably not raped by an adult. A full review of the facts suggested that the 10-year-old had raped the younger boy himself and concocted the story to incriminate someone else. Reviewing the case, the Queens district attorney dismissed the charges against Daniels. The detective who originally arrested him—and was awarded a departmental citation for his work on the case—was still convinced that Daniels had committed the crime.

In a 1984 out-of-court settlement, the City of New York awarded Mr. Daniels $600,000 to compensate him for the "huge chunk of time" he spent in prison, wrongfully convicted of and imprisoned for a crime he clearly did not commit (Raab, 1985).

Gordon Hall was the out-of-wedlock child of servants who worked for a wealthy family in a castle in England. He is described as having had incomplete sex organs of both sexes. His grandmother treated him as a girl, and everyone else treated him as a boy. During adolescence, he experienced menstruation. As a young man, Gordon inherited a fortune from a distant relative on his mother's side. He began writing, and became the successful author of 17 books, mainly about celebrities, including the royal family. In time, he was informally adopted by Dame Margaret Rutherford, a British actress, now deceased. Gordon settled in a mansion in Charleston, South Carolina, and enjoyed the attention of privileged, polite Charleston society as the genteel, wealthy author of respectful biographies of respected figures. One day, Gordon Hall issued a two-part bulletin to the Charleston community: He was going to become a woman. Hall insisted, however, this would not make him, now her, a transsexual, because, she insisted, she was always female. And second, as the "reconstituted" Gordon Hall, Dawn, she would marry a Black man who worked in a local garage, one John-Paul Simmons, a former mental patient.

Charleston society did not take the news well. After the wedding, her house was bombed, her wedding presents were set on fire, and she was beaten and thrown from a third-story balcony. The insurance on the house was cancelled, she lost the mortgage, her husband sold her antiques for next to nothing, and he temporarily abandoned her while she lived in a welfare hotel. She now claims to be divorced from Simmons, with whom she still lives in a vermin-infested hovel in upstate New York, and to be engaged to Lemuel Smith, a convicted multiple rapist and murderer, now currently residing at Great Meadow Correctional Facility in Comstock. She says her interest in Smith began when her late adoptive mother, Dame

Rutherford, appeared to her in a dream, saying, "Go and help Lemuel." Smith, the most frequently visited inmate at Great Meadow, says that Dawn Simmons's interest in him is not reciprocated (Agus, 1984).

At the age of 7, Leonard Ross passed an examination for a ham radio operator's license. By 11, he had won $164,000 on two television quiz programs, answering questions about the stock market. Lenny graduated from high school at 14, from college at 18; he entered Yale Law School when he was four years younger than nearly all his classmates. He taught at Harvard, Columbia University Law School, and Boalt Hall, the University of California at Berkeley's law school. Ross also worked on the successful gubernatorial campaign of Jerry Brown and at the State Department and the Civil Aeronautics Board in Washington. His last job was with a small law firm in San Francisco.

Lenny Ross was brilliant; his mind worked like "quicksilver." Said the dean of the Columbia Law School, "I've never seen anybody grasp problems as quickly and see the implications on so many different levels." Even his ordinary conversations with friends were studded with dazzling insight and originality. He drew parallels between seemingly unrelated phenomena such as James Joyce and McDonald's commercials, ancient history and comic books. Even normally intelligent friends often had difficulty following his conversations, so daring, brilliant, and original were his ideas.

One spring evening, Lenny climbed over a fence surrounding the pool area of the Capri Motel in Santa Clara, California, just a mile and a half from his brother's house. He took off his glasses and shoes and went into the water. Ross did not know how to swim. At 10:30 the next morning, the motel manager found his body lying face down, arms crossed, at the bottom of the pool. Ross was 39 years old.

Lenny Ross, while seemingly so successful, continually left "a trail of unfinished projects through much of his life." He studied at Yale's graduate school of economics for three years after law school but failed to write his doctoral dissertation. He undertook a number of writing projects, but always collaborated with authors who were willing to finish what he began. "He had great ideas," said one of his co-authors, "but no follow-through." During the last dozen or so years of his life, his behavior became increasingly erratic. He spoke faster and faster, often leaving sentences unfinished, leaping from thought to thought without supplying connections. His mind was full of brilliant ideas, many of which made no sense to his listeners. A compulsive dieter and overeater, Lenny often wolfed down food while it was still frozen because he was too impatient to defrost it. Once, depressed over a failed romance, he tried to cut his throat with a broken bottle.

Ross was not a successful teacher at Harvard, Columbia, or Berkeley. One of his colleagues said, "His mind moved so fast, he tended to skip over the intermediate premises . . . without articulating them. The students found him a little bewildering." At Boalt Hall, he was unable to complete several of his courses. He once came to a lecture and stood in front of the class, unable to speak a single word for a half hour; finally, his students straggled out, leaving him standing, completely mute, in front of the room. One morning, Ross was found lying underneath a parked car, rehearsing a lecture. Following this incident, he was hospitalized briefly; he resigned from the Boalt Hall faculty soon afterward.

Ross's life "had begun to shatter." His brilliant mind began to spin out of control as "his attention span grew shorter and shorter." Said a lawyer friend, seeing Lenny disintegrate was "like standing in front of a great painting that melts in front of your eyes. . . . It has defective pigments and disappears. There's an enormous sense of waste." Ross realized his brilliance would not help him out of his depression. He began to look on suicide as a relief, a deliverance from his unbearable misery. Toward the end, he was unable to hold down a job, and his mother and brother were caring for him.

At his memorial service, a Columbia Law School professor summed up his life by saying: "What could account for Lenny's remarkable decline and despair? What is it about a world that made a genius like Lenny find it so intolerable? I do not know. I do not want to know" (Dowd, 1985).

It's called the "empty box" scam, and it's usually done with small, expensive items, such as jewelry. It works like this. A customer makes a purchase at a store. In New York State, the sales tax is 8.25 percent. On a $100,000 purchase, this amounts to $8,250, a substantial sum. The customer complains about the size of the tax. The sales clerk mentions the tax does not have to be paid if the item is sent to an out-of-state address. "Do you have a residence in another state? Or do you know someone to whom the item may be sent?" the customer may be asked. The customer, however, does not want to wait for the mailed item to arrive; he or she wants it immediately; in fact, wants to walk out of the store with the item. Well, the salesperson explains, we could let you have the item immediately, and without paying the tax. We'll mail an *empty box* to an out-of-state address of your choosing. We'll pretend to the tax people that we actually mailed the item in the box, and you can walk out with your purchase.

The scam is, of course, illegal, and it costs New York State precisely the amount of the tax the customer avoided paying. It is a tax burden that must be shouldered by all other New York State taxpayers. An obvious aspect of the scheme is that the rich purchaser makes the most use of it, while the average working person has to pay more in taxes in order to make up for the tax the rich avoided paying. In a recent state investigation, the stores mentioned as participating in the empty box scam included Cartier, Van Cleef & Arpel's, and Bulgari, among the most expensive and exclusive of Fifth Avenue jewelry stores. Some purchasers who were snared in the recent audit include:

- Adnan Khashoggi, a billionaire Saudi Arabian arms dealer, at one time reputedly the world's richest man, purchased several silver items from Bulgari costing $200,000. The empty boxes were mailed to Switzerland. Tax saved: $17,000.

- Frank Sinatra purchased about $30,000 worth of jewelry from Bulgari. It was delivered to his Waldorf Towers suite. The empty boxes were sent to casinos in Las Vegas and Atlantic City. Tax saved: about $2,500.

- Donald Trump, one of New York's biggest builders and property owners, purchased $65,000 worth of jewelry from Bulgari, including a $50,000 necklace. The empty box was sent to Trump's former attorney in Connecticut. Tax saved: over $5,000.

- Leona Helmsley, owner of half of a $5-billion husband-and-wife real estate empire, made 10 purchases from Van Cleef & Arpel's, including a $375,000 diamond necklace and a $105,000 platinum-and-diamond clip. The empty boxes were sent to Helmsley's Florida address. Tax saved: $38,000 on these two items alone.

The state's commissioner of taxation and finance estimated that New York City loses approximately $100 million per year on the tax evasion scheme. According to the commissioner, this scam "has existed for some time," it is "pervasive and widespread," a "systematic practice"; and it "involves all levels of store employees." Customers at luxury stores expect to be treated royally; they have spent a great deal of money, and know that the store's mark-up and profit on their purchase are substantial. Generally, the more expensive the item, the greater the margin of profit. Customers also know that the sales staff is aware they could take their business elsewhere and they expect special treatment. The store managers and sales staff want to retain their business; stores earn as much on a single luxury purchase as they do on 100 routine purchases. Why not treat the big-spending customers in a special way? The tax evasion scheme is one way that such stores have of holding onto favored customers (Purnick, 1985; Bastone, 1986a, 1986b).

Dorrian's Red Hand is a popular bar on New York's fashionable Upper East Side; it caters mainly to a young crowd, many of whom are teenagers—underage by the state's drinking law, but usually able to provide fake documentation that they are at least 21. After a long summer evening of talking, drinking, and flirting with friends, Jennifer Dawn Levin, 18, a freshman at an expensive two-year college, and Robert Chambers, 19, an unemployed college dropout, left Dorrian's together. Less than two hours later, Ms. Levin's body was found by a jogger several blocks away in Central Park. Her clothes were in disarray, and she had been strangled.

Levin and Chambers were part of the same social circle of friends and acquaintances—students and graduates of exclusive private schools, the sons and daughters of the privileged elite. Theirs is a world without material want, in which cars, lavish vacations, expensive clothes, and a fashionable address are taken for granted. It is a world in which teenagers move with the sophistication, experience, and blasé, easy assurance of adults. Said a close friend of the victim, "We're like 35-year-old people.... We act like we're adults. Most of us have credit cards; we all drink; and we fool around, have [sexual] flings" (Stone, 1986: 48). It is a world in which the consequences of accidents, misdeeds, and the many errors of judgment to which the young are typically prone can be erased through the intervention of well-connected, well-healed parents. And in this world, violence is as remote as the six o'clock news.

Chambers had a consistently dismal academic record. He was not asked back to Choate, an exclusive prep school, after a less-than-mediocre freshman year. The following year, he managed to get into a somewhat less exclusive New York prep school, but was expelled for drug use and theft from a teacher. After getting into an even less distinguished prep school, he managed to graduate with borderline grades and to enter a program at Boston University geared to students who had academic problems in high school. After one semester, Chambers flunked out of the program. He went to live with his mother, did odd jobs for pocket money, and frequented bars and discos five or six nights a week. Theft apparently had been a pattern for Chambers throughout his high school

years. The police claim he engaged in far more serious crimes following the demise of his academic career at Boston University—specifically, a string of a dozen or more burglaries with a partner, netting tens of thousands of dollars. In addition "money was disappearing from pocketbooks at Dorrian's and from the apartments of Chambers's friends, and Chambers was the main suspect" (Stone, 1986: 49). Once, several girlfriends caught him with someone else's ID in his wallet, clearly stolen; another time, friends found him with a stolen radio. "Yet there were few consequences to the discoveries. Chambers continued to hang out at Dorrian's and he continued to socialize with the very people he had victimized" (Stone, 1986:49).

Chambers also had a drug problem. He was a chronic cocaine user until his mother found drug paraphernalia while she was cleaning his room. After her discovery, he checked himself into a drug rehabilitation clinic. Released after a month, Chambers counseled his friends against the use of cocaine, but he drank heavily and smoked marijuana regularly.

Chambers was over 6 feet tall and more than 200 pounds. Teenage girls typically found him extremely atractive and charming and were drawn to him. Indeed, many of his friends said that Chambers's biggest problem in life was that he still believed he could get by in life solely on good looks and charm.

In Dorrian's the night of August 25 and the early morning August 26, Chambers was arguing with his current girlfriend, after which Jennifer Levin, an attractive, popular, high-spirited young woman, began flirting with him. They talked for several hours and then left together about 4:30 A.M. They sat down in a grassy area in Central Park and began sex play. Chambers claims that Levin became too rough and aggressive, and that he accidentally killed her in his attempt to fend her off. (The claim clearly has no credibility whatsoever; Chambers outweighed Levin by 100 pounds.) The autopsy found that Levin had been strangled for at least 20 seconds. Apparently, Chambers stood over

Levin's body for some time, then he left her there. She was found less than an hour after Chambers killed her. Making no effort to summon help or the police, he went home and slept for several hours. At 2:00 P.M. that afternoon, the police, who learned that Levin left Dorrian's with Chambers, began questioning the young man about the killing.

His version of the story sounds very much like the classic blaming the victim defense: It was her fault she was killed. More specifically, the cause of her death was supposedly her active, adventurous sex life. When it was believed that she may have been killed by a stranger, the New York press began their stories on the Levin murder on a sympathetic note. When it was learned, however, that she died at the hands of a male companion whom she willingly accompanied to a secluded area of the park, the stories became vicious. New York's tabloids competed with one another in "blaming the victim" stories. The *News* ran one story under the headline, "Sex Play Got Rough"; and another, under the even more accusatory, "How Jennifer Levin Courted Death." The *Post*, not to be outdone, ran "Wild Sex Killed Jenny." For the killer, the tabloids had little but sympathy. The *Post* ran stories under the titles "Inside Preppie Suspect's Mind" and "Secret Agony of Preppie Suspect." One of the *Post*'s stories displayed a photograph of Chambers's parents with the caption "The secret grief of *his* parents" (my emphasis), ignoring the far greater grief Levin's parents must have felt.

The New York newspapers "savaged Levin because she was a lively young woman, who willingly left a bar and headed for the bushes, with a young man, in the early morning hours. And since sex, especially female sexuality, is filthy and disgusting, she deserved whatever she got—even after she died" (Stokes, 1986: 8).

In the middle of jury deliberation, in the spring of 1988, Chambers entered a plea of voluntary manslaughter, an offense less serious than murder, admitting that he had caused her death. He will serve at least five years in prison.

In April 1987, Gary Hart, former senator from Colorado, was the front-runner for the 1988 Democratic presidential nomination by a wide margin. Polls show that in the crucial state of Iowa, with its early primary, 65 percent of the Democratic voters favored Hart. His nomination seemed highly probable, if not almost certain. Then one day early in May, his presidential aspirations were dashed. The *Miami Herald* ran a front-page headline story claiming that an attractive young woman, Donna Rice, had stayed overnight with Hart in his Capitol Hill townhouse while Lee, his wife of 28 years, was ill in Colorado. The media had previously hinted at the politician's "womanizing," but in response, he challenged reporters to substantiate their claims. "Follow me around," he said. Several did, and quickly discovered the indiscretion.

Hart and Rice insisted their friendship was platonic. It was, however, a claim much of the public was not prepared to accept. Though a clear majority believed Hart had been treated unfairly by the press, most also thought he and Ms. Rice were lying about the nature of their relationship. Moreover, even those who had no moral qualms about adultery felt that Hart's brazenness showed a remarkable lack of judgment and, above all, character. Polls showed a sharp decline in support for Hart. His campaign was dogged by questions about his extramarital affairs. Once, Hart was asked point-blank if he had ever committed adultery. Five days after the *Herald*'s headline story and less than a month after Hart had announced his candidacy, he announced his withdrawal from the race. "Under the present circumstances," he said, "this campaign cannot go on." Turning to a counterattack, he blamed the press for his demise. "I refuse to submit my family and my friends and innocent people and myself to further rumors and gossip. . . . It's simply an intolerable situation." "The American system of campaigning for the presidency," Hart said, "is just a mockery" that "reduces the press of this nation to hunters and presidential candidates to being hunted. . . . And if it continues to destroy people's integrity and honor, then that system will eventually destroy itself" (Morganthau et al., 1987: 22). Some observers argued that placing the blame on the press was like killing the messenger who brought the bad news. Said one of Hart's friends, "He never seemed to understand that it was his behavior that was the problem."

Most insiders agreed that Hart had brought about his own self-destruction, that his campaign was a scandal waiting to explode. His extramarital affairs disturbed his friends, supporters, and campaign workers for years, and were widely known among the press corps. "You can't get away with saying you made one mistake if that mistake is actually part of a pattern," said an aide (Morganthau et al., 1987: 28).

It is not clear exactly what Hart had expected the press to do, especially given the challenge he had thrown down earlier. Perhaps he imagined he was invulnerable, beyond the rules that restrain ordinary mortals. Perhaps he loved taking risks, playing with fire. Perhaps he felt adultery is overlooked nowadays, or overlooked for a privileged few. Rumors abound about the extramarital affairs of a number of presidents and presidential candidates, including Franklin Delano Roosevelt, Dwight Eisenhower, John F. Kennedy, Kennedy's brother, Robert, and Lyndon Johnson. Perhaps, Hart felt, if they got away with it, why can't I? It's possible Hart was a victim not so much of the press as a combination of his own bad judgment and a shift in what is regarded as legitimate areas of scrutiny by the press. In the past, adultery was more or less off limits to the press, at least for respectable figures. It was a private area not considered appropriate for gazing and snooping; the public preferred to swallow myths about its heroes than to learn the seamy truth. We have evolved into an age when myths are less acceptable; the public would prefer to see the wrinkles, the soft, white underbelly, and the dirt that used to be swept under the rug. We live in a time of kiss-and-tell biographies, a time in which nothing is sacred, and privacy has been sacrificed for the insatiable thirst to know. Hart was simply a victim of our society's growing pains.

One commentator suggested another factor in Hart's demise: the rise of feminism. We live in a transitional period, this argument goes, between the past chauvinistic and patriarchical standard, when married men could do just about whatever they pleased, and the evolving contemporary view that women should be treated with dignity and respect and as equal partners in a marriage. Philandering is incompatible with the equality of women. Though feminists have felt this for some time, a "strange shield" existed to protect adulterous politicians from scrutiny and criticism. In the Gary Hart–Donna Rice scandal, that shield dropped to reveal a man who does not treat women as full human beings. Hart's adultery, this view holds, represents a form of sexual exploitation—of his wife and family, of Donna Rice, and of the female half of the American public. Such behavior casts serious doubt on the candidacy of a man who seeks to represent the electorate as a whole. More than anything else, Hart's downfall reveals the death throes of the sexual double standard and the emergence of sexual equality (Lessard, 1987).

Lying, cheating, stealing, betrayal, murder, corruption, decadence, harming others, graft, crime, taking drugs to get high, engaging in "immoral" sexual practices (Cohen, 1966: 1)—these and other equally disapproved acts of wrongdoing are what this book is about. Clearly, deviance is about good and evil, morality and immorality, social rules and their violation, and approval and disapproval. Whenever anyone engages in an activity that attracts widespread social disapproval, the interest of the sociologist of deviance is aroused. Whenever members of a society feel impelled to punish or condemn someone for doing—or even for being—something that seems "not right," the behavior or that condition falls within the scope of the sociology of deviance. The field that studies deviance includes the behavior itself and those who engage in it, and reactions to the behavior and those who engage in it, as well as the many explanations for why the behavior occurs.

Clearly, in some way or another, the behaviors we have just described are deviant. What is it about these behaviors, and others like them, that attracts our attention? And how does the sociologist study behavior—and why?

What's your reaction to the behaviors described in the preceding examples? Do you agree they all are instances of deviance or deviant behavior? If so, why? If not, what is the quality that some lack or have that excludes them from qualifying? Do adulterous liaisons by prominent figures qualify as deviant behavior? Or being accused of a crime one did not commit? Transsexualism? Fabricating scientific findings? Going crazy and committing suicide? Engaging in a tax-evasion scheme? Shooting teenagers who may or may not have been trying to rob you? Accidentally—or on purpose—killing a sexual partner? What is it that makes these actions, or reactions, instances of deviance? Does explaining concrete illustrations of the general concept bring us any closer to what deviance is? How may we answer the question: *What is deviance?*

Deviance is an area of social life that readily engages our emotions; thus, controversy is unavoidable. Questions dealing with deviant behavior are inevitably questions of ideology, morality, and politics. Not everyone agrees that certain actions are right or wrong, good or evil. Likewise, not all social scientists agree about the essential reality of deviance, or even how to go about studying or thinking about it. This should be expected. Prior to reading a study dealing with a certain deviant activity, or encountering the behavior in real life, we may have strong feelings about it. Perhaps we have religious or moral objections to extramarital sex and would look with disfavor upon a study that reports it may actually strengthen a marriage. We might have a son or daughter and fear that he or she will become a homosexual; consequently, we may approach the subject of homosexuality with certain prejudices. Possibly, a close relative was murdered and because of this, we cannot look on the subject of criminal homicide without bias. Perhaps we believe pornography is repugnant and, hence, are extremely favorable about any and all manner of evidence suggesting it is objectively harmful. Perhaps our general political orientation is conservative—or liberal, or radical—and this colors the way we think about the entire topic of deviance.

Complete objectivity is probably an impossibility in any subject dealing with human behavior; this holds even more strongly for so controversial a field as deviant behavior. Nonetheless, it is necessary to put aside some prejudices and examine deviance with a keen eye and an unbiased mind. This may entail thinking about the subject in unconventional ways, adopting concepts and insights that may seem uncomfortable or inappropriate at first. These new ideas will show us things we might not have seen or thought about before and lead us to a valid or accurate understanding of the reality of deviant behavior. This book represents an attempt to present the student with just such an eye-opening discussion of this exciting phenomenon.

CHAPTER
2

What Is Deviance?

What is it, specifically, that *makes* the examples in Chapter 1 instances of deviant behavior? *Why* are they deviant? Although most of us would agree that they exemplify the general territory of deviance in one way or another, it is a bit more difficult to isolate exactly what it is that *makes* them examples of this phenomenon.

Is shooting four Black teenagers who are standing over you a form of deviance? Should what Rev. Bakker did—from financial irregularities to a 20-minute liaison with a church secretary—be regarded as deviant? Was it really all that reprehensible? Why study a medical experimenter faking data in a course devoted to deviant behavior? If falsely accused of a crime, a crime you did not commit, did you engage in any deviance at all? Clearly, Gordon Hall and Lenny Ross were not mentally well; is mental illness, properly speaking, a type of deviance? Can we really call tax evasion by affluent citizens

and the employees of respectable retail stores deviant in the same way that street crime is? Isn't adultery extremely widespread in our contemporary society—and if so, then what's so deviant about Gary Hart's peccadillo?

Before deciding certain specific acts qualify—or do not qualify—as instances of deviance, perhaps it would be fruitful to step back a bit and decide what we *mean* by deviant behavior in the first place. What is it that makes these actions deviant? What is the specific quality that certain acts have in common, which others that are not deviant lack, that leads us to decide they are deviant?

If asked, almost anyone can come up with a number of examples of what he or she regards as deviant, as we saw earlier. Although we can think of many *specific* examples of deviance, it is more difficult to locate the *general* property or characteristic that qualifies an act as such. According to what definition or criterion do we decide behavior is or is not an instance of deviance? What is the defining quality all such acts have in common? Is it social disapproval? Its illegal or criminal status? That it violates certain religious or moral codes?

Not everyone will answer these questions in the same way. For one person, the key defining element in deciding what's deviant is if that certain behavior harms others. A second person will say an act that offends God, or is a violation of certain religious principles, makes it deviant. A third person will argue it is the criminal code that decides: Whatever is against the law constitutes deviant behavior.

However we define deviance, clearly we are in the realm of *undesirable* behavior or characteristics. Deviance implies negativity of some sort. Whatever else it is, to nearly everyone, deviance is not a good thing. Deviance is an *inherently invidious* concept; that is, it is offensive or repugnant. Some commentators have suggested that "good," positive, or acceptable deviance exist as well as bad, negative, or unacceptable deviance (Wilkins, 1964: 45). Examples of good deviance would be sainthood or being the perfect student. In the study of deviant behavior, these observers complain, there has been an "exclusive fixation on the objectionable, the forbidden, the disvalued"; to see deviance exclusively as that which is "offensive, disgusting, contemptible, annoying or threatening" is overly restrictive (Dodge, 1985: 17). To most sociologists, this objection makes no sense whatsoever. Good, positive, or acceptable deviance is an *oxymoron,* that is, a contradiction in terms (Sagarin, 1985). To the vast majority of sociological observers and to the author of this book, deviance is *always and by definition negative*. There is no such thing as good, positive, or acceptable deviance.

And yet, we still have not answered the question: Negative in what way? Precisely where does the negative quality reside? Is deviant behavior *bad by its very nature?* Or is it generally *thought of as bad?* Is deviance bad because it violates God's law? Or a law of nature? Because it is immoral behavior? Because it is inherently, intrinsically evil? Because the individuals who engage in it are sick, pathological, psychotic? Or because it violates the rules of society? Because it invites or stimulates hostility and condemnation by members of a particular society? In exactly *what way* is deviance "bad, negative, unacceptable"?

THREE BASIC PERSPECTIVES

There are three basic ways to define deviance: from the absolutist, the normative, and the reactive perspectives.

The Absolutist Perspective

The absolutist perspective argues that the quality or characteristic of deviance resides in the very nature of an act itself. Deviance is intrinsic to certain actions; it dwells within them. The evil of deviance, this view holds, is inherent to the behavior itself. If something is deviant, it is wrong now and forever, here and everywhere else. Deviance is an action that is wrong in the abstract, regardless of how it is judged. It is an offense against the order of the universe, in the same way that adding up two and two and getting a total of five is. Something is deviant if it violates an absolute, eternal, final law. The feeling on the part of the Moral Majority that abortion is an abomination and constitutes murder is an example of the absolutist perspective toward deviance. Even if it takes place in a society that accepts and condones it, abortion would still be murder, as well as an instance of deviant behavior. According to the absolutist perspective, what is deviance is decided not by norms, custom, or social rules. Wrong and right exist prior to and independent of these artificial, humanly created agents. What is or is not deviant behavior, according to this view, is an objective fact and not an arbitrary social judgment.

Some time during the nineteenth century, as a result of recognizing that members of different societies practiced customs that are markedly different from our own, a certain measure of *cultural relativity* came to be accepted in the social sciences with respect to what is deviant. Relativity is exactly the opposite of absolutism. Judgments of right and wrong, it was realized, varied from one place to another and from one historical time period to another. What is right in Tibet is wrong in France; what was wrong in the thirteenth century was right in the nineteenth. Rather than regard a single standard of right and wrong as correct, most observers grew to recognize the relativity in deviant behavior. Today, except for some utopian Marxists (I'll explain various theories of deviance in Chapters 3 and 4), sociologists have largely abandoned the absolutist perspective in the study of deviance. The view that there is an absolute right and wrong that exists independently of social custom, norms, and human judgment is now regarded as archaic, although, outside the field of sociology, some observers still believe it.

The Normative Perspective

The normative perspective locates the quality of deviance not in the actions themselves but in the fact that they violate the norms of the culture in which they take place. According to this view, we can tell when an action is deviant by consulting the customs of a society; when it runs counter to those customs, it is an instance of deviant behavior. To the normative sociologist, deviance is the *formal violation of the norms*.

The normative perspective implies relativity. An action that may be praised in one place or time may be condemned in another. What makes a given action deviant is the fact that it is a violation of the customs or laws where it occurs. We know, for example, that the norms of Soviet society frown on private economic enterprise and that the norms of Wall Street approve of, even encourage, this type of behavior. Consequently, engaging in profit making is deviant in the Soviet Union but not in the United States. Specific actions about whose deviant status we are wondering do not have to be witnessed or judged by the members of a society for us to determine this question. We know what the norms are, and we can decide when they are violated by a given action. If we know that, in a certain

society, having sex with a partner of the same gender is regarded as wrong, when this happens it is automatically an instance of deviance. (Of course, if that same act were to take place in a society where it is not regarded as wrong, it would not constitute deviant behavior.) In short, the normative view locates deviance *in the discrepancy between an act and the norms of a society.*

Although the normative view of deviance is the most commonly accepted perspective among sociologists in the field, there are serious problems with looking at the phenomenon in this fashion. Here are some of them (Goode, 1981a: 49–50).

First, the normative view assumes that "the norms" cause behavior in some abstract, unspecified fashion. In fact, most people engage in conventional behavior and avoid deviance not because they blindly follow the norms of their society but because they anticipate negative reactions from the people they care about if they did otherwise. This perspective implies a kind of automatic quality in the norms, without considering just how they translate into action.

Second, the normative view underplays exceptions. Not èveryone in a society agrees that normative behavior is right or behavior that violates the norms is wrong. This perspective assumes a normative consensus, which does not exist for many forms of behavior.

Third, the normative view does not adequately allow for contingencies or extenuating circumstances that alter observers' judgments of whether an individual or an act will in fact be regarded as deviant. For instance, driving considerably over the speed limit is a violation of the norms governing driving and will typically draw a punishment—a speeding ticket from a traffic officer. However, what if the driver is "transporting a seriously wounded individual to a hospital" (Gibbs, 1972: 46)? The extenuating circumstances of this act make it necessary for us to reclassify the act not as an act of deviance, but as an act of altruism and bravery. The normative view does not give sufficient importance to such contingencies.

Fourth, the normative view ignores the

distinction between violations of norms that generate no special attention or alarm and ones that cause audiences to punish or condemn the actor. For instance, a bank teller who is a petty bureaucrat, a "stickler for the rules," who "does everything by the book" is breaking a norm that dictates that he or she help customers. Likewise, the bank robber who holds up that same teller with a gun is also violating the norm against stealing. According to the normative view, both actors are breaking the norms, and thus, both are equally guilty of deviant behavior. However, the behavior of the teller does not raise alarm in the community, and he or she will not be punished for these actions, whereas the robber will generate a great deal of attention, concern, and other types of public reaction (Erikson, 1962: 10). It is difficult to call both an instance of deviant behavior simply because each has violated a norm.

The Reactive Perspective

Normative theorists believe that deviance can take place in secret; an act that nobody except the actor knows about is no less in violation of the norms than is an act that is witnessed and judged by others. Reactive sociologists disagree. They adopt a position that is even more radically relativistic than the normative sociologists. The reactive perspective argues that the characteristic of deviance can be found in *how actual behavior is judged*. To qualify as deviance, an act must (1) be observed or at least heard about and (2) generate concrete punishment for the perpetrator. Many acts that are committed are not observed by others or never come to light in any way. Even acts that become known about do not necessarily result in condemnation or punishment for the individual who engaged in them. According to reactivists, these acts are not examples of deviance at all. In other words, reactive sociologists deny that people react to *types* of acts or acts "in the abstract" (Gibbs, 1972: 40). It is impossible, they say, to know beforehand whether a man who admits to being a homosexual, or who is observed engaging in homosexual acts, will be regarded negatively by

"straight" observers (Kitsuse, 1962). It is not homosexuality per se that is reacted to, they say, but specific individuals or acts in specific situations by specific observers.

What makes an act deviant is how it, and the individual who engages in it, are reacted to by actual people. They key criterion in the reactive perspective is *concrete social disapproval toward specific actions and actors*. Reactivists argue that behavior is not deviant until it has been condemned; the quality of deviance rests within the actual condemnation itself. This means that if someone gets away with committing "the perfect murder" (even if the murderer knows that it is an act of murder), it is neither deviant nor murder at all, because it did not result in punishment of the perpetrator. Actual, concrete punishment is what constitutes deviance to the reactivist. Deviance is behavior that has *already* attracted negative reactions from the members of a society. There is no deviance apart from this negative response from the community. Deviance exists when and only when there is a negative reaction to an act and to the individual engaging in it by observers or others who may have heard about it. It is these negative reactions that *constitute* deviance. No reactions, no deviance (Pollner, 1974).

Most sociologists today adopt the normative, not the reactive view of deviance. Reactivists are in the distinct minority among researchers of deviant behavior. There are, it must be said, strengths and weaknesses of each perspective. Here are a few problems with the reactive view.

First: *It ignores secret behavior that would be reacted to as deviance, were it known to the community.* In fact, most deviance is enacted in secret. Yet, to the reactive theorist, there is no such thing as secret deviance; it is a contradiction in terms. If we were to adopt the reactive perspective, we must give up studying behavior that is enacted in secret or that does not result in punishment. As far as deviance is concerned, the life of the professional thief whose illegal activities are never suspected by the community or who is never apprehended by law enforcement is exactly the same as the life of the ordinary, law-abiding, conventional citizen. Many observers would regard this view as erroneous and unproductive, and at least one observer has dubbed it a "cop out" (Polsky, 1969: 110–112).

Second: It ignores secret behavior that would be reacted to as deviance, *even where the actor knows that it would be condemned by the community.* In other words, the reactive perspective ignores the views and the definition of the individual engaging in the behavior itself. Most people who enact behavior that breaks the rules or the law are aware of the potential reactions their behavior would touch off in others. They may or may not agree that it should be punished, but they are usually aware of how others would treat them and their behavior in the event of discovery.

Third: *It denies the possibility that there is any predictability in the reactive process.* Reactivists make the assumption that the sociologist cannot predict which concrete acts will be reacted to negatively. We cannot know for sure whether a given instance of robbery, let's say, will be ignored, condoned, or praised or will generate punishment. Let's wait until we see what observers actually do before we decide that a given act is or is not deviance, the reactive sociologist seems to be saying, because such outcomes are too unpredictable to know beforehand. But in fact, "reactions are not idiosyncratic. No one would assert, for example, that reactions to completely naked individuals strolling down a sidewalk would be indistinguishable from reactions to fully clothed individuals. Stated more generally, in all social units there is some degree of association between types of acts and types of reactions" (Gibbs, 1972: 43). If we followed the implication of the reactive view to its logical conclusion, we would have to admit that we are in no position to predict whether murdering an infant in its crib or chewing gum is more likely to be regarded as deviant in real life. Both may be accepted or punished, and thus, we must reserve judgment until we see what actually happens. But, of course, to different acts we can attach a certain *likelihood* of punishment

or toleration, a possibility that the reactivists seem to be denying.

Fourth: *It ignores the reality of victimization.* The reactive perspective ignores the fact that deviance that is not punished *may have real victims.* For instance, a very low proportion of all rapes are detected, and a very low proportion are reported to the police. Of the ones that are reported, a minority result in the apprehension and arrest of the perpetrator. A woman is sexually assaulted, the man who did it escapes and is never caught or punished. *Does this mean that the woman was not raped?* This view is impossible to agree with, and yet, this is precisely what the reactivists seem to be saying.

A MODEST RESOLUTION OF THE DILEMMA

We are ensnared in a true dilemma here. On the one hand, it is true that we cannot know for sure if a given act will be punished by a given audience, because so many exceptions and contingencies abound, as Kitsuse (1962) argues. On the other, as Gibbs (1972) points out, we do have some idea in advance which behavior is likely to generate punishment of the actor: Sanctioning is not a random process. Consequently, some sort of blend between the normative and the reactive approaches becomes necessary.

In my view, a way out of this dilemma is to adopt a "soft" reactive view and thereby avoid the weaknesses and capitalize on the strengths of each perspective. This view, a compromise between the normative and the reactive perspectives, would contain the following particulars (Goode, 1981a: 50–51).

First, norms do not by themselves cause or inhibit behavior. What "the norms" are is a set of inferences constructed by sociologists as a result of adding up and averaging out reactions that they have observed for behavior in many situations and contexts, in the presence of a wide range of audiences. That is, the sociologist should be able to say, regarding a certain act, "To me, this looks very much like an example of the type of behavior I've seen punished just about everywhere. Therefore, I'll call it an instance of deviance. From this, I can infer what the norms are." The normative sociologists have got the whole process backward: They work from the supposed norms to societal reactions. "Soft" reactive sociologists do the reverse: They build up an image of what the norms look like as a result of observing societal reactions.

Second, no rule is absolute. Not even the most rigid determinist can possibly expect perfect predictability to be necessary to identify group norms. Consequently, the "soft" reactive theorist must adopt a *probabalistic* approach to deviance: "behavior is deviant if it falls within a class of behavior for which there is a probability of negative sanctions subsequent to its detection" (Black and Reiss, 1970: 63). If the sociologist is sufficiently perceptive, he or she will be able to discern whether the specific audience witnessing or evaluating the behavior in question will judge that it belongs to that general class of behavior that has generated negative reactions in the past. But no such prediction will be infallible.

Third, because most behavior that would earn the actor punishment is never detected, let alone sanctioned, any reasonable observer is forced to ask the question, "What is the *actor's* perception of how the audience feels regarding his or behavior?" "How does this perception influence the actor's further behavior?" "His or her self-image?" The enactor of deviant behavior must operate in a sea of imputed negative judgements regarding his or her behavior (Warren and Johnson, 1972: 77). The actor's sense of how others would react cannot be ignored in the equation of deviance.

And fourth, the societal reactions of audiences do not necessarily create the behavior in question out of thin air. Psychiatrists do not, all by themselves, generate mental disorders as a result of their judgments of who is mentally ill; the police do not conjure up criminal acts where they did not exist before by making arrests. Clearly, the behavior would have existed with or without these imputations of deviance. However, such judgments are part of the process that makes certain actions deviant in the first place. They impart to certain acts a uniquely deviant quality.

Although societal reaction does not create the actual behavior that is defined as homosexuality, it does lend to it a stigmatized status and influences certain features of that activity and the lives of men and women who engage in it that would be lacking in the absence of negative labeling.

This dilemma and its resolution are acknowledged among several proponents of the interactionist or labeling school (which I'll discuss in Chapter 4). If deviance is constituted or created by negative reactions, then "secret" deviance cannot exist; it is a contradiction in terms to refer to deviance that is secret. If it is secret, there cannot have been any negative reactions to punish the actor; if there were no such reactions, then it cannot be secret. We cannot have deviance in the absence of detection and negative labeling, the "hard" reactive school argues, because it is what creates deviance in the first place. According to at least one labeling theorist (Kitsuse, 1962, 1972, 1975, 1980) and the proponents of a related school, ethnomethodology (Pollner, 1974), deviance exists when and only when there is concrete, real-life condemnation.

On the other hand, Becker seems to have one foot in the "hard" and one in the "soft" reactive view discussed here. It should be clear, he writes, "that insofar as a scientist uses 'deviant' to refer to any rule-breaking behavior and takes as his [or her] subject of study only those who have been *labeled* deviant, he [or she] will be hampered by the disparities between the two categories" (1963: 14). In addition, Becker's delineation of secret deviance (1963: 20–22) admits to the possibility that deviance can exist in the absence of literal labeling. Becker also writes, "We cannot know whether a given act will be categorized as deviant until the response of others has occured" (1963: 14). In short, to Becker, "whether a given act is deviant or not depends *in part* on the nature of the act (that is, whether it violates some rule) and *in part* on what others do about it" (1963: 14; emphasis mine).

Erikson, too, endorses a view of deviance that is close to what I've spelled out here as the moderate or "soft" reactive stance; that is, that deviance can exist as a general category of behavior, in the absence of literal, concrete labeling. He writes, "It is the audience which eventually determines whether or not any episode of behavior *or any class of episodes* is labeled deviant" (1964: 11; emphasis mine). This indicates that, to Erikson, certain acts are highly likely to be regarded, among specific audiences, as instances of a general category that is seen as deviant in nature. We can, according to this view, refer to acts that are likely to be regarded as deviant *even before they are so labeled by specific audiences*. To Erikson, then, and to Becker, the concept of "secret deviance" makes sense—as it does not to the hard or more radical reactivists.

THE MENTAL EXPERIMENT

To answer the question, "What behavior is deviant?" we have to perform a *mental experiment*. Imagine behavior being enacted in many different settings before many different audiences. How do these audiences react? How do they treat the actors? Are they hostile and condemnatory? Neutral? Or do they applaud and praise what's been done and those who do it? Imagine a mother walking past the bathroom in her home and seeing her daughter shoot heroin into her arm. Or a father witnessing his son fellating another young man. Or imagine seeing your best friend robbing then stabbing an 80-year-old man. Or a neighbor savagely beating a 3-year-old child. What would go through your mind? What would you do? If we are perceptive, our mental experiments will sensitize us to what is deviant—behavior that attracts censure and punishment from numerous, or from influential, people.

In these cases, we have behavior of a certain kind enacted by an individual. This behavior, and the individual, are evaluated—

or would be evaluated, if known about—in different ways by different observers, parties, or *audiences*, real or potential, direct or indirect. These audiences include:

1. The actors or participants
2. Victims, if any
3. Social intimates of the participants, who are not necessarily direct observers on the scene, but whose opinion the participants value greatly
4. Direct observers, witnesses, bystanders, if any, who may impinge upon, constrain, or perhaps encourage further deviance
5. The members of the town, village, tribe, or the general society in which the participants live, who are socially and emotionally a bit more distant or removed from the actor than the social intimates are
6. Agents of formal social control, such as the police, the courts, prison officials, welfare case-workers, psychiatrists, teachers
7. The "detached" or distant observer, the person who reads or hears about the behavior from such a vast social distance that the participant is not influenced by his or her judgment in any way.

Naturally, these parties or audiences may overlap some. And people who would belong in one category in one case might belong in a different one in a different case.

What makes a given activity deviant? Why would it fall within the scope of our attention and interest as students of deviant behavior? Simply for this reason: *From someone's point of view, it is regarded as a reprehensible act; the actor, it is felt, is worthy of punishment of some kind.* Certain parties or audiences, from the participant to the detached observer, would condemn the behavior, the actor, or both, were they to come face to face with one or the other. In determining what is deviant behavior, it is important to identify the party judging the behavior. The point is to locate the relevant audience.

What is seen as reprehensible and worthy of punishment to one audience will be innocuous or even praiseworthy to others. Does this mean that "everything is relative," as we often hear? This sophomoric cliché is a crass oversimplification; it is erroneous for a number of reasons. Saying that what is regarded as deviance is a matter of judgment and evaluation, and varies from one audience to another, may appear to imply certain conclusions that aren't true. Taken literally, it means that almost any behavior is deviant to some people and that no behavior is deviant to everyone. Since deviance exists only as a description of what some people believe, or how they do or would react to some behavior, almost anything could be deviant. This is literally true, but it is not very useful. Because different people and groups are not equally powerful, neither are they equal in a numerical sense. Consequently, someone who enacts behavior that is opposed by a small number of relatively powerless individuals stands a *low* likelihood of being condemned, whereas someone who enacts behavior that is opposed by a large number of relatively powerful individuals is *highly* likely to be condemned. Thus, the "everything is relative" cliché is wrong because not all acts stand the same chances of being condemned as deviant.

Attitudes toward, and reactions to, potentially deviant behavior are held and expressed by people with vastly differing degrees of power—power to have their views of what is right and wrong win out over those of other people. We are not interested in a mere patchwork mosaic of different beliefs and customs in a given society. Rather, we have to direct our attention to the *dominant moral codes*. Looking at different definitions of deviance, as if they all got equal time, as if they existed side by side without impinging upon one another, as if they existed in a kind of ethical "free enterprise system," belies the hierarchical nature of deviance. What we would like to know here is *which forms of behavior stand a high chance of being condemned and punished*. Different acts have differing probabilities of exciting moral outrage in a given society.

Thus, although it is possible, for example, to locate some people in the United States who believe that dancing is a degenerate, evil practice—probably followers of an extremely strict, orthodox, fundamentalist religious sect—our likelihood of running across them, and being subject to the punishment that flows from their belief, is extremely slim. Therefore, we can say that dancing is not a deviant act; this is a shorthand way of saying that it is not deviant *to most Americans.* This does not deny that to some people dancing *is* a deviant practice. If we were members of a Hutterite commune, we would attract condemnation if we were to dance to popular music with a member of the opposite sex. Since most of us are not Hutterites, it is a simple matter to discount the minority view. But we should never make the mistake of slipping over into the assertion that the dominant view is the only one. We still have to examine the social scene in which the behavior we are interested in takes place. If we are studying the customs of the Hutterites—of if we happened to be an adolescent growing up among the Hutterites—it is *that* definition which we would have to pay attention. Is going to school deviant? To most American parents, if their children do *not* want to go to school they are chastised. But there may be exceptions:

Sonia would slip out of the house at six-thirty in the morning before her father was awake and then would sit in front of a nearby public school until it opened for classes. Her father thought she was out early selling flowers or begging, a daily task she was first sent into the street to perform when she was eight. He began grumbling when the amount of money she brought home at night dropped off . . . , and her education was abruptly terminated, complete with a beating, when her father caught her doing homework. After that she was placed under strict supervision. An older sister and some cousins were assigned to teach her more sophisticated thievery (Maas, 1976: 22–23).

So some form of behavior may be deviant to a tiny number of people. It is still deviance— *to those people.* It is only out of numerical significance that we concentrate on behavior that many people consider deviant.

How many people are necessary to condemn a behavior as deviant? There is no clear-cut answer to this question. If we were to answer this by saying a majority, or over 50 percent, the next logical question would have to be, how intense does their negative reaction have to be? People can be mildly disapproving of some acts, while they may react in a violently hostile fashion toward others. Also, disapproval and condemnation take many forms. Can these different faces of hostility and punishment be measured, reduced to a single dimension, to a precise score? How does a slap in the face compare with not saying hello to someone who has done something someone else regards as deviant? Or gossiping about him or her? Or reporting the behavior to the police? Can an official execution by the state be compared with a lynching? If a wife divorces a man for something he does, something she disapproves of, is this equivalent to, or more or less serious than, losing his job? The point is, all these reactions are forms of social disapproval and condemnation. They vary in seriousness, but their weight varies according to the person whose behavior touches off the response. Where do we draw the line and say one reaction is serious, but another isn't serious enough to qualify as "condemnation"? There can never be an exact or final answer to the question. Deviance is clearly a matter of degree. People who are punished, whose behavior is disapproved of, will evaluate the negative reactions of others. They will sense that disapproval is headed their way. Deviance is just about anything that touches off reactions such as these. But how serious and how intense these reactions have to be is a bit arbitrary and not easily measured.

In the end, we are left with three dimensions that determine what is deviant in a society. The first is *numbers*. How many people are likely to punish a certain form of behavior defines, in part, its degree of deviance. The higher the number of people that do and will disapprove of something, the greater the chances of being punished for doing it, and therefore, the "more deviant" it is. The second dimension is *power*. The greater the power of those who disapprove of something, the higher the probability of being punished for doing it, and therefore, the more deviant it is. And last, we have the *intensity* dimension: The more extreme

the negative reactions, the more severe the penalty that is likely to be touched off by committing a certain act, the more deviant it is judged. Just where you wish to draw the line between "more deviant" and "less deviant" is up to you. As long as we keep in mind the idea that deviance is a spectrum, with shades of gray, and not a polarity, not a matter of black or white, then we will not run into any difficulty on this point.

TYPES OF RELATIVITY

The "everything is relative" cliché blurs distinctly different types of relativity. Things are "relative" in different ways. Too often they are lumped together. Basically, there are three broad types of "relativity": relativity from one *audience* to another, from one *actor* to another, and from one *situation* to another.

By audience relativity, I mean that the judgment as to what is good or bad, conventional or deviant, depends on the observer who witnesses and evaluates the act. Some observers will or would condemn a given act, while others will or would not do so. This is what most people mean when they refer to "cultural relativity." But it is, itself made up of different kinds of relativity. By actor relativity I mean that observers and audiences alter their evaluations as to whether behavior is good or bad according to *who is doing it.*

Situational relativity simply means that the *circumstances of the act*—where it is committed, how it is committed, why it is committed, and so on—alter most audience's reactions to and evaluations of the behavior. Cannibalism would be the classic example, but there are more common examples closer to home.

Audience Relativity

As far as audience relativity is concerned, the most variation occurs *from one specific individual observer to another*. There are certainly no absolute universals in human behavior. There is almost no act that is literally practiced by no one and condemned by literally everyone. Almost any form of behavior, however bizarre or statistically unusual, is attractive to some people, however small that number may be. So in the sense of an ultimate, absolute, literal prohibition on certain activities, universals simply don't exist. The variations in who condemns what are enormous. So the very first type of audience relativity is the variation from one individual person to another who does or would witness the act. *Some* people can be found who do not condemn almost any action we could possibly dream up.

Actors are also observers; they evaluate their own actions. There are many forms of behavior that attract participants who do not condemn—and even praise—what they themselves do that would attract widespread condemnation from others. On the other hand, there are some forms of behavior that are carried out by actors who feel enormously guilty about what they do. Even though they engage in a certain form of behavior, they do not feel good about participating in it and feel that it should legitimately be condemned, along with anyone (including themselves) who takes part in it. So if we are to understand variations in evaluations of behavior, perhaps one place to begin would be what the actor thinks of it. This is still a form of audience relativity, because the actor is being self-reflective, is looking upon his or her own behavior, reflecting upon it, and judging it.

Greenwald and Greenwald report the case of a woman who found herself becoming sexually aroused by her 12-year-old son. In spite of the strength of the incest taboo, an intimate mother-son relationship developed. The woman reportedly felt that there was nothing wrong with "complete family love" and that she had a "more richly satisfying sex life than the majority of 'morally perfect' women" (1973: 120).

Clearly what this woman did would be regarded by the overwhelming majority of people more or less everywhere as deviance. Her behavior would fit our definition of deviance: To most people, mother-son incest would be seen as "morally offensive." But the woman involved claimed to feel positive about it. Even behavior we think would be universally condemned often attracts participants who see themselves and what they do in a positive light.

Quite a different picture is presented by child molesters. As observers, they condemn their own actions. In fact, so repulsive is child molesting behavior to those who participate in it that they find it necessary to "explain" their behavior in terms that deny their responsibility in it. ("I was too drunk to know what I was doing" or "I didn't seduce her—she seduced me!") On the whole, child molesters will strongly condemn other child molesters and will deny their *their* rationalizations for their behavior are valid. On the other hand, many child molesters will deny that they even took part in the behavior for which they are sitting in a prison cell (McCaghy, 1967, 1968). Thus, not all people who practice deviant behavior approve of it in general; they may justify their own participation in it by invoking extenuating circumstances. Or they may deny that they did it at all. (For a different view, see Rossman, 1976.)

The first and most important observer or "audience" of one's own behavior, then, is oneself. People who participate in a form of behavior others condemn may or may not condemn it themselves. This is a form of relativity, a type of variation in what is seen as deviant or not, what is considered good, bad, or otherwise.

Another type of audience relativity is variation in condemnation of behavior from one group to another within the same society, from one *subculture* to another. If you conducted an experiment with different audiences watching actors perform an act, chances are their reactions would vary somewhat. The young adult is less likely to condemn marijuana use than are the middle-aged and the elderly. The urban dweller is far more tolerant of homosexuality than is the resident of a small town. Members of orthodox religious sects more readily and severely condemn a wide range of unusual and nontraditional behavior. Priests, in general, disapprove of premarital sex, while young adults somewhat distant from organized religion are much more likely to approve of it.

Another type of "audience" relativity is variation from one society or civilization to another. This is the usual meaning of "cultural relativity," the fact that what is deviant in Scarsdale isn't in the jungles of South America, what is expected on Wall Street may be condemned in China.

Aside from individual, group, and societal variations in what is considered deviant, we also have historical differences. What is condemned today may not have been yesterday, and vice versa. Participating in the ancient Aztec ceremony involving human sacrifice would be thought the actions of a lunatic in contemporary Mexico and would bring down swift reprisals upon one's head. In Puritan New England, adulterers could be, and were, put to death; today, adultery is both widely practiced and widely tolerated. Conceptions of right and wrong change over time. Any relativistic view of deviance must also be dynamic. Change is a vital element in all deviant behavior. This also means that what is deviant today may not be tomorrow; what is conventional today may be deviant tomorrow. These definitions are in a constant state of flux.

Actor Relativity

The second type of relativity is that based on *actor* variability. It is still true that the only thing that makes acts deviant is the audience judging them. But audiences also react differently according to who is enacting the behavior being evaluated. There is a Latin saying, "What is permitted to Jove isn't permitted to the cow." This means, simply, that high-status individuals are allowed a great deal more leeway in what they do; their behavior isn't judged quite so harshly as that of lower-status occupants. This isn't always true (the public drunkenness of a clergyman is more likely to be condemned than the public drunkenness of a garbage collector, for example), but as a generalization it is fairly sound. And it does point to the fact that who the actor is makes a great deal of difference as to how audiences judge the behavior in

question. In a sense, the acts are not the same, because they meet with a more tolerant audience. Just as we must specify the audience when dubbing an act as deviant, likewise, we must specify the actor being evaluated as well. Clearly, status is not the only actor dimension that shifts the degree of deviance of a given act. An act may be considered deviant, in the abstract, to most people, most of the time, if committed by most actors—but not, in fact, actually condemned in certain specific instances. Often a generally offensive, typically punished act will only create some sense of discomfort among upright conventional folk, but will elicit no punishment or even denunciation if kept within the bounds and reasonably secret, simply because the actor is a valued, familiar member of the community.

Some forms of behavior are deviant *specifically* because of the characteristics of the actors involved. Wearing a diaper is deviant behavior—specifically for an adult. Consider the following episode:

Geraldine Parrish . . . was alone in . . . her convenience store Tuesday night when she saw a man in his mid-20s get out of his car. The man was wearing a pink baby's hat tied under his chin. . . . "I knew something was wrong," Mrs. Parrish said. . . . She ran behind the counter to get her gun, and when she looked up, she noticed something even more unusual. "He had on a diaper, baby powder on his body, socks with no shoes, that stupid hat and . . . huge diaper pins." The man asked for a pack of cigarettes, but when she pulled the gun out, the man threw up his hands and yelled, "I'm going, I'm going." He ran out of the store, got back in his car, pulled out quickly, and caused another person to run off the road. . . . "I was more afraid of this nut than I was of the man who had been here to rob me," Mrs. Parrish said, "At least I knew what the other guy was going to do" (Anonymous, 1976).

The degree of deviance of adults wearing diapers (except to a masquerade party) is obvious. We generally don't think of this as a kind of "relativity" at all. Every position we occupy, every characteristic we have, every group we belong to, has attached to it a number of expectations as to how we are supposed to act. When we do something that departs radically from those expectations, our behavior is often condemned by others. Different positions, characteristics, and groups bring forth different expectations, and hence, different conceptions as to what constitutes deviant behavior. The deviance of a great deal of behavior inheres not in its abstract, formal properties, but in whether it is considered appropriate for certain kinds of people.

Situational Relativity

Last, there are *situational* variations that produce relativity in judgments as to what is considered deviant. The setting makes a great deal of difference; people will allow certain actions in one setting, but the same actions, if enacted in a different setting, will be condemned as deviant. Nearly all behavior could, conceivably, be considered deviant in one setting but not in another, as "normal" in one setting but not in another. Casually eating a meal is, in most situations, thought of as normal; no one takes note of such an act. But if a raging lion is on the prowl in one's house, such an activity would be thought of by most of us as cause for suspicion of one's sanity. In fact, much deviant behavior consists of "normal," conventional behavior enacted *in an inappropriate situation*. Nearly everyone would, under most circumstances, consider an act of flinging a baby out of a 10-story window an act of insanity, even if the child happened to land safely and was not injured by the fall. But if the building were in flames, if the stairs leading to safety were on fire, if the person who threw the baby out the window were a firefighter, and if a safety net were below, this would be thought of as an act of heroism, not insanity. Likewise, it is the norm for respectable folk not to be publicly intoxicated. But the rule is relaxed for certain occasions—New Years Eve, for instance. Clearly, then, the social embeddedness of the behavior in a certain context drastically alters the character of that behavior—from deviant to conventional, and vice versa. Sex between husband and wife is typically an instance of conventional behavior; when it takes place in the lobby of a busy hotel, it is an instance of deviance. The same behavior in two different settings is cause for reinterpretation on the part of audiences; there is a degree of relativity in judgments of deviance from one setting or situation to another.[1]

Audience, actor, and situational relativity, taken together, do not mean that there is no such thing as a rule or a norm. But it does mean that norms and rules have to be determined by crystallizing out of innumerable real-life reactions to behavior (or, second best, statements people make about how they feel or would react to certain actions). Even after toting up and averaging out all these reactions, we still cannot be absolutely certain what the rules and the norms are, because we do not know *all* of the extenuating circumstances that will convert tolerance into punishment, or vice versa. Consequently, there is a measure of ambiguity and unpredictability in deviance. Observers and students who are intolerant of ambiguity and unpredictability should not study devi-

---

[1]In the first edition of this book, I wrote:

Starting in 1973 farmers and ranchers in the Midwest and Rocky Mountain states began finding their cattle dead and mutilated. Expert and precise surgery had been performed on their bodies; "night surgeons" had crept into fields and removed their tongues, eyes, ears, tails, genitals, or udders. These cattle mutilations have continued into the late 1970s, and the motive, as well as who the culprits are, remain a mystery at this writing. One observer (Sanders, 1976, 1977) opined that these ghastly operations were conducted by the U.S. government under the cloak of "clandestine chemical/biological-warfare research." Other observers feel that they are the product of a bizarre religious sect. If it is government or U.S. Army officials or operatives, how would most Americans react to the individuals involved? Most likely they would say, "They're only doing their job." They would not regard the behavior as deviant. On the other hand the same behavior *would* be regarded as offensive were it to stem from an unauthorized, unofficial body of practitioners of a strange movement or cult.

Since that writing (1978), the "cattle mutilization mystery" has been solved (Rorvik, 1980). It is a case of *collective delusion* (Stewart, 1980). In fact, the "surgery" performed on the cattle was the work of animal scavengers, mainly blowflies and small mammals, such as coyotes.

ant behavior, for they may be motivated to impose more order than actually exists. But the rest of us will find a scrutiny of deviance fascinating and instructive.

WHAT IS DEVIANCE?
A BRIEF SUMMARY

In sum, by *deviance* I mean one thing and one thing only: *behavior that some people in a society find offensive and that excites—or would excite if it were discovered—in these people disapproval, punishment, condemnation of, or hostility toward the actor.* Deviance is behavior that is likely to get you into trouble. It is based on a judgment made by somebody. It isn't simply behavior, but behavior that is evaluated in a certain way. As to whether some act is or is not an instance of deviance cannot be known at all until we know something about what specific people think and feel about it. What we have to find out is, *deviant to whom?* Acts and people are *labeled* deviant. They aren't deviant according to some abstract, artificial absolute, universal standard.

Deviance is a kind of relationship between behavior and literal or potential negative reactions. Without these reactions, literal or potential, we do not have deviance. It is in the territory between behavior and reactions that we find the phenomenon of deviance.

To most people, the term "deviant" conjures up an image of individuals who are not only evil but psychologically abnormal as well; "deviance" implies behavior that is both immoral and "sick." It must be emphasized that the sociologist does *not* use these terms in this way. "Deviance" and "deviant" are completely nonevaluative terms. Sociologically, they mean individuals who, or behavior that, attracts widespread public scorn, condemnation, or punishment. In order to understand these phenomena, we must purge the terms of their automatic taint of pathology. Some forms of deviant behavior will be regarded as a manifestation of a disordered mind; some individuals who are considered as deviants are mentally ill. But mental pathology or illness is not an as-

pect of a sociological definition of deviance. The two dimensions are independent of one another. Mental illness is a form of deviance not because mentally ill individuals have "sick" minds, but because their condition and their behavior attract stigma. And most deviant behavior is enacted by individuals who, by any conceivable measure, are perfectly "normal." Abnormality, sickness, and pathology have nothing to do with a sociological definition of deviance.

ONCE AGAIN: WHAT IS DEVIANCE?

Going back to the examples in Chapter 1, we are now much better able to answer the question of whether or not they are instances of deviance, and if so, why—and if not, why not? In all of them, there is a probability that the actor will be condemned or punished—or already has been condemned or punished. When we refer to a type of action, we have a fairly good idea in advance as to the likelihood that the actor will be condemned or punished, given our knowledge of the audience in the picture. When we refer not to a general or hypothetical behavior, but to a specific, concrete act that, in fact, took place, we do not have to speculate on the likelihood of condemnation by audiences—we already *know* how at least one specific audience reacted. Of course, other audiences might have reacted differently. Still, the reactions of real-life audiences tell us a great deal about deviance in general.

Because Bakker was dismissed from his post as television preacher indicates to us that, among fundamentalist or evangelical Christians in the United States, certain actions are regarded negatively. Certainly the Seventh Commandment, "Thou shalt not commit adultery," comes into play here. Threatening the viability of a religious enterprise through financial excesses and irregularities is bound to generate disapproval. That Bakker was actually dismissed represents a concrete condemnation of his actions, hard evidence that his behavior was considered deviant in significant and substantial quarters. Although he still has some supporters who continue to defend him, this does not alter the belief that, to many Christians, Bakker committed a series of deviant actions.

Public opinion polls suggest that much of the public does not regard what Bernhard Goetz did as deviant or punishable; indeed, in some social circles, he is regarded as a hero and a victim. That he was acquitted of the charges of attempted murder and assault with a deadly weapon lends further support to this position. Contrarily, that a significant minority of the public disagrees shows that deviance is not a black-or-white affair but is a matter of degree, that different audiences look upon an action such as Goetz's in different ways. This does not mean that one audience is right and the other wrong in some abstract sense—just that there is substantial disagreement on this question.

Dr. Cort had his research grant taken away, was fired from his job, and has been discredited as a scientist, which shows that, among his employers and in the scientific community, faking data is a serious violation of acceptable behavior. It is important that this act would not be so seriously regarded by the general public, but it is not entirely related to the question of whether Cort's behavior is deviant or not. Certain actions can be deviant *mainly or exclusively to certain specific audiences;* those audiences can be so crucial in an actor's life that it is they, and not the general public, who define what constitutes deviant behavior.

The case of Charles Daniels shows that an accusation, however false, can have serious consequences. Daniels did not engage in the—clearly deviant—behavior of which he was accused. He was, however, punished for engaging in it, and he suffered from the punishment, which was very real and very painful. This punishment cannot be wiped away simply by asserting that Daniels was innocent. Even the financial restitution cannot cancel the painful and stigmatizing experience he suffered. Mr. Daniels is a classic case of a falsely accused deviant. On the other hand, to many sociologists, although Daniels was, for a time, *a* deviant (albeit a falsely accused deviant), *he did not engage in deviant behavior,* at least, not the behavior of which he was accused and convicted. He is a good example of "a deviant without deviance."

Most observers would no doubt see Gordon/Dawn Hall's complicated journey through life as deviant. Many Americans would interact with a transsexual only with a certain amount of discomfort and awkwardness. Hall's marriage to a Black man led to a variety of negative reactions in the community in which he/she lived, which clearly demonstrates the deviance of his/her actions. And his/her relationship with a convicted rapist and murderer clearly would not sit well with many of the readers of this book. It would be difficult to claim that Hall led a traditional or conventional existence.

Lenny Ross's friends tried to help and protect him all his life. His brilliance gave him a great deal of leeway; because of it, most of the people with whom Ross interacted accepted him and his unusual, eccentric behavior. But at some point, eccentricity becomes madness, and the fund of tolerance one's brilliance generates in others is expended. The madder one becomes and the less acceptable one's behavior, the less others want one to be around. Although this tolerance does demonstrate that a certain degree of relativity exists according to who one is, this relativity does have its limits.

It is true that Cartier, Van Cleef & Arpel's, and Bulgari—and their customers—are respectable. It is also true what they did is illegal—not just technically illegal, like jaywalking, but illegal enough for New York City agencies to initiate official action against them. That these acts are not criminal—that is, no one will be arrested for engaging in them or serve a jail or a prison sentence; the worst that can happen is a small fine—means that the acts committed are only *mildly* deviant. Since no customer will suffer any consequences except a little easily shrugged off bad publicity, and having to pay sales tax in the future, it tells us their behavior is fairly conventional, and not really deviant. That fact should tip us off to an important insight: Deviance and social harm or cost are only loosely related to one another. A scam costing millions of dollars is hardly punished, while far less costly acts, such as theft, may result in arrest and possibly a prison sentence, then social cost is not the only factor designating what or who is deviant. In a way, then, the empty box scam, like the Goetz attempted murder case, represents something of a *negative case*, interesting more because it is *not* regarded as deviant than because it is. If we want to know what deviance is, we also have to investigate what it isn't. Such attitudes, just or unjust, help explain the basis for judgments of deviance.

The Chambers-Levin case tells us a great deal about the dynamics of deviance. It shows that some people, if they are seen as charming and good-looking, can get away with a great deal of behavior that would ordinarily be regarded as deviant if engaged in by others. With Chambers and with the brilliant Lenny Ross, it is important to realize that audiences' reactions to an actor and his or her behavior are not automatic. There is always a certain amount of leeway built into what people do when faced with clearly unacceptable behavior. Moreover, the Chambers case shows that, under certain circumstances, a victim may be condemned even more than the perpetrator. The condemnation may be unjust, and tolerance of the perpetrator's behavior is unconscionable. It is our job to understand *how* this process of condemnation and tolerance works. Only by seeing it in action can we hope to grasp the phenomenon of deviance.

Was Hart engaged in deviance with his philandering behavior? Doesn't a majority of married couples—or at least, a majority of married men—do the same thing? John F. Kennedy got away with it. Why not Gary Hart? As we saw, how rare or common an act is does not define its deviant quality. Most people lie occasionally, but if we are caught in a lie, the person we are telling it to will become upset with us. Lying is common, but deviant nonetheless. Likewise, taking three showers a day is uncommon, but not condemned; no one will get into trouble for taking three showers a day. Because adultery is common does not mean it is not deviant. The fact that most individuals become upset

if they discover their spouses engaging in sexual infidelity demonstrates the act's deviant character. In the past, politicians suffered no consequences for adulterous behavior, while today they are more likely to be condemned, which simply proves behavior itself is not the only determinant of an audience's reactions. Hart is not Kennedy, and then is not now. That Hart was hounded out of his candidacy is living proof that *his* adulterous behavior was regarded as deviant. Again, the justice or injustice of this disparity does not alter the picture one bit, though it does emphasize the variability of judgments of what is deviant.

Another crucial point is made by these examples. In recent years, it has become fashionable within sociology to claim that too many sociologists who study deviance have been overly concerned with "nuts, sluts, and perverts," that is, with scandalous, seamy, immoral behavior, often of despised minorities, in preference to the unethical and damaging practices of the rich and the powerful (Liazos, 1972). Or that a certain wing of sociologists who study deviance have focused on stigma to the detriment of looking at the process of domination, the exercise of power, and the revolt against injustice (Piven, 1981).

Such topics are, indeed, fascinating and sociologically revealing. To the extent that domination is relevant to rule-making and rule enforcement, this is, indeed, a relevant criticism. And while the revolt against injustice has often generated the machinery of social control throughout the history of the world, it may not be widely regarded as wrongdoing by the general public. Often, injustice does not generate much social disapproval. It would be difficult, therefore, to study domination, power, and injustice as instances of deviant behavior.

On the other hand, and more importantly, it would be sociologically insensitive of us to dismiss scandalous, "immoral" behavior from our scope. As the Jim Bakker–Jessica Hahn, Gary Hart–Donna Rice, and other examples reveal, such behavior often generates much public disapproval and may have important consequences. An investigation of such behavior and the reactions to it, far from representing an indulgent wallowing in the trivial, the scandalous, and the inconsequential, can reveal profoundly important sociological processes. Too often, criticism comes from a "politically correct," rather than an empirically and theoretically relevant, stance. Throughout this book, we will focus on how things work rather than what seems to be right.

CHAPTER
3

Traditional Theories of Deviance

Do you wonder about why the men and women whose behavior was described in Chapter 1 acted the way they did? Don't you wonder why a religious figure would risk respectability, credibility, and control of a multimillion dollar empire for a 20-minute fling with a church secretary? Why a mild-mannered engineer would shoot four Black teenagers who "stood over" him in a subway? Why a scientist would fake research data and thereby destroy his career, ending up on an unemployment line? How a completely innocent man could possibly be accused and convicted of a truly heinous crime, serving several horrendous years in prison before the mistake was corrected? Why a brilliant mind disintegrated to the point of suicide? Why exclusive, expensive stores collaborate in tax-avoidance schemes, thereby cheating the public of millions of dollars a year? How a college dropout could kill a young woman companion with whom he has just made

love? What reasons would impel a front-running presidential candidate to risk his candidacy to engage in indiscretions with a young, attractive, would-be model?

The question *Why do they do it?* has been and continues to be asked about individuals who stray beyond moral and legal boundaries. "What kind of person would do such a thing?" we ask. After all, most subway riders do not carry guns and shoot fellow passengers who might be threatening them, most scientists do not fake data, most people convicted of a crime are not falsely accused, most people with brilliant minds do not commit suicide, most men who make love with women do not then kill them immediately afterward, and so on. What is it that makes some people stray while most of us do not?

Moreover, you might think about how these individuals would be treated by others as a result of their behavior. How do others relate to them after finding out what they did? And what is their fate at the hands of law enforcement? Some of the actions I described are against the law, while others are simply regarded as socially unacceptable. Goetz and Chambers were arrested; Bakker and Hart were not. Goetz, after attempting to murder the four Black teenagers—and after admitting having done so—was acquitted of the crime of attempted murder; Daniels, on the basis of nonexistent evidence, was convicted and imprisoned. Bakker lost his lucrative position; Hart was forced to step aside as a presidential candidate. Why? What acts are regarded as criminal in nature and which ones represent violations of a normative or moral code? What accounts for criminalization—passing laws against certain forms of behavior? Against which actors are these laws enforced? Which specific, potentially criminal acts result in conviction for the perpetrator and which do not? What are the consequences of moral and social disapproval of someone's actions? Do some people get away with disapproved acts, while others are severely punished for the same behavior?

Over the years, many theories have been advanced to explain *rule making, rule breaking,* and *reactions to rule breaking* (Sutherland and Cressey, 1978: 3). In other words, theories of deviant behavior attempt to answer one or several of the following questions:

1. Why do they do it?
2. Why is it (or isn't it) regarded as wrong?
3. Why is it (or isn't it) against the law?
4. What happens when somebody engages in it? How do other people react? And why?

The questions of why rules and laws are made, and what accounts for reactions to breaking rules and laws, are fairly recent endeavors. In contrast, the earliest theories of deviant behavior typically concentrated on: Why do they do it?

Everywhere and at all times, rules have existed. Wherever there are rules, wherever there are laws, they will be broken, even if occasionally. Everywhere, virtuous, lawabid-ing, conventional members of society wonder what leads certain people to engage in acts of wrongdoing—adultery, blasphemy, embezzlement, theft, witchcraft, heresy, murder, incest, cowardice, treason, plagiarizing, suicide, aberrant and mentally deranged behavior, lying, and so on. Throughout history, speculation as to the causes of deviant behavior has been a major concern of the members of cultures just about everywhere. And everywhere, explanations and theories as to why some members of society break its rules have been put forth.

WHAT IS A THEORY?

The earliest speculations on the why of deviance and crime could not be called theories as we understand the term, even in the broadest sense in which that word might be understood. As we'll see in this chapter, from time immemorial until roughly the seventeenth century, the most popular explanation for why they did it was possession by evil spirits. In addition, for centuries, most people used popular, at-hand, commonsensical explanations that did not necessarily invoke demons or evil spirits. Beginning roughly with the Industrial Revolution, theological and commonsense speculation were replaced by more rigorous ways of looking at society. More specifically, people began applying evidence to arguments in a more systematic, empirical fashion.

The term "theory" has different meanings to different individuals; hence, it is best to begin this chapter with a brief discussion of what I mean by the word. The popular meaning of theory, that which is held by the man and the woman on the street, is an assertion that has not been verified empirically or factually, something more than a guess but far less than a fact. Fact and theory can be arranged, according to this view, along a unidimensional continuum of degrees of certainty or confidence, with fact at the top and theory near the bottom. Facts are statements that are factually true and are supported by such convincing evidence that someone would be a fool to assert otherwise. "George Bush was elected president of the United States in 1988" is just such a statement. On the other hand, most people regard a theory as a statement for which there is little evidence, which might be, but in all probability is not, true. Some people go even further and assume a theory is simply empty, wild speculation, with no basis in fact whatsoever. To call something a theory is not to take it seriously, to dismiss it out of hand.

To the scientist however, a theory is an entirely different kettle of fish. The dictionary defines theory as "an explanation for a general class of phenomena." A given theory may be factually verified and widely accepted by experts in a given field, dismissed as nonsense, or lie somewhere in between. In other words, according to the biologist Stephen Jay Gould, facts and theories are two different things, not "rungs in a hierarchy of increasing certainty. Facts are the world's data. Theories are structures of ideas that explain and interpret facts" (1984: 254). Some theories are facts *and* theories simultaneously; that is, are both general explanations *and* factually verified at the same time. Gould regards evolution as an example of a theory that is also a fact. In contrast, some theories are plausible, but not yet factually verified or disconfirmed; for example, that alcoholism is genetic—that is, that some people drink excessively and destructively because they inherited this tendency from their ancestors. And lastly, there are theories that are empirically unverified and totally implausible—those that the facts, once they have been gathered, are extremely unlikely to verify. Here, we would have to include astrology—a theory that the sun, the moon, and the stars control our destinies—or the "lunar cycle"—a theory that phases of the moon cause people to commit crimes (Lieber, 1978). Such theories are not explanations for facts or observations but supposed explanations for pseudofacts and nonobservations (Hines, 1988; Abell and Singer, 1983).

To qualify as a scientific theory, an explanation must have the following characteristics. First, it must be *empirical*—it must refer to phenomena in the material world and it must point to the data of the five senses, supplemented, of course, by instruments that measure our human senses. We must be able to see, hear, smell, touch, or taste what it refers to. Moreover, other people must also be able to see, hear, smell, touch, or taste these things. In other words, the observations must be capable of being confirmed. If what an explanation refers to are not data of the senses, the theory is not scientific. For instance, some people believe that crystals have a wide range of powers because they give off an energy field. Since this energy cannot be located or measured empirically, and because crystals cannot be shown empirically to have any curative powers whatsoever, scientists conclude that this theory is not scientific.

Second, a theory or scientific explanation must be *systematic*. This means the evidence testing and verifying the theory should not be scattered, anecdotal, or hit-or-miss; it must be gathered in a planned, disciplined fashion, spelled out in advance so that statements or propositions can be determined as true or false. Evidence must not be selected specifically to verify a hypothesis. It is scientifically improper to pick and choose one's cases to show that one is right.

Third, a theory must be *falsifiable* (Popper, 1959); it must be stated in such a way that it can be disconfirmed. You must be able to state exactly what evidence will make your statement false, what will prove you wrong. If you say, for example, that you have spiritual powers that enable you to predict the future, you must construct your predictions in such a way that, if things turn out differently, you will be forced to say, well, I'm wrong, that's all. Many supposed theories are so vague that they are virtually untestable. For instance, if you say, American society will go through a spiritual malaise in the future, you can define "spiritual malaise" so broadly that anything will qualify. This would not represent a scientific theory.

Fourth, a theory must supply a *causal mechanism*. It must account for why things happen the way they do. A theory cannot be a simple description, such as recreational drug use increased in the United States in the 1960s. Why did it increase? What accounts for the rise? A theory must explain *why* this rise occurred, what accounts for it, and what is the precise cause-and-effect sequence.

Fifth, a theory must be fairly *general.* An explanation does not qualify as a scientific theory if it refers to a single event, such as why Martin Luther King was assassinated, why George Bush was elected president, or what caused the defeat of U.S. military forces in Vietnam. A theory is an explanation for a general *class* of events or phenomena; for example, why did the dinosaurs die out (not one specific dinosaur—dinosaurs in general)? What are the factors contributing to teenage suicide (not one specific teenager, but teenager suicides in general)? What causes violence (not the violence of a specific person, but violence in general)?

Technically, theories can never be totally confirmed. It is a far simpler matter to *disconfirm* a theory, to demonstrate conclusively that it is false (Popper, 1959). Suppose someone proposes that the lunar cycle causes an increase in murder and other aggressive acts because the effect of the moon's gravitational pull on fluids in the body causes changes in human personality (Lieber, 1978). Disconfirming evidence would be a simple matter: There are no differences in rates of criminal homicide and other violence between periods of the month corresponding to the lunar cycle. On the other hand, if there were such differences, would that definitively confirm the theory? Not necessarily; there may be an infinity of potentially valid alternative explanations that could account for the variation. There is no possibility of disconfirming *all* the possible alternative explanations that could account for observed empirical variation. Explanations or theories come to be accepted as true not because the evidence supporting them is definitive, but because they account for the most observations and are more plausible than competing explanations or theories.

Even what are called facts cannot be regarded as definitive beyond a shadow of a doubt. As Stephen Jay Gould says, "fact" does not mean "absolute certainty." Absolute certainty exists only in logic, mathematics, and theology. Any statement describing the material or empirical world must retain a measure or degree of uncertainty, small though it may be, for statements widely regarded as facts. Natural and especially social scientists do not make a claim to eternal, perpetual truth. What is called a fact is that which has been "confirmed to such a degree that it would be perverse to withhold provisional assent" (Gould, 1984: 255). Sociologist Ben-Yehuda has been challenged by students who ask him, triumphantly, "Can you *prove* that while talking with you, I have not been to the moon and back again?" Such a claim could have been accomplished using unknown powers; no known empirical test can ascertain *with absolute certainty* that the student did *not* visit the moon (Ben-Yehuda, 1985: 85). The correct answer to the student's question is that science generally, and sociology specifically, is not about certainty. We never know anything with absolute confidence. We have to settle for varying *degrees* of certainty. Some assertions are more plausible than others; we have more confidence in them because the evidence supporting them is more abundant and convincing. Says Gould, "I suppose that apples might start to rise tomorrow [instead of fall], but the possibility does not merit equal time in physics classrooms" (1984: 255).

THEORIES AND PERSPECTIVES

In sociology generally, and in the sociology of deviance specifically, the term "theory" is used a bit more broadly than in the natural sciences. There are sociological theories that conform to the classic scientific definition; they are explanations for a general class of phenomena. For instance, arguing that punishment increases, rather than decreases, further commitment to deviant behavior because it intensifies a deviant identity, is an example of a theory or explanation that can be confirmed or falsified. I suspect this theory is false more often than it is true; no matter—it qualifies as a scientific theory because it possesses the five criteria mentioned above.

On the other hand, many sociological approaches are not theories in the sense proposed above. Rather, they are *perspectives* or *orientations* toward the phenomena they examine, *paradigms* or models outlining in a general way how the world works. A perspective directs us to certain aspects of a phenomenon we want to examine. A painter does not look at the sea in the same way a biologist does; a poet will describe love differently from a psychologist; police officers and criminologists are concerned with crime, but the models of what that phenomenon is to them are radically different.

Most of the perspectives or paradigms we will look at here and in Chapter 4 are not, in the strictly scientific sense of the word, theories at all, even though they are widely referred to as theories. They tell us what to look for, what to notice; they alert us to concepts, processes, mechanisms, and relationships that are likely to have relevance in the real world. They say, "A lot of things in the social world work this way, although often, they don't." They will not withstand rigorous operationalization or scientific testing. Robert Merton said, in reference to approaches to deviance: "When sociologists speak of 'theories,' they only adopt a convenient abbreviation. Strictly speaking, none is a theory in the exacting sense. . . . Rather, they are general theoretical orientations that indicate *kinds of sociological variables* to be taken into account in trying to understand deviance. They do not state definite relationships between sets of specific variables" (1976: 31). Still, they are useful in that we might often miss interesting observations if we did not look at the world through the lens of these perspectives.

The dominant theories of deviance—anomie theory, functionalism, labeling or interactionist theory, the theory of differential association, control theory, conflict theory—are all perspectives rather than rigorous scientific theories. They all make some interesting observations, but all are limited, partial views of deviant behavior; all fail to account for vast ranges of phenomena, and aspects of all are stated in such a way that they can be confirmed or disconfirmed, given the right data. At the same time, each provides a set of sensitizing concepts rather than a rigorous scientific explanation. Yet, scientific propositions and explanations—real theories—can be gleaned from these broad perspectives. Thus, I will refer to these perspectives as "theories," since that is the way they are generally discussed.

PERSPECTIVES IN THE SOCIOLOGY OF DEVIANCE

Most discussions of sociological theories of deviance present them, one by one, much like different-colored eggs in a carton. They are treated as equivalents, as comparable, as covering more or less the same territory, as asking more or less the same kinds of questions, and as competing with one another. This is an erroneous view. In fact, these theories or perspectives are not at all equivalents; they do not cover the same territory or ask the same questions, and, for the most part, do not compete with or directly contradict one another. "Sociologists of deviance have progressively spread out into a loose network of factions and social worlds. . . . Intellectual prominence [in the field] has become increasingly parochial: radical criminologists discuss each other's ideas, discounting criticisms and works of outsiders as trivial and ideologically laden; interactionists do not embark on debate, being reluctant to trade on a metaphysical plane; applied criminologists may have no commerce with the fanciful and irrelevant abstractions of the theorists. Such a drift toward closure has insulated one schismatic group against its fellows, permitting diverse ideas to be aired without effective challenge. The result has been only the most superficially controlled growth, a growth which moves thought in very different ways and toward very different goals" (Rock, 1980: 292).

Sociologist Nanette Davis (1980: 13) explains that the various theoretical perspectives in the study of deviance should not be seen as contradictory. "To say that one theory . . . contradicts another," she says, "is like saying that tools in a toolbox contradict one another." Instead, each can be looked at as *appropriate for a different purpose*. This point can be made even more strongly. Going back to the egg analogy, rather than seeing the various theories in the study of deviance and crime as different-colored eggs, but all eggs nonetheless, one theory should be seen as a piece of an eggshell, another as a yolk, a third as an omelette, a fourth as the frying pan, a fifth as a feather on a chicken, a sixth as the carton, a seventh the person who eats the egg, an eighth the salt and pepper that add flavor to the egg, and so on. These theories cannot be lined up and examined as if they were engaged in dealing with the same issues. Though they all look at the phenomenon of deviance, they look at different *aspects* of this phenomenon, and they approach it on their own special terms, and therefore, not at all on the terms of the other perspectives. They are not even rough equivalents, and should not be regarded as such.

Of course, *from the point of view of each perspective*, the other perspectives *are* commensurable—that is, they are all lacking to the extent that they do not share that perspective's concerns. For instance, a Marxist could analyze all non-Marxist theories and find that none fosters revolution the way Marxism does; to that extent, they are all inadequate. An interactionist will fault all other theories to the extent that they fail to take the actor's definition of the situation into account. In other words, each theory *sets up relevant criteria* for evaluating the other theories, and *according to these criteria*, all other theories can be arranged along a dimension corresponding to how well they measure up. Only in this extremely biased sense can the current theories of deviance be considered equivalents.

Another way of saying this is that the different perspectives on the sociology of deviance and crime are *incommensurable* (Wright, 1984). Their practitioners look at different aspects of the phenomenon; they are concerned with different issues; they attempt to answer different questions; they use different types of evidence; they read and cite different researchers and theorists; they do not, for the most part, read the writings of practitioners of other schools and, when they do, it is only to supply them with relevant quotes to criticize and critique their work; they think that practitioners of other schools are, or at least should be, concerned with their own questions and issues, and when they criticize the other perspectives, they believe these criticisms are devastating, even fatal; and, for the most part, they ignore the criticism that practitioners of other schools direct at their own school's writings, believing them to be irrelevant to their concerns.

In short, what we have in the sociology of deviance and crime is a kind of "communications breakdown." There is a "lack of resonance" between the various perspectives, a "lack of reciprocal understanding of the meaning associated with the basic concepts employed." These perspectives are possessed of "radically disparate worldviews as to the nature of social life" (Wright, 1984: v–vi). No amount of evidence presented by the practitioner of a given perspective could disconfirm a different perspective to the satisfaction of *its* practitioners, because the questions and issues that each is concerned with are incommensurable, incompatible, in different dimensions—and because they are perspectives, not theories.

DEMONIC POSSESSION

Historically, the oldest explanation for deviant behavior has been *demonic possession*. For millennia, evil spirits, including the devil, were thought to cause men and women to engage in socially unacceptable behavior. A half a million years ago, Stone Age humans drilled holes into the skulls of individuals who engaged in wrongdoing of some kind—

who, today, would be recognized as being mentally ill—so evil spirits could escape (Davison and Neale, 1986: 7). The ancient Hebrews, Egyptians, Greeks, and Romans performed rites of exorcism to cast out demonic beings dwelling in the body and soul of transgressors. In the Middle Ages, thousands of women and men were burned at the stake for making a pact with the devil and supposedly engaging in wicked deeds because of it. Among both the fairly well educated and much of the mass of society, the theory of demonic possession was a dominant explanation for wrongdoing in Renaissance Europe (Ben-Yehuda, 1985: 23–73)—very roughly, the 1400s to the 1600s—and in the Salem colony in Massachusetts in the 1600s (Erikson, 1966). By the 1700s in Western Europe and North America, however, it had almost completely died out.

SHADOW CRIMINOLOGY

In legal commentary, plays, poems, sagas, literary and intellectual essays, and even in everyday talk among ordinary members of a society, there has been "a prolonged attempt to make sense of the existence of wickedness"; in societies everywhere, individuals "have repeatedly dwelt on the conflict between good and evil." This speculation has been dubbed "shadow criminology" or "proto-criminology" (Downes and Rock, 1982: 50); it began long before academic disciplines began devising theories of deviance and crime, indeed, long before universities even existed. Such speculation, however, has always been unsystematic, diffuse, and ad hoc—made up for the moment on an act-by-act or crime-by-crime basis. These explanations tend to be commonsensical and usually without empirical foundation. In a given murder, for example, it may be speculated that he did it out of passion; or, in a robbery, he was too greedy for his own good; or if a woman becomes a prostitute, she was just a whore at heart. Such explanations do not add to our store of knowledge about deviance or crime (though it may be interesting to try to understand why such explanations are devised). Thus, shadow criminology need not concern us here.

FREE WILL AND RATIONAL CALCULATION

The first sophisticated, academically respectable perspective or theory of criminal behavior is the "free will" or *classical* school of criminology (Vold and Bernard, 1986: 18–34) and is associated with the name of Cesare Beccaria (1738–1794), an Italian scholar who was strongly influenced by the French rationalists, such as René Descartes (1596–1650), and the laissez-faire economist Adam Smith (1723–1790).

The eighteenth century in Europe is generally referred to as the Age of Enlightenment or the Age of Reason. Philosophers and scientists had long ago abandoned the idea of the intervention of spirits to explain worldly phenomena and, instead, concentrated on material forces. Rather than being seen as a result of seduction by demons, violations of rules, norms, and laws were thought to be caused by free will—a rational calculation of pleasure and pain. Individuals choose among a number of alternative courses of action according to benefits they believe will accrue to them. They avoid activities they believe will bring them more pain than pleasure. This model, then, sees people, criminals included, as free, rational, and hedonistic (Barlow, 1987: 75). Actions that bring pleasure to an individual will be enacted and continued; those that are painful will be abandoned, eighteenth-century thinkers believed. The way to ensure conformity to society's norms and laws is to apprehend and punish offenders, thereby making the pain following a violation greater than the pleasure derived from it.

The classical school made a number of assumptions that are now regarded as false. It ignored obvious disparities in wealth and power and thereby failed to recognize forces that make certain kinds of crimes more likely among the poor and less likely among the rich. In addition, we now see that people are not completely rational in their behavior; they engage in deviance and crime for a number of reasons aside from pursuing pleasure and avoiding pain. In addition, what is pleasurable to one person may be painful to another, and vice versa. Homosexuality and heterosexuality provide relevant examples here: To someone who enjoys sex solely with members of the same gender, sex with the opposite gender would not be pleasurable, and vice versa. Moreover, most of the time that a rule or a law is violated, the offender is not caught—thereby making the offender's calculation of pleasure and pain far more complicated than these early thinkers believed. In addition, detection of crimes and enforcement of laws are quite often erratic, this muddying the cost-benefit analysis the potential criminal must make. Overall, the classical school of criminology held a faulty view of human behavior.

In the 1800s, the *neoclassical* school made its appearance; its assumptions were basically the same as those of the classical school, with the exception of certain necessary modifications to apply the original theory to the actual administration of justice (mainly in France). One of the classical school's principal tenets was that every criminal was to be treated identically—the same punishment for the same crime. The neoclassical school modified this rigid assumption so that age, mental condition, and extenuating circumstances were taken into account (Vold and Bernard, 1986: 26–27).

The free will perspective has made something of a comeback in recent years, in more sophisticated forms than its original version: The *rational choice behavior* school (Cohen et al., 1980) and the strictly economic model (Becker, 1968; Warren, 1978) are based on some of the classical school's basic assumptions. Unlike the classical school, however, these contemporary models do not encompass all crimes within their scope; instead, they focus almost entirely on economic crimes. The rational choice behavior school argues that criminal motivation need not be considered; it is a given. Criminal behavior, it argues, is a *purposive* and *rational* means of attaining an end—acquiring money more efficiently than by any other method. People act according to the *utility* that the outcome of their actions have for them. An assumption of both the rationality and the economic models is that all individuals, when faced with the same alternatives, would make essentially the same choice. It is possible that too many assumptions have to be made for the model to work. In real life, there are too many constraints and contingencies that push and pull individuals in various directions for us to assume that utility will dominate their choices of action, whether in a deviant and criminal, or in a conventional, law-abiding direction. Although rationality certainly enters into the crime and deviance equation, the fact that jails, prisons, and reform schools are full of young, and not-so-young, men who committed crimes impulsively, without planning, and got caught as a consequence, indicates that the free will factor is not a totally reliable explanation.

THE POSITIVE SCHOOL

The nineteenth century was characterized by a shift away from viewing people as rational actors, who fully understood causes and consequences of their actions, to seeing behavior as being determined by forces beyond their control, understanding, and rational will (McCaghy, 1985: 8ff). *Positivism,* the dominant scientific perspective in the second half of the nineteenth century, argued that the only valid information is that gathered in a strictly scientific fashion, which meets all five criteria outlined above; that is, it is empirical, systematic, falsifiable, general, and explanatory. Nineteenth-century positivists believed that behavior is determined or strictly caused by specific factors or forces that can be discovered and explicated only by the scientist.[1]

In the nineteenth century, the positive school assumed that deviant and criminal behavior is caused by a biological pathology or defect of some kind. Wrongdoing, such as criminal behavior, was thought to be traceable to something organically and constitutionally wrong with the offender, an inborn defect of some kind. One variety of this theory assumed that deviants were simply too feebleminded to understand society's rules, and this is why they violated them. The most well-known and influential of the nineteenth-century positivists writing on deviance and crime was Cesare Lombroso (1835–1909), an Italian physician and scholar, who argued that the physical abnormalities of certain individuals forced them into committing crimes. The criminal represented an evolutionary throwback to a more primitive or apelike human, an "atavism," according to Lombroso. Clearly, the theory owed much to Charles Darwin's evolutionary theory, as spelled out in *On the Origin of Species*, (1859). (Most observers today would argue that Lombroso's application of Darwinian theory represents a distortion of its main ideas.) In short, the nineteenth-century positive school of criminology argued that physical defect or pathology was the major explanation for criminal and deviant behavior. By the late 1800s and early 1900s, however, most researchers realized that physical abnormalities could not explain all, or even most, deviation from laws and social norms. Even Lombroso modified his theory over the years, granting to biological pathology an increasingly smaller role. (The definitive critique of Lombroso's positivistic criminology may be found in Gould, 1981: 123–143.)

There has been something of a revival of biological and constitutional theories of deviance and crime (Wilson and Herrnstein, 1985: 69–172). This approach tends to focus on conventional street crimes, such as murder, robbery, and rape, which require risk-taking and physical exertion. Thus, the biological position rests on the argument that criminal and conventional activities requiring risk and physical exertion are more likely to be committed by people who are more willing to take risks and are capable of greater physical exertion. Obvious candidates are men and the young (Gove, 1985). It should not astonish us that this is so. In fact, it would be truly remarkable if it were not. More specifically, any departure from relationships that would be predicted according to this model is what requires explaining. For instance, if physical strength and daring account for deviance and crime and men are stronger and more daring than women, then what accounts, for example, for the fact that the proportion of women arrestees varies so much from one society to another (Simon, 1975a: 111–119; 1975b: 89–96; Adler, 1979; Conklin, 1981: 129)? Clearly, in an advanced industrial society, physical strength counts for less than it did in hunting-and-gathering and agrarian societies (Gagnon, 1971). Biological factors must always be mediated through a social and cultural environment and must be counted as being of limited utility in explaining wrongdoing.

SOCIAL PATHOLOGY

failure of the individual

"Social pathology" is the name given to the late nineteenth- and early twentieth-century perspective that argued that (1) *society is very* much like an organism and (2) deviance is very much like a disease (Mills, 1943, 1963: 525–552; Davis, 1980: 31–55; Rubington and Weinberg, 1977: 17–24). The social pathology school abandoned physical defect as the major cause of deviance and crime. Rather, the deviant is seen as the individual who cannot or will not adjust or adapt to the laws, standards, values, and norms of conventional society. Deviance represented the inability to fit into the normal, healthy social body, according to social pathologists. For the most part, the most basic cause of deviant behavior specifically, and all social problems generally, is a failure in socialization.

Most social pathologists distrusted the large city. A healthy society was seen as harmonious, homogenous, and slow moving; cities, in contrast, generated conflict, diversity, and rapid social change. All this encouraged nonconformity and unhealthy behavior. In addition, social pathologists generally saw middle-class values as normal, and those of the lower and working classes as pathological and abnormal. Deviance was seen as an almost exclusively underclass phenomenon. The solution to the adjustment problems of the poor—poverty, "vice," crime, unemployment, delinquency, violence—was to socialize the deviant into the wisdom of accepting conventional middle-class society's values and encouraging conformity to its standards of behavior.

Social pathology had its heyday in the period roughly between 1890 and 1910. By the end of World War I, the perspective had declined sharply among sociologists studying deviance and other social problems. Society is not really very much like a biological organism, and deviance cannot be regarded as even remotely like a disease. To argue that behavior that strays from respectability and conventionality is necessarily abnormal or pathological is to make a value judgment, not a statement of objective fact. The same behavior can be viewed as acceptable or immoral, depending on one's perspective. What the social pathologist approach lacked in viewing deviance is a sense of relativity.

SOCIAL DISORGANIZATION AND THE CHICAGO SCHOOL

Just after World War I, a school of thought emerged that both replaced and to some extent grew out of the social pathology perspective. It has come to be called the "Chicago School," because its most prominent practitioners were teachers and their graduate students at the University of Chicago. This viewpoint shifted the location of the pathology from the individual to the social structure. While social pathologists argued that the problem resided in the failure of some individuals to adapt to the society in which they lived, the Chicago School argued that entire neighborhoods had become so disorganized that adapting to them inevitably entailed engaging in certain forms of deviant behavior. Social disorganization, the principal variable explaining deviance according to the advocates of the Chicago School, was caused primarily by urbanization. As cities grew, their residents increasingly came into contact with strangers. This encouraged impersonality, social distance, and a decline in social harmony. People no longer shared the same values or cared about how others felt about them and what they did. As the city grows, its sense of community breaks down. And as social disorganization in an area increases, deviant behavior increases correspondingly (Traub and Little, 1985: 41–43, 44–68).

Not all neighborhoods are equally disorganized, however, and therefore, rates of deviance vary from one area to another. Certain neighborhoods of a city "give licence to nonconforming behavior" (Suchar, 1978: 74). Those areas in which the population is geographically unstable, moves a great deal, is composed of a variety of different racial and ethnic groups, has a high proportion of immigrants, and lacks neighborhood controls are those in which deviant behavior frequently occurs. In other words, Chicago sociologists insisted that deviance varies systematically by physical and geographical location. Where someone is residentially determines the likelihood of that person committing deviant and criminal acts. Deviance is relatively absent in certain neighborhoods and extremely frequent, even routine, in others. The Chicago School placed a heavy emphasis on *social ecology*—the view that physical spacing and interdependence determine human behavior. And the specific degree of social disorganization—high in some neighborhoods and low in others—is what causes deviance and crime.

Eventually, the strong emphasis by the Chicago School on social disorganization was abandoned in the study of deviant behavior. Later researchers found that poor slum neighborhoods often exhibit a high degree of cohesion and social organization (Whyte, 1943), which the Chicago School adherents failed to recognize simply because it was different from that which prevailed in more middle-class areas. The Chicago School suffered from what is now regarded as a middle-class bias in assuming that behavior that departed from that of comfortable, respectable, small-town folk was "disorganized." Many socially disapproved activities are committed as much by the affluent, middle-class members of society as by representatives of the lower and working classes. The Chicago sociologists made the erroneous assumption that deviance was almost exclusively an underclass phenomenon. They examined street prostitution without considering the middle-class call girl, the skid row alcoholic but not the drunk whose family and friends cover for and take care of him, the street narcotic addict but not the middle-class recreational drug user. The Chicago School displayed much the same kind of bias and parochialism that marked earlier theories. By the early 1940s, the Chicago School, with its emphasis on social disorganization, was regarded as obsolete.

However, this line of thinking did make at least one major contribution to the study of deviance: it emphasized firsthand, up-close observation of a wide range of deviance. The early Chicago sociologists used the city of Chicago as their natural laboratory, studying such topics as slum neighborhoods, juvenile delinquency, drug addiction, mental illness, race and ethnic relations, and alcoholism among homeless vagrants. The work of these early researchers was marked by a distaste for what they saw and the desire to improve existing conditions. At the same time, one of their major contributions was *empirical:* to view society realistically, as it really is. Chicago sociologists rejected "armchair" research, which is conducted without any contact with the real world; they insisted that to find out what society is like, it is necessary to get out into the streets and study the social world as it exists.

FUNCTIONALISM

Functionalism is a theoretical perspective that emerged in the 1930s, primarily as a product of the writing and teaching of Talcott Parsons (1902–1979), who systematized the ideas of several European sociologists, including Vilfredo Pareto (1848–1923), who set forth the idea of society as a social system, and Emile Durkheim (1858–1918), who emphasized the causes and consequences of social cohesion as well as a phenomenon he termed the "collective conscience." Functionalism asked the basic question, "How is social order possible?" The answer that it gives is that societies, in a more or less unintended, nonconscious fashion, have protected themselves over the years by prohibiting harmful activities and encouraging beneficial ones. Social customs and institutions that persist over time are good for society because they serve one of these two functions (Parsons, 1951; Davis, 1949; Davis and Moore, 1945).

Deviance, according to the functionalists, can be either beneficial ("functional") or harmful ("dysfunctional") to society as a whole. Certain activities will promote social stability, integration, and cohesion—and will be functional; others, by their very nature, will generate hostility and discord among the members of a society and thereby make the society more unstable and less viable—and they, therefore, will be dysfunctional for the society. Certain taboos will be more or less universal around the world, because the activities they prohibit will inherently sow the seeds of conflict. Specific activities will be regarded as deviance everywhere because they threaten the social order.

However, the main contribution of the functionalists lay not in their analyses showing that certain forms of deviance are harmful, or dysfunctional, and their prohibition is therefore beneficial, or positively functional. Rather, functionalism represented a considerable advance over the previous perspectives in large part because it stressed that certain forms of deviance have a positive or integrative effect on society. "Overwhelmingly," functionalists "stressed the functions—not the dysfunctions—of deviant" behavior (Matza, 1969: 55). Of course, often, most members of a society will not recognize these effects, positive or negative; they may be hidden, unacknowledged, or, in functionalist terminology, *latent* consequences of deviant behavior.

Deviance, the functionalists argued, is often beneficial for society, a kind of "blessing in disguise." For example, Kingsley Davis (1937, 1971) argued that prostitution serves a positive function for society: "Enabling a small number of women to take care of the needs of a large number of men, it is the most convenient sexual outlet for armies and the legions of strangers, perverts, and physically repulsive in our midst. It performs a role which apparently no other institution fully performs" (Davis, 1971: 351). By diverting the sexual energy of a large number of men onto "disreputable" women and away from "respectable" women, Davis argues, the traditional family is preserved and society benefits as a consequence. Robert Merton, probably the most prominent functionalist sociologist writing today, argued that political bossism and the local party machine, although corrupt, inefficient, favoristic, and deeply involved in criminal activities, fulfills the crucial social function *"of humanizing and personalizing all manner of assistance* to those in need" (1957: 74). This solidifies the neighborhood and strengthens the society as a whole.

Where social pathologists saw deviance as almost inevitably producing *undesirable* effects on a society, functionalists argued that the effects that nearly everyone recognized as desirable often flowed from deviant behavior.

Where earlier perspectives saw deviance as *untenable,* as something that could (and should) be gotten rid of through firm and authoritarian intervention, functionalists argued that deviance provided a tenable, viable way of life for many members of society. The *persistence* of deviance—the fact that it exists everywhere, throughout history—indicates that it makes positive contributions for both the members of society that engage in it and for society as a whole.

And last, where earlier perspectives saw a *disjunction* between deviance and conventionality, a gap or space separating the "good guys" from the "bad guys," functionalists pictured a *continuity* between them. Deviance, the functionalists argued, shades over into conventional behavior. Much of what ordinary law-abiding folk think and do borders on, but doesn't quite become, deviant behavior. There is deviance *in miniature* in the most conventional of behavior and an incipient deviant in even the most conformist of souls. We should look at deviance in *linear* terms rather than in either-or, dichotomous, or black-or-white terms. There is an unbroken continuum between the respectable and the disreputable. A clear break between them simply does not exist. The relationship between vice and virtue is devious rather than simple, continuous rather than dichotomous (Matza, 1969: 68, 74, 77).

Functionalists offered insight into why rules—and therefore deviance—exist in the first place, as well as into some of the major consequences of deviant behavior. In its time and in its modest way, functionalism did make at least one major contribution: It purged the field of the automatic implication of pathology (Matza, 1969: 31). Functionalism was the first major perspective historically to argue that deviance is not necessarily a result of an undesirable or abnormal condition and that it does not always produce negative consequences. Deviance is, in fact, part and parcel of the normal functioning of any society.

At the same time, the functionalist perspective has suffered sustained, and in the view of many critics, fatal criticism (Gouldner, 1970). Functionalism is accused of justifying the existing status quo, of being incapable of analyzing or predicting social change, of glossing over and ignoring conflicts between groups and social classes, as well as failing to take note of profound differences in power and wealth, and the implications this has for deviant behavior. Functionalism was dominant in sociology generally from the 1940s into the early 1960s. (It never became a dominant perspective in the study of deviant behavior specifically.) Since the 1960s, this theoretical orientation has undergone a steady decline in influence. Today, functionalism, as a perspective studying the sociology of deviant behavior, has importance primarily as an historical footnote.

ANOMIE OR STRAIN THEORY

Anomie theory was born in 1938 with the publication of "Social Structure and Anomie," written by Robert K. Merton (1938). Influenced by the nineteenth-century *Suicide* by French sociologist Emile Durkheim, Merton was struck by the insight that deviant behavior could be caused by a disturbance in the social order, which sociologists call *anomie*. Merton wondered why the frequency of deviant behavior varied so dramatically from one society to another, and from one group to another in the same society. He assumed that the answer could be found in the way that *"social structures exert a definite pressure upon certain persons in the society to engage in non-conforming rather than conforming conduct"* (Merton, 1957: 132). These pressures could produce very *unconventional* behavior from very *conventional* origins and motives, Merton reasoned. Anomie theory is also called *strain* theory, because deviant behavior is hypothesized to result from a certain kind of strain.

What sorts of social pressures would tend to produce high rates of deviant behavior? Merton locates them in the society's *culturally defined goals,* which are "held out as legitimate objectives for all or for diversely located members of the society" (1957: 132). These goals, Merton claims, are widely shared; more or less everyone in the society wishes to attain them. What are these goals in our society? Primarily monetary and material success. "Making it," within the scope of the American Dream, involves being affluent. We are bombarded on all sides by messages to achieve, to succeed. This is an almost universal American value, a basic goal toward which nearly everyone aspires.

Every society also places certain limitations on how to achieve culturally defined goals. While everyone may value wealth in our society, it is a separate question as to how we are permitted to acquire that wealth. Groups, institutions, and societies differ in their restrictions as to how to reach certain goals. For instance, beating up, bribing, or having sexual intercourse with a professor are not considered legitimate means of achieving the goal of receiving an "A" in a course. Although any one of these methods or means might work from time to time, the social system of higher learning in America frowns on them. They are not "acceptable modes" of reaching out for the goal of a high grade.

However, in some other social settings, the importance of the specific means that are selected to attain a certain goal may be of little or no consequence. Some societies place an extremely heavy emphasis on attaining a given goal, but remain fairly tolerant about exactly how one goes about attaining it. Here we have a case of "winning at any costs." Merton maintains that we have just such a situation in contemporary America. Contemporary American culture "continues to be characterized by a heavy emphasis on wealth as a basic symbol of success, without a corresponding emphasis upon the legitimate avenues on which to march toward this goal" (1957: 139). We have an acquisitive society, in which "considerations of technical expediency" rule supreme. The basic question becomes: "Which of the available procedures is most efficient in netting the culturally approved value?" (1957: 135).

In other words, it is less important just *how* one makes it; the important thing, above all, is *making it* (Krim, 1961: 32–38).

In contemporary America, we have a conflict between the culture (what people are taught to aspire to) and the social and economic structure (the opportunities they have to succeed). We have, in other words, a *malintegrated* society. Aspirations cannot possibly be met by the available material resources. While the aspirations of the population are unlimited, their actual chances of success are quite limited. This creates pressure in the direction of deviant behavior. "It is only when a system of cultural values extols, virtually above all else, certain *common* success-goals *for the population are large* while the social structure rigorously restricts or completely closes access to approved modes of reaching these goals *for a considerable part of the same population,* that deviant behavior ensues on a large scale" (Merton, 1957: 146). "It is . . . my central hypothesis," Merton wrote, "that aberrant behavior may be regarded sociologically as a symptom of disassociation between culturally prescribed aspirations and socially structured avenues for realizing these aspirations" (1957: 134).

How do people who are subject to these conflicting pressures adapt to or react to them? What styles of conflict resolution should we expect from dwellers of this type of social structure? Just what types of deviance should we predict for success-hungry Americans? Merton drew up a typology of different responses to goal attainment and legitimate versus illegitimate means of attaining these goals.

The conformist mode of adaptation, accepting both legitimate cultural goals of success and the institutionalized or conventional means for reaching these goals, is not of interest to the student of deviant behavior except as a negative example. It is in the typology simply for the purpose of comparing with various forms of deviance. Becoming a lawyer, an accountant, or a physician and striving for material success by achieving in one's profession—becoming affluent through a legal, legitimate profession performed in a law-abiding, respectable fash-

ion—is an example of the most common mode of adaptation: *conformity.* In fact, given the strength of the values of success in this society, and given the relatively limited opportunities for genuine success for the population at large, it is surprising that so many Americans choose the "conformist" route. Conformity is not, in any case, deviance.

The mode of adaptation Merton called *innovation* involves accepting the goal of success but choosing to achieve it in an illegal, illegitimate, or deviant fashion. This adaptation is clearly the most interesting of all modes to Merton. He devoted more space to describing it than to all of the other modes combined. The innovative mode of adaptation occurs when someone has "assimilated the cultural emphasis upon the goal without internalizing the institutional normal governing ways and means for its attainment" (1957: 141). An innovative mode of adaptation to the pressures of American culture and society would encompass most types of money-making criminal activities, for example, white-collar crime, embezzlement, pickpocketing, running a confidence game, bank robbery, burglary, prostitution, and pimping.

The *ritualist,* in Merton's scheme, has abandoned lofty success goals but "continues to abide almost compulsively by institutional norms" (1957: 150). The ritualist plays it safe, plays things by the book, doesn't take chances. The mode of ritualism as an adaptation to American society's heavy emphasis on success is a kind of *partial* withdrawal—an abandonment of the goal of success, but a retention of the *form* of doing things properly, following all the rules to the letter. In many ways, ritualism is a kind of *overconformity.* "It is, in short, the mode of adaptation of individually seeking a *private* escape from the dangers and frustrations which seem to the inherent in the competition for major goals and clinging all the more closely to the safe routines and the institutional norms" (1957: 151). A petty bureaucrat, who insists that all rules and regulations be followed in every detail, would exemplify this mode of adaptation.

Retreatism, a rejection of both goals and

institutionalized means, is a *total* cop out. It is a "retreat" from the things that society values most. These people are "true aliens." "Not sharing the common frame of values, they can be included as members of the *society* (in distinction from the *population*) only in a fictional sense." In this category Merton places "some of the adaptive activities of psychotics, autists, pariahs, outcasts, vagrants, vagabonds, tramps, chronic drunkards and drug addicts" (1957: 153). This mode occurs, with most who adopt it, because the individual values the success goal, but cannot attain it, being either unwilling to use illegitimate means or a failure even after attempting to achieve success by using illegitimate means. Retreatism, then, is brought on by repeated failure, such failure causing severe personal conflict. "The conflict is resolved by abandoning *both* precipitating elements, the goals and the means. The escape is complete, the conflict is eliminated, and the individual is asocialized" (1957: 153–154). Merton feels that this mode of adaptation is the least frequent of the four discussed so far.

Rebellion "involves a genuine transvaluation." It is an attempt to deal with the dominant goals and means by overthrowing them altogether. While the retreatist merely rejects them and puts nothing in their place, the rebel renounces prevailing values and introduces an alternative social, political, and economic structure, one in which the current stresses and strains presumably would not exist. The act of revolution would be a clear-cut instance of rebellion. Merton devotes the least attention to this mode.

Although the anomie theory of Robert K. Merton exerted an enormous impact on the field of the sociology of deviance for decades after its initial publication in 1938, there are very few, if any, studies being conducted today that are significantly influenced by this perspective. This is true for a number of reasons.

Middle-class bias. Anomie theory suffers from the same middle-class bias that distorted all earlier theories of deviance: it made the assumption that lower- and working-class people commit acts of crime and deviance significantly more frequently than do members of the middle class. Today, most observers readily admit that violent "street" crimes are committed more often by individuals at the bottom of the class structure than is true of those at the top. Yet—and here is where the problem enters—there are many criminal and deviant activities engaged in by the more affluent, prestigious, well-educated, and powerful members of society. Although official police statistics on who commits crimes show that crime is a predominantly lower-class phenomenon, it is now clear that the specific crimes that middle-class people commit are those that are far less likely to result in official police attention than are the ones that lower- and working-class individuals commit.

Irrelevance of anomie for most forms of deviance. Although the malintegration between means and goals that characterizes contemporary American society will typically put pressure on certain members to engage in certain forms of deviance, *most forms of deviant behavior will not be produced by the pressure of such malintegration*. Thus, Merton's theory is not an "explanation" of deviant behavior at all, but a delineation of some of the possible outcomes of a certain kind of social and economic strain. But the anomie scheme turns out to be largely irrelevant to *most* forms of deviant behavior. Activities such as nonaddicting recreational drug use, assault, criminal homicide, petty gambling, homosexuality, adultery, child molestation, holding deviant beliefs, and so on *are completely unexplained by the anomie scheme.*

Can the primary locus of the origin of mental illness truly be placed at the feet of frustrated success strivings? Did the "alternate life-styles" and counterculture movements really arise out of the need to escape the rat race? Or did its adherents simply find it a more viable and comfortable way of living? Did the bohemian of the 1920s, the "beat" of the 1950s, the hippie of the 1960s arise out of an "adaptive response" to the disjunction between the goals and means dictated by American society? Is financial disaster behind the alcohol consumption and destructive behavior of most alcoholics? Does the delinquent fit into the means-ends scheme at all? These questions emphasize that there are serious problems with all the forms of deviance claimed by Merton to fit into the anomie paradigm[2]—*with the exception of innovation*. It seems almost intuitively apparent that when a heavy emphasis is placed on a goal, and less attention is paid to just how one achieves that goal, a lot of people are going to figure out a not quite approved technique of achieving it rather than resort to a thoroughly approved technique that doesn't work.

Deviance: normative violation or social disapproval? Closely related to the point made about most varieties of deviant behavior is the problem that much behavior that is classified as deviance by the anomie scheme—in all modes, not simply retreatism—*is not really deviance at all.* Because if only a minor stress is placed on how one reaches the major goals in a society, then one will not be condemned for employing "illegitimate" means. To the extent that one's choice of the means to attain a given goal is irrelevant or morally neutral, employing those means is not a form of deviant behavior. To the extent that choosing certain means to attain a given goal (for instance, cheating on an exam to receive an "A" in a course) is mildly disapproved of, it is an act representing only a mild form of deviance. Merton defines deviance as the violation of institutionalized expectations. But he is really discussing a situation where formally enunciated rules exist ("don't cheat on exams"), the institutionalization of which has partly or completely broken down on the private level. If cheating does not bring down denunciation or punishment upon the head of the cheater,

then it is no longer a form of deviant behavior, regardless of what the formal rules state.

In the generation or two following its initial publication, anomie theory was criticized, extended, added to, and amended. Perhaps the two most well-known additions to Merton's anomie theory have been Cohen's status frustration and Cloward and Ohlin's illegitimate opportunities theories. Both focus more or less exclusively on juvenile delinquency.

Albert Cohen: Status Frustration

Albert Cohen (1955) agrees with Merton and argues that American society indiscriminately measures members of all social classes according to middle-class criteria. And, like Merton, Cohen argues that individuals at the bottom of the class structure are less likely to be successful according to these criteria; they will, therefore, experience pressure. For Merton, however, *material success* is the main focus of middle-class values; when Americans fail to achieve material and monetary success, they feel strain. For Cohen, in contrast, the failure to achieve *status* is the main source of strain for many individuals located in the lower and working classes.

Why are members of the lower and working classes most subject to strain? Although they are under the same pressure to succeed as the middle and upper classes, they are less equipped and less well connected to be able to do so. The cards are stacked against the lower-class boy, Cohen argues. The status system (that prevails in the school system, for example) is totally dominated by middle-class figures and middle-class values. The lower-class boy grows up in a middle-class society and is judged by a "middle-class measuring rod." Middle-class values include academic achievement, rationality, the control of physical aggression and violence, delaying gratification, wholesomeness, a respect for property, and displaying manners and courtesy toward others. In contrast, the lower-class masculine culture cultivates irrationality, impulsiveness, a display of physical aggression and violence, and carelessness with property. How can the lower-class boy possi-

[2]At one point, Merton claims that anomie theory "is designed to account for some, not all, forms of deviant behavior, customarily described as criminal or delinquent" (1957: 178). Yet in other places (1957: 134, 146), Merton makes a case for anomie being the major cause of deviance in general. In other words, Merton "is vague as to which behavior is covered by this explanation and which is not" (Clinard, 1964: 19).

bly achieve status in a society in which everything he has learned is disvalued, and the opposite of what he has learned is specifically what generates status? It is a system in which lower-class boys are doomed to failure.

As a consequence of ending up at "the bottom of the heap," the lower-class boy faces a status problem: how to achieve dignity, respect, and status in such a ranking system. According to Cohen, the answer is to overturn the dominant, middle-class status system by regarding as good that which is disvalued and regarding as bad that which middle-class society values. Everything is turned on its head. Since lower-class boys are "denied status in the respectable society because they cannot meet the criteria of the respectable status system," they value status criteria that they *can* meet (Cohen, 1955: 121). This entails giving free reign to violence and aggression, destroying property, gratifying their hedonistic impulses, failing in school—and being proud of it—being nasty and impolite to others, especially middle-class authority figures. In Cohen's scheme, *the delinquent gang is a solution to the lower-class boy's problem of status frustration*. It is a way of substituting a new value system for the traditional middle-class one—a value system that has criteria on which the lower-class boy can now achieve status.

There are at least three major differences between Merton's original anomie theory and Cohen's addition to it. One, as I said above, Merton stresses the achievement of material success, while Cohen stresses the achievement of status.

Two, Merton's most important adaptation to the stress of anomie, innovation, is *utilitarian* in nature; that is, the lack of material success is the problem, and Merton's innovators go out and achieve material success in a rational, pragmatic fashion, albeit unconventionally. In contrast, Cohen stresses a *nonutilitarian* adaptation to status frustration—destroying property, failing in school, fighting, and so on. To Cohen, the stealing that the lower-class boy engages in is not a utilitarian attempt to acquire material goods, because, he believes, the boy is casual with

those goods, often destroying or discarding them soon after they are acquired.

The third difference between Cohen's status frustration and Merton's anomie is that Merton's scheme is atomistic or *individualistic;* in contrast, Cohen's theory is tightly focused on how solutions to the problem of status frustration are hammered out in a group of interactional setting. For Merton, people work out adaptations to anomie more or less in isolation. He does not supply any group or interactional mechanism for working out solutions to the problem of blocked success strivings. For Cohen, it is only by experiencing status problems *in the presence of others who share the same problems* that these solutions are arrived at.

Although Cohen's status frustration theory is regarded as interesting and elegant and is often cited in the delinquency literature, few researchers nowadays take it seriously as an explanation of the origin of the delinquent subculture. There are at least two major problems with the theory.

First, it is clear that lower-class boys are not so totally wrapped up in the middle-class value system that they feel themselves to be failures as measured by it. While material success is a widely shared American value and is strongly held at the bottom of the class system, few of the other accompaniments of middle-class culture discussed by Cohen are of much concern to the lower-class boy. Cohen has clearly overestimated the power of middle-class culture on the values of the lower-class boy. Walter Miller's theory of the lower-class subculture, to be discussed shortly, which posits a certain independence between lower- and middle-class cultures, seems more accurate on this point.

The second serious, indeed, fatal flaw in Cohen's theory is that it fails completely in delineating lower-class delinquent culture as materially nonutilitarian, malicious, and destructive. It is possible that Cohen's portrait was true in past generations. Today, however, lower-class delinquent boys, if anything, are even more materialistic than members of the middle class. They steal (and today, sell drugs) specifically to acquire material goods—expensive sneakers and clothes, 10-speed bikes, even cars, gold chains, watches and other jewelry, and electronic gadgets. Far from destroying or discarding them, they value them no less than the middle-class individual. Their orientation is clearly highly utilitarian and super-materialistic. The lower-class boy embraces and adapts some middle-class values, while he simultaneously discards others. There is anything but a wholesale rejection of middle-class values in the lower-class delinquent subculture. In short, Cohen's theory of status frustration seems not to explain or characterize delinquency very well.

Cloward and Ohlin: Illegitimate Opportunities

A second major extension of Merton's anomie theory may be found in Richard Cloward and Lloyd Ohlin's *illegitimate opportunity* scheme (Cloward, 1959; Cloward and Ohlin, 1960). Cloward and Ohlin agree with Merton in insisting that the lower and working classes have been encouraged to strive for material success; they agree that they are more likely than the middle classes to find this goal blocked and frustrated, to have far more restricted access to legitimate opportunities for success, and to feel more strain because of it; and they agree that these strains and pressures produce more deviant behavior, at least of the innovative type, on the part of lower- and working-class occupants. So far, their respective theories are much the same. Where Cloward and Ohlin depart from Merton is in insisting that, while *legitimate* opportunities for success are more accessible to the middle classes, *illegitimate* opportunities are *not* equally accessible to all lower- and working-class individuals. Merton simply assumes that all lower- and working-class individuals have equal opportunities to engage in illegal, illegitimate, criminal, and deviant activities. You want to rob a bank? Just go out and do it! Prostitution, pimping? No problem—just find your customers!

As Cloward and Ohlin point out, it is not easy to engage in illegal, illegitimate, crimi-nal, and deviant activities, especially innovative ones. In fact, opportunities to do so are differentially distributed; they are abundant in some neighborhoods and scarce in others. Some slums are what Cloward and Ohlin called "integrated"; that is, adult professional gangsters and criminals live and operate there and are visible community figures. The talented, daring, ambitious youth living in such a neighborhood will be recruited from a delinquent gang that specializes in money-making crime, eventually to graduate to full-time, full-fledged careers in theft and other professional crime. Youths living in neighborhoods that lack such figures, or who have little talent for crime, will perceive themselves as failures in the illegitimate opportunity structure. They cannot "make it" as a criminal. For those who do make it, who graduate from criminally oriented delinquent gangs to professional thievery, the institutionalized goal, material success, is retained, but it is acquired illegitimately. This is, of course, Merton's innovative adaptation. Lacking such illegitimate opportunities, this adaptation is far more difficult to devise on one's own; and hence, success-striving will, in all likelihood, remain unfulfilled.

In slums where networks of gangsters, racketeers, and other professional criminals are lacking, youths who feel strain to achieve have no real illegitimate opportunity structure to satisfy that need. So, a second type of subculture or gang that may serve to satisfy success strivings is the *conflict* gang. Again, such subcultures are differentially available to lower-class youngsters. The lower-class youngster whose aspirations are blocked both by the legitimate and illegitimate achievement structures may have the opportunity to achieve status through violence in gang warfare. The lower-class youngster who lives in a neighborhood where such gangs do not exist, or who cannot meet the requirements of violent activities, will be defined as a failure. Again, illegitimate opportunities to achieve are not available to all. Violence can be an answer to some youngsters' otherwise blocked achievement aspirations; but for others, this is not an available option, owing to the lack of illegitimate opportunities in certain neighborhoods.

Youngsters who have failed to make it in the legitimate, law-abiding world, in the crime- and conflict-oriented illegitimate world, turn to drugs. A third subculture or type of gang that may provide a solution for blocked aspirations is, according to Cloward and Ohlin, the so-called *retreatist* gang. The retreatist subculture is a drug-using gang; they "retreat" into the dreamy, undemanding endeavor of getting high. Retreatists are double failures because of their failure in the legitimate and the illegitimate opportunity structures. There is nothing left for them to do but to get high. Their aspirations are totally blocked. Using drugs in a gang setting provides an escape for them, a way of relieving the strain they feel for their across-the-board, catastrophic failure.

Like Cohen's theory, Cloward and Ohlin's is more noteworthy for its theoretical innovations and conceptual elegance than for its empirical support. In fact, the evidence to verify the illegitimate opportunity structure explanation for delinquency has been found to be more or less totally lacking. The theory predicts that blocked economic aspirations are the source of delinquent behavior, but nearly all studies on the subject have found that juvenile delinquents tend to have significantly *lower* aspirations than nondelinquents—the opposite of what Cloward and Ohlin predict. In addition, although many lower-class youths do, indeed, have relatively high aspirations, nearly as high as middle-class youths, most make a distinction between aspirations and realistic expectations—that is, anticipated success, what they expect to achieve monetarily and occupationally. Cloward and Ohlin (as well as Merton and Cohen) assume that youths' aspirations are what determine their involvement in illegitimate activities. In fact, what we see is that having realistic material expectations inhibits the kind of felt strain that these theorists predicted would result in criminal activity. Moreover, the *discrepancy* between aspiration and expectation seems to be roughly the same for delinquents and nondelinquents.

Another problem with Cloward and Ohlin's theory is that it mistakenly assumes delinquent gangs are specialized as to activity—theft, violence, and drug use. In fact, this turns out to be a fantasy; gangs do not specialize as the theory predicts. Money-making crime, violence, *and* drug use are pervasive in most delinquent gangs.

Finally, the real measure of the value and validity of a theory is whether researchers use it in their work. Illegitimate opportunity theory is not cited among contemporary researchers, is not used in their work, and seems not to explain delinquent behavior to their satisfaction. Like Cohen's status frustration theory, Cloward and Ohlin's theory of illegitimate opportunities is cited for historical reasons, not as a valid current explanation for delinquent behavior.

DIFFERENTIAL ASSOCIATION

In 1939, in the third edition of a criminology textbook written by sociologist Edwin Sutherland (1883–1950), a major theory of deviance and crime was propounded for the first time (Sutherland, 1939). It was called the theory of *differential association,* and it has become one of a small number of important perspectives in the field.

The first and most fundamental proposition of the theory of differential association states that criminal behavior, and by extension, deviance as well, is *learned.* This proposition is directed against biological theories, which assert that crime is caused by genetic, metabolic, or anatomical defects, and against the view that criminal activities are hit upon accidentally or through independent invention. No one simply stumbles upon or dreams up a way to break the law, according to Sutherland; this must be passed on from one person to another in a genuine learning process. The theory of differential association also opposes the view that mental illness or an abnormal, pathological personality is a major causal factor in the commission of criminal behavior. Rather, Sutherland argues that crime is learned in a straightforward, essentially normal fashion, no different from the way in which members of American society learn to speak English or brush their teeth.

A second proposition of the theory of differential association is that criminal behavior, and, by extension, deviance as well, must be learned through face-to-face interaction between people who are close with one another. People are not persuaded to engage in criminal behavior as a result of reading a book or a newspaper, seeing a movie, or watching television. Criminal knowledge, skills, sentiments, values, traditions, and motives are all passed down as a result of interpersonal—not impersonal—means. Two major factors that intensify this process are *priority* and *intensity*. The earlier in one's life one is exposed to attitudes and values (which Sutherland called "definitions") favorable to committing crimes, the more influenced in that direction one will be. And the closer and more intimate the friends, relatives, and acquaintances that endorse committing crimes, likewise, the more swayed one will be to break the law.

Sutherland's theory, then, argued that people who embark upon engaging in criminal behavior *differentially associate* with individuals who, through word or deed, endorse violations of the law. Notice that the theory does not say that one needs to associate with actual criminals to end up breaking the law oneself—only that one is more heavily exposed to *definitions* favorable to criminal actions. One can be exposed to law-abiding definitions emanating from criminals and criminal definitions emanating from law-abiding individuals (though, of course, it usually works the other way around).

In sum, Sutherland's theory of differential association holds that a person becomes delinquent or criminal because of an excess of definitions favorable to the violation of the law over definitions unfavorable to the violation of the law. The key to this process is the *ratio* between definitions favorable to the violation of the law to definitions that are unfavorable. When favorable definitions *exceed* unfavorable ones, an individual will turn to crime (Conklin, 1981: 255).

The theory of differential association has been criticized for being vague and untest-

able (Gibbons, 1977: 224; Conklin, 1981: 256–257; Sutherland and Cressey, 1978: 91). Later efforts to refine and operationalize the theory (Burgess and Akers, 1966; DeFleur and Quinney, 1966) were not successful in rescuing it from imprecision. Exactly how would a researcher measure this ratio of favorable to unfavorable definitions of violations of the law? And exactly how could "favorable" and "unfavorable" be indicated or measured? Even one of the staunchest defenders of the theory admits that Sutherland's formulation of the differential association process "is not precise enough to stimulate rigorous empirical test" (Cressey, 1960: 57).

A great deal of research and anecdotal evidence demonstrates that much crime is, indeed, learned interpersonally. However, it seems at least as overly ambitious to assume that all criminal behavior is learned as it is to assume that all noncriminal behavior is learned. Many actions, criminal and noncriminal alike, are invented anew by individuals in similar situations. For instance, adolescents need not learn how to masturbate from other adolescents; many discover the activity as a result of exploring their own bodies. All behavior is not learned, at least not directly. Much of it, deviant or otherwise, may be devised in relative isolation. There is a great deal of independent invention of certain forms of deviance and crime. The human mind is, after all, almost infinitely creative. The idea to do something, and its eventual enactment, almost certainly had a cultural or learning foundation, but it was not necessarily directly learned in detail. One can, by oneself, "put the pieces together."

Moreover, many criminal activities do not fit the differential association learning model: check forgery (Lemert, 1953, 1958, 1972: 150–182), embezzlement (Cressey, 1953), child molestation (McCaghy, 1967, 1968), wartime black market violations (Clinard, 1952), as well as certain crimes of passion (killing a spouse and/or his or her lover) and crimes involving psychiatric compulsion (such as kleptomania). In addition, it should be emphasized that some forms of deviance and crime are not approved of by a majority of the people who engage in them (such as alcoholism, drug addiction, mental illness, child molestation) and, consequently, could not be learned in anything like the fashion that Sutherland suggests, that is, by being exposed to definitions favorable to engaging in these forms of behavior. While it is true that much criminal and deviant behavior is learned, much of it is not. As a partial theory, differential association is valuable; as a complete theory, it is clearly overly ambitious. Rather than being a theory of explaining all crime, delinquency, and deviance, differential association, instead, should be regarded as a concept that helps us to understand a particular process that some rule breakers go through and some do not. Learning, for example, is not *the* cause behind why some people become prostitutes or homosexuals. Rather, *in becoming* a prostitute or a homosexual, one is typically involved in a learning process. Seen in this more limited light, differential association offers insight into the dynamics of deviant and criminal behavior.

Sutherland's theory of differential association has been revamped by contemporary theorists and cast into a behaviorist or social learning framework (Burgess and Akers, 1966; Akers, 1985: 40–52). This perspective attempts to explain the deviance learning process in terms of *operant conditioning*. That is, people are rewarded or are reinforced for certain behavior by others and are punished for engaging in different behavior; people will learn deviant behavior to the extent that reinforcement takes place for engaging in it in groups that value deviance. This contemporary version of Sutherland's theory is more sophisticated than the original and incorporates some of the variables and processes discussed in the next chapter into the theory. However, social learning or behaviorist theory has been attacked for ignoring social, structural and economic factors, for being unable to explain why certain things are rewarding or reinforcing to some people and not to others, and for not being a real explanation but a *tautology*, or a statement that is simply true by definition but cannot be proven empirically. While learning is a major aspect of all sociological theories or perspectives toward deviance, behaviorism as a total theory does not have a large following among sociologists of deviance.

The idea that crime, delinquency, and deviant behavior can be learned in a direct, straightforward fashion in certain social groups or circles has been explored and elaborated by a number of researchers. One extension of Sutherland's theory of differential association is the "culture transmission" paradigm set forth by the anthropologist Walter Miller (1958). Miller argues that at least one form of deviance—gang delinquency—is a direct by-product of lower-class culture. "The lower class way of life," Miller writes, "is characterized by a set of focal concerns—areas or issues which command widespread and persistent attention and a high degree of emotional involvement" (1958: 6). These "focal concerns" are trouble, toughness, smartness, excitement, fate, and autonomy. Each concern pressures young lower-class males into direct conflict with the law and with agents of law enforcement. For instance, an emphasis on toughness often leads to a desire to demonstrate one's masculinity by engaging in fights, assaultive behavior, and belligerent confrontations with the police. A desire for thrills, fast-paced excitement, and danger make "hanging out," gambling, fighting, bar hopping, and heavy drinking particularly appealing. Miller argues that simply by being a member of a lower class and participating member of its culture, one "automatically violates certain legal norms" (1958: 18). One is expected to break the law in many situations (which would call for law-abiding behavior for middle-class members of society). Lower-class culture, Miller writes, "is a distinctive tradition many centuries old with an integrity of its own"—and that tradition includes the routine violation of the criminal law (1958: 19). Miller's argument is that lower-class adolescents "get into trouble because they remain faithful to cultural standards learned from their parents" (Empey, 1982: 199).

A number of critics have questioned Miller's analysis. As we'll see in more detail a bit later on, some researchers find that self-reported delinquent behavior does not vary significantly by social class at all. Many observers argue that lower- and working-class adolescents are no more likely to engage in illegal, and delinquent acts than are middle-class youths (Akers, 1964; Voss, 1966; Empey and Erikson, 1966; Tittle et al., 1978). One sociologist believes the view that the lower and working classes are more likely to commit crime than members of the middle class is an aspect of "popular wisdom," a view that "has existed for many years," probably based on the fact that lots of people "avoid slum areas after dark" (Conklin, 1981: 139).

The studies that show no differences between the classes in this regard are self-report studies; that is, they are based on asking people if they have engaged in certain kinds of behavior. And although self-report studies on deviant and criminal behavior are generally fairly valid and reliable, researchers must know how to interpret their findings. In the studies that show no differences in delinquent behavior between socioeconomic strata, the problem is that they did not distinguish between *degree of seriousness* of delinquent acts, as well as their *frequency of commission* (O'Brien, 1985: 63–79). While middle-class youths probably have no higher rates of *trivial* acts of delinquency, lower- and working-class adolescents *do* have significantly higher rates of *more serious* delinquent acts, and they tend to engage more frequently in those acts they do commit (Elliott and Ageton, 1980). The "no difference" hypothesis seems not to hold up after all, and people avoid slum areas for a very good reason (slum dwellers would, too, if they could): Crime, especially predatory crime, is more likely to take place there. (We'll have more on the no difference hypothesis shortly.) Thus, Miller's hypothesis that delinquent and criminal behavior are more common in the lower and working classes—indeed, that these social classes are a "generating milieu" for such behavior—probably does have some basis in fact. The

argument that lower- and working-class males are no more delinquent than those from the middle classes is clearly based on a serious methodological fallacy.

However, even if lower-class adolescent delinquent and criminal behaviors were more prevalent and frequent than were those of the middle class, this still would not explain why a fairly low proportion of lower- and working-class boys are involved in serious violations of the law. Miller's theory, in short, overexplains: If we were to follow out its implications strictly, we would predict that all lower-class adolescents would be delinquent, a clearly false assertion. Moreover, some argue, the supposed "focal concerns" that Miller claims characterize lower-class culture seem to be just as much a feature of middle-class attitudes and values (Valentine, 1968: 135–138; Hirschi, 1969: 212 ff.). Many observers do not find Miller's "culture transmission" theory entirely convincing. On the other hand, Miller does a service to the field by emphasizing the importance of learning, and that of social class, in the commission of delinquent, criminal, and deviant behavior.

CONTROL THEORY

Control theory is a major theory in the fields of deviant behavior and criminology; however, it is used almost exclusively in the study of delinquency (Nye, 1958; Hirschi, 1969; Wiatrowski et al., 1981; Agnew, 1985). While most theories ask, Why do they do it?—that is, what process *encourages* deviant behavior—control theory turns the question around and asks, Why *don't* they do it? In other words, control theory assumes that we all are encouraged to break the rules, that deviance-making processes are strong, obvious, and almost commonsensical. This theory does not see a departure from the norms as problematic and takes for granted the allure of deviance and crime. What has to be explained, control theorists argue, is why most people *don't* engage in deviance, why they don't engage in delinquent behavior, why they don't break the law and engage in a life of crime. What causes deviant behavior is the absence of the social control that causes conformity. Most of us do not engage in deviant or criminal acts because of strong bonds with or ties to conventional, mainstream social institutions. If these bonds are weak or broken, we will be released from society's rules and will be free to deviate. It is not so much deviants' ties to an unconventional group or subculture that attracts them to deviant behavior, but their lack of ties with the conforming, mainstream culture, which frees them to engage in deviance.

Of course, delinquency, deviance, and criminal behavior are matters of degree. Nearly all of us engage in some deviant and criminal acts at least once during our lives. Control theory does not state that individuals with strong ties to conventional society will *never* engage in *any* deviant or criminal action, regardless of how mildly unconventional it is. It does, however, assert that both deviance and control are matters of degree: The more attached we are to conventional society, the lower the likelihood of engaging in behavior that violates its values and norms. A strong bond to conventionality does not absolutely insulate us from mildly deviant behavior, but it does make it less likely.

Control theory has four basic components: *attachment, commitment, involvement,* and *belief.* The more *attached* we are to conventional others—parents, teachers, clergy, employers, and so on; the more *committed* we are to conventional institutions—family, school, religion, work; the more *involved* we are in conventional activities—familial, educational, religious, occupational; and the more deeply we *believe* in the norms of conventional institutions—family, school, religion, and occupation—the less likely it is that we will violate society's norms and engage in deviant behavior. Deviance is "contained" by bonds with or attachments to conventional people, institutions, activities, and beliefs. The stronger these bonds or attachments, the more conventional and conformist one's behavior. If they are strong, deviance and crime are unlikely.

TWENTIETH-CENTURY POSITIVISM: CAUSAL ANALYSIS

The last perspective to be discussed is not generally regarded as a theory by most observers of, or commentators on, theories of deviance and crime (Liska, 1981; Davis, 1980; Clinard and Meier, 1985; Traub and Little, 1985; Douglas and Waksler, 1982; Farrell and Swigert, 1988). Indeed, in the sense of containing specific substantive propositions gathered around a coherent, integrated explanation, positivism is not, strictly speaking, a theory at all. Instead, positivism must be looked upon as an orientation, a perspective, similar in that respect to the other sociological orientations and perspectives discussed here and in Chapter 4.

As we saw, in nineteenth-century criminology, the term "positivism" (synonymous with "the positive school") referred to the perspective that held that the major cause of criminal behavior was biological pathology. The term usually refers to Lombroso and his followers. Nowadays, biological pathology has not disappeared as an explanation factor, in the study of deviant and criminal behavior (Wilson and Herrnstein, 1985: 69–103, and *passim*), but it plays a much-reduced role compared with a century ago. Thus, we must always keep the distinction between what was called positivism in criminology in the nineteenth century, which had a very narrow focus, and what is referred to as positivism today, which is a far broader orientation.

What is positivism? *It is the application of the strict scientific method in the study of human behavior.* The practitioners of positivism maintain that sociology and criminology are not essentially different from the natural sciences, such as biology and physics. They believe that deviance and crime can be studied in basically the same way that natural phenomena, like stars, chemicals, and ocean tides can be studied (making the necessary adjustments in research methods for subject matter, naturally). The scientific method can be applied equally to social and to natural phenomena.

The positivistic approach in the study of social reality generally, and deviance and crime specifically, is based on the following assumptions or axioms:

1. The sociologist can—and must—be objective in the study of the social world, as well as in the study of deviance and crime.
2. Social phenomena, generally, and crime and deviance, specifically, are *objectively real.*
3. Phenomena and events in the social world, generally, and in the world of deviance and crime, are *determined,* that is, linked together in a specific *cause-and-effect* fashion.
4. The ultimate goal of all scientific endeavors is *explanation.*

Positivistically inclined sociologists believe that they can be just as objective in the study of the social world as the physicist is in studying the natural world. By employing the scientific method, the social scientist can transcend the problems of bias and subjectivity and view the world as it really and truly is. Science, the positivist says, has little or nothing to do with questions of ideology or politics (though the social scientist can *study* questions of ideology and politics—objectively, of course). They exist in totally separate realms. Putting aside ideological and political considerations is a necessary component in scientific objectivity. One must follow the famous saying of the late eighteenth- and early nineteenth-century French diplomat Talleyrand, who said, "I do not say it is good, I do not say it is bad, I say it is the way it is."

Saying that deviance and crime are objectively real means that they possess specific objective characteristics that clearly distinguish them from conventional, conforming, law-abiding behavior. In other words, all of the many forms of deviant behavior *share a common thread,* a *differentiating trait,* that distinguishes them from conventional, conforming behavior. At the very least, *each specific type* of deviance or crime (such as homosexuality, robbery, drug use, mental illness, or homicide) shares key characteristics in common. It is the scientist who deter-

mines what is deviance or crime, and what each specific type is, by observing the behavior in question and classifying it appropriately according to its objective characteristics. The characteristics of deviant and criminal behavior *are contained within the actions themselves.* It is their possession of certain observable properties that makes them deviant or criminal in nature. Positivists argue that behavior is not deviant or criminal simply because it is labeled as such. Rather, they assert, deviant and criminal behavior is objectively real just as stars and water and frogs are objectively real; the reality of specific forms of deviance, likewise, exists independent of the labeling process.

The third axiom of positivism is its adherence to strict *causality* or *determinism.* This means that things in the real world happen in a cause-and-effect fashion. Things do not happen accidentally or randomly; things are the way they are because of specific forces or factors acting in a predictable, almost mechanical fashion. Factor A causes or has an effect on B. The positivist argues that social factors or variables are related to one another in the same causal fashion as in the physical realm. If you deprive a tree of light and water, it will die; if you reward a rat with food for pressing a bar, it will continue to press that bar; if you mix certain chemicals, an explosion will occur. Likewise, the same cause-and-effect sequence is said to take place in the social world. Urbanization increases the crime rate; strong ties to conventional others decrease rates of deviance; anonymity increases the likelihood of committing crimes. Conditions such as these cause specific forms of behavior. It is the scientist's job to locate the cause-and-effect chains that exist in the world. People's behavior, to the positivist, is caused by conditions and factors. In fact, a key building block of the positivist approach to human behavior is that human behavior is determined, to some extent, *by forces beyond our control* (Vold and Bernard, 1986: 45).

The ultimate goal of all scientific endeavors is *explanation.* Why is the world the way it is? What caused it to be so? More specifically, in the sphere of deviance and crime, the positivist searches out causes for the commission and incidence of deviant and criminal behavior. Why do certain individuals, or certain categories of individuals, violate the norms and break the laws? Why do they engage in certain forms of criminal and deviant behavior? What are the causes of rape, murder, alcoholism, mental illness, robbery, homosexuality, prostitution, white-collar crime, and so on? The positivist is principally interested in *why one person, or one category of persons, commits deviant and criminal acts while another does not.* According to the positivist, the avenue to discovering the cause or causes of deviant behavior, or specific forms of it, is by isolating the key factors that deviants share in common. All deviants, they say—or at least, all deviants of a certain type—share a specific trait or set of traits that sets them apart from people who do not violate the norms or break the law. Even if a single trait cannot be found that all deviants share, certain traits will be found that are *more common* among deviants than among nondeviants. It is these traits, factors, variables that cause the commission of deviant behavior. Isolate them, the positivistically inclined social scientist believes, and we will have explained the behavior in question.

Even though positivism cannot be termed a theory, several propositions can be teased out of the work of sociologists who adopt this orientation (Gibbs and Erickson, 1975; Gove, 1980, 1982a, 1985; Nettler, 1984; Gibbs, 1981; Stark, 1987: 166–223). These propositions sound very much like the commonsensical maxim, "Cream rises to the top," or, since we are examining deviant behavior, "Mud falls to the bottom." To put things simply, positivisim says *people get pretty much what they deserve.* Another way of saying this is *the relationship between action and reaction is rational and nonproblematic.*

What does this mean? Two things.

First, norms and laws represent a rational attempt to protect society from the harm that deviants and criminals can do. Rules, norms, and laws, therefore, do not vary much from society to society; we can examine criminals and deviants to discover cross-

cultural, transsocietal, and international regularities among them. The positivist rejects the central place that relativity has in labeling theory's approach. Deviance and crime are not relative, the positivist says, or at least not nearly so relative as the interactionists claim (Newman, 1976). The observed similarities from society to society indicate that there are strong commonalities in the norms and laws societies devise to protect their members from the objective harm deviants and criminals can do. Norms and laws are *taken for granted* to the positivist. To put it another way, the creation of norms and laws is neither interesting nor worthy of study to the positivist; the norms and laws that exist, positivists believe, are there for some very commonsensical and obvious reasons. Why study this process when we already know what the answers are? If the positivist were to be asked, Why study crime? chances are he or she would answer more or less as follows: I study crime not simply because it distresses people, but also because it hurts people, tears at the social fabric, and damages society in a clearly observable, objectively determinable fashion. As a general rule, crime does not distress people aribitrarily or irrationally; rather, people tend to be concerned about crime because of the objective damage it does to them, to their loved ones, and to society.

The second proposition that can be found in the positivist's approach to the study of deviance and crime takes the process a step further. Not only are norms and laws rational and their enactment nonproblematic, but, likewise, the *enforcement* of norms and laws is rational and nonproblematic. In other words, people are evaluated on the basis of what they do. Contingencies, positivists hold, are not an important source of labeling or stigma. Deviants and criminals are labeled because they violate the norms and laws of a society, not because of certain ancillary characteristics they might have. In short, the only really important question in this field is: Why do they do it?

For instance, many interactionist theorists have been concerned with the process whereby some mentally disordered individuals are regarded by the public and by psychiatrists as mentally ill, while others, equally as disordered, are not. In short, interactionists study the *contingencies* involved in being labeled mentally ill (Goffman, 1961: 135, passim; Scheff, 1966, 1974, 1984; Lemert, 1951: 387–443; 1972: 246–264). In contrast, the positivists claim that the psychiatric diagnostic process is fairly accurate and that individuals diagnosed as mentally ill, objectively speaking, actually are. The role of contingencies in the diagnostic process is insignificant. What counts is how crazy someone actually is (Gove, 1980, 1982). In short: "Some people are more crazy than others; we can tell the difference; and calling lunacy a name does not cause it" (Nettler, 1974: 894).[3]

CRITICISMS OF POSITIVISM

The positivistic perspective in the study of deviance and crime, as with all other perspectives, has sustained criticism from adherents of other theories. First, the objective approach adopted by the traditional social sciences, its critics say, ignores the crucial dimension of the *subjective experience* (Blumer, 1969: passim, esp. 2–6, 22–23, 37, 127–139; Matza, 1969: passim; Thio, 1988: 18–20; Goode, 1975: 571–576). The most important quality of all behavior, the antipositivists say, is its *meaning to the participants*. To study deviance primarily as objective behavior is to

concentrate on the superficial features of actions. Behavior becomes seen as mechanical movements and not actions that are meaningful in a certain way to all concerned.

To equate two actions that are similar outwardly and mechanically is to lose sight of the fact that they may be seen and reacted to in radically different ways; they may *mean* different things to the participants involved. *What something is,* say the subjectively oriented sociologists, is entirely dependent on how it is interpreted by the relevant audiences, including the actor. In short, "Meaning is not inherent in the act; it must be constructed" (Douglas and Waksler, 1982: 24). An act "is" nothing until it is categorized, conceptualized, and interpreted. It is the subjective process that creates the act as an example of a general type of behavior. In one society, incest is defined by sex with both close and very distant relatives, encompassing half the population of the society, village, or tribe in question. In another society, incest is committed only by having sex with a very small number of relatives, includings parents, siblings, grandparents, aunts and uncles by blood, and first cousins on only one parent's side. The same act may take place in each society, but one calls it incest and the other doesn't. In other words, we may know very little when we know the "objective" features of an act; to know it in a truly sociological fashion, critics of positivism say, we must know it subjectively as well.

A second objection that the more subjectively oriented theorist of deviance has to the positivistic study of the field is a high degree of *skepticism toward determinism*. The notion of causality is extremely complex in human behavior and may, some say, not be valid at all. To say that one thing caused or causes another cannot be determined with any degree of precision. In the case of an automobile accident, for example, is the cause the fact that the driver was intoxicated, that the road was slick from a sudden downpour, the fact the driver swerved to avoid hitting a child on a bicycle who came shooting out of a side street, a recent feeling of depression in the driver's life, the fact that the driver was going over the speed limit, or the fact

[3]A strong parallel can be seen between the positivist's position on deviance and crime—that people get pretty much what they deserve—and the functionalist's position on stratification. Functionalists argue that rewards, such as prestige and income, are given to occupants of "functionally important" jobs, that is, that contribute most to society's "functioning." In other words, in stratification, the deserving are rewarded and those who are not deserving are accorded little prestige and low pay (Davis and Moore, 1945; Davis, 1949; 366–368). To put it another way, the poor deserve their economic fate because they don't contribute much to society. Both the positivist view of deviance and punishment and the functionalist view of stratification conform to what psychologist Melvin Lerner (1980) calls the "just world hypothesis," which he dubs "a fundamental delusion": the belief that virtue is rewarded, evil is punished, and the fortunate deserve their good fortune; the unfortunate, likewise, deserve their misfortune.

that the driver was a beginner behind the wheel, having driven for less than six months? Are all these factors "a" cause? Or some combination of them? Unraveling the cause or causes of a fairly simple occurrence such as a single automobile accident is an extremely problematic and subjective question (Douglas and Waksler, 1982: 27–29). How much more difficult it is to do so for a general phenomenon, such as crime, homosexuality, or alcoholism, that is participated in by millions of actors and reacted to by even more observers. Some sociologists (Hirschi and Selvin, 1966, 1967: 114–136) argue that the complexity of the social world merely makes the job of tracing out causality in the social world difficult—but not impossible. However, some critics of the idea of causality in the study of deviance argue that this means that the researcher should be extremely skeptical of the whole idea of causality in the social world.

Third, positivists have been accused of being overly naive concerning the question of "objectivity." Many sociologists argue that true objectivity is an impossibility; every observer is to a degree contaminated by personal, political, and ideological sympathies. We cannot avoid taking sides, this position argues (Becker, 1967). Studying street crime automatically entails ignoring and implicitly deemphasizing the importance of white-collar crime. Studying a prison from the point of view of the convicts entails accepting their view of reality as true and setting aside the view of the guards and other correctional officials. Conducting research on the factors that lead to revolutions in South America may result in supplying information to repressive regimes that will be helpful to them in quelling those revolutions. Deciding to publish findings from a study that are technically true but might be damaging to certain oppressed groups or to the cause of justice always entails making a political choice—against the people and in favor of "science for its own sake." Choosing to publish damaging but true findings is no more "objective" than is choosing to suppress those findings. Deciding to work on atomic weaponry because one wishes to "advance

scientific knowledge" also automatically entails advancing the cause of the military.

One selects sociological issues to study on the basis of subjective criteria, not simply to advance knowledge in some abstract, pure scientific fashion. And choosing to study one topic instead of another, and in a certain way, always has political and ideological implications as well as consequences. One can never remove oneself form the question of ethics in doing social research.

One of the more revealing criticisms of positivism can be called the "wake up and smell the coffee" problem. Positivists typically insist they have a monopoly on empirical truth. They claim the social scientist is in a better position to know what's going on in the social world than the ordinary man and woman in the street. Social scientists have studied the world in a systematic, empirical fashion, and it is they who are the experts. Whom do you ask about the stars and the planets—an astronomer with a Ph.D. in the subject or someone you bump into on the street? Whom would you trust to do a brain operation on you—a brain surgeon or your roommate, who knows next to nothing on the subject? The answer is obvious, right? Well, positivists say, it's the same thing with the social world. It is the social scientists who have conducted the studies that tell them about the world we all live in. They devise indicators of concepts, measure variables, determine relationships, establish correlations, analyze data, determine causality, and, in the end, draw conclusions and come up with answers to important scientific questions. So, after conducting a scientific investigation, many researchers are convinced their conclusions are definitive, absolutely true, and without flaw. They become wedded to their findings—and no wonder, since they went to so much time, trouble, and cost to establish them in the first place. Often, social researchers lose sight of the fact that scientific findings are always tentative, always subject to error and revision.

Some studies conducted by scientifically inclined researchers have come up with counterintuitive findings—that is, those that contradict common sense—which actually turn out to be correct. After all, common sense is not an infallible guide to the real world; often, what many of us believe to be true is a myth, a fallacy. Systematic, reliable evidence is a more valid guide to the way things are than what "most people" believe to be true. Many introductory sociology textbooks present true-false quizzes that ask students questions on issues about which most people are misinformed. (For an example, see Goode, 1988: 10–11.) Here, sociological research presents accurate information that contradicts what most people—incorrectly—"know" to be true.

On the other hand, it occasionally happens that even carefully conducted scientific studies come up with conclusions that are wrong—obviously wrong in ways that can be clearly determined, wrong in ways that anyone using his or her senses systematically can determine. In other words, the researchers failed to "wake up and smell the coffee." They failed to walk outside their university offices and look around and see that the world doesn't work the way they claimed it does, the way their data told them it did. Here, we have an example of *vulgar empiricism*—that is, a simpleminded, ignorant faith in the specific findings from a specific study, while ignoring the richer, more valid data of our own senses. Vulgar empiricism is the fallacy of believing absolutely anything the data say, regardless of what one sees in the real world. Positivists may be especially prone to commit such a fallacy.

A good example of this "wake up and smell the coffee" fallacy is the claim made by certain positivistically inclined sociologists, which we mentioned briefly, that there is no relationship between social class and crime and delinquency. Now, certain crimes *are* more likely to be committed by members of the middle and upper classes—that is, white-collar or corporate crimes. However, this is not the point the no relationship researchers are making. Their claim is that there is no relationship between social class and street crime—the crimes most of us think of when we picture the usual sorts of crimes: burglary, theft, violence, vandalism, arson, robbery, auto theft, and so on. These researchers claim it is a "myth" that lower- and working-class individuals commit crimes more than middle- and upper-class individuals. There is, they say, only a "slight negative" correlation here; we should have "serious doubts" about the assumption of class differences in criminal behavior. Moreover, according to this line of thinking, the social classes are converging in their patterns of criminal behavior; that is, they are becoming more similar over time (Tittle and Villemez, 1977; Tittle, et al., 1978). This finding has spawned a virtual industry of writings on the subject, some agreeing with the no relationship conclusion (Hindelang et al., 1979, 1981; Stark, 1987: 179; Weis, 1987), and others strongly disagreeing (Clelland and Carter, 1980; Braithwaite, 1981; Kleck, 1982; Elliott and Ageton, 1980; Elliott and Huizinga, 1983).

It might seem that the no relationship thesis would be defended by the Marxist school, which we'll discuss in Chapter 4. After all, if the powerful and the wealthy—the bourgeoisie—are the "bad guys" and the members of the working class—the proletariat—are the "good guys," then it makes sense that ascribing a high crime rate to the working classes would be called a "bum rap" by Marxists. In fact, this is not what Marxists say. Marxists argue that social behavior grows out of the economic conditions in which people live; arguing that middle- and working-class individuals commit the same kinds of crimes at the same rate would be admitting that social class has no impact on important dimensions of behavior. The Marxist view that there are no class differences in criminal behavior is not typically Marxist, in spite of what some misinformed observers have claimed (Toby, 1980). No, it is the conventional sociologists, the positivists, not the radicals who make this claim (Mankoff, 1980: 141).

Now, the idea that there is no association between socioeconomic status and criminal behavior (remember, for the time being, we're only talking about street crimes) does not merely violate common sense, it simply makes no sense whatsoever. It contradicts what everyone can determine for themselves. Although those who support the no relationship position claim this objection is irrelevant, it is obvious the rate of street crime is *vastly* higher in poor than in wealthy neighborhoods. Stores located in poor neighborhoods are far more likely to be "ripped off," and, therefore, to pay higher rates for theft insurance. Unless middle-class individuals come in large numbers to lower-class neighborhoods to commit crimes, the conclusion is inescapable: Poor people are simply a lot more likely to commit street crime than more affluent individuals. Anyone who believes differently has never lived in or visited a poor neighborhood, or talked to the residents of one. Saying otherwise violates the life experience of the poor, who are vastly more likely to be the victims of street crimes. Advocates of the no relationship school are denying the data of their senses and the wisdom of everyone who has lived in a stratified society. Instead, they have absolute faith in the data that appear on their computer printouts—again, the fallacy of vulgar empiricism.

In addition, the differences between the races in ordinary criminal behavior are substantial. Every study ever conducted has shown that blacks are more likely to commit—and be the victim of—street crime than whites; and these differences do not disappear when the possible role of prejudice in getting arrested is taken into account (Hindelang, 1978). This is especially true of robbery. Since race is so strongly correlated with class, if class had no impact on criminal behavior *within each racial category* and if there were no relationship overall, either middle-class blacks would have to have a higher crime rate than lower-class blacks, or middle-class whites would have to have a higher crime rate than lower-class whites. "We know of no reason to expect patterns of this kind" (Greenberg, 1981: 65). Adherents of the no difference or no relationship line of reasoning cannot explain why the race/class/crime patterns run totally contrary to their findings.

What was the problem with the studies whose findings showed no difference in patterns of criminal behavior between individuals variously located in the class structure? Why, in their studies, were lower-class people no more likely to commit street crimes than middle-class individuals when this is not true in the real world? As I said in my discussion of Miller's theory of lower-class culture as a generator of delinquency, it turns out that researchers demonstrating that class and crime are not related, or only weakly related, used an extremely poor measure of criminal behavior. They made up an index of criminality by throwing together trivial offenses and serious crimes. Some of the "peccadillos" Clelland and Carter (1980: 326) included in their index of delinquency and crime were driving a car without a license or a permit, skipping school, defying parental authority, taking something worth less than $5, underage drinking, disobeying teachers, walking on grass, cheating on an exam, and breaking someone else's pencil! Real—that is, serious—crime, such as rape, robbery, murder, and assault does not take place frequently enough to study easily in a self-report design without a very large sample. Thus, all the no relationship researchers have shown is that middle- and lower-class individuals commit extremely trivial offenses in roughly equal proportions. Yet, it is the serious crimes that everyone is interested in and refers to when discussing the issue of criminal behavior. In fact, lower-status individuals commit *serious* crimes far more often than middle- and upper-status individuals; and as the seriousness and the frequency of the offenses increase, the class discrepancy also increases (Elliott and Ageton, 1980; O'Brien, 1985: 76).

Again, the problem here was having too much faith in one's data, of thinking the findings from one's own study are more conclusive and definitive than the data available to every observing, thinking individual. Although practitioners of all schools of thought are prone to this error, it is the positivists who may be especially inclined to it. To the positivist, the researcher knows better than the ordinary man and woman on the street, and sometimes, this leads to embarrassing blunders, as the no relationship between class and crime shows very clearly.

CHAPTER
4

Contemporary Sociological Theories of Deviance

All early perspectives on deviant behavior, from demonic possession to anomie theory and differential association, examine the factors that lead individuals to break the rules. Two later perspectives, both largely developed in the second half of the twentieth century—labeling theory and conflict theory—part company with this tradition and demand a radically different emphasis.

Labeling theory focuses on *reactions to* rule breaking. It deals mainly with the question of "what happens to people *after* they have been singled out, identified, and defined as deviants." This tradition, for the most part, abandons the investigation of why some individuals break the rules and shifts its attention, instead, to "the important role of social definitions and negative social sanctions in pressuring individuals to engage in further deviant actions" (Traub and Little, 1985: 277; 1980: 241). The perspective begins with the view that we tend to be influenced by

what that others think of us. How is the wrongdoing and rule breaking of individuals reacted to by others? How is rule breakers' further behavior influenced by their image in the eyes of others? To simplify things a bit, these are the central questions of labeling theory.

Conflict theory also abandons the question of why some people break the rules. Instead, it deals with the issue of *making* the rules, especially the criminal law. Why is certain behavior outlawed? And why is other, often even more damaging behavior, *not* outlawed? Conflict theorists answer these questions by arguing that laws are passed and rules are approved because they support the customs or the interests of the most powerful members of a society. In a large, complex society, no rule or law is accepted or believed as right by the whole society—only certain segments of it. Likewise, no rule or law protects everybody's rights or interests—

again, only those of certain social groups or categories. It is the powerful groups that are able to impose their will on the rest of the society and make sure that laws and rules favorable to themselves, and possibly detrimental to other, less powerful groups, are instituted. That, in a nutshell, is the central concern of conflict theory.

LABELING THEORY

In the 1960s, a small group of researchers wrote a small body of works that came to be looked upon as a more or less unified perspective that is referred to as *labeling theory*.[1] (It is also called "interactionist" theory and "reactive" theory, but labeling theory is the most commonly used term.)

The model or approach toward deviance the members of this school adopt is the *reactive* perspective spelled out in Chapter 1. Some labeling theorists prefer the "hard" reactive perspective, and some the "soft," but all adopt some version of the reactive approach. Labeling theory was built on the work and writings of two principal precursors—Frank Tannenbaum and Edwin Lemert. The first, Tannenbaum, cannot be regarded as a member of the labeling school, since he wrote so long ago, had no firsthand contact with its other proponents, and did not work out the implications of his early insights. Tannenbaum can be regarded as the "grandfather" of labeling theory. The second, Lemert, is much closer in time to current labeling theorists, is a sociologist (while Tannenbaum was a historian), and wrote in a much more sophisticated fashion than did Tannenbaum; some of his writing is squarely in the labeling tradition, and some criticizes it sharply. Lemert may be regarded as the "godfather" of labeling theory.

Labeling theory grew out of a more general perspective in sociology—*symbolic interactionism*. This approach is based on "three simple premises." First, people act on the basis of the *meaning* that things have for them. Second, this meaning grows out of *interaction* with others, especially intimate others. And third, meaning is continually modified by *interpretation* (Blumer, 1969: 2). These three principles—meaning, interaction, and interpretation—form the core of symbolic interactionism, and, likewise, labeling theory as well. People are not robots, symbolic interactists are saying; they are active and creative in how they see and act on things in the world. They are not simple "products" of their upbringing or their environment, but arrive at what they think, how they feel, and what they do, through dynamic, creative processes. And one of these processes is what people make of the reactions of others toward who they are and what they do. Strictly speaking, labeling theory is not a separate theory at all, but an application of symbolic interactionism to deviant phenomena.

Labeling Theory: The Precursors

The year 1938 marked the publication of a book written by Frank Tannenbaum, a professor of history and a Latin American specialist; it was entitled *Crime and the Community*. Tannenbaum argued that in a slum area, nearly all boys engage in a wide range of mischievous behavior—getting into fights, skipping school, stealing apples, and throwing rocks at windows. These actions, normal and taken for granted by the boys themselves, are regarded as deviant and criminal by the authorities—by teachers, the police, and the courts. In an effort to curtail this behavior, the police will apprehend and punish some of these boys. If the boys persist in this behavior, they will be sent to reform school.

However, punishment does not always

[1]Two of the major labeling theorists, Becker (1973: 178) and Kitsuse (1972: 233), have rejected both the term "labeling" and the title "theory" as a valid description of their perspective. Both prefer the term "the interactionist approach" (Becker, 1973: 181, 183; Kitsuse, 1972: 235). Their approach is not, they explain, strictly speaking a theory—that is, a general explanation for why deviance occurs in the first place—and the term "labeling," they say, implies too simpleminded a connection between stigma and its outcome. Unfortunately, in the field of deviance, the perspective is widely known as "labeling theory," and it is difficult to refer to it as anything else.

curtail these activities. In fact, it often has the ironic effect of escalating the seriousness of the deeds that these boys commit. Arrest and incarceration will typically result in the community regarding a boy as not merely mischievous, but as incorrigible—a budding criminal in the flesh. By being treated as a delinquent and forced to associate with slightly older and more experienced young criminals in reform schools, the trouble-maker comes to see himself as a true delinquent.

Tannenbaum was the first observer of deviance to focus more on reactions to behavior than on the behavior itself. He argued, in fact, that the key factor in escalating an individual's behavior from mildly to seriously deviant was the punishment that he or she received. It is possible that Tannenbaum did not believe that punishment always and inevitably resulted in this escalation process, but he certainly wrote as if he believed it.

About a dozen years after the publication of Tannenbaum's *Crime and the Community* (1938), a textbook with the inappropriate and anachronistic title *Social Pathology* appeared; written by sociologist Edwin Lemert (1951), it pursued Tannenbaum's insights, but with considerably more sophistication, complexity, and detail. Lemert distinguished between *primary* and *secondary* deviation. Primary deviation is simply the enactment of deviant behavior itself—any form of it. Lemert argued that primary deviation is *polygenetic* (1951: 75–76; 1972: 62–63); that is, it is caused by a wide range of different factors. In fact, Lemert asserted, the original cause or causes of a particular form of deviance is not especially important. What counts is the social reaction *to* the behavior from others.

Secondary deviation occurs when the individual who enacts deviant behavior deals with the problems created by social reactions to his or her primary deviations (1951: 76), "The secondary deviant, as opposed to his actions, is a person whose life and identity are organized around the facts of deviance" (Lemert, 1972: 63).

Not all primary deviation results in punishment or condemnation. Some communities or social circles display more "tolerance"

for rulebreaking, behavior than others do (Lemert, 1951: 57–58). When primary deviation is punished, however, the individuals engaging in it are stigmatized, shunned, and socially isolated. They are forced into groups or circles of other individuals who are also stigmatized. The social isolation reinforces the individual's commitment to these groups and social circles and the deviant's commitment to the behavior itself.

Lemert, like Tannenbaum, emphasized the ironic consequences of condemning and punishing rule breakers: it can make further deviance more likely. However, Lemert, unlike Tannenbaum, discussed both sides of this process. One possible outcome of negative social reaction to primary deviation is to "eliminate the variant behavior" altogether. Certain radical or revolutionary groups in Europe "have at times been ruthlessly hunted down and destroyed"; in the United States, the practice of polygyny, or multiple marriages, "was stamped out" (Lemert, 1951: 63). Although the repression of deviance can result in its elimination, the ironic effect of strengthening it and making it more likely has captured far more attention of labeling theorist over the years.

Labeling Theory: The Main Points

Tannenbaum may be regarded as the "grandfather" of labeling theory and Lemert, the "godfather." They may be regarded as forerunners or precursors of the perspective. Most observers regard Howard Becker (1963,1964), John Kitsuse (1962), and Kai Erikson (1962, 1966), labeling theory's principal contemporary proponents.[2] Although Becker (1973) and Kitsuse (1972, 1975, 1980) later elaborated their original formulations, for the most part, what is now known as labeling theory was spelled out in the short span of time between 1962 and 1966. It should also be said that, although labeling

[2]Plummer (1979: 86) found that, in a large number of commentaries on labeling theory, only the names of Tannenbaum, Lemert, Becker, Kitsuse, and Erikson were mentioned as representative theorists by more than half; only Becker and Lemert were mentioned by nearly all.

theorists have been depicted by most commentators, particularly critics, as consistent in their views, in reality, they represent a remarkably diverse group of thinkers (Goode, 1975: 570; Plummer, 1979: 87). Still, there are some ideas these theorists do have in common; just as important, they are *regarded* as a school whose representatives agree about the phenomenon of deviance in nearly every detail. Thus, labeling theory should be discussed as a "theory," school, or perspective in the sociology of deviance.

According to Becker (1973: 177–208; 1981) and Kitsuse (1972, 1980), labeling theory is not so much an explanation for why certain individuals engage in deviant behavior as it is a perspective whose main insight tells us that the labeling process is crucial and cannot be ignored. Labeling "theory" is not so much a theory as it is an orientation, "a useful set of problems" centered around the origins and consequences of labeling (Plummer, 1979: 88, 90). The labeling approach shifts attention away from the traditional question Why do they do it? to a focus on how and why judgments of deviance come to be made and what their consequences are—a very different enterprise. Why are certain acts condemned at one time and in one place, but tolerated at another time, in another place? Why does one person do something and get away "scott free," while another does the same thing and is severely punished for it? What happens when someone is caught violating a rule and is stigmatized for it and what consequences does the stigma have for that individual's subsequent behavior (McCaghy, 1985: 79, 82, 84; Clinard and Meier, 1985: 78–80)? These are some of the major issues labeling theorists have concerned themselves with.

The labeling perspective emphasizes the following concepts in the drama of deviance: *relativity, the construction of moral meanings and definitions, the inner world of deviance, labeling* and *stigma, audiences, contingencies, reflexivity,* and *the "stickiness" of labels and the self-fulfilling prophecy.*

Relativity. The most important characteristic of an act, according to labeling theorists, is how a society views it and how people react to it and to someone who enacts it. Behavior is not deviant in itself; it only becomes deviant when it is seen and reacted to in a given society. Is adultery deviant? Not in some societies, like the Lepcha of Sikkim, a tiny state in northern India. The Lepcha tolerate and even encourage adultery (Gorer, 1967). In other societies, like Saudi Arabia, adultery is most decidedly deviant; couples caught engaging in it are severely punished, and may even be stoned to death. What is crucial here is not the nature of the act itself, which represents the same outward or mechanical actions in both places, but the *meaning* of the action to those who witness and evaluate it and the actual or potential reactions by others to the act and its perpetrators.

It might seem that this is a noncontroversial and universally accepted notion, that every sociologist agrees that definitions of right and wrong vary from one society to another. This is not entirely true. Some approaches emphasize the universals in deviance rather than the variation. Functionalism, for example, has argued that some actions are more likely to be punished—that is, regarded as deviant—in societies around the world because they are *dysfunctional*, because tolerating them would lead to their widespread enactment and, hence, a weaker, less cohesive and less viable society. Incest is just such an act: Cultures almost everywhere prohibit incest because it undermines the foundation of the society, the family (Davis, 1949: 401–404; 1976: 226). Likewise, certain actions are highly likely to be regarded as crimes in nearly all societies with a penal code because they are inherently harmful; any society that did not discourage them would be seriously jeopardized (Newman, 1976). Hence, although most other perspectives are, at most, only *moderately* relativistic in that they are more likely to stress the universals in deviance—the similarities from one moral code to another—the labeling perspective may be called *radically* relativistic in that it is more likely to emphasize differences, the variation or relativity in moral and legal codes from one society to another.

In addition, the labeling approach emphasizes relativity from one group, subculture, or individual to another within the same society. Some social circles approve of marijuana use, for instance, while others condemn it (Becker, 1963: 70, 72–78). Some individuals condemn homosexuality while others do not (Kitsuse, 1962). The negative labeling of an activity that is widely condemned in a given society cannot be assumed or taken for granted. We will almost always be able to locate certain circles of individuals who tolerate or accept forms of behavior that are widely or more typically stigmatized. Relativity from one group to another is an important element of the labeling theorists' approach. In contrast, more conventional perspectives argue that, though some variation does exist, the degree of agreement within the same society about what should be condemned is extremely high (Rossi et al., 1974; Klaus and Kalish, 1984). Again, this becomes a question of emphasis: Labeling theorists emphasize the variation; adherents of other perspectives emphasize the agreement. And once again, labeling theory emerges as the more radically relativistic position. Far from being trivial and unoriginal, the labeling perspective can be seen as bucking the tide of mainstream consensus.

Audiences. The labeling process is effected by *audiences*. An audience is an individual or any number of individuals who observe and evaluate an act or the person who engages in an act. An audience could be one's friends, the police, teachers, a psychiatrist, bystanders—even oneself, for you can be an observer and an evaluator of your own behavior (Becker, 1963: 31; Rotenberg, 1974). It is the audience that determines whether something or someone is deviant: no audience, no labeling, therefore, no deviance. However, an audience need not directly view an act; audiences can witness behavior "indirectly," that is, they can be told about someone's behavior. "The critical variable in the study of deviance . . . is the social audience rather than the individual actor, since it is the audience which eventually de-

termines whether or not any episode of behavior or any class of episodes is labeled deviant" (Erikson, 1964: 11).

This means that no act is deviant in the abstract, as we saw in the point on relativity; behavior is deviant only *to* specific audiences. Deviance is not a property contained in specific actions; rather, it is a relational or transactional term that spells out a certain kind of relationship between an act and specific audiences. It says, members of audiences A, B, and C are likely to find this behavior offensive and may wish to punish the perpetrators, even though most of audiences X, Y, and Z are unlikely to have this reaction. Thus, *to* audiences A, B, and C, a specific form of behavior is deviant; *to* audiences X, Y, and Z, it is not.

Some audiences include the following: first, society at large (Schur, 1971: 12). It can be said that a majority of the American public finds adulterous sex morally unacceptable and therefore deviant. Thus, to most Americans, that is, to the audience of American society generally, adultery is deviant. A second audience is one's significant others (Schur, 1971: 12–13), those people with whom one interacts most frequently and intimately, with whom one has a close relationship and whose opinions one values. It could be that in your social circle, sex by a married person with someone other than his or her spouse is perfectly acceptable; thus, to the audience of your significant others, adultery is not deviant. On the other hand, in my significant social circle, adultery is an abomination; thus, to the audience of my significant others, adultery is decidedly deviant. And a third type of possible audience is official and organizational agents of social control (Schur, 1971: 13). Can you get into some kind of formal, official trouble for engaging in the behavior in question and getting caught at it? Can you be arrested for it? In most law enforcement agencies, at least in the United States, adultery is not a legitimate cause for arrest. Thus, to the audience of the agents of formal social control, adultery is not deviant. Clearly, whether an act is deviant or not depends on the audience that does or would evaluate the act. Without specifying a specific audience, the question of an act's deviance is meaningless.

The construction of moral meanings and definitions.

Acts are not intrinsically deviant; they can be looked upon and judged in various ways. How does a particular type of behavior come to be regarded as deviant, that is, morally undesirable? Moral meanings are *constructed*. That is, notions of right and wrong come to be defined over time within specific social and cultural contexts. They do not arise accidentally; specific processes and structures generate certain moral codes. At the same time, the construction of certain notions of right and wrong could have happened otherwise—this outcome is not inevitable. For instance, at one time in U.S. history, marijuana use was not condemned; it was a morally neutral activity. By the 1930s, however, its use came to be defined as deviant. Why? What causes an activity like smoking marijuana to be defined as deviant?

Although there are many factors that play a role in construction of moral meanings, labeling theorists stress the following two.

First, the role of *moral entrepreneurs*. If persuasive, legitimate, active, credible figures launch a campaign to discredit an activity, it stands a high chance of being widely regarded as wrong or immoral—in a word, deviant (Becker, 1963: 147–163). Just such a process took place in the 1930s with marijuana (Becker, 1963: 135–146). In the 1980s, antidrug sentiment was revived, with First Lady Nancy Reagan acting as a "moral entrepreneur" (Goode, 1989: 35).

A second factor facilitating the definition of an activity as deviant is the *social status and power* of individuals who engage in an activity (Becker, 1963: 15–18, 145; Lofland, 1969: 14). Relatively powerless, low-status individuals are more likely to find their activities defined as morally unacceptable—deviant— than those who have more power and a higher status. In the 1930s, for instance, marijuana was more likely to be used by racial and ethnic minorities, the young, and jazz musicians—all politically marginal social categories. This made it easier for moral entrepreneurs to categorize their behavior as morally undesirable and therefore deviant.

The inner world of deviance.

Moral entrepreneurs are never completely successful: Not everyone accepts the definition of certain activities as deviant. No society is uniform with respect to its moral code; some individuals will always be found in every society who have notions of right and wrong that differ from that of the majority. More specifically, individuals who engage in a certain behavior usually define it quite differently from those who do not. One major endeavor of the labeling theorist is to attempt an understanding of *how deviants define their behaviors*. What, in other words, is the *inner world* of deviance like? For instance, how do homosexuals see their behaviors? What is their attitude about being homosexual? How do they experience being gay? How do they define the "straight" world? What is the construction of *their* moral meaning like? How do they define right and wrong with respect to sexuality? What does it *feel* like to be a member of a minority that is looked down upon by the straight majority? To know how the world of homosexuality is lived, it is necessary to enter that world and listen to those who actually live it.

Labeling and stigma.

The key elements in the deviance process are labeling and stigmatizing. This entails two steps. First, an *activity* is labeled deviant, and second, an *individual* is labeled a deviant. In this labeling process, if no one labels something or someone deviant, no deviance exists. An act cannot be deviant in the abstract; it must be defined by the members of a society or a group *as* deviant; in other words, it must be *labeled* as morally wrong. Likewise, a person cannot be regarded as a deviant until this labeling process takes place.

Labeling involves attaching a *stigmatizing* definition to a person or an activity. Stigma is a moral stain, a sign of reproach or social undesirability, an indication to the world that one has been singled out as a shameful, morally discredited human being. Someone who has been stigmatized is a "marked" person; he or she has a "spoiled identity." Interestingly enough, Erving Goffman, who wrote a book on stigma that strongly influenced the labeling theorists, stated, "I do not think all deviators have enough in common to warrant a special analysis" (1963: 141). A stigmatized person is one who has been labeled a deviant. Once someone has been so discredited, relations with conventional, respectable others become difficult, strained, problematic. In other words, "being caught and branded as a deviant has important consequences for one's further participation and self-image.... Committing the improper act and being publicly caught at it places [the individual] in a new status. He [or she] has been revealed as a different kind of person from the kind he [or she] was supposed to be. He [or she] is labeled a 'fairy,' 'dope fiend,' 'nut,' or 'lunatic,' and treated accordingly" (Becker, 1963: 31, 32).

So important is this labeling process that, in some respects, it does not much matter whether or not someone who has been stigmatized has actually engaged in the behavior of which he or she is accused. By the lights of labeling theory, falsely accused deviants are still deviants (Becker, 1963: 20). In many important respects, they resemble individuals who really do commit acts that violate the rules. For example, women and men burned at the stake for witchcraft in the sixteenth century were deviants in the eyes of the authorities and the community (Currie, 1968) and were burned no less crisply for not having engaged in a pact with the devil. Two men are stigmatized in a certain community for, let's say, sexual behavior with young boys. One is guilty, the other is innocent. Labeling theory would hold that these two men will share important experiences and characteristics in common, *by virtue of that labeling process alone,* even though they are poles apart with respect to having committed the behavior of which they were accused.

Can a *class* or *category* of behavior be regarded as deviant in the absence of the labeling of specific enactors of that behavior as deviant? In other words, can someone who engages in behavior that is widely condemned—like homosexuality, heroin addiction, or robbery—be said to engage in "deviant" behavior without having actually been caught and condemned? (I touched on this issue in Chapter 2 when I discussed the reactive definition.) The labeling theorists split on this issue. Erikson (1964: 11; 1966: 13) refers to a "class of episodes" as deviant, implying that a category of behavior can be labeled deviant even though someone who engages in it may not be so labeled. Becker (1963: 14, 19, 20–21) waffles on the issue; in some places he implies this is possible; in other places, he seems to say that it is not. For instance, he refers to "secret deviance" and the "secret deviant" (1963: 20–21). Clearly, these are unlabeled acts and individuals; but if deviance is defined by labeling, how can someone, or something, be deviant *in the absence of labeling?* They can't, if we are entirely consistent on this issue. In contrast, Kitsuse (1962) is consistent on this issue: Until a specific, concrete individual engaging in a specific, concrete act is caught and punished, we cannot refer to deviance at all. To Kitsuse, a class of behavior per se—for example, homosexuality—cannot be regarded as deviance; only specific instances of it that have been concretely detected and punished can be so regarded.

This division among the major labeling theorists on the judgment of deviance of *categories* of behavior versus concrete *instances* of behavior is nicely captured by Plummer's distinction between *societal* deviance and *situational* deviance (1979: 98). "Societal" deviance is made up of widely condemned classes or categories of behavior. It would be difficult to argue that robbery, homosexuality, transvestism, or alcoholism *per se* are not regarded by a high proportion of Americans as censurable, unacceptable, deplorable behavior. One is far more likely to be stigmatized than praised for engaging in them. For most people, they are not "normal" patterns of behavior. One need not agree with this judgment, or its appropriateness, justice, or fairness, to recognize that it is true. "Situational" deviance, in contrast, ignores such a broad consensus and examines only concrete negative judgments of behavior and individuals *in context*. Not all alcoholics are condemned for their excessive drinking; though most are, there are specific situations and contexts in which one may interact where the majority judgment is not followed. Looking at situational deviance focuses exclusively on judgments of deviance in real-life, micro-interactional settings (Plummer, 1979: 98).

Thus, among the early labeling theorists, Kitsuse believes *only* situational deviance can legitimately be called instances of deviance; Erikson admits both societal and situational deviance exist; and, in places, Becker implies societal deviance exists, and in other places, he suggests only cases of situational deviance constitute authentic examples of deviant behavior.

Becker's distinction between being publicly labeled and enacting "secret deviance" was simultaneously paralleled in the work of Goffman (1963: 41–42) in his distinction between being *discredited* and having *discreditable* characteristics. A "discredited" person is one who has been stigmatized, whose stigma is known or evident to the conventional others with whom he or she interacts. These others may ignore the stigma, avoid the stigmatizing subject, or reject the person because of it. Still, being discredited means that one's interaction with others is likely to be strained, spoiled, awkward. On the other hand, possessing "discrediting" characteristics means that one passes oneself off to others as "untainted" when one knows that others would not accept oneself for what one is. One controls information about oneself, knowing that others would react in a punishing, condemning, or at least condescending fashion if they had access to it. The "secret deviant," then, is an individual with discreditable characteristics who is engaged in "passing" as a conventional person in a conventional world.

Most people find being stigmatized painful; typically, they attempt to avoid it. While most members of a deviant minority are aware of the hostile feelings the majority has for their group and activity, they tend not to share those feelings. At the same time, it is difficult to avoid interacting with members of the majority. Hence, they must either insulate themselves to some degree from majority members, or keep their deviant membership and activities a secret from them. In Goffman's terms, they must engage in "passing" and in "information control." Most people who engage in deviant behavior are not punished or *sanctioned* for it; most, in other words, can be said to be *secret deviants*. Anticipating punishment for their identity and behavior, they conceal information about themselves to the nondeviant world (Warren and Johnson, 1972).

Contingencies. Not everyone who violates a rule or a law will be criticized or punished by those who witness the deed (Kitsuse, 1962; Becker, 1963: 11–13; Erikson, 1964: 10, 12). Labeling theorists argue that rule breakers are not punished or condemned *simply* because they have violated society's rules. Actions that are regarded as deviant to most people in a society may be tolerated by certain individuals or groups within it. Ideas about what behavior should be tolerated or punished are not necessarily held in common by all members of a large, complex society. In other words, we should not assume uniformity and homogeneity with respect to what's deviant. Even when people disapprove of behavior in general, or even specific, concrete instances of it, they do not always condemn or punish those who engage in it (Becker, 1963: 12; Kitsuse, 1962). Labeling theorists emphasize the role of *contingencies* in the labeling process.

A contingency is a seemingly incidental or accidental feature of an event or a phenomenon. In the world of deviance, a contingency is anything that logically shouldn't influence the labeling process, but actually does. Two people are mentally ill; one lives in a rural area very far from a mental hospital, a second lives very near one. The first is allowed to live out his life among people who tolerate him and his behavior, while the second is institutionalized (Goffman, 1961: 135). In this case, the distance one lives from a mental hospital represents a contingency.

In fact, in general, the labeling theorist would say, that it could be said that "mental patients suffer distinctly not from mental illness, but from contingencies" (Goffman, 1961: 135).

During a particular evening, at different times, the police happen upon two drunks on skid row. When they encounter the first man, they have plenty of room in their van; so they apprehend the man, arrest him, take him to the police station, put him in a cell, and make him sleep off his drunk. When they encounter the second man, their paddy wagon and their cells are full. As a result, they tell him to go home and go to sleep. In this case, police resources represent a contingency influencing whether or not the drunks are arrested (Bittner, 1967).

The Saints are a gang composed mainly of middle-class boys; the Roughnecks, a gang made up of working- and lower-class boys. Both engage, more or less equally, in a variety of delinquent activities. None of the Saints is ever arrested, while all of the Roughnecks have been arrested, some of them frequently. Here, the socioeconomic status of their parents is a contingency determining whether or not they get arrested (Chambliss, 1973a).

One specific type of contingency is what are called *ancillary* or *auxiliary characteristics.* These are all the seemingly secondary characteristics or traits of individuals, such as power and status, that shouldn't influence the labeling process, but actually do. As a general rule, the greater the prestige and power of the deviator, the greater his or her likelihood of avoiding or resisting being stigmatized as a deviant. The less prestige and power the deviator has, the higher the likelihood of being successfully stigmatized or negatively labeled. In short, the application of the label "deviant" is strongly influenced by factors that lie outside the deviant behavior itself. Other ancillary or auxiliary traits include appearance, age, sex, and race. For instance, blacks who murder whites are more likely to receive the death penalty than those who murder another black (Garfinkel, 1949; Becker, 1963: 13; Barlow, 1987: 147). Here, race is an ancillary characteristic of a victim that should be incidental or irrelevant in the sentencing the offender receives. Yet it is a powerful contingency in the ultimate stigma—execution. Labeling theorists emphasize the role ancillary characteristics play as contingencies in the labeling process.

Reflexivity. Reflexivity simply means looking at ourselves in large part through the eyes of others. It is what is widely, although a bit mechanically, called the "looking glass self." Labeling theory is based on a seemingly simple but fundamental observation: "We view ourselves through the eyes of others, and when others see us in a certain way, at least for long enough or sufficiently powerfully, their views are sure to have some effect" (Glassner, 1982: 71). Being stigmatized by others is certainly not the only factor that influences what people do in the drama of deviance, but it is a crucial one. In addition, not everyone who enacts behavior that would usually be punished if it were discovered is caught—nor, for that matter, punished. At the same time, nearly all people who violate society's major norms know they would be punished, condemned, stigmatized, and labeled as deviants if they were discovered. Thus, they move around in a world in which they are aware that their identities and their behavior are potentially punishable. In other words, both direct and indirect labeling operate in the world of deviant behavior (Warren and Johnson, 1972: 76–77). People who violate norms have to deal with the probable and potential, as well as the actual and concrete, reactions of the respectable, conventional, law-abiding majority. All violators of major norms must at least ask themselves. "How would others react to me and my behavior?" If the answer is "They will react with criticism, hostility, condemnation, punishment—they will attempt to stigmatize you," then the rule breaker must try to avoid detection or be prepared for being labeled.

The "stickiness" of labels and the self-fulfilling prophecy. Labeling theorists argue that stigmatizing someone as a socially and morally undesirable character has important consequences for that person's further rule breaking. Under certain circumstances, being labeled may intensify one's commitment to a deviant identity and contribute to further deviant behavior. Some conventional, law-abiding citizens believe "once a deviant, always as deviant." Someone who has been stigmatized and labeled "is ushered into the deviant position by a decisive and often dramatic ceremony, yet is retired from it with hardly a word of public notice." As a result, the deviant is given "no proper licence to resume a normal life in the community. Nothing has happened to cancel out the stigmas imposed upon him" or her; the original judgment "is still in effect." The conforming members of a society tend to be "reluctant to accept the returning deviant on an entirely equal footing" (Erikson, 1964: 16, 17.)

Deviant labels tend to be "sticky"; and the community tends to stereotype someone as, above all and most importantly, a deviant. When someone is identified as a deviant, the community asks, "What kind of person would break such an important rule?" The answer given is "one who is different from the rest of us, who cannot or will not act as a moral human being and therefore might break other important rules" (Becker, 1963: 34). Once a deviant label has been attached, it is difficult to shake. Ex-convicts find it difficult to find legitimate employment after being released from prison; ex-mental patients are carefully scrutinized for odd, eccentric, or bizarre behavior; a young woman who is seen as sexually promiscuous (the label may or may not have been earned as a result of her actual behavior) will, in all likelihood, continue to be so viewed until she leaves the community.

Such stigmatizing and stereotyping tends to deny to deviants "the ordinary means of carrying on the routines of everyday life open to most people. Because of this denial, the deviant must of necessity develop illegitimate routines" (Becker, 1963: 35). As a consequence, the labeling process may actually increase the deviant's further commitment to deviant behavior; it may limit conventional options and opportunities, strengthen a deviant identity, and maximize participation in a deviant group. Labeling someone as a deviant, thus, may become "a self-fulfilling prophecy" (Becker, 1963: 34); that is, *someone becomes what he or she is accused of being*—even though that original accusation may have been false (Merton, 1948, 1957: 421–436; Jones, 1986). The ex-con may find it impossible to go straight and will return to a life of crime; the ex-mental patient may buckle under the strain of having to act normal; the sexually permissive girl may find that the only reason that boys want to date her is for short-term sexual gratification, and so she ends up satisfying their demands.

Nonetheless, labeling theorists are careful to point out that negative labeling does not always or inevitably have this self-fulfilling outcome. "Obviously," says Becker, "everyone caught in one deviant act and labeled a deviant does not move inevitably toward greater deviance" (1963: 36). Indeed, such labeling could very well "stamp out," repress, or cause a discontinuation of the deviant behavior that was punished—as has been the case with marijuana use (Becker, 1955, 1963: 59), political radicalism in Europe, and polygyny (a man having several wives) in Utah (Lemert, 1951: 63). Still, the more interesting prediction is that social control will lead to an intensification of a commitment to deviance, not a discontinuation of it, which is the proposition that labeling theorists have usually focused on.

Criticisms of Labeling Theory

Perhaps what is most remarkable about labeling theory is not so much what it says but what has been said about it. If we were to examine only the original basic texts—one book and an anthology by Becker (1963, 1964), one article by Kituse (1962), and one article and a book by Erikson (1962, 1966)—we would find they have attracted commentary running into hundreds of works. There are few examples in the history of sociology of so much having been written about so little. Moreover, the overwhelming majority of this commentary on labeling theory has been negative; it represents, in the words of one defender of the perspective, "a major industry of criticism" (Plummer, 1979: 119). If this commentary had died down over time, it would indicate that labeling theory had been refuted, discredited, and was no longer valid or useful. In fact, these comments, criticisms and "critiques" keep coming practically unabated, suggesting that the theory may resonate with meaningful themes in the sociology of deviance (Conover, 1976: 229).

Most contemporary observers agree that labeling theory's shift away from an exclusive focus on the question of the etiology of deviance to broader concerns, including the issue of judgments of deviance, is all to the good. At the same time, as I just pointed out, the labeling perspective has encountered a great deal of criticism on a number of grounds from a wide variety of sources.

Perhaps the most common criticism of labeling theory—and it has come mainly from sociologists working in the positivist tradition—is that it is not a theory at all. It does not explain the etiology or cause of acts such as rape, criminal homicide, homosexuality, robbery, drug addiction, and child molestation. Instead, its critics charge, it is only concerned with *reactions to* these acts—not why they occur in the first place. Social scientists with a positivistic orientation want to know *Why do they do it?* On this issue, they say, labeling theory is silent—in fact, useless (Gibbs, 1966: 11–12; 1972: 44; Hirschi, 1973: 168–169; Clinard and Meier, 1985: 81). Labeling "does not create the behavior in the first place" (Akers, 1968, 1985: 31). Therefore, these critics charge, the perspective cannot account for why the behavior was enacted; it is, in short, inadequate with respect to the most basic requirement of any theory—explanation.

Labeling theorists actually agree that their perspective does not deal with the question of etiology or cause. Labeling theory was never intended to be an explanation of primary deviation (Kitsuse, 1972; 236; Becker, 1973: 179)—or why people engage in deviant behavior initially. In the words of Becker, the original proponents of labeling theory "did not pose solutions to the etiologic question." Labeling theorists agree that the perspective should not be thought of as an explanatory theory in the strict sense.

Rather, it is an orientation, a perspective that guides the social scientist to interesting processes, variables, and observations. Thus, the criticisms along these lines have tended to be misguided and irrelevant. Critics are insisting that labeling theory should do something its proponents never set out to do in the first place.

A second commonly leveled criticism is that the act of labeling does not inevitably produce an intensification of the actor's commitment to deviance, deviant behavior, or a deviant identity. Critics often charge that punishment is often effective; it causes wrongdoers to give up rule breaking and return to conventionality and conformity (Mankoff, 1971; Akers, 1985: 30–32; Gove, 1980a, passim; Bordua, 1967). In addition, some critics aver, it is possible for individuals to engage in rule-breaking behavior *prior to* or *in the absence of* labeling or stigma (Scull, 1972: 284). In other words, a career of enacting certain forms of behavior can develop *in the absence of* labeling (Clinard and Meier, 1985: 82–83). Many, perhaps most, individuals who engage in deviant behavior, even routinely, are never apprehended, stigmatized, or labeled, and yet they continue the behavior in question (Warren and Johnson, 1972).

However, as we saw earlier, labeling theorists concur with this line of commentary, too. The perspective never asserted that labeling necessarily produces further deviant behavior, they say. Nor is labeling necessary for deviance to take place or to be continued. As I explained earlier, Lemert pointed out that a number of practices (the two examples he provided were political radicalism and polygyny) were "stamped out," rather than stimulated by effective social control (1951: 63). Becker, too, emphasized that pursuing a deviant path may be facilitated best by an *absence* of social control; being apprehended and condemned for engaging in deviant behavior often results in a *discontinuation* of the practice. For instance, Becker pointed out, the marijuana smoker must learn to "contend with the powerful forces of social control" in order to continue the use of this drug (Becker, 1955, 1963: 59). When nonusers punish or apply sanctions to the user, the latter may simply decide to give up the grass. These sanctions often have the effect of rendering the activity "distasteful," "inexpedient," or "immoral," and users are pressured to become nonusers; the user can continue only if he or she is able to render these sanctions ineffective (1963: 60–62). Social control, then, *according to labelists,* may actually function to *prevent* some deviant behavior. The view that labeling theorists claimed everyone who is labeled inevitably moves toward greater deviance, though widespread, is clearly erroneous. It is a view of the perspective that has been "vulgarized into a narrow theory"; it attributes to labelists a position that they simply did not support (Plummer, 1979: 89).

Another criticism, usually stemming from critics holding a radical or a Marxist persuasion, argues that labeling theory indirectly assists the oppression of powerless groups and solidifies the rule of the powerful. As a result, the perspective contributes to oppression, exploitation, imperialism, racism, and sexism (Gouldner, 1968; Thio, 1973; Smith, 1973). It does this in two ways: first, by concentrating on the condemned and stigmatized behavior of powerless individuals— "nuts, sluts, and preverts" (Liazos, 1972)— that is, the dramatic and "immoral" varieties of deviance that capture the conventional imagination and outrage the general public. And second, as a consequence, it ignores the truly dangerous and damaging individuals and forms of behavior, "the unethical, illegal, and destructive actions of powerful individuals, groups, and institutions in our society" (1972: 111). Here, Marxists would include the exploitation of workers by factory owners and managers; selling shoddy, dangerous merchandise to the public; denying qualified workers jobs on the basis of their gender or race; failing to install safety devices in mines, killing miners as a result; polluting the atmosphere with factory waste; and so on. Why haven't the labeling theorists studied actions such as these? Why have they concentrated on the mentally ill, sexually unconventional, drug users, and skid row alcoholics—in short, individuals who are so-

cially marginal and politically powerless, who are acted upon, but who have relatively little impact on society? Why haven't the labeling theorists concentrated on the real movers and shakers, the manipulators, the high-level criminals in capitalist society—the business elite?

This line of criticism has two aspects to it. First, it is true that sociologists identified as belonging to the labeling school have not investigated the destructive actions of the powerful in society. The forms of behavior that Marxists and radicals study, those that they criticize labeling theorists for ignoring—oppression, exploitation, racism, sexism, imperialism, and so on—certainly do more harm to human life than do most (or even any) acts of obvious deviance. But labeling theorists have not studied them because they are not deviant. It is ironic that behavior that falls under their umbrella is not generally regarded as deviant. Many of us feel that such behavior *should* be condemned by the public. And yet, deviance is behavior that is widely condemned; a study of deviant behavior is not *about* oppression and exploitation, it is *about* condemnation and punishment. Oppression and exploitation may be found in some deviant actions, and may be lacking in others. In other words, oppression and exploitation vary independently of deviance; they cannot be equated with one another by decree. Certainly they can be studied, but not under the rubric of deviance. To be condemned is to be disvalued; to be disvalued is to be rendered powerless. One cannot be a respectable business executive engaging in actions that are widely seen as "just business" and be regarded as a deviant at the same time. *"The study of deviance is the study of devalued groups, and devalued groups are groups which lack status and prestige."* A sociology of deviance "which does not focus centrally on powerless groups is likely to be a very odd sociology of deviance" (Plummer 1979: 110).

The other aspect to labeling theory's neglect of unethical, damaging, even technically illegal actions of the powerful, however, is that it is possible to study such actions within the labeling paradigm *through the back door,* so to speak. The perspective can insist on raising the question of why certain actions tend to be condemned while others are not. An adequate understanding of labeling theory demands that damaging but conventional, respectable (that is, nondeviant) behavior be studied. The disjunctions between public condemnation and objective social damage should intrigue us. If we define deviance by public condemnation, we have to find out both the why of it—why some behavior attracts condemnation and punishment—as well as the why not—why other forms of behavior are not considered deviant. We can never fully understand what is deviant until we get a look at what it isn't. By looking at both, we realize it is not social harm or any "objective threat to society" that accounts for behavior being labeled as deviant. We couldn't deal with this issue adequately if we concentrated exclusively on deviant or criminal behavior.

According to U.S. Surgeon General C. Everett Koop, cigarettes kill over 300,000 Americans every year; deaths from heroin addiction probably account for 1 percent of that figure. In one study, selling heroin was regarded as the third most serious crime listed—deemed more serious than all forms of forcible rape and the planned killing of one's spouse. Even *using* heroin in this study was more strongly comdemned than killing someone in a barroom brawl. Selling marijuana ranked as more serious than the forcible rape of one's former spouse and "killing a spouse's lover after catching them together" (Rossi et al., 1974). And in another study, someone who runs a narcotics ring is condemned more severely than is a person who plants a bomb in a public building, a man who rapes a woman, or a woman who stabs her husband to death (Klaus and Kalish, 1984).

Selling the cigarettes that kill so many Americans is never widely regarded as reprehensible by the American public; indeed, cigarette executives are respectable individuals, holding prestigious jobs. Although labelists cannot magically regard selling cigarettes as deviant, they *can* ask the basic question: *Why isn't this behavior condemned?* If selling cigarettes is so destructive to human life, why do those who engage in it enjoy the cloak of respectability? How does the construction of meaning arise whereby the *more* damaging activity is *not* condemned and the *less* damaging activity is *strongly* condemned? Such questions should not be construed to represent a plea to legalize heroin, or to criminalize cigarettes. They are, however, an effort to understand why definitions of deviance arise and are maintained. Issues like these can be raised within the labeling framework; they are, in fact, intrinsic to it.

Nonetheless, the radicals and the Marxists are correct in their criticism that labeling theorists *have not,* historically, studied the conventional, destructive actions of the powerful that their perspective implies could and should be conducted. While it is fascinating to ask, Why do some actions attract stigma? it is equally as interesting to ask, Why do other, far more damaging, actions *not* attract stigma? And this is a task labeling theorists have not undertaken. Viewed in this light, it can be said that the perspective itself is blameless, but its practitioners are guilty as charged.

And last, one problem that many observers have with the implications of the labeling perspective is its laissez-faire or "live and let live" approach to deviance and crime. It seems to extend a hand of tolerance and acceptance—indeed, even *appreciation*—toward all manner of harmful activities. Labeling theory's stance seems to be that harm, like deviance, is in the eye of the beholder; it's all a matter of definition as to whether a given form of behavior is harmful or not.

When first formulated in the 1960s, labeling theory seemed quite radical. Its message was that individuals who are criticized, condemned, ridiculed, persecuted, and even arrested and imprisoned should not be the focus of attention. No; instead, we should take a hard look at the condemners, the persecutors, the self-righteous framers and enforcers of the law. Perhaps, labeling theorists seemed to imply, deviants aren't nearly so harmful to society as conventional, law-abiding folk said. Maybe deviants are a problem to society just because a lot of people *think* they are a problem. The epigraph to

Howard Becker's (1963) classic *Outsiders*, taken from William Faulkner's *As I Lay Dying*, read, in part: "It's like it ain't so much what a fellow does, but the way the majority of folks looking at him when he does it." The clear implications seemed to be that the "problem" of deviance would disappear if we were to accept a wider range of unconventional behavior.

From today's vantage point, it is clear this approach works better for some forms of behavior than for others. If we tolerate the marijuana smoker and the jazz musician (two examples of deviants in Becker's *Outsiders*), the homosexual (the subject of Kitsuse's classic article), and the Puritan lawbreaker (Erikson's focus of attention), what about the rapist and the murderer? The man who beats his wife and children to a bloody pulp? Or racists who rove in gangs and beat up Blacks who are caught walking in predominantly white neighborhoods? The drunk driver who runs a red light and plows into another car, killing an entire family? Are they just misunderstood? Are they condemned simply because of society's prejudices and preconceptions? Should the mantel of acceptance and tolerance be extended to cover them, too?

In the early 1960s, it may have seemed extremely important that we understand how labeling and stigma work to discredit perfectly harmless behavior and individuals; today, it is equally important to recognize that deviance may have real victims. Not all deviance is objectively harmful, it is true; but by the same token, not all deviance is harmless, either. The labeling theorists performed an important service in the 1960s in showing that condemnation does not necessarily fall on the most harmful members of a society. At the same time, taking this argument to its logical extreme implies that *all* deviants are misunderstood and mistreated; that *all* condemnation is irrational, and based on prejudice; that, in a sense, deviants are *always* society's victim. Clearly, no labeling theorist meant to say this, but their focus of attention on "soft" deviance to the exclusion of "hard" deviance (Ben-Yehuda, 1985: 2, 3) implied this. Today, we know better and can

take the labeling perspective for what it is: an incomplete, only partial look at an important, controversial phenomenon.

CONFLICT THEORY

Social scientists can be divided according to how much *consensus* or *conflict* they see in contemporary society. Theorists who see a great deal of consensus argue that the values and beliefs of the members of society are more or less consistent with one another, that there is a high degree of consensus about basic or core values. This view is influenced by the French sociologist Emile Durkheim (1858–1917), who believed that societies possessed a "collective conscience," or a shared sense of morality. In other words, most people agree with one another about most values. In addition, people tend to be *interdependent*—they need one another to get along in life. Consensus theorists tend to see social life as fairly harmonious, and societies as more or less cohesive and stable. Societies display a kind of inherent and unconscious wisdom; many social institutions that might seem destructive and repressive actually benefit the society as a whole. Examples include social stratification (Davis and Moore, 1945; Davis, 1949; 366–368); prostitution (Davis, 1937); bossism and the corrupt political machine (Merton, 1957: 73–78, 80–82); deviance and crime (Merton, 1957: 78–80; Bell, 1961: 127–150; Hawkins and Waller, 1936); and even conflict itself (Coser, 1956). The functionalists discussed in the Chapter 3 are a good example of consensus theorists.

In contrast, conflict theory—and there are several distinct schools within this broad tradition—do not see a great deal of consensus, harmony, or cohesion in contemporary society. They see groups with competing and clashing interests and values. They see struggles between sectors of society, with resultant winners and losers. They see tension, struggle, and conflict between groups, categories, segments, and classes in society. Most social institutions, they argue, do not benefit the society as a whole; rather, they benefit some groups *at the expense of* others. For instance, stratification does not benefit society as a whole, but only the rich and the powerful, at the expense of the poor and the weak. In addition, it is to the advantage of the rich to have the economically disadvantaged *believe* stratification is for the good of the entire society; that way, the disadvantaged will be less likely to threaten the interests of the rich.

Groups struggle to have their own definitions of right and wrong enacted into law. The key word here is *hegemony,* or dominance: Groups struggle to legitimate their own special interests and views and to discredit and nullify those of competing groups. For instance, pro- and antiabortionists hold rallies and demonstrations and lobby in Washington to get laws passed, have laws taken off the books, or keep existing laws on the books. Such is the order of the day according to the conflict theorist, who sees a constant struggle among competing groups in contemporary society.

Perhaps the most conflict-oriented of all the conflict theorists are the Marxists. Their ideas are sufficiently different from the non-Marxists conflict theorists to merit a separate discussion. Conflict theorists who do not work within the Marxist paradigm are often called *interest group* theorists (Orcutt, 1983: 311, 316–322) or *pluralistic conflict theorists* (Pfohl, 1985: 341–344). I will use conflict theory, interest group theory, and pluralistic conflict theory more or less interchangeably and will refer to Marxist theory as separate from this tradition. In fact, while the Marxists obviously draw their main theoretical inspiration from Karl Marx and his followers, the conflict theorists are most influenced by the writings of Max Weber (1864–1920). Within the field of criminology, conflict theory is associated with George Vold (1958; Vold and Bernard, 1979, 1986); Joseph Gusfield (1963, 1967, 1981); Austin Turk (1969, 1972, 1976, 1977, 1980); Charles McCaghy (1985; Denisoff and McCaghy, 1973); Clayton Hartjen (1978); Stuart Hills (1971, 1980); and Jerome Skolnick and Elliott Currie (Skolnick et al., 1969; Skolnick and Currie, 1985: 447–488; Currie, 1968, 1985; Currie and Skolnick, 1984: 410–449). In addition, Richard Quin-

ney (1970); Anthony Platt (1969); and William Chambliss (1964; Chambliss and Seidman, 1971) wrote early works within the conflict tradition, but later turned to the more radical embrace of the Marxist paradigm.

The central issue for all conflict-oriented criminologists is the emergence and enforcement of norms, rules, and, especially, laws. How do laws get passed? Which groups manage to get their own special interests and views enacted into law? Who profits by the passage of which laws? Which laws are enforced and which are passed but never enforced—and why? Why are certain activities regarded as deviant while others are regarded as conventional by the members of a given society?

The answer provided by the conflict approach is that laws, rules, and norms grow out of a power struggle among interest groups, factions, and social classes. The most powerful group or groups in society are the ones that are successful in having their own special views of right and wrong accepted by the society as a whole or formulated into criminal law. Likewise, the enforcement of the law represents the application of power against the powerless by the powerful.

Conflict theorists explicitly reject two commonly held views concerning the law. The first is that the law is a "reflection of the social consciousness of a society," that laws make up a "barometer of the moral and social thinking of a community" (Friedman, 1964: 143). Instead, conflict theorists argue that public views on what is regarded as conventional or deviant, law-abiding or criminal, vary strikingly from group to group in a large, complex society. Even where there is consensus on a given issue as to what behavior should be against the law, the conflict theorist asks how and why it is achieved (Turk, 1980: 83–84; Chambliss, 1976: 3). For most issues, there is no majority consensus—only different views held by different social groups. The point of view held by the most powerful of these groups is the one that becomes law.

The second widely held view of conflict theorists is that laws are passed to protect society as a whole, to protect all classes and groups in society more or less equally. The conflict theorist argues that laws do not protect the rights of the many, but the interests of the few. There is no such thing as "the society as a whole," the conflict theorist would argue. Societies are broken upon into segments, sectors, groups, or classes that have very different interests. Very few laws have an equal impact on all segments of society. The earliest laws of vagrancy in England, for example, were passes to protect the interests of the wealthiest and most powerful member of English society—the landowners in the 1300s, and the merchant class in the 1500s (Chambliss, 1964). The laws of theft in England, again, were interpreted in the 1400s mainly to protect the property of merchants (Hall, 1952). The laws regulating the quality of meat sold to the public were supported by, and served the interests of, the largest meat packers (Kolko, 1963).

It is true that legal systems attempt to cloak the special interest character of the law and crime by invoking "the common good." A crime is said to represent an offense against "the state," against "the people." Indeed, some laws *do* serve the common good, as the three above examples attest. Still, this was not necessarily why the laws were passed in the first place, and it does not account for the fact that a given law does not have an equal effect on everyone in a given society. For instance, laws against theft protect people with property far more than people without property; if you own nothing, you can lose nothing to theft.

In sum, the conflict perspective on the passage and the enforcement of law holds that in contemporary society:

1. Groups or segments of society differ significantly in their possession of power.

2. The more power a social group or segment of society has, the greater the likelihood it will be successful in getting its views translated into law; the less power a group has, the lower is this likelihood.

3. Societies are not unified or homogeneous; they differ significantly in economic interests, views of right and wrong, definitions of deviance and conventionality, and

stake in the ongoing system of prestige and honor. The notion that a given outcome will have equal impact on society as a whole, that anything can be "in the interests of society" or for "the public welfare," is a fiction.

4. Individuals and groups tend to be motivated to maximize their own self-interests and worldview through the criminal law—by attempting to engineer laws that maximize their own special interests and worldview.

5. The relationship between "social harm" —that is, outcomes that are widely agreed upon to have done damage to large numbers of people—and criminalization is oblique. Many laws are passed and enforced that criminalize relatively harmless activities; and many dangerous and damaging activities are not criminalized at all, or are formally criminalized, but the laws controlling them are not enforced. In large part, laws tend to be passed and enforced for reasons other than the protection of the members of society from harm.

6. The protection of society will typically be invoked as a reason for the passage of nearly all laws by their supporters; often, although not always, people involved in passing these laws will believe in this protectionist rhetoric.

7. Criminal laws tend to be passed and enforced specifically because they serve the economic, political, and ideological, and status interests of groups or segments in a society that hold the most power—that is, groups who control the resources of the society.

8. The consequences of the law are typically unrelated to the public welfare. Laws rarely have the protective effects claimed for them when they are passed. It may happen that many people benefit from them, but this is atypical.

9. Law enforcement tends not to be directed at the illegal activity of the powerful and, especially, not at illegal activity in which the powerful alone are engaged.

Laws, then, are not seen by the conflict school as an expression of a broad consensus, or as an altruistic desire to protect a large number of the members of a society from objective, clear, and present danger.

Rather, they are the embodiment of the beliefs, life-style, and/or economic interests of certain segments of society. In other words, they are the product of the lobbying of *special interest groups*. Thus, the law is a means of forcing one group's beliefs and politics on the rest of society. Laws are passed (and enforced) not because they protect society in general, or because many people believe in their moral correctness, but because they uphold the ideological or material interests of a certain sector of society. This serves to stop certain people from doing what others consider evil, undesirable, or unprofitable; or to make them do something that others consider good, desirable, or profitable. The passage of a law could represent the triumph of a point of view or an ideology associated with a particular group, social category, or organization—even if that law is not enforced. The passage of law represents the crystallization of one group's economic or ideological interests into the criminal code. In the usual case, "criminal law marks the victory of some groups over others" (Quinney, 1970: 43). The conflict school takes the passage and enforcement of laws out of the public sphere of public safety and the collective conscience, and places it squarely in the arenas of morality, ideology, politics, and economics.

In addition to being interested in the passage and enforcement of criminal laws, conflict theorists also examine—although to a far lesser extent—the question of the causes of criminal behavior. What causes criminal behavior according to the conflict perspective?

Before answering this question, the conflict theorist is careful to point out that the issue is not explaining criminal behavior as such, but explaining forms of behavior that have *a high likelihood of being defined as criminal*. And what forms of behavior are these? As we saw earlier, the behavior of the poor and the powerless stand a higher likelihood of being defined as crimes, while behavior of the rich and the powerful stand a considerably lower likelihood. Thus, the street crimes that the poorer strata are more likely to commit are those actions that are criminalized, while the harmful, unethical, and even technically illegal corporate or white-collar crimes of the wealthier strata are not seen as criminal, and are not studied by the criminologist *as* crimes. When someone asks what causes criminal behavior, he or she invariably means what causes people to engage in a particular *type* of criminal behavior— namely, street crimes such as robbery, rape, and murder.

It seems almost intuitively obvious that being at the bottom of the heap economically in a highly stratified society will lead to many problems of living, which, in turn, make certain criminal actions more likely— most notably, street crimes. In a society in which money is the measure of a person, if one has no money, one will clearly be more likely to seek to obtain it in whatever way one can—illegally if necessary—than someone who already has a great deal of money. Very few wealthy executives grab a gun and hold up a neighborhood liquor store, but then if they already earn $500,000 a year, why should they? In addition, if one faces countless problems, many of them economic, in just getting through each day, it seems obvious that anger and rage will occasionally erupt into actual interpersonal violence. If a person has a great deal of money, power, and status—and money, power, and status answer many of life's most pressing problems—again it seems obvious that he or she is less likely to feel a sense of frustration and rage and, hence, engage in violence, than if he or she is poor, powerless, and disvalued. The conflict theorist has no problem looking at the origins of crime within the class structure—indeed, such a perspective is entirely consistent with conflict theory.

More specifically, conflict theorists find that sharp *economic inequality* is associated with a high rate of crime. In the United States, cities with the greatest economic differences between rich and poor and Black and white have the highest rates of street crime, especially violent crimes (Currie and Skolnick, 1984: 441; Currie, 1985: 144–179). Likewise, in nations around the world, countries with the greatest measure of inequality between rich and poor tend to have the highest rates of street crime and violence (Braith-waite and Braithwaite, 1980). In the welfare states of Western Europe, which show fairly small economic differences between rich and poor, and in Eastern Europe, crime rates are quite low. In the United States, with greater economic differences between rich and poor, crime rates are much higher. And in economically developing Third World countries, especially those in which the tra-ditional culture has been disrupted, crime rates are higher still. "The evidence for a strong association between inequality and crime is overwhelming" (Currie, 1985: 146).

The glaring economic differences be-tween rich and poor, then, produce a high crime rate, especially violent street crimes. What's the solution to a nation's high crime rate? To the conflict theorists, the answer seems clear: a redistribution of the economic pie. Make the rich poorer and the poor richer; make the powerful more powerless and the powerless more powerful. Make the economic and political differences between the top and bottom strata less glaring, less pronounced, more equalitarian (Currie, 1985; Chapter 5; Braithwaite, 1979: 230–255). This solution is likely to anger conserv-atives, because they believe social and eco-nomic *equality* produces crimes (Davies, 1983), or believe, in any case, that crime is not strongly related to economic inequality (Wilson, 1985: 6–7, 13, 126, 251). It will also anger Marxists, who believe true equality cannot be attained outside the context of a communist revolution. (For Braithwaite's re-sponse to this objection, see 1979: 239–244.) Still, many conflict theorists will argue that the only way to significantly reduce street crime is to generate more economic equality.

Conflict or interest group theorists agree with Marxists on a number of points, as we'll see. Marxists also say that the criminal law is the creation of the most powerful segments of a society. They agree that the interests of the powerful tend to be translated into, and are protected by, the criminal law. They agree that a consensus rarely prevails with respect to the activities the public feels should be criminalized; in any case, if such a consensus should prevail, it is rarely the

principal reason why the law is passed in the first place. Moreover, Marxists agree that criminalizing certain forms of behavior rarely protects the interests of society as a whole; rather, some segments will profit while others may be hurt by the enforcement of many laws. Laws and their enforcement rarely have a uniformly positive—or a uni-formly negative—impact on all classes or segments in any society.

These two schools of thought part com-pany on a number of important points, how-ever. In contrast to Marxists, non-Marxist conflict theorists argue as follows.

Not all important conflicts are between eco-nomic classes. Marxists regard the economics as paramount, of central importance, and conflicts between the haves (the bourgeoisie or capitalist class) and the have-nots (the pro-letariat) as the primary determinant of social change in a capitalist society. In contrast, the conflict theorists, following Max Weber, re-gard the economic institution as one of sev-eral important dimensions in a society. The question of which institution influences which other ones—whether it is religion in-fluencing the economy, the family influenc-ing politics, the economy influencing the ed-ucation, and so on—depends on the issue and the circumstances in question. Not only can the various institutions influence one another, but also, the world of ideas can in-fluence the material world and vice versa. Ideas are "codeterminant" with economic forces (Hinch, 1983, 1984). In Marx's scheme, the material world is paramount, and the ideational world, the world of ideas, is dependent upon it and caused by it—not an equal to it. For example, Max Weber's theory, expressed in *The Protestant Ethic and the Spirit of Capitalism,* that religious ideas could have been influential in bringing about industrial capitalism, is almost univer-sally rejected among Marxists because it gives the ideational world equal power with the material or economic world. Conflict theorists do not see one sphere as dominant over the other, while Marxists most emphati-cally do.

Interest group theorists insist there are

sources of conflict that cannot be traced directly to economic and social class factors. For instance, feminist criminologists argue that sexism and the oppression of women is behind the passage of many laws (for instance a man cannot legally rape his wife in most states), the nonpassage of other laws (for instance, the Equal Rights Amendment), and the nonenforcement of still others (such as wife-beating). These laws have little or nothing to do with the struggle between the bourgeoisie and the proletariat; instead, they represent a conflict between one relatively powerless category in the population (women) and a relatively powerful one (men). Many other struggles—for instance, that between young and old, or between different racial or ethnic groups—may not represent a simple clash of class and economic interests.

For instance, during the 1920s, a series of unusually harsh laws was passed in Canada criminalizing opium possession. Anyone convicted of selling or giving narcotics to a minor was to receive a mandatory whipping. Convicted narcotics offenders were denied the appeals usually extended to other convicted offenders. The police looking for narcotics were given the "drastic right to search" certain establishments, a right not normally extended to the majority of suspects. It turns out that the brunt of this narcotics legislation was directed at the Chinese, who were suspected of passing on their supposed opium-smoking habit to whites. Majority whites were not, for the most part, engaged in an economic struggle with Chinese-Canadians; many did, however, hold certain racist beliefs about the Chinese, which found their way into the drug laws passed at the time. Here, we have a struggle not between social classes but different racial groups (Cook, 1970).

Some conflicts are over symbolic issues. Marxists insist that struggles between classes and factions in capitalist society are typically "rational" and relate to the distribution of resources and economic power. Non-Marxist conflict theorists insist that, while many issues are of this type, a substantial proportion is over questions that can be classified as "symbolic" or "irrational"; they have to do with matters of status more than of power or economic interests.

For instance, in 1919, the sale of alcoholic beverages in the United States was prohibited. But by 1933, the national ban on alcohol was regarded as a failure and was abandoned. Conflict theorists argue that both the original passage of the law, the Volstead Act, and its later repeal can be explained by power differences between segments in the population with differing views of right and wrong.

Early in the twentieth century, rural dwellers, Southerners, and the "old" middle class consisting of prosperous farmers; local business merchants; white, Anglo-Saxon Protestants; and native-born Americans of native-born parentage wielded a great deal of power in U.S. politics relative to their numbers in the population. And these segments favored Prohibition. They tended to regard total abstinence from alcohol as respectable, a sign of virtue; they felt drinking was distinctly disreputable—in fact, deviant. The triumph of Prohibition represented the triumph of a certain life-style and the moral virtue of the groups that bore that life-style. "Some of the deepest struggles in American politics have emerged over issues which are not directly related to economic divisions in society" (Gusfield, 1963: 13).

By the early 1930s, Prohibition was regarded as failure. Why? The segments of the population that came to exert more power in national politics than previously consisted of urban dwellers, non-Protestant ethnics—mainly Italian and Irish Catholics and Jews—as well as residents of the Northeast, and sons and daughters of immigrants. Among these segments in the American population, abstention from drinking was seen as no particular virtue. They tended to favor drinking, opposed Prohibition, and supported its repeal. Prohibition was repealed not because it didn't work, according to conflict theorists, but because the groups that supported it lost power, and those that opposed it became significantly more influential in the political process. The law had a symbolic function as well as practical consequences: It asserted that the group that favored it and whose life-style it affirmed were respectable and dominant. When Prohibition was in effect, conservative, rural, white Anglo-Saxon Protestants were told, it is your beliefs that are law, your life-style that is dominant; you are legitimate, and all other groups and categories are less than respectable. When Prohibition was repealed, drinkers—the supporters of repeal—were told, you are respectable, your life-style is legitimate, acceptable, nondeviant. As much as anything, Prohibition and its repeal were about status and respectability.

The law, in short, has a symbolic function to many conflict theorists: "Public affirmation of a norm through ... government action expresses the public worth of one subculture vis-à-vis others.... It demonstrates which cultures have legitimacy and public domination, and which do not. Accordingly, it enhances the social status of groups carrying the affirmed culture and degrades groups carrying that which is condemned as deviant" (Gusfield, 1967: 175). To a non-Marxist conflict theorist, many issues pertaining to deviance and crime, to norms and laws, have little or nothing to do with rational, instrumental, economic questions, but are noninstrumental, or *symbolic*. In contrast, the Marxist tends to look for economic conflict, particularly class struggle, behind the important issues of the day.

Deviance and crime exist and will continue to exist in socialist societies. Conflict and rule breaking are omnipresent and universal; they will exist and flourish, even in a socialist society. Interest group theorists, following Max Weber, tend to emphasize the continuities and similarities between capitalism and socialism; Marxists emphasize their differences. As we'll see below, the more simple-minded Marxists insist that crime and deviance will not exist under "true" socialism; Marxists with a more complex view of how the world works argue that crime and deviance will probably be drastically reduced under a mature socialist regime. Adherents of all Marxist schools believe crime and devi-

ance will look very different under socialism compared with capitalism. In contrast, non-Marxists tend to emphasize their similarities.

All brands of Marxism contain a strain of utopianism (although in varying degrees, depending on the brand). That is, they all believe when capitalism is overthrown and abolished and the age of socialism is ushered in, society will look a lot better than it does today. Many of society's basic problems will be solved, or at least ameliorated. Capitalism is based on a competitive ethic, with individuals and groups struggling with one another to take resources away from others to obtain more for themselves. This competitive ethic, many Marxists believe, lends an atmosphere of opposition, hostility, conflict, and brutality to capitalist society, which, in turn, stimulates high rates of crimes such as robbery, murder, and rape. (For such an argument for rape, see Schwendinger and Schwendinger, 1983.) In addition, under capitalism, certain relatively harmless activities, like homosexuality, are stigmatized; under socialism, laws discrediting certain harmless minorities will not be necessary and will not exist. Severe conflict between groups, so rife and deep-seated under capitalism, will subside when true socialism is institutionalized.

Non-Marxist theorists disagree. They argue that conflict is endemic to all social relations; transforming a society's economic base from private to public hands will not eliminate conflict, violence, and differences in interpretation of the law. Crime, deviance, and delinquency are probably ineradicable features of all societies, capitalist or socialist. For instance, the high rate of alcoholism that existed in Czarist Russia remains in the Soviet Union today, under socialism. True, certain actions are and will be considerably more common in some societies than in others, but the nature of a society's economic base has very little to do with this. Socialism, they insist, will not eliminate, or probably even drastically reduce the incidence of deviance or crime or the impulse to legitimize norms, pass laws, stigmatize the deviant, or arrest and punish the lawbreaker. Of course, if a society's laws are drastically different, its crimes will be different, too. In some socialist societies, buying and selling for a profit are illegal; clearly, such economic crimes do not exist under capitalism. But a society's legal and normative structure is not likely to change very much under socialism, most interest group theorists insist. Much the same forms of deviance and crime that exist under capitalism will remain under socialism.

MARXIST CRIMINOLOGY

Karl Marx (1818–1883) is, worldwide, the most important social scientist who ever lived. More than a third of the earth's population lives under some sort of Marxist regime, and most contemporary social thinkers and writers have been profoundly influenced by Marx's theories. In the United States, his theories are less influential than elsewhere; nonetheless, a vigorous band of Marxist sociologists continues to influence students in colleges and universities around the country.

Almost every imaginable subject has been analyzed from a Marxist perspective—photography, art, love, sex, marriage and the family, the mass media, religion, education, politics, the population problem, social movements—even Donald Duck. There is not one single Marx, but several: Marx's early work is more humanistic; his later work is more deterministic. Marx and Engels together wrote some 13 million words; although there is some consistency in that huge body of writing, there are contradictions and irresolvable complexities. Moreover, there are dozens of different Marxist schools of thought; some of them disagree almost violently with what others have to say about how the world should be viewed. Thus, to characterize Marxist thought in a few pages inevitably does injustice to the complexity of the man, his thought, and the writings of his followers. Marxism, however, is a more or less coherent body of thought, a perspective, an orientation; there are some common threads in it—otherwise, we would not be able to use one term to cover it all.

Marxism stresses the importance of the role of economic factors in human affairs. More specifically, Marx argued two points. First, society's economic stage determines its general character. Economic stage is determined by a society's *mode of production*—how a society organizes its labor. There are five basic modes of production in human history: egalitarian, or "primitive communism"; slave; feudal; capitalist; and socialist. Capitalism, a society based on private property and the pursuit of profit, exhibits all of the features of a competitive, greedy, exploitative social order. Such a society will have a culture that reflects the distinctive stamp of its economic base, capitalism. Thus, its system of justice will be a capitalist system of justice, its family system will be adapted to the needs of a capitalist economic order, its art will be a capitalist-derived art, and so on.

Second, Marx said, the members of a society relate to one another primarily as representatives of their economic position—that is, because they belong to a certain social class. People's beliefs, their political views, and their ideology will tend to reflect their social class. To Marx, ideology is extremely important because it usually justifies and rationalizes people's economic interests. The rich tend to believe they deserve their favored position in life because it is to their advantage to do so. Social classes that receive more of a society's riches will attempt to retain their privileges; those that receive less will attempt to obtain more. One way of keeping the have-knots down is physical coercion—swords, guns, tanks, billy clubs. Actually, physical coercion isn't a very good way of keeping the poor in their place, because regimes based on it tend to be unstable. Successful regimes convince the poor they deserve their fate, and that the rich deserve theirs; they tend to be more stable and, therefore, more capable of effectively exploiting the poor.

Marx stressed *conflict* in societies, generally, and in capitalist society, specifically. He argued that harmony and a correspondence in economic and social interests between the social classes were not possible under capitalism. It is in the workers' best interests to organize, destroy the capitalist order, and institute socialism. It is in the business elites' best interests to repress and exploit the working class and prevent all moves toward socialism. The two classes are always and inevitably at odds and in conflict with one another. It is an opposition that must inevitably result in violent clashes, outright revolution, and the establishment of a socialist order.

In the early 1960s, the late C. Wright Mills (1962; 96–99) distinguished between three varieties of Marxists: vulgar Marxists, sophisticated Marxists, and plain Marxists. The term "vulgar," as used here, means *crude* and *ignorant;* many Marxists have ignored the complexity and subtlety of Marx's own ideas and have turned them into a simpleminded cartoon, a system of thought that is far more rigid and simplistic than Marx intended. Vulgar Marxists "seize upon certain ideological features of Marx's political philosophy and identify these parts as the whole" (1962: 96). They can be "typified by political and intellectual rigidity"; they "substitute narrow-minded and blind application of . . . rhetoric, slogans, and terminology for rigorous analysis" (Thomas, 1982: 313).

Sophisticated Marxists "are mainly concerned with Marxism as a model of society." They are not particularly interested in accumulating evidence to test the validity of their model. Instead, they are fascinated with the abstract model itself as if were holy writ, something along the lines of a sacred artistic masterpiece, not to be tampered with. When evidence comes along that seems to contradict the model, they tack complex and convoluted explanations onto it as to why the evidence does not "really" demonstrate Marxism's weaknesses. Their sole interest seems to be in supporting the view that Marx was infallible and that no evidence yet accumulated could possibly challenge his theories (Mills, 1962: 96–98). In short, sophisticated Marxists "see Marx's writings as sacred text and argue . . . over their true meaning and how these meanings should be translated into sensible statements, given contemporary changes" (Thomas, 1982: 313).

Plain Marxists, into which category Mills placed himself, "work in Marx's own tradition." They ground Marx in the body of classical sociological thinking. Marx's work, like that of all other social scientists, is historically specific; Marx was, after all, a creature of his own time—not a talismanic figure to be worshipped and defended at all cost. Plain Marxists are not rigid, dogmatic thinkers, but ones who see Marx's body of work as raw material from which to build living theory and research about an everchanging social and economic world—a world Marx could not have foreseen in detail. They see tension and dilemmas in Marx's work and in its varying ability to confront social reality (Mills, 1962; 98–99). In sum, the plain Marxists "attempt to develop the methodological, conceptual, theoretical, and political value of a Marxian position . . . , to recognize and resolve the conceptual and theoretical difficulties of a Marxian framework while developing it also as an empirical research tool" (Thomas, 1982: 313).

Marx and his collaborator Friedrich Engles (1820–1895) wrote very little specifically on deviance and crime. Consequently, anyone putting together a Marxist perspective toward the subject must extend, extrapolate, and fill in the gaps, rather than rely on what Marx himself said. The lack of Marx's writings on deviance and crime has not deterred Marxist scholars from writing on the subject, however, for the criminological literature adopting the Marxist approach is immense.

In looking at Marxist writings on crime and deviance, Mills's scheme is at least partly useful. To me, it appears there are least two Marxist approaches to deviance and crime, roughly paralleling Mills's typology: *vulgar utopian Marxism* and *plain Marxism.* "Vulgar utopian Marxists" have qualities similar to the first two categories Mills delineated, the vulgar Marxists and the sophisticated Marxists; thus, I have collapsed them into a single category. And the plain Marxists who study crime and deviance correspond to Mills's category of the same name.

Vulgar Utopian Marxists

In the 1970s, a school of criminologists arose in Britain and in the United States whose representatives published a large number of books and articles. They called themselves "critical" criminologists, "new" criminologists, and "radical" criminologists. They even called themselves "anticriminologists," thereby making the point that they opposed traditional criminology. By denouncing capitalism, they believed, they would assist in its downfall and eliminate crime and, hence, the need to study it; they imagined themselves "abolitionists" of criminology (Cohen, 1988). Their work was extremely influential in the study of deviance and crime; the writings commenting on their works in the field of criminology are voluminous. They regarded themselves as legitimate Marxists, called themselves Marxists, used a number of Marxist categories, wrote as radicals and revolutionaries, and were vigorous critics of capitalism and staunch defenders of socialism. At the same time, many Marxists attacked, first, their credentials as Marxists and, second, their arguments as shallow, misleading, and invalid.

I call this school of sociologists the "vulgar utopian Marxists," and use the term "vulgar" because, it is now generally conceded by many Marxists and non-Marxists alike—indeed, now, even by several of the individuals who were so designated at one time—that their work in the early 1970s was simplistic, crude, and ignorant of what Marx himself said. I call it "utopian" because adherents of this school were more concerned with how the world *ought* to look, in their view, and with what is wrong with contemporary capitalist society, according to their abstract ideal, than how the world actually *does* look. Their gaze was so strongly fixed on a nonexistent future—a future nearly all now concede neither *will* or even *can* exist—that they lost sight of social realities right in front of their noses. The most well-known representatives of this perspective include Richard Quinney (1972a, 1972b, 1973, 1974a, 1974b, 1975, 1979, 1980a; Quinney and Wildeman, 1977):[3] Anthony Platt (1973, 1975);

Herman and Julia Schwendinger (1970, 1974, 1975, 1977); and Ian Taylor, Paul Walton, and Jock Young (1973, 1975).

Most of the practitioners of this approach have gone on to adopt a different point of view from that which they expressed in the 1970s. Quinney, for example, began his career in the 1960s as a criminologist adopting a fairly conventional approach (1965, 1966, Clinard and Quinney, 1967); in fact, he did his dissertation on prescription violations among pharmacists, adopting strain as his explanatory variable (1963). In 1970, he authored a book that took a conflict or interest group perspective. His Marxist phase ran through the 1970s. In the early 1980s, he came under the influence of Christianity, attempting to reconcile Marxist with Christian though (1980b, 1982). Finally, in the mid-to-late 1980s, he seems to have been strongly influenced by Buddhism (1986). No one can predict what his next phase will be.

The same can be said of Taylor, Walton, and Young. All have turned away from abstract, utopian reasoning to empirical examinations of real-life, grassroots crime and punishment, and specific systems of deviance, crime, and justice. Moreover, their current work displays a certain measure of skepticism, a quality distinctly lacking in their earlier, more idealistic writing. For instance, in the early 1980s, Taylor produced a complex, subtly nuanced analysis of "law and order" (1981), light years away from the simplistic propagandizing of *The New Criminology* (Taylor et al., 1973). Young has since co-

---

[3]Quinney poses special problems that are not, for the most part, presented by the other theorists mentioned; that is, he tends to be inconsistent and contradictory in his approach. On the one hand, he claims to be a "historical materialist," that is, a Marxist. And yet, on the other hand, he adopts the contrary, or idealist, position by saying that *even if the material conditions for revolution do not exist,* if we all think good and right and pure thoughts, we can bring socialism about (1980a, passim, esp. 166ff; 1979: 398–399; Quinney and Wildeman, 1977: 171–172). Marx was especially hostile to this idealistic fallacy. Knowing that a strain in Quinney's approach is idealistic and otherworldly,—that is, unconcerned with social and material conditions—makes it understandable that, first Christianity (1980b) and then Buddhism (1986), would eventually have a special appeal for his thinking. After all, if the material world does not cooperate with one's analysis and predictions, one can create a fantasy world that will correspond.

authored a book on the politics of abortion in Britain (Greenwood and Young, 1976), which takes a reformist stand that is completely contrary to the absolutist, revolutionary stance expressed in that earlier volume (Taylor et al., 1973). He has also penned an essay, again, supporting the idea of reformism, with the revealing subtitle "From New Criminology to Marxism" (1979), suggesting that the "new" criminology was not squarely within the Marxist tradition. Platt (1978) came to argue—from a Marxist position—that members of the lower and working classes are themselves mainly the victims of street crime; and the Schwendingers (1977) and Young (1979) ended up reputiating their earlier romanticization of criminal behavior.[4]

Thus, while a specific school of Marxist sociologists crossed paths in examining deviance and crime, arriving at more or less the same place in the early-to-mid 1970s, soon thereafter they all took off in somewhat different directions. Yet, it is the works I characterize as belonging to the vulgar utopian Marxist school that will be remembered when the history of theories of criminology is written.

What characterizes vulgar utopian Marxism in the field of criminology and the study of deviance? This approach takes as its starting point that the social world as it exists—that is, capitalist society—is an inauthentic, illegitimate reality, and that phenomena that exist in it do not *deserve* to exist. Therefore, they should be treated *as if* they did not exist. They agree with the Catholic theologian Thomas Aquinas (1225–1274) and the English statesman and Catholic martyr Thomas More (1478–1535), who said, centuries later, that an unjust law is not a true law, and therefore not a law that should be treated *as* a true law. Taking off from this assumption, the vulgar utopian Marxists make at least the following points.

1. Practioners of *all other approaches*—that is, non-Marxist, nonutopian approaches—are deluded, partial in scope, and ensnared by ideological traps; they are, therefore, *irrelevant or harmful* and should be ignored (Taylor et al., 1973, passim). Only Marxism (and this particular brand of Marxism) is capable of seeing social reality as it really is. There is only one legitimate, authentic truth here (Quinney, 1974a: 1–16, 17ff).

2. Criminologists (that is to say, traditional, conventional, non-Marxist criminologists) are engaged in repressing "those who threaten the social system." Criminology "continues to be dominated by a single purpose: preservation of the existing order" (Quinney, 1974b: 13, 15). It is therefore among "the agents of the capitalist state" (Quinney, 1980a: 176). "Theories of deviance—sometimes enhanced by research—serve a single purpose: They justify the existing social order" (Quinney, 1972a: 317).

3. "We know best": If criminals, victims of a crime, individuals who are defined as oppressed or exploited, do not adopt our point of view, they are exhibiting *false consciousness*—that is, acting against their own best interests. If they knew better, they would agree with us. Accepting people's subjective views as if they were valid is counterrevolutionary; it is theoretically and politically unacceptable. The problem with such subjectivity is that it takes all views of reality as equally valid; it fails to provide "a yardstick for judging the goodness of one reality over another." In short, it lacks the critical perspective that can only be found with Marxism (Quinney, 1974a; 5–8).

4. The law and other conventional definitions of crime and deviance are products of capitalism and reflections of an unjust social order. They arose out of the need by the capitalist class to maintain its power, control, and profits. The ruling elite is responsible for the criminal laws; the police and the courts are instruments of ruling-class domination. All law in capitalist society is repressive. The legal system exists for a single purpose: to repress the working class, deprive it of social justice, and attempt to prevent the socialist revolution from taking place. Law is

---

[4]For an intelligent analysis of the excesses of the vulgar utopian Marxists in the early 1970s by an insider, see Cohen (1988). For two critiques of vulgar Marxism by Marxists, see Greenberg (1981: 2–13, 59, 63–64, 69, 191, 412–417; 1986) and Hinch (1983, 1984). This section is heavily indebted to these discussions.

an "arm" of the ruling class in capitalist society (Quinney, 1974a: 24, 55f; 1974b; 24). *All law in capitalist society is, by its very nature and irrespective of its consequences, contrary to the interests of "the people"*: "Until law is the law of the people, law can be nothing other than official repression" (Quinney, 1972b).

5. Deviance and crime exist *solely* because of economic oppression of the working class under capitalism; they will not exist under true socialism. Every detail of capitalist society is saturated by capitalism; nothing of any consequence can be changed without destroying capitalism's economic foundation—that is, capitalism itself. Only under true socialism will human freedom blossom and human destiny be able to unfold (Quinney, 1974a: 16). Under socialism, people will not longer be alienated, classes will no longer have need "to dominate one another," and there will therefore be no need "for a legal system to secure the interests of a capitalist ruling class." As a result, "there will no longer be the need for crime" (Quinney, 1974b: 25).

6. Since deviance and crime exist because of the "contradictions" of capitalism, it does no good to reform the capitalist criminal justice system without eliminating capitalism altogether; in fact, making people more comfortable in a repressive system only helps capitalism survive and therefore intensifies the repression. Thus, liberal reformism is an evil and should be denounced (Platt, 1975: 97; Quinney, 1974a: 84, 171, 178, 179; 1974b; 15, 390–391).

7. The only truly important job of any student of crime is to contribute to the downfall of capitalism—that is, to take part in the revolution; this can be accomplished only by exposing the injustices of capitalist society. A Marxist analysis of crime "shares in the larger *socialist struggle*. One commitment is to eliminating exploitation and oppression. Being on the side of the oppressed, only those ideas are advanced which will help transform the capitalist system. The objective of the Marxist analysis is change—revolutionary change" (Quinney, 1979: 398).

8. The empirical world is inauthentic and therefore of no real importance. Quinney (1972a: 320) refers to "the absurdities of empiricism." The way things are is not the way things will be in the future; that which exists will inevitably perish. Thus, in effect, what we seem to see before us does not really exist and should not concern the politically correct observer. Criminal behavior, as such, is simply a by-product of capitalism and, therefore, is of trivial concern; it is, in Marxist parlance, *epiphenomenal*. In other words, the "ought" is more important than the "is." To put it another way, the *real* or *true* or *authentic* "is" is really the "ought." We live in a world in which our "essence" has been cut off from our "existence." Therefore, our understanding must be "prophetic," one in which the "is" and the "ought" are unified (Quinney, 1980a: 2).

9. Since the law is an agent of repression in capitalist society, "criminality in itself is a threat to the capitalist system"; crime and criminals are seen "as laudible forces in the class struggle" (Hinch, 1983, 1984). Thus, crime and deviance are political statements, and the deviant and the criminal should really be regarded as heroes. Since deviants and criminals reject social and legal definitions that are products of an unjust, repressive social order, they are, in their own way, fighting against capitalism. All that is needed to turn the criminal into a revolutionary hero is a "development of political consciousness" (Hinch, 1983, 1984). Therefore, criminals ought to be revered, not punished (Taylor, et al., 1973: 169, 221; Quinney and Wildeman, 1977: 166–168; Quinney, 1974a: 116, 118; 1979: 120; 1980a: 61–62, 65–66; for a Marxist critique of this view, see Wenger and Bonomo, 1981). In some work in this tradition, a distinction is made between the "lumpen" crimes of the lower classes and the political crimes of the true working classes (Quinney, 1980a: 59–66). Young (1975: 64) accuses practitioners of the labeling perspective of romanticizing the deviant, which seems to be precisely the vulgar utopian Marxist's problem at this point.

10. At the same time, crime should be *redefined* to mean violations of human rights—sexism, racism, exploitation, imperialism—

in short, anything that contributes to human misery and deprives people of their human potential—*those are the true crimes*. The people who should be locked up are members of the capitalist class, not ordinary street criminals (Liazos, 1972; Smith, 1973; Platt, 1975: 103; Schwendinger and Schwendinger, 1975).

Criticisms of Vulgar Utopian Marxism

It is clear from our contemporary vantage point that the vulgar utopian Marxist approach to deviance and crime was more ideology and dogma than analysis. The claim that one cannot separate politics from one's view of reality is now seen as glib, a cop out, not thought through very carefully. Vulgar utopian Marxists have sustained almost as much criticism from Marxists as from non-Marxists. In fact, many of the criticisms from these two approaches have been similar. Perhaps the most important and fundamental of these criticisms is that vulgar Marxists adopt a "unicausal approach," an oversimplified view that capitalism is the cause of all crime—indeed, the root of all evil (Mankoff, 1978: 295–298; Shichor, 1980b: 201; Gibbons, 1982: 148). These critics find, for example, the vulgar Marxist assertion that crimes of violence, such as rape, are a simple product of capitalism (Schwendinger and Schwendinger, 1974; 1983), an absurdity and not in accord with the facts. Crime and deviance—rape included—and social problems of all kinds, including oppression and exploitation, predated capitalism and will exist long after the demise of capitalism.

The more simpleminded Marxist criminologists are faulted for the naive view that crime will be eliminated with the advent of socialism and are called to task for the deliberate avoidance of facing the existence of crime and deviance in socialist and communist nations (Greenberg, 1979; Klockars, 1980; 109–110). To focus exclusively on crime in capitalist countries and ignore its existence in nations based on Marxist principles is to abdicate the sociologist's responsibility to study deviance and crime in the real world (Mankoff, 1978: 297). In their defense, many utopian Marxists claim that so-called socialist societies such as the Soviet Union and China do not represent "true" socialism. Unfortunately, "true" socialism exists only in their heads, not anywhere in the real world—not exactly the most valid basis from which to launch such an important argument.

Vulgar utopian Marxists have also been criticized for their lack of interest in actually studying the empirical reality of crime and deviance (Nettler, 1984: 196ff). Crime is, in utopian Marxist terms, *epiphenomenal*—that is, it is a secondary, pathological by-product of capitalism that will disappear when the illness is cured; it is, therefore, of no real importance in itself. In the Marxist's eyes, the "illness" is capitalism, and the "symptoms" include crime and deviance, along with oppression and exploitation. According to this logic, there is no point in studying crime and deviance in their own right. Utopian Marxists, their critics argue, are ignorant regarding the details of criminal behavior per se. Studying criminal behavior itself becomes reduced to "a political preoccupation of bourgeois criminology" (Klockars, 1980: 108). After all, the utopian Marxists claim, criminology has "served a single purpose: legitimation of the social order" (Quinney, 1974a: 26). Non-Marxist observers do not agree. They regard the understanding of criminal behavior as an end in itself; and that, by ignoring crime, the utopian Marxist has simply ceased to function as a criminologist.

The utopian Marxist perspective on deviance and crime is unconcerned with studying the world as it actually exists but claims to be very concerned with changing it (Quinney, 1979: 422). In fact, utopian Marxists believe the world "as it is" is not really the way it will be in the future; and thus, to examine current conditions, structures, and behavior is to get bogged down in an illegitimate, inauthentic present and to legitimate unreal phenomena as real. As a consequence of this dominance of advocacy over description and analysis, some critics charge, utopian Marxist criminologists have adopted an ideological, not a factual, position. It matters not what the details of the facts are, but how pure one's ideological position is. "Don't confuse me with the facts" is the vulgar utopian Marxist's watchword. In this way, argument is reduced to assertion, anecdote, association, and analogy, rather than based on systematic evidence (Turk, 1980: 80–81). The world the utopians see in the future is in reality a world they wish existed, but wishing doesn't make something true. And willing the present into unreality, likewise, cannot be achieved through an act of faith. Crime exists, it has a real impact on real people's lives, and it is very much worth studying. It is specifically this task that criminologists undertake to accomplish.

Last, many critics object to the tendency of utopian Marxists to see criminal law and society's norms as illegitimate, being impositions from the capitalist power structure. In addition, the utopian Marxist tends to regard any effort to study them as if they were real as bourgeois and counterrevolutionary (Smith, 1973; Quinney, 1972a: 317). Utopian Marxists object to any acceptance of existing categories of reality as an acceptance of the status quo; this lends support of the official version of reality (Quinney, 1973: 183; 1974a: 26). Utopian Marxist criminologists contend that more traditional criminologists and sociologists of deviance accept the dominant definition of law and norms by studying activities defined as "crimes" and "deviance" according to the prevailing moral and legal order; they therefore legitimate the reality of these definitions (Friedrichs, 1980: 39). By studying but neither criticizing nor attempting to destroy the structure that produces these laws and norms, the traditional sociologist helps to make them real and thereby cooperates in the oppression of the people. Utopian Marxists wish to *redefine* crime as the violation of human rights (Liazos, 1972; Quinney and Wildeman, 1977: 6–14; Schwendinger and Schwendinger, 1975); they wish to take the definition of what a crime is out of the hands of the capitalist elite, they contend, and put it into the hands of "the people."

Non-Marxists regard this view as so much windy rhetoric. They separate studying a phenomenon from accepting its legitimacy. Saying that crimes share a common status with respect to the law means specifically this and nothing more. Our personal feelings and ideological views about the legitimacy, fairness, or justice of a given law are irrelevant. When we call an act a crime, we don't necessarily agree that it ought to be a crime—only that it is. It happens to be a legal fact that someone apprehended by a police officer with a hundred kilos of cocaine in his or her possession stands a very high likelihood of being arrested. It doesn't much matter what we, as observers, might think or feel about the laws against the possession of cocaine; they exist as a legal reality.

The irony of vulgar utopian Marxists is that, in seeking human liberation, they end up binding themselves into an intellectual straightjacket. In his "Theses on Feuerbach," Marx said: "The philosophers have only *interpreted* the world, in various ways; the point, however, is to *change* it." The vulgar utopian Marxists managed to misinterpret the world—and they did not succeed in changing it either. Although we can admire their idealism, we must, at the same time, recognize that it takes more than thinking good thoughts to build a legitimate perspective with which to view the world.

As I said earlier, this school has been attacked as much by Marxists as by non-Marxists. One Marxist, in the pages of a radical journal, attacked one vulgar utopian Marxist's writings in the following words: "I would say Quinney discredits a Marxist approach in criminology. He has put forth a text that is dogmatic in that it expounds a single position that is very much under debate without mentioning its problematic nature, and pursues an argument that is patently untenable in a number of respects and overtly illogical in places. Often he has not checked his points empirically and where he has he has done so in a way that is open to question. His dangerously simplified analysis leads to an over-optimistic picture.... There is little to be said for verbal radicalism and neglect of the task at hand which, for criminologists, is to produce solid and well-reflected information about social control and crime" (Steinert, 1978: 313).

Plain Marxists

The legitimate, or in Mills's phrase, the "plain" Marxists offer a much more complex and interesting—and less naive—view of crime than the vulgar utopian Marxists. Marxism is a valid and worthwhile perspective in criminology, but its serious adherents have only begun to put together a well-rounded view of criminal behavior; moreover, when the critics of Marxism attack the paradigm, they either point to positions that Marxists do not hold or they focus entirely on examples of vulgar Marxism (Mankoff, 1980; Beirne, 1979; as examples, see Toby, 1980; Akers, 1980; Klockars, 1980). There is a tradition of Marxist criminology, but it is only now beginning to take shape. Moreover, plain Marxists view Marxist research as an ongoing enterprise subject to revision and discovery, rather than as dogma or eternal truth engraved in stone, as the vulgar utopian Marxists do.

As we saw earlier, Marx and his collaborator Engels wrote very little on crime; a Marxist criminology must be constructed from the general framework of Marx's writings on economics and society. Marxism begins with the general postulate that *a society's mode of production is the basis for its social order;* its patterns of economic organization shape its patterns of social organization (Michalowski, 1985: 16, 21). This means that the nature of a society's economy shapes its criminal behavior and its criminal justice system. For instance, in a small tribal hunting- and-gathering society, theft will rarely occur because property is owned collectively; the concept of private ownership is alien. In addition, everyone knows everyone else, and anonymity is impossible—no one can disappear into a crowd with anyone else's goods. In this type of society, when crime does take place, justice is not typically *retributive*—that is, punishment of the offender as we know it usually does not occur—but rather *restitutive*—that is, the offender has to restore to the victim what is seen as rightfully his or hers.

Capitalism, too, has its own distinctive style of criminal behavior and criminal justice system; the way the law is framed and enforced and the way it is violated are influenced by the fact that our economic system is based on the private ownership of the means of production and the pursuit of profit. Unlike the vulgar utopian Marxists, however, plain Marxists do not draw a rigid or deterministic connection between capitalism and crime and justice. All social institutions are "partly autonomous" from their economic base or infrastructure. Marx himself analyzed the relations between the economy and the other aspects of society as "a set of *asymmetric but reciprocal* determinations" (Greenberg, 1981: 16; my emphasis). This means that, although capitalism influences the form and content of both the criminal justice system and criminal behavior, it does not determine them in every minute detail; in fact, they may even act back on the economy and influence it in significant ways. This is a very long way from saying, as the vulgar utopian Marxists do, that the *only* purpose of the criminal law is to satisfy capitalist interests (Quinney, 1974b: 19, 21, 24). In short, contemporary Marxists have tried to "formulate less simplistic conceptions of the state and law" (Greenberg, 1986) than those that prevailed in earlier Marxist texts.

A second feature of contemporary Marxist criminology is that, unlike vulgar utopian Marxism, it recognizes that the capitalist class—though it does attempt to use the law in a self-interested fashion to further its own interests—does not always get its way. Capitalists "sometimes fail to achieve their legislative goals" (Greenberg, 1986). The ruling elite is far from unopposed in its will; other classes struggle against its efforts and sometimes achieve partial victories. The subordinate classes have some measure of power. Clearly, the ruling elite in capitalist society has more power and usually gets its way, but not every detail of legislation can be explained by its support by the bourgeoisie. There is no need to seek a conspiracy working in the interest of the capitalist class behind the passage (or nonpassage) of every law, because it often happens that laws are passed, or laws fail to get passed, *contrary* to the interests of the capitalist class. Contemporary Marxists do not make the assumption, so dear to the vulgar utopian Marxist's heart, that all law in capitalist society is repressive. The police, the courts, and the prisons do not always operate to the benefit of the ruling class alone (Greenberg, 1986). Marxists now recognize that if "law is to achieve its ideological function by appearing to be fair, it must sometimes *be* fair" (Beirne, 1979). Early work in the Marxist tradition was "overly conspiratorial"; current work attempts to break away from this simplification (Greenberg, 1986).

But let's be clear about this: The plain Marxists do not retreat to the consensus position and say the capitalist system is fair, all classes contribute equally to the shaping and the administration of the law, and democracy works well under capitalism. Nothing could be further from the truth. Marxists insist the capitalist class has the overwhelming and usually decisive edge in any class conflict—although it sometimes loses in a given struggle with other classes. Moreover, all struggles that take place in a capitalist society are marked by the fact of their capitalist context. One cannot abstract any struggle— and this applies strongly to the passage and enforcement of the criminal law—from its historical, that is, capitalist context (Greenberg, 1986).

A third aspect of the plain Marxist's thinking about crime and deviance is that there may be division and factionalism within the capitalist class itself. Vulgar utopian Marxists tend to exaggerate the unity and the wisdom of the capitalist elite. As Marx himself showed (for instance, in *The Eighteenth Brumaire of Louis Bonaparte)*, a given issue may attract shifting alliances, with members of the same class being on different sides, and members of different classes being on the same side. Not all struggles align the bourgeoisie on one side and the proletariat on the other. *Ultimately,* when the revolution

comes, there will be only two classes, and they will align themselves into two massive and hostile forces; but this is only the final outcome of a long history of struggles that will align the classes in factions that cannot be predicted from revolutionary theory alone. In short, divisions within capitalism are important; intra- *and* interclass alliances may operate to secure one set of interests at the expense of others.

Fourth, contemporary Marxist criminology is based on a *legalistic* definition of crime. Vulgar utopian Marxists ignored existing law as illegitimate and strove to redefine crime according to their own views of right and wrong; studying existing laws and their violation collaborates with injustice and stabilizes oppressive capitalist regimes (Smith, 1973; Liazos, 1972; Quinney, 1972a: 317ff; 1974b: 13ff). In contrast, Marx himself rejected the "human rights" definition of what a crime was and adopted a legalistic conception of law in capitalist society; "he pointed out that the concept of theft made sense only in relation to a juridically defined concept of property" (Greenberg, 1981: 27–28). For the most part, contemporary Marxists "use a legal definition of crime; they treat crime as a violation of the criminal law. . . . When radical criminologists write about crime, they generally write about the same categories as other criminologists" (1981: viii).

Crime is a legal reality. Whether a law is just or unjust, it has real consequences for real people's lives if enforced; to ignore it demonstrates contempt for both victims and offenders. Moreover, there are specific reasons why certain laws come into being; if we ignore criminal law as a mere by-product of capitalism, *we cannot investigate the very process that Marxists consider crucial*—that is, the economic and social origins of the law. Such a view assumes that all law comes about in the same deterministic, mechanical fashion, a proposition that is demonstrably false.

A fifth feature of plain Marxism that contrasts with its more vulgar varieties is that contemporary authentic Marxists are *empirical* in their orientation; that is, they use real evidence to document their case, rather than simply asserting they are right and exhorting their readers to believe them. Vulgar utopian Marxists argued that since conventional social scientists have "only" served the interests of the ruling elite and evidence can be interpreted any way the viewer intends (Quinney, 1972a: 317; 1974a: 5, 6, 7, 8, 12–13, 26, 32, 39; 1974b: 4, 13, 15; 1980: 2ff), then what's the point of gathering evidence? The main thing is thinking politically correct thoughts.

Nothing could be further from the authentic Marxist's approach. Contemporary Marxist studies—including Marxist criminology—are marked by an impressive marshalling of empirical evidence. After all, states one Marxist criminologist: "There would be little value in having a criminology that is Marxist unless it added to our ability to understand crime, criminal law, and criminal justice" (Greenberg, 1981: vii). Thus, rather than theorizing about capitalist society in the abstract, without reference to actual concrete contexts, today's Marxist criminologists deal with more delimited, specific phenomena in a more empirical fashion. Whose interests did the emergence of the system of plea bargaining serve? Was Prohibition in the United States simply a struggle among status groups, or did economic interests play a role in its emergence and its demise? Why are there vastly more arrests and incarcerations today than in the 1950s? How and why did the urban police system expand rapidly in the late nineteenth century? Is juvenile delinquency a response to the deprivation of wage earning teenagers? Is antimonopoly legislation enforced? How effectively? These are examples of the kinds of questions that Marxists with an empirical orientation might ask and attempt to answer. As noted earlier, several of the Marxist criminologists of the early 1970s who attempted to theorize abstractly (Quinney is a major exception) have turned to the analysis of more concrete phenomena (Greenwood and Young, 1976; Platt, 1978; Schwendinger and Schwendinger, 1983).

Sixth although the earlier, more superficial Marxist perspective disdained the study of the causes of conventional criminal behavior as collaborating with definitions of crime concocted by the power structure, more contemporary Marxists do not automatically dismiss such a venture (Greenberg, 1981: 57–75). In fact, the young Karl Marx looked at the economic reasons for the theft of wood by displaced peasants in the nineteenth century (Linebaugh, 1981). Examining the causes of crime is neither an empty nor a counterrevolutionary exercise; the economic conditions of a society both limit certain people's actions and present specific opportunities to others. It is within a specific economic context that people violate the law; they powerfully influence who violates the law, which laws are violated, and how frequently they are violated. It should be emphasized that Marxists are quite emphatic on the issue of the *historical specificity* of statements on crime: Criminal behavior always takes place within a specific historical context, and statements about crime apply only to that historical context. For instance, if the lower classes are more violent in contemporary capitalist society, this does not necessarily mean they are also more violent in feudal societies as well (Greenberg, 1981: 18). On this point, Marxists and the more traditional criminologists, especially positivists, disagree. But admitting this qualification, contemporary Marxists are no less interested in the causes of crime than are the practitioners of other perspectives. Of course, they have quite different explanations as to why criminal behavior takes place and investigate a far wider range of crimes, especially the crimes of the powerful, than is true of the conventional criminologist. And Marxists tend to be far more likely to point a finger at the organization of capitalism itself as a major cause of criminal behavior (the "macro" level), while conventional criminologists are more likely to look at the individual lawbreaker and the characteristics he or she has (the "micro" level) as the explanatory variable here.

Plain Marxists, no less than vulgar utopian Marxists, consider capitalism an evil. They foresee, too, that capitalism will be destroyed by its own internal contradictions. They argue that socialism will radically transform the nature of social relations among people, including crime and criminal justice. Socialism, Marxists believe, will provide a far less exploitative and less oppressive society in which to live. On these issues, all Marxists agree; that is what makes them Marxists. At the same time, the contemporary Marxist is more realistic about how to characterize crime and justice in capitalist society, what the chances are for a socialist revolution, and what crime and justice are likely to look like in that future socialist society. It is possible that, with a body of systematic, empirical work behind it, Marxist criminology will have to be taken more seriously by the practitioners of the other perspectives in the field.

CHAPTER
5

Drug Use as Deviant Behavior

"Execute Drug Dealers, Mayor Says," "Brutal Drug Gangs Wage War of Terror," "Flood of Drugs—A Losing Battle," "The Battle of Drug Testing," "Surge of Violence Linked to Narcotics," "War on Drugs Shifting to Street," "Drug Violence Erodes a Neighborhood," "Drug Production Soars"—these and other headlines fairly scream out the public's anxiety over the drug abuse issue.

Fear of and concern with the threat of drug use has waxed and waned over the years in the United States. One measure of that fear and concern is the number and content of news stories on the subject. In the 1930s, hundreds of sensationalistic newspaper and magazine articles detailed the supposed horrors of marijuana use. In the 1940s and 1950s, such stories declined in number and stridency. In the second half of the 1960s, literally thousands of news accounts were published and broadcast on LSD's capacity to make users go crazy and do danger-

ous things. In the early 1970s, heroin was in the news. By the mid-1970s, the media had quieted down on the drug front. But the mid-1980s witnessed a rebirth—indeed, something of an explosion—of public concern over the use and abuse of illegal drugs.

The Reader's Guide to Periodical Literature indexes all the articles published in a number of large-circulation magazines in the United States and Canada. In March 1979 to February 1980, only 15 articles were published in all of the magazines indexed by *Reader's Guide* on drug abuse and six other drug-related topics. In the 1980–1981 period, there were 37 such articles; in 1981–1982, 29; in 1982–1983, 38; in 1983–1984, 48; and in 1984–1985, 76. In 1985, the *Reader's Guide* changed the period included in the tally to coincide with the calendar year; in 1985, there were 103 articles on drug-related topics. But in 1986, there were 280, substantially more than a doubling in only a year, and a sixfold increase in less than three years. Clearly, 1986 is the year drug use and abuse exploded as a social problem in the United States (although the situation had been growing throughout the 1980s). This flood-tide of public concern is certain to continue at a high level in the 1990s.

So intense was this latest wave of public concern and fear of drugs and drug use that I dubbed it a "moral panic" (Goode, 1989: 26–35; see also, Kerr, 1986b; Jensen et al., 1987; Ben-Yehuda, 1986; Cohen, 1980). A moral panic is a widespread, explosively up-surging feeling on the part of the public that something is terribly wrong in their society because of a moral failure of a specific group of individuals, a subpopulation defined as the enemy. In short, a category of people has been *deviantized* (Schur, 1980). This is pre-cisely what happened with drug use and abuse in the mid-1980s. By 1986, American society was experiencing something of a moral panic about drug use and abuse.

Moral panics do not emerge entirely as a result of a public awareness of an objective threat that the condition or behavior the public is concerned about poses. There may be far more serious conditions or more dan-gerous behavior that attract little or no con-cern. In fact, as a general rule, the public has an extremely hazy notion of how threaten-ing or damaging certain conditions or forms of behavior are. Why is radon contamina-tion, a cause of 5,000 to 20,000 deaths in the United States each year from lung cancer alone (Eckholm, 1986), a matter of little or no public concern—or even awareness? Why did the absurd rumor that the former Proc-ter & Gamble logo—the face of the man in the moon on a field of 13 stars—was a sym-bol of satanism provoke some 12,000 to 15,000 calls a month to the company, forcing P&G to drop the logo from its packaging and advertising? Can anyone seriously claim the logo posed a greater objective threat to American society than radon poisoning, about which most Americans have not even heard?

Which causes more deaths—accident or disease? The public judges them to be equally frequent, in spite of the fact that dis-ease takes 15 times as many lives as accidents (Slovic, et al., 1980). Events that are dramatic and easy to recall are judged by the public to be more common, other things being equal, than those that are less dramatic and more difficult to remember. The media play a role in this process; more dramatic events are more newsworthy, more likely to be re-ported, more likely to be recalled by readers and viewers, and therefore more likely to be thought of by the public as frequent. Though disease takes 100 times as many lives as homicide, newspapers contain 3 times as many articles on death from homicide as death from disease (Slovic et al., 1980). One study found that the public perception of the extent of crime in a community corre-lated more strongly with the amount of crime news in the local newspapers than it did with the actual crime rate (Davis, 1952). It is clear, then, that people become aroused by certain conditions or behavior and re-gard them as a social problem only in part because of the objective danger they pose or the damage they do to a society. Certainly, most people have a wildly inaccurate notion of the extent of a given danger or damage; they may become riled up by objectively triv-ial conditions or behavior and may ignore objectively serious ones. Hence, we must look at the current drug panic not as the rec-ognition of an objectively serious problem (which drug use and abuse may very well be), but the product of a variety of social, cul-tural, and economic forces. Indeed, at the very period when the drug panic was build-ing and eventually exploded on the social scene, drug use in the United States was ac-tually declining (NIDA, 1986; Johnston et al., 1987).

Humans have ingested drugs for thou-sands of years. Significant numbers of nearly every society have used one or more drugs to achieve certain mental or physical states. Drug use comes very close to being a univer-sal, both worldwide and throughout history. Some of these drugs include beer and wine; the peyote cactus, which contains mescaline; the "magic mushroom," which contains psi-locybin; marijuana and hashish; opium; the coca leaf, which contains some cocaine;

morning glory seeds; nutmeg; various medicinal substances, both natural and synthetic; and the nicotine contained in the tobacco leaf.

Most of the time drugs are used, it is in a culturally appropriate and approved manner (Edgerton, 1976: 57). Sometimes, the drug use that some members of a particular society engage in its unacceptable to its more conventional members: The wrong drug is taken, it is taken too often or under the wrong circumstances, or it is taken with undesirable consequences. In that case, we have an instance of deviant behavior.

WHAT IS DRUG USE?

Before we embark on an exploration of the issue of drug use as deviant behavior, we must answer a seemingly simple question: What is a drug in the first place? Most of us assume the term "drug" refers to a set of substances with clearly identifiable chemical properties or biological effects. It is a common belief that specific characteristics are *intrinsic to* or *dwell within* the substances that are called drugs. A commonly used definition of a drug is "any substance, other than food, that by its chemical or physical nature alters structure of function in the living organism" (Ray, 1978: 94). However, a moment's reflection tells us that this definition, although widely used, is far too broad and all-encompassing to be of much use; a cup of coffee would qualify, as would oxygen, water, vitamin C, penicillin, perfume, ammonia, beer, automobile exhaust fumes—even a bullet fired from a gun.

The inadequacy of this definition has been recognized even by some of the observers who originally proposed it (Ray and Ksir, 1987: 4). The point is, whether something is a drug or not depends on the *context* in which the term or the substance is used. All chemical substances have a number of characteristics or dimensions. Which one is relevant or important to us in a given context? There are several equally legitimate definitions of what a drug is, each one valid for a specific and somewhat different con-

text or dimension. Is penicillin a drug? Yes, if we are interested in its medical utility; no, if we are interested in its effects on the human mind. Is alcohol a drug? Yes, if we are interested in its effects on the human mind; no, if we are interested in its legal status. There is no single valid definition of what a drug is, but several, depending on what *aspect* or *dimension* of the substances in which the observer is interested.

At least four aspects of chemical substances are relevant to the student of deviance. The first is *psychoactivity:* Can the substance get a person high? Does it have subjective effects? Does it influence the workings of the human mind—mood, feeling, emotion, thinking, cognition, how people see and perceive the world?

The second is the *recreational* dimension or aspect: Do people actually *take it* to get high—and *how many* do so? Do they use the drug to achieve the subjective effects that it is capable of delivering? Clearly, we are far more interested in the psychoactive drugs that are widely used for the purpose of getting high than those that *can* have an effect, but are unknown and unused.

Illegality is the third: Clearly, substances whose use, possession, and sale are against the law are more relevant to the student of deviance than those whose use is officially accepted and openly and legally sold and distributed. Clearly, arrest and imprisonment is one way someone may be punished for drug use and possession. If the possession of a given drug is illegal, students of deviance are more interested in it than one whose possession is perfectly legal.

And fourth is the *public definition:* how the general public sees and defines the substance and its users. What substances come to most people's minds when they are asked to provide examples of drugs? The users of which substances are thought of when individuals are referred to as "drug users"? What are the public stereotypes of the substances and their users? Few people think of alcohol as a drug, or of moderate drinkers as drug users; but when drug use and drug users are mentioned, for many, heroin *will* come to mind. In the sense of the public definition, heroin is a drug and alcohol is not. Even though two substances may have similar objective effects, the fact that one is publicly regarded as a drug and the other isn't may create a category of potential deviants—the users of a substance widely regarded as a "drug."

The point is that some substances may be a drug according to one definition but not according to another, equally valid definition. It is the aspect or dimension of chemical substances in which we are interested that defines them as drugs, not the simple chemical properties or pharmacological effects the substances have. When we speak or write of drugs, we are referring to a social and linguistic category of phenomena, not simply to a natural, objective, chemical, or pharmacological category. This does not mean that drug effects are imaginary, that people just think that they occur, that there is no such thing as objective or "real" drug effects. The effects are quite real; we just have to consider them important enough to pay attention to and to use as the basis for our definition.

FACTORS THAT INFLUENCE DRUG EFFECTS

It is misleading to discuss the effects of drugs without emphasizing that drug effects are dependent or *contingent* on a number of key factors. These factors can literally determine whether the effects that a given drug is capable of producing *will actually take place*. What a drug does to the minds and bodies of individuals who take it depends on *how* it is taken in the first place. Although drugs do have a certain *potential* for specific effects, it is not a simple question of biochemistry whether this potential is actually realized. All drug use takes place within a certain social context or setting. Factors such as custom and personality determine how the drug is taken and, hence, what effects it has. Just because a given drug *can* have certain effects on humans or animals in a laboratory or hospital setting is no assurance it will actually do so in more naturalistic settings, in

actual drug-taking situations, simply because people in the street may not take it the way that experimenters administer it to their subjects. For instance, if monkeys are forced-fed marijuana smoke in many times the quantity or doses that humans use in real life, they will undergo some brain damage. But if no human uses it in this way or in these quantities, are the findings of such research relevant to actual usage patterns? Clearly, *a drug's effects are totally dependent on the actual context of use.*

Some of the most important factors that influence drug effects are (1) identity, (2) dose, (3) potency and purity, (4) drug mixing, (5) route of administration, (6) habituation, and (7) set and setting.

Identity. The identity of a drug is simple yet fundamental: *Is the drug as advertised?* What is the actual substance or chemical being used, taken, or administered? Many substances sold on the street as a type of drug actually turn out to be, on chemical analysis, something altogether different. For instance, many pharmacological look-alikes are sold on the street, or even by mail order, as amphetamines—and are thought to be amphetamines by their users—but they contain nothing but caffeine. Even though expectations and social definitions that the substance being taken will have an impact on the user, it still makes a great deal of difference just what specific chemical is being ingested. Many people who claim to have taken a certain drug have not had any experience at all with the drug in question.

Dose. The dose of a given drug makes an absolutely crucial difference. Any discussion of drug effects is completely meaningless without a discussion of this fundamental factor. A drug's pharmacological properties remain only a potentiality until the matter of dose is considered. There are dosage levels at which no drug would have any discernible effect on anyone, and there are other levels at which all drugs would have a deadly effect. Someone could take heroin every day for life without any adverse effect—indeed, without a discernible effect of any kind—if it is taken in extremely minute quantities, say, two micrograms per dose. Likewise, marijuana, which hardly ever causes a drug overdose in real life, could be fatal—if two pounds were forced down someone's throat. Of course, heroin is almost never taken in doses of two micrograms, and hardly anyone ever eats two pounds of marijuana at a sitting; thus, these drugs do not have the effects—or noneffects—I described. These are extreme examples, but still, think of the effects that alcohol has if someone consumes one can of beer versus those that one experiences after consuming half a quart of vodka. Here, the effects of alcohol will vary according to the *dosage* taken. The same principle holds for the effects of all drugs.

Potency and purity. Potency refers to the quantity of a drug that will produce a given effect. The lower the dose it takes to produce a given effect, the higher the potency of that drug. Marijuana is naturally variable in potency. Some batches will contain only 1 percent THC (or tetrahydrocannabinol, which is the psychoactive agent in marijuana, the chemical that triggers the marijuana "high"), while others will be as potent as 10 percent THC. Clearly, the effects of these two batches, which are at such different points on the potency spectrum, will elicit quite different effects. If we were to ask users of each batch what marijuana's effects are, we would get very different answers.

Purity refers to the percentage of the ingested substance that is composed of the actual drug under consideration. Street drugs typically vary enormously in purity. It is misleading to discuss people simply taking certain drugs. Rather, they take specific batches or samples that contain varying amounts and proportions of the drug in question. Until fairly recently, the heroin sold on the street typically contained 3 to 5 percent actual heroin; the rest was made up of inert substances such as quinine, lactose (or milk sugar), and mannitol. Today, samples of street heroin are much purer and often contain 30 to 50 percent (sometimes 70 percent) actual heroin. One result is that, although fewer people are taking heroin nowadays than in the early-to-middle 1980s, more are dying of overdoses.

Drug mixing. Many users who take one drug will take another simultaneously, in combination. A drug that will have one set of effects when taken alone will have an entirely different set of effects when taken in combination with specific other drugs. For instance, cocaine and heroin are often taken together, an often lethal combination known as a "speedball." This pharmacological phenomenon is known as *synergy:* Certain drugs taken simultaneously, will have stronger effects than if taken separately. Alcohol and barbiturates exhibit synergistic effects; the chances of dying of an overdose as a result of taking them together is greater than taking twice as much of either separately. This *multiplier* effect is characteristic of certain drug combinations. The more users mix drugs when taking them, the more the effects they experience will differ from those that would occur taking each drug separately, at different times.

Route of administration. The *way* in which a drug is taken influences what effects it will have on users. Some drugs are taken almost always in only one way by users in a given society. In large part, the culture determines a certain route of administration as proper and customary. In the United States, marijuana is nearly always smoked. In other cultures, it is more commonly consumed differently: baked or sprinkled in foods, as in India and the Middle East, or brewed in tea, as in Jamaica. Smoking cocaine in its "crack" or freebase form is an extremely rapid, efficient, potent, and reinforcing means of getting the drug into the bloodstream; and many more users who smoke cocaine become dependent (or "addicted") on it than is true of those who snort it. Snorting or inhaling cocaine through the nostrils is slower, less efficient, less potent, and less reinforcing; hence, users who employ this method are far less likely to use the drug compulsively and become dependent on it. Intravenous injection, likewise, is a rapid and highly pleasurable route of administration, and produces effects that less efficient and less reinforcing routes do not produce. The least efficient means of taking a drug is oral ingestion or swallowing; it takes more to get high or to have a given effect this way, and consequently, the doses must be larger than for other routes. In addition, the high or euphoria is more muted, less powerful. Route of administration is an extremely crucial factor when considering a given drug's effects.

Habituation. Habituation refers to how accustomed one is to taking a certain drug or drug type. Since the continued use of most drugs leads to tolerance, or a build-up of the quantity necessary to produce a given effect, habituated users can and will take far more of a drug than will the drug-inexperienced individual. Junkies inject a quantity of heroin that produces euphoria in them, but would bring a painful death by overdose to half a dozen nonusers. In addition to the pharmacological factor of tolerance, there is the factor of *behavioral tolerance:* People who become increasingly experienced with a drug learn better how to handle its effects. Drinkers can handle complex physical tasks under the influence better than alcohol novices can—although, obviously, not as well as they could when sober. Clearly, the effects a drug has is partly dependent on how experienced with that drug the individual is.

Set and setting. "Set" refers to the psychic, mental, and emotional state of the person taking the drug. It includes expectations, intelligence, imagination, mood, and so on. "Setting" refers to the social and physical environment in which drug use takes place. It could be the immediate surroundings, such as one's own living room, or it could include the broader social and cultural scene, for instance, the legal climate of a country with respect to drug use and possession, or the degree of society-wide condemnation of use and users. Setting also refers to whether one takes a drug with friends or strangers, in comfortable or uncomfortable surroundings, or engaged in activities compatible or incompatible with the drug state—such as driving, talking with strangers, and so on. Clearly, one's setting in part determines one's set. And just as clearly, set and setting

significantly influence drug effects—especially psychic effects.

A CLASSIFICATION OF DRUGS AND THEIR EFFECTS

There are many ways of looking at drug effects. One is to divide them into those that are "objective" and those that are "subjective." *Objective* effects can be perceived and measured by an observer. Examples would be heartbeat rate and pupillary dilation. Here, it does not matter what the user thinks or says happens; what happens is what external observers actually see. *Subjective* effects are experienced internally by the user and can be known to those who do not take the drug themselves only secondhand, by means of verbal reports from users or, even more indirectly, from the behavior of users. Both objective and subjective effects are equally "real"; however, subjective effects are more difficult to study, although usually more interesting—at least to the sociologist.

All classifications of drugs and their effects are at least a bit misleading. A drug does not "belong" together with other drugs in a certain category and apart from other ones as a result of an edict from reality, science, or medicine. In fact, humans construct drug classifications; we latch onto certain traits as a relevant basis for a classification scheme. One of the basic principles in pharmacology is that *all drugs have multiple effects.* There is no drug with a single effect. This means that one effect of a given drug will lead a scientist to place it in one category, while a second effect of that same drug will cause another scientist to place it in an altogether different category. In which category does the drug "belong"? The answer is that it depends on what is of interest to the observer; it does not depend solely on the objective characteristics of the substance itself. For instance, cocaine has a stimulating or a speeding-up effect on many of the body's organs and functions; it can, in short, be classified as a stimulant. But it also has the property of being a local anesthetic: it numbs the sensation of pain upon contact with tissue. This pain-killing property puts it in a category in common with many depressants that have, in nearly all other ways, the *opposite* effect to stimulants. In which category does cocaine belong: stimulants or local anesthetics? Again, it depends on which of these effects of cocaine we are interested in.

Still, while drug classifications are fuzzy around the edges, the picture is not totally without a certain pattern. Several drugs classified in one way do have some—although not all—properties and effects in common that are, at the same time, markedly different from the properties and effects other drugs have. Classify we must, for, as misleading as classification is, it is also necessary; the human mind cannot work in any other way.

One way of classifying drugs is to look at their effect on the central nervous system (CNS)—that is, the brain and the spinal cord. Some drugs directly stimulate or speed up signals passing through the CNS; others depress or slow down these signals; still others have little or no impact on the speed of CNS signals; and lastly, some have a complex and contradictory effect.

Central nervous system *stimulants* produce arousal, alertness, even excitation; they inhibit fatigue and lethargy. Stimulants speed up signals passing through the CNS. Examples include cocaine, of course, amphetamines, caffeine, nicotine, and Ritalin.

Depressants have the opposite effect: They inhibit, slow down, retard, or depress signals passing through the central nervous system. There are two basic types of depressants. The first is the *analgesics,* which inhibit mainly one principal action of the CNS—the perception of pain. For our purposes, *narcotics* are the most important type of analgesic. This category includes opium and its various derivatives: morphine, heroin, and codeine. And it also includes the various synthetic and semisynthetic narcotics, called *opioids* (or "opium-like" drugs), such as Percodan, methadone, and meperidine (or Demerol). Currently, all narcotics are also physically addicting (although scientists are currently at work searching for a nonaddicting nar-

cotic—a "bee without the sting"). There are also several nonnarcotic drugs that have some of the narcotics' pain-killing property but do not induce dependence, euphoria, or mental clouding on administration. Nonnarcotic analgesics include aspirin, Darvon, Talwin, Tylenol, and ibuprophin. As might be expected, nonnarcotic analgesics are far less potent painkillers than narcotics.

Unlike narcotics, which have a depressive effect on one main bodily function—the perception of pain—*general depressants* have a depressive effect on a wide range of body organs and functions. They tend to induce relaxation, inhibit anxiety, and, at higher doses, result in drowsiness and, eventually, sleep. The most well known of the general depressants is alcohol, which is known to scientists as ethyl alcohol or ethanol. Other examples include sedatives (or sedative-hypnotics) such as barbiturates and methaqualone (which has brand names such as Quaalude and Sopor), and tranquilizers, such as Valium. Originally, pharmacologists thought that tranquilizers relived anxiety without producing mental clouding, drowsiness, and physical dependence, which are characteristics of the sedatives such as the barbiturates. Today, however, it is clear that tranquilizers are far more similar to sedatives than was previously believed; often, mental clouding and drowsiness result from their use and, if the drug is taken at a high enough dosage for a long enough period of time, an actual physical dependence. Also, as with all general depressants, it is possible to die of an overdose of tranquilizers. Tranquilizers are used for such "minor" mental problems as anxiety, insomnia, and various neuroses. Valium, once the number-one prescription drug in America, is a tranquilizer, as are Librium, Equanil, and Miltown.

Hallucinogens (once also called psychedelics) have effects on the central nervous system that cannot be reduced to a simple stimulation-depression continuum. They occupy their own unique category and include LSD, peyote and mescaline, "magic mushrooms" (which contain psilocybin), the mushroom *Amanita muscaria,* morning glory seeds, the chemicals DMT (dimethyltripta-mine) and DET (diethyltriptamine), and a drug called MDMA, or "ecstasy." Today, in the United States, LSD and ecstasy are the only hallucinogens used on anything like a widespread basis. The principal effect of hallucinogens is not, as might be expected from their name, the inducement of hallucinations, but *extreme psychoactivity*, a loosening of the imagination and an intensification of emotional states. Most recent classifications include a drug called PCP or Serinyl, referred to as "angel dust" on the street. Used as an animal tranquilizer, this drug has almost none of the properties associated with hallucinogens. I prefer to classify it as a sedative with paradoxical and unpredictable effects.

Marijuana has, at different times, been classified as a depressant, a stimulant, and, until fairly recently, a hallucinogen. Many observers now feel that it belongs in a category by itself.

Scientists pay close attention to two phenomena associated with drugs: *cross-tolerance* and *cross-dependence*. As a general rule, drugs that are put into a specific drug category can replace or substitute for one another. For instance, if one is addicted to heroin, does not take the drug for four or five hours, and the effects begin to wear off, one can avoid undergoing withdrawal symptoms by taking another narcotic, such as morphine. This is an example of *cross-dependence*. If a person takes LSD every few hours for several days, tolerance will set in: It will become harder and harder, and it will take more and more of the drug, to get high, unless the user stops taking it for a while. (One can still get high on different category of drugs, however.) After one takes LSD every few hours for several days and then takes a different hallucinogen, for example, mescaline, one still won't be able to get as high as one did with the initial dose; it will have the same diminished effect as LSD does. The individual has become tolerant to the effects of all the hallucinogens by taking one of them frequently. This is an example of *cross-tolerance*. Marijuana is not cross-tolerant with any of the

hallucinogens, which is why most observers feel that it does not belong in this category.

THE EXTENT OF DRUG USE IN THE UNITED STATES

There are four fairly readily identifiable types or "circles" of drug use in the United States: (1) medical use, (2) legal recreational use, (3) illegal instrumental use, and (4) illegal recreational use.

Medical Use

Medical use includes drugs, called *prescription* drugs or *pharmaceuticals*, prescribed by physicians to patients and taken within the context of medical therapy, as well as the less potent *over-the-counter* (OTC) drugs purchased by the general public without benefit of a prescription. Roughly 1.5 billion prescriptions are written for drugs in the United States each year, about half of which are new prescriptions; the other half are refills. Between one in six and one in seven of all prescription drugs is psychoactive; that is, they influence mood, emotion, and other mental processes. Prescription drugs comprise $30 billion-a-year industry in the United States at the retail level. Examples of over-the-counter drugs include aspirin, No-Doz, Sominex, Allerest, and Dexatrim. By 1990, the annual retail sales of OTC drugs in the United States totaled roughly $10 billion. OTC drugs are not strongly psychoactive, cannot generate a true physical dependence in users, and have a fairly low level of toxicity—that is, it is difficult to overdose on them; they are hardly ever used for recreational purposes. Moreover, their use is not regarded as deviant by most of the public.

While the sales of prescription drugs generally have remained fairly stable at 1.5 billion prescriptions per year for a decade or more, the sales of *psychoactive* prescription drugs have dropped sharply in the past decade or two. For nearly every legal psychoactive prescription drug on record, the number or prescriptions written in the late 1980s was significantly below that written each year for the 1960s and 1970s, according to IMS America, a firm that tabulates drug sales each year. For instance, *one-fifteenth* as many prescriptions were written for the fast-acting barbiturates (Amytal, Seconal, Nembutal, and Tuinal) in 1986 as in 1966, and *one-thirteenth* as many as in 1971. For the amphetamines (Benzedrine, Dexedrine, Biphetamine, and Desoxyn), one-eighth as many prescriptions were written in 1986 as in 1966 and 1971. The number of prescriptions for methaqualone (Quaalude and Sopor) skyrocketed over 10 times between 1966 and 1971 to 1976 but by 1981, this figure fell by two-thirds, and by 1986, prescriptions were not being written for methaqualone at all. Two amphetamines, methedrine and benzedrine, are no longer prescribed in the United States. This decline is not counteracted by an increase in the number or the size of the doses prescribed, because, for nearly all prescription drugs, the number of doses prescribed per day and the size of each dose have also declined over time.

The decline in prescription drug use in the past decade or two is one of the most remarkable and significant of all changes that have taken place on the drug scene in America. This decline has come about as an indirect consequence of drug manufacturers' aggressive marketing strategy in convincing physicians to adopt pharmaceuticals without adequate testing and to overprescribe them for their patients, which has resulted in numerous adverse medical consequences, including physical dependence and deaths by overdose and the diversion of these drugs into street recreational use. Because of the negative publicity that resulted from both medical misuse and overuse and street use, pressure was put on the medical establishment to reduce the number of prescriptions written for psychoactive pharmaceuticals. For instance, in the 1960s and 1970s, amphetamines were widely prescribed by physicians to combat obesity—indeed, in many cases, were written for patients (mainly women) who were barely overweight. Today, because of such abuses and their attendant medical consequences,

legal prescriptions for this purpose have been brought to a virtual halt. As we saw, methaqualone, hugely prescribed in the 1970s and widely used recreationally and billed on the street as an aphrodisiac (once frequently called the "love drug"), is not being prescribed at all today. In short, overprescribing was defined as deviant behavior within the medical fraternity; and, as a consequence, the excesses of the 1960s and 1970s were brought under control by informal and formal sanctions, including the arrest of physicians who continued to overprescribe and their patients who insisted on continuing to use the banned or more tightly controlled substances.

Legal Recreational Use

Legal recreational use is the legal use of psychoactive substances to achieve a certain mental or psychic state by the user. The most commonly used legal recreational drugs are alcohol, cigarettes, and caffeine. Some 85 percent of the American population has at least tried alcohol, and about 6 Americans in 10 age 12 or older have drunk alcoholic beverages in the past month—some 113 million individuals. Roughly a third of all Americans have smoked a tobacco cigarette in the past 30 days—some 60 million individuals (NIDA, 1986). Americans consume approximately 16 pounds of caffeine per person per year, mainly in coffee, tea, cola, chocolate, and No-Doz.

Clearly, then, the extent of legal recreational drug use is immense. The most popular legal recreational drug, alcohol, is used by a majority of the U.S. population. Even the second most commonly consumed legal drug, tobacco, is used by more individuals than are *all illegal recreational drugs combined.* In fact, tobacco, in the form of cigarettes, is used most frequently among all drugs: Smokers use their drug of choice, on average, 10 to 20 times a day—or more—whereas users of no other drug do so as frequently. Drinkers, for example, do not use alcohol as much, on average, during an entire *week* as smokers do in a *day.* Clearly, in the total picture of drug use, legal instrumental use looms extremely large. At the same time, the moderate use of legal recreational drugs by adults is not considered deviant behavior in most quarters, and the moderate use of legal recreational drugs by adults is not considered a form of deviant behavior by most Americans.

Illegal Instrumental Use

Illegal instrumental use includes taking various drugs without benefit of prescription for some instrumental purpose—such as driving a truck cross-country, studying for exams through the night, calming feelings of anxiety, and so on. Individuals who purchase prescription drugs illegally, without a physician's prescription, do not think of themselves as "real" drug users. They do not seek a high or intoxication but rather a goal of which most conventional members of society approve. These users regard their behavior as only technically illegal and, therefore, not criminal in nature and decidedly nondeviant. They do not make a sharp distinction between the use of legal over-the-counter drugs and the use of pharmaceuticals without a prescription; both are for the purpose of attaining a psychic or physical state of which society approves. One simply happens to be technically illegal.

Illegal Recreational Use

The illegal drug trade is an enormous economic enterprise. One journalist wrote: "There is more money in illegal drug traffic than in any other business on earth" (Gonzales, 1985; 104). Another agreed: "The inhabitants of the earth spend more money on illegal drugs than they spend on food. More than they spend on housing, clothes, education, medical care, or any other product or service. The international narcotics industry is the largest growth industry in the world. Its annual revenues exceed half a trillion dollars—three times the value of all United States currency in circulation" (Mills, 1987: 3). I suspect this figure represents an overestimate. Indeed, it is possible that the total amount of money spent on illegal drugs is not even remotely knowable. Nonetheless, the many estimates of the size of the American drug trade at the retail level hover around the $100 billion mark, "more than the total net sales of General Motors, more than American farmers take in from all crops" (Lang, 1986: 48). It should be sufficient to say simply that a great deal of money is spent on illegal drugs in the United States, certainly tens of billions of dollars. And the huge sums involved represent a correspondingly huge demand for illicit drugs.

Where there is smoke, there is fire. The figures on drug sales tell us that the use of illegal drugs for the purpose of getting high encompasses a sizable proportion of the U.S. population. One study, conducted in 1985, found that well over a third of the population age 12 and over (37 percent, or 70 million individuals) has at least tried one or more illegal drugs; and one in eight (23 million people) has used once or more within the past month and would be considered a "regular" user (NIDA, 1986). As a source of criminal and deviant behavior, drug use is formidable and impressive.

The most frequently used illegal drug in America is, as we might expect, marijuana; a third of all Americans over the age of 11 have at least tried it, and 1 in 10 has used it within the past month. For cocaine, the next-most popular illicit drug, these figures are 12 and 3 percent. Stimulants (aside from cocaine), tranquilizers, hallucinogens, analgesics, and sedatives cluster together in popularity: between 6 and 10 percent of all Americans have tried each drug type, and about 1 percent used each once or more in the past month. Of all drugs or drug types used recreationally in the United States, heroin is the one that is least likely to be used: Only 1 percent of all Americans have tried it, and less than .5 percent used it within the past month (NIDA, 1986). A study of drug use among high-school seniors found pretty much the same patterns, except the average level of use was somewhat higher for nearly all drugs, and stimulants were the number two illicit drug rather than cocaine (Johnston et al., 1987).

Legal and illegal drugs vary considerably

in user loyalty, or continued use. Some drugs are much more likely to be "stuck with"; others are more likely to be used extremely infrequently or episodically, or to be abandoned after a period of experimentation. Of all drugs, legal or illegal, *alcohol* attracts the highest degree of user loyalty—nearly 7 out of 10 (69 percent) of all individuals who have used alcohol once or more in their lifetimes are still using it; that is, they say they used it at least once within the past month. Slightly over 4 in 10 of all at least one-time cigarette smokers (42 percent) smoked a cigarette within the past 30 days. Of all illegal drugs, marijuana attracts the highest proportion of loyal users who "stuck with" the drug: Not quite 3 in 10 of all individuals who have at least some experience with marijuana (29 percent) used the drug within the past month. For cocaine, the figure was a shade over a quarter (26 percent). For all the other drug types except hallucinogens, this figure varied between 15 and just under 20 percent. For hallucinogens, it was only 7 percent, and for heroin, the number of users was too small to calculate the percentage of recent users (NIDA, 1986).

MARIJUANA

Effects of Marijuana

Technically, what is referred to as marijuana is not actually a drug, but a vegetable substance containing a whole series of chemicals. What is sold on the street in the United States is made up of the dried leaves and flowering tops of the plant *Cannabis sativa*, or, less commonly, *Cannabis indica*. Hashish, a related substance, contains only the resin and flowering tops of the cannabis plant, with no leaves; it is typically (although not always) more potent than marijuana itself. The cannabis plant contains hundreds of chemicals; of these, 61, called cannabinoids, are unique to itself (Turner, 1980: 83–84). The primary psychoactive agent in marijuana is, as we saw, tetrahydrocannabinol, or THC for short. It is generally agreed that the THC gets the user high. Street marijuana

varies between 1 and 10 percent THC, the average centering roughly around 4 percent; it is generally agreed that high-potency marijuana gets the user higher than low-potency varieties.

In considering the effects of any drug, "acute" and "chronic" effects must be distinguished. "Acute" effects take place under the influence of the drug, within the context of immediate use. "Chronic" effects take place over the long run, after an extended period of use. Marijuana causes an increased heartbeat rate, redness of the eyes, and dryness of the mouth; these are acute effects. In addition, motor coordination is impaired, raising the possibility of an increased risk of automobile fatalities under the influence. Short-term memory also deteriorates under the influence; one has a harder time remembering things that just happened, for instance, what he or she was saying in the very middle of a sentence. These are all acute effects of marijuana. They are also objective effects; that is, they can be determined by an external observer. Examples of chronic effects are the heavy, long-term consumption of alcohol, which causes cirrhosis of the liver, and heavy, long-term cigarette smoking, which causes lung cancer. These are regarded as chronic effects because they take place not during the immediate context of a given episode, when the user is under the influence, but over the long run, after a considerable period of use.

One of the interesting things about the use of specific drug use is that, in different periods of history, different claims are made as to the effects of each. In the 1930s, newspaper and magazine stories alleged that marijuana caused users to go crazy, engage in promiscuous sex, and commit violent acts. Today, these claims are hardly ever made even by the strongest antimarijuana propagandists. It is not the acute effects of marijuana that attract most critics today, but the chronic, long-term effects. It is feared that the long-term use of marijuana will prove to be medically damaging. At the same time, these are the effects of the drug that are the most controversial.

In 1974, Senator James Eastland, chairman of the Senate Judiciary Committee, organized a series of hearings on what he called the "Marihuana-Hashish Epidemic and Its Impact on United States Security." He assembled two dozen expert witnesses, most of them physicians, who could be counted on to claim that marijuana is a dangerous, medically damaging drug. No other point of view was presented at these hearings. "We make no apology," said Senator Eastland, "for the one-sided nature of our hearings—they were deliberately planned that way" (Eastland, 1974: xv). Some of marijuana's medical ravages included, these witnesses claimed, brain damage, "massive damage to the entire cellular process," including chromosomal abnormalities; the drug also supposedly "adversely affects the reproductive process," causing sterility and impotence; it causes cancer, paranoid thinking, and a life of lethargy and sloth, called the "amotivational syndrome." Senator Eastland concluded from this testimony that if the "cannabis epidemic continues to spread . . . we may find ourselves saddled with a large population of semi-zombies." Are Eastland's witnesses correct in viewing marijuana's effects as pathological? What is the consensus in the scientific and medical community on marijuana's long-term chronic effects?

Perhaps it is a copout to say the jury is still out on the marijuana medical question. Remember, no drug is completely safe. There is no chemical substance, no drug, no activity known to humankind, that is completely without harm to anyone. Some damage can be found with the ingestion of every drug—in some people, at some time. So, the question should not be Can some damage be found if we look hard enough? After all, one can die of an "overdose" of water: It's called drowning. Does that mean water is dangerous and damaging? Of course not. Thus, when assessing damage, the question should be What is the *likelihood* of damage in a wide range of situations and instances of use—both acute and chronic? And with respect to the pathological effects claimed by some observers from marijuana—a damaging impact on the brain, testosterone, white blood cells,

chromosomes, the female reproductive system, and so on (Mann, 1985, 1987; Jones and Lovinger, 1985)—the most honest conclusion that can be reached is that these findings remain controversial and contradictory. Every study demonstrating a pathological effect can be matched by at least one documenting that marijuana does not have this effect. Only by focusing exclusively on the pathological findings and ignoring the nonpathological ones can one say marijuana is truly medically damaging and dangerous. The only medical pathology that has been independently confirmed by several observers and is unmatched by nonpathological findings is impairment to the functioning of the lungs. Heavy, long-term marijuana use decreases the capacity to take in, utilize, and expel air. Daily marijuana use "leads to lung damage similar to that resulting from heavy cigarette smoking" (Petersen, 1980: 19). However, its more general impact awaits further study.

So far, we've looked only at marijuana's objective effects, some acute, some chronic. What about its subjective effects—that is, what it feels like to experience the marijuana intoxication? After all, the subjective effects are why the drug is used in the first place. Marijuana is used, overwhelmingly, because individuals who use it want to get high and because they like the feelings associated with being high. Although it may serve the interests of propagandists to claim the drug's subjective effects are mainly unpleasant, even painful (Lord, 1971), or that using the drug actually diminishes the body's capacity to feel pleasure (Jones and Jones, 1977; Jones and Lovinger, 1985: 398; Mann, 1985: 183), it does not serve the interest of truth.

In fact, the overwhelming majority of individuals who smoke marijuana, especially regular smokers, find the effects of the drug pleasurable. Individuals who have unpleasant experiences under the influence typically discontinue their use of the drug.

Many studies have been conducted that ask users to describe the effects marijuana has on them. The most common response in a study I did (Goode, 1970) was that users felt more peaceful, more relaxed under the influence; 46 percent mentioned this effect spontaneously, without any prodding on my part. Thirty-six percent said they felt their senses generally were more "turned on," that they were more sensitive in almost every way on marijuana than was true normally. Thirty-one percent said they felt their thoughts were more profound, deeper, that their minds ran in a more philosophical and cosmic vein. Twenty-nine percent said everything seemed funnier than usual—they laughed much more than they did when they were straight. A quarter (25 percent) said they felt all their emotions were subjectively exaggerated; 23 percent said time seemed to move much more slowly; 22 percent said they became more withdrawn, introverted; 21 percent said their mind wandered, they experienced a kind of stream of consciousness; 20 percent said they felt dizzy, lightheaded; 19 percent said they felt tired, lazy, lethargic; 18 percent said they felt light, airy, floating; 18 percent said their short-term memory deteriorated, they tended to forget things easily; 18 percent said they felt freer, more uninhibited; 18 percent said the stimulation of their senses was more pleasurable; 17 percent said they become hungrier; 17 percent said their musical ear was sharper. Not all of the effects described were judged pleasurable—fully 15 percent said they often felt paranoid—but most of the effects were experienced as positive in nature.

What is the impression conveyed by this and the many other studies on marijuana intoxication? The most obvious and dominant impression is that users overwhelmingly describe their marijuana experience in favorable and pleasurable terms; in short, most users, most of the time, enjoy what they feel when they get high. A second impression is that marijuana use is a distinctly recreational activity. The vast majority of the effects reported by users are whimsical in nature—happy, silly, euphoric, relaxed, hedonistic, sensual, foolish, and decidedly unserious. Moreover, marijuana is commonly used in conjunction with pleasurable activities—eating, sexual intercourse, listening to music, watching a film or television, attending a party, socializing, and so on. The most common episodes for most marijuana smokers are specifically these recreational moments. The high is deliberately sought as a means of intensifying enjoyable experiences. The drug tends not to be used during more serious moments, such as studying or reading. Moreover, serious activities were felt to be *impaired* while the user was high; for instance, in my study, two-thirds said their ability to read something was worsened under the influence.

Marijuana Use in the United States: 1960–1990

In 1960, less than 1 percent of youths age 12 to 17, less than 5 percent of young adults age 18 to 25, and less than .5 percent of all adults over the age of 25, had tried marijuana; by 1967, these figures had nearly quadrupled, to over 5 percent for youths and over 15 percent for young adults (Miller and Cisin, 1980: 13–16). The percent trying and using marijuana increased throughout the 1960s and the 1970s, and reached its peak roughly in 1979, when nearly a quarter of youth age 12 to 17 (24 percent), close to half of young adults age 18 to 25 (47 percent), and nearly 1 in 10 of older adults age 26 or older (9 percent) had used the drug within the past year. In addition, in 1979, slightly over half of high-school seniors (51 percent) used marijuana in the past year. But throughout the 1980s, these percentages declined: By 1985, to 20 percent for youths and 37 percent for young adults; among older adults, the figure increased slightly (to 9.5 percent); for high-school seniors, there was also a decline in annual prevalence throughout the 1980s; by 1986, to 39 percent, and in 1987, only 36 percent (NIDA, 1986; Johnston et al., 1987: 47–49; University of Michigan, 1988). Clearly, marijuana use has become less and less common since the 1970s; just as clearly, its use has also become decreasingly acceptable and increasingly deviant. This decline may become a long-term trend. Nonetheless, even today, for late adolescents and young adults, regular (or at least, monthly or so) marijuana use is the norm, statistically speaking.

Marijuana Use as Deviance and Crime

The use and the criminal status of marijuana have had a remarkable and an extremely complicated history in the United States. Before the 1930s, very few Americans had even heard of marijuana or knew anyone who used it and, consequently, very few thought of it as deviant. Until well into this century, the few who did know of the drug thought of it as a kind of medicinal herb; George Washington grew it on his plantation, probably for this purpose. During the decade of the 1930s, however, marijuana became the subject of countless sensationalistic newspaper and magazine articles. The drug was dubbed the "killer weed," and "weed of madness," a "sex-crazing drug menace," the burning weed of hell," a "gloomy monster of destruction." Journalists and propagandists allowed an almost unlimited reign to the lurid side of their imagination on the marijuana question. Every conceivable evil was concocted concerning the effect of this drug, the principal ones being insanity, sexual license, and violence. A popular film distributed in the 1930s, *Reefer Madness*, illustrates this "marijuana causes you to go crazy, become promiscuous, and want to kill people" theme; it is now shown to pro-marijuana audiences, who find it so ludicrous as to be hilarious.

By 1937, partly as a result of the hysterical publicity surrounding marijuana, laws criminalizing its possession and sale were passed in every state and at the federal level as well. Several observers argue that racism against Mexican-Americans was one principal reason for the public's belief in the drug's evil effects and the swiftness with which these laws were passed (Bonnie and Whitebread, 1970: 1011, 1015; Musto, 1973: 220). The majority of the states that passed the earliest marijuana laws were Western states with the largest concentration of Mexican-American populations. It is likely the racial and ethnic characteristics of some users, along with dominant white attitudes toward the ethnic group that was thought to be most likely to use the drug—Mexican-Americans—were more significant in influencing the antimarijuana legislation of the 1930s than what scientists believed at that time were the objective properties and effects of the drug. It is plain that an activity can be condemned not so much because of its objective impact, but because of the majority feeling about the group that is thought to practice it.

Marijuana use remained completely illegal and deviant throughout the 1930s, 1940s, and 1950s. In the 1960s, the popularity of this drug increased rapidly; and the community became aware that it was not simply the poor or members of minority groups, but the sons and daughters of affluent, respectable, middle-class folk, who used it. Marijuana acquired a mantel of, if not respectability or conventionality, then at least not complete deviance either. Attitudes began to soften and, in the 1970s, possession of small quantities of the drug was no longer a crime in 11 states, which made up a third of the U.S. population. Then, in the early 1980s, possibly beginning with the election of conservative Ronald Reagan to the presidency in 1980, the tolerant sentiment toward marijuana that was growing during the 1960s and the 1970s dissipated, and a new mood set in. No states decriminalized small-quantity marijuana possession in the 1980s, and public opinion hardened against legalization and strengthened for complete criminalization; increasingly, the public saw the drug as dangerous, and a decreasing proportion of Americans actually used it. Marijuana, its possession, use, and sale had become strongly deviant once again. For certain activities, then, deviance and crime are cyclical.

Accompanying this public concern was a dramatic shift in attitudes toward all drugs, but most especially toward marijuana. Between 1977 and 1986, the proportion of high-school students who felt marijuana possession should be entirely legal declined by half—from 34 to 15 percent; at the opposite end of the spectrum, the proportion who favored keeping the possession of any quantity of the drug a crime doubled, from 22 percent in 1977 to 43 percent in 1986. Moreover, the proportion who believed smoking marijuana regularly entails "great risk" more than doubled during 1977 to 1987, from 35 to 74 percent. Thus, in the sense of supporting the arrest and imprisonment of users and believing regular use is a dangerous activity, "beyond the pale" medically, America's high-school students moved away from seeing marijuana use as conventional and ordinary to seeing it as deviant. The percentage of high-school students saying they "disapprove" of the use of marijuana increased consistently between 1977 and 1986 (Johnston, et al., 1987: 118–132; University of Michigan; 1988).

HALLUCINOGENIC DRUGS

Hallucinogenic drugs are those that produce severe "dislocations of consciousness" (Lingeman, 1974: 91–92), that act on the nervous system to produce significant perceptual changes (O'Brien and Cohen, 1984: 114). As we saw earlier, there are many hallucinogenic drugs, but today, the most widely used representatives of this category are LSD and MDMA ("ecstasy"). Hallucinogenics were once also called "psychedelics," to indicate that the mind is "made manifest"— or works better than ordinarily—under their influence; but this term is hardly used at all today. It is in the mental, psychic, and "subjective" realm that the effects of LSD and other hallucinogenics have their most profound, dramatic, and interesting effects.

LSD: Subjective Effects

Extreme *emotionality* is probably the most central of all the effects of hallucinogenic drugs: a marked heightening of the significance and impact of much of experience that would otherwise, in a "normal" frame of mind, be regarded of no special significance. Great, enormous mood swings tend to dominate the typical "acid" trip. Something typically experienced as somewhat uncomfortable, slightly annoying, or a bit unpleasant will assume the dimension of utter dread and total negativity. And that which would be felt as mildly pleasant when not under the influence may become a voluptuous, totally encompassing experience.

The term "hallucinogens" implies that drugs of this type generate hallucinations— that this is, indeed, their most significant effect. The term implies that, under the influence, users see things that "aren't really there." This designation isn't quite accurate. Users very rarely report having full-blown, authentic hallucinations while they are on an acid trip. Much more commonly, they report "seeing" things that don't exist, but they are fully aware that it is the drug that is inducing the visions. In my own interview study of users of LSD (Goode, 1972: 101–109), after describing a vision they had under the influence, they nearly always added, "But I knew that I was imagining it." These visions included the following: "My eyelashes grew and became like snakes," "I saw a man with a frog's head walking down the street," "The first thing I noticed was that my arm was made of gold," "In the mirror, I saw my clothes change into costumes from different periods of history." Perhaps the term "virtual hallucination" or "pseudohallucination" would be more accurate to describe the hallucinogenic drug experience. Unlike schizophrenics, individuals under the influence of a hallucinogenic drug almost never have auditory hallucinations.

A commonly described effect of LSD and the hallucinogens is *eidetic imagery:* unusually rich, vibrant, extremely lifelike, and exquisite images that are seen with one's eyes closed; usually they are in motion, and they are commonly called "eyeball movies." One of my interviewees said: "Closing my eyes, I saw millions of color droplets, like rain, like a shower of stars, all different colors." Another said he saw "hundreds of fleurs-de-lis, repeating themselves, moving several lines. . . . Another . . . was hundreds of iron crosses, repeating themselves in four lines at right angles to one another, receding into some point on the horizon."

An extremely common effect of LSD and other hallucinogens is *synesthesia,* or the translation of one sense into another, the experience of several senses being stimulated simultaneously. Users report "hearing" color, or "seeing" sounds. Users would see someone clapping hands, hear the sound, then "see" a burst of color coming out of the hands. Or hear music and then experience making love to the notes.

Many users of psychedelic or hallucinogenic drugs perceived the physical world as being fluid, dynamic, in constant flux, shimmering, wobbling, flowing. Said several respondents: "Things were oozing as if they were made of jelly," "A brick wall wobbled and moved," "Paint ran off the walls," "I saw wriggling, writhing images," "I saw flowers on the window sill, blowing in the breeze. I went to touch them, but there was no breeze, and the flowers were dead."

Hallucinogenic Drugs: A Thumbnail Sketch

Psychedelic drugs were taken, in the form of peyote, the psilocybin (or "magic") mushroom, and the bark of the yage vine, mainly for religious and ceremonial purposes, by Native American Indians long before the coming of Europeans to North and South America. Although some intellectuals experimented with mescaline and peyote just before and just after the turn of the nineteenth century, it was not until the second half of the twentieth century that hallucinogenic drug use became fairly widespread. Of course, a number of hallucinogenic drugs occur in natural substances—for example, mescaline in peyote and psilocybin in the "magic mushroom." Still, hallucinogens did not become popular until they were available in a synthetic chemical—lysergic acid diethylamide (LSD).

In 1938, Albert Hofmann, a Swiss chemist, synthesized LSD; at the time, he merely noted its existence and set it aside. In 1943, he accidentally inhaled an extremely minute quantity of the drug, felt dizzy, and left the lab to go home and lie down. He experienced a "stream of fantastic images of ex-traordinary plasticity and vividness ... accompanied by an intense, kaleidoscopic-like play of colors." Hofmann was, in fact, experiencing the first LSD trip in human history. He suspected that his unusual experience was the result of the chemical he was working on. The following Monday, he returned to the lab and took 250 micrograms of the drug, a dose that, for most drugs, would have had no effect whatsoever. He was, once again, forced to discontinue his work and, accompanied by an assistant, go home and lie down. He later described his experiences in some detail. They included most of the effects described above, as well as a feeling of timelessness, depersonalization, a loss of control, and a number of others. "I was overcome with fears that I was going crazy," Hofmann said. "This drug makes normal people psychotic!" he declared. During the 1940s and 1950s, a few researchers picked up on Hofmann's insight and speculated that the hallucinogenic drug experience might be the key to insanity. In time, they found the differences outweighed the similarities, and this line of research was eventually abandoned.

The use of LSD might have remained almost totally confined to hospitals and laboratories had it not been that in 1954, a British novelist and essayist, Aldous Huxley, famous for his classic novel *Brave New World,* took mescaline and described his experiences in a slim, poetic volume entitled *The Doors of Perception.* Though he did draw the parallel with insanity, he also added a new twist to the growing literature on hallucinogenic drug use. Being normal, Huxley wrote, is learning to shut out or eliminate most of the distracting, overwhelming, disturbing, confusing stimuli that take place all around us. Psychedelic drugs, he claimed, wash away the many years of rigid socialization and programming we have been exposed to and permit us to perceive that we have learned to ignore. Taking psychedelic drugs, Huxley wrote, can bring about a kind of transcendence, much like religion.

Huxley's book was read by Timothy Leary, a Ph.D. in psychology and a lecturer at Harvard University. Vacationing in Mexico in

1960, he took a dose of the psilocybin mush-room and had what he described as a "vi-sionary voyage." "I came back a changed man," he declared. With several colleagues, he administered doses of hallucinogenic drugs to hundreds of volunteers, including Harvard undergraduates, theology students, and convicts; with all of them, Leary claimed, it "changed their lives for the better." The experiments, many observers felt, were casu-ally administered, unscientific, and aimed mainly at proselytizing; usually a physician was not present. By the fall of 1962, Harvard's administration voiced acute concerns about the experiments, which Leary brushed off as "hysteria" that was hampering his research. In the spring of 1963, Leary was fired, an event that touched off headline stories.

One indication of the excitement stirred up by the use of LSD and other psychedelic drugs was the enormous number of articles that were published in popular magazines and newspapers on the subject. It is a phe-nomenon confined almost entirely to the 1960s. The first article listed in the *Reader's Guide to Periodical Literature* was published in *Look* magazine and was entitled, ominously and prophetically, "Step into the World of the Insane." In 1962, a popular article ap-peared reporting that LSD was being used on the street. In the entire decade before February 1963, only 11 articles on LSD had been published in all of the popular maga-zines indexed by the *Guide*—only one per year (not counting those appearing in *Science,* which, although listed in *Reader's Guide,* is not really a popular magazine). But beginning with Leary's dismissal from Har-vard, the stories on LSD mounted quickly. From March 1966 to February 1967, 50 pop-ular articles were published on LSD and in-dexed in *Reader's Guide.* In March 1967, a re-search article appeared that purported to show that LSD damaged human chromo-somes. (Later, it was revealed the research was flawed and its conclusions fallacious.) That angle proved to be a major theme in the 33 articles published in the subsequent year. But by 1968, LSD had declined in news-worthiness; only 13 articles appeared from 1968 to 1969, and less than half that in each

subsequent year. Only one article on LSD was published in 1974 and 1975. Clearly, by the mid-1970s, as news, acid had had it.

The pre-1967 magazine (and newspaper) articles on LSD conveyed the distinct im-pression that anyone who ingested the drug stood an unwholesomely strong likelihood of losing one's mind—temporarily for sure, and possibly permanently as well. The ef-fects of LSD were described as "night-marish"; "terror and indescribable fear" were considered common, routine, typical. *Life* ran a cover story in its March 25, 1966, issue entitled "The Exploding Threat of the Mind Drug That Got out of Control." *Time* ran a feature essay on LSD emphasizing the drug's "freaking out" aspect. "Under the in-fluence of LSD," the story declared, "non-swimmers think they can swim, and others think they can fly. One young man tried to stop a car . . . and was hit and killed. A maga-zine salesman became convinced that he was the Messiah. A college dropout committed suicide by slashing his arm and bleeding to death in a field of lilies." Psychic terror, un-controllable impulses, violence, an uncon-cern for one's own safety, psychotic epi-sodes, delusions, and hallucinations formed the fare of the early articles on the use of LSD. The newspaper articles on LSD were even more sensationalistic, lurid, and one-sided than were those published in popular magazines. Newspaper headlines screamed out stories such as "Mystery of Nude Coed's Fatal Plunge," "Strip-Teasing Hippie Goes Wild on LSD," and "Naked in a Rosebush" (Braden, 1970).

After 1967, the chromosome-breakage angle dominated articles on LSD in the pop-ular press. One article, which appeared in the *Saturday Evening Post,* displayed photo-graphs of distorted babies, explaining that "if you take LSD, even once, your children may be born malformed or retarded" and that "new research finds it's causing genetic damage that poses a threat of havoc now and appalling abnormalities for generations yet unborn" (Davison, 1967). This wave of hyste-ria was not quite so strong or as long lasting as the "insanity" theme, but it did convince many users of LSD that perhaps the drug was far more dangerous than they had thought. As we now know, the whole issue proved to be a false alarm. LSD is an extremely weak gene-altering agent, exceedingly unlikely to cause chromosomal abnormalities in the doses typically taken (Dishotsky et al., 1971).

In the 1960s, LSD use appeared to many to possess a *uniquely deviant potential;* to some, the threat it seemed to pose was massive. In 1966, the New Jersey Narcotic Drug Study Commission declared LSD "the greatest threat facing the country today" (Brecher et al., 1972: 369). And yet, this hysteria and hostility evaporated in what was probably record time. Today, the use of hallucinogens is no longer a public issue, at least, not apart from the use of drugs generally. LSD has been absorbed into the morass of drug taking in general—less seriously regarded than heroin use, but more so than marijuana. LSD never really *materialized* into the threat to society that many people claimed it would. The drastic, dramatic, cosmic, philosophical, and religious claims originally made for the LSD experience now seem an artifact of an antiquated age. The psychedelic movement, which never made up a majority of users, even regular users, of LSD, simply disappeared. The fear of the conventional majority that users would go crazy, drop out, or overturn the social order also never came to pass. LSD has become just another drug taken occasionally by multiple drug users for the same hedonistic, recreational reasons they take other drugs—to get high.

Patterns and Trends in LSD Use

In the United States, LSD and the other hallucinogens are taken extremely episodically. As we saw earlier, of all drugs or drug types for which we have detailed, systematic information, LSD is used with the greatest infrequency. This does not mean there are fewer individuals who have used LSD than is true of any other drug; it means that, among at least one-time users, LSD is used least frequently. Only 7 percent of all individuals who had taken LSD once or more in their lives took it during the previous month (NIDA, 1986). If we compare this figure with 29 percent for marijuana, 26 percent for cocaine, and 69 percent for alcohol, we realize just how infrequently LSD is used among those who do or did use it. "The most important fact about chronic or long-term psychedelic drug use is that there is very little of it" (Grinspoon and Bakalar, 1979: 176). There are three possibilities for this episodic pattern of LSD use: (1) tolerance sets in rapidly, producing diminishing effects; (2) unlike most drugs, the effects of LSD are extremely unpredictable and inconstant so the user doesn't know what to expect; and (3) a LSD trip is often difficult, exhausting, strenuous, emotionally draining, and not an experience one usually wishes to undertake regularly.

It is common belief among the public that the use of LSD and other psychedelic drugs peaked in the late 1960s and plummeted in the 1970s. This belief is probably due to the intense media attention devoted to hallucinogens—as we saw, a phenomenon confined almost entirely to the 1960s—and most people think there is a close connection between media attention and the frequency of a phenomenon (Slovic, et al., 1980). Actually, the two are very loosely connected (Davis, 1952). The truth is the use of LSD lagged considerably behind its media image. Use was, in fact, extremely low—but growing—in the 1960s, when a great many stories in newspapers, magazines, and television were reported by the media; and use reached a peak in the late 1970s, at a time when media attention had practically died out.

According to a series of Gallup Polls reported in the February 1972 issue of *Gallup Opinion Index*, only 1 percent of American college students had ever taken LSD or any other hallucinogenic drug by 1967; by 1969, the figure reached 4 percent; in 1970, it was 14 percent; and in 1971, 18 percent. It is clear, then, that at least in colleges, the use of LSD rose dramatically from the late 1960s to the early 1970s—at precisely the same time media attention actually dropped off sharply. In a series of studies on drug use patterns among the American population, likewise, hallucinogenic drug use peaked for most age groups roughly in 1979, and declined during the 1980s. For instance, in 1974, among 18- to 25-year-olds, 16.6 percent had ever used a psychedelic drug; in 1979, this figure was 25.1 percent; in 1982, it was 21.1 percent; and by 1985, it had fallen to 11.5 percent. With some variation, this pattern prevailed for other age categories (Miller et al., 1983; NIDA, 1986). High-school LSD use peaked a little earlier—roughly 1975—and declined during the late 1970s and throughout the 1980s (Johnston et al., 1987; 47, 48, 49). LSD use declined more or less consistently throughout the 1980s and may do so into the 1990s.

The use of LSD in the United States should teach us some very important lessons about the perception of social problems and the imputation of deviance to an activity. First, the public hysteria generated over an activity or a condition may be totally disproportionate to its objective threat to society. Some activities or conditions attract considerably more than their fair share of public hysteria, while others attract far less. Second, media attention does not necessarily reflect how common or frequent an activity is; some common activities receive little or no media attention, while some rare or infrequent activities receive a great deal. An activity could very well rise in frequency at a time when media attention is declining, or decline in frequency when media attention rises. Third, it is likely that people base their notions of the frequency of an activity, the commonness of a condition, and the threat both pose to society more on how well known they are than on the objective facts of the matter. In many ways, a study of LSD is more instructive for what it tells us about deviance in general than about what it specifically tells us about drug use.

COCAINE AND CRACK

Although the general trend in illegal recreational drug use throughout the 1980s has been downward, the use of cocaine and its crystalline product, crack, increased during the decade. That would seem to qualify it as a worthy object of study in any course on deviant behavior.

Cocaine is a stimulant. Its most commonly described effect is exhilaration, elation, euphoria, well being, a voluptuous, joyous feeling. Probably the second most frequently described effect is confidence, a sensation of mastery and competence in what one is and does; and third, increased energy and the suppression of fatigue, a stimulation of the ability to continue physical and mental activity more intensely and for a longer than normal period of time.

The early medical uses of cocaine were to offset fatigue and to cure morphine addiction. Later, it was used as a local anesthetic. Freud experimented with the drug on himself to overcome fatigue and depression, and it worked: After taking it, he felt cheerful, euphoric, and energetic. He also published his first scientific papers on cocaine, and came under attack for presenting a too-positive view of its effects and advocating its use. In time, he became dependent on the drug and had to break himself of his craving for it (Byck, 1974). At least one contemporary observer argues that some of Freud's more fanciful theories were born out of a cocaine-dependent brain (Thornton, 1983).

At the end of the nineteenth and the beginning of the twentieth centuries, cocaine, like morphine and opium, was a major ingredient in many patent medicines. Import figures indicate that some 26,000 pounds of cocaine were brought into the country, legally, as late as 1919. Cocaine was also an ingredient in many soft drinks—including Coca-Cola—until 1903, when it was deleted because of pressure applied "by Southerners who feared blacks' getting cocaine in any form" (Ashley, 1975: 46).

A major reason for the downfall of cocaine was racism. Although there is no reliable information documenting that blacks were more likely to use cocaine than whites, it was feared by some whites that this was so—and that blacks were especially dangerous and violent under the influence. That this was believed by much of the white majority brought the drug under state and federal control. Numerous articles were written just after the turn of the century claiming that cocaine stimulated violent behavior among blacks. In 1903, the *New York Tribune* quoted one Colonel J. W. Watson of Georgia as saying that "many of the horrible crimes committed in the southern states by the colored people can be traced directly to the cocaine habit." A Dr. Christopher Koch asserted, in an article published in the *Literary Digest* in 1914, that "most of the attacks upon white women of the South are a direct result of a cocaine-crazed Negro brain." Even the staid *New York Times* published an article in 1914 entitled "Negro Cocaine Fiends Are a New Southern Menace," which detailed the "race menace," "cocaine orgies," "wholesale murders," and "hitherto inoffensive" blacks "running amuck in a cocaine frenzy." (Summarized in Ashley, 1975; Grinspoon and Bakalar, 1976; and Musto, 1973.)

"All the elements needed to insure cocaine's outlaw status were present by the first years of the twentieth century: It had become widely used as a pleasure drug . . . ; it had become identified with despised or poorly regarded groups—blacks, lower-class whites, and criminals; and it had not . . . become identified with the elite, thus losing what little chance it had of weathering the storm" (Ashley, 1975: 74).

By the time of the passage of the Harrison Act in December 1914, which included cocaine as a narcotic (as we saw, pharmacologically, cocaine is not a narcotic), 46 states had already passed state laws attempting to control cocaine. (Only 29 had done so with the opiates.) This indicates that cocaine use was seen by many legislators as a major drug problem at the time. There can be no doubt this was related to racial hostility toward blacks by the dominant white majority.

It is impossible to know with any degree of accuracy just how frequently cocaine was used in the years following its criminalization in 1914. We have anecdotes and often hysterical and sensationalistic newspaper stories, not reliable information. It is frequently mentioned as the drug of choice among elite social circles in the 1920s, but after that came "The Great Drought." Writes one cocaine expert, "Virtually every source

I have consulted agrees that cocaine use was insignificant during the 1930s" (Ashley, 1975: 105). Its use remained insignificant and confined to a very tiny number of Americans more or less into the 1960s. And then the explosion occurred—paralleling the marijuana explosion, though on a smaller scale.

We have four reliable, systematic sources for recent increases in cocaine use and abuse in the United States. Not all of their indicators point upward for cocaine use—although most do. More significant, however, is *the rise in the frequency of cocaine use among those who use the drug.* Although there may not be a continuous rise in the number of people who use it, there *is* a consistent rise in the amount used by those who do use it.

In the national survey cited earlier (NIDA, 1986), the annual use of cocaine remained more or less stable for 12- to 17-year-olds between 1979 (4.2 percent) and 1985 (4.4 percent); decreased slightly for 18- to 25-year-olds (19.6 to 16.4 percent); and doubled for adults age 26 or older (2 to 4.2 percent). Use within the past month also doubled for the over-26 age category. The number of Americans who had used cocaine during the previous month rose from 4.2 to 5.8 million between 1982 and 1985.

In the second source, the high-school survey cited earlier (Johnston et al., 1987: 47–50), cocaine use was remarkably stable between 1979 and 1986—15 to 17 percent for lifetime prevalence; 12 to 13 percent for annual prevalence; and stable at 6 percent for 30-day prevalence. However, the proportion of *daily* cocaine users in this study doubled, from .2 to .4 percent. The use of cocaine dropped slightly but significantly between 1986 and 1987: For annual prevalence, for high-school seniors, from 13 to 10 percent; for young adults beyond high school, from 20 to 16 percent; and for college students, from 17 to 14 percent. This was the first time any indicators of cocaine use declined in this ongoing survey since the 1970s (University of Michigan, 1988).

A third data source indicating trends in cocaine use and abuse is the federal Drug Abuse Warning Network (the DAWN program), which counts both fatal and nonfatal drug overdoses in medical examiners' reports and major hospitals in 26 cities around the country. Although there are problems using DAWN's data (Ungerleider et al., 1980), it is reasonable to infer drug abuse *trends* from this information. DAWN indicates a massive increase in cocaine abuse in recent years. In 1986, excluding alcohol, cocaine was the second most frequently mentioned drug in nonlethal emergency room overdoses (17.3 percent of all cases) and the second most frequently mentioned drug in medical examiners' reports of fatal overdoses (13.3 percent of all cases). Only heroin and the narcotics made a larger contribution to drug overdoses in 1986. What is so remarkable is how swiftly cocaine rose to the number two position. Between October 1979 and September 1980, DAWN recorded 3,757 nonfatal emergency room cocaine-associated episodes, and 127 cocaine-related deaths. In 1981 to 1982, there were 5,830 emergency room mentions, and 198 lethal cocaine-associated cocaine overdoses, a substantial increase. During 1985, there were 13,501 emergency room episodes and 643 lethal overdoses attributed to cocaine, a massive increase. And in 1986, cocaine emergency room mentions numbered 24,847, an increase of 84 percent from the previous year; and medical examiners reported 1,092 lethal overdoses in which cocaine was present, an increase of 70 percent from 1985 (DAWN, 1987: 26, 53). Since both lethal and nonlethal cocaine overdoses occur mainly in the very heavy user, and specifically when the drug is smoked or injected, these figures, however flawed, point to a *massive* increase in heavy cocaine use by means other than snorting.

The fourth source indicating recent changes in cocaine abuse comes from the study results of drug testing of arrested criminal suspects. Clearly, the drug is being used on a startlingly frequent basis by men (and women, but mainly men) who make their living committing predatory street crimes. One study showed that among men arrested for serious crimes in New York's Manhattan borough, the proportion who tested positive for cocaine *nearly doubled* between 1984 and 1986. When they were guaranteed anonymity, 85 percent of the men arrested for felonies agreed to be tested for the presence of drugs. In 1984, 42 percent tested positive for cocaine use; in 1986, 78 percent did. Among all categories of arrestees, robbers were most likely to have cocaine in their bodies: 90 percent tested positive for the drug! The rise was especially sharp among the young. For 16- to 20-year-olds, in 1984, 28 percent tested positive, but by 1986, this had risen to 71 percent; for 21- to 25-year-olds, the respective figures were 43 and 91 percent (Bronstein, 1987).

In short, regarding heavier and more frequent use by street criminals and causing more overdoses, cocaine is becoming a more deviant drug over time.

Many recreational users of cocaine claim the drug is safe and extremely nontoxic. This is partly true and partly false. Powdered cocaine, sniffed and used occasionally—less than weekly—in moderate doses, causes little if any physical or mental damage (Petersen, 1979; Van Dyke and Byck, 1982). The problem is that many cocaine users find it difficult to moderate their use; in fact, roughly 1 in 10 begins using the drug more and more frequently, in larger and larger doses, and through increasingly more dangerous routes of administration (Siegel, 1984). Many moderate recreational cocaine users find themselves taking the drug so frequently and in such high doses that they spend all of their money, sacrifice their savings and property, lose their jobs, destroy relations with loved ones, and endanger their own lives. Any drug having this effect on users, even if only 1 in 10, cannot be called safe.

In its powdered form, cocaine is usually sniffed, or *snorted*, that is, inhaled sharply through a nostril. To do this, the user often chops the drug into fine lines with a razor blade on a smooth surface, such as a mirror, and snorts each line up one nostril per line with a tiny tube, such as a short, chopped-off soda straw or a rolled-up bill. Other users prefer to scoop up the powder with a tiny spoon, place it near the nostril, and then snort it. As we saw earlier, snorting is slower, less efficient, less reinforcing, and less intensely pleasurable than smoking the drug.

During 1985 and 1986, the principal means of smoking cocaine was freebase. Freebase is cocaine that has been chemically purified by soaking it in ether, which removes the adulterants, thereby producing a more or less pure cocaine "base" that is smoked. After 1986, crack became the principal smoked cocaine product. In contrast to freebase, crack is made by soaking cocaine and baking soda in water and heating the mixture; the crystals precipitated out of this solution are what is called crack. Freebase is relatively pure cocaine, but crack is impure by its very nature, containing only 30 to 40 percent of the psychoactive drug; most of what's in crack is baking soda or sodium bicarbonate. Taking powdered cocaine intranasally produces a high that takes roughly 3 minutes to occur and lasts perhaps 30 minutes. There is no real rush or intense orgasm-like explosion of pleasure. Injected, the rush will take only 12 to 15 seconds to appear, and it is described as far more intense and voluptuous than the high that occurs when cocaine is snorted. When cocaine is smoked, either in freebase or crack, the onset of the drug's impact is even faster, a matter of 6 to 8 seconds; and the intense, orgasmlike high or rush lasts for perhaps 2 minutes, followed by an afterglow that lasts 10 to 20 minutes. The euphoria achieved in this experience is extreme, and it impels the user to want to use the drug over and over again.

One indication of the recency of crack use on the street is that, from its founding until mid-1985, the national telephone hotline for cocaine information and assistance (1-800-COCAINE) had received no mentions of crack at all out of a total of a million calls. A year later, *half* of its calls dealt with crack (Chatlos, 1987: 12).

As with nearly any new drug, sensationalistic exaggeration in the media accompanies its use. Newspaper headlines and television stories imply that all teenagers in the country have either used crack or are in imminent danger of doing so, that every community nationwide has been saturated by the drug. Although crack is indeed a frightening drug, the facts on the scope of its use are considerably less unsettling than the news would have us believe. In the 1986 nationally representative high-school survey cited earlier, questions on crack were included for the first time; that year, 4 percent of those questioned said they had used crack at least once during the year (Johnston et al.: 1987, 16–17, 38); in 1987, the figure was at the same level, with a lifetime prevalence of 5.6 percent. (Unfortunately, the study could not study high-school dropouts, whose crack use is almost certain to be higher than currently enrolled high-school students.) Crack is significantly more likely to be used among students who do not plan to go to college than among those who do; to be used in large communities than in small ones; and to be used in the Northeast and the West more than in the Midwest and the South. Roughly half of the high schools in the study showed no crack use at all. One 1 percent of all college students in this survey had used crack (Johnston et al., 1987: 16–17; University of Michigan, 1988). Thus, the drug is used by far fewer young people than the media suggest.

A June 16, 1986, story in *Newsweek* claimed that using crack immediately impelled the user into "an inferno of craving and despair." "Try it once and you're hooked!" "Once you start, you can't stop!" These and other slogans are repeated so often about crack that they seem to take on a truth of their own. In fact, these slogans are serious distortions of reality. Crack may be the most reinforcing drug we know, and compulsive patterns of use probably build up for it more explosively than for any other drug. Still, most users do not take it compulsively and destructively. In one Miami study of 308 heavily involved drug users age 12 to 17, 96 percent of whom had used crack at least once and 87 percent of whom had used it regularly, only a minority, 30 percent, used it daily, and half used it once a week or more but not daily. A majority of the daily users limited their use to one or two "hits"— "hardly an indication of compulsive and uncontrollable use. Although there were compulsive users of crack in the Miami sample, they represented an extremely small minority" (Inciardi, 1988: 26). Crack is a very scary drug with some serious medical consequences, not the least of which is chemical dependence. At the same time, the hellish experiences described in the media do not typify what most users go through when they take this drug. Once again, the drug user is characterized as a deviant by the media, a characterization that becomes a reality for much of the public.

HEROIN AND THE NARCOTICS

As we saw earlier in a summary of the American drug scene, of all well-known drugs or drug types, heroin ranks the lowest in popularity. Assuming the polls are reasonably accurate, only about 1 percent of the U.S. population has so much as tried heroin (NIDA, 1986); most estimates hold that there are roughly half a million addicts in the United States. Only 1 percent of the high-school class of 1987 in the United States has ever taken heroin, and .5 percent used it during the previous year; among college students, the annual prevalence was *only .2 percent* (University of Michigan, 1988). Although the high-school survey does not sample dropouts, who are certainly more likely to use heroin than currently enrolled students, and the national survey tends to miss the hard-to-track-down individual, also more likely to use heroin, it is true that heroin is a very rarely used drug compared with the others we've been discussing.

The question that arises, then, is Why study heroin use at all? If it is so rarely used, why discuss it? One answer is that, until the advent of crack, heroin use—and especially addiction—has been the most deviant form of drug use in the minds of most of the public. It is usually regarded as the *ultimate* form of drug use known. And second, heroin seems to create social problems of great seriousness and magnitude—if not in absolute terms (for surely alcohol is more socially, personally, and financially damaging than heroin in its total impact), then at least in terms of how much of an impact each drug user has on society.

One of the problems that heroin creates is medical in nature: Addicts overdose a great deal, especially compared with other recreational drug users. Heroin shows up with remarkable frequency in the Drug Abuse Warning Network (DAWN) statistics. Between the 1979 to 1980 and the 1986 periods, the number of nonlethal emergency room overdoses involving heroin doubled (from 7,784 to 15, 832), and the number of lethal overdoses reported by medical examiners tripled (from 474 to 1,549). Roughly 18 percent of all nonlethal drug overdoses reported by DAWN involved one or more of the narcotics, and about 60 percent of these entailed heroin. A whopping 30 percent of all lethal drug overdoses involved narcotics, again, about 60 percent of these were with heroin (DAWN, 1987: 30, 54). Considering how few people use heroin, its contribution to medical overdose statistics is massive. Even among the narcotics, the part that heroin plays in contributing to drug overdoses is enormous.

Another reason why a study of heroin is crucial in any course on deviance is that the potency of the drug sold on the street has been increasingly dramatically. For decades, the heroin available at the retail or user level has been only 3 to 5 percent pure; the rest was made up of adulterants and fillers, such as mannitol, lactose, and quinine. In 1986, though, the New York City police were confiscating heroin with a purity of 30 to 70 percent. Much of this is "China White" heroin—derived from opium grown in Southeast Asia and imported from Hong Kong by ethnic Chinese. In 1983, only 3 percent of the heroin confiscated on the streets of New York was China White; in 1986, 40 percent of it was; and by 1987, the police estimate, this had reached 70 percent. In addition, between 1983 and 1986, a new strain of Mexican heroin, called "black tar," with a purity of 60 to 70 percent, showed up with great frequency across the country. And third, a synthetic "designer drug," a narcotic called fentanyl, with a potency of 20 to 40 times that of heroin, began to appear on the street all over the country, especially in California; it was a special favorite of physician addicts (Kerr, 1987b, 1987c; Brinkley, 1986; Gallagher, 1986). A greater range of ethnic and national groups is importing heroin now than was true in the past; and partly as a consequence, a wider range of different types of narcotics is available today than was previously.

It is likely that the number of individuals who use and are addicted to heroin is declining, even though the number of overdoses is increasing; since users are taking more potent forms of the drug, each occasion of use is becoming increasingly more dangerous. Probably the young people who would have used heroin in 1982 to 1987 are now using cocaine, especially crack. Thus, recruitment into heroin addiction definitely seems to be declining. On the surface, the data on overdoses, which show increases, as we saw, do not seem to bear this out. Closer inspection shows that the overdose figures, in fact, confirm this view. There are several indications of this. In emergency rooms around the country in 1981, more than 50 percent of heroin users seeking treatment were in their twenties, and 35 percent were in their thirties. In 1985, less than 40 percent were in their twenties, and just under 45 percent were in their thirties (Kerr, 1986a). In 1981, 48 percent of all drug abusers seeking treatment listed heroin as their drug of choice; only 11 percent listed cocaine. In 1986, only 13 percent mentioned heroin; a majority, 52 percent, named cocaine or crack (Kerr, 1987a). Clearly, then, what seems to be happening is that heroin use is declining, and in order to attract a dwindling clientele, dealers are now selling increasingly potent samples of the drug. And the more potent samples are causing more overdoses.

The History of Narcotic Addiction

Narcotic addiction was extremely widespread in the United States even before heroin existed. Some time between 1803 and 1805 (the exact date is uncertain), morphine was chemically isolated from opium, and a practical hypodermic needle and syringe was devised in 1854. Morphine is, of course, an effective analgesic or painkiller, and it was used during the Civil War (1861–1865) for extremely serious and painful operations, such as the amputation of limbs. As a result, a small wave of unwitting medical addicts was created.

Opium and morphine (and cocaine as well) were ingredients in many patent medicines that were sold legally and openly in the United States before 1914. Mrs. Winslow's Soothing Syrup, Mother Bailey's Quieting Syrup, McMunn's Elixir of Opium, Koop's Baby Friend, Paregoric Elixir, Godfrey's Cordial, Ayer's Cherry Pectoral, Hamlin's Wizard Oil, along with 50,000 other readily available preparations were sold to the American public in the nineteenth and early twentieth centuries (Inciardi, 1986: 2–3; Brecher et al., 1972: 3–16; Berridge and Edwards, 1987: 62–72). These patent medicines were dispensed in pharmacies and drugstores, by physicians, in grocery and general stores, in bookshops, by tobacconists, in department stores, through mail order catalogs, and at traveling medicine shows—to anyone, for any reason, without benefit of prescription. (The 1897 edition of the Sears, Roebuck catalog offered hypodermic kits for sale.) In fact, prior to 1906, it wasn't even necessary to *list* the contents of these nostrums. Nineteenth-century America was truly "a dope fiend's paradise" (Brecher et al., 1972: 3).

Medicines containing narcotics were used for just about any ailment that plagued humankind: teething pains, menstrual cramps, toothaches, insomnia, nervousness, depression, rheumatism, athlete's foot, diarrhea, dysentery, consumption, the common cold, and even baldness and cancer. They were panaceas, or ineffective cure-alls. In 1898, heroin was synthesized, and it quickly joined the ranks of the ingredients in the pseudo-medicines freely available to the American public. It is important to stress that *most* of the narcotics users in the United States a century ago took drugs for medical, pseudo-medical, or quasimedical reasons, not for the purpose of attaining a high or euphoria.

They were used by people to cure, or alleviate the pain of, ailments and illnesses. Since most diseases are self-limiting and cure themselves eventually without medical intervention, these panaceas appeared to work. Often, however, after the disease had passed, the user of the patent medicine was left with a physical dependence.

It is impossible to estimate with any degree of accuracy just how many medical addicts patent medicines called into being. Records kept at the time were extremely unreliable and unsystematic; in fact, in the nineteenth century, the very concept of addiction was not clearly understood. Estimates ranged from a low of 100,000 addicts to a high of several million. In 1919, the Treasury Department issued a report claiming that roughly a million individuals were addicted to narcotics at the turn of the century. Other estimates, based on extrapolations from several local surveys, range from less than a quarter of a million (Terry and Pellens, 1928) to just under half a million (Kolb and DuMez, 1924).

Medical addicts at the turn of the century were, for the most part, respectable folk. The heavy users of patent medicines were disproportionately drawn from the middle and upper-middle classes (Brecher et al., 1972: 18). Although some criminals did use narcotics—mostly they smoked opium—the vast majority of narcotics users were users for medical reasons, and they were not involved in a life of crime. There was no necessary connection between the heavy, chronic use of narcotics and criminal behavior. The addict was not a deviant, an outsider, or an outcast. He or she usually carried on conventional, everyday activities—marriage, a family, a job, friendships, an education—and was not cut off from polite society, as is the case today. The addict then was seen as a sick person in need of medical attention, a helpless victim, but not a criminal or a deviant. The public didn't approve of drug addiction, but it was considered an unfortunate affliction rather than a manifestation of immorality and depravity; addicts were pitied rather than scorned. There was no isolation or stigmatization of the addict before the turn of the

century. Moreover, there was no *subculture* of addiction: Addicts did not associate with one another because of their habits; they did not behave differently from nonaddicts; there was nothing particularly remarkable about them except for their addiction (Terry and Pellens, 1928; Lindesmith, 1965, 1968; Duster, 1970; Griffin, 1976; Musto, 1973).

In addition, the nineteenth-century addict was more likely to be a woman than a man, the reverse of today's picture; in studies conducted at the time, roughly two-thirds of the medical addicts surveyed were female. Users tended to be middle-aged rather than young (Brecher et al., 1972: 18). Blacks were underrepresented among addicts then; again, the reverse of the contemporary scene. And in the past, users were not drawn mainly from large cities, but from the entire rural-urban spectrum. In short, the narcotic addict population of a century ago was almost totally different in nearly every respect from the addict of today.

In December 1914, Congress passed the Harrison Act. It banned the sale of all over-the-counter narcotics (along with cocaine, which the law defined at the time as a narcotic). In order to purchase a medicine containing a narcotic drug, it became necessary to secure a prescription from a physician. Since many physicians were willing to write prescriptions for narcotics, this, by itself, did not pose a serious problem for the addict. At the time, maintaining addicts on narcotics, thus keeping them from the agony of withdrawal, was considered acceptable medical practice. The Harrison Act expressly stipulated that the law did not apply to, and therefore should not have criminalized, the dispensing of narcotics by a physician "in the course of his professional practice," and that a prescription can be written "for legitimate purpose" and if "prescribed in good faith."

However, after 1914, the police did begin arresting addicts, as well as physicians dispensing prescriptions to addicts for drugs containing narcotics; the legal appeals of some of these cases went all the way to the Supreme Court. In a series of Supreme Court cases between 1919 and 1922, it was declared that maintenance of the addict on narcotics was *not* part of legitimate medical practice; "the court ruled that such prescriptions were illegal regardless of the purpose the doctor may have had" (Lindesmith, 1965: 6). According to one estimate, in the dozen years following the passage of the Harrison Act, roughly 25,000 physicians—1 out of 10 of all the physicians in the country!—were arrested for issuing prescriptions for narcotic drugs to addicts. About 3,000 actually served a jail or prison sentence for this new crime. Fairly quickly, most physicians abandoned treatment of the narcotic addict, leaving them to fend for themselves. By the 1920s, addicts, too, began to be arrested in large numbers; in 1921, there were only 1,000 federal arrests on narcotics charges; by 1925, there were more than 10,000 (Lindesmith, 1965: 143).

Although the criminalization of addiction did reduce the size of the addict population, most estimates hold, it also had another effect: the generation of an addict subculture—a criminal class that had barely existed previously. Some criminals smoked opium, but the number was tiny; most addicts, as we saw, were medical addicts. What the law and its enforcement did was to forge a link between addiction and crime. The addict was a criminal, first by definition, by using, possessing, and purchasing an illegal substance, and second, by virtue of having to commit crimes to secure drugs. It was the criminalization of addiction that created addicts as a special and distinctive group, and it is the subcultural aspect of addicts that gives them their recruiting power. The majority of medical addicts probably did give up their habits when narcotics became a crime, but some turned to the emerging addict subculture for their drugs and committed crimes to pay for them.

Heroin Addiction and Dependence

Everyone knows that heroin is an addicting drug, certainly one of the most addicting drugs known. In addition, it is common knowledge that heroin addicts are "enslaved" by their habit; they commit money-making crimes to pay for the drug they take so they can continue their addiction and avoid the agony of withdrawal. They have to take heroin just to remain normal. And since heroin is illegal, it is difficult to obtain and costly to buy; because of this, it is profitable for the underworld to sell it. Like most pieces of conventional wisdom, this picture isn't entirely accurate.

There are many theories as to why addicts continue to use heroin, in spite of the many painful and life-threatening experiences they have as a result of taking the drug, and even after many episodes of "kicking" the drug habit. Two of these theories are based on the mechanism of *reinforcement,* or the rewards subsequent to a given act. *Positive* reinforcement theories explain the continued use of heroin by the pleasurable sensations that come with using the drug. *Negative* reinforcement theories explain continued heroin use by the avoidance of pain that taking heroin produces. Which of these two theories explains heroin use, abuse, and addiction better?

The argument invoking negative reinforcement goes more or less like this. Initially, the use of heroin may not be pleasurable at all. In time, the user learns how to take heroin and how to interpret its effects, so that its use is pleasurable. In the first few weeks or months of use, pleasure is a major motivating force in continuing to use heroin; this period could be called the "honeymoon" phase. However, the user gradually becomes physically dependent on the drug, usually without realizing it. Because of the tolerance mechanism, the user, in order to continue receiving pleasure, must increase the doses of the drug; eventually, physical addiction takes place. At some point, the attainment of euphoria becomes problematic, for all practical purposes, an unreachable goal. If use is discontinued, painful withdrawal symptoms wrack the addict's body. But even though addicted, the user is not yet a true addict, because withdrawal, though painful, may not necessarily be associated in the user's mind with taking the drug. To become a true addict, the user must, first, recognize that continued administration of heroin has produced physical dependence;

second, that discontinuing the heroin use produces agony and pain; and third, that taking heroin *will alleviate painful withdrawal distress.* It is this dramatic, three-step process that fixes in the individual's mind the need to keep taking narcotics. This is what makes an addict a true addict.

According to Alfred Lindesmith (1947, 1968), the earliest proponent of this theory:

The critical experience in the fixation process is not the positive euphoria produced by the drug but rather the relief of the pain that inevitably appears when a physically dependent person stops using the drug. The experience becomes critical, however, only when an additional indispensible element in the situation is taken into account, namely a cognitive one. The individual not only must experience withdrawal distress but must realize that his [her] distress is produced by the interruption of prior regular use of the drug. (1968: 8)

In short, "The perception of withdrawal symptoms as being due to the absence of opiates will generate a *burning* desire for the drug" (Sutter, 1966: 195).

In contrast, the positive reinforcement theory holds that the majority of drug users, abusers, and addicts continue to take the drugs because of their "extremely potent reinforcing effects" (McAuliffe and Gordon, 1980: 138); that is, because of the intense pleasure they generate. According to positive reinforcement theory, continued, compulsive drug use, heroin included, does not require that the user be physically addicted; users take drugs day after day, year after year, because of their positive reinforcing effects, because they derive intense pleasure from doing so. Why don't all people who experiment with a given drug become compulsively involved with it? Many drug users are reinforced—that is, they experience euphoria—from their very first drug experience onward, and the more they use the more intense the sensation and the greater the motivation to continue. There are, therefore, individual differences in the reinforcement value of a given drug or of drugs in general.

Which explains heroin addiction better— the negative or the positive reinforcement theory?

The negative reinforcement theory holds that the pleasure addicts derive from the administration of heroin declines over time; it becomes harder and harder to get high—to the point where euphoria is no longer a factor. The primary motivation in continued use is the reinforcement heroin offers in alleviating pain. Recent evidence however, suggests that addicts and other compulsive drug abusers do, in fact, experience euphoria, and that this is a major factor in their continued drug use. In one study of addicts, all of whom used heroin at least once a day, 98 percent of the sample said that they got high or experienced euphoria at least once a month, and 42 percent got high *every day.* For nearly all respondents in this study, euphoria was consciously desired and sought. In fact, 93 percent said that they wanted to be high at least once a day, and 60 percent wanted to be high *all the time* (McAuliffe and Gordon, 1974: 807). Clearly, most heavy, compulsive heroin users continue to seek, and many in fact achieve, euphoria; its attainment is a major motivating force behind their continued use.

These two perspectives may not be as far apart as they seem. In fact, there are two quite different types of addicts, the behavior of each ruled by a distinctly different mechanism: the *maintainers* and the *euphoria seekers.* The maintainer takes just enough heroin to avert withdrawal distress. Some addicts lack the financial resources, and are insufficiently willing to engage in a life of crime, to obtain enough heroin to attain euphoria. They are simply staving off the agony of withdrawal, "nursing" their habit along. To achieve the high they really want would require taking such a substantial quantity of the drug that their lives would be utterly and completely transformed. They would have to work very hard and run a substantial risk of danger and arrest to do so. Not all users want to commit crimes, and certainly not to live a life of crime, to get high; not all think the chances of arrest are worth threatening such valued features of their lives as their jobs, family, and freedom. They prefer to "maintain" a habit over risking what they have in order to achieve euphoria.

They have retained most of their ties with conventional society, and "let loose only periodically" (McAuliffe and Gordon, 1974: 822).

In contrast, the pleasure-seeking addict takes narcotics in sufficient quantities and at sufficiently frequent intervals to achieve euphoria. Such a habit is extremely expensive, and typically requires illegal activity to support it. In addition, the life-style of the euphoria-seeking addict is sufficiently disruptive that a legal job is usually not feasible; he or she must resort to criminal activity instead. It is also difficult for the nonaddict to fit in with and be capable of tolerating the addict's life-style, so that marriage and a family are typically not possible—or are, at best, extremely chancy propositions. Further, since heavy opiate use depresses the sexual urge, intimate relations with the opposite sex are difficult.

In short, the euphoria-seeking addict has sacrificed conventional activities and commitments for the hedonistic pursuit of pleasure; and to engage in this pursuit, a commitment to a deviant and criminal life-style is necessary. Such sacrifices make no sense "if they were directed solely toward reducing withdrawal symptoms, which could be accomplished with much less effort, as every addict knows. . . . *For it is the frequency of euphoria, more than anything else, that stratifies the addict social system.*" In the addict subculture, the greater the success in achieving euphoria, the greater the prestige. "In this sense, hard-core addicts are the true elite, and the addict stratification system itself points to the fundamental importance of euphoria" (McAuliffe and Gordon, 1974: 828).

In short, the negative reinforcement theory works better for the maintainer-addict, while the positive reinforcement theory works better for the euphoria-seeking addict. Which theory works best depends entirely on how much heroin the addict takes and what motivation is the primary mover in his or her actions.

Since positive reinforcement is the major reason why many heroin addicts use narcotics, it forces us to face an extremely crucial point: The line between addiction and use is not sharp or clear-cut. If positive reinforcement is a (possibly *the*) driving force behind most dependence, then it does not much matter whether users are technically addicted for them to be long-term, compulsive users. Many users continue taking heroin because they have been powerfully rewarded with repeated administrations of the drug over a long period of time. They *have* to take heroin because their bodies are attuned to the euphoria they have experienced. They aren't necessarily physically dependent on heroin—that is, they wouldn't undergo withdrawal symptoms if they stopped—but the psychological dependency is just as strong as if they were. Dependency is a *linear* dimension, a spectrum, not an either-or proposition. Physical dependency or addiction is simply the end or extreme point of a continuum.

This conclusion is verified by a study of some 200 New York heroin abusers (Johnson et al., 1985), which found that doing what one has to do to survive is a common theme in heroin users' lives. Most of the "addicts" in this study were not addicted in the physical sense. They were psychologically and behaviorally dependent on heroin; they used it as much as they could, week after week, and their lives pretty much revolved around procuring the money to pay for it, getting the drug itself, and using it. Most regular users of heroin are not addicted in the strictly physiological sense; that is, they would not suffer painful withdrawal symptoms if they were to discontinue use. Most regular, even compulsive, users of heroin take their drug often, but not necessarily several times a day, day in and day out, in classic junkie fashion. Instead, they use twice one day, once the next, not at all for three days, four times the day after that, and so on. The classic junkie may be a relative rarity compared with the number of nonaddicted compulsive heroin abusers. It is entirely possible that the 500,000 figure commonly quoted for the number of addicts in the United States refers to technically nonaddicted heroin abusers rather than to addicts who are physically dependent on heroin.

This means that most "addicts," that is,

most compulsive heroin abusers, are not driven by the need to avoid withdrawal. The popular image of the addict being impelled by the physiological drive to avoid withdrawal symptoms ("I need a fix") is highly likely to be a myth. Psychological dependence is every bit as powerful a drive as—and may even be more powerful than—physiological dependence. The heroin abusers in the study of Johnson and his colleagues (1985) *do* "need a fix." But for the most part, they do not need it to avoid withdrawal since most of them are not taking enough heroin or any other narcotic sufficiently frequently, or in large enough doses, to be physically dependent.

Is experimenting with heroin an automatic ticket to addiction or even compulsive abuse? Does trying and then using heroin always lead to physical or even psychological dependence? Is there any such thing as a "recreational" heroin user? Is there any such thing as "controlled" opiate use? The heroin users I've just described are compulsive users; their lives revolve around the drug, and they would take more of it if they could. But is there a different heroin user who takes the drug on a regular but noncompulsive basis—that is, on a fairly *controlled* basis? Until fairly recently, it was not recognized that controlled opiate use was possible; one was considered either an addict or an abstainer. Recent research suggests the occasional yet regular controlled user of narcotic drugs is more common than the addict. The term used in the world of street narcotic use to describe this limited use is "chippying" or "chipping": to fool around with heroin, to use it once in a while or even more often without getting hooked, without developing a true habit. How common is this pattern of heroin use?

We all recognize that the controlled use of alcohol is possible—it is in fact the majority pattern. Most drinkers are moderate in their consumption of alcohol and do not become alcoholics. Alcohol, as we'll see in Chapter 6, is every bit as dependency-producing—is as physically addicting—as the narcotics. How much and how often people in a given society use a certain drug, including

alcohol, and what proportion are physically dependent on it are not a simple function of the pharmacological properties of the drug itself, but depend in part on the people—their culture and society—using the drug. For instance, in the United States roughly during the 1800 to 1840 period, about *three times* as much alcohol was consumed per capita as is true today (Lender and Martin, 1987: 205–206)—same drug, different rules, different patterns of use, and differing proportions of alcoholics in the population. It is the people who take drugs, not the drugs themselves, that control people. All drug use is surrounded by values and rules of conduct; these values and rules spell out sanctions—penalties for misuse and rewards for proper use—and these values, rules, and sanctions have an impact on how drugs are actually used. Some of these values may be society-wide and some may be distinctive to special groups or subcultures within the larger society. All have an impact on the behavior of the members of the culture or subculture who take them seriously.

Is it really possible to use heroin or any of the other opiates on a moderate or controlled basis? One study (Zinberg, 1984) located a number of controlled opiate users and examined their patterns of use—what made them distinctive, how they accomplished this seemingly impossible feat. They had been using opiate drugs on a controlled basis for an average of four and a half years. For the year preceding the study, about a quarter (23 percent) used opiates sporadically, or less than once a month; a third (36 percent) used one to three times a month; and four in ten (41 percent) used twice a week. None used daily or more. Their pattern of use and the length of time they had sustained this pattern showed "without question that controlled use can be stable" (1984; 69).

It might be objected that stable, nonaddicted opiate users have simply not yet reached the stage in their drug careers when use inevitably becomes uncontrolled and compulsive. This objection is easily countered by comparing the length of time of the opiate use of the controlled users with the length of time of the addicts in the sample of this same study; they were not substantially different. In addition, most compulsive users and addicts had never had a period of controlled use. And third, the length of time these controlled users had been taking narcotics represents ample time for them to have developed an addiction or a pattern of compulsive use (Zinberg, 1984: 69–70). Clearly, controlled use is a stable pattern for a significant porportion of narcotics users; experimentation or moderate use does not necessarily or inevitably turn into compulsive use or addiction. Addiction is a phenomenon that must be understood in its own right. At the same time, without more information, we cannot be sure exactly how typical or frequent controlled use is.

This study also compared and contrasted the patterns of use that characterized controlled users of narcotics with compulsive users and found interesting differences. They did not differ in their route of administration—for example, snorting versus intravenous injection—or personal acquaintance with someone who died of an opiate overdose. They *did* differ from controlled users in that, they (1) rarely used more than once a day; (2) often kept opiates on hand for a period of use without immediately using them; (3) tended to avoid using opiates in the company of known addicts; (4) tended not to use opiates to alleviate depression; (5) rarely or never used opiates on a "binge" or a "spree"; (6) usually knew their opiate source or dealer personally; (7) usually used opiates for recreation or relaxation; and (8) tended not to use opiates to "escape" from the difficulties of everyday life (Zinberg, 1984: 69–81).

In short, some users of opiates manage to set rules for themselves—norms—and stick to them; for them, regular use does not necessarily lead to compulsive use or addiction. Again, it is the people who take drugs, not the drugs themselves that control people; in many ways, patterns of drug use are determined more by *who* takes the drugs than by the intrinsic characteristics of the drugs themselves—by what the drugs *are*, in some abstract sense. In fact, what drugs "are" is determined by how they are used and what happens to whoever uses them; and, in turn, this is determined by just who it is that uses them in the first place. If we forget the social and personal dimensions of drug use, we are distorting its fundamental reality.

LEGALIZE DRUGS?

In the latter half of the 1980s, a drastic and unusual proposal to solve some of the disastrous consequences of illicit drug use and abuse has become popular in some circles: to *legalize* all or most currently illegal drugs. Taking the profit out of drug sales and making drugs more or less readily available, this view holds, would sharply reduce the crime, violence, and devastation that has taken place in many urban neighborhoods as a result of drug use and abuse (Gonzales, 1985; Kerr, 1988; Church et al., 1988; Hamill, 1988; Fletcher, 1988). This proposal has no realistic hope of becoming law, so the debate it has stirred up is in many ways a theoretical exercise, not one based on anything likely to happen. Still, since this argument is taken seriously among some observers, it is worthwhile to respond to it.

The fatal flaw in the prolegalization argument is that drug use is almost certain to increase after legalization, but the impact of legalization is likely to be variable, depending on the drug. It would be least for marijuana: Studies suggest that in the states in which small-quantity marijuana possession is not a crime (there are 11), decriminalization has not resulted in an increase in use (Cuskey et al., 1978; Single, 1981; Johnston, 1980). There are probably three reasons for this: (1) a condition of near-saturation has been reached for marijuana; nearly everyone who wants to use already does; (2) the odds of being arrested on marijuana possession charges are extremely slim (there are some 400,000 marijuana arrests in the United States each year—but, annually, well over 25 million Americans who use); and (3) the effects of marijuana are pleasant, but not as immensely reinforcing as those of some drugs (heroin and cocaine, for example).

The legalization, and thus the ready availability, of marijuana would have a greater impact than mere decriminalization, but not much.

Cocaine is altogether different. As we saw, cocaine is an *immensely* reinforcing drug, both for animals and for humans; it is, in fact, the most reinforcing drug known. It offers so much pleasure—direct, immediate, sensuous pleasure, unmitigated by learning or acquired taste—that it is reasonable to expect many more users would be attracted to it if it were legally available. In a 1985 national survey, just under 6 million Americans took cocaine in the past month and were therefore defined as "regular" users (NIDA, 1986); it is possible that 1 in 10 of these are compulsive, uncontrolled users. In contrast, 113 million Americans drank alcohol during the previous month, of whom, again, roughly 1 in 10 is a compulsive, uncontrolled drinker; they could be called alcoholics. Doesn't it make sense that we should expect at least as many compulsive cocaine users as alcoholics if cocaine were readily available?—in fact, certainly more, since alcohol is far less reinforcing and far more of an acquired taste. Can we afford to have more than 10 million cocaine addicts in our midst?

Even the medical control and dispensation of heroin are unwise. They have been phased out in England, and there are some 50,000 unregistered addicts there—a huge explosion of addiction during the 1980s. The reason maintenance programs cannot be successful in eliminating addiction is that the primary motive addicts have in using narcotics is euphoria. They want that orgasm-like rush coursing through their veins, and that is one thing maintenance programs do not supply. Maintenance programs appeal mainly to the older, burnt-out, used-up addicts who have a couple decades of addiction behind them. On the other hand, giving junkies exactly what they want can only balloon the number of heroin addicts.

Drug profits do not create drug users and abusers; eliminating drug profits will not diminish the number of users or the quantity of use; quite the reverse. It will eliminate *some* drug-related problems, as its proponents suggest—the murders, much of the crime, many of the medical maladies of junkies. It is society's choice as to which we want: a relatively small number of sick, violent, criminal addicts or a much larger number of healthier, less violent, and less criminal addicts. Most Americans would choose the former.

The current somewhat punitive policy has not worked because it has not eliminated drug use and abuse. But it has worked in at least one extremely crucial respect: *containment*. It has kept certain highly reinforcing drugs out of the hands of millions of Americans who would otherwise become involved with them. Actually, there is no politically acceptable, nondrastic means of eliminating or sharply reducing drug use in the United States. Viewed in that light, current policies have worked, in their clumsy, limited, even damaging way. Clearly some medium-scale reforms would work better, but any major change on the scale of outright legalization is likely to be a disaster.

Legalize Drugs?

In 1988, in a nationwide poll conducted by ABC News, 9 out of 10 Americans said they rejected the legalization of all currently illegal drugs. Over half (51 percent) said they believed that legalization would lead to increased drug use; 11 percent said use would decrease; and 38 percent said it would make no difference. Legalization was favored for marijuana somewhat more often (25 percent of those polled) than for cocaine (7 percent) and heroin (6 percent), but for no drug did the prolegalization sentiment even remotely approach a majority. By a margin of two to one, those polled believed that legalization would lead to an increase in crime: 47 versus 23 percent.

SOURCE: *The New York Times*, September 15, 1988, p. 26.

CHAPTER

6

*Alcohol Use and Alcoholism**

In terms of its impact on the workings of the human mind, alcohol is a drug in precisely the same sense that LSD, heroin, and cocaine are: They are all *psychoactive*. Likewise, in the sense that alcohol is used in large part, although not entirely, for its effects on the drinker (the user takes it to get high)—alcohol is drug not essentially different from marijuana and cocaine: It is a *recreational* drug. With respect to its capacity to induce a *physical dependence* in the drinker, alcohol is a drug in the same way that heroin and the barbiturates are: Alcohol is "addicting," that is, it generates severe withdrawal symptoms when the heavy, long-term drinker discontinues its use. In fact, alcoholism is by far our most common form of drug addiction. Estimates hold that there are roughly 10 million

*This chapter is reprinted, with permission, from Erich Goode, *Drugs in American Society* (3rd ed.), New York: McGraw-Hill, 1989, pp. 108–136.

alcoholics and only half a million heroin addicts in the United States. The typical drug addict, then, is an alcoholic, not a street junkie. In that a sizable minority of drinkers displays a pattern of *behavioral dependence*—they continue to drink heavily in spite of the social cost to themselves and to others that they care for—alcohol is a drug no different from cocaine, amphetamines, and heroin.

In the bodily sense, then, *all drinkers are drug users*. There is no internal, chemical feature of alcohol that sets it off from the substances people think of as drugs. There is no biochemical aspect of drinking that is qualitatively different from what most of us regard as "drug use."

There are two ways in which alcohol cannot be regarded as a drug, however: First, most of the public does not consider alcohol a drug (Abelson et al., 1973: 512; Abelson and Atkinson, 1975: 97), and second, legal controls on the purchase of alcohol are minimal, which is not true for most drugs. Almost any adult may buy it almost anywhere in the country. This chapter will consider some of the similarities and differences between alcohol and the substances that are universally regarded as drugs and what relevance these similarities and differences have for human behavior. To us, how a drug is regarded and what it does to us physically are equally important; moreover, the two mutually influence one another. Still, in many respects, there is a yawning chasm between the "objective" properties of some drugs and their image in the public mind. Alcohol is one of these drugs.

Alcohol has an ancient and checkered history. Fermentation was one of the earliest of human discoveries, dating back to the Stone Age. Alcohol emerges spontaneously from fermented sugar in overripe fruit; the starch in grains and other food substances also readily converts to sugar and then to alcohol. Because this process is simple and basic, the discovery of alcohol by humans was bound to be early and widespread. It is also no accident that alcohol's "remarkable and seemingly magical properties as the ability to induce euphoria, sedation, intoxication and narcosis" (Health, Education and Welfare, 1971: 5) and its "great capacity for alleviating pain, relieving tension and worry, and producing a pleasurable sense of well-being, relaxation, conviviality, and good will toward others" (Straus, 1976: 184) have made it an almost universally acceptable and agreeable beverage. Consequently, we have been ingesting beverages containing alcohol for something like 10,000 years. It is also the most widely used drug in existence; alcohol is ubiquitous, almost omnipresent the world over.

Actually, what is generally referred to as "alcohol" is one of a whole family of alcohols. Pharmacologists call it *ethyl alcohol,* or *ethanol.* Other representatives of this family include wood alcohol (methyl alcohol) and rubbing alcohol (isopropyl alcohol), which are outright poisons, even in small quantities. It is therefore no accident that ethyl alcohol, the most pleasant and one of the least toxic of all the alcohols, has come to be

identified with the general term. I will refer to ethyl alcohol simply as "alcohol."

Societies differ vastly in their average level of alcohol consumption. What proportion of their members drink at all, and how much each drinker consumes on the average, varies enormously from one nation to another, and even from one group to another within a country. In addition, every society that has some acquaintance with alcohol has devised and institutionalized rules for the proper and improper consumption of alcohol. There is, then, intersocietal variation on the behavioral and the normative levels. Although there are indeed biochemical "effects" of alcohol, both short-term and over the long run, most of them can be mitigated or drastically altered by the belief in and the observance of these cultural rules. Heavy, long-term alcohol use is associated with certain medical maladies, but the extent to which intoxication leads to troublesome, harmful, or deviant behavior varies considerably from society to society. In many places, alcohol use poses no social problem according to almost anyone's definition. The drug is consumed in moderation and is associated with no untoward behavior. In other places, alcohol use has been catastrophic by any conceivable standard. The overall impact of alcohol, then, is not determined by the biochemical features of the drug itself, but by their *relationship* to the characteristics of the people drinking it. This is not to say that alcohol can have any effect that the members of a society expect it to have. There is a great deal of latitude in alcohol's effects, but it is a latitude within certain boundaries.

As with illegal drugs, the effects of alcohol can be divided into short-term or *acute* effects while under the influence, and long-range, or *chronic* effects. Even this breakdown is crude. The actue effects can be further subdivided into those that rest within the "objective" or strictly physiological and sensorimotor realms; the realm of behavior under the influence, called *drunken comportment;* and the "subjective" realm, or what it feels like to be drunk, how the intoxication is experienced. The sensorimotor effects are fairly specific and easily measured in mechanical and mental performance, such as motor coordination, memory, and the ability to achieve a given score on certain psychological tests. Drunken comportment, in contrast, refers to the vast spectrum of free-ranging, real-life behavior: what people do with and to one another while under the influence. A sensorimotor effect would be driving more poorly under the influence; drunken comportment might refer to whether or not one even gets into a car while drunk in the first place. The long-range effects can be divided, at the very least, into *medical* effects and *behavioral* effects—what happens to one's daily life after ingesting certain quantities of alcohol over a lengthy period.

ACUTE EFFECTS OF ALCOHOL

The potency of alcoholic beverages is measured by the percent of *absolute alcohol* they contain. Pure ethyl alcohol is 100 percent absolute alcohol. Beer contains about 4 or 5 percent. Wine is about 12 percent; it is the most potent drink we can concoct through the natural fermentation process. ("Fortified" wine, in which alcohol is added to the natural substance, may be no higher than 20 percent alcohol. The wines skid-row alcoholics drink are usually "fortified." Sherry is a wine fortified with brandy.) However, the process of distillation (boiling, condensing, and recovering the more volatile, alcohol-potent vapor from the original fluid, and adding an appropriate proportion of water) produces drinks, like Scotch, vodka, gin, rum, and tequila, that are about 40 to 50 percent alcohol, or 80 to 100 "proof." Consequently, in order to consume roughly an ounce of absolute alcohol, someone would have to drink two 12-ounce cans of beer, or two 4-ounce glasses of wine, or a mixed drink containing about $2\frac{1}{2}$ ounces of Scotch or gin. According to *the rule of equivalency*—which states that the effects of alcohol are determined mainly by the volume of absolute alcohol that is drunk, rather than the type of drink itself—these drinks would be roughly equal in strength,

and would have approximately the same effects on one's body.

Alcohol, when it enters the body, is translated into what pharmacologists call *blood-alcohol concentration* (BAC), or *blood-alcohol level* (BAL). This corresponds fairly closely to the percent of one's blood that is made up of alcohol after it is ingested. There is a relationship between blood-alcohol concentration and what we do under the influence. The effects of alcohol are, to a large degree, dose-related: The more that is drunk, the greater the effect it has. There are, of course, person-to-person variations in this respect. And there are many qualifications that must be noted.

The effects of alcohol are influenced by many factors. Some of them are directly physiological. Since alcohol registers its impact via the bloodstream, the *size* of the drinker influences blood-alcohol concentration; the larger the drinker, the more alcohol it takes to make him or her drunk. The presence of food and water in the stomach will retard and space out over time—by as much as two times—the rate of absorption of alcohol into the bloodstream. Consequently, the less one has in one's stomach, the less it takes to get one drunk. The *faster* one drinks, the less able the body is to metabolize the alcohol within a standard period of time, and the drunker one will become. One can drink small quantities of alcohol continually without demonstrating any effects at all, if the drinks are taken slowly enough. The presence of carbonation in an alcoholic beverage—as, for example, in champagne or sparkling Burgundy—will speed up the metabolism process and can make one drunker more quickly.

As with practically all drugs, alcohol builds pharmacological tolerance: It takes more to have an effect on a regular drinker than on an abstainer, more on a heavy drinker than an infrequent drinker. Much of this is behavioral tolerance: simply learning to get used to alcohol's effects. But biochemical tolerance does develop as well. There is a kind of "plateau," however; it requires something like twice as much alcohol to have an effect in the sensorimotor realm in the heavy, long-term drinker as in the moderate drinker.

Alcohol's strictly physiological effects include cellular dehydration (a major reason for a hangover the day after), gastric irritation (which may lead to an upset stomach after drinking too much), vasodilation (an increase of blood flow through the capillaries), a lowering of body temperature (though the surface of the skin does become flushed, creating an illusion of greater body warmth), some anesthesia, and a depression of many functions and activities of the organs of the body, especially the central nervous system. Alcohol also disorganizes and impairs the ability of the brain to process and use information.

One ounce of alcohol consumed in less than an hour will result in a blood-alcohol concentration of roughly .05 percent in a person of average size (see Table 6.1). This produces in most people a mild euphoria, a diminution of anxiety, fear, and tension, a corresponding increase in self-confidence and, usually, what is called a "release" of inhibitions (an effect I'll have to qualify shortly). Decreased fear also typically results in a greater willingness to take risks; this effect has been demonstrated in laboratory animals (Health, Education, and Welfare, 1971: 39). Alcohol is, for most people, at low doses, a mild sedative and a tranquilizer. This is by no means universally the case, however. There are many people for whom alcohol ingestion results in paranoia, distrust, heightened anxiety, and even hostility. These "effects," however, typically occur, when they do, at high doses. And at low doses, alcohol will result in little or no diminution of motor and intellectual performance.

Alcohol's effects on motor performance are familiar to us all: clumsiness; an unsteady gait; an inability to stand or walk straight; slurred speech. One's accuracy and consistency in performing mechanical activities decline dramatically as blood-alcohol concentration increases. And the more complex, the more abstract, and the more unfamiliar the task, the sharper the decline. The most noteworthy example is the ability to drive an automobile. It is crystal clear that

TABLE 6.1 Alcohol Intake and Blood-Alcohol Level (BAL) (for a 150-pound individual, in one hour of drinking)

Absolute Alcohol (ounces)	Beverage Intake	Blood-Alcohol Level (BAL) (grams/100 milliliters)
$\frac{1}{2}$	1 can beer (12 oz.) 1 glass wine (4 oz.) 1 oz. distilled spirits	.025
1	2 cans beer (24 oz.) 2 glasses wine (8 oz.) 2 oz. distilled spirits	.05
2	4 cans beer (48 oz.) 4 glasses wine (16 oz.) 4 oz. distilled spirits	.10
3	6 cans beer (72 oz.) 6 glasses wine (24 oz.) 6 oz. distilled spirits	.15
4	8 cans beer (96 oz.) 8 glasses wine (32 oz.) 8 oz. distilled spirits	.20
5	10 cans beer (120 oz.) 10 glasses wine (40 oz.) 10 oz. distilled spirits	.25

Note: The less someone weighs, the higher the BAL, other things being equal; the more someone weighs, the lower the BAL. The BAL of males tends to be slightly lower than that of females.

SOURCE: Adapted and simplified from Ray and Ksir, 1987: 155.

drinking, even moderately, deteriorates the ability to drive, and contributes to highway fatalities.

How intoxicated does one have to be to lose the ability to perform mechanical tasks? What does one's blood-alcohol level have to be to display a significant decline in motor coordination? And how many drinks does this represent? The answers depend on a number of factors, as I just said, experience with alcohol being crucial. It is true that seasoned drinkers can handle themselves better at the same blood-alcohol level than novices can, but experienced drinkers are typically far too overconfident about their ability to function while under the influence. In fact, since alcohol tends to dull anxiety and tension, drunk drivers typically think that they perform better than they actually do—and are surprised, even incredulous, when their ineptitude is demonstrated to them—so that the problem becomes more than a simple deterioration in mechanical ability. All drinkers experience a loss of motor skills at a certain point, and it occurs at a fairly low BAC. However, many drivers are quite willing to get behind the wheel while intoxicated: In 1987 in the United States, there were 1.7 million arrests for drunk driving.

There is a kind of "zone" within which alcohol impairment occurs. At about the .03 percent blood-alcohol level, some very inexperienced and particularly susceptible individuals will display significant negative changes in the ability to perform a wide range of tasks. (See Table 6.1 for an indication of how much alcohol this entails for a 150-pound person.) The Federal Aviation Administration (FAA) sets a .04 percent BAC as representing an alcohol-influenced condition, and prohibits pilots from flying at this level of intoxication. As we can see from Table 6.1, this is less than two typical drinks. At the .10 level, even the most hardened, experienced, and resistant drinker will exhibit some impairment in coordination. Most states set a BAL of .10 as constituting legal intoxication—a far too conservative a level, in the view of most experts. At the .04 percent level, for most people, there is no measurable increase in the likelihood of having a highway accident. But at the .06 percent level, the risk doubles. As we can see, this is only slightly more than two typical mixed drinks, or two beers, or two glasses of wine. At the .10 level, one's driving ability deteriorates by 15 percent, and one's likelihood of having an accident shoots up six or seven times, according to one estimate (Brodie, 1973: 32). According to another estimate, at a .08 BAL, one's risk of being involved in a fatal car crash triples, and at .12, it increases fifteenfold (Ray and Ksir, 1987: 157). At the .15 level of blood-alcohol concentration, which constitutes "driving while intoxicated" (DWI) everywhere in the United States, one's skill at handling an automobile drops by one-third and one's chances of smashing

up increase by between 10 to 50 times (Brodie, 1973: 32).

Motor-vehicle crashes are the most common cause of "nonnatural" death in the United States; they account for more fatal injuries than any other type of accident. The proportion of drivers involved in fatal crashes whose BAL tested at .10 or higher was 50 percent in 1980. This figure declined through the 1980s to 38 percent in 1985 (Brooke, 1986), but in 1986, the number of deaths from drunk driving increased a bit (Stevens, 1987). Taking all traffic fatalities together—drivers, passengers, pedestrians, and cyclists—42 percent were alcohol-related in 1983. The National Highway Traffic Safety Administration reported that 60 percent of fatally injured drivers of motorcycles had a BAC of .10 or higher; for fatally injured drivers of heavy trucks, this was only 20 percent. Even pedestrians vastly increase their chances of being killed by an automobile—more than fivefold!—if they are intoxicated. A third of pedestrian fatalities in one study had a BAC of .15 or higher, whereas only 6 percent of the control group randomly selected at the same time and place were this intoxicated (Brodie, 1973: 32).

Automobiles are not the only source of fatal alcohol-related accidents. The National Transportation and Safety Board estimates that nearly 70 percent of drownings are alcohol-related. The U.S. Coast Guard estimates that of all boating accidents that result in a drowning, 88 percent are alcohol-related. Nearly half (46 percent) of all burn victims had been using alcohol at the time of their injury. In roughly a quarter of all suicides (23 percent), a measurable level of intoxication was found in the victim's body (Health and Human Services, 1987: 8–11). In an unpublished study supplied by the chief medical examiner of North Carolina, the following figures represent the percent of people who died of each cause who registered a BAC of .10 or higher: drowning, 41 percent; fire, 58 percent; stabbing, 68 percent; firearms, 40 percent. Another study examined a thousand consecutive violent or accidental deaths in New York City in 1972. A BAC of .10 or higher was found in a third of all victims—33 percent for victims of falls, 44 percent for vehicular drivers or passengers, and 32 percent for pedestrians (Haberman and Baden, 1974). Numerous studies (Combes-Orme et al., 1983; Abel and Zeidenberg, 1985; Goodman et al., 1986) show that close to half of all homicide *victims* were drinking at the time they were killed, and one-third had a BAC of .10 or higher. Adding it all up, one estimate holds that in 1980 alone, alcohol was responsible for nearly 60,000 premature deaths from accident (38,000), suicide (8,000), homicide (12,000), and other non-disease-related sources (Ravenholt, 1984; Health and Human Services, 1987: 6). Thus, in one year, alcohol was responsible for the loss of more American lives—not even counting the illnesses it caused—than was the Vietnam War.

Beyond the .15 blood-alcohol level, one's ability to function plummets. At the .20 level, the drinker is somewhat dazed, confused, and distinctly uncoordinated; any movement at all becomes risky and problematic. Driving is extremely hazardous. At the .30 level, any response to the stimuli of the outside world becomes an insurmountable chore. One's ability to perceive and comprehend what is happening is reduced to a bare minimum. At the .40 level, most people pass out and lose consciousness; this is regarded as the LD-50—the point at which half of all drinkers die from an overdose. At .50 percent, if the drinker is still alive, he or she has entered a coma, from which he or she can be aroused only with the greatest difficulty. At .60 percent, overdoses are increasingly common; death occurs as a result of the inhibition and paralysis of the respiratory centers. Almost anyone whose blood is .80 percent alcohol will die.

DRUNKEN COMPORTMENT

When we look at alcohol's effects, we must be careful to distinguish clearly those that are more or less standard from those that manifest themselves in almost endless variation. There is no doubt at all that alcohol,

if drunk in sufficient quantity, results in a significant and measurable impairment in the drinker's ability to perform sensori-motor activities. In this sense, alcohol's effects are to a large degree specific. But in another realm, they are more or less completely dependent on the individual who is drinking and the culture in which drinking takes place. Does alcohol make the drinker depressed or euphoric? Gregarious or withdrawn? Vicious or pleasant? Energetic or passive? Most of us feel that alcohol universally "releases inhibitions," allowing us to show our uglier, more animalistic side, ordinarily kept in check by the restraints of our civilization. Alcohol, this homespun view theorizes, acts in a fairly standard fashion on the human animal.

An extensive survey of the impact on human behavior that alcohol has in many of the societies of the world was undertaken by two anthropologists, Craig MacAndrew and Robert B. Edgerton, and reported in a book entitled *Drunken Comportment* (1969). MacAndrew and Edgerton demonstrate that this folk view of alcohol universally acting as a "releaser of inhibitions" is false. Human emotions and behavior are far more subtle and labile than that. People are not simply under the control of alcohol; the precise effects of alcohol are under the control of the society in which drinkers grow up and live. Behavior under the influence, or drunken comportment, is sensationally and dramatically different from one society to another. MacAndrew and Edgerton report, for example, that when drunk, the Yuruna, an Indian tribe living in South America's tropical rain forest, become withdrawn, acting "much as though no one else existed" (1969: 17). In Takashima, a tiny rural fishing village in Japan, drunkenness results in "camaraderie, laughter, jokes, songs and dances" (MacAndrew and Edgerton, 1969: 33). The residents of Aritama, a village made up of mestizo, or part-Indian, part-Spanish people, in northern Colombia, are a somber, controlled, almost morose people. And, "regardless of the degree of intoxication that is achieved" by Aritama drinkers, their "rigid mask of seriousness stays in place"; they remain "unobtrusive and silent," seemingly incapable of enjoying themselves (1969: 25–27). The Camba of Bolivia, another mestizo people, drink a concoction they call, appropriately enough, "alcohol"; it is a sugar cane distillate that is 89 percent alcohol—almost 180 proof! In the early stages of their intoxication they are convivial, high-spirited, gregarious, voluble. The more they drink, the more stupefied and thick-lipped they grow, staring silently at the ground. Many simply pass out and fall asleep. Throughout their drinking bouts, there is a complete absence of verbal or physical aggression.

The Mixtecs of Mexico drink, we are told, truly prodigious quantities of alcohol, frequently to the point of passing out, stupefied. Along the way to becoming drunk, do they become violent? Angry? Hostile? Dangerous? These Indians specifically deny that alcohol is capable of producing violent behavior in them. And that is, indeed, exactly what happens: They are never observed to become loud, aggressive, or violent. Drinking coconut toddy among the Ifaluk, residents of a tiny island in the Pacific, results in no anger or violence either. Instead, a "warm feeling of good fellowship" spreads through everyone, "and every man becomes a brother and the world is a paradise" (MacAndrew and Edgerton, 1969: 29).

Not only is drunken behavior markedly different from culture to culture, but it also varies strikingly in the same culture *from one social setting to another*. Among traditional Papago, an American Indian desert-dwelling people, a cactus wine was drunk ceremonially to await the coming of a brief, sparse rainy season. The people became drunk, often hopelessly so, and vomited copiously. Drunkenness was approved during this period and no one acted unruly; fighting was entirely absent. The most violent activity observed was singing. With the intrusion of whites into Papago territory, initiating the ready availability of liquor and its use during times other than the rainmaking ceremony, the Papago became violent during drunkenness. Getting drunk took on a nontradi-

tional, nonceremonial, and even deviant character. Here we have two kinds of drinking, leading to precisely opposite behaviors under the influence. Clearly this difference cannot be explained simply by the nature of alcohol itself (MacAndrew and Edgerton, 1969: 37–42).

Beer drunk in tribal villages by South Africans results in behavior that is "free of rancor" and lacking in physical aggression. But the very same beer drunk by the very same tribespeople when they migrate to the urban South African slums frequently results in arguments, fights, brawls, and stabbings. "While the beverage of the South African Bantu has not changed, the circumstances surrounding its consumption most certainly have. And as these circumstances have changed, so, too, has their drunken comportment" (MacAndrew and Edgerton, 1969: 53). In rural Okinawa, the Japanese residents drink sake. There are, however, two distinctly different types of drinking occasions. When men and women drink together, behavior is "completely free of drunken aggression." When men drink by themselves, they become quarrelsome, noisy, and often physically violent. When the Indians of Tescopa drink pulque among themselves, the result is harmony and contentment, a feeling of fellowship; violence is unheard of. When Tescopans drink with outsiders, violent, bloody fights frequently erupt (1969: 55–57).

Exactly the same pattern that we observe with violence prevails with regard to the connection between drinking alcohol and sexual licentiousness. In some societies, drunkenness produces no departure at all from the usual puritanical sex code. This is true, for example, of the Abipone of Paraguay and the Pondo of South Africa. The Camba of Bolivia, when sober, stress "interpersonal harmony" and a "rigorously enforced puritanical approach to all things sexual." Does intoxication produce a dissolution of these inhibitions? Not only does alcohol "fail to produce tidal waves of aggression and sexuality, it does not even produce ripples" (MacAndrew and Edgerton, 1969: 33).

In other societies, when alcohol is drunk, a normally reserved people may become amorous—but always within certain specific limits. The Tarahumara of Mexico, normally an extremely chaste, puritanical, and timid people, when drunk engage in mate swapping, a practice that is absolutely unheard of and never engaged in when they are sober. Or alcohol may make some amorous peoples even more so. The Lepcha of Sikkim are one of the most sexually active and permissive people on the face of the earth. They have intercourse extremely early in life, at age 10 or 12 and continue to do so vigorously into old age. Adultery is common, even expected, and no cause for anger on the part of the spouse. Sex, it has been said, constitutes the principal recreation among the Lepcha. It is their main topic of conversation as well as an inexhaustible wellspring of humor. During the annual harvest festival, large quantities of home-brewed liquor are drunk. The normally relaxed sexual customs blossom into almost unbridled promiscuity. Lepcha theory is that the more couples that copulate, and the more often they do so, the richer the harvest. If someone sees his or her spouse having sex with someone else, it is bad form to interrupt or even to mention it to anyone later. Four- or 5-year-old children imitating copulation with one another are encouraged by adult onlookers. Yet, throughout this festival of carnality, the incest taboos are never broken. The Lepcha feel a sense of horror about incest: It is believed that if enacted by even one couple, it will bring disaster to the whole community. What is interesting is that the Lepcha have an extremely broad interpretation of incest, one that encompasses a very high proportion of the population, including second, third, and fourth cousins (what we would call "kissing cousins"), any in-laws no matter how remote, blood relatives on the father's side for nine generations, and so on. Every child of 10 has learned and knows which members of the community are legitimate sex partners and which ones are to be shunned sexually. Even when the Lepcha are drunk, these rules are never broken, in spite of the huge number of relatives with whom one may not

have sex, and in spite of the very powerful norms propelling almost every Lepcha into the arms of many partners of the opposite sex. Alcohol may relax sexual custom, but when it does, it does so only in a pattern that is socially and culturally approved.

There is, then, a time, a place, and an object selectivity, both for violence and for sex under the influence: Disinhibition takes place within limits set by the community. In other words, "however great the difference may be between persons' sober and drunken comportment . . . it is evident that both states are characterized by a healthy respect for certain socially sanctioned limits" (MacAndrew and Edgerton, 1969: 85). By itself and in and of itself, "the presence of alcohol in the body does not necessarily conduce to disinhibition, much less inevitably produce such an effect" (1969: 87–88). It is possible, then, to speak of *the socially organized character of drunken comportment.* How does socially approved drunken behavior arise? "Over the course of socialization, people learn about drunkenness what their society 'knows' about drunkenness; and, accepting and acting upon the understandings thus imparted to them, they become the living confirmation of their society's teachings" (1969: 88). There is in nearly every society a zone of behavior that is permissible *only under the influence.* Being drunk is considered a kind of time out. The norms of what is acceptable behavior while intoxicated—and what is not—are already spelled out well before one gets drunk. The behavior may be thoroughly reprehensible if one is sober, but if committed while drunk, one may *invoke* the disinhibiting effect of the alcohol one has drunk. The otherwise deviant act becomes an excused transgression. This doesn't work for all behavior. Societies allow the excuse of drunkenness for some forms of behavior but not others. It matters not to the law of the United States that one is drunk when murdering one's spouse, though it may count in one's own mind. In some other societies, drunkenness may be a mitigating circumstance in homicide, considerably reducing the penalty one will receive.

Behavior under the influence, then, does

not follow a predetermined, biochemically fixed pattern. It, too, has its norms, although they may be a bit different from those that influence behavior when one is sober. It is not the drug, alcohol, that truly *makes* anyone do anything. Alcohol is merely one component in a vastly intricate scheme.

With regard to alcohol use and violent behavior in the United States, two facts are clear: The first is the enormous range in the drug's impact on Americans, and the second is that alcohol is associated with a great deal of violence here. Clearly, many Americans view being drunk as a legitimate occasion for engaging in brawling and sexually aggressive behavior. It is far too simple to say that alcohol consumption is *the* or even *a* cause of violent behavior. But in our society, alcohol consumption and violence often appear together. The more violent the crime, the greater the likelihood that the offender was drunk while committing it. One classic study reported that in 60 percent of all murders the killer had been drinking prior to his attack on the victim (Wolfgang, 1958). A later study, conducted in Chicago, found this figure to be 53 percent (Voss and Hepburn, 1968). Thus, although alcohol cannot be said to *cause* people to kill one another, it is certainly involved in an extremely high proportion of all homicides in the United States.

The same holds true of sexual aggression. The massive study conducted by the Institute of Sex Research (the "Kinsey Institute") on convicted, incarcerated sex offenders indicated that alcohol plays a significant role in sex crimes—especially those involving force, as well as those against young children. In about 40 percent of all acts of male sexual aggression against adult women (mostly rape and attempted rape), the offender was classified as drunk. Exactly two-thirds of all aggressive sexual offenses against young girls, or child molestation, involved drunkenness (Gebhard et al., 1967: 761–763, 813). Another study found that 45 percent of the men arrested in the city of Cincinnati on the charge of rape had a blood-alcohol concentration of .10 percent or higher (Shupe, 1954).

ALCOHOL CONSUMPTION AND CONTROL IN THE UNITED STATES

Alcohol consumption should be interesting and instructive to any student of human behavior for a variety of reasons. For one thing, legal controls have been applied to the manufacture and sale of alcoholic substances, with mixed results. Moreover, the use of alcohol has been regarded as respectable during most of the nation's history—indeed, to refuse to drink has been seen as unacceptable, unfashionable, even slightly deviant. Yet during the period between roughly 1850 and the 1920s, drinking became an atypical, minority activity. The typical American disapproved of it on principle. Perhaps equally important, "respectable" Americans were *most* likely to oppose alcohol consumption; the less prestigious, less affluent, and less powerful social and ethnic groups tended to be more favorably inclined toward drinking. The dominant attitude of conventional Americans was that moderate drinking was not possible: One either abstained altogether or become an incurable alcoholic—there was no in-between territory.

During this period, there was an attempt, as there invariably is today in other areas of life, to demonstrate a *moral* point by mobilizing credibility and a rational-sounding argument. The fact is, Prohibitionist elements in America opposed the use of alcohol on moral grounds: They considered the practice evil, an abomination. In their denunciations of drinking, the line between what the drug does to the user and the inherent degeneracy of the practice itself was extremely fuzzy. In order to see drinking as a morally tainted activity, Prohibitionists wished to convince others that it was an irrational, illogical, damaging activity as well, that it had consequences in the real world that any reasonable person would disapprove of. All that was necessary was the dissemination of the "correct" point of view.

Thus alcohol has had a fascinating cyclical history in America. The Indians who greeted Columbus brewed and drank beer. (They were not, however, acquainted with distilled spirits.) The Puritans, although remembered for their abhorrence of sensual and physical pleasures, arrived on the shores of New England with ample supplies of beer, wine, and hard liquor. The *Arbella*, which arrived in the Boston area only a few years after the *Mayflower*, "set sail with three times as much beer as water, along with 10,000 gallons of wine." In addition, most settlers brought along a supply of distilled spirits as well. "So liquor was more than a luxury in the colonial mind; it was a necessity to be kept close at hand" (Lender and Martin, 1987: 2). Increase Mather, a Puritan minister of some distinction and the author of *Woe to Drunkards* (1673), while warning against overindulgence, said, "Drink is in itself a good creature of God, and to be received with thankfulness." Drinking "constituted a central facet of colonial life. Indeed, two of the key characteristics of early drinking patterns were frequency and quantity. Simply stated, most settlers drank often and abundantly" (1987: 9).

Drinking in colonial America was "utilitarian, with high alcohol consumption a normal part of personal and community habits." Beer and cider were common at mealtime, with children often partaking; collective tasks, like clearing a field, were typically accompanied by a public cask. Farmers usually took a jug into the fields with them each morning. Employers often gave their employees liquor on the job. Political candidates usually "treated" the electorate to alcoholic beverages, including at polling places on election days. The Continental Army supplied its troops with a daily ration of 4 ounces of rum, when it was available, or whiskey. Drinking was extremely common in seventeenth- and eighteenth-century America, considerably higher than it is today. One estimate holds that in 1790, when the first national census was taken, the per capita alcohol consumption for the American population age 15 and older was 5.8 gallons of absolute alcohol per year, more than twice its present level (Lender and Martin, 1987: 9–10, 205).

Drinking in seventeenth- and eighteenth-century America was rarely considered a serious social problem; in fact, there was a remarkable lack of anxiety about it. While heavy drinking and even alcoholism certainly existed, most drinkers consumed alcohol in a family or a community setting, and strong social norms kept excessive drinking within acceptable bounds, and prevented unacceptable and potentially dangerous behavior under the influence from getting out of hand. Drinking, though heavy by today's standards, was fairly well socially controlled. "As the colonial period drew to a close, most Americans still held to the traditional view of drinking as a positive social and personal good" (Lender and Martin, 1987: 34).

High as alcohol consumption was at the turn of the eighteenth century, it actually rose significantly into the nineteenth—from 5.8 gallons of absolute alcohol per person age 15 and older per year in 1790 to 7.1 in 1830. Moreover, the proportion of the alcohol consumed in the form of distilled spirits, in contrast to beer and wine, was 40 percent in 1790; in 1830, it was 60 percent. Said one observer in 1814, "the quantity of ardent spirits" consumed in the United States at that time "surpasses belief." Drinking "had reached unparalleled levels." The notion "that alcohol was necessary for health remained firmly fixed. It was common to down a glass of whiskey or other spirits before breakfast. . . . Instead of taking coffee or tea breaks," Americans customarily took breaks at eleven and four for a few pulls on the jug. "Even school children took their sip of whiskey, the morning and afternoon glasses being considered 'absolutely indispensable to man and boy.'" Distilled spirits "were a basic part of the diet—most people thought that whiskey was as essential as bread." In the early nineteenth century, "the idea that the problem drinker could cause serious social disruption had occurred to relatively few people; drinking behavior, even when disruptive, remained largely a matter of individual choice" (Lender and Martin, 1987: 205, 46, 47, 53).

Reacting to these apparent excesses, the temperance movement began to take shape.

Perhaps the most influential of the early advocates of prohibition, who wrote when he was but a voice in the wilderness, was Benjamin Rush, Philadelphia physician, signer of the Declaration of Independence, surgeon general of the Continental Army, and author of *An Inquiry into the Effects of Ardent Spirits on the Human Mind and Body* (1784). Rush challenged the conventional view that drinking was an unmixed good. Rush did not condemn drinking per se, only heavy, uncontrolled drinking, nor did he condemn alcoholic beverages per se—his primary target was hard liquor. "Consumed in quantity over the years," he wrote, distilled spirits "could destroy a person's health and even cause death." Rush was the first scientist or physician to label alcoholism a disease characterized by progressively more serious stages; it was accompanied, he said, by addiction. Rush felt that community constraints on drinking in late eighteenth- and early nineteenth-century America had broken down, destroying drinkers' lives, families, and ability to function as breadwinners and citizens.

Although he conveyed a powerful sense of urgency, Rush was not optimistic about reform. However, he had friends who were influential in religious affairs, and "he had sown the seeds of reform movements to come." The first temperance society was founded in 1808, and by 1811, the temperance movement, uniting a number of scattered and independent organizations, was formed. In 1826, the American Society for the Promotion of Temperance (later the American Temperance Society) was founded. Initially, the society, like Dr. Rush, preached the gospel of moderation. It "helped organize local units, sent lecturers into the field, distributed literature (including Rush's *Inquiry*), and served as a clearinghouse for movement information." Within three years, more than 200 state and local antiliquor organizations were active. By 1830, temperance reform "constituted a burgeoning national movement" (Lender and Martin, 1987: 68).

By the 1830s, the adherents of local abstinence carried the day in the movement. The Temperance Society boasted 1.5 million members who proselytized righteously for their cause. Employers stopped supplying liquor on the job. Politicians ceased being so free and easy about "treating" their constituency and supporters with alcohol. An extremely effective tactic of the temperance movement was to influence local and county politicians to refuse granting licenses to taverns, undercutting major centers of heavy drinking. Although the movement lost some steam before and during the Civil War, while more pressing matters were settled, the 1870s and 1880s witnessed a rebirth of even stronger prohibitionist activity.

Alcohol consumption plummeted between 1830 (7.1 gallons of absolute alcohol per person age 15 and older per year) and 1840 (3.1 gallons). Between 1850 and 1920, when national alcohol prohibition took effect, alcohol consumption remained, with relatively small decade-to-decade fluctuations, at about 2 gallons per year for every adult age 15 and older in the population.

The Volstead Act, bringing about a complete national prohibition on the sale of alcohol, took effect in 1920. After its passage, the author of the Volstead Act, Senator Morris Sheppard, representing the state of Texas, uttered the classic statement: "There is as much chance of repealing the Eighteenth Amendment as there is for a hummingbird to fly to the planet Mars with the Washington Monument tied to its tail." But by 1933, Prohibition had been declared a failure and was abandoned as a social experiment. (The Eighteenth Amendment is the only one ever to be repealed in American constitutional history.) What happened in the historically brief intervening 15 years?

During Prohibition, at a time when people were actually drinking less than they did before, *drinking alcohol was becoming considered more and more respectable.* Attitudes and behavior are not always perfectly correlated. So the question becomes: What happened socially, economically, and politically during the course of Prohibition? I contend that people's attitudes toward the use of alcohol per se were tangentially related to whether Prohibition worked or not. And they were not based on the medical effects of this drug. Something else changed the people's minds. What was it?

Many forms of behavior that become criminalized pose no direct threat in any way to their practitioners, nor to the other members of a society. But they may be considered deviant by self-righteous, morally indignant conventionals. The struggle between alcohol drinkers and Prohibitionists in the years before the passage of the Volstead Act can be looked at primarily as a struggle between status groups and lifestyles. Supporters of Prohibition were primarily rural dwellers, native-born members of the native-born parentage, either white-collar or middle class or owners of farms, and overwhelmingly Protestant. Opponents of Prohibition were far more likely to be urban dwellers, immigrants or the sons and daughters of immigrants, manual laborers, and Catholic. "Prohibition stood as a symbol of the general system of ascetic behavior with which the Protestant middle classes had been identified" (Gusfield, 1963: 124). A number of historical changes took place during the twentieth century that directly impinged upon the issue of alcohol and Prohibition. First, the old Protestant middle class suffered a serious decline in prestige as a social group. Second, urban dwellers, Catholics, the non-Anglo-Saxon ethnics, all secured far more political power than they had held previously. Third, the "new" middle class rose in numbers, in power, and in status. The urban, cosmopolitan, college-educated, technically trained executive working for a nationally based corporation became the symbol of the middle class. The old-time locally based entrepreneur lost hold on the American consciousness as the model representative of the middle class. *And it was specifically this "new" middle class that abandoned abstinence and took to recreational drinking.* The Volstead Act was passed because abstinence was identified with a prestigious and powerful group in American society. Prohibition failed because it was the powerful, prestigious middle class that

abandoned abstinence as a legitimate and respectable way of life. Temperance ceased to be necessary to a respectable life; its symbolic connection with respectability was severed. And lastly, the Depression loomed before the American public and the government and relegalizing alcohol manufacture and sale brought with it the prospect of jobs and tax revenue (Gusfield, 1963: 111–138).

By the time that repeal actually did take place, the idea of Prohibition had become so unpopular that the population of no area of the country wanted to retain the Volstead Act. A study conducted in 1932 by a magazine of the time, the *Literary Digest,* found that adults favoring the retention of Prohibition ranged from a scant 19 percent in the populous, urban northern states of New York, New Jersey, and Pennsylvania to 41 percent in the rural Bible-belt southern states of Mississippi, Alabama, Tennessee, and Kentucky. Thirty-nine states actually voted on the repeal of Prohibition in 1933. Repeal carried by three to one (15 million for, 5 million against). Again, as with the *Literary Digest* poll, in northern, urban, and heavily Catholic states like New York, New Jersey, and Rhode Island, repeal was chosen by more than 80 percent of the voters. But in rural, Protestant southern states like Alabama, Arkansas, and Tennessee, the vote was between 50 and 60 percent for repeal. Only in North and South Carolina did a majority vote to retain Prohibition.

We've all learned that Prohibition was a catastrophic failure, perhaps the least successful effort to control behavior in the nation's history. Many of us even believe that alcohol consumption rose during this period—after all, we say, outlawing an activity will only encourage people to engage in it. In fact, the truth is exactly the opposite from this gem of conventional wisdom: All indications point to the fact that alcohol consumption declined sharply during Prohibition, and rose once legal restrictions were lifted.

Of course, we do not have hard data on alcohol consumption between 1920 and 1933; since sales were illegal, no record of them was kept. We must, therefore, make inferences about use by relying on more indirect indicators of alcohol consumption. One such indicator is the incidence of cirrhosis of the liver, which is very closely correlated with alcohol consumption in the population. The rate of death from cirrhosis of the liver remained between 12 and 17 per 100,000 in the population each year between 1900 and 1919. But it dropped to between 7 and 9 per 100,000 in the 1920s and early 1930s, a reduction of almost half. In the mid-1930s, it began to rise again (Grant et al., 1986).

In addition, the number of people arrested and jailed in the state of Connecticut on the charge of public drunkenness fell from more than 7,000 in 1917 to fewer than 1,000 in 1920. And the number of automobile fatalities—also strongly correlated with alcohol consumption—declined 40 percent between the years immediately preceding Prohibition and the 1920–1933 period (Burgess, 1973: 152). Putting together a number of indicators, two authors (Lender and Martin, 1987) estimate the yearly adult per capita alcohol consumption in the United States for the 1920–1930 period at .9 gallons of absolute alcohol, less than half of what it had been in 1916–1919. Use did not skyrocket immediately after Prohibition; most people simply got out of the habit of drinking and it took several years for them to resume the habit. In 1934, consumption rose to .97 gallons; by 1935, to 1.20, and the prewar 1936–1941, to 1.54. In fact, alcohol consumption rose steadily between the end of Prohibition and the late 1970s, as we'll see shortly.

Why do many people believe that drinking increased rather than decreased during Prohibition? That's not hard to answer: It's a much more entertaining and interesting story. We tend to focus on "speakeasies" and honky-tonks, jazz clubs, secret passwords, bathtub gin, silver hip flasks, Al Capone, gang warfare, corruption, payoffs, a few honest, crusading crime-fighters—all of this is exciting stuff. It sticks in our minds. We tend to exaggerate the frequency of the unusual and underplay that of the routine, the everyday. We assume that most people were engaged in these exciting alcohol-related activities that we've heard so much about. People living in a given age often think that every-

one who lived at a different time was engaged in that period's most memorable and noteworthy activities. In fact, people who actually lived through another time will tend, upon recollection of it, to exaggerate their participation in these unusual activities. The truth about Prohibition is, therefore, relatively unexciting. In general, most Americans did not drink during Prohibition, and those who did drank significantly less, and less often, than they did before or after.

Today, Americans age 15 or older consume about 2.58 gallons of absolute alcohol per person per year (Lender and Martin, 1987: 206). This is a fairly "hard" or reliable statistic because it is based on sales and not simply what people say they drink. This works out to just under 1 ounce of absolute alcohol per person age 15 or older per day. Of course, some people drink a lot more than this, some less, and some not at all. Roughly one-third of all Americans are more or less total abstainers. Thus it makes sense to tabulate the quantity of alcohol consumed specifically for drinkers, and leave abstainers out of the picture entirely. Adult drinkers consume a bit more than $1\frac{1}{2}$ ounces of absolute alcohol per day. This represents two and a half 12-ounce bottles or cans of beer *or* three 4-ounce glasses of wine *or* one 3- or 4-ounce drink of hard liquor per day for every drinking adolescent and adult in the country.

During the 1980s, the American population become more moderate in its use of psychoactive substances. We saw earlier that the use of illegal drugs (except cocaine) declined between 1979 and the late 1980s. More or less the same has been true of alcohol consumption. The use of alcohol rose more or less steadily from the end of Prohibition (an average of 1.20 gallons of absolute alcohol in 1935) to 1978 (2.82 gallons), and declined after that. In 1980, the per capita yearly alcohol consumption for Americans 15 and older was 2.76 gallons of absolute alcohol per year; in 1985, as I just said, it was 2.58 (Lender and Martin, 1987: 206). It is likely that this downward trend will continue for the foreseeable future.

Recorded yearly alcohol sales can be

backed up with information on the proportion of the American population who says that it drinks. Every year or so, the Gallup Poll asks a sample of Americans the following question: "Do you have occasion to use alcoholic beverages such as liquor, wine, or beer, or are you a total abstainer?" This question was first asked in 1939, when 58 percent defined themselves as drinkers, 42 percent as abstainers. In 1945, 67 percent said that they drank; the percentage declined between 1945 and 1949, then rose steadily throughout the 1950s and 1960s, and reached a peak of 71 percent in 1976 and 1978. It declined thereafter, and stood at 64 percent in 1984, but rose slightly to 67 percent in 1985 and 1986 (Gallup, 1980: 236; 1986: 80–81; 1987: 18–19).

The National Institute on Drug Abuse survey (NIDA, 1986) also contains information on alcohol consumption. The questions NIDA asks are a bit different from Gallup's; NIDA is more specific about the time periods in which the alcohol consumption took place—that is, has the respondent ever drunk alcohol, and has he or she drunk alcohol within the past month. As can be seen in Table 6.2, there has been a noticeable decline in self-reported alcohol consumption between 1979 and 1985 for all ages.

For youth age 12 to 17, the proportion who ever drank dropped from 70 to 57 between 1979 and 1985, and from 37 to 32 percent for those who drank within the past month. For young adults age 18 to 25, the decline was less substantial, from 95 to 93 percent and from 76 to 72 percent, respectively. For older adults, there was a decline in the "ever" statistic, from 92 to 89 percent,

but the proportion drinking within the past month remained stable at 61 percent (Fishburne, et al., 1980: 89; NIDA, 1986). Clearly, then, the NIDA survey, like the sales figures and the Gallup Poll, shows a significant decline in alcohol consumption during the 1980s. The trend, then, must be regarded as real and not the artifact of one particular measuring device. Moreover, it must be taken as part of a more general trend in the decline of the use of all psychoactive drugs (except cocaine) in the 1980s.

What accounts for this recent decline in alcohol consumption? Partly a shift to lighter, lower-alcohol-content drinks. In 1977, distilled spirits accounted for 40 percent of the alcohol consumed in America; in 1985, this figure had decreased to 35 percent. Correspondingly, wine increased from 48 to 52 percent. While in principle this would not necessarily decrease the nation's overall alcohol consumption—drinkers might conceivably consume more wine to get the same amount of alcohol—in practice, the switch has resulted in decreased use. In addition, many young drinkers are turning to wine "coolers," with an alcohol content of 5 to 6 percent. To the extent that wine coolers are being substituted for regular wine, this represents a decline in the total quantity of alcohol consumed by the drinker; on the other hand, if wine coolers are substituting for beer, there is a very slight increase.

Another significant development in the 1980s is the fact that all states in the United States have instituted a 21-year-old drinking age, while in 1979, only 14 had such a law. Although conventional wisdom says that

TABLE 6.2 Alcohol Consumption, 1979–1985

	1979		1985	
	Ever	Last Month	Ever	Last Month
Youth (12–17)	70%	37%	57%	32%
Young Adults (18–25)	95	76	93	72
Older Adults (26+)	92	61	89	61

SOURCE: Fishburne, Abelson, and Cisin, 1980: 89; NIDA, 1986.

young people will find a way to drink in spite of legal restrictions (for an article making this claim, at least for college students, see Ravo, 1987), the same fallacy applies here as to Prohibition: When legal controls exist and are enforced, drinking will decline significantly for the relevant age group; although many will break the law, enough will comply to bring down the average level of alcohol consumption significantly. According to one study, a year after New York state raised its drinking age to 21, alcohol purchases among 16- to 20-year-olds declined by 50 percent, and use itself declined by 21 percent. When the legal age was 18, 25 percent of 17-year-olds and 20 percent of 16-year-olds said that they had purchased alcohol during the previous month. When the drinking age was raised to 21, more than a quarter of the 19- and 20-year-olds surveyed said that they had purchased alcohol within the last month; but only 9 percent of the 18-year-olds, 14 percent of the 17-year-olds, and 6 percent of the 16-year-olds said that they had done so. The same systematic tendency toward a decline prevailed for use, and, other studies indicate, the same pattern holds for the country generally (Kolbert, 1987).

The most important reason for the decline in the consumption of absolute alcohol, however, has been a consistent decline in drinking overall. As we saw, it is not simply a reduction in the use of lower-alcohol-content beverages that has brought these consumption figures down; that would reduce the sales and total consumption figures, but not the proportion of the population who have ever drunk or the proportion who drank within the past month. The simple fact is, fewer people are drinking, and, among those who drink, a higher proportion is drinking less when they drink, and less frequently as well. The same pattern prevails as with the illicit psychoactives: Americans are using fewer psychoactive drugs nowadays than they were a decade ago.

The decline in drinking in the population generally, and for teenagers specifically, along with stricter law enforcement with respect to drinking and driving, have translated into a significant decline in alcohol-related deaths in auto accidents. The National Highway Traffic Safety Administration estimated, as I said above, that 38 percent of all drivers in a fatal automobile accident in 1985 had a BAL of .10 or higher, a significant decline from nearly 50 percent in 1980 (Wald, 1986). In 1982, the administration estimated, 16,790 drunk drivers were involved in fatal crashes, whereas the figure for 1985, with more total cars on the road, was 14,650. A survey by Louis Harris in 1983 found that 32 percent of those questioned said that they had driven a car after drinking during the past year; by 1986, this figure had declined to 26 percent. In Minnesota, random roadside checks indicated that roughly 5 percent of all drivers on the road at night were legally drunk in 1976; in 1986, the figure was 2.5 percent. In that same state, in 1976, only 14,000 drivers lost their licenses in connection with alcohol-related offenses; in 1986, the figure was more than 45,000. Clearly, the result of increased police enforcement of the drunk-driving laws has been to reduce the number and proportion of drunks on the road and, consequently, alcohol-related deaths. However, such actions have mainly had an impact on the more moderate social drinkers. Heavy drinkers and alcoholics are undeterred by the crackdown; as a result, a higher proportion of alcoholics are now being arrested on the road than in the past. Said a Maine highway official, "We're getting into the hard-core alcoholics now. Before, they bagged social drinkers, and heavy drinkers got by. . . . Now that social drinkers aren't out there, the alcoholics are getting caught" (Malcolm, 1987).

WHO DRINKS? WHO DOESN'T?

Just as interesting as the overall figures on alcohol consumption and their changes over time is group-to-group variation in drinking. Who drinks and who doesn't? Are certain groups or categories significantly and consistently more likely to drink than others?

A study by public-opinion pollster Louis Harris and his associates (summarized in

Armor et al., 1976: 53–62), explored the social correlates of drinking.[1] Two basic measures of alcohol consumption were used: the percent of abstainers in each group, and the mean daily alcohol consumption among nonabstainers for each group. There was a relationship between what percent of each population drank at all (that is, the percent of nonabstainers in each group) and the average quantity consumed, but the correlation was far from perfect. In fact, a major finding of this study was that for many groups there was a high proportion of abstainers, but among those who did drink, their average level of consumption was surprisingly high; among other groups, it was exactly the reverse.

Social class, or socioeconomic status (SES)—a combined measure made up of income, occupation, and education—also showed a complicated relationship with drinking. The higher the social class, the greater the likelihood of drinking at all: 79 percent of upper-class respondents drank, as opposed to 66 percent of middle-class people and only 48 percent of the lower-class respondents. Yet, among those who did drink, the daily ethanol consumption did not vary much across class lines. Education alone correlates very strongly with drinking, too. The 1985 Gallup Poll found that only 49 percent of respondents who were not high-school graduates said that they drank; 69 percent of high-school graduates did so; 74 percent of respondents with some college did; and fully 80 percent of college graduates said that they were drinkers. Clearly, then, there is a strong and powerful correlation between drinking and education and SES in general. The higher the SES the greater the chances that someone will drink. However, this relationship makes an interesting flip-flop when it comes to drinking to excess or getting into trouble as a result of drinking. When these same respondents were asked, "Has drinking ever been a cause of trouble in your family?" 24 percent of those who had not graduated from high school said yes, but only 17 percent of college graduates did so, with the in-between categories also in between on their answers to this question. Clearly, while high-SES people are more likely to drink, they are also less likely to get into trouble for drinking, while for lower-SES individuals, the reverse is true (Gallup, 1986: 80, 81).

The Catholic-Protestant difference in drinking tends to be large nationally. In the Louis Harris poll (Armor et al., 1976: 53–62), 42 percent of the Protestants were total abstainers, nearly twice as high a figure as for the Catholic respondents (22 percent). This statistic was also backed up by the Gallup Poll: 60 percent of Protestants said that they drank, and 78 percent of Catholics did so. The majority of Southern Baptists, a highly abstemious denomination, said that they were abstainers—only 45 percent drank at all. However, interestingly, Southern Baptists were also more likely to get into trouble for drinking, possibly indicating a lower degree of acceptance of any level of drinking whatsoever in the Southern Baptists milieu.

Both the Harris and the Gallup polls consistently find a strong correlation between geographical residence and drinking. In the Harris Poll, a majority (54 percent) of all southerners were abstainers, while this was true of only about half as many northerners (28 percent). In the Gallup Poll, the results were not quite so striking: 56 percent of all southerners said that they drank, but about seven respondents in ten from the other regions of the country drank—72 percent for easterners, 70 percent for midwesterners, and 73 percent for residents of the West (Gallup, 1986: 80). Although the exact mag-

[1]The rather large discrepancy between these figures on the average daily alcohol consumption and those just cited for the national average is due to the fact that the national average figures are based on alcohol *sales*, a reliable set of statistics, while the figures cited here are *self-reports*, in which consumption tends to be underestimated by more than half. In a paper delivered at the San Diego Symposium on Alcohol and Cardiovascular Disease, Dr. Charles Kaelber reported that a comparison of self-reports of alcohol consumption from national household surveys with figures on alcohol sales revealed the former figure to be less than half (less than 0.40 ounce of alcohol per day) the latter (close to 1.0 ounce per day). This study was summarized in the October 3, 1980, issue of *ADAMHA News* (vol. VI, no. 20).

nitude of the figures differs, the same relationship can be observed: Southerners drink significantly less than northerners.

Gender or sex, too, correlates strongly with drinking. In fact, of all variables, perhaps gender correlates most strongly with alcohol consumption. Men are consistently more likely to drink than are women, and they drink more when they do drink. In the Harris Poll, three-quarters of the men (74 percent) were drinkers, while only a slight majority (56 percent) of women were. Likewise, men who drank consumed considerably more than—in fact, twice as much (.91 ounce of absolute alcohol per day) as—women (.44 ounce). In the Gallup Poll, again, the differences were not quite so striking: 72 percent of the men said that they drank, while 62 percent of the women did so.

Age, too, strongly predicts drinking. In the Harris Poll, the vast majority of under-30 respondents drank: Only 23 percent were abstainers. The older the respondent, the greater the likelihood of being an abstainer: Almost half (49 percent) of the over-50 respondents said that they had not consumed any alcohol in the previous year, twice as high a percentage as in the youngest category. More or less the same pattern prevailed in the Gallup Poll: 74 percent of the 18- to 29-year-olds, and 74 percent of the 30- to 49-year-olds drank, and 54 percent of the over-50-year-olds did so—again, twice the proportion of abstainers in the older category.

Drinking's correlation to race and ethnicity has been studied extensively and in detail, and clear-cut differences among groups remain in spite of generations of assimilation (Greeley, et al., 1980; Cahalan and Room, 1974; Health and Human Services, 1987: 18–20; Health, Education, and Welfare, 1971: 23–25). Consistently, individuals of the following ethnic backgrounds are highly likely to drink: Irish, Italians, Jews, northern WASPs (white Anglo-Saxon Protestants), Slavs, Scandinavians, and Germans. Members of the following ethnic groups are more likely to be abstainers and not drink at all: Blacks, Latins, southern WASPs, and Asians.

Of all groups, the Irish are most likely to drink a great deal, and to get into trouble when they drink. In one study (Health, Education, and Welfare, 1971), fully a third of individuals with an Irish-born father were defined as heavy drinkers, far higher than the proportion for any other category. In another study (Greeley et al., 1980: 9, 10), Irish-Americans were most likely to drink two or more times per week (42 percent versus 15 percent for Italians and Jews and 24 percent for WASPs), and most likely to drink three or more drinks at a sitting (33 percent versus 11 percent for Jews, 14 percent for Italians, and 24 percent for WASPs). Another study (Cahalan and Room, 1974) devised several measures of heavy drinking and getting into trouble as a result of drinking. Jews were extremely unlikely not to drink at all (only 8 percent were abstainers), but they were also extremely unlikely to drink heavily or to get into trouble as a result of drinking. Irish and Italian Catholics had almost exactly the same proportion of drinkers (only 4 and 5 percent abstainers, respectively). But Irish-Americans were far more likely to drink heavily and to get into trouble when they drank (Cahalan and Room, 1974: 101). Clearly, some alcohol-related aspect of Irish culture seems to be preserved even after one or more generations of residence in the United States. In a survey of 22 countries by the Gallup organization, a majority of the Irish surveyed (51 percent) answered yes to the question "Do you sometimes drink more than you think you should?" The average for the respondents from all countries was 29 percent, and it was 32 percent for residents of the United States (Gallup, 1986: 186).

THE PROBLEM DRINKER

By defining the alcoholic simply as someone who drinks a given average quantity of ethanol per day over a certain period (with all due respect to the qualifications registered earlier), we avoid the trap of thinking that alcoholism necessarily means any more than that. What *else* it means is an empirical question, something we have to investigate, not something we can define in the first place. By defining alcoholism along a single line we can actually determine whether this behavior, heavy drinking, is related to other things in the drinker's life. What most people mean when they refer to the alcoholic is actually what might better be called the *problem drinker* (Cahalan, 1970).

Are alcoholics and problem drinkers the same population, different points along the same spectrum, or totally different groups? Heavy drinkers may (and often do) become problem drinkers; problem drinkers are usually (but not necessarily) heavy drinkers. Getting into various kinds of trouble is one possible outcome of drinking a lot, but not a necessary one. The notion of the problem drinker is sociologically useful because it is the opposite of one "objective" definition of alcoholism that has been proposed—the consumption of 15 centiliters of absolute alcohol per day. The notion of a problem drinker is based on *how people see what happens to the drinker's life,* supposedly as a result of unwise or excessive drinking. Being considered a problem drinker is a result of a combination of drinking and how this behavior is reacted to by others as well as by the drinker.

Heavy drinking is associated with a number of social and legal problems, but these problems will vary in kind and in intensity. And part of the reason for the variation can be traced to the social and cultural context in which heavy drinking takes place. Alcohol may or may not directly cause these problems. They are closely connected with alcohol's social image, with conventional drinking practices in a given culture, with what one generally does or is expected to do when drunk, with the demands placed on one's performance, and with how the drunk is dealt with by other members of a society, particularly his or her intimates. In other words, when we examine the problem drinker, we have to understand *the social organization of alcohol-related trouble.* It is absolutely crucial, however, to keep in mind that *what is considered a problem in the first place* and *what*

specific problems we are considering will vary from place to place. A problem drinker, then, is quite simply someone who gets into trouble—directly or indirectly—because of consuming alcohol.

Problems come in many forms, and drinking, likewise, assumes a number of guises. When we discuss "problems," we are referring to anything that is connected to values and conditions that are threatened, damaged, or destroyed (or thought to be) as a result of drinking. One can be a problem drinker because one has a glass of wine at meals from time to time in a completely abstemious community: One can be labeled a deviant because of it, and be condemned or ostracized. "Problems" are socially defined and created; alcohol consumption can be measured independently of what anyone thinks. The two may or may not be related in a given case. That is for us to find out—in terms of where, when, and how.

The "consequences" of one's drinking depend in part on what one does when drunk and in part on community standards regarding drunkenness and intoxicated behavior. Breaking the drinking codes of one's group, or threatening strongly held values by being drunk, gets one assigned to the category of alcoholic more swiftly than the bare fact of drinking. In a study of the drinking practices of a nationally representative sample of men age 21 to 59, Don Cahalan and Robin Room (1974) found some impressive correlates of heavy drinking and problem drinking. They found, among other things, that getting into trouble as a result of drinking was not a simple function of the quantity of alcohol consumed; other factors played a role as well. They devised a scale of "problems" that drinkers sometimes become entangled in—problems on the job, problems with their wives, problems with friends and neighbors, financial problems, problems with the police and so on. One of the factors related to problems among drinkers was local attitudes toward drinking and drinking customs. The "drier" the community—the less the per capita alcohol consumption, and the more opposed a certain proportion of the community was to drinking—*the less drinking it took to get a man in trouble*. The "wetter" the community was, and the greater the tolerance there was for heavy drinking, the greater the quantity of drinking it took to get a man in trouble (Cahalan and Room, 1974: 81). For instance, drunk-driving arrests were significantly *higher* in states where there was *less* drinking. This was because community standards were stricter with regard to drunken driving (1974: 82).

WHO IS THE ALCOHOLIC?

The writings and research on alcoholism are controversial, contradictory, and confusing. Most of the major and pressing questions as yet have no definitive answers. Is alcoholism a disease? Can recovered alcoholics drink in a moderate, controlled fashion? On what criteria should a definition of alcoholism be based? Can the cause of alcoholism be located primarily in the substance, alcohol, itself, or in the characteristics of the drinker? Is biological make-up a major component in the etiology of alcoholism? For any imaginable answer to these questions, there are fervent supporters and critics. Very little is conclusively agreed upon in this field.

There are four common definitions of or criteria for alcoholism (Schuckit, 1985: 5). First, the *quantity* and *frequency* of alcohol consumed (DeLindt and Schmidt, 1971): Alcoholics are individuals who drink a substantial quantity of alcohol over a period of time. Second, *psychological dependence* (see the essays in Blane and Leonard, 1987): Someone is an alcoholic if he or she "needs" alcohol psychologically, cannot function without it, suffers extreme discomfort and anxiety if deprived of it under specific circumstances. Third, *physical dependence:* Someone is an alcoholic to the extent that he or she would suffer *withdrawal symptoms* upon discontinuation of drinking (Mendelson and Mello, 1985: 265–269). And fourth, the *life problems* definition (Schuckit, 1984): Whoever drinks and incurs "serious life difficulties" as a consequence—divorce, being fired from a job, being arrested, facing community censure,

harming one's health, being accident-prone, and so on—and continues to drink in spite of it, is an alcoholic.

Each of these definitions poses serious problems, and has been criticized for its deficiencies.

Defining alcoholism by the quantity of alcohol consumed has the drawback that the same amount of alcohol may be relatively innocuous for one person (for instance, a healthy 28-year-old) but harmful to another (an ill 68-year-old). Further, someone may drink no alcohol at all, but have the potential for developing a pattern of heavy consumption subsequent to taking up drinking. Is this individual to be regarded as exactly the same animal with respect to alcohol as the abstainer whose potential alcohol experience is likely to be positive and moderate?

Psychological dependence has been criticized for being vague and difficult to test. Questions supposedly tapping the "signs" of alcoholism include: "Do your friends drink less alcohol than you do?" "Do you drink to lose shyness and build self-confidence?" "Do you occasionally drink heavily after a disappointment, a quarrel, or when the boss gives you a hard time?" "Are there certain occasions when you feel uncomfortable if alcohol is not available?" A yes answer to these and similar questions is supposedly a sign that one is dependent on alcohol—and therefore an alcoholic. The problem is that many moderate drinkers could also give a yes answer to such questions. Psychological dependence on alcohol is extremely difficult to pin down; in the words of one expert, "determination of this attribute is very subjective" (Schuckit, 1985: 5).

The physical dependence or withdrawal criterion of alcoholism is an absolutely certain sign of the condition—but it is far too restrictive. Indeed, anyone who is physically dependent on alcohol must be regarded as an alcoholic by any reasonable definition, but many other drinkers who would also be called alcoholics are not physically dependent on the drug.

The life-problems definition is dubious because it is contingent on the nature of one's social milieu, as we saw in the previous section. In some areas, one can get into a great deal of trouble with an extremely moderate amount of alcohol consumption—as, for example, in contemporary Iran or in a fundamentalist Christian community. On the other hand, many communities and cultures worldwide tolerate extremely high levels of alcohol consumption, and "cushion" the drinker from many serious problems and consequences that drinking may entail elsewhere. Moreover, medical complications consequent to high levels of drinking appear on a statistical, rather than an absolute, basis. Not all heavy drinkers develop cirrhosis of the liver. Is one who does an alcoholic and one who drinks just as much, but doesn't contract the disease, not an alcoholic?

Alcoholism is one of those phenomena that is difficult to define, but most experts would say that they "know it when I see it." The four above criteria overlap in practice; most drinkers encompassed by one definition will also be encompassed by the others. A clear, reliable, and valid definition is far more important for theoretical purposes than for practical or clinical reasons.

Perhaps the bitterest controversy in the field of alcohol research in the last decade has been the question of whether or not recovered alcoholics can drink in moderation after treatment. The controversy has, in fact, spilled over into the courts and scientific review panels in both Canada and the United States, as one team of researchers accused other investigators of scientific fraud, and filed a $96 million lawsuit against them for their study and its results. While the charges of fraud were dismissed (Maltby, 1982; Boffey, 1982b, 1984), the debate rages on.

On one side of the controversy stand researchers who argue that formerly heavy and problem drinkers, and even a substantial proportion of victims of severe alcoholism, can learn to drink sensibly, in moderation, and in a controlled fashion. Uncontrolled, heavy, damaging drinking, they contend, is a *reversible behavioral disorder;* behavior that is learned can be unlearned, at least, in a substantial proportion of cases. These research-

ers do not claim that all alcoholics can drink moderately—some say one in ten, others say a majority—but that controlled drinking is not only possible, but a feasible long-term treatment goal for many alcoholics. This approach is especially likely to be endorsed in Europe (Boffey, 1983; Heather and Robertson, 1981) and in Canada (Sobell and Sobell, 1978, 1984), although some American researchers accept it as well (Armor et al., 1976; Polich et al., 1980).

On the other side, the more traditional and orthodox approach, and the one most likely to be adopted in the United States, is that alcoholics are incapable of drinking in a controlled, moderate fashion; the only possible alternative is total abstinence (Pendery et al., 1982). Alcoholism, say the advocates of this position, is an *irreversible disease;* the alcoholic is sick, and *cannot* return to drinking. The National Institute on Alcohol Abuse and Alcoholism (NIAAA) has consistently adhered to the view that "abstinence is the appropriate goal of alcohol treatment." In a 1981 report to Congress, the NIAAA stated that, "while a substantial minority of alcoholics are capable of engaging in controlled drinking for a short period of time, it is difficult to predict in advance who they are and it is not likely that they can control their drinking over the long run" (Boffey, 1983: C7).

The abstinence-only school argues that studies showing the possibility of controlled drinking are flawed—that they rely on self-reports of drinking by alcoholics, who lie notoriously about their alcohol consumption; they select heavy drinkers and problem drinkers, but not true alcoholics as subjects (so-called gamma, or physically dependent, alcoholics); they do not use a long enough follow-up period to determine whether their subjects have relapsed into dangerous drinking behavior; they have been careless about following up their subjects and often fail to record the disastrous lives these individuals are leading, even the fact that some of their subjects have died of alcoholism. (Pendery et al., 1982, summarizes most of these points.) These objections, says the abstinence-only faction, render valueless and misleading the results of studies showing that controlled drinking is possible.

Some of these objections are valid for some of the controlled-drinking studies that have been conducted. However, enough such studies have been done without these flaws to make it clear that some alcoholics can drink in a moderate, controlled, non-problem fashion. The only question is the size of this category. Is it one in ten, as a report by the National Academy of Sciences suggested in 1980? Or six out of ten, as others argue? (Boffey, 1983, summarizes several of these studies.) Perhaps future research will yield better data than we have today.

In one study, alcoholics were studied four years after their release from a variety of federal treatment programs. These programs were not geared specifically toward training recovered alcoholics to drink sensibly, so its results must be taken as a conservative estimate. More than half of the nearly 1,000 subjects in the study (54 percent) were still drinking heavily enough to be considered problem drinkers. More than a quarter (28 percent) had abstained completely from alcohol during the six months prior to the study, and thus fit the "abstention-only" model. The remainder, less than a fifth (18 percent), were drinking in a more or less moderate or "nonproblem" fashion, half drinking an average of 3 ounces of absolute alcohol per day; the other half, less than 2 ounces per day (Polich et al., 1980: 51).

Abandoning the "abstention-only" model for treated alcoholics—even if they constitute only a substantial minority—represents something of a revolution in thinking about the subject. If the notion of the alcoholic's inevitable "irreversible impairment" when drinking has to be abandoned, then the very idea of alcoholism as a disease must also be rejected, and the notion of alcoholism as a modifiable behavior has to be introduced (Heather and Robertson, 1981: 247–248). Given the fundamental systems of thought on which these two assumptions are based— the medical model and the learning-theory model of alcoholism—it is likely that this controversy will be with us for some time to come.

ACCOUNT: ALCOHOLISM

The contributor of this account is an electrician in his forties.

I started drinking when I was about 12. I used to go out with a bunch of other guys and we'd find some wino from the neighborhood and we'd give him a half a dollar and have him go into a store and get 4 or 5 quarts of beer. Then we'd go to the park and we'd drink there. Most of the guys, when they'd fill up, they'd leave and go home. But with me and maybe one or two other guys, if there was something left, we'd drink it up. Or if it was gone, I'd try to go out and get some more. Most of the time, I'd get drunk. I'd do this at least once-twice a week, usually more. My whole social life was drinking. I'd just hang around guys who drank. Or I'd be with girls who had babysitting jobs. I'd go with them and drink the booze that was around the house. During this time, I'd black out quite a bit. Later, the next day or something, I'd be told the funny and not-so-funny things I did when I was drunk—and I wouldn't even remember. I'd climb a pole or a tree, or I'd wind up getting in a fight, or getting nasty, and I wouldn't remember any of it. I didn't know it at the time, but I was having blackouts.

When I was 16, I forged my birth certificate and I enlisted in the Army. They found out after four months and I got a minority discharge. Right after my discharge, I got drunk one night and I stole a car. I wasn't aware of stealing the car. In fact, I wasn't even aware I was in a *car*. I woke up when I smashed into the rear end of a police car waiting for a red light. The cops got out and asked me for my license and registration. I didn't have it. No license, no registration, I was driving a stolen car, and I had smashed into a police car. They put me in a juvenile detention home for three or four weeks. When I turned 17, I enlisted in the Air Force for four years.

For most the time I was in the Air Force, I'd drink whenever I could. I drank a lot. The booze was plentiful. I'd drink maybe four to five times a week, probably. Like a fifth of Seagram's or if it was beer, maybe 24 bottles or cans. I'd drink from five in the afternoon to two or three in the morning. I used to get in a lot of fights. I got one court-martial. I drank like that until the age of 25.

Basically, I was a periodic drinker for most of this time. I'd drink for four or five weeks, and then I'd quit for a week, and then I'd drink again. During this time, I got married. I'd stay out all night and I'd drink. I'd drink rather than pay my bills, just to feed my drinking habit. Relations with my wife were strained, to say the least. If she tried to admonish me, I'd say, "I drank before I knew you, and I'll probably die drinking." I never thought it was a problem. I thought the problem was with my wife, not me.

I was getting into a lot of car accidents. I'd wake up in a smashed-up car and not remember where I was. I had one really major car accident and that's when I swore off alcohol, for good, I thought. It was only for five-and-a-half years. And after all that time, when I picked up the first drink, it was just like it was before. I drank a beer at 10 A.M. and I kept drinking all day, till late into the evening, until I passed out on my brother's living room floor. I went right back into my periodic drinking pattern. I'd go for a few weeks and then give up for a week or two. And then I'd try to see if I could drink one or two drinks, and I could, that night, and then I'd go back the next night and drink till I had another blackout. This got worse and worse for the next eight-and-a-half years. It came to the point where I no longer wanted to go out and have a drink. Then, I *needed* it, just to clear the cobwebs out. It got to be where it was a hopeless thing. When I picked up one drink, there was no telling what would happen— where I'd go, what I'd do, who I'd end up with.

The last three years of my drinking were almost daily—there were no off days. I did nothing but drink. I'd work only a couple days a week. My relationship with my wife was gone by then—she was just beaten down by it. The emotional turbulence in the lives of my six children was tremendous. A lot of pain was involved there. My teenage daughter would have to answer the phone, and it would be some woman I had wound up with—I would just go somewhere and the next day, I'd find myself with someone. My kids had to deal with that. I was never a father to my children. I just didn't bother coming home. And when I did, I'd get into an argument with my wife about the whole thing, and I'd want to go out and drink again. I'd wake up with guilt and remorse, and want to drink to drown it out.

One night, I sat down at my kitchen table and started going into a crying jag. I knew I was in trouble. The bottom had fallen out. My wife was in Al-Anon, which is an organization for the relatives of alcoholics. She suggested that I go to AA. She even dialed the phone for me. I went to a meeting that night. I listened to three speakers, and I thought they were nuts. I couldn't wait to get out of there and get a drink—which is what I did. I drank for three more months. That was the pits. I knew my life was really messed up. So I stayed off the booze for ten months. Still, my mind wasn't functioning properly. I couldn't concentrate, I couldn't work on the job. I'd work 15 hours a day just to wear myself out. My marriage had fallen apart. I was still miserable. See, I was fighting it. I had quit drinking on my own, and I thought I was a self-sufficient person. I now realize I wasn't. So once again my wife suggested that I go to another AA meeting, and I went. I sat down and talked to some people I could talk to. This fellow shared his life with me. I realized that I wasn't unique, that I wasn't a freak. I came to see that I could have a decent life without booze, and that it was alcohol that was causing my problems. I saw that I had the choice of destroying the rest of my life or staying sober. I could have ended up on the Bowery or killing someone. That day was my last drink—August 13, nine years ago.

I lost my wife and kids. I lost a house. My business was down the drain. I was $40,000 in debt in back taxes and bills. I owed everybody. I even owed the garbage man—he wouldn't come and pick up my garbage. If I heard the phone ring, I wouldn't want to pick it up. I was afraid it was another bill collector. At the age of 38, I woke up and found out what life was all about.

In the beginning, I went to a lot of AA meetings. For three-and-a-half years, I went to an AA meeting almost every day. I had a lot to work on. I had to learn to live with some kind of humility and self-acceptance. My life took a complete turn around. Everything is right in my life now. I'm out of debt. I can put in a full day's work. I'm a responsible person. I've gotten remarried. Today, I feel good about my life.

If I were to give someone advice, I'd say, if you see the roadsigns coming down the pike, use them. When you pick up a few drinks and you can't tell what's going to happen—don't drink. Drinking robbed me of any kind of a relationship with anybody. I didn't know what it was like to be with somebody because I didn't know who I was. The only social occasions I wanted to go to was where booze was going to be served. If there was no booze, I didn't go. So if booze is pulling you away from what's out there, don't drink. I didn't care about the consequences of my drinking—sickness, the accidents, the fights, the destruction of my marriage, causing my kids nothing but misery. That's another sign: If you drink and don't care what happens, you're in trouble.

And another thing. When I drank, I thought I was the person I wanted to be. It increased my self-confidence. I could always blame somebody else for what went wrong, put everything off on the external world. It wasn't me, it was everybody else. If I'd get something bad off somebody, I'd just go away from the people who were bothering me about my drinking, and I'd go to another bar and drink there. If you can't be who you are without drinking, don't drink. If you need booze to cover up your problems, don't drink. If you have to change your circle of friends because of your drinking, you need help.

In my heart I knew I didn't want to drink. But I suppressed it, I pushed it down. And what made it possible for me to do that—was drinking. I say these things not just to talk about my life. I would like to share my life with other people to help someone. I'd like someone to learn from my life. If they can't handle it, stay away from it. That's what I would tell them—don't drink.

The last thing I want to say is the most important—in fact, it's the point of the whole thing: I couldn't have stopped drinking without God's help. I could never stop drinking before. Only when I asked God for sobriety, to be relieved of the obsession to drink, was I able to quit. It was God who gave me the strength to stay sober. [From the author's files.]

CHAPTER

7

Heterosexual Deviance

Clearly, sexual behavior provides one of the more frequently cited arenas from which examples of deviance are drawn. When individuals are asked to provide concrete instances of deviance, sexual acts often come to mind with many. When I asked the members of my last class in deviant behavior for concrete examples of deviance, an extremely high proportion gave sexual examples. Many of these answers involved acts of violence, such as rape and child molestation. Homosexuality was the third most commonly mentioned instance of deviance, after murder and rape (53 out of 230 students); 31 cited prostitution; 23, incest; 7, a man wearing women's clothes; 6, sexual abuse; 4, lesbianism; 3, sodomy; 3, "sleeping around"; 2, masturbation and adultery; and 1 each, nymphomania, voyeurism, oral sex, fetishism, sex with animals, sex with a corpse, sex in public, transsexualism, bisexuality, and pornography.

Of all sexual acts, pornography (though mentioned only once) and prostitution are widely condemned and widely practiced, which makes them reasonable subjects for sociologists to investigate. Moreover, they are also instructive for the sociologist of deviance to study because, in this society, we experience a certain *ambivalence* toward them—that is, they are tolerated and condemned, although not always by the same individuals or segments of society. And both are also sociologically crucial to study because they generate a *social structure* (Gagnon and Simon, 1967: 9–11)—that is, a network of individuals whose actions are patterned, predictable, normatively governed, and routinized. With both, specific individuals in particular positions are expected to do certain things—and for the most part, they actually do them. People in the social structures of prostitution and pornography have commitments, obligations, mutual expectations, individuals with whom they have more or less ongoing reciprocal relations; there is a "community" of prostitution (Prus and Irini, 1980), just as there is a community of pornography.

It is not simply a number of isolated individuals, each doing his or her own thing, or even sets of isolated pairs of individuals doing their own thing together, but a *social organization* surrounding both activities. Each is, in a sense, a social *institution*. In prostitution, these individuals include not only the prostitute and her customer, but also, at the very least, other prostitutes, pimps, the police and judges, hotel owners, clerks, and bellboys, landlords, and madams. The actors on the stage of pornography include the male and female actors or models, producers, photographers, and camera and sound persons; customers, viewers, and purchasers of the pornographic material; and distributors, owners, and employees of the retail stores or shops that sell, rent, or distribute the material. Thus, one of the more interesting aspects of these two forms of sexual deviance is that they are a result of a number of people acting more or less together to produce an institution and behavior that are widely condemned and socially disvalued.

PROSTITUTION

Prostitutes can be male or female; they can sell sexual favors to the same or to opposite-sex customers. However, in terms of frequency, there are far more female prostitutes selling sexual favors to male customers than all other forms combined. In a sexist society, women can more readily earn a high income selling sexual favors than engaging in most other economic enterprises. Where women are treated primarily as sex objects, where their achievements have been at least partially blocked in other areas, and where men can easily separate sex from affection, the institution of prostitution will flourish.

In many ways, prostitution is an extension and a reflection of the values, activities, and institutions of conventional society. Prostitution upholds and reflects at least four basic values of American society. One is *the double standard* by which men and women are judged by two different sets of sexual rules. Women who sell their bodies (or even have sex with a number of different men) are regarded as "tramps," "sluts," and "whores," earning widespread public scorn, while men who purchase sexual favors (or who sleep with many women) are socially and morally acceptable, even respectable. The double standard necessitates the existence of a relatively small number of women who service a very large number of men. The lust of men finds its outlet in "bad" women, outcast women—prostitutes. They are condemned; they are deviant. They are, according to this ideology, markedly different from the virtuous wives, mothers, and sisters who comprise the population of "good" women, the conventional women who tolerate the animal nature of their men, their husbands and sons.

The institution of prostitution also affirms the commercial money-making ethic of capitalist society. Engaging in sex, like selling used cars, is a commercial transaction. Women, like cars, become treated as commodities, as salable objects. The sign of a true capitalist economy is that human relations become reduced to a cash connection. The basic reason why much human contact takes place is that someone expects to profit from it in a monetary sense.

Third, our economy is based on *alienated labor:* millions of workers are engaged in jobs they do not enjoy, jobs that are simply a means of keeping them alive, jobs with no joy in them. A society whose members expected and demanded work that enriched them would not have the forms of prostitution that exhibit themselves in our own society.

Fourth, this society devalues women; what they do is not held in the same regard as what men do. Women receive their reward primarily through men; their role is secondary—to serve men. Men find it difficult to regard women as fully human, whether they are mothers or whores. Prostitution is the outward manifestation of a male-dominated society: an institution designed to cater to the desires and delusions of men and to exploit women, keeping them in their place.

The institution of prostitution, then, rests on and grows out of the double standard, the commercial ethic, alienated labor, and the inferior status of women. As such, it reflects and upholds the status quo rather than challenges it. Prostitution is not a manifestation of a "permissive" society, but a restrictive one. While it is true that in severely repressive societies, prostitution is rare, it would also be rare in a society in which true sexual freedom prevails. In fact, sexual repression and prostitution seem to go hand in hand. "I see it as a symptom . . . of the kind of sex we have here now," a former prostitute writes. "I think as long as you're going to have compulsive marriage and compulsive families, you're going to have prostitution. . . . Monogamy and prostitution go together" (Millett, 1973: 50, 51). The motives of the customers who frequent prostitutes demonstrates this fact.

The Prostitute's Clients

The simple fact is, prostitution is based on many men paying for the sexual favors, often of anonymous women, that they are unable to obtain noncommercially, in ordinary human relationships with women. These men are sexually deprived, not sexually free. Although prostitutes will report that some of their customers are young, attractive, and sexually desirable men, the large bulk of the men who frequent the services of prostitutes are middle-aged and most often married. This indicates a number of things, one being that their marriages are probably sexually unsatisfying in some way. Perhaps their wives are less than enthusiastic about performing certain sexual acts that these men want, such as fellatio, or perhaps these men feel guilty about demanding such acts of their wives—who, after all, are "good" women—but not of a "bad" woman, a whore.

It may be that these men are incapable of asking, or even unwilling to ask, their wives to perform or take part in certain acts *they themselves* consider deviant and "dirty." If

their wives were to agree to the behavior they want, according to their standards, this would demean their wives in their eyes. They wouldn't want their wives to do "immoral" sexual acts, because they believe in the sexual double standard. One prostitute described a somewhat unusual act one of her customers wanted to try out (one, he discovered, that didn't turn him on at all, and which he abandoned midway into the act for ordinary intercourse). She says,

He absolutely could not try this with his wife . . . the wives might be horny to try it, but the whole marriage scene—husbands and wives just don't open up this way to each other. And this man, I have a feeling he would be disappointed if he would do this with his wife and she went along with it. I think he probably has a certain amount of contempt for me because I will do these things, but I'm a whore, I'm supposed to do these things. He wouldn't be so pleased if his wife were in this position, and he had contempt for her. He wants her, if not on a pedestal, at least a long ways from being a hooker (Wells, 1970: 111).

Said another prostitute:

These men [Johns] couldn't have their wives do these things [that prostitutes do] because their wives would think that there was something wrong with them, and they would want a divorce. Some guys just can't get turned on by normal sex. This is the only way that they can get off (Zausner, 1986: 61).

Perhaps the prostitute's clients crave "variety" through intercourse with a number of women and cannot attract women sexually unless they pay them. Or perhaps they do not wish to risk emotional commitment in a meaningful relationship.

Perhaps they have not paid too much sexual attention to their wives, and, consequently, their wives have become turned off by their lackluster performances. Or perhaps because their wives have begun to expect sexual satisfaction—which these men feel inadequate and inept at dealing with—they seek the company of women who will put on a show of faking orgasms to bolster up the sagging male ego. Men do not feel it as necessary to apologize to a prostitute for their inability as a lover.

Perhaps these men have become successful in their careers and have become persuaded that they are "worth" more on the sexual marketplace than their wives are. In the equation of a sexist society, a man's desirability is largely tied in with his success, particularly in the economic sphere; a woman's desirability tends to be measured by her surface physical attributes. Prostitution is one social institution designed to handle this disparity.

Or perhaps the customer comes to the prostitute as an unintended consequence of the so-called sexual revolution. A sexually deprived man will wonder, since everyone says that sex is easily available, why he can't get any. A painful thought like this can be partially assuaged by visiting women who offer sex for pay.

Perhaps the client is starved for companionship and intimacy—for someone with whom he can say absolutely anything without fear or embarrassment. Many men do not have any "anything goes" relationship with a woman, any woman; they may be trapped in verbal, emotional, and behavioral games of masculinity that involve bragging, lying, and pretending invulnerability. The prostitute's room may serve as a kind of confessional. As Wayland Young says about the prostitute, "Listening next to fucking is the thing she does most of " (1966).

There are men who simply prefer sex for pay—because they want things clean, neat, and uninvolved; or because they enjoy hiring a woman to do their sexual bidding—engaging, that is, in a watered-down version of the master-slave relationship; or because they feel that sex is basically dirty, and paying for it alleviates some of the guilt.

Of course, these do not exhaust all the clients' reasons for visiting a prostitute. There are many men who travel a great deal—sailors, salesmen—and are frequently in a town in which they are strangers. Or there are men who work in an area that is located far from an even-sexed population—such as lumberjacks, members of the armed services, oil workers, and so on. Rather than face the prospect of an empty hotel room, or all-male companionship, or the unlikely success of a "one-night stand," they seek out the services of prostitutes. Some men have just recently moved to a new location and have not yet found female companionship. There are physically deformed or handicapped men, who through fear of rejection by some women, turn to prostitutes for sex and companionship.

And there are what British prostitutes call "kinkies"—men whose sexual interests are so bizarre that it would be almost impossible to locate women whom they would not have to pay to take part in their requests (or men who are too ashamed to request their wives or lovers to take part in them). Sadomasochism, with the man as the "submissive" partner and the woman as the "dominant" partner, is probably the most common single form of "kinky" sex requested of the prostitute. Various fetishes—clients dressed as women, masturbating in front of the nude prostitute, a fixation on overcoats, articles of rubber, high heels and nylon stockings, and so on—also make their appearance. Nearly all prostitutes, if they have been plying their trade for any significant length of time, encounter kinkies.

Xaviera Hollander, author of a number of books, classifies freaks into, first, sadists and masochists, "who need to inflict pain or have it inflicted," and, second, "weirdos, or sickies, whose preference is for more subtle, way-out fantasy." A freak, writes Ms. Hollander, is basically anyone who needs fantasy, degradation, or punishment in order to achieve his interpretation of erotic gratification (Hollander, 1972: 208).

How Do Prostitutes Feel about Their Work?

Many conventional men think that the prostitute is attracted to the profession because she enjoys sex and wants as much of it as she can get. This is male mythology, plain and simple. Participants in the prostitution scene—prostitutes themselves, pimps, madams, everyone except customers—will almost universally say that a woman's enjoyment of intercourse (on those extremely rare occasions when it occurs) with clients *gets in her way;* it does not make her a more effective prostitute. This is true both of the specific sex act as well as of sex with customers generally. One woman, Joyce, a prostitute, explains it this way:

I would say that nothing could prompt me to have an orgasm or even become excited with a John.... I doubt that I would be able to manage it.... I will always pretend to be excited, and to come at the moment he comes, but if I really got excited I would be all involved with myself, and the timing would be thrown off, and actually he wouldn't have as good a time as if I were faking it. It's funny to think of, but he gets more for his money if it's a fake than if he were to get the real thing (Wells, 1970: 139).

Women who enjoy sex with their customers do not make good prostitutes, according to those who are acquainted with this institution firsthand. Instead of thinking about the most effective way of making money at the job, they would be doing things for their pleasure and enjoyment. For instance, if they met a man who pleased them in bed, they would want to stay with him a protracted length of time, thereby extending their turnover time and hence cutting down on how much they can earn. Or they would allow a man to perform cunnilingus on them, which is time-consuming; it is not considered a money-making activity. It is relevant only insofar as it pleases the customer and induces him to pay her more. If a woman treats it as an avenue to her pleasure, she is being a poor businesswoman. "It's terrible if they enjoy their work," says Silky, the pimp. "I think that anyone who would love it has a problem" (Gootman and Mekleburg, 1973: 32). When asked about whether prostitutes have a touch of "nymphomania" in them, Sheri, a madam, replied, "No, definitely not. A nymphomaniac couldn't make it in this business for a number of reasons. For one, she likes sex too much to use it for financial gain. For another, she is constantly thinking, 'Maybe this is finally the man who is going to help me reach *my* climax.' Conse-

quently, she is totally worthless in the profession" (Wolman, 1973: 111). A woman who is a prostitute and is concerned about her own enjoyment is contemptuously referred to by others, on the scene as a "come freak."

Few prostitutes enjoy their work. While the major inducement is money, the major "unpleasantry," according to one study, is having to engage in sex with their customers (Gray, 1973: 411). Most look upon having sex with many strangers with distaste; most in fact disdainfully view the men they have sex with. "Usually I can't stand tricks," one prostitute explains. "It's sex with tricks I hate. Sex is horrible. Just horrible. I used to be able to stand it, but now I close my eyes and keep thinking it's a dog fucking me. It's just disgusting. If I didn't have a strong mind, I would go off—crazy.... When I get a guy up to the apartment, I get the money and then I light a cigarette and put it in the ashtray. I clean the guy off and fuck. When the cigarette burns out, I know the time is up" (Hall, 1972: 100, 102). One prostitute, nicknamed "Juicy," put the matter bluntly and plainly: "I never enjoy sex while I'm working. I'm only interested in one thing, money" (Zausner, 1986: 43).

The reasons for this are not difficult to come by. It is just about impossible to develop and maintain a positive and affectionate attitude toward hundreds of strangers engaging in the most intimate act possible with them. Prostitutes feel that commercial sex is a gruesome mockery of the love relationship. Nearly everyone in this society, regardless of how cynical, has been taught, and still to some extent believes in, the romantic ideal. Where tenderness, affection, even passion, are absent in behavior that is supposed to be dominated by them, it becomes an embittering experience. When this is multiplied hundreds of times over, the result can be positively numbing to the participant.

"One day and then another day, and all the days are the same. It's just one thing after another, one man after another. I see this endless parade of penises. Coming at me. Just an endless parade of marching penises," one prostitute explains. Eventually, she says, she just thinks of the customer "as a penis with a body attached." The only way to deal with this alienating experience, she explains, is to remain: "Absolutely . . . detached. Removed. Miles and miles away." (Wells, 1970: 88, 92, 97)

A woman interviewed by Kate Millett, feminist author of *Sexual Politics*, explains her reactions to her former life as a prostitute. "The worst part about prostitution is that you're obliged not only to sell sex only, but your humanity. That's the worst part of it: that what you're selling is your human dignity." This woman, an exprostitute (now a psychologist with a Ph.D.), tells us that the specific aspect of sex for sale was only one part of the indignity; mainly it was "being a bought person," having to play at a charade of being polite, agreeable and charming to men who were unappealing and odious to her. "That's the most humiliating thing," she says, "having to agree with them all the time because you're bought." It is true that other businesses also require a certain prostitution of the soul—being agreeable to a boss whom one does not respect, selling products that people don't really need. "But there's a special indignity in prostitution," this woman explains, "as if sex were dirty and men can only enjoy it with someone *low*. It involves a type of contempt, a kind of disdain, and a kind of triumph over another human being" (Millett, 1973: 57, 58).

The prostitute typically harbors a great deal more contempt for her client than he for her. The term "trick" expresses this contempt: Her customer has been "tricked" out of his money, out of his dignity, out of his manhood—the very things he tries so hard to demonstrate. He has been deceived into thinking of himself as sexually desirable while being relieved of his money. The prostitute usually thinks of her customer as basically stupid; he believes practically everything she tells him. "The hardest thing to learn is the vulnerability of the man. You have to make yourself believe that this man is stupid enough to believe anything you tell him. And he is" (Hall, 1972: 59). The prostitute feels that she sees the John *as he really is*, but he sees only the social façade of her—the illusion she constructs to part him with

his money. He is doubly contemptible, first, for being "tricked" out of his money and, second, for believing in the phony act the prostitute devised to take it. The John tells the prostitute his troubles, secrets he keeps from his own wife, she sees him at his weakest moments, she sees his vulnerability, his insecurities, he has shown her he needs her enough to pay for what she has. She is seeing the *true self* of the man she beds down with—or so it seems to her. *He* sees precisely the opposite side of her—the side that is publicly available, to anyone, for hire, the phony side of her. A man who goes away from such an encounter thinking that the way the prostitute presented herself to him is the real her is, by her lights, a stupid person worthy only of ridicule and condemnation.

Also remember what the customer of a prostitute is: a man who cannot (or does not want to) attract a woman to his bed unless she is paid. "I'll always say it," Laurie, a prostitute, exclaims. "Johns are fools. They're just suckers to me. . . . They're bigger fools than us because I feel as though *any* man could get *any* woman they want for a girlfriend" (Coleman, 1971: 23–24). An indication of this negative attitude toward Johns is manifested in a study conducted by one of the co-authors of the famous Kinsey studies, Paul Gebhard. A clear majority of the prostitutes in this survey said that they *never* liked one of their clients; only 5 percent said that they liked a quarter or more of them (Gebhard, 1969).

Of course, this can too easily and facilely be reduced to the formula, "prostitutes hate men." It is legitimate to ask the chicken and egg question: Do women hate men first, and become prostitutes because of it, or do they become prostitutes first and then come to hate men—some men, anyway—because of their experiences as prostitutes? Observers like psychiatrists and psychoanalysts who believe that personality is formed early, endures throughout one's lifetime, and manifests itself in nearly all of one's behavior will feel that the man-hating came first. Sociologists are more likely to believe that attitudes are more malleable than this, and often, feelings are specific to certain situations and rarely apply across-the-board. As evidence, it will often be maintained by those who favor the "man hater" argument that prostitutes are frigid, that they only fake orgasms—if they even do that—with their customers. Who but the most naive would believe that a woman should, or could, have orgasms routinely with many middle-aged strangers in the space of 15 minutes for each sexual encounter? One woman, Faith, a prostitute, comments on this male illusion: "Can they really think you take a girl right off the street and give her fifteen, twenty dollars and give her a quick little fuck in a dirty hotel room, and figure this is gonna' make her come?" (Wells, 1970: 68). One study found that prostitutes were considerably more orgasmic with their boyfriends, lovers, and husbands than the average woman is (Gebhard, 1969).

How Do Women Become Prostitutes?

A great deal of research on prostitution has attempted to answer the question of what factors are associated with entering "the life." An economically deprived background is one of the most commonly cited of such factors. It is no doubt true that prostitutes are more likely to be recruited from the poorer segments of society, but this has to be qualified. There are many women who are not, and never were, poor, and who become prostitutes. The "blue-collar" street prostitute is far more visible than is the middle-class, college-educated call girl. The former's visibility makes it easier for her to be both arrested and studied. So it is easy to underestimate the number of women who come from a middle-class background (who are more likely to end up being semivisible call girls) and to exaggerate the number of women who come from working-class backgrounds (who are more likely to end up working on the street, and to be highly visible). Furthermore, relatively affluent women may be more likely to engage in activities that very few people would label actual prostitution, and that never officially or unofficially get counted as prostitution, but that are similar to it in many ways: like marrying

for money; or receiving gifts, entertainment, and wining and dining in exchange for intercourse. The last chapter in Gail Sheehy's (1973) book on prostitution is entitled "The Ultimate Trick," and it chronicles one woman's climb to great wealth through the wise and shrewd use of her body.

It may not be that working-class women engage in prostitution more, but that the type of sexual exchanges they make are more likely to be called prostitution by middle-class standards. Middle-class women are, perhaps, less likely to make the leap from sex for gifts to sex for outright cash than working-class women are because they have been more firmly convinced that the former isn't nearly as "bad" as the latter. Perhaps the difference between the two is the more hardheaded, no-nonsense, and realistic attitude on the part of the working-class women. After all, most men, even today, whether they are Johns or seducers, do not respect the women with whom they have intercourse. In a sexist society, there is an element of oppression in much heterosexual contact—especially if it is specifically sexual in nature.

Another factor that the available research links with prostitution is sexual contact with many partners on a superficial basis at a relatively early age.

Nanette Davis, in an exploratory study of 30 prostitutes selected from three correctional institutions (1971), characterizes the process of drifting from casual sex with many boys (often called "promiscuity") at an early age into the young woman's first few acts of prostitution. The average age of first intercourse for Davis's women was 13.6. Petting experiences were almost entirely absent; their first sexual contacts typically involved intercourse right from the beginning. And for 28 out of the 30, that first sexual experience was felt as either meaningless or distasteful. The average age of this sample's first prostitute experience was 17.3. What happened during the in-between three or four years? This is a "preliminary period of vague, floating promiscuity," of an "increasing irrelation to society" (Young, 1966: 132). All except 2 of Davis's sample of jailed women reported that they had been regarded by parents, teachers, and neighbors as troublemakers, as "slow learners," as misfits—in short, even before they became prostitutes, as deviants. All except 7 had been confined to a juvenile home or training school as adolescents for truancy, incorrigibility, or for sexual delinquency. Davis speculates that this process of typing and labeling is a contributing condition that facilitates a deviant identity to emerge: "In the interactional process with significant others ... , the girl achieves an identity of one who is different. She is expected to behave in unconventional ways" (Davis, 1971: 303). The girl who was confined to a training school engaged in acts of prostitution for the first time significantly *earlier* than nontraining school girls—15.8 versus 21.3.

Many studies indicate that a very high proportion of women who become prostitutes were the victims of incestuous sex with their fathers or stepfathers, violence within their families, and rape or other coerced sex at an early age (James and Meyerding, 1977; Rosenblum, 1975; Pines and Silbert, 1983; Zausner, 1986: 5). Early victimization seems to figure prominently in the lives of prostitutes. Perhaps these experiences contribute to a young woman's loss of self-esteem and to a view of herself as "sexually debased," as someone who is the inevitable target of sexual exploitation and objectification. Rather than turn her negative feelings stemming from these experiences on her oppressors, some victims turn them inwardly, feeling, somehow, responsible for her victimization. Many such women see prostitution as a natural and inevitable alternative (James and Meyerding, 1977: 1384).

Many sensationalistic articles are published each year that claim that a high proportion of young women who become prostitutes enter the life as a result of being forced against their will by being beaten, tortured, and raped by pimps (Tomlinson, 1981; Adams, 1981). It would be a mistake to think that this never occurs. However, it is also relatively rare. It serves a propagandistic purpose to disseminate the claim that pimps are active corruptors and women,

their passive victims. This would, however, be a distortion of reality. One study of 32 teenage prostitutes found that not only were none of them forced into prostitution but that none of them even claimed to know anyone who had been started in prostitution in this fashion. "Generally, charm, flattery, the promise of money, protection, companionship, and emotional closeness are enough to initiate girls into the world of prostitution" (Bracey, 1979: 23).

It would be foolish to think that a single generalization can serve as a universal explanation as to why some women become prostitutes. There is no single factor. But many women do go through one or another, or several, of a fairly limited set of common experiences. There are a number of different *paths* to prostitution. We do know for sure that nearly all women see prostitution as a form of deviance; to them, it is disvalued, worthy of condemnation. Most women who eventually become prostitutes at one time looked down upon prostitution. For them it was an undesirable thing to do and to be. And moreover, it is a publicly condemned activity. All women at the very least know of its deviant status, even if they do not share in the generally negative attitude toward it. So to become a prostitute, it is necessary for a woman to look upon prostitution with enough favor to allow herself to participate in it. In other words, they have to *neutralize the stigma* attached to prostitutes and prostitution in their own minds. They have to reconcile a halfway positive and desirable self-image with their participation in an activity and a profession they look upon with scorn. (There is another possibility: They maintain a negative self-image, and participate in prostitution because of it. Psychoanalysts are fond of this explanation.)

I pointed out earlier that this process of neutralization is common; it takes place among participants of a number of deviant activities. Few of the women in the Davis study launched themselves straight from a few initial acts of prostitution into a full-time career of selling sex. For a majority (21 out of 30), there was a transitional stage involving occasional acts of prostitution or a zigzag pattern—vascillation between deviant and conventional lives and identities. Conventional attachments are not yet denied; their self-definition as a prostitute was delayed, not willingly or easily incorporated. There seemed to be a kind of internal struggle. During this process of vascillation, attempts are made to adopt the deviant identity without self-condemnation. What is needed to progress further is a successful effort at a *normalization* of prostitution (Davis, 1971: 312). Processes of accommodation take place to incorporate a once condemned, publicly deviant status into one's own conception of oneself. The movement into accepting sex as a vocation (1971: 315) is made only as a result of resolving this struggle of self-acceptance, this problem of self-respect. There will be an emphasis on other values—values that prostitutes achieve at—mainly monetary success. Straight people will be looked upon with increasing distaste. "I can't cope with square people" (1971: 316), the prostitute will say to herself. "All the square people I meet are pale. You get hooked on this life and nothing else satisfies you" (Hall, 1972: 176). What becomes necessary, then, is a twofold process: the normalization of engaging in acts of prostitution, and the denial of legitimacy and validity of conventional behavior and values. Prostitutes "develop a set of beliefs which counteract the social anathema attached to their way of life" (Jackman et al., 1963). Facilitating this process is an identification with the criminal or "hustler" life-style and seeking out, or falling into the company of, individuals who reward and who believe in deviant, unconventional values.

Many women are initiated into prostitution over a period of time through a step-by-step process. They do something that bothers their conscience only slightly, something that demands that they redefine themselves, revise their self-image. This allows them to participate in another type of behavior that they see as only a bit more "deviant," something they condemn only slightly more strenuously. But their attitude has already been revised toward that behavior because they took part in something that wasn't really too

different from it. Eventually they step over into a realm they have to admit is truly deviant. Most of us do things that could be seen, even by ourselves, as very much like prostitution. Men may act obsequious to a boss for career advancement, or may spend eight hours a day at jobs they dislike. Often this shades over into unethical and even illegal behavior. The steps may be quite small and almost imperceptible.

One woman, Bernice, explains her initiation into prostitution in the following manner. She worked as a model for a garment manufacturer who was married and had four children. She had an affair with him that eventually sputtered to an end. One afternoon a number of models, including herself, modeled a line of clothes for several buyers for a chain of Midwestern clothing stores. Later, her boss came into the dressing room and told her that one of them expressed an interest in her. "Look," he said, "this fellow thinks you're really beautiful, and he'd like to go out with you. You do what you want to do, but if you want to go out with him—well, it might be good for business" (Wells, 1970: 29). She asked her boss to point the man out, and Bernice decided that he was "not bad looking." She says that she didn't think "about any sex part to it. Not immediately." But while on the date, she realized that if the man liked her, he would naturally want to make love to her. "Here I was actually going out on a date with a John, that's what it really amounted to, and I didn't see it in those terms at all" (1970: 30).

After coming to work the next day, her boss took her aside and gave her an envelope with three $10 bills in it. Bernice was shocked. "I asked him what kind of a girl he thought I was. Can you imagine a line like that? But that's what I said." Her boss looked chagrined. He explained that she had "showed this fellow a good time, and maybe he'll be grateful in the future." He explained that he had given her presents in the past— why not now? "It's funny," Bernice remarked, "how you won't mind doing something, but you will mind the name, the label." The next occasion, a week later, her boss set up a date with another buyer. She knew that she would get extra money for it, plus, this time, the next day off. And she was not naive this time; she knew that sex would be involved. So she gradually began accepting dates with buyers, working for the same boss. And later, some were buyers and some weren't—some were just friends of her boss. And later still, she began accepting dates from these buyers on her own, independent of arrangements her boss had set up—and was paid for it. Finally, her boss told her that it would be a good idea if she stopped coming to work altogether and concentrated entirely on being "available if someone wanted to see her."

At each step, Bernice said, "I would keep being amazed at the way I could just shrug off the changes I was going through. . . . And I look myself in the mirror, and . . . I'm amazed to see that I'm still me" (Wells, 1970: 33–34).

Prostitution and AIDS

It might seem reasonable to assume that a major reason for the wildfire spread of AIDS in the 1980s and into the 1990s has been sexual encounters between prostitutes and their clients. Writing in the *Journal of Acquired Immune Deficiency Syndrome,* Dr. Mindell Siedlin states: "It is likely that those heterosexuals with the largest numbers of anonymous partners would be most likely to be exposed" to the AIDS virus. Prostitutes, she said, should be similar in this respect to homosexual men (Lambert, 1988: B5). Indeed, in a number of countries worldwide, this is true. One recent study of 1,000 prostitutes in Nairobi, Kenya, found that 85 percent were infected with the AIDS virus (Lambert, 1988: B5). In the United States, in contrast, only a minority of prostitutes who are not intravenous drug users or the sex partners of IV drug users are infected with AIDS. In fact, prostitutes are more likely to get AIDS from their lovers and customers than they are to give it to them. In one study of prostitutes in eight areas of the country, 13 percent tested positive for the AIDS virus. The figure was 21 percent for the self-admitted needle-using

drug takers in this study, and only 5 percent for those who denied injecting drugs, which indicated that most of the latter had had drug-using sex partners (Lambert, 1988: B5).

There are at least two reasons why AIDS is rarely spread from prostitutes to customers, aside from the relatively low rate of infection among prostitutes. The first is that nearly all prostitutes use condoms. (All the women interviewed by Zausner (1986) stated that they insist their customers use condoms for all sex acts, including fellatio and even masturbation.) Infection is considerably less likely if a condom is used. A second reason why there is a low likelihood that infection will travel from a prostitute to a customer is that heterosexual intercourse—both vaginal and oral—is not an efficient spreader of the AIDS virus. The chance of contracting AIDS in one sexual encounter with a member of a high-risk category not using a condom is estimated to be between 1 in 1,000 and 1 in 10,000. Using a condom brings this likelihood down to between 1 in 10,000 and 1 in 100,000 (Boffey, 1988a). One-time sexual intercourse without a condom with a partner who is not in a high-risk group but whose infection status is unknown carries a risk of infection of 1 in 5 million, or "about the same as the risk of being killed in a traffic accident while driving 10 miles on the way to that sexual encounter" (1988a: A18).

Although prostitution cannot be dismissed as a potential future source of AIDS—especially given what we know about the tragic experience in other countries—in the United States, for now, prostitution is not a major, or even a minor, source of AIDS.

PORNOGRAPHY

There are strong parallels between pornography and prostitution. In fact, the word "pornography" stems from the ancient Greek, meaning writings about prostitutes or harlots. For the most part, prostitution and pornography entail the use of women's bodies for men's pleasure. Both cater largely, almost overwhelmingly, to the desires of men;

that is, most customers of prostitutes are men, and most consumers of pornography are men. Both are based on alienated labor: women pretending to enjoy themselves while engaged in activities they find distasteful or, at best neutral. (As Marx said, much the same also applies to most men and women who work at licit jobs in a capitalist society.) Both prostitution and pornography grow out of women's inferior status; both entail treating women as objects. In prostitution and pornography, equality is usually absent: They represent the expression of a certain kind of power of one individual, or category of individuals, over another.

Prostitution expresses sexual repression, not liberation; likewise, in most pornography, sexual repression is the rule because women are depicted stereotypically, not as she is or wants to be. Both prostitution and pornography entail an inaccurate representation of women and are, in complex and interesting ways, forms of deviant behavior. The prostitute and the actress or model for pornographic fare are deviant, condemned, morally beyond the pale. (Generally, men who act in porno movies or videos are not condemned nearly as much as the women, and they may even be admired.) Also, the man who supports the activity—the customer of the prostitute and the man who purchases pornography—is usually a respectable individual, usually working at a decent job, a member of the community, often married with children.

What Is Pornography?

As with other behavior, the definitional question must be answered before an intelligent discussion can follow. One problem is that pornography has always been a battleground of controversy, as we'll see shortly. On one side of the controversy, it is opposed and criticized by conservatives and moralists (Hudson, 1986), and, since the 1970s, by the antipornography faction of feminism (Lederer, 1982), Women Against Pornography (WAP). As we've seen with other deviant behavior, in any area where controversy is intense, even defining the relevant phenomena can be a problem.

Most antipornography feminists make a clear distinction between "erotica," which they see as good, and pornography, which is bad. Erotica is the representation of "a sexual encounter between adult persons which is characterized by mutual respect" (Longino, 1982: 28), mutual affection, and desire between equals. In contrast, pornography is sexually explicit material that entails "clear force, or an unequal power that spells coercion ... no sense of equal choice or equal power" (Steinem, 1982: 23). Interestingly, antipornography advocates seldom offer concrete examples of erotica.

According to some observers, this distinction between erotica and pornography "sounds promising, but it doesn't hold up." Erotica, which is literature or pictures containing sexual themes, may actually be used for pornographic purposes. In fact, the term "erotica" is widely used as a euphemism for "classy porn." If it is expressed in "literary language" or esthetically-pleasing photographs or videos and is used and consumed by the educated—by members of the upper-middle class—it is called erotica; if it is esthetically trashy and "can't pretend to any purpose" except sexual arousal, it is called pornography—by its very nature "smut." The "erotica versus porn" distinction evades the "question of how porn is *used*. It endorses the portrayal of sex as we might like it to be and condemns the portrayal of sex as it too often is, whether in action or in fantasy. But if pornography is to arouse, it must appeal to the feelings we have, not those by some utopian standard we ought to have.... In practice, attempts to sort out good erotica from bad porn inevitably come down to 'What turns me on is erotic; what turns you on is pornographic'" (Willis, 1983: 463).

In short, as Gagnon and Simon observe, the category pornography "is as elusive as mercury" (1973: 281). Thus, rather than insisting on a single definition of pornography as valid, it makes more sense to isolate several *dimensions* that capture specific angles or aspects of the phenomenon. Since some observers will see as pornography works others would regard as innocuous or even innocent of sexual meaning, it becomes necessary to determine *how pornography is defined by different audiences.* At least three definitions could be used.

1. The *functional* definition: *works consumed for the purpose of sexual excitation.* This definition looks at material from the point of view of the *consumers* of the material—primarily their use of it and the responses it generates in them.

2. The *labeling* definition: *works that much of the public think of as obscene*—that is, material that, it is believed, excites "lustful" thoughts and is therefore sexually vulgar, offensive, shameful, and disgusting. This definition looks at pornography from the point of view of the disapproving public, or segments of the public.

3. The *genre* definition: *works that are created primarily for the purpose of arousing the lust of an audience or customers and that conform to a narrow and distinct formula.* This definition takes the point of view of the *creators* and the *producers* of pornographic works (who, in turn, are trying to figure out what the audience wants). They assemble, manufacture, and sell commercialized sex; they want to turn on as many men as possible and to make a profit doing so.

These definitions lead us to two inescapable conclusions: (1) *Something may be pornographic in one sense, but not in another.* (2) *Something may be pornographic to some people, but not to others.*

Any meaningful look at pornography must necessarily be relativistic. Some works can arouse sexual excitation in one individual but not in another; many people are sexually bored and unresponsive to material that may wildly excite others. Most men do not find pictures of women being bound and gagged, dressed in uniforms or leather attire, wearing masks or spike heels, or brandishing whips sexually exciting. On the other hand, a minority are so wildly turned on by such photographs that an entire industry is based on supplying them to customers (Becker, 1963: 20–21). In addition, standards as to what is pornographic change over time. In the pre-*Playboy* era, when photographs of

nude women were more difficult to obtain than they are today, many young men found photographs of bare-breasted native women in *National Geographic* extremely arousing and used them to masturbate with. Today, with more revealing and explicit material far more readily available, adolescents rarely find these pictures exciting or use them for masturbation. Thus, in the past, such pictures *were* pornographic to many adolescents; today, they are not. The pictures haven't changed very much, but the responses to them have.

Can great works of art be pornographic? Of course: *Insofar as they are offensive to some* and *are used for the purpose of arousal and masturbation,* they *are* clear-cut instances of pornography. To the extent that neither is true, they are not pornographic. The "work of art" and "pornographic" categories do not inhabit separate worlds; they overlap and crosscut one another (Peckham, 1969). In 1814, a painting of a nude woman, entitled *Venus,* by Diego Velásquez (1599–1660)—one of the greatest painters who ever lived—was described by a Spanish inquisitor general as "obscene." In 1914, while hanging in the National Gallery of London, this work was slashed by a feminist demonstrator because she regarded it as obscene (Troutman, 1965: 42). Thus, *to this inquisitor general* and *to this early feminist,* Velasquez's *Venus* was obscene—a pornographic painting. That it would not be so regarded by hardly anyone today does not detract from the fact that it *was* so regarded at one time by some observers. To select an even more extreme example, the antiporn feminist Susan Griffin labels as pornographic the works of the German painter Franz Marc (1880–1916), a judgment nearly all art historians and critics—not to mention ordinary, run-of-the-mill appreciaters of art—would find totally baffling, indeed, outright bizarre (Griffin, 1981: 4, 8ff). To focus on the second dimension, that many art works are not only sexually exciting, but have been used for the purpose of sexual arousal—specifically masturbation—can be verified by interviewing any number of sensual men and women of artistic taste.

Are such mainstream and readily available magazines such as *Playboy* and *Penthouse* pornographic? Again, clearly and unquestionably, the answer is yes—and certainly for far more men than is true for works of art. We must get away from seeing the term "pornography" as negative or pejorative. Individuals who say the images found in such magazines are not "dirty" or offensive will insist they are not pornographic; those who insist they are, indeed, offensive and degrading will insist they are, by their very nature, pornographic. Clearly, *Playboy* and *Penthouse* are *regarded* by many Americans as offensive—and in that sense, they are *clearly* pornographic. Since many adolescents and young adults purchase and use the pictures in these magazines as masturbatory aids, they are, in that sense, pornographic. Our feelings about the goodness or badness of such magazines should not prevent us from recognizing how they are viewed or used by others.

Our last definition of pornography—the genre definition—looks at works differently. Those in the business of supplying material that is used for sexual arousal must have some sense of what it is that turns customers on; if not, they will go out of business. Thus, producers and manufacturers of sexually explicit material rely on formulas and conventions that, they believe, arouse consumers and will stimulate them to purchase the product in question. However, rather than a single convention, there are a number of them, each catering to the tastes of different *segments* of the pornography market.

What might be regarded as "classy" or middle-class, "soft-core" photographic pornography is one such convention; the pages of *Playboy* and *Penthouse* are examples. If these magazines violated the canons spelled out by the genre, their readers would be disappointed, and their sales would suffer. The women whose photographs appear in the pages of these magazines are, overwhelmingly, young—late teens to middle twenties. They are, in conventional terms, extremely attractive. No blemishes appear on their faces and bodies. They tend to be slim and long-legged, and, in recent years, with busts of a certain size (not too small, not too large). Nearly all are white; all are, or seem to be, middle-class—"the girl next door." These women are photographed in various stages of undress—some of them are fully clothed, some are partially nude, and some are completely nude. The conventions regarding fully nude photographs are fairly clear-cut and detailed. For instance, although pubic hair has been allowed since 1970, pictures flaunting the woman's inner labia are not acceptable in "classy" soft-core photographs. Men sporting an erection never appear in these pictures; in fact, most, at least in the main pictorials, the centerfolds, are of a woman alone, very rarely accompanied by a nude male. And overt violence hardly ever appears in the photographs in these magazines (though it may be in their cartoons or stories). These are some of the current conventions that guide middle-class, soft-core photographic pornography. (The canons for working-class, soft-core pornographic photographs, exemplified by those in *Hustler,* are somewhat different.)

"Hard core" is an altogether different convention. In hard core, sexual explicitness reigns supreme. Hard core contains sex and little else; its sex is out in the open, leaving little or nothing to the imagination. Erections bloom like flowers in springtime; intercourse is depicted explicitly, as are anal and oral sex. To pander to the sexual cravings of a large number of men, it is necessary to get to sex fairly quickly, without much ado. The proportion of explicit sex relative to everything else is extremely high in hard-core genre pornography. The ratio of photographs or footage depicting total nudity to those depicting clothed subjects is extremely high. Within hard core, there are a variety of genres. *Mainstream* hard core focuses on activities that many, if not most, couples are likely to engage in, such as intercourse, fellatio, cunnilingus, and anal sex. But there are deviations from this genre as well; minority sexual expressions find their way into pornographic fare in "golden showers," sex with animals, S/M (sadomasochism), sex with amputees, sex with children, and so on. Each sexual expression, however repugnant to most of us, has generated pornography that is produced, distributed, and sold to an audience who wants it to look a certain way.

In spite of this diversity, however, most of what is produced, distributed, sold, bought, and used as hard-core pornography, possesses at least five basic characteristics. First, there is an illicit, "naughty" element: *What society represses is actually good.* "It may be bad, but I like it," seems to be the message in all pornography. Second, *everyone is really obsessed with sex, whether or not they admit it.* Third, all women, or at least, many women, are *always sexually available and are limitlessly responsive,* "are lusty and free in both surrender and enjoyment" (Gagnon and Simon, 1973: 267). Fourth, under the right circumstances with the right woman, a man will become potent almost beyond belief, infinitely arousable, infinitely responsive. Fifth, ordinary, mundane relations, activities, and interactions—between a boss and his secretary, a nurse and her patient, between mother and son, neighbors, clerk and customer, salesman and housewife—*are saturated with sexual meaning.* In short, "sexual encounters can happen at any moment, to anyone, around almost any corner" (Gagnon and Simon, 1973: 266).

These, then, are the outlines of pornography. What effects does pornography have on the viewer, the reader, the consumer?

The Effects of Pornography: Definitions and Concepts

What happens to people who read or view pornography? What effects does it have? Although any of dozens of possible effects could be studied, most research and commentary on the subject in recent years have focused on aggression and violence. Specifically: Does exposure to pornography stimulate men to become more violent against women—that is, more likely to engage in rape and other forms of assault, including mutilation, torture, and murder? There are at least three possible models regarding the

effects of pornography on male aggression against women: (1) the *catharsis* theory, (2) the imitation or *modeling* theory (McCormack, 1978), and (3) the "no-effects" theory.

The catharsis theory, which is now generally regarded as obsolete, is that pornography acts as a kind of "safety valve," permitting men to harmlessly express "antisocial" sexual impulses. Through one of his characters, the writer Truman Capote voices this theory in the following words: "Pornography, in my opinion, has been misunderstood, for it doesn't develop sex fiends and send them roaming alleyways—it is an anodyne for the sexually oppressed and unrequited, for what is the aim of pornography if not to stimulate masturbation? And surely masturbation is the pleasanter alternative for men 'on the muscle'" (1988: 50).

Pornography arouses the viewer sexually; by satisfying this arousal through masturbation, there is less sexual energy left over for aggressive encounters with the women in the man's life (Polsky, 1969: 183–200). The same argument has been applied to prostitution (Davis, 1937). Although masturbation is a frequent, practically universal accompaniment of exposure to pornography among men (see the two accounts at the end of this chapter), such experiences by no means exhaust the consumer's total output of sexual energy. It is entirely possible that, following such masturbatory episodes, the consumer of pornography will then seek to sexually aggress against women. Moreover, violence against women need not express itself exclusively in the act of rape; other forms of violence are entirely possible. Indeed, many rapists are totally or partially impotent when they attack women. The catharsis model is based on two completely fallacious assumptions: (1) that rape is mainly, even exclusively, a sexual act and only secondarily an act of violence; and (2) that each man has a more or less finite and fixed quantity of sexual energy that is partially used up by exposure to pornography.

The imitation or *modeling* theory argues that viewers of porn imitate or model their behavior after what they read in books and see in pictures and on the screen. Pornography, the advocates of this approach claim, stimulates unwholesome impulses that might otherwise rest dormant in the male. In pornography, women are treated as sexual objects to be exploited and debased. According to the proponents of this school, the message in pornography is not sexual liberation; it is that in sexual encounters, women should be subordinated, humiliated, dehumanized, degraded, injured, raped, and mutilated. In pornography, women are depicted as creatures who enjoy and invite all of these things; in real life, men who are exposed to this message will treat women in the same manner that they see women being treated in pornographic depictions. Conservatives and moralists have argued this position for centuries, and it is consistent with conventional, mainstream opinion. A poll conducted by *Newsweek* in 1985 found that nearly three-quarters of the American public (73 percent) believes "sexually explicit" materials "lead some people to commit rape or sexual violence," and roughly the same proportion (76 percent) believes they also "lead some people to lose respect for women." The *Attorney General's Commission on Pornography: Final Report* (Hudson, 1986) exemplifies this line of thinking on the subject.

In the 1970s and 1980s, the modeling approach received a great deal of support from a wing of the women's liberation movement (Griffin, 1981; Lederer, 1982; Dworkin, 1981). Pornography, according to this view, is "the ideology of cultural sadism" (Barry, 1984: 205–252), "the undiluted essence of antifemale propaganda" (Brownmiller, 1975: 394). In the words of the principal slogan feminists chant at antipornography rallies: "Pornography is the theory; rape is the practice" (Morgan, 1982). The feminist view adds a *political* dimension to the imitation model: Pornography specifically and explicitly serves the function of defining women as "dirty whores" so that men can better keep them in a subservient position in real life; pornography reflects, reinforces, and stimulates hostility, aggression, and violence in men against women, who become terrorized by the assaults that result. What pornog-

raphy is "about," say some feminists, is men subjugating and dominating women and women being held in a subservient position; what pornography is about, they say, is *power*.

The no-effects theory holds that the evidence does not support the contention that pornography causes men to become more aggressive or violent against women. Some adherents of this model hold that the evidence is insufficiently compelling or is conflicting; others hold that the evidence is fairly strong—but in a no-effects direction: Men specifically do *not* become more violent against women after being exposed to pornography.

In 1967, Congress passed Public Law 90-100, mandating an extensive study of obscenity and pornography, in part to answer the question of the impact of this type of material on actual behavior. Dozens of experts conducted a large number of detailed research projects. In 1970 and 1971, the Commission on Obscenity and Pornography released its findings in a nine-volume report (with one summary volume). More than 75 separate monographs, articles, papers, and studies were published in the full report, some 20 of them dealing specifically with the effects of pornography on its consumers and viewers. The researchers included sociologists, psychologists, and psychiatrists. The findings of the many studies that made up this report were strikingly consistent with one another. Sexually explicit material, the report concluded, has an extremely superficial and short-lived impact on the lives and behavior of the persons exposed to it: "Established patterns of sexual behavior were found to be very stable and not altered substantially by exposure to erotica" (Commission on Obscenity and Pornography, 1970: 25; see also Goldstein and Kant, 1973). Pornography, the report concluded, does not make people more aggressive or violent, or men more likely to assault or rape women. The 1970 Commission on Obscenity and Pornography represents the classic statement of the no-effects theory.

The no-effects conclusions of the commission's report have been widely attacked. One of the critics' main objections has been that the report did not distinguish between "erotica," or "good" sexually explicit material, and "pornography," or "bad" sexually explicit material (Bart and Jozsa, 1982: 214; Russell, 1982c: 216–217). As we've already seen (Willis, 1983: 463), this distinction is difficult to maintain. However, more to the point, except for one minor study, the 1970 commission *did not study reactions to violent pornography.* Nearly all the pornography in its studies depicted nonviolent, consensual sex. Clearly, then, the 1970 commission failed to study what is probably the *central* issue in the pornography studies of the 1980s—the impact of violent pornography on men's behavior and attitudes toward women and the causal mechanism behind this impact; that is, whether it is the sexual explicitness or the violence that produces the observed impact.

Perhaps a more clear-cut and fruitful distinction than that between pornography and erotica is one that could be made between sexually explicit materials that *contain* violent images and those that do *not.* It might be assumed that such a distinction would be easy to make, that everyone would agree as to what violence is and which specific images contain it and which do not. *Most* pornography contains no clear-cut, overt violence, just depictions of nude women or nude couples engaged in various consensual sexual acts; it would be "hard to make a convincing case that such images are violent" (Rubin, 1984: 298). Not all observers agree, however. Some feminists argue that, since we live in a sexist society in which women are not free to do what they wish, *all* sexually explicit images of women produced by and for men, are *by their very nature* violent (Dworkin, 1981; 1982c: 286–287).[1]

Given this approach, it is not clear exactly how we could make any kind of meaningful distinction between violent and nonviolent sexually explicit material. By means of this definitional trick, one is able thereby to define all sexually explicit images as violent, sides, such reductionism allows women no basis for distinguishing between consensual heterosexuality and rape." To feminists such as Dworkin, "In a patriarchy, all sex with men is pornographic" (1983: 464–465). And if there's no difference between ordinary heterosexual intercourse and rape, then what does one mean when one says that pornography causes rape and violence? In an age when nearly all feminists are making a clear distinction between consensual intercourse and rape, one of their principal and most outspoken spokespersons is doing exactly the opposite—claiming that consensual intercourse and rape are basically the same thing. To Dworkin, the male sexual urge is fueled by hostility toward the woman and the need to commit violence against her. Dworkin has written: "Men love death. In everything they make, they hollow out a central place for death.... Men especially love murder. In art they celebrate it, and in life they commit it" (1982a: 141). She has also said: "... sex and murder are fused in the male consciousness, so that the one without the imminent possibility of the other is unthinkable and impossible." The "annihilation of women is the source of meaning and identity for men.... The fact is that the process of killing ... is the prime sexual act for men in reality and/or in imagination" (1982c: 288–289). Ms. Dworkin's theory to explain why men "need" pornography—and why it is inevitably linked to murder—is twofold. First, "the sons" (younger men, presumably) because they fear anal rape, "phallic power," and being murdered by their fathers, "bonded with the fathers who had tried to kill them. Only in this alliance could they make certain that they would not again be bound on the altar for sacrifice." (Her documentation for this assertion is the biblical story of Abraham and Isaac.) And second, having experienced episodes of impotence and waning virility, and, feeling rage because of it, they wished to "revenge themselves on the women who had left them." Her conclusion is that "the perfect vehicle for forging this alliance was pornography" (1982a: 146). It is not clear what one should make of this bizarre and deranged theory, or if it was even meant to be taken seriously in the first place. It is a literary, not a scientific, theory, more metaphorical than empirical. It violates most of the criteria for meaningful, serious, systematic, scientific thinking spelled out in Chapter 3. Whether her theories are deranged or not, Ms. Dworkin has had a great deal of influence on feminist thinking about pornography, and she and her writings have received the endorsement of such important authors and feminist figures as Gloria Steinem, Erica Jong, Phyllis Chesler, Robin Morgan, and Mary Daly. Thus, she and her writings, however bizarre and easily dismissed, deserve attention.

[1] In fact, perhaps the most influential antipornography feminist, Andrea Dworkin, regards *all heterosexual intercourse,* by its very nature, as "penetration," an invasion, an act of mutilation, domination, humiliation and brutality (Dworkin, 1987). This raises the inevitable question, if all consensual heterosexual intercourse is by its very nature a brutal act of violation and subjugation, *then how does it differ from rape?* As feminist Ellen Willis says: "If all manifestations of patriarchical sexuality are violent, then opposition to violence cannot explain why pornography ... should be singled out as a target. Be-

because they do not depict perfect reciprocity. For instance, a *Playboy* centerfold is defined as "violent" because it is a photograph of a nude woman that is purchased and ogled by young men who use it for masturbatory purposes, without any possible reciprocity on the woman's part. Of course, that is not how most people would define violence, but this is how the Women Against Pornography feminists define it. The next stage that Women Against Pornography takes in this definitional process is to present slide shows of women who are bound, gagged, and tortured in pornography (Dworkin, 1982b: 255), claiming this is what pornography is all "about." Again, this is a definitional trick—very little pornography depicts such sadomasochism—but it has not been entirely successful, as we'll see.

Of course, not everyone shares the view that no such distinction between violent and nonviolent pornography should be made; in fact, even most feminists would reject it. (More to the point, most feminists do not support the view that pornography should be criminalized; for a "pro-sex" feminist position, see Snitow, Stansell, and Thompson, 1983, and Vance, 1984.) In fact, one anthology of feminist writings on pornography (Ellis et al., 1988) is replete with pornographic photographs. So, perhaps, we can make a distinction between sexually explicit material that would be *widely* and *conventionally* regarded as violent and sexually explicit material that would *not* be so regarded. For us, the presence of *overt, clearly ascertainable, widely agreed-upon* violence is what defines pornographic material as violent. (We'll let the philosophers answer the question of whether or not a picture of a nude woman, intrinsically and by its very nature, implies violence.) For example, in one study of pornography, violence was defined as "rape, sadomasochism or exploitative/coercive sexual relations" (Scott and Cuvelier, 1987a: 535). To us as sociologists, we have to be able to see concrete violence to define an image as violent—and others have to see it as well; we cannot simply define violence into existence.

Defining pornography as violent if it contains fairly explicit and widely agreed-upon acts of violence allows us to determine objectively the proportion of pornography that is violent versus that which is not. Defined this specifically and concretely, we can say violence tends to be fairly rare in sexually explicit material. One study (Scott and Cuvelier, 1987a, 1987b) found the ratio of violent pictorials to all pictorials in *Playboy* between 1954 and 1983 was 8.6 per thousand; to total pages, it was .78 per thousand. The *Attorney General's Commission on Pornography* (Hudson, 1986), an antipornography document, conducted a study that examined the imagery in sexually explicit material, but refused to report its findings. As the American Civil Liberties Union reveals, only .6 percent of the material the commission examined contained "force, violence, or weapons" (Lynn, 1986: 42). My own examination of advertisements for 500 pornographic videos (see pages 159–162) shows that about 4 percent of these ads describe scenes of simulated rape or forced sex, and 11 percent describe sadomasochism, domination, or humiliation. (Slightly more ads featuring domination depict men being dominated by women than the opposite.) Thus, although violence in pornography is not *extremely* rare, it is *relatively* so; it is far from typical. Interestingly enough, one study (Palys, 1986) found the most hard-core or sexually explicit ("triple X") videos contained less violence and depicted more egalitarian and mutual sexual behavior than *less* sexually explicit "adult" videos.

It is often asserted that, over time, nonviolent pornography is becoming "old hat," passe, and boring to most consumers, and that violent pornography is becoming far more widespread (Longino, 1982: 31–32; Smith, 1976; Malamuth and Spinner, 1980). In fact, recent tabulations (Scott and Cuvelier, 1987a, 1987b; Donnerstein et al., 1987: 88–93) have shown this is not the case; if anything, there was some increase in the proportion of violent pornography from the early to the late 1970s and a decrease since then. There is almost certainly an increase in the *total volume* of violent pornography since the early 1970s, because there has been

Themes in Advertisements for Pornographic Videos

I obtained 27 brochures advertising pornographic videos distributed by seven different firms. Five-hundred separate videos were offered for sale and were described in capsule summaries detailing the activities that took place in them. (I would like to thank the necessarily anonymous pornography collector who assisted me in obtaining this material.) I read the advertisements and coded the themes in these descriptions. All the brochures (except one) were in color; more than half of the capsule descriptions of the videos were accompanied by a tiny still photograph depicting the principal action that takes place in each one. These descriptions tended to be fairly short, containing some five to seven sentences. There were 2,246 themes in these 500 ads, or roughly four-and-a-half themes per ad. There is no way of knowing whether these ads are representative of pornographic videos in general; however, because I obtained them from a wide range of sources gives us some confidence this may be so.

Themes are mentioned in an ad to attract customers; the more frequently certain themes are mentioned in ads, the more likely it is that a wide audience wants to view the action described by that particular theme. Minority themes are, in all likelihood, of interest only to a small minority of potential customers. The correlation between the frequency of themes mentioned and the popularity or desirability of that theme to the mainstream pornography-viewing public is not perfect (although it is likely to be quite strong). Still, if a pornography distributor offers videos for sale that customers do not want to watch, they will not respond to these ads or purchase the videos described in the ads. Of course, minority themes may be extremely desirable to some viewers; but in all likelihood, they are in the minority among pornographic video viewers and purchasers.

As an example of the relationship between the nature of the materials offered for sale and the popularity of those materials, consider the questionnaire asking about customer preferences that was sent out recently by a pornography distributor. "In our endeavor to bring you better videos," the introductory paragraph read, "we need your feedback. We need to know what is good or bad about our videos and what we can do to make them better." The questionnaire asks about the content, quality, and price of specific videos the distributor sells—whether they are superior, good, or poor. At the bottom of the questionnaire, space is provided for comments: "Please list your suggestions on how we may improve our upcoming videos." Clearly, meeting customer demand means selling more videos and earning a greater profit. Just as clearly, the casettes offered by mainstream, high-volume video distributors reflect widespread interest, desire, and satisfaction. What is sold the most is what most customers want and get turned on by. Thus, if certain themes are common, they are the themes reflecting what most pornography viewers want; if certain themes are absent, they simply are not turn-ons for most viewers. Of course, again, minority themes represent minority interests, though they may be highly arousing for that minority.

It can be assumed there is a strong correlation between the action described in an ad and the action that actually takes place in the video itself. Although it is important to study the content of the actual videos (which I did not do), it is also important to know what themes are presented in the advertising brochures, because they indicate what the distributor *thinks* customers want and demand and what, in all probability, they actually *do* want and demand. It seems warranted to assume, if an ad mentions a particular theme, that activity is almost certain to be featured in the video; if a theme is not mentioned, that activity may be depicted in the video, but the likelihood is lower than if the theme were mentioned.

As can be seen in Table 7.1, some themes are present in a high proportion of the ads for hard-core pornographic videos, and some are fairly rare. Only two themes were mentioned by a

TABLE 7.1 Advertisement Themes for Pornographic Videos*

Adultery: 17 (3%)
Anal Sex: 120 (24%)
Analinctus: 5 (1%)
Breasts, large: 28 (6%)
Breasts, sex between: 9 (2%)
Cunnilingus: 48 (10%)
Dildos: 30 (6%)
"Doggie style": 43 (9%)
    Intercourse doggie style: 20 (4%)
    Oral sex doggie style: 23 (5%)
Exhibitionism: 3 (1%)
Fellatio: 280 (56%)
Homosexuality, Male: 3 (1%)
Incest: 15 (3%)
    Father-daughter: 2**
    Mother-son: 2**
    Sisters: 2**
    Brother-sister: 3 (1%)
    Not clear: 6 (1%)
Intercourse: 270 (54%)
Interracial sex: 70 (14%)
    Black man/white woman: 26 (5%)
    White man/black woman: 14 (3%)
    Black woman/white woman: 8 (2%)
    Asian woman: 19 (4%)
    Not clear: 3 (1%)
Kinky sex (not specific): 51 (10%)
Lesbianism: 177 (35%)
Masturbation of the man: 33 (7%)
    Man does it: 5 (1%)
    Woman does it: 28 (6%)
Masturbation of the woman: 33 (7%)
    Man does it: 5 (1%)
    Woman does it: 28 (6%)
Obese woman: 3 (1%)
Objects in vagina (fruit, vibrator, etc.): 8 (2%)
One man, two or more women: 50 (10%)
One woman, two or more men: 43 (9%)
Orgy: 68 (14%)
Penis, huge: 68 (14%)
Pregnant woman: 4 (1%)
Prostitution: 9 (2%)
Rape, forced sex: 18 (4%)
    Man forcing woman: 11 (2%)
    Woman forcing man: 3 (1%)
    Woman forcing woman: 4 (1%)
"Sandwich": 5 (1%)
Semen on woman: 126 (25%)
    Semen on woman's body generally: 69 (14%)
    Semen in woman's face: 57 (11%)
    Woman drinks semen: 1**
Shaved vagina: 5 (1%)
Sit-intercourse: 15 (3%)
"Sixty-nine": 14 (3%)
S/M, domination, humiliation, etc.: 56 (11%)
    Man dominant: 16 (3%)
    Woman dominant: 21 (4%)
    Not clear: 13 (3%)
    Lesbian domination: 6 (1%)

Teenage ("cheerleader," schoolgirl, etc.): 22 (4%)
    Teenage girl: 18 (4%)
    Teenage boy: 4 (1%)
Testicles, licking: 28 (6%)
Transsexual, transvestite, hermaphrodite, etc.: 12 (2%)
Virgin, girl: 11 (2%)
Virgin, boy: 5 (1%)
Voyeurism: 18 (4%)
Younger man or boy with older woman: 6 (1%)
Ads not classifiable as to theme: 41 (8%)
Total number of themes present: 2,246
Total number of videos advertised: 500
Total number of brochures from which these 500 ads were taken: 27

Major Themes in Pornography

Fellatio: 56%
Intercourse: 54%
Lesbianism: 35%
Semen on woman: 25%
Anal sex: 24%
Interracial sex: 14%
Huge penis: 14%
Orgy: 14%
S/M, domination: 11%
One man, two or more women: 10%
Kinky, bizarre: 10%
Cunnilingus: 10%
Doggie Style: 9%
One woman, two or more men: 9%
Masturbation of the woman: 7%
Masturbation of the man: 7%

*Percentages are the percent of the 500 ads that contain each theme.

**Less than one-half of one percent

majority of these ads—fellatio (56 percent), and straight intercourse (54 percent). Lesbianism was also very popular; it appears in over a third of the ads (35 percent). It would be more accurate to describe this action as "pseudolesbianism," since it is not only typically simulated—very few of the women in these videos are actually lesbians—but also, the lesbian action in porno movies and videos is serving heterosexuality: Its message is that some women think they prefer other women sexually, but when they meet the right man, he will convert them to liking men. Semen spurting onto the woman's body is also specifically mentioned in these ads (25 percent); nearly half of the time it is mentioned, it is described as landing on or in the woman's face. (The term used to describe semen spurting onto the woman's body or face is a "splash-off.") Anal sex is mentioned nearly as much as spurting semen (24 percent). Interracial sex, a man with a huge penis, and an orgy each attracted a mention in one out of seven ads (14 percent). Some form of sadomasochism or domination (11 percent), one man having sex with two or more women (10 percent), sex described as "kinky" or "bizarre," or some other comparable term (10 percent), cunnilingus (10 percent), sex "doggie style" (9 percent), and one woman with two or more men (9 percent) were mentioned in roughly 1 out of 10 of these ads.

Overt violence tends to be fairly rare; only 4 percent of the ads featured simulated rape or forced sex (and only 2 percent featured a man raping a woman). And the bondage/domination/sadomasochism theme, though fairly popular, was a minority of the themes mentioned. (Again, the woman acting in the role of dominatrix was more common than the man dominating the woman.) It is also likely that some sadomasochistic action appears in the videos described as "kinky," with no further specification, but the fact that exactly what that entailed was not mentioned is probably significant. All in all, it has to be agreed, the action antiporn feminists describe in their presentations and writings—women "bound, gagged, sliced up, tortured in a multiplicity of ways" (Dworkin, 1982b: 255)—is rare or nonexistent in mainstream hard-core videos. As I said earlier, however, although these activities tend to be rare in pornography, they are common in "slasher" movies and videos.

On the other hand, we cannot doubt that women are used for men's sexual purposes in these videos. There is little or no reciprocity here. Moreover, male dominance in the sex act is a very strong subtext in nearly all pornography that turns men on. The theme of a woman "servicing" a man orally is over five times as common (56 percent) as that of a man "servicing" a woman (10 percent). Women are highly likely to be anally penetrated (mentioned in 25 percent of the ads), an activity which, if it is not done gently, is apt to be painful. The significance of the huge penis theme is that the bigger the man's penis, the more the man can domi-

nate and subdue the woman. The theme of the semen on the woman's body is, likewise, an act of domination and subjugation. The symbolic significance of "doggie style" intercourse or fellatio is that such a position symbolically represents the woman's subservience, that she is, again, *serving* the man sexually. Even the lesbian theme reinforces the idea that the man is the master of the woman in the sexual act. For instance, lesbianism is very rarely the final porn act directed at men—it is almost always followed by the man having intercourse with the woman, thereby demonstrating the sexual superiority of men over women.

Most of the themes in these ads describe acts that imply, either directly or indirectly, male domination. Taken by itself, each act does not *intrinsically* express the dominance of the man and the subordination of the woman. It is in the *context* of the predominance of the male-dominant positions in these videos: that these videos are produced *by* and *for* men—and the context of a sexist society generally—and that the dominance-subordination themes may be inferred from the action described. "The very meaning of representation is largely determined by its social context. For instance, a photo of a woman kneeling down to perform fellatio on a man has a very different social meaning than a picture of a man kneeling down to perform cunnilingus on a woman. The first picture implies subordination, while the second merely implies that a man is giving a woman pleasure" (Valverde, 1987: 126–127).

It would be startling if porno videos did *not* express sexist values. In real life, most men are dominant in their relations with women and in the sex act, and they want things to stay that way. In fact, most men are probably not nearly so dominant in the sex act in real life as they would *like* to be—many more want to engage in the acts portrayed in these videos than we might infer if we imagined the action they contain to represent a slice of real life. But these videos are not an engine of sexism; they are merely a mirror of it. The sexism in these videos does not automatically translate into rape or other acts of brutality; in fact, it does not even cause men to become dominant in their real-life sex acts. Pornography is a distorted reflection of the sexism already deeply entrenched in our society; it is not an independent cause of it. Pornography is not "about" power as the anti-porn feminists claim; that is, these pornographic videos are not manuals to teach men how to subdue women sexually and in other ways. Unequal power in relations between men and women *is* most decidedly reflected in the action in these videos. But as such, the depicted action represents a fantasy that men who purchase them have about how they want their sex lives to be led, and, in some ways, a slice of their actual sexual lives, which is highly likely to be sexist. If porn were to be eliminated overnight, this sexism, both in its milder and everyday forms and its more brutal, vicious forms, would remain. If, one fine day, we were to achieve a sexually equalitarian society, it is highly likely that most of our pornography would be more equalitarian than it is now.

In short, we see in these ads, and presumably in the video tapes themselves, a great deal of sexual domination of women by men. However, we see very little clear-cut, explicit, overt sexual violence. Some feminists regard depictions of sexual domination as symbolic violence and argue that such depictions translate into violence in real life. In doing so, they make three conceptual and empirical leaps of faith: (1) that depictions of phenomena are the same thing as the phenomena themselves, (2) that depictions of (what is to them) symbolic violence is the same as depictions of real violence, and (3) that viewing depictions of (what is to them) symbolic violence results in real-life violence against women. In contrast, most researchers of pornography, who use evidence to document their assertions rather than relying on philosophical assumptions and literary analogies, take the first two assumptions to be false and the third to be an empirical question that can't be assumed in the first place.

an increase in the overall total volume. Still, it is important to make a distinction between violent and nonviolent pornography, to have some sense of how common violent pornography is, and to understand the impact violent and nonviolent pornography have on male consumers.

The Effects of Pornography: Research Findings

Does viewing violent, sexually explicit material cause men to become more violent toward women? Does sexually explicit material by itself, without any violent imagery, cause men to become more violent toward women? Does material depicting violence itself, with no sexually explicit images, cause men to act more violently toward women?

How do we study these questions? Clearly, social scientists cannot show pornographic films or videos to men and then follow them around to see if they engage in aggressive or violent acts against women in real life. Studies on this issue are usually conducted by looking at certain types of aggressive behavior in a laboratory setting. There are at least three problems with this research. First, the men in these experiments are not necessarily the men, or even the *kinds* of men, who actually purchase pornography in real life and on whom the effects of this material are most relevant; the effects of pornography may be significantly different for these two sets of men. Second, the behavior of men in the immediate setting of the laboratory may not necessarily carry over into everyday life. And third, some aggression against women could be noted in these experiments simply because, in them, young men are being sexually aroused by explicit material, but are not afforded the opportunity to satisfy their arousal, which results in some frustration.

Nonetheless, experimental conditions may be the most practical way to study this question. Moreover, research has shown there is a strong correlation between men's behavior in laboratory experiments and their behavior in everyday life (Donnerstein et al., 1987: 101–103, 111; Malamuth et al., 1986). Clearly, such research affords a *clue* to what kind of an effect violent and nonviolent pornography may have on how men treat women.

Since a fair proportion of pornography contains explicit violence, we should be interested in the question of whether it is the sexually explicit nature of pornography, or its violence, that produces any effects on viewers whom we might observe. So we should ask, Does viewing sexually explicit but nonviolent pornography cause men to become more aggressive or violent toward women?

The relationship between viewing *nonviolent but sexually explicit* material and aggressing or acting violently toward women is extremely complex. Sapolsky (1984: 86–95) summarized 10 studies that researched this relationship; the conclusions of some of these studies supported the "hostility-aggression" hypothesis, while those of others did not. In addition, several studies have been conducted since then (Donnerstein et al., 1987: 38–73), with equally inconclusive results. At this point, the best generalization we could make on this relationship is that "there is not enough evidence from laboratory experiments to conclude that exposure to nonviolent pornography leads to increases in aggression against women under most circumstances." Moreover, the "research outside the laboratory is even less conclusive" (Donnerstein et al., 1987: 72, 73). As a general rule, when such inconsistent results are obtained in research, the hypothesized effect tends to be weak and appears only under certain conditions and in some individuals. Clearly, sexual explicitness in pornography, by itself, is not a major determinant of male aggression against women—if it is a determinant at all.

The violence depicted in some pornography (again, a minority genre) is an altogether different matter. It is possible to state conclusively that "exposure to violent pornography will increase aggression against women"; in addition, "it also plays a part in changing the way men think about women" (Donnerstein et al., 1987: xi)—that is, believing more strongly in rape myths (for instance, that all women yearn to be raped), becoming more tolerant and accepting of rape and

other violent acts against women, and believing rapists should receive more lenient punishment or no punishment at all.

In one experiment, men who watched films depicting sexual violence were more likely to administer more electrical shocks to partners than those who watched nonviolent sexual films. In addition, the former administered more shocks specifically to women than the latter (Donnerstein, 1981; Sullivan, 1980; Goleman, 1984). Another study asked 120 male undergraduate volunteers to rate the essays written by partners in an experiment (who were actually confederates of the researcher); they were also instructed to administer shocks to their partners for writing a poor essay. Once again, viewing films depicting violent sex increased the likelihood of administering more shocks and shocks with greater intensity (Baron and Bell, 1977). Another study tested the connection between viewing acts of violence against women and attitudes toward this violence by showing matched groups of students two different types of films—one depicting male aggressive sexual behavior and the second containing no violence at all. A week later, the students in the study filled out a questionnaire. Men who had seen the violent movies, compared with those who had not, were significantly more likely to believe myths about rape (for instance, that women have an unconscious wish to be raped) and to hold more positive attitudes toward aggression against, and the domination of, women (Malamuth and Check, 1981).

In short, "violent pornography can increase aggression against women in a laboratory situation" and can change men's attitudes toward women for the worse (Donnerstein et al., 1987: 96, 100). It has this effect, first, because it presents "the idea that women find sexual violence arousing; second, because it *desensitizes* the viewer to violence through repeated exposure; and third, through the process of *misattribution*—that is, by linking sexually explicit images with violence—the viewer is aroused and misattributes his arousal to the violence, not the sex, thereby associating the two (Donnerstein et al., 1987: 88, 112ff). Significantly, however, depictions of violence against women *devoid of sexual content,* or containing only mildly sexually explicit depictions, also tend to increase men's aggression and hostility toward women as much or nearly as much as violence *with* sexual content. Violence "against women need not occur in a pornographic or sexually explicit context to have a negative effect on viewer attitudes and behavior" (Donnerstein et al., 1987: 112).

One of the principal objections to the findings of the 1970 Commission on Obscenity and Pornography was that the findings of the surgeon general's report on television violence showed that exposure to aggression and violence increased the aggressive and violent acts of viewers, especially children (Donnerstein et al., 1987: 35–36; Diamond, 1982). Thus, the reasoning went, if the media have an impact on aggression and violence, then why doesn't pornography have a similar effect? But this reasoning holds up only if we are looking at *violent* pornography; we should expect an impact here. (Of course, if we regard pornography violent by definition, then our puzzlement should be understandable.) In fact, why should nonviolent erotica result in increases in violence among viewers? In the media studies, the impact of media violence on real-life violence was studied; here, the activities in the media and the activities in real life correspond. On the other hand, in the pornography studies focusing on nonviolent material, how can we assume the depiction of an activity in photographs, film, or video will result in an altogether different activity in real life? Defining something as violent when others do not view it that way means we will make mistaken assumptions about the effects it has on them.

The Question of Criminalization

One major goal in the antipornography agenda is to criminalize violent pornography specifically and all pornography generally because, its advocates claim, porn causes men to act more violently toward women. Yet, as the above studies show, it is possible the emphasis some feminists place on banning pornography may be entirely "misguided." By stressing the pornographic content of pictures, films, and videos, say three psychologists who specialize in studying the impact of pornography, "we ignore the substantial quantity of violence against women contained in R-rated movies. What is particularly troubling about these depictions is their tremendous availability. It is safe to assume that many more people have been exposed to violence against women in this form than have been exposed to violent pornography" (Donnerstein et al., 1987: 112).

If nonsexual violence, or violence with a very mildly sexual content, including that in "slasher" or "splatter" films such as *Texas Chainsaw Massacre, I Spit on Your Grave, Halloween, Friday the 13th, Maniac, 2000 Maniacs, Blood Feast, Color Me Blood Red,* has as strong a negative impact on how men treat women, but is seen by many times the number of men, than is true of violent pornography, then why has the latter and not the former received the attention of feminists? Moreover, the violence in pornography is typically so stylized, artificial, and clearly simulated that it seems incredible anyone would be influenced by it in his or her everyday life; on the other hand, the violence depicted in "splatter" films is extremely realistic and brutally graphic—why not attempt to ban the latter first? Why attempt to criminalize pornography—pornography generally, not just violent pornography? Why not mount a campaign to criminalize "slasher" films, as well as depictions of *all* violence against women in the media—in nonsexual as well as sexual material? Why not attack and criticize violence on television, in advertising, in fiction, and in films generally? What is it about sexually explicit images that moves one wing of the feminist movement to protest against all pornography, whether it is violent or nonviolent? Why are sexual images "fused" in some feminists' minds with violence?

It is unlikely that magically eliminating pornography overnight would have any impact on violence against women. It is, as some "pro-sex" feminists have said, a "false hope" that "without porn, there will be far less male violence," because the elimination of pornography would "leave the oppressive structures of this society perfectly intact" (Snitow, 1988: 16). If "*Hustler* were to vanish from the shelves tomorrow, I doubt that rape or wife-beating statistics would decline," says another "pro-sex" feminist author (Willis, 1983: 463). As human rights activist Aryeh Neier says, there is practically no pornography in many countries of the world (the example he used was El Salvador) where rape and other forms of brutality toward women are common (Brownmiller et al., 1984: 36). The truth is, pornography, especially that which abuses, humiliates, and degrades women, is a *symptom* of female powerlessness, not an independent cause of it. Pornography will become more equalitarian to the extent that the structure of power and wealth are equalitarian; somehow, antipornography feminists have mistaken a symptom for a cause, attacked a reflection of something rather than the thing itself. The question is: Why?

Certainly many feminists are genuinely outraged by pornography, by the very fact it exists, regardless of its impact—especially so by depictions of sexually explicit acts of violence against women, but by sexually explicit images generally. They are puzzled and angered that so many men would so readily and unthinkingly purchase and become aroused by such material. Partly out of ignorance, partly out of a diffuse sense of rage, they become fixated on examples of the more extreme and violent sexual acts in pornography—sadomasochism, rape, depictions of mutilation and murder—imagining that they are typical, that men could possibly pay to watch and become aroused by them. These examples, however rare, are indeed distressing; and they cause one to wonder about the men (and women, if there are any) who experience them as sexually exciting. It would be a mistake to dismiss the rage some feminists feel about pornography and the direct relationship of that rage to the intrinsic nature of pornography itself. And rage, as one politically active "pro-sex" feminist says, is "empowering," it opens the eyes and cleanses the blood; "today's antipornography campaigns achieve their energy by mobilizing a complex amalgam of female rage, fear, and humiliation" (Snitow, 1988: 10). Many antipornography feminists, however mistaken, genuinely *believe* that pornography is the foundation stone of male dominance and male violence against women.

Again, the question is: Why? A "frustration engendered by two decades of working against the most egregious expression of sexism, male violence against women, has led many women, often unfamiliar with pornography . . . , to scapegoat sexual images in their search for the real cause of this seemingly incurable social evil." The elimination of "these pervasive assaults on all women's freedom seems maddeningly distant" (Ellis, O'Dair, and Tallmer, 1988: 6). In their inability to solve the fundamental, very real, day-to-day problems women face in a sexist society, some feminist leaders and theorists have focused on an issue that seems respectable, and the target, disreputable. Pornography seems like a *winnable* issue because it is vulnerable to criminalization and censorship; legitimate, mainstream, conventional industries, like advertising, television, and film, are more influential, more powerful, and, therefore, less vulnerable to reform. In the words of feminist author Lisa Steele (in Burstyn, 1985), pornography may be an easy target compared with the rest of the feminist agenda—equal rights, abortion, and economic justice. It is the very *stigma* that adheres to pornography that is a factor in influencing feminists to attack it.[2]

Contrary to Andrea Dworkin, who believes that all men love pornography and that it is entirely acceptable and consonant

[2]A good contrary example of a critical feminist analysis of the mainstream media is Betty Segal's three-part videotape, *The Power of Suggestion*. Daytime television soap operas are "the most widely consumed form of entertainment in the Western world," and, Segal argues, their hidden message is the legitimation of violence against women. It is possible that soap operas prepare women to accept the violence men inflict upon them far more than pornography stimulates men to inflict violence upon women. If this is so, does it not seem reasonable that soap operas should be a far greater target of criticism and analysis by feminists than pornography?

with the values of our violent, sexist, patriarchical society, most Americans believe pornography is a deviant, stigmatized phenomenon. As we saw earlier, a 1985 *Newsweek*–Gallup Poll revealed nearly three-quarters (73 percent) of all Americans believe pornography leads some people to commit rape, and about the same proportion (76 percent) feel it leads some people to lose respect for women. These figures represent an increase since 1970, when the comparable statistics were 49 and 43 percent, respectively, which shows that pornography is becoming less reputable and more deviant over time. Moreover, the percentage of Americans who want to totally ban sexually explicit materials depicting violence is 73 percent for magazines, 68 percent for films, and 63 percent for videos. For magazines, theaters, and videos that simply show adults having sexual relations, the comparable figures were 47, 40, and 32 percent (Hudson, 1986: 927, 933).

Interestingly enough, Women Against Pornography has capitalized on conventional, moralistic antipornography sentiment by forging an alliance with conservatives, the Far Right, and Christian fundamentalists, who oppose many items on the feminist agenda, such as the Equal Rights Amendment and abortion. Many liberals and radicals have criticized the movement for this alliance, arguing that it hurts progressive reforms generally, even though it may give WAP a great deal of power and clout in the short run (Duggan, 1988; Duggan et al., 1988; Willis, 1983). Answers Dworkin, "When women get raped they're not asked first whether they're Democrats or Republicans." She takes help where she can get it, she says, because "pornography shows clearly how the Left has betrayed women— they're entirely corrupt" (Press et al., 1985: 66). Tactics aside, this uneasy alliance provides strong evidence *against* the position of Women Against Pornography, since their position is that pornography is a cornerstone of patriarchy, or male dominance— and the conservative right *supports* patriarchy and strongly *opposes* pornography!

In fact, most Americans are ambivalent about pornography. "They want access to conventional erotica while suppressing more extreme forms" (McGrath, 1985). On the one hand, most of the public—both male and female—doesn't like pornography, at least, its more violent forms; doesn't purchase it; wishes it would go away; and feels it does bad things to men and women. On the other hand, a sizable proportion of the public believes that if a phenomenon or an activity does not pose a clear, present, or immediate danger to society, certain constitutional rights should be respected. Although some feminists (Dworkin, 1982b) have explicitly stated they have little but contempt for freedom of speech and other constitutional guarantees if these conflict with their own personal or political goals, most Americans do not agree.

One indication of the conflict between the goals and methods of the antipornography movement and the Constitution is the law (which is summarized in Donnerstein et al., 1987: 139–141; and Ellis et al., 1988: 88), written by two leading feminist antipornography spokespersons, Andrea Dworkin and Catherine MacKinnon (1987). Designed to permit all women to sue producers and distributors of pornography because it is a form of sex discrimination, it was vetoed by the mayor in liberal Minneapolis in 1983, declared unconstitutional in conservative Indianapolis in 1984, and voted down by the moderate Suffolk County legislature in 1984. These defeats of antipornography legislation show that, in spite of the stigma that adheres to pornography, many legislators and jurists are not convinced that its less violent forms are truly harmful. Moreover, enough political representatives of the U.S. electorate believe a clamp-down on pornography represents a sufficiently serious violation of constitutional rights that legislation should not be used to eliminate it. More important, the proposed law would have included violent and nonviolent sexual images and would have resulted in banning not only truly harmful pornography and soft-core porn such as *Playboy*, but also works of art, sexually explicit but relatively innocuous images, and some medical and psychological material (Duggan et al., 1988; Duggan and Snitow, 1984). In short, the definitional reach of the antiporn feminists is far too broad. Relatively little pornography contains the violence they claim is typical. Although the examples of violent pornography they parade in their antiporn presentations and demonstrations are truly disturbing, they simply have not convinced enough Americans, or some American lawmakers and judges, that they are typical of pornography in general.

The pornography issue is fascinating for a number of reasons. One is that it is a textbook case of a movement's attempt to generate or strengthen the public's sense of moral outrage over a specific issue. If the movement really did have criminalization as its goal, it is possible the effort was doomed to fail; it is also possible the effort has been handled badly. In any case, one interesting aspect of this effort is that some of the very things that outrage feminists and, they believe, strengthen their case actually make their job more difficult. It can be stated as a dilemma, a dilemma that faces all movements attempting to mobilize the support of the general public. On the one hand, public outrage is a valuable resource in mobilizing the goals of Women Against Pornography—that is, removing violent and sexist images from the media—and nothing mobilizes public outrage more than the claim that the evil is widespread. On the other hand, *if images that exploit women are as widespread as the antipornography feminists say, then those images must be an integral part of conventional society.* And if this is true, then it is much more difficult to eradicate them. If violence has seeped into advertising, mainstream films shown in family theaters, even television programming, then a movement that has far more support than Women Against Pornography would be necessary to eliminate it. If low-key sex is used to sell cars, cigarettes, even household products, what herculean effort would it take to remove it from advertising? Speaking out against the conventionalization of sexism and violence in the media may make theoretical sense, but it does not make tactical sense; attacking conventional, deeply entrenched institutions and practices simply underscores the impossibility of the task.

Pornography is one of those activities and institutions that is *deviant but tolerated.* There are at least three different forms of toleration that blunt the antipornographers' efforts. The first is *constitutional tolerance.* Even many individuals who wish pornography would disappear from the face of the earth do not support vigorous antiporn criminalization and censorship because they believe such actions would infringe on individuals' rights of free speech. (Child pornography, incidentally, is not protected by the First Amendment.) Second is the *tolerance of related material.* The question is Where do we draw the line? Many Americans are not able to etch a specific type of pornography out of the universe of sexually explicit material and feel comfortable about banning it. If violent porn is banned, then what about only mildly erotic, but far more violent, "slasher" films? If *Hustler* is to be banned, then what about *Playboy?* If *Playboy,* what about pornographic art? Mainstream advertising that suggests violence against women? Medical texts? Nudist magazines featuring photos of families playing volleyball in the buff? In spite of feminist claims, it is not possible to draw a sharp line between types of sexually explicit material to the satisfaction of most observers. The third is *tolerance of pornography itself.* Most Americans do not purchase pornography, but a substantial minority does. Soft-core and nonviolent hard-core pornography is big business; whenever an activity is participated in by a substantial segment of the population, it is difficult to criminalize. Roughly 40 percent of all VCR owners bought or rented an X-rated cassette during all of 1985 (Press et al., 1985: 61); the figure is certainly substantially higher in 1991. Antiporn feminists expressing outrage at the size of the pornography business simply emphasize that their efforts to eradicate it will almost inevitably fail.

The example of pornography teaches us that stigma is often ambivalent and rarely total in any large, complex society, and that the effort to criminalize an activity often contradicts other values that society holds dear. In their crusade to ban a certain activity, moral entrepreneurs must encounter a feeble or divided opposition, command an extremely powerful following, or violate few widely accepted, conventional values. The antipornography movement has failed to mobilize enough negative sentiment against pornography to criminalize it, partly because most Americans simply do not believe it is as bad as radical feminists say it is.

Antiporn feminists have made three mistakes in interpretation. The first mistake is assuming "because it offends me, it must have bad effects." In fact, many patently offensive phenomena do not have effects that all of us would agree are noxious. The second mistake is the assumption that "if it offends me, it must be equally as offensive to most other people—or at least, it *ought* to be." This has not proven to be the case. People interpret things differently, and no amount of haranguing will make someone feel something when that feeling is not already there. And the third mistake of antipornography feminists is imposing an interpretation on pornography that participants do not necessarily share. Feminists cannot understand why anyone would find pornographic material sexually arousing; and so they interpret it in a way they *can* understand—that is, the subordination and humiliation of another human being. How can that be sexy? they ask; it's not sexy *to me.* Therefore, it must have a nonsexual meaning. Or, the sexual meaning must derive from a nonsexual source—it's sexy *because* the woman is dominated by the man. What I see there is the exercise of *power* by one individual over another; therefore, that's what it must mean to anyone who looks at it and enjoys it—that must be the reason *why* men read, look at, or view pornography. This is a fairly basic and fundamental fallacy, yet it is extremely common. We cannot make the assumption that others will always understand or experience a given activity or phenomenon as we do. Unless we put ourselves in the shoes of those who participate in an activity, our understanding of it will be hollow and meaningless.

The efforts of antipornography feminists to demonologize pornography have not, for the most part, been successful. If their goal, however, is to make the American public more aware of the dangers of pornography, their efforts have been successful; antipornography sentiment is much stronger today than it was in the late 1960s and early 1970s, possibly due in part to the efforts of Women Against Pornography. On the other hand, if antipornography feminists wish to criminalize pornography and make it significantly more unobtainable, clearly they must rethink their theory and tactics.

It is clear from their writings that the antiporn feminists do not consider the impact of pornography the main issue. Indeed, it is even beside the point. Naturally, they assume pornography, which is offensive to them, will have undesirable consequences—the old "evil causes evil" fallacy. This is, of course, an empirical issue and cannot be assumed in the first place. Suppose it were demonstrated, conclusively and convincingly, that pornography does not have the consequences attributed to it by its critics? Most would say it doesn't matter. The issue of the impact of porn is, in reality, empirical window dressing, a logical-sounding argument to shore up a deeply felt moral and ideological position. Pornography, the Women Against Pornography supporters would say, *does not deserve to exist*—regardless of its impact. *Its very existence* is an offense against women, they say, and for that reason alone, it should be criminalized. A parallel here can be seen in the reaction to Salman Rushdie's book *The Satanic Verses* in 1989. Many Muslims around the world found the book an offense against the prophet Muhammad and against Islam generally. Not because it was likely to arouse anyone to do anything evil, they said, but because the very existence of certain phrases in the book was *inherently* offensive to the faithful. The central fact of pornography for the antiporn feminist is that it is a *blasphemy* against women. And this is specifically why their campaign is doomed to failure: A substantial proportion of the American public and the legal community do not regard the fact that certain depictions or materials are offensive to some as a sufficiently compelling reason to prohibit their distribution. Most Americans, and most legal scholars, would say that these materials must do some real-world damage to justify their prohibition—and it is this empirical damage that has not been adequately documented. Perhaps it never will be.

ACCOUNT: INTERVIEW WITH A PORNOGRAPHER

The informant is 30 years old and works in the entertainment industry. I am the interviewer. ("Q" indicates my questions; "A" indicates the answers the respondent gave to my questions.)

Q: Why don't you tell me a little bit about this movie that you made.

A: I feel, like many men, that I've been treated badly by women and that the more I try to be nice to them, the more license it gives them to treat me worse. And I think many men feel this way. Basically, the idea of the movie was to concentrate on the damsel in distress: girls tied up, girls being knocked around, spat upon, kicked around, punched, beaten up. The movie is a soft-core kind of a pornography, a soft X rather than a hard X: There's no nudity. In my movie, women are terrorized. Women are not fucked in the movie at all—they're *fucked over*. Every scene has a woman being taken advantage of against her will, forced to do something sexual, like a strip-tease or suck a dildo or take a punch. It's an exploitation movie. The idea is to appeal to the darker side of the prurient interest of men. I think more exciting than naked girls and stuff like that is the resistance—you know, the rape fantasy, forcing a girl against her will. That's a more striking screen image than the touching, sensitive love story, which I find terribly boring. Another thing is, they're all women in the movie. There are no men in the film, not even an off-screen voice of a man.

Q: Give me a typical scene, a couple of scenes.

A: Okay, one typical scene is a woman who is dressed for the Governor's Ball comes to the door: full evening gown, red, very nice and tight and clinging; bouffant hairdo; long white gloves; too much make-up; big, long ear-rings. She goes to the door and a lady cop bursts in the door, knocking her down, throwing up her skirt so you can see her legs and all that. Before the woman can protest, she's tied up and frisked, with the hands passing all over her, underneath the skirt. The victim is not enjoying it at all, but the lady cop's enjoying herself tremendously, much the same way a lascivious man cop would. So the lady cop talks about how much she digs it and then she frisks her, ties her up, spanks her, accuses her of some ridiculous crime, like, selling heroin to kindergarten kids, before she discovers, ah-hah! big surprise—that she's got the wrong woman. The cop turns aside and goes. "Hey, don't tell her, but I knew it all the time." She turns back and says, "Sorry lady—these things happen," and she walks out. That's one of the scenes in the movie.

Q: What about another one?

A: Another one involves what I call the CARLA—Computerized Anthropomorphic Responding Love Automaton: C·A·R·L·A. One of the first uses that somebody will consider in making robots, artificial people is, you know, the sex dolls. Similar to the sort of thing that you buy in Times Square and blow up, except *infinitely* more sophisticated. This is a device, a machine, that any man will be proud to own. In the office, it never forgets appointments. It never shows up late. It's completely reliable, 100 percent efficient. Also, it can be a personal bodyguard. It has faster reflexes than a real person. Somebody pulls out a gun and points it at you, it steps in front of you. It's 10 times stronger than a real girl. It can easily double as jack for your car, but its real purpose of course is to jack up your spirits. At home, it's the perfect housekeeper and the equivalent of a master chef. And, of course, at your leisure, it can be programmed to have any kind of sexual response you want. You can program it to occasionally give you a hard time. And if it gives you too bad a time, you can knock it around and not have any fears of hurting anybody, 'cuz it's not a body, it's a *thing*. It can be programmed so that, like, 15 to 20 times a year, it won't let you fuck it no matter *what* you do. You can take your frustrations out on her. It's the perfect wife. Not only that, but the longer it lives with you, the more hip it becomes to your personal idiosyncracies, so the longer you own the machine, the more personal it becomes to you. So after a while, it'll put real women out of business.

Q: Was it hard to get women to act in this movie?

A: It was a big problem at first. I jerked around for a long time trying to ask women that I knew personally or guys who knew women that they could turn me on to. They'd get three or four pages into the script and they'd, like, run screaming into the night. Well, not literally, but figuratively. I'd have to stop and change the subject and then forget all about it.

Q: What do you think they were reacting against?

A: Well, the dialogue is actually what they were turned off about it, because the dialogue is one long, nonstop profanity. You never hear girls talking like that, at least, not unless they're, like, in the bathroom with themselves or something. But the thing was, when I found the right medium to advertise for actresses, I had no trouble whatsoever getting girls to act in the film. I had many more women than I needed. I realized that the type of woman I would have to use would have to be a regular actress. I simply approached them as an actress-type gig. I said, this is an exploitation film, but here's the criteria: there's a lot of profanity and so on. And for them, it was strictly a job.

Q: Do you think that this profanity that's in your movie is what's appealing to some men who would [go to] a movie?

A: I don't *think* it's appealing to some men—I *know* it's appealing to *a great many men.*

Q: Dirty talk?

A: *Absolutely!* The most popular pornographic film ever made was a movie called *Talk Dirty to Me.* That's what the boys'll buy.

Q: How do you think women would react to your movie?

A: Most women wouldn't go for this type of stuff. I think most women would watch the movie I made for a few seconds before they put their fist through the screen. Even most so-called levelheaded or even-tempered women would be *deeply offended* by this film. Actually, the feminists wrote my script for me. Everything that they complain about is *just* what I wanted to put in the movie. The last bit, the bit about the CARLA, is where women are *literally reduced* to sexual toys for the pleasure and amusement of men. I mean, that's the bottom rung of the ladder, that's as low as you can go.

Q: If you were to tell somebody about this movie, like a friend, or a woman you met in a bar or something, what would you say?

A: I wouldn't necessarily discuss my project with just anybody that I'd meet. You see, I'm pretty closed-mouthed about my private life, and I consider this my private life. It's something hot for me to jerk off to in the middle of the night, 'cuz I *love* pornography. With me, it's the last drug I'll give up after Coca-Cola. It's very much like a drug for me. I hafta have it, and quite a bit of it. Usually the stuff that's available is weak. It gets me very high, but only for a short time. And then I need more. I never get any of the good stuff. So I decided I could do it better.

Q: So what you're saying is that there's a personal connection between your own tastes and what gets you excited and what you're doing to make money.

A: Absolutely. There's no way I can say that I'm coldly detached from the whole thing. No. I picked this particular subject and topic because I knew it would have to be something that I liked and something that would, you know, turn me on, too.

Q: Well, one time I was at your house and you had this stack of, um, bondage magazines. Looking at those magazines is what turns you on?

A: Yeah. Ever since I was a kid, maybe 15. It's only in bondage magazines and a few other specialized magazines that you get women in glasses, women in lingerie, skirts, costumes, uniforms—*anything.* What's suggested in the bondage magazines is that somebody's being taken advantage of or somebody using their body to take advantage of a situation. In some of these magazines, with the pure bondage, women strive to be, like expressionless on their face. You get the very, very beautiful women in the absolute, strict bondage. The face, and the expressions, even when one woman's tying up another one, would be completely blank, or eyes closed. Never struggling against the bonds, only *in bondage.*

Q: That's interesting. I think, well, I guess most men, if they wanted to jerk off, they'd want to look at a picture of a woman who's completely naked.

A: How can you say that about most men? Most of the guys I hang out with, all they ever talk about is kink. *High* heels (bangs on the table), *make*-up (bang), *lip*stick (bang), *ear*rings (bang), *slit* skirts (bang). Yeah, man. Absolutely.

Q: Okay, so how does this carry over into your personal life?

A: It doesn't. I never get a chance to tie up any of the women that I go out with. They'd think I was nuts and wouldn't go out with me. So I pretty much stick with the fantasy.

Q: Interesting. What would you do if you met a woman who'd go along with it? Would that make it more exciting than the pictures?

A: Gee, it's hard to say. There's a real danger in realizing your fantasies. I'm pretty happy the way it is now. Occasionally, I think almost anybody gets a little rough in their lovemaking. It's a very loving kind of a thing. You understand that what I'm talking about in bondage and lovemaking is not beating people up or anything like that, but it's, like, tying your girlfriend to a chair while you feel her up, or tying her to a chair while you fuck her in the face, or tying her to the bed while you make love to her, or something like that. It can be stimulating, it can be a turn on. I think a lot of men have it in the back of their minds, even the most civilized and gentlemanly of men, that, one or two times, when, boy, if I could have given that bitch a good (slaps his hands together) *crack,* boy, I sure would'a felt a lot better! And believe me, I'm not a physical person or anything; I've never been in a fight in a bar. It's the monsters from the id. That's why we have laws and religion—we're all monsters in our subconscious. And women, the most liberated of women, will wink at the boss to get by a tough situation. And when it comes to that, *so much* for your ERA. Women will still occasionally use their physical attractiveness to take advantage of a situation. Don't you agree?

Q: I think that there's a certain proportion of women who don't do it at all.

A: (Angrily.) *Bullshit!* Oh, well, the ones that are physically unattractive, yeah.

Q: I've met a number of women who are beyond this stuff.

A: Unless you spend your entire life with all of those women, you can't say that. Because maybe they would never do it to you. Maybe with you, they know that intellect or wit or charm will work a lot better.

Q: So you think this feeling of, like, hostility toward women gets translated into a certain kind of sex act?

A: (Loudly, almost shouting.) *Am I the first guy to tell you that there's a lot of hostility involved in male sexuality?*

Q: I'm getting you to spell it out. I'm being naive on purpose. It's an interviewer's tactic.

A: Oh, I see. I'm being manipulated. That's okay; manipulate away, man.

Q: So what I'm asking is whether you see a connection between this feeling of hostility that you sometimes feel toward women and the type of sexual acts that you were describing before involving bondage and things like that—do you see any connection there?

A: It's pretty obvious, really. There's an old, established connection between sex and violence. You have only to look as close as the animal kingdom. Attacking and biting each other is part of the courtship and mating ritual. So there's really no reason why it shouldn't extend to *Homo sapiens* as well. Basically, there's still that hunter-killer thing there. All we have to do is walk down the street and see the hickeys on people's necks and scratches on people's backs and stuff and then you have exactly what it is I'm talking about. This fetish thing, though, I'm appealing to what would be probably a very small minority of men. But such guys would be willing to pay for it as long as they could get what they wanted.

Q: Did you ever work these routines into your actual lovemaking?

A: No. Let me tell you more about the movie than about my personal life. (From the author's files.)

ACCOUNT: ENCOUNTER WITH PORNOGRAPHY

The informant is a 40-year-old writer. His reaction to an experience in a Times Square pornography parlor was quite different from the attitude described by the first informant.

I had a meeting with one of my publishers in an office on Fifth Avenue in the forties, and after that one was over, I had a couple hours to kill before my next appointment, so I decided to wander around Times Square and check out the scene. I had seen a couple of porno movies before, and I had seen hookers propositioning customers in various parts of the city, but nothing I had ever witnessed prepared me for what I saw that day. I walked into the biggest porno parlor on 42nd Street and started looking around. As far as I could tell, there were three activities going on there.

The first was the booths. You step in, close the door, face a small screen, and insert a quarter into a slot and watch a few minutes of a crude, grainy, scratchy, silent porno movie. When the time is up, the screen goes dead. You can keep watching one till the end, paying another quarter each time the movie stops, or you can move on to another booth and watch a different movie. Outside of each booth on the door, there's a still shot depicting the movie's main theme—bestiality, bondage, a woman with huge breasts, a man with a huge penis, a sex scene between a black and a white person, and so on. To give you some idea of what goes on in these booths, there were several men walking around the place, with mop and pail in hand, cleaning up what the guys had left behind on the walls and the floors of the booths. Leaving a booth, I passed by an employee who had just made change for a customer. He turned to me and smiled and said, "I don't know what that guy had on his hand, but it was wet and sticky." Okay, these movies were pretty much what you'd expect—sleazy porn.

The second thing that was going on there was that there were scantily clad women wandering around the halls of this joint asking the men to join them in four-by-four glass stalls, where they'd draw the blinds and do whatever it is that they do. I imagine it's all negotiable—the activity and the amount the man pays. All that was was prostitution in glass stalls, so I wasn't all that shocked by that, either.

Upstairs, there were more booths, just like the porno booths, but with no pictures on the doors. Loud rock music was playing inside, on the other side of the back wall of the booths. You step in and close the door. Facing you is a small window maybe one foot wide and two feet high, covered by some sort of a yellow shield. You put a quarter in a slot, and the shield lifts up, and you find yourself staring into a room occupied by maybe five or six women, completely naked, sort of swaying to the music. The thing is, when the shield lifts up, there's no pane on the window—the shield was the pane—so you can just reach right into the room where the women are swaying to the music. And it's not just you, but there's maybe ten other guys staring into the room from the other booths.

A woman came over to me, stood right in front of the open window, and asked, "Would you like to touch me?" I was stunned—shocked, really. I'm not sure why. It all seemed so raw, vulgar and, well, *dirty*. I shook my head and she wandered off, looking for other potential customers. Four or five of the other guys in the booths reached their hands into the room, grabbing the women, clutching their breasts, fingering their vaginas, stroking them all over, as they bobbed and swayed to the music. To me—and this is going to sound *melodramatic* or something—it seemed like a vision of *hell*. The lights were bright and harsh, the music was blaring, and all these men were reaching through these small windows to fondle women who were clutching huge wads of one-dollar bills, as they bobbed up and down to the music, pretending, in a halfhearted way, to be enjoying themselves.

After a few minutes, the yellow shield closed, and I left the booth, walked down the stairs and out onto 42nd Street, feeling sick. I kept thinking: This whole thing is so *degrading,* why would anyone, man or woman, want to do something like that? Does that make me a prude? I don't know. All I know is, that scene made me feel that the human body and spirit were being degraded. (From the author's files.)

CHAPTER
8

Male and Female Homosexuality

Considering how frequently homosexual acts are engaged in and how common male and female homosexuals are in the population, the depth of public misconceptions concerning both should be astonishing. In one of the most popular books on sex ever published, *Everything You Wanted to Know About Sex But Were Afraid to Ask,* physician David Reuben displays his abysmal ignorance on the subject of homosexuality, parading myth and misconception as truth. Lesbians, Reuben claims, commonly use a dildo, or artificial phallus, "held in place with an elastic harness," so that "an unreasonable facsimile of heterosexual intercourse is possible" (1969: 218). Male homosexuals, he writes, because they "find their man-to-man sex unfulfilling," frequently masturbate while forcing a carrot or cucumber, lubricated with vegetable oil, into their anus, or have intercourse with a melon, a canteloupe, or, "where it is available," a papaya (1969:

129, 142, 147). It is not altogether clear just how Dr. Reuben gathered this information; it is at any rate, nonsense—although instructive of the prevailing ignorance on the subject. Although some lesbians do engage in dildo sex (Byron, 1985), it is a small, minority phenomenon. And my guess is that having intercourse with fruit (and here, a watermelon seems a likely target!) is more common among heterosexual than homosexual males.

HOMOSEXUALITY: ESSENTIALISM VERSUS SOCIAL CONSTRUCTIONISM

There are two basic ways to view the reality of homosexuality: through the *essentialist* model and through the *social constructionist* model (Goode, 1981: 58f; Plummer, 1981a: 54f; Troiden, 1988: 101–122; Greenberg, 1989). Most psychiatrists and other physi-

173

cians, many psychologists, a few sociologists, and, for the most part, the man and woman on the street, see homosexuality through the essentialist model. Most sociologists and anthropologists, and some psychologists, see the reality of homosexuality through the prism of the social constructionist model.

The essentialist argues that homosexuality, like heterosexuality, is a natural, universal category that exists independent of culture, time, or situation. It exists a priori or *before* it is defined by any particular society; it is a *pregiven* entity, much like stars, frogs, or orchids. Homosexuality is a concretely real phenomenon with more or less identical basic properties the world over. Just as "a rose is a rose is a rose," to the essentialist, a homosexual is a homosexual is a homosexual—a specific type of being, identifiable by hard, reliable measures or indicators. Somewhere lurking within each homosexual are clear-cut manifestations of his or her "homosexualness." Every scientifically informed observer should agree as to the exact nature of someone's sexual classification. It is nature that accurately divides the human world into homosexuals and heterosexuals, not members of the culture, the subculture, or the particular scene in which these humans live and act. In this sense, homosexuals and heterosexuals are as clearly distinguishable from one another as apples and oranges or rubies and diamonds (Troiden, 1988: 101). Essentialists typically apply the disease analogy to homosexuality and see it much like a *condition* that one "has." In medicine, for example, experts diagnose patients to determine whether they have cancer, diabetes, or an ulcer; experts can determine whether someone "has" homosexuality in the same way. (The difference is that homosexuality is usually regarded by essentialists as a condition that *saturates* the person, that is thoroughly and completely "in" someone, whereas diseases are generally seen as external invasions, not an aspect of someone's "true," indwelling self.)

Essentialists regard the fundamental reality of homosexuality as residing in *sexual orientation*, sexual *preference*, or sexual *feelings*. To them, sexual behavior is secondary; what

counts is erotic desire. Some men and women have sex with persons of the same gender in contexts that call for it—in prison, for instance, or in some societies in ritualistic contexts. Likewise, some men and women have sex mainly or exclusively with members of the opposite gender, but lust after same-sex partners—for example, "closet" gays who are married and keep their desires hidden. Essentialists are concerned with the question of whether or not someone is a "true" homosexual or a "pseudo" homosexual (Socarides, 1978: 100–101). Someone who engages in situational homosexuality may not be a "true" homosexual—that is, does not have the homosexual's fundamental motivation or etiology, or display the homosexual's essential traits. Contrarily, someone who never engages in homosexual behavior may actually be a "true" homosexual, because he or she harbors those traits. What is crucial about homosexuality to the essentialist is the etiology of sexual orientation—that is, what *causes* someone to prefer same-sex partners. Little else is of any consequence about the phenomenon of homosexuality (Whitam, 1977, 1983; Whitam and Mathy, 1986).

In contrast, the social constructionist believes homosexuality is not a concrete, universally agreed-upon reality, but a phenomenon that exists because of the way it is defined socially, culturally, and situationally. What homosexuality "is," social constructionists argue, is what collectivities believe it to be. Its "essential reality" is not a constant or a universal, but varies according to the settings within which it appears. There are no definitive, absolute criteria for what homosexuality "is" or who "is" a homosexual. Rather, there are *dimensions* of homosexuality, which are regarded as crucial in defining its reality; those dimensions vary in importance from one society or culture to another, one social context to another, or one historical time period to another. Also, the *content* of homosexuality varies enormously—the norms, values, and practices that are accepted among homosexuals are characteristic in one time and place and absent in others. In other words, "being" a homosexual is experienced differently, according to the social context within which it takes place. And what it means to "be" a homosexual also varies considerably: It is a savagely stigmatized category at one time and in one place, tolerated in another, encouraged in a third, and required in a fourth.

The constructivist argues that homosexuality can be looked at as a social *role* (McIntosh, 1968; Goode, 1981; Weeks et al., 1981)—that is, a set of norms, beliefs, and practices one learns as a member of a particular culture or subculture. In some societies, this role is lacking; same-gender sexual context appears, and may even be, extremely common, but there is no such thing as homosexuality as such—no such homosexual role. In other societies, some men and women are called homosexuals and are expected to do, and not to do, certain things; if not, they are punished by others called homosexuals and by the heterosexual majority. And in the many contexts in which the role exists, homosexuality manifests itself differently—here, one set of rules, and there, a different set. Same-gender sexual behavior does not assume universal outlines everywhere. In ancient Greece, men who made love with individuals of the same gender chose adolescent boys as partners, not other adult men. Yet they were expected to marry, have sex with women, and raise children (Dover, 1978; Hoffman, 1980). In the United States, adult male homosexuals have sex with one another and rarely have sex with women once they decide they are gay; in this country today, homosexuality and heterosexuality are seen as mutually exclusive, one precluding the other. Both institutions are called homosexuality, and they are similar in that same-gender sex is involved; but what homosexuality *means* and how it is *experienced* in these two settings are radically different.

Among the Sambia (Herdt, 1987), same-gender sex is required of *every single male* for a period of 10 to 15 years (see "Ritual Homosexuality among the Sambia of New Guinea," pages 176–177). In contrast, the straight majority in the United States prefers that *no one* engage in homosexual behavior, and most Americans look on homosexuals with con-

tempt. In prison, men who act as the aggressor or insertor in sex with other men are regarded as supremely heterosexual; men who act out or are forced to play the passive or insertee role are regarded as girlish, effeminate, weak, and therefore homosexual (Wooden and Parker, 1982). The social constructionist would argue that what homosexuality "is" is how it is regarded and defined in its many contexts. In prison, it is the insertee who is regarded as homosexual, not the insertor; most people who have no knowledge of sex in prisons would see both as homosexual behavior. What the Sambia do would be seen by most Americans as homosexual in nature, even though the Sambia would define as homosexual only same-gender sexual contact that takes place outside a ritualistic context. To the social constructivist, there is no universal essence that defines the reality of homosexuality, only these varying cultural, social, situational, and historical definitions.

In a sense, the argument between the essentialists and the constructionists is an argument not only about what is true but what is crucial to look at; in this sense, they are talking past one another. Phenomena that constructionists regard as important and interesting essentialists dismiss as irrelevant and trivial. Essentialists focus on sexual preference; in contrast, constructionists examine a wide range of phenomena revolving around same-gender sexual contact. Says one essentialist: "Homosexuality is . . . a sexual orientation and no useful purpose can be served by regarding it as anything else" (Whitam, 1977: 2). In other words, it matters not that men and women who are "truly" heterosexual have homosexual sex in prison; that supremely masculine men—pirates, warriors, bandits—have often engaged in homosexual acts when they are in exclusively same-gender company, but are otherwise exclusively heterosexual; that the content of the homosexual role or subculture varies so much from one society to another; that "homosexuals" are bisexual in their behavior in one place and exclusively homosexual in another; that in some societies, boys and adolescent men are expected to be,

Ritual Homosexuality among the Sambia of New Guinea

New Guinea is a large island north of Australia and southeast of Southeast Asia; the eastern half of the island is called Papua New Guinea. Formerly a protectorate of Australia, Papua New Guinea is now an independent country. Until fairly recently, most of the cultures of New Guinea were extremely warlike and had engaged in combat with their neighbors for centuries. The former colonial Australian government banned traditional warfare that took place among tribes in their territory, and, for the most part, its efforts were successful.

Sambia society, like most of New Guinea, is based on warfare; in spite of the ban on fighting among their traditional enemies, every Sambia man regards himself as a warrior who stands ready to engage in lethal combat if necessary. As a general rule, warrior societies are profoundly mysogynist—that is, based on hostility toward women and the inherent superiority of men. As with nearly all societies based on warfare, the contrast between male and female is the foundation of Sambian beliefs and practices. The men fear their loss of strength and virility—what they regard as their masculinity. Masculinity, Sambia men believe, is easily depleted; it must be constantly renewed through ritual. Women contaminate and weaken boys, prevailing Sambia beliefs hold; they must be protected and envigorated by adult men. The key to infusing masculinity into young boys is ritual homosexuality.

From age 7 to 10, Sambia boys are separated from the women and children of their village and initiated into an all-male society, located in its own exclusive hamlet, where the boys remain for the next 10 to 15 years. During that time, they regularly engage in homosexual activities, "first as the fellator (insertee) and then as the older fellated (insertor)." At marriage, which takes place between the ages of 18 and 25, youths are bisexual, engaging in sex with both initiated boys and women. With the advent of fatherhood, when a Sambian man's wife gives birth to his first child, all homosexual activities cease; he becomes exclusively heterosexual. However, when the new cycle of initiating boys into the all-male cult begins, he engages in ritual homosexuality with the new crop of boys (Herdt, 1987: 6). Adult men never have sex with other men, and their homosexuality with boys and adolescents is usually dominated by its ritual significance. Some Sambian men continue to have sex with adolescents, a deviant practice there, but always as the insertor, never as the fellator. Fellating boys "is strictly forbidden, is immoral, and would be regarded as unspeakably unmanly" (Herdt, 1981: 252).

In American society, in contrast, *most* of the homosexual behavior between older and much younger males takes place with the older male acting as the fellator and the younger man, the insertor. In contrast to the prevailing (and mistaken) view that predominates in the United States, the Sambia do not see homosexuality as a denial of masculinity; in fact, to them, it is "the only means through which it is attained" (Herdt, 1987: 10). The male body is seen to be incapable of manufacturing its own semen; it must be externally acquired and renewed. Fellatio is the concrete means by which boys attain semen and, therefore, their strength and masculinity. Prior to initiation into the warrior cult, boys are seen as being polluted by their mothers and, therefore, soft and weak. For boys to reach puberty requires semen, which, in turn, requires the cult initiations based on homosexual practices. Without exception, every single Sambian man is initiated into the cult; there are no exceptions. "No Sambia man exists who is uninitiated" (Herdt, 1987: 111), and this includes a mentally retarded man, another who is regarded as mentally ill, and a third who is blind.

The Sambia do not see homosexuals as effeminate; in fact, there are no effeminate homosexuals among the Sambia. More specifically, in Sambia, there are very few homosexuals as such; there are boys and young men who, following custom, practice exclusive homosexual relationships for more than a decade, then practice bisexuality for a time, and then, finally, are exclusively heterosexual. In short, although behavior we would see as homosexual exists among the Sambia—behavior between two males that entails genital arousal—*homosexuality as we know it* is not a feature of this behavior. It is not stigmatized; in fact, to engage in *anything but* this behavior during a certain period of the Sambian male's life is savagely stigmatized. It is not part of a homosexual role; in fact, it does not separate the enactors from those who are not, since all males engage in homosexual behavior. There is no homosexual subculture among the Sambia; all men are part of the all-male villages for their adolescence, and no men are in their adulthood. The practice does not lead to a lifetime of homosexual behavior; in fact, it leads to bisexuality, which, in turn, leads to heterosexuality. In short, in nearly all respects, this behavior, which we call homosexuality, contrasts almost violently with homosexuality in Western society. It is so different, in fact, that it is difficult to regard the two as belonging to the same category.

and are, exclusively homosexual in their behavior for a substantial stretch of their lives in ritual contexts, and then, as adults, are exclusively heterosexual—*none of this matters.* To the essentialist, there is one thing and one thing only that is of any consequence: sexual preference. Everything else is an exercise in obscurantism and irrelevancy. The reality of homosexuality is exhausted by a single dimension or criterion. To discuss anything else on the same level is to confuse what is secondary with what is primary (Goode, 1981b: 59). Thus, because of this disagreement concerning what is important, there is no possibility of resolving the argument between the essentialists and the constructionists. It is a semantic and definitional issue that has no conceivable solution.

HOMOSEXUALITY AS DEVIANCE

Recall that our definition of deviance conveys no negative or pejorative overtones whatsoever. It does *not* mean immoral, sick, unnatural, or pathological. It is necessary to issue this reminder because the public seems to hold this obsolete and sociologically invalid meaning of deviance more for homosexuality than for any other form of behavior.

Roughly halfway through a course in deviant behavior that I taught recently, a student used the term "deviance" in the pathological sense to apply to homosexuals. I was thunderstruck. I asked how, after my elaborate explanations as to the meaning of the term, she could use it in such an antiquated sense. She replied that the term just seemed to her to apply to homosexuality because, in spite of what I said, she regarded it as unnatural. No amount of evidence could persuade her otherwise. At the other end of the spectrum, soon after the publication of the previous edition of this book, I received a half-dozen letters from a self-proclaimed gay activist in the Midwest who claimed my classifying homosexuality as a form of deviance implied that it was unnatural and pathological. Again, no amount of attempts at persuasion would alter his position. So let's be clear about this: Homosexuality is a form of deviant behavior because most members of this society do not approve of it, and because this disapproval takes the form of condemnation and punishment of homosexuals and strained, difficult relations between straights and gays.

Homosexual behavior and desires and a homosexual identity and orientation typically attract *sexual stigma* (Plummer, 1975; Troiden, 1988: 52–57). How do we know this? How exactly can we measure the deviant status of homosexuality? What clear-cut indicators or manifestations of homosexuality's deviant status do we have? What can we point to that will permit us to *see* that homosexuality is a form of deviant behavior?

In some ways, homosexuality provides an almost perfect or "ideal" model for what deviance is all about. (There are ways the status of homosexuality departs from this deviant ideal, which we'll look at momentarily.) In many social circles, homosexual practices are regarded as an abomination: People who are known to engage in them are treated as outcastes. Wisely, most who practice homosexuality keep the fact hidden from the heterosexuals they know. The prohibition against homosexual behavior, for westerners, stretches back to the story of Sodom and Gomorrah in the book of Genesis, cities destroyed by the wrath of God because their citizens practiced "unnatural" acts. Typically, parents consider the question Would you want your son or daughter to become one? with trepidation and fright. Many jobs are closed to known homosexuals—especially those involving children or the national security or those demanding respectability and conventionality. Some of the most derogatory words in the English language address themselves to known or suspected homosexuals: "faggot," "queer," "punk," "cocksucker," and "fairy," for example.

One civil liberties lawyer compared public hostility against homosexuals ("homophobia") with the persecution of Jews in Nazi Germany (Glasser, 1975). It is not widely known that, in spite of the fact many high-ranking Nazi officials were homosexuals (Bleuel, 1974), thousands of male homosexuals were arrested for their sexual orientation (lesbians were spared this fate), put into concentration camps, forced to wear their badge of stigma—the pink triangle—castrated, and even killed (Rector, 1981; Plant, 1986). One civil libertarian estimates the total number of homosexuals who died in Nazi camps at 250,000 (Glasser, 1975), while a historian more conservatively estimates the figure is closer to 5,000 to 15,000 (Plant, 1986). Although even a roughly accurate figure is probably impossible to come by, it is clear that, at times, homosexuals have been savagely persecuted.

American public opinion is also strongly negative concerning homosexuals and homosexuality. In a study based on a nationally representative sample, two-thirds of the respondents regarded homosexuality as "very much obscene and vulgar"; two-thirds said they have never liked homosexuals; two-

thirds said homosexuals should never be allowed to practice medicine or enter government service; three-quarters said they should be prohibited from being judges, schoolteachers, or ministers. A clear majority disapproved of decriminalizing homosexual acts. Nearly half agreed that "homosexuality is a social corruption which can cause the downfall of civilization" (Levitt and Klassen, 1974).

We might be tempted to argue that recent changes in public opinion have reduced the intensity of some of these feelings, but, alas, for the most part, this is not the case; if anything, most Americans are more negative toward homosexuals and homosexuality than they were in the recent past. Each year, Gallup polls have been conducted on the American public's attitudes toward homosexuals and homosexuality; one question the Gallup organization frequently asks is "Do you think homosexual relations between consenting adults should or should not be legal?" In 1982, 45 percent of those questioned said homosexual relations should be legal, while 39 percent said they should not—a slight edge for the liberal, tolerant, accepting position. But in only five years, in Gallup's 1987 poll, American sentiment had turned against homosexuality: 33 percent said homosexual relations should be legal (a drop of 12 percentage points), while a clear majority, 55 percent, said they should not be legal (a rise of 16 percentage points). The 1987 poll represented the first time that a majority of the American public opposed the legalization of homosexuality.

In these polls, there was a clear-cut relationship between education and attitudes toward the legalization of homosexual relations, with better-educated individuals being far more likely to favor making or keeping them legal, and less well-educated individuals favoring making or keeping them illegal. In 1987, 53 percent of college-educated respondents said homosexual relations should be legal; 36 percent said they should not be legal. Support for the "should be legal" position declined, and support for the "should not be legal" position rose, as education declined. Only 21 percent of the respondents with less than a high-school education said homosexual relations should be legal, while nearly two-thirds (65 percent) said they should not be legal (Gallup, 1986: 284–285; Gallup, 1988: 64, 65, 66).

Public opinion favoring the criminalization of homosexuality is only one of a vast array of concrete measures, indicators, and manifestations of the deviant status of same-gender sexual orientation. Nearly everywhere we turn, we are reminded of the homosexual's second-class citizenship; nearly everywhere, heterosexuality is expected, preferred, favored, taken for granted, and regarded as superior. Homosexuals are unwelcome in many quarters. They tend to be regarded as morally inferior, looked down upon, made fun of, and stigmatized—in a word, they are seen as deviants by the straight majority.

When the issue of a male homosexual teaching adolescent boys is considered, most heterosexuals will raise the question of whether he will seduce his students. (Most Americans wish to restrict homosexuals' access to the teaching profession more than any other occupation.) That this possibility holds at least equally for male heterosexual teachers of adolescent girls rarely enters the minds of most heterosexuals; somehow, they will say, homosexuals are "different."

Lesbian mothers are often asked if they "brainwash" their daughters to become lesbians. Heterosexuals, however, are engaged in an almost daily, nonconscious campaign to "brainwash" their children to become heterosexuals. In any case, the evidence from empirical research suggests that children raised by lesbian mothers are just as likely to grow up to be heterosexual as those raised by heterosexual mothers (Gutis, 1987).

When the question of repealing the laws against homosexual acts is debated, a cry often goes up that this will open the doors to homosexual assaults upon young boys. Consider this diatribe published in the *Humbard Christian Report* in 1972 (not 1872!): "Here in Youngstown, we are shocked by a terrible crime against a young boy by a sex pervert which resulted in the boy's murder, yet our lawmakers passed a bill legalizing this crime . . . ! What insanity! This is giving a green light to more and worse sex crimes. This is bringing out into the open what the law and moral standards have always condemned. . . . This bill, if it passes the Senate, will open a Pandora's box of crime and filth unparalleled in the history of the United States" (Petras, 1973: 102). Why one case of sexual violence by a man against a boy is any more typical of homosexuality in general than one case of a heterosexual rape-murder is of heterosexuality in general is not clear. But the fact that this equation is taken seriously in some circles emphasizes that the same rules of logic do not apply to the same forms of behavior for many heterosexuals.

When he asked a sample of respondents to name persons they regarded as deviant, Simmons (1965) found that the most common response (49 percent) was "homosexuals." Of the deviant groups listed, the sample was most intolerant of, and wanted to place the greatest social distance between, themselves and homosexuals. ("Lesbians" were next most rejected.) The characteristics attributed to homosexuals were by far the most negative and consistently stereotyped: 72 percent of the sample said homosexuals were "sexually abnormal," 52 percent felt they were "perverted," and 40 percent said they were "mentally ill" (Simmons, 1969: 28, 33). When I asked the students enrolled in a recent course on deviance which forms of behavior came to mind as examples of deviance, homosexuality was third most often mentioned, after murder and rape and ahead of robbery.

Even today, many—perhaps most—practicing psychiatrists and psychotherapists feel homosexuality is, in and of itself, a form of emotional illness, or at the very least a *manifestation* of an emotional illness. Perhaps for no other form of deviant behavior is there so strong an urge by scientific researchers and clinicians to *pathologize* homosexuality. It is clear that, for homosexuality, scientific and medical stigmatization is strong and widespread. The pathology perspective seems to be most clearly exemplified by professional writings on homosexuality. Albert Ellis, a clinical psychologist, states: "Every gay person I've seen is . . . pretty nutty. . . . I think that 50 percent of them are borderline psychotics" (Karlen, 1971: 223). Ellis's mentor, Eli Siegel, founder of the therapeutic school of Aesthetic Realism, stigmatizes all homosexuality by claiming—without presenting a shred of evidence—that its fundamental cause is contempt for everything outside of oneself (Reiss, 1986).

In spite of the American Psychiatric Association's 1973 ruling that homosexuality is not in itself a sign of a mental disorder, many psychiatrists and other therapists continue to adhere to the view that homosexuality is pathological. In 1977, the journal *Medical Aspects of Human Sexuality* distributed questionnaires to psychiatrists on the issue of homosexuality. Two-thirds of the respondents (69 percent) answered yes to the question "Is homosexuality usually a pathological adaptation (as opposed to a normal variation)?" Seven in 10 answered yes to "Are homosexuals' problems in living a result of personal problems more than stigmatization?" And a clear-cut majority (60 percent) believed homosexual men are "generally less capable than heterosexual men of mature, loving relationships." Slightly less (55 percent) believed the same of lesbians when compared with heterosexual women (Lief, 1977). It is unlikely that these attitudes have changed substantially in recent years.

In 1979, the House of Bishops of the Episcopal Church voted overwhelmingly to ban homosexuals from becoming Episcopal priests. Voting 99 to 34, the ecclesiastical body declared: "We affirm the traditional teaching of the Church on marriage, marital fidelity and sexual chastity as the standard of Christian morality. Candidates for ordination are expected to conform to this standard. Therefore we believe that it is not appropriate for this church to ordain a practicing homosexual" (Sheppard, 1979). In 1988, the primary policy-making body of the United Methodist Church voted to retain its standard that homosexuality is "incompatible with Christian teaching" and therefore a bar to the ordained ministry. Motions to

change the church's position were rejected by two-thirds of the voting delegates. A similar proportion voted to keep the church's current prohibition on using church funds for projects advocating the acceptance of homosexuality (Steinfels, 1988).

"Sodomy" is defined as "unnatural" copulation; it refers most particularly to anal sex, although some definitions include oral sex as well. (A disparaging term to describe homosexuals is "sodomite.") Clearly, both heterosexual and homosexual sex can entail sodomy; although the term does not refer exclusively to homosexual actions, typically, the implication is that sodomy is what homosexuals engage in. Sodomy is a crime in 24 states of the United States; in 19 of these, the act may be either heterosexual or homosexual, and in 5, the law refers specifically to homosexual actions. In Georgia, an antisodomy state, oral or anal sex between any two people, heterosexual or homosexual, is a crime. In Atlanta, in August 1982, a police officer, armed with a search warrant for an investigation of a public drunkenness offense, was admitted to Michael Hardwick's residence. He noticed, through the crack in a door that was ajar, the man having oral sex with another man. The officer promptly arrested Hardwick, who contested the constitutionality of Georgia's sodomy law all the way to the Supreme Court.

In 1986, in a five-to-four decision, the Court decided that the states' antisodomy laws are constitutional—that a state may legally prohibit sodomy among homosexuals—even if it is practiced among consenting adults in the privacy of their own homes. Individuals engaging in homosexual acts, the Court declared, do not enjoy the right of privacy accorded those who practice more conventional sexual behavior. The majority opinion declared that the argument claiming individuals have the right to practice homosexual relations is "insupportable" and "facetious." To give homosexuals the "fundamental right to engage in homosexual" sodomy, wrote Justice Byron White, is something the Court was "quite unwilling to do." Laws against homosexual acts, he said, have "ancient roots" and therefore should not be tampered with (Greenhouse, 1986; Taylor, 1986; White, 1986).

Of course, the sodomy laws are very rarely enforced; hardly anyone is ever arrested in the United States for this crime. In fact, Hardwick was not convicted of sodomy, but he chose to challenge the law's constitutionality so that it would be stricken from the books, not to escape punishment. At the same time, the sodomy laws do spill over into other crucial areas. For instance, custody and adoption: Social welfare agencies cannot award custody or the adoption of a child to a household in which one or more biological or potential surrogate parents are engaging in specifically criminal actions. This means the custody or adoption of a child cannot by law be awarded to a known homosexual in nearly half of the states of the United States. In addition, professional licences granted to candidates based on their "good moral character" could be denied because they practice a criminal act. The case could also "impede counseling and research into AIDS," license police harassment of gays, and slow the advance of homosexual rights. A spokesman for a homosexual rights organization said of the Court ruling, "It's a major disaster from our point of view." Said the Reverend Jerry Falwell, a fundamentalist minister, "The highest court . . . has issued a clear statement that perverted moral behavior is not accepted practice in this country" (Rohter, 1986).

In May 1981, a 19-year-old University of California at Los Angeles student, Timothy Curran, was expelled as an adult leader of a California Boy Scout troop because a newspaper photograph depicted him attending a local dance with a male date. Mr. Curran attended the dance as a homosexual to make a political statement. A spokesperson for the Boy Scouts of America stated that as a homosexual, Mr. Curran "was not a good moral example to be emulated by younger scouts." (This episode was reported by the Combined News Services and appeared in newspapers on May 1, 1981.)

Thus, all around us, we see countless indicators of homosexuality's deviant status. Most heterosexuals want to keep or make homosexual acts illegal—indeed, in nearly half the states of the United States, they *are* illegal, a long-standing tradition recently upheld by the highest court in the land. Homosexuals are readily and spontaneously thought of when heterosexuals are asked to provide examples of deviants. Many, perhaps most, psychiatrists and practitioners of other therapeutic traditions regard homosexuality as abnormal, a pathological condition. Being a homosexual has been grounds for dismissal from a leadership position in the Boy Scouts, exclusion from ordination as a priest or minister, expulsion from the armed services (Egan, 1988), being deemed unfit for adoption (Dullea, 1988), and for not gaining custody of one's own children (Gutis, 1987). And gangs of youth, to demonstrate what they see as their manhood, beat up homosexuals (see "The Violent Practice of 'Gay Bushing,' " pages 203–204). In other words, homosexuality provides us with an almost perfect example of a deviant status. Being publicly known as a homosexual in the United States today almost inevitably entails attracting hostility and stigma, being condemned and punished—in short, being labeled as a deviant.

Given the widespread hostility, fear, and denunciation facing known homosexuals, it should come as no surprise that most keep their sexual identity hidden from heterosexuals. Contrary to popular stereotypes, most gays, male or female, are not readily detected by straights. Their sexual orientation is probably known to their gay friends, but is hidden from the heterosexual community. Much of what the homosexual does—and this is true of most self-admitted "deviants"—involves deception, playacting, information control, an elaborate *presentation of self* to the outside world (Goffman, 1959, 1963: 41ff). Typically, homosexuals must negotiate, navigate, and interact in a world of (usually correct) *imputed hostility* (Warren and Johnson, 1972: 76–78).

Most homosexuals keep their sexual preferences hidden even from the heterosexuals

they are close to. In one study of male homosexuals, only slightly more than a quarter of
the sample (27 percent) said their mother
"definitely knows" they are homosexual;
only one-fifth of the respondents said their
father definitely knows. Half of the mothers,
they said, do "not seem to know or suspect,"
and this was true of 62 percent of the fathers. Just under half of the respondents' sisters (48 percent) and brothers (48 percent)
definitely did not know. *Only 10 percent of the
respondents said most of their heterosexual friends
know,* and half (52 percent) said "only a few"
know or suspect. About 1 in 10 (11 percent)
said *none* of their heterosexual friends know
about their sexual orientation (Weinberg
and Williams, 1974: 105).

When asked, "From how many heterosexuals do you try to conceal your homosexuality?", 30 percent said *all,* and 38 percent said
most; only 1 in 10 said "only a few" (10 percent) or "none" (9 percent). This secrecy and
deception is based on a solid foundation.
These male homosexuals sense that homosexuality is saturated with public scorn. Only
7.5 percent of this study's sample of male homosexuals said "most heterosexuals in general" would feel tolerant and accepting of
their homosexuality; the figure was only 29
percent for most of their heterosexual
friends of the same sex; and it was roughly
half (53 percent) for their "best friend of the
same sex" (Weinberg and Williams, 1974:
106). A quarter of this sample (26 percent)
said "most people" feel *disgusted or repelled* by
homosexuals, while an additional 4 out of 10
said most people simply "dislike" homosexuals.

Given the strong suspicion of, discrimination against, and hostility toward homosexuals, many observers view homosexuals as one
of a number of *oppressed minority groups*
(Humphreys, 1972; Adam, 1978: 24–27; Yearwood and Weinberg, 1979) whose members
are struggling to obtain civil rights granted
to the majority. Hatred of homosexuals is
called "homophobia" (Lumby, 1976) and is
considered no different from racism, sexism,
or antisemitism—or an irrational prejudice
against any other group or category in a society. (But see Plummer's (1981b: 61ff) qualifi-

cations of the homophobia concept.) Homosexuals are discriminated against in hiring,
gay spokespersons insist, excluded from
housing in certain areas, sometimes attacked
by gangs of youths who need fear no reprisals for their acts of violence ("gay bashing"),
avoided socially by many respectable, conventional members of society, and often deprived of honest portrayals in the mass media. We can argue that the parallels, while
they are not perfect, between minority status
for racial and ethnic groups and for homosexuals are extremely strong. In any case,
hostility toward homosexuals is one of the
reasons why this identity, orientation, and
behavior are studied in a course on deviance.

HOMOSEXUALITY AS DEVIANCE:
SOME AMBIGUITIES

There is no doubt then, that homosexuality
is a form of deviance. Any behavior, identity,
or characteristic that generates such public
condemnation is, by definition, a form of deviance. At the same time, there are aspects
of homosexuality that run in the opposite direction, which contradict its generally deviant character. First, although the general status, homosexual, is widely condemned by
the heterosexual public, the majority of homosexuals, as individuals, are not themselves condemned. In fact, the quality of homosexual "deviantness" stems not from
direct face-to-face condemnation, but from
symbolic stigma (Warren, 1974: 146) or what
might be called *indirect labeling.* Second, in
spite of the Supreme Court's anachronistic
1986 ruling, over half the states have repealed their laws against homosexual acts.
(The first of these was Illinois, in 1961.) In
addition, very few men (and no women) are
ever arrested for committing homosexual
acts in private. Almost all such arrests take
place when men solicit the attention of the
wrong men in public places. One observer
estimated there are approximately 6 million
acts for every 20 convictions for homosexuality (Hoffman, 1968: 91). Of course, any estimate of this type is chancy, but it should be

clear that, in terms of the enormity of the ratio of apprehended to unapprehended culprits, homosexuals are far ahead of marijuana users.

Another factor that makes homosexuality a less than clear-cut case of deviance is that the United States is almost alone among the nations of the Western world in keeping the statutes against sodomy and other homosexual acts on the law books. Alfred Kinsey said the citizens of practically no European nation "have become as disturbed over male homosexuality as we have here in the United States" (Kinsey et al., 1953: 477); the statement applies with equal force today. Moreover, engaging in homosexual behavior is morally neutral in most of the societies of the world. A survey of 76 societies found in 49 of them (64 percent) "homosexual activities of one sort or another are considered normal and socially acceptable for certain members of the community" (Ford and Beach, 1951: 130). Indeed, in some societies, homosexual behavior is not only tolerated, it is encouraged, even expected, not only for some members of the society but for *all* of its male members (as we mentioned earlier for the Sambia). Of course, because it is accepted elsewhere does not make homosexuality any less deviant here. It merely underscores my earlier point concerning the relative and subjective nature of judgments and evaluations of human behavior.

In addition, not all of the heterosexual majority accepts the traditional definition of homosexuality as immoral and depraved. Many see homosexuality as a variant of normal sexual expression, with no particular moral significance. Although it is true *all* homosexuals would face condemnation by at least *some*—indeed, most—of the "straights" in their lives were they to reveal their orientation to everyone they knew, it is also true *some* of their heterosexual peers accept homosexuality and homosexuals without qualms. This means that, while declaring oneself as a homosexual often (probably usually) results in censure from the straight majority, this is not always the case. It is almost certain, for instance, that a publicly proclaimed homosexual could not get

elected president of the United States—at least, not for the foreseeable future. Yet, a handful of openly gay politicians have gotten elected to public office in recent years. For instance, in 1983, Gerry Studds, a Massachusetts Democrat, acknowledged his homosexuality after disclosures revealed he had had a sexual relationship with a teenage page in the House of Representatives; Congressman Studds has been reelected twice since his admission. Clearly, a majority of his constituency did not hold such negative views of homosexuality that this revelation damaged his candidacy.

An acceptance of homosexuality in some social circles does not mean it is not a form of deviance to the majority of the members of our society. It just means some people can be found who feel otherwise. A very different case is presented by Robert Bauman, a conservative Republican congressman from Maryland, who did not enjoy the same fate as Congressman Studds. In 1980, his homosexual behavior and orientation were revealed to the voters of his district, who promptly voted him out of office. Bauman also lost his wife, his family, his house, and "most of his powerful friends." In his memoirs, *The Gentleman From Maryland: The Conscience of a Conservative,* Bauman said, "I might have been Speaker of the House—who knows. . . . Instead, I'll be remembered for different things" (Leersen, 1986).

DIMENSIONS OF HOMOSEXUALITY

As in any other area of human life, homosexuality is, in large part, a matter of definition. Put plainly and simply, there is no possible definition of who is a homosexual, or even what is homosexual behavior, that will satisfy everyone. It is more fruitful to examine different *dimensions* of homosexuality—dimensions that are often, but not necessarily, found together. In short, homosexuality must be regarded as a *multidimensional* phenomenon (Troiden, 1988: 15–16). Past observers have attempted to attach a precise label to specific people and specific acts, thinking they could be unambiguously classi-

Public Stereotypes of Male Homosexuals: Are They Accurate?

The public stereotype of the male homosexual among the "straight" or heterosexual majority is that of a man who displays effeminate mannerisms and appearance—who looks and acts like a caricature of a woman. Limp wrists, a falsetto voice, a lisp, and a dress are presumed to be characteristics of most homosexual men. (Interestingly, most men who delight in wearing women's clothes—transvestites—are heterosexual, not homosexual; see Brierley, 1979; Talamini, 1982). Although there are some gay men who display obvious effeminate mannerisms, they constitute a small minority of all male homosexuals. Someone who consistently displays this style is called a "nellie" or a "nellie queen"; such mannerisms are called "swishy." One study found that approximately one homosexual in six (16 percent) fits this stereotype—that is, both described himself and was described by the interviewer as being "obviously feminine" in behavior and demeanor (Saghir and Robins, 1973: 106–107). It is almost superfluous to point out that women themselves do not act in this fashion; it is a caricature or a distortion of femininity (Newton, 1972). Actually, many homosexual men will "camp" or "swish" on occasion or in appropriate circumstances, but usually act completely masculine.

Why does the majority hang onto such inaccurate stereotypes of homosexual men? "More than sheer ignorance seems to be involved," writes one sex researcher. "The higher the taboo on homosexuality . . . , the more incomprehensible homosexuality becomes as anything other than some sort of impaired masculinity. But when a high amount of homosexuality is expected . . . there is little or no tendency to assume that homosexuality implies effeminacy, or that effeminacy necessarily indicates homosexuality" (Tripp, 1976: 160). Of course, it is the obviously and exaggeratedly effeminate homosexual who is most *visible* to the straight world, which leads many heterosexuals to believe in the validity of the inaccurate stereotype.

"Homosexual" indicates a love of one's own sex, and it is men whom the homosexual male loves, not women. A much more common style among homosexuals is a macho or manly style; in fact, this virile or "butch" style is becoming increasingly common among gay males (Humphreys, 1971; Sage, 1975). *Extremely* macho, supermasculine homosexual males, like those who are extremely effeminate or "swishy," are very conspicuous and visible. A walk through a heavily gay neighborhood, such as Christopher Street in New York's Greenwich Village, verifies that the supermasculine style is at least fairly common among homosexual men. Many of these men are heavily muscled and are clearly involved in bodybuilding. Some wear tight leather outfits with silver studs, heavy wrist bands, motorcycle boots, sleeveless denim jackets, and thick studded belts. A few have shaved their heads completely bald; many sport full beards or handlebar moustaches and a tattoo or two on their arms and shoulders. Many can be seen lounging against a huge 1000 cc motorcycle. Some wear quasimilitary regalia or sadomasochistic leather outfits; some try to look like lumberjacks or cowboys.

These macho men are every bit a caricature of masculinity as the swishy "queens" are of femininity; neither is typical of the gay community. In fact, there is no single typical homosexual style, any more than a single heterosexual style. A high proportion of homosexual men, however, have adopted a virile, although not supermacho style. Many wear their hair short, wear jeans, tennis shoes or running shoes, or, in cooler weather, boots, a T-shirt or a short-sleeved knit shirt, and, again, in cooler weather, a lumber jacket or other type of heavy wool shirt. Most appear to be in excellent physical condition. The overwhelming majority would be invisible as homosexuals to most heterosexuals; they could "pass" as straight. Many heterosexuals who are knowledgeable concerning the gay scene can spot them as gay, not because they are especially effeminate, but because the style of masculinity among gay males is somewhat different from the heterosexual style of masculinity. However, many features once unique to the gay subculture have been adopted by the straight world (the use of amyl nitrite during sex, for example, disco music and dancing, the word "camp," many clothing styles, and so on). And meanwhile, a high proportion of the heterosexual majority still clings to the stereotype of the typical homosexual male being effeminate.

fied as either homosexual or heterosexual. Anna Freud wrote that the ultimate criterion of sexual orientation was the sex of one's masturbatory fantasies. While this might be one of a number of useful criteria, I would like to suggest something quite different.

First, that there is no such thing as *a* "homosexual." And, second, that there is no such thing, strictly speaking, as "homosexual behavior." By these statements, I do not mean that homosexuals and homosexuality do not exist, but merely that who and what fall into these categories are to some degree arbitrary, not absolute, fixed, or final. We should keep in mind that:

1. Categorizing depends on selecting specific criteria for defining people and their behavior.
2. These criteria cannot be justified scientifically—they can only be justified according to what one or another observer considers important.
3. The nature of one's sexual commitment may change over time, sometimes drastically.
4. There are many dimensions of homosexuality; some people will be classifed as "homosexual" according to some of them, but not according to others.
5. Homosexuality is a matter of degree on a spectrum from complete homosexuality, through mixed homosexuality, to complete heterosexuality. The two polar types are rare; most of us fall in between them.

Let's look at a few examples to show what we mean.

Consider George, a subject of Laud Humphreys's study, *Tearoom Trade,* a married truck driver in his mid-thirties. He and his wife have seven children; they are Roman Catholic and do not use contraception. "How often do you have intercourse with your wife?" Humphreys asked George. "Not very much in the last few years," he replied. "It's up to when she feels like giving it to me—which ain't very often. I never suggest it. . . . She's afraid to have sex but doesn't believe in birth control. I'd just rather not be around her! I won't suggest having sex anyway—and she just doesn't want it anymore" (1970: 114, 115). George is a participant in "tearoom" sex—same-gender sexual contact with strangers in public restrooms. George plays the role of the insertor in his homosexual contact: He never reciprocates after a man has performed fellatio on him. George considers himself a heterosexual; indeed, his self-image is unambiguously masculine. Performing fellatio on another man would threaten that image of himself. George has no friends who are gay and shuns the homosexual subculture. For him, sex with men in urinals serves as a substitute for sexual contact with his wife. He chooses not to have sex with, nor can he afford, prostitutes, and a heterosexual affair would threaten an already shaky marriage and threaten him with separation from his children. George is regarded by frequenters of "tearooms" as *trade:* predominantly heterosexual men who come to be serviced, but who do not reciprocate. Trade, says Humphreys, "en route from the din of factories to the clamor of children, . . . slip off the freeways for a few moments of impersonal sex in a toilet stall" (1970: 117).

George's case reminds us that some men's behavior prior to their homosexual activity can be exclusively heterosexual, their identity can be unambiguously heterosexual, their subcultural involvement entirely heterosexual, and, in all likelihood, their masturbatory fantasies heterosexual as well. But at the moment they describe their experiences, their behavior is predominantly homosexual. That is, their behavior is technically homosexual in the sense that it involves genital contact with a member of the same sex. In the case of prison homosexuality, it wouldn't be *regarded* as homosexual by anyone in the social scene in which it takes place. The behavior of the so-called passive partner, the man into whose body is inserted the other man's penis, would be thought to be homosexual, even if it involved coercion. Those of us outside the prison community would think of *both* as engaging in homosexual behavior, but prisoners wouldn't agree. George would probably not see what he is doing as "homosexual" behavior. He would see what the men who service him do as homosexual in nature. Other denizens of the tearoom scene would probably divide on the issue. Which is it? Is George engaging in "homosexual behavior" or not? It's a question of perspective, not one of solid, indisputable fact.

Of course, the reverse is also possible: a man or boy who does not engage in "homosexual" behavior could be regarded as homosexual along the other dimensions. An adolescent boy is thought by his peers to be effeminate—a "queer," a "pansy," a "fruit." A role and a public label exist even before the actual activity it supposedly designates actually occurs, if indeed it ever does. As with other stereotypes, the public notion of the homosexual role is both in part false and in part true—that is, it can have an effect on people's behavior. Let's say a boy so labeled begins to think that he is, perhaps, a homosexual. He explores the possibility by visiting a gay bar. He is sexually excited by pictures and even the thought of handsome, muscular men. Whenever he masturbates, he fantasizes sexual contact with another man. And yet he has not, as yet, engaged in sexual behavior with another man. He has, however, had, and continues to have, intercourse with two girls with whom he maintains a close and affectionate friendship. Would it be correct to say this boy is a homosexual? Again, the only accurate answer that could be given to this question is that it depends on what you mean. He is in some senses, but not in others.

Alfred Kinsey and his colleagues (1948) took a giant step in this area by looking upon sexual orientation as a continuum. He devised a "heterosexual-homosexual rating scale," which classified men from zero to six in their degree of being one or the other. This scale was based on: (1) "physical contacts which result in erotic arousal or orgasm" and (2) "psychic response." The zeroes were exclusively heterosexual, and sixes were exclusively homosexual; the ones through fives were, in varying degrees, in between. Commenting on the scale, Kinsey wrote:

Males do not represent two discrete populations, heterosexual and homosexual. The world is not to be divided into sheep and goats. Not all things are black nor all things white. It is a fundamental of taxonomy that nature rarely deals with discrete categories. Only the human mind invents categories and tries to force facts into pigeonholes. The living world is a continuum in each and every one of its aspects. The sooner we learn this concerning human sexual behavior the sooner we shall reach a sound understanding of the realities of sex.

One of the most often cited statistics in the social literature is from Kinsey's research: Over one-third, or 37 percent of all American males, have at least one homosexual experience that results in orgasm from the onset of adolescence to old age. An additional 13 percent of Kinsey's sample said they had felt homosexual urges or desires—they had been physically aroused by another man—without actually engaging in homosexual behavior. In addition, about 60 percent of the sample said they had engaged in preadolescent sex play with another boy. About 6 percent of the total of all Kinsey's respondents' orgasms were derived from homosexual contact. Only 4 males in 100 could be regarded as exclusively homosexual: They had never had any sexual contact with women and had never been aroused by them. Kinsey rated the men with no heterosexual and only homosexual contact and arousal as a six; those with no homosexual and only heterosexual contact and arousal as a zero. Thus, 54 percent of American males could be called "monosexual." The rest were "bisexual" in varying degrees. Three men in 10 (30 percent) had at least incidental homosexual experience or reactions during a period of at least three years. One out of 6 (18 percent) had at least as much homosexual as heterosexual activity and/or desire during three years or more of their lives. And 1 out of 13 of the men in the sample (8 percent) was exclusively homosexual for three or more years (Kinsey et al., 1948). As I pointed out earlier, many current observers and experts (Hunt, 1975: 303–315, summarizes these views) feel Kinsey's figures represent an exaggeration, that the prevalence of homosexual behavior was, and still is, considerably below the level they indicate. But even if the magnitude of the figures are scaled down, there are several lessons we can learn from them.

The first is that a sizable proportion of American men—and precisely how large this proportion is continues to be the subject of debate—has had homosexual experiences and has felt erotic desires toward other men. When these data were first published in 1948, a storm of outrage greeted the study because it seemed to be saying "everybody's doing it, and it's not really so bad." What had been hidden from public view for so long had become public knowledge almost overnight. But not only had many men—remember, males during and after puberty, not two 6-year-olds playing "doctor"—engaged in homosexual activity at least once in their lives, but also a huge proportion *continued* to engage in homosexual behavior during *a considerable period of time* in their lives. And a third lesson is that *homosexuality seems not to be a fixed "condition."* Kinsey's figures demonstrated that there is a great deal of shifting of the object of one's sexual activity over time. Half the men who were exclusively homosexual in their behavior during three or more years had sex with women at a different time in their lives.

Kinsey's study of the sexual practices of women published five years after the "male" volume, *Sexual Behavior in the Human Female* (Kinsey et al., 1953), revealed a parallel picture for lesbian behavior, although the figures were considerably smaller. The results he obtained regarding the sexual activity of American females were not nearly so dramatic as those he elicited in his study of males. Nevertheless, it was found that 13 percent of all American women had at least one homosexual experience to orgasm from the onset of adolescence to old age. An additional 7 percent of the female population had engaged in one or more homoerotic episodes after puberty, but without achieving orgasm. Roughly 2 or 3 females in 100 could be regarded as exclusively homosexual: They had neither had sexual contact with men nor were they sexually aroused by them. Their only source of sexual contact and arousal had been with other women.

Self-identity

Although Kinsey's research represented a considerable advance over the literature prior to the late 1940s and early 1950s, today we realize that the picture is even more complex than his scheme allows. To begin with, Kinsey did not consider *self-identity* as a crucial dimension of homosexuality. How men and women define their own gender sexual preferences has an enormous impact on their behavior, their sense of ease with their lives, their social relations with others, what they think, how they feel, their experiences, both external and internal. This is not to say that people who don't think they are homosexual, but who are in all other respects, therefore aren't homosexual. All it means is that this particular dimension of homosexuality is lacking in their makeup. In the sense of self-identity, they simply aren't homosexual; in other respects, they may be. If we fail to consider this dimension, our understanding of homosexuality will necessarily and inevitably be shallow and incomplete.

The Homosexual Subculture

A second crucial dimension any careful observer of the sexual scene must consider is subcultural involvement. This means association with others who are homosexuals—who consider themselves as such and who practice homosexual behavior. Subcultural involvement refers to one's immersion in a specific social "scene." As with any category of humanity, homosexuals do not form a tightly knit group—but they are a kind of group nonetheless, a "quasigroup" or a "near group." Think of any social category: police officers, the very rich, marijuana smokers, birdwatchers, people with red hair, Quakers, residents of Chicago. Some of these categories will form the basis for group cohesion; others will not.

In speaking of a group or a subculture, I mean that (1) its members interact with one another more frequently and more intimately than they do with members of other social categories, (2) its members' way of life, and their beliefs, are somewhat different from members of other social categories, and (3) its members think of themselves as belonging to a specific group, and they are so defined by those who do not share this trait. In these three senses, then, homosexuals do form a subculture, or group. But not all men or women who practice homosexual behavior are involved in the subculture. In fact, they are differentially involved, some almost to the complete exclusion of "straight" people, others absolutely not at all. The degree to which a given person who practices homosexual behavior is involved in and with the homosexual subculture determines many crucial facets of his or her life, both sexual and nonsexual. To ignore this dimension would be suicidal.

Subjective Behavior Judgments

A third crucial dimension of homosexuality often lacking in past analyses is the subjective meaning that both participants and nonparticipants attach to behavior, people, and roles people play. By "subjective meaning," I mean simply whether or not homosexuality is considered part of what's going on. This isn't dictated by the formal properties of what people are or do; it grows out of certain definitions and judgments that vary from place to place, from time to time. Recall that among prisoners what the sexual aggressor does it not considered "homosexuality" by him, by his partner, or by his fellow prisoners. The same goes for our married man, George, who engages in tearoom sex in public lavatories. If George were to be asked, "Have you ever engaged in homosexual behavior?" he would probably answer in the negative. Many young men "hustle" homosexuals for money. They allow themselves to be fellated, but they never reciprocate. They do this only if they are paid, and they maintain a rigid emotional barrier between themselves and the men who fellate them. To break any of these rules would threaten their masculinity and invite their being defined as a homosexual. But within the boundaries of what they do, they do not see their behavior as homosexual. Most have girlfriends and eventually drift out of hustling to get married (Reiss, 1961).

In short, engaging in technically homosexual behavior—that is, genital contact to the point of orgasm—does not necessarily entail the subjective meaning of homosexuality for all involved. We may not all agree on what we see as "homosexual behavior"; conceptions as to what constitutes homosexuality follow different rules. And each perspective has to be examined separately, in its own right.

Sexual Preference

To make our investigation complete, it is necessary to look at sexual preferences. Now, it is never the case that everything is equal. No one is faced with the alternative of two sexual partners who are exactly the same except for gender. So we have to visualize gender preference as hypothetical rather than real. We all encounter many people during the course of our day, some of them men, and some women. How does it come to pass that we end up in bed with a member of one or the other sex? Is it because of availability?

Men in prisons do not choose the gender of their partners; it is forced on them by circumstance. If they had the power of choice, nearly all would have intercourse with women, not men. It is relatively easy to find willing male sex partners in an urban center after a few minutes of "cruising" in the right place; talking women into bed is generally much more difficult. Many men prefer the sexual company of women, but don't want to be subject to the "hassle" it would entail. They end up having sex with men because men are far more readily available. On the other hand, many men prefer to abstain from sex altogether than have intercourse with other men. So we have a spectrum along the dimension of same-sex preference: from the preferential homosexual, the man who, in the face of almost unlimited options available, consistently chooses men over women; through the situational homosexual, who engages in same-sex intercourse only where women are not to be found, or where men are far more readily available then women; over to the confirmed heterosexual, who prefers no sex to sex with men. Certainly sexual preferences comprise an absolutely crucial dimension of sexuality.

Also, romantic preferences, or the potential for becoming emotionally involved with men or women, should be considered in any definitional scheme. The ability to fall in love with someone of the same sex must be counted as one out of a number of ways of determining sexual orientation. Some people can be said to be *homoemotional.*

Sexual Arousal

Likewise, the ability to be turned on physically is important: Whether or not one becomes sexually aroused by men or by women has to be taken into account in constructing a complete picture of homosexuality. Men and women who are homoerotic are homosexual along this particular dimension. We agree with Anna Freud in this respect: The gender of the object of one's masturbatory fantasies, which fuel sexual excitement, is basic in deciding whether one is homosexual or heterosexual. But again, it is only one dimension out of a number of important dimensions.

Public Definition

And last, the public definition of one's sexual role and preference cannot be ignored when understanding the phenomenon of sexual orientation. This does not mean that if anyone else thinks you are a homosexual, therefore you are. But it does mean that being labeled as a homosexual will make a great deal of difference to your sexual life, and to your life in general, in a large number of ways. The secret homosexual and the overt homosexual do not lead the same sort of lives; likewise, the man who is falsely thought to be a homosexual by everyone in a community will not lead the same sort of life as the one who is correctly assumed to be "straight." By itself, the public labeling of our gender preference will have an impact on many other things we consider important. At the very least, it is crucial in influencing one's self-identity and definition.

Summary

Perhaps the main point to emerge out of this discussion is that *no single dimension of homosexuality alone determines a person's sexual orientation.* A person may be a "homosexual" in a number of different ways. And second, these dimensions are not necessarily found together in the same person. In other words, a given person may be a homosexual in one way, but not in another. Although these dimensions are often found together, and are generally correlated with one another, it doesn't always happen. We have to examine various combinations of characteristics, and the kind of consequences these combinations have for people's lives, both sexual and nonsexual.

This approach insists that there is no such creature as a "true" homosexual (Omark, 1978; Goode, 1981b). Each dimension may be taken as a kind of *indicator* of homosexuality. The connections between the various dimensions are *statistical,* not absolute. Given the fact of one's homosexuality alone or in a combination of these dimensions, we can make predictions regarding the *likelihood* of the others. Among all these dimensions, however, probably the best such indicator is identity. Given the fact that someone declares a homosexual identity, the chances are very good (although not certain) that he or she will "be" homosexual along the others—for instance, will also have had far more sex with same-gender partners. The reverse is also true, but probably not quite as powerful a predictor: Someone who has had far more sex with members of the same gender has usually, but far from always, adopted a homosexual identity. A long history of intercourse with same-sex partners may or may not lead one to adopt a homosexual identity—although it often does. Naturally, the more dimensions along which one "is" homosexual, the greater the likelihood of successfully predicting homosexuality in the remaining dimensions.

Does this mean that there is no such thing as homosexuality or a homosexual *along one or another of these dimensions?* No; all it means is that we should not solidify or reify these dimensions into absolute, ironclad realities that tell us everything we need to know about someone's homosexuality—or the entire phenomenon of homosexuality. But we should not fall into the opposite trap, either. Homosexuality is not like clothing that can be put on or cast off at will. Sagarin tells us that *acts,* not people, should be labeled as homosexual. To think that one *is* a homosexual, independent of what one *does,* is a fallacy, according to this line of reasoning. One is not a tennis player until one plays tennis, and one is not a tennis player after one quits the game; one is a tennis player only by virtue of the fact that one plays tennis. People are homosexual in no more meaningful a sense than one is a tennis player: only because one engages in homosexual acts. If someone doesn't so engage, one isn't a homosexual. There is absolutely no indwelling trait of homosexuality outside the acts themselves, any more than there is in "being" a tennis player. To think so, this author declares, is to fall victim to "the tyranny of isness" (Sagarin, 1973, 1975: 144–154).

Another commentator writes concerning this view that, at first reading, this position "appears to make a great deal of sense" (Humphreys, 1979: 239). But on further reflection, it can be seen to be something of an exaggeration. Being thought a homosexual both by the "straight" majority and the gay minority is a *master trait* or a *master status* (Becker, 1963: 33). That is, this characteristic, being a homosexual, *overwhelms* all others. It is regarded as more fundamental, more important, more *consequential,* than being a tennis player. This label, since it is profound and tenacious, will have real-life consequences and will influence how others treat one, how one regards oneself, and what one does in response. And a sexual identity of regarding oneself *as* a homosexual, likewise, even independent of the public label, will impact upon the many facets of one's life. It is an identity that influences and determines many other things about oneself, including aspects of one's personality, behavior, and many less momentous identities. It is not so easily discarded as an identity based on the ability to swing a tennis racket (Humphreys, 1979: 239). Although it is easy to fall into the trap of "the tyranny of isness," in reading more into behavior than is actually there, likewise, it is equally as easy to fall into the trap of the "tyranny of isn'tness"—of not seeing what is actually there (Humphreys, 1979: 242). Just because labels and identities are applied, constructed, or adopted in a less than straightforward fashion, and are based on ideas rather than material circumstances, does not mean that they can be thought away. They are very real because they are regarded as real.

HOMOSEXUALITY: DISEASE OR WAY OF LIFE?

It is very difficult for the psychoanalytically trained, pathology-oriented psychiatrist to accept the meaningfulness of this array of dimensions. First, it is imperative that sexuality be defined in *either-or* terms. Seeing the world in a complex fashion blunts and diffuses condemnation of it and labeling it as a clear-cut syndrome.

Second, not only does the sociological point of view claim that there are *degrees* of homosexuality, but it also says that there are a number of dimensions of sexual orientation. This is threatening to the pathologist who wants to capture the essence of a supposedly "sick" category in a single criterion.

Third, the traditional psychoanalytic orientation toward homosexuality is *essentialistic*. That is, it attempts to put forth the notion that the *essence* of homosexuality can be captured in some distinct formula, that there is such a thing as "true" homosexuality, which can be distinguished from "pseudo," "adaptive," "reactive," "secondary," or "situational" homosexuality. Saying, as I do, that what homosexuality "is" depends on what you mean, that it can "be" different things according to your definition or orientation, robs the phenomenon of some essential, basic, indwelling character. Saying that it is real when it is defined, variously, as real, is a retreat from saying that it is a solid quality resting firmly somewhere.

Fourth, many of the dimensions of homosexuality I spell out are outside the scope of traditional psychiatry. The psychoanalyst wishes to define the reality of homosexuality alone, to monopolize the definition of what it is, and who is a homosexual. Psychoanalysis is an esoteric orientation; that is, only the person who is trained in the craft may speak on the subjects it addresses itself to. No one else, it is claimed, has the competency to speak or write on the subject of human behavior. And in the past, the psychoanalyst could be counted on to pathologize a wide range of unorthodox behaviors. Consequently, threats from other observers' interpretations could be neutralized with an ad hominem argument. Only the psychoanalytic view is labeled "scientific" (Socarides, 1978).

Commenting on a study by Martin Hoffman (1968), one psychiatrist objects to the method used in the study—interviewing homosexuals in their natural habitat, in gay bars, in steambaths, on the street, in their dwelling places: "Data collected in this manner and in such settings cannot be taken seriously, studded as they are with rationalizations and devoid of rigorous scientific methodology on the part of the author" (Socarides, 1975: 94). This critic is saying (1) only information collected in the process of psychoanalysis is valid and (2) only conclusions claiming homosexuals are sick are valid.

Only in the consultation room does the homosexual reveal himself and his world. No other data, statistics, or statements can be accepted as setting forth the true nature of homosexuality. All other sources may be heavily weighted by face-saving devices or rationalizations or, if they issue from lay bodies, lack the scientific and medical background to support their views. The best that can be said for the well-intentioned but unqualified observer is that he is misguided because he does not have and cannot apply those techniques which would make it possible to discern the deep underlying clinical disorder or to evaluate the emotional patterns and interpersonal events in the life of a homosexual (Socarides, 1970: 1199).

As with any other area of human sexuality, particularly sexual deviance, the debate on homosexuality can become rancorous and even hostile. We might have supposed that, after centuries of writings on homosexual behavior, some sort of consensus about its nature would be emerging. This appears not to be the case. Perhaps still the most vigorously contested question is whether or not homosexuality is normal or abnormal, an alternative life-style or a manifestation of psychic pathology, a viable form of behavior or a mental illness. On one side, taking the "pathology" position, are many—perhaps, even now, most—psychiatrists, other physicians, such as endocrinologists, some psychologists, and, of course, most of the public. On the other, we have younger psychiatrists, some other physicians, and most behavioral scientists—principally anthropologists, psychologists, and sociologists. The second faction would hold to the "alternative life-style" notion.

The Pathologist's Viewpoint

Even the most rigid of the sexual pathologists makes a distinction between exclusive or "obligatory," homosexuality (sometimes called "true" homosexuality), and episodic, temporary, or situational homosexuality. However, exactly where the line is drawn between these two groups isn't altogether clear. Irving Bieber, perhaps the foremost spokesman for the pathology position, stated, "An isolated homosexual experience doesn't define a man as homosexual; but if he has one such experience every year, he would have to be considered homosexual" (Bieber et al., 1971). This means that a heterosexually active male, 1 percent of whose experiences are homosexual, 99 percent of which are heterosexual, would be considered homosexual, according to this view.

The first premise of the pathologists is that obligatory homosexuality is the manifestation of a psychosexual disorder, equivalent to a disease. They do not say merely that many homosexuals are neurotic or that homosexuals are more likely to be sick than heterosexuals. They say that exclusive homosexuality is always and by definition a sign of disordered sexuality. Socarides expressed this position when he stated, "There is no obligatory homosexual who can be considered to be healthy. The very existence of this condition precludes it" (1970: 1201).

Bieber, the most influential of all medical figures to write on homosexuality, says, "We consider homosexuality to be a pathologic, biosocial, psycho-sexual adaptation consequent to pervasive fears surrounding the expression of heterosexual impulses" (Bieber et al., 1962: 220). And again, "All psychoanalytic theories assume that adult homosexuality is psychopathologic" (1962: 18). Socarides, another homosexuality pathologizer, has stated, "True obligatory homosexuality is a form of psychiatric or emotional illness" (1970: 1200).

In a debate with another psychiatrist before the American Psychiatric Association, Bieber put it this way:

The central question is: Is homosexuality a normal sexual variant that develops like left-handedness does in some people, or does it represent some kind of disturbance in sexual development? There is no question in my mind: Every male homosexual goes through an initial stage of heterosexual development, and in all homosexuals, there has been a disturbance of normal heterosexual development, as a result of fears which produce anxieties and inhibitions of sexual function. His sexual adaptation is a substitutive adaptation.

Bieber goes on to make a medical, or pathology analogy: "What you have in a homosexual adult is a person whose heterosexual function is crippled like the legs of a polio victim." While denying that homosexuality is a mental illness, Bieber claims that it is the manifestation of a psychiatric disorder. (Some may feel that the distinction is one of form rather than of substance.) In an interview with *Playboy*, as part of a panel of experts on homosexuality, Bieber states,

Heterosexuality is part of normal biosocial development, while homosexuality is always the result of a disordered sexual development.... It is not normal for a man to make love to a man. It doesn't disorder sexual development for two men to make love to each other. It is merely evidence that their sexuality has already *been* disordered.... I should like to underscore the point that it isn't easy to sidetrack a male from a heterosexual destiny. It takes a lot of trauma.

Pathologists reject the idea that homosexuality is culturally defined, that it is acceptable in one place and "deviant" in another only because of the historical accident of culture. Homosexuality, Bieber says, "is maladaptive because it is based on fears that are not realistic, and not because of cultural unacceptability. It would be no less abnormal if it were culturally accepted." Homosexuality, according to this view, "is a type of heterosexual inadequacy." It "is never unrelated to fears and inhibitions associated with heterosexuality." It is totally incorrect "that normalcy can only be culturally defined and that homosexuality would not be pathological in a society that accepted it." This implies "that if our society accepted it, homosexuals wouldn't suffer any more psychological problems than heterosexuals. During the Victorian era, frigidity was regarded as normal. Can we therefore assume that frigidity created no psychological problems for a woman or for her husband because it was culturally defined as normal? I think not" (Bieber et al., 1971: 63, 67, 68, 69, 70).

The precise location of the abnormality of homosexuality is not altogether clear, however. An answer to the question "Wherein lies the inherent pathology of exclusive homosexual behavior?" is not immediately forthcoming. There is, pathologists would say, a heterosexual destiny. However, just how this exhibits itself cannot be spelled out with much clarity—in our instincts, perhaps? A heterosexual instinct that is sidetracked by early childhood traumas? Since Freud himself insisted on human bisexuality at birth, psychoanalysts do not make use of the mythical concept of heterosexual instincts. But since they must ground their view of homosexuality as a sickness, the notion of a heterosexual destiny still has to be affirmed. One analyst correctly notes that "there is no inevitable genetic or hormonal propensity toward a partner of either the same or opposite sex." What, then, naturally impels people toward members of the opposite sex? What is it that is abnormal about homosexual love?

The . . . male-female design . . . is anatomically determined, as it derives from cells which in evolutionary scale underwent changes into organ systems and finally into individuals reciprocally adapted to each other. This is the evolutionary development of man. The male-female design is thus perpetually maintained, and only overwhelming fear can disturb it (Socarides, 1975: 99).

Homosexual object choice is not innate or instinctual nor is heterosexual object choice since both are learned behavior. The choice of sexual object is not predetermined by chromosomal tag-

ging. Heterosexual object choice . . . is supported by universal concepts of mating. It is further determined by 2½ billion years of human evolution and is a product of sexual differentiation, at first solely based on reproduction but later widened to include sexual gratification (Socarides, 1970: 1201).

Men and women, then, are "reciprocally adapted to each other anatomically, endocrinologically, psychologically, and in many other ways," according to this view (Socarides, 1970: 1201).

However, the meaning of "reciprocally adapted," "the male-female design," and "anatomically determined" is still murky. It seems that what is being asserted is the ancient Aristotelian idea of the "nature" of living beings and the function of their organs. What is "anatomically determined" is that which is "natural" for an organ or an organism; what violates that organ or organism's destiny is "unnatural," an *offense against nature.* In his *Metaphysics,* Aristotle explains that living things have *essences* or attributes that characterize what they truly are. Every living being contains within itself a destiny or life force that will be realized naturally over time. Forces within an acorn, for instance—its "nature"—assure that it will become an oak tree, and not an orchid or a bullfrog. The essence of the acorn is realized by the process of becoming what is contained within itself to become (Hoffman, 1968: 104–106).

Nature decrees that the mouth be used for eating, the eyes for seeing, the nose for smelling, and so on. In reacting to a statement by William Masters that expressed the opinion that anal intercourse was a viable sexual activity, Socarides angrily retorted, "What was, until then, a purely excretory organ had become a genital one" (1975: 121). It is the nature of the anus to be used solely for excretory purposes; to do otherwise is "unnatural" and "abnormal." Homosexuals are subverting their own destiny and that of their bodily organs by (sometimes) practicing anal intercourse. This is one of the things that makes homosexuality a psychiatric abomination. Of course, the same holds true for *heterosexual* anal intercourse and for oral sex as well; the mouth, after all, was not "anatomically determined" to perform fellatio or cunnilingus, although it is clearly capable of doing it. In a survey conducted in 1972, about half of all married high-school-educated men and women and two-thirds of the married college-educated men and women said that they had engaged in cunnilingus or fellatio with their spouse during the previous 12 months (Hunt, 1975: 198). According to the view that activities of organs are "determined" by nature, most married couples engage in "unnatural" behavior in the sex act.

It could be that what is considered "unnatural," "unhealthy," or "abnormal" about the practice of homosexuality is that homosexuals fail to reproduce themselves, that their sex is, in toto, lacking in biological fertility. "Not all cultures survive," writes Socarides; "the majority have not, and . . . serious flaws in their sexual code have undoubtedly played a significant role in their demise" (1975: 11). Abram Kardiner, an influential psychiatrist, has stated:

There is an epidemic form of homosexuality . . . which generally occurs in social crises or in declining cultures when boundless license and boundless permissiveness dulls the pain of ceaseless anxiety, universal hostility, and divisiveness. . . . This is . . . one facet of the tidal wave of egalitarianism and divisiveness that is sweeping the country. . . . But this egalitarianism is bound to exact a high price from the community . . . [for it is a] symptom of a social distress syndrome. . . . Homosexuals cannot make a society, nor keep ours going for very long. It operates against the cohesive elements in society in the name of a fictitious freedom. It drives the opposite sex in a similar direction. And no society can long endure when either the child is neglected or when the sexes war upon each other (quoted in Socarides, 1975: 89–90).

It is clearly true that homosexual *acts* do not lead to biological reproduction; it is not true that homosexual men and women do not and cannot reproduce themselves. There are many homosexual men and women who are heterosexually married and who care for children in much the same way that heterosexual couples do (Ross, 1972; Dank, 1972; Klemesrud, 1973). The rate of heterosexual marriage among homosexuals is certainly lower than it is among heterosexuals; their rate of fertility is unquestionably lower as well. But homosexuality is certainly no bar to marriage or childbearing and child rearing. But is childbearing inevitable and "natural"; is *not* bearing children "unnatural"? In a period of history when survival of the tribe and the human race depended on producing large numbers of offspring, it certainly had evolutionary significance, significant survival value. Today, however, in a period when overpopulation in the rest of the world is a problem rather than underpopulation, and when American society is edging toward zero population growth, can we assert that not having children is "unnatural"? This assertion seems difficult to accept today. Moreover, many forms of nondeviant, heterosexual sex lead to nonreproduction and yet they rarely become a target for pathology seekers. Innumerable heterosexual couples have decided not to raise children; males undergo vasectomies, and females, tubal ligation. Is the sexual behavior of these couples "unnatural"? Some observers of the current sexual scene argue that the so-called sexual revolution includes the option for many people at some time during their lives of leading a celibate existence. Is this nonactivity abnormal? Again, those who write that homosexuality is unnatural do not see that the general argument that they use to pathologize it also applies to other forms of nondeviant sex. And this necessarily vitiates their argument.

Refuting the Pathologist's Viewpoint

I believe, therefore, that the view of homosexuality as unnatural and a form of sickness is distinctly archaic. It is, in my opinion, refuted by the available evidence.

First, the assumption as to the inherent desirability of heterosexuality is merely, solely, and exclusively a value judgment, couched in the form of a pseudoscientific medical fact. It is a judgment that anyone is free to accept or reject, according to one's personal feelings and taste.

Second, while pathologists decree that homosexuality represents a kind of inadequate or disordered heterosexual functioning, they never consider the opposite—that heterosexuality represents an inadequate or disordered homosexual functioning. Male homosexuality is no more a fear or a hatred of women than is heterosexuality a hatred or fear of men; likewise, lesbianism is no more a fear or a hatred of men than is heterosexuality a hatred or fear of women. If obligatory homosexuals exclude half the available population from their sexual scope—then obligatory heterosexuals do likewise; they refuse to consider sex with any and all members of their own sex. And the faithfully married couple represents the most restrictive of all forms of sexual behavior aside from celibacy. The least restrictive sexual pattern would be displayed by the bisexual—or better yet, the "polymorphous pansexual," the man or woman who is willing to entertain the notion of sex with anyone, or even anything.

In fact, we could make a third point by taking this argument a step farther: Men and women who are self-designated homosexuals as a general rule have had far more heterosexual contact than heterosexuals have had homosexual contact. The overwhelming majority of homosexuals have at the very least given heterosexuality a try; relatively few heterosexuals, at least after adolescence, have experimented with homosexuality. We might therefore, see heterosexuality as "compulsive" and homosexuality as freely chosen!

Fourth, there is no evidence whatsoever that there is anything like a "heterosexual destiny." The pathologist's concepts of "male-female design," "anatomically determined," inexorable "evolutionary development," and "anatomical and biological capacities" are vague, almost mystical, and highly biased. Exactly what they mean in precise terms can never be determined. The anatomic equipment of men and women certainly *permits* heterosexual intercourse—but it does not dictate it. Likewise, the anatomical equipment of men permits homosexual behavior; the hands, the mouth, and the anus are as capable of sexual stimulation and satisfaction as is the vagina. And the same may be said of the anatomical equipment of women. Male and female homosexuality is as anatomically "rational" as is heterosexuality.

Fifth, just how the personalities of homosexuals are "disordered" is not altogether clear. Psychologist Evelyn Hooker subjected a number of homosexuals and matched heterosexual controls to personality tests and then asked a panel of psychiatrists and clinical psychologists to pick out which were which on the basis of their test scores. The panel did not do any better than guessing—indicating either that the tests couldn't tap whatever personality differences these two groups supposedly displayed or that there were no such differences (Hooker, 1957, 1958). Of course, it is always possible to declare by fiat that adequate heterosexual functioning is a necessary definition of mental health. Then homosexuality is by definition a sign of a disordered sexuality. But statements that are true by definition don't help us understand the world at all, since literally anything may be declared to be true by defining it that way.

Sixth, if homosexuals actually are sick, and if homosexuality actually is a manifestation of a psychosexual disorder, psychiatrists would be the last of all researchers to know it. To bolster their expertise in this area, psychotherapists claim their patients represent a cross section of all homosexuals, that whatever ailments they complain of are characteristic of homosexuals in general. But some thought renders this claim invalid. It is only homosexuals suffering from psychic distress who seek help of psychiatrists in the first place. What about those who are happy, well adjusted, satisfied with their lives? Why should they seek psychotherapy? The fact is, they wouldn't. And psychiatrists would not know of such people, of how typical they might be, or how atypical their own patients are. And their theories do not for the most part take this simple fact into account. They reason solely and exclusively from their own patients. Imagine if a psychiatrist tried to claim that all shoe salesmen suffer from mental illness. When pressed for evidence, the reply is, "Because all of my patients who are shoe salesmen suffer from mental illness!" Of course; that's why they see a psychiatrist in the first place! Absurd as this whimsical example is, it corresponds exactly to the type of evidence that has been presented when the personalities of homosexuals are described. Psychiatric descriptions and explanations of homosexuality are almost without exception based on this fundamental fallacy.[1]

COMING OUT

The term "coming out" does not have a precise meaning in the gay world; in fact, it has several meanings. One is to decide that one is, in fact, a homosexual—to accept a homosexual *identity* for oneself. Another meaning of the term is to make a public disclosure of one's homosexuality among other homosexuals, to "come out of the closet." And a third meaning is to participate in the homosexual subculture. Hooker (1965: 99) and Gagnon and Simon (1973: 143–145) define "coming out" as including self-identity *and* public exploration of the homosexual community. Dank (1971) uses the term to mean "identifying oneself as being homosexual"; this self-identification, he writes "may or may not occur in a social context in which other gay people are present" (1971: 181). One aspect of "coming out," then, is *accepting a homosexual identity* (Troiden, 1979, 1988: 35ff; Plummer, 1975; Cass, 1979, 1984; Ponse, 1978). Regarding oneself as gay—in the vocabulary of some, recognizing that one *is* a homosexual—is not something that happens automatically. Translating the erotic feelings one

holds for others of the same sex, or translating same-gender sexual behavior that one has experienced, is a long, often difficult, and socially patterned process.

There is a considerable independence between engaging in homosexual behavior—and even recognizing that what one is doing is, in fact, "homosexual" behavior—and adopting a homosexual identity. Dank (1971) reports a six-year interval between a person's awareness of his first same-gender sexual arousal and the decision that he is a homosexual. Homosexuality is not an orientation that one learns directly from one's parents, or from any other agency of childhood socialization. Nearly everything one learns from the heterosexual majority about homosexuality is negative. It is such an uncomplimentary image that no one would want to embrace it. In fact, not only is the homosexual role saturated with stigma, but so is homosexual behavior and erotic desires toward someone of the same gender. Consequently, very few young people who do actually feel sexual desires toward members of the same sex will identify these desires as specifically "homosexual." In addition, very few who engage in homosexual behavior will, at its initial inception, define it as "homosexual." So the first two processes that must take place for men and women who eventually say to themselves, "I am a homosexual," is that their *desires* and their *experiences* must be specified as, essentially, homosexual in nature.

Initially, such experiences will be defined away as adolescent horseplay rather than as a prelude to adult homosexuality. (In fact, this is usually actually the case: what they do usually *is* adolescent horseplay.) Such desires will be seen as "a passing phase," a "childhood crush," meaningless and not indicative of anything in general. The public stereotype of homosexuality is so denigrating and unattractive in our society that, most young people will reason, no self-respecting human being would want to be identified with the label. What someone who feels homosexual desires or who derives pleasure from homosexual contact will say is something like, "I know that homosexuality is an ugly, dirty

---

[1]Occasionally a psychiatrist will study groups of unconventional people "chosen at random." However, their casual and anecdotal use of evidence and their insistence that their techniques, alone of all research tactics, yield the truth, makes their claims suspect. For example, see Hendin, 1975.

thing, so this can't be a homosexual experience, since it feels good and I like this person." Identification of gay experiences will bring about a crushing feeling of guilt, a sense that "there's something wrong with me." Consequently, their gayness must be explained away. "I started to realize that I felt a sexual attraction for other men.... I passed the attraction off as being due to the circumstances—the loneliness and the need for female companionship," explains a man who was enlisted in the military service at the time. "I rationalized my feelings as indicating ... deep friendship.... The possibility that I might be gay terrified me" (Troiden, 1977).

Once experiences and feelings have been identified as homosexual in nature, the next step is seeing oneself as homosexual. Just as it is possible to say to oneself, "Yes, I lied, but I'm not a liar," or "I did get drunk last night, it's true, but I'm not an alcoholic," likewise, many men and woman can (and do) say, "I had a homosexual experience, but I'm not a homosexual." Being a homosexual is condemned in our society far more than is engaging in homosexual acts. Being a homosexual means, to most of us, adopting the homosexual role, of being saturated through and through with a stigmatizing and shameful identity. An act is what one *does;* it is possible to distance oneself from it. But an identity is what one *is:* Distancing oneself is impossible in every sense of the word. It is part of one's *essence,* the core of one's being. So this is a very basic step. Seeing one's experiences as homosexual is a necessary but not a sufficient condition for seeing oneself as gay. It is only one step, far from the final one. At some point, men and women begin to "suspect" that they might be gay. Being continually *aroused* by members of one's own sex is one element in this process. Having homosexual fantasies also ushers in the process. And engaging in homosexual activities—and especially enjoying it, in spite of the guilt that often accompanies it—also will commonly cause one to question one's sexual orientation. But remember, probably most men and women have had sexual desires toward a member of their own sex at least once, most have had same-gender sexual fantasies, and at least a significant minority of both sexes have had homosexual experiences. But only a tiny proportion of this total comes to see themselves as being *a* homosexual. What, then, precipitates the gays out from the straights?

The answer is a combination of several things. One is *a persistent lack of erotic and/or emotional interest in the opposite sex.* Second is the continuing failure of one's ability to explain away one's homosexuality. Third is having a deep, significant, meaningful homosexual experience with someone whom one respects and loves. Fourth is having an intimate, particularly one who is gay, explain to one that one *is,* in fact, gay. And last is dramatically realizing that there are many attractive, desirable, "normal" men or women—who don't fit one's preconception of the homosexual—who are gay. In some as yet unknown combination, these factors come together to bring someone who *suspects* that he or she is gay to gradually *accept* and *incorporate* it into his or her identity. Being introduced to a particular homosexual scene in which one meets large numbers of desirable, attractive people who destroy the public stereotype of what it means to be gay— that there are many likeminded individuals—can be particularly electrifying.

I knew that there were homosexuals, queers and what not; I had read some books, and I was resigned to the fact that I was a foul, dirty person, but I wasn't actually calling myself a homosexual yet.... I went to this guy's house and there was nothing going on, and I asked him, "Where is some action?" and he said, "There is a bar down the way." And the time I really caught myself coming out is the time I walked into this bar and saw a whole crowd of groovy, groovy guys. And I said to myself, there was the realization, that not all gay men are dirty old men or idiots, silly queens, but there are some just normal-looking and acting people, as far as I could see. I saw gay society and I said, "Wow, I'm home" (Dank, 1971: 187).

What is necessary is for the individual to be able to neutralize the stereotype of what it means to be a homosexual—to "change

... the meaning of the cognitive category homosexual before they can place themselves in the category" (Dank, 1971: 189). Homosexuality must be seen as a morally and psychiatrically neutral or even desirable status. A vocabulary of motives has to be adopted that places one's actions and status in the realm of normalcy—even if this interpretation is rejected among the heterosexual majority: "Being a homosexual does not label a person as sick or mentally ill. In every other capacity I am as normal or more normal than straight people. Just because I happen to like strawberry ice cream and they like vanilla, doesn't make them right or me right" (Dank, 1971: 190). In short, what is at stake here is the individual's sense of esteem and self-worth. And this necessitates "an entire transformation in the meaning to the concept of homosexual for the subject." In the words of one subject, "I had always thought of them as dirty old men that preyed on 10-, 11-, 12-year-old kids, and I found out that they weren't all that way.... It was a relief for me 'cause I found out that I wasn't so different from many other people.... I thought I was mentally ill. Now I accept it as a way of life, and I don't consider it a mental illness.... I consider myself an outcast from general society, but not mentally ill" (Dank, 1971: 191).

I met a straight guy when I was in college.... As our friendship developed, I realized that I was falling in love with him and that I had never cared for anyone as deeply as I cared for him.... One night we were out drinking with a bunch of guys at a college bar. We both got rather high and when we returned to the dorm I went with him to his room. It was the beginning of a very beautiful night. I walked over to him, put my arms around him, and kissed him. He reciprocated. We eventually masturbated each other to orgasm. He is now married and has a family. This incident led to a fateful resignation that I was irrevocably gay. Due to the beauty of the experience ..., I was able to rid myself of any doubts that I had regarding my being a homosexual as negating the possibility of being a good person (Troiden, 1977).

Heterosexual conceptions of homosexuality not only define it in negative terms; they also make a "big deal" out of it. As men and women who gradually come to the realization that they are gay begin to "come out," they also come to see that being gay is not the "big deal" they have been taught it is. One male homosexual explained it to me in the following words: "Before you come out, you see being gay as this huge, monstrous thing. In fact, the sexual side of being gay is no more a big deal in one's life than it is for straight people." So not only does the homosexual neutralize the stigma of being gay in his or her vocabulary of motives, he or she also minimizes its *weight*. It assumes manageable proportions.

DIFFERENCES BETWEEN MALE AND FEMALE HOMOSEXUALS

Heterosexuals tend to view aspects of the life of the homosexual more or less in its entirety as stemming from its uniquely homosexual character. The homosexual's gender choice is a "prepossessing concern" on the part of nonhomosexuals (Gagnon and Simon, 1973: 137). Many heterosexuals forget that what homosexuals are and do may have nothing to do with their sexual preferences. Actually, although there are parallels between male and female homosexuals by virtue of the fact that their behavior and their character are widely condemned by "straights," and by virtue of the fact that they are alienated from many mainstream institutions, actually, the differences between them are in many ways far more striking. In most crucial respects, the lesbian is more similar to her heterosexual sister than she is to the male homosexual. Consequently, the differences between male and female homosexuals should be instructive.

Perhaps the most striking difference between male homosexuals and lesbians has to do with the nature of their sexual—and emotional—relationships. Typically, the male homosexual has had intercourse with many partners on a relatively anonymous, impersonal basis. In a reanalysis of the original Kinsey data, two researchers show about half of the male homosexuals in the sample reported that 60 percent or more of their sexual partners were men with whom they had had sex with *only once*. And for four-fifths of the sample, their longest homosexual affair lasted less than a year (Gagnon and Simon, 1973: 139, 140). Every study that has ever been conducted on the subject has found that male homosexuals tend to be extremely promiscuous. (Not every one is, and many are involved in long-term monogamous relationships, but the general tendency is difficult to deny.) In a study I was involved in, 23 percent of the sample said that they had had intercourse with 500 or more partners; the point at which the category designating respondents who had slept with the *least* number of partners was drawn at under 100 partners (Goode and Troiden, 1979). Another study found that 43 percent of the white male homosexuals and 33 percent of the black homosexuals said that they had had 500 or more homosexual partners; 79 percent of the whites and 51 percent of the blacks said that more than half of their partners were strangers (Bell and Weinberg, 1978: 308).

Lesbians, in contrast, tend to have fewer sexual relationships, the relationships tend to last much longer, and both partners tend to be far more romantically involved than is true for male homosexuals. In the Kinsey volume on women, it was found that the number of sexual partners that homosexual and heterosexual women had been involved with was almost identical—for both, about half had had sex with only *one* partner, and a bit over 10 percent had had sex with six or more partners (Kinsey et al., 1953: 336, 492). No doubt for both groups, the figure is different today, but the male-female differences are still marked. In a much more recent comparison between male and female homosexuals (with heterosexual controls) the same basic pattern was uncovered. Nearly all the male homosexuals (94 percent) had had sex with 10 or more partners, but this was true of only a tiny minority of the lesbians (15 percent). Although only one of the male homosexuals in the sample had had sexual contact with three or fewer partners, this was true of 30 percent of the lesbians and 60 percent of the heterosexual women (Saghir and Robins, 1973: 59, 229). Another way of saying this is that female homosexuals tend to be more interested in much more of the *total person* of their sex partners. For them, sex is more than just sex. Their more romantic and intense commitment inclines them to be concerned with all aspects of their partner's personality and being. Most heterosexuals—particularly men—fixate on, and exaggerate the importance of, the specifically *sexual* side of lesbianism. In fact, lesbians see their orientation as primarily a *romantic* matter, a holistic approach toward women, a life-style, a way of being. The sexual side is only one facet of that life-style. Male homosexuals, in contrast, tend to be far more interested in their sex partners specifically *as* sex partners. There is, in fact, a more intense *genital fixation* for male homosexuals.

The comparative number, intensity, and duration of their relationships also has a reflection in the twin phenomena of *cruising* and the *locales* of sexual activity (Delph, 1978). Male homosexuals, especially those who live in large, urban areas, are often "on the lookout for some action." Between a third and a half of the adult male homosexuals in one study, depending on their age, customarily had sex both in public and private settings. In comparison, "no homosexual women ever engaged in sexual activity in a public place" (Saghir and Robins, 1973: 236).

Cruising as a purposeful activity aimed primarily at finding sexual partners is a very different behavior when practiced by the homosexual women compared to the homosexual men.... Cruising among the men is an intense activity involving a multiplicity of places and hangouts, many of them public facilities like parks, beaches, movie houses, streets, bars and numerous other locales. Among the homosexual women, cruising of public places is almost nonexistent and, when it occurs, it is usually done within the framework of a socially acceptable setting. To find a sex partner, the homosexual women usually embark on establishing a relationship over a period of weeks or months before any sexual contact occurs (Saghir and Robins, 1973: 234).

Male homosexuals are typically much more impatient and wish to start (and end) the sexual side of the relationship at the first meeting.

Perhaps the two locales that represent an extreme version of the impersonal sex that characterizes many homosexual encounters are certain steam baths and public urinals in large cities, which acquire a reputation for places that are frequented by men interested in quick, easy, impersonal sex. (Not all—or even most—of the men that visit the "tearooms" are self-admitted homosexuals, remember.) In the baths, one gay author explains, "verbal foreplay is rare" and "the accent is on genitalia. . . . Romance is removed from the sex act and is reduced to lust." One bath house attempted to cater to lesbians, in addition to male homosexuals. "Instead of zeroing in on each other, the women preferred to chat in the television lounge. There was hardly any stalking, very little sex transpired. After a month, the place reverted to an all-male policy." The sex that goes on in the baths involves men who are, "like the extras in *Quo Vadis*, . . . faceless and nameless" (Bell, 1976). One sociologist observed sexual encounters between men in public restrooms. Of 50 such encounters on which he took notes, in only 15 of these was there any exchange of words *at all* between partners, so impersonal were they (Humphreys, 1970: 12).

It is true that sex in public places like "tearooms" (public urinals) and the baths represents the most impersonal of all homosexual encounters that could be engaged in. But it is also true that such encounters are almost totally absent among lesbians. The willingness of many male homosexuals to engage in completely impersonal sex with many other men marks them off from lesbians in a distinct fashion. Entire institutions are supported by the casual sex of male homosexuals. The gay bar, for instance, is *primarily* for the purpose of meeting and picking up new sex partners. "A gay bar where you couldn't pick anyone up would stay in business around a day and a half," a gay man explained to me. This is not true of lesbian bars—lesbian bars are primarily for the purpose of socializing with friends—and it is true of only a minority of bars where heterosexuals mingle. But it is also true that cruising and promiscuity among gay males *is a distinctly male phenomenon*. It is not specific to *gay* males. Were heterosexual females as willing to engage in casual sex as men are, then the world of heterosexuality would be as marked by casual sex as the world of male homosexuality. It is only because most heterosexual females keep the cruising tendencies of heterosexual males in check that heterosexuality is not marked by the volume of casual sex that prevails among male homosexuals.

Male homosexuals also begin their sexual activity much earlier in their lives than female homosexuals. When asked about the age of the "onset" of mutual masturbation, 60 percent of a sample of male homosexuals said that it began at age 13 or earlier; only 15 percent said age 20 or older. For fellatio, 24 percent began it at age 13 or younger, and 32 percent said 20 or older. But for lesbians, the percentage saying that the onset of mutual genital stimulation was at age 13 or younger was only 9 percent; 51 percent said 20 or older. For cunnilingus, it was 2 percent at age 13 or younger, and 72 percent age 20 or older (Saghir and Robins, 1973: 51, 219, 221).

Lesbians have also had a great deal more *heterosexual* contact than male homosexuals have. In one study, slightly under half (48 percent) of the male homosexuals said they had had intercourse with a woman, but over three-quarters of the female homosexuals (79 percent) said they had had intercourse with a man at least once. In fact, the lesbians were more likely to have had heterosexual intercourse than the *heterosexual* women were—79 percent versus 58 percent (Saghir and Robins, 1973: 88, 246). Of those women who did have intercourse, about the same proportion said that they had had it with five or more men—69 percent for lesbians and 60 percent for the heterosexual women. As many homosexual as heterosexual women had been maritally proposed to by a man (Saghir and Robins, 1973: 250), a fact that resoundingly refutes the notion that lesbians are, in some way, "failed" women with respect to their sexual desirability to men.

Goode and Haber (1977) found that college women who had had at least one homosexual experience (not necessarily self-admitted lesbians) were strikingly more likely to have had intercourse than women without homosexual experience; they were also more likely to have had intercourse with a larger number of male partners. The median number of men that the homosexually experienced women had had intercourse with was 5, and the mean was 7.4; for the homosexually inexperienced women, these figures were 2 and 3.6. They also tended to have been more heterosexually *precocious*, that is, they had had intercourse for the first time between a year and a year and a half younger in their lives. The two groups of women did differ significantly on the dimension of the experience of loveless heterosexual relationships in which they had intercourse, the enjoyment of fellatio, and the source of their most pleasurable orgasm. Women who had had homosexual experience were far more likely to have ever had intercourse with a man they were not in love with—80 percent versus 53 percent. They were less likely to say that they usually enjoyed fellating a man (20 percent versus 46 percent), and more likely to say that they usually did not enjoy it (27 percent versus 8 percent). And they were less likely to say that the source of their most pleasurable orgasm was intercourse with a man (21 percent versus 52 percent).[2]

What these and other data seem to point to is the fact that women who eventually say to themselves, "I am a lesbian" are highly likely to have at least given men a try sexually. Relatively few were totally turned off to men sexually even before they engaged in heterosexual intercourse. For the majority of lesbians, their awareness of their lack of sexual, erotic, and emotional interest in men comes from *their experiences with men,* and not their prior and relatively fixed notions of what men are like in the absence of that experience. With the awareness that they are gay, lesbians will eventually lose interest in men and stop having intercourse with them. After their early twenties, heterosexual contact among homosexual women drops off sharply. But generally this does not occur until they have sexually experimented with men.

This pattern is in strong contrast to homosexual men, who are far less likely to have had intercourse with women, especially with a number of women. This pattern emerges in part because male homosexuals come to see themselves as gay much earlier in their lives than female homosexuals do. And in part it is due to the fact that, even today, the male is expected to take the initiative sexually, and heterosexual males tend to be more sexually aggressive and even insensitive than heterosexual women; they are more likely not to "take no for an answer." Consequently, they will sometimes pressure women to have intercourse with them, women who may be only half-interested.

This leads us to another difference between homosexual men and women: their *public image* in the straight majority's eyes. There is considerably less fear and hostility on the part of the heterosexual majority toward the lesbian than toward the male homosexual. (At least this is true in contemporary America. Anthropological data indicate that in many other societies there is more outrage at female homosexuality than male.) The reasons for this are complicated. To begin with, the prevailing sexist attitude dictates that the lesbian simply hasn't met the right man yet, that she can be converted to heterosexuality by an aggressive, expert lover. (And many men fantasize that they could be that lover!) They see the lesbian as a challenge, a test to their manhood, a potential means of demonstrating their virility. They think of lesbianism as a primarily *sex-*

---

[2]Using a variety of indicators, Goode and Haber surmised that the women with at least some homosexual experience formed a very mixed group. Some could be called sexual "adventurers," and their experiences with other women were simply one out of a number of viable sexual experiences that they wished to try—and actually did try. It is out of this group that women who come to see themselves as bisexuals will emerge. And others will eventually decide they are lesbians and will abandon intercourse with men altogether as a viable option for them.

ual orientation rather than a whole emotional approach to men and women.

To many heterosexual males, the lesbian is actually erotic—at least, the stereotype is, since most of them would not know a lesbian if they met one. Scenes of two or more women making love (or pretending to) with one another comprise a high proportion of pornographic fare, and prostitutes are often employed to put on a lesbian love-making scene by Johns, for whom such scenes are highly stimulating. Heterosexual women typically find lesbians a puzzlement, but not a threat. (And they typically ask lesbians questions about their *emotional* life far more than about its specifically *sexual* side, which is the side men are so curious about.)

Yet both male and female heterosexuals seem unusually threatened by male homosexuals. Perhaps both sense a threat to what they see as the very basis of manhood. Or perhaps both think that they can easily envision what male homosexuals do in bed, but they cannot conjure up a comparable image of what lesbians do. Perhaps, too, in our chauvinistic tradition, it is considered degrading for a male—the dominant sex—to play the role of the subordinate sex, by playing at femininity. (Of course, remember, there is no inherent link between femininity and male homosexuality, but most straights don't know this. They feel that the androgynous male lowers his status more than the androgynous female does—toward whom a kind of begrudging respect must be extended.) In addition, since the male homosexual's style is so much more conspicuous, more blatant, and more public, and the lesbian's is more low-key, unobtrusive, less overt, and obvious, he comes to the public eye more and, consequently, is available for, and attracts, more public condemnation. All of this is not to say that female homosexuals do not meet with widespread and strong disapproval, denunciation, and hostility from the straight majority. Indeed they do. But it does not have quite the savagery that the male homosexual faces. But notice: It is primarily because of *sexism* that this is the case. It is only because the dominant heterosexual male does not take lesbianism seriously that it is not condemned to the same degree as male homosexuality. Ironically, it may be the case that the more seriously lesbianism is taken by heterosexuals the greater the threat they will see from it, and consequently, the more they will condemn and sanction those who practice it.

HOMOSEXUALITY AND AIDS

As we saw, in some ways, public attitudes toward homosexuality are worsening: In 1987, more Americans felt homosexual relations should be illegal (55 percent) than felt that way in 1982 (39 percent). We cannot doubt the AIDS crisis has a great deal to do with this trend. In 1985, the Gallup Poll asked the American public whether the recent AIDS epidemic changed their attitudes toward homosexuals. Over a third (37 percent) said it changed them for the worse, whereas only 2 percent said it changed these feelings for the better (Gallup, 1986). Clearly, to understand the feelings of the heterosexual majority toward homosexuality and homosexuals, we have to know something about AIDS.

AIDS—acquired immunity deficiency syndrome—was not diagnosed until 1981, and the virus that causes the disease was not isolated until 1983. Once again, the media attention focused on the subject indicates a measure of the public's concern. In the 1981 to 1982 period, there are no articles listed in *The Reader's Guide to Periodical Literature* on AIDS, meaning no articles on the subject appeared in any of the popular magazines and newspapers published in the United States and Canada that *Reader's Guide* indexes. In 1982 to 1983, there were 9. In 1983 to 1984, the real beginning of media attention to the disease, there were 68. In 1984 to 1985, 70 were listed in the *Guide*. In the full year 1985, 175 were indexed by *Reader's Guide*. In 1986, this had risen to 225; and in 1987, it jumped to 593. Two conclusions can be reached from this tally: (1) public concern, like the disease itself, is extremely recent; and (2) it is growing at an explosive rate.

There are some good reasons for the pub-

The Violent Practice of "Gay Bashing"

James Chavez, a 26-year-old homosexual, tried to enter what he thought was a gay bar in Portland, Oregon. It turned out he was wrong, and two teenagers swiftly beat Chavez to death. In New York City, a former police officer and the son of a minister, sprayed two well-known gay bars in Greenwich Village with gunfire from an arsenal of weapons, including an Israeli-made Uzi submachine gun; two men were killed and six were wounded. "I just don't like faggots," the man explained after being arrested. Four University of California baseball players in Riverside attacked a campus gay activist and were temporarily suspended. "Almost every gay I know has been mugged," says a recent victim of a San Francisco attack. "It's random, senseless fag bashing by young kids who think they can get away with it" (Reese, 1981).

Maine has one of the lowest rates of violence in the country; in the past decade, there had been only six murders in Bangor. And yet, one day in July, three teenage boys accosted Charles Howard, a flamboyant 23-year-old gay man, began punching him, and dragged him to the railing of a bridge over a stream. "No! No! I can't swim," Howard screamed, but the boys threw him into the water and watched him drown. "He attracted abuse and derision by his appearance and manner," said a friend. "Many of us who knew him admired his courage. He died of it" (Butterfield, 1984).

Two young men, Barry Finnegan, age 19, and David Frank, age 20, were crossing a Manhattan street when they were approached by six teenagers, who began shouting "Homos!" and "Fags!" The young men ignored the taunts and continued walking, but the boys assaulted them with knives, bats, and fists. Finnegan, who was stabbed twice in the chest, suffered a collapsed lung and had to be taken to the hospital; Frank was treated for a fractured elbow and was released. The police could not locate any suspects. A spokesperson for the New York City Gay and Lesbian Anti-Violence Project said such assaults increased 36 percent between 1987 and 1988. "Last year, we are more likely to see people struck or punched. . . . This year,

we're getting more cases of physical assault with a real weapon, like a gun, or a knife, or a bat." He added that in half of the incidents that took place during the first six months of 1988, derogatory references were made by the attackers to AIDS; in 1987, this was only 30 percent (Hays, 1988).

A systematic interview of male and female homosexuals conducted in Philadelphia in 1987 revealed that gays are subjected to far more criminal violence than is the American population as a whole. Nearly half of the gay men in the sample (46 percent) and a fifth of the women (20 percent) reported they have experienced at least one episode of criminal violence during the preceding year because of their sexual orientation. For the men, this was almost 12 times higher than the average rate for men in the general population; and for women, it was 9 times higher than for women generally. Nearly three-quarters of the men (73 percent) and 4 in 10 of the women (42 percent) said they experienced at least one episode of criminal violence during their lifetime because they were gay. Moreover, the rates of criminal violence for gays in 1987 were twice as high as they were for gays in 1984, when a comparable study was conducted (Gross et al., 1988: 9).

One of the ways people defined by the majority as deviants may experience their deviance is that they are more likely to be the victim of verbal and even physical attacks than is true of conventionals. Moreover, they are less likely to be protected by either the police or by the conventionals who do not attack them. Perhaps no deviant minority is as subject to physical attacks as male homosexuals; perhaps no deviant minority is as unlikely to be protected.

Why is there so much violence against homosexuals? Some argue, rightly or wrongly, that gay men are perceived to be an easy target, too effeminate to fight back. Others cite the rise of a more conservative, even reactionary mood in the country, legitimating violence against unpopular, unconventional minorities. Add to this mixture that many attackers of gays see themselves as failures, increases the possibility of violence. "The have-nots are frustrated, angry. . . . Anyone considered a deviant is a perfect scapegoat" (Reese, 1981).

Although mainstream conservatives do not condone such violence, some far-right political and religious figures have defended and encouraged it. In 1982, the Reverend Jimmy Swaggart, a television evangelist who was recently in trouble for his own sexually deviant acts, published a pamphlet in which he declared, "God is saying here that not only is the homosexual worthy of death, but perhaps also those who approve of homosexuality." The Reverend Ernst Rueda, a Roman Catholic priest, in a book distributed to state and federal legislators, defended individuals who attack gays "as social agents of the majority." Noach Dear, a New York City politician and Orthodox Jew, declared on television that homosexuals wouldn't be beaten up if they did not let straight people know they are gay—"blaming the victims, not the perpetrators of violence." The message that these figures "and other so-called leaders send is quite clear: Beating up gay people is O.K." (Martin, 1988: A25).

One of the more dramatic and tragic of recent events demonstrating that some heterosexuals condone gay bashing—indeed, even killing homosexuals—was the ruling of a Texas judge in a murder case. One night in Dallas, a group of nine teenage boys drove to a section of town "to pester the homosexuals." It is a common practice for teenage boys in this area to spend evenings in neighborhoods known to be frequented by gays for the purpose of harassing and beating them up. Tommy Lee Trimble, age 34, and Lloyd Griffin, 27, drove to a street corner where these boys were standing and invited them into their car. One of them, Richard Lee Bednarski, 18, got into the car and, after it reached a secluded spot, ordered Trimble and Griffin to remove their clothes. When they refused, Bednarski drew a revolver and began firing, killing both of them. The Judge, Jack Hampton, who decided the case, declared he gave the youth a more lenient sentence than the prosecutors sought because the victims would not have been killed "if they hadn't been cruising the streets picking up teenage boys. . . . I put prostitutes and gays at about the same level," he said, "and I'd be hard put to give somebody life for killing a prostitute." Judge Hampton added, "I don't care much for queers cruising the streets. I've got a teenage boy" (Belkin, 1988).

The most widely used theory to explain this violence is that many assailants are angry and insecure regarding their own sexual identity. They hate gays because they fear they are not themselves sufficiently masculine, or might be "queer" themselves. Their inner turmoil and hostility turn outward to obvious homosexuals, attacking what they fear most in themselves. And since, in our society, masculinity is associated with violence, they reason that they can't be homosexual because they beat someone up—and a "queer" to boot! One indication this may be true for many perpetrators of violence against gays is that, in a homicide involving a homosexual male, the victim is rarely simply shot as is the case with most killings. Murders involving a gay male are often vicious and gruesome. "He is more apt to be stabbed a dozen or more times, mutilated and strangled" (Miller and Humphreys, 1980: 179).

lic to be concerned about AIDS. As far as experts are able to tell, no one recovers from the disease; seven years after a victim is infected, the fatality rate is 100 percent. AIDS kills its sufferers by destroying the body's immune systems, making fatal infection from a host of other diseases inevitable. It is possible that no disease in recent memory has been as feared as AIDS, and none has had as great a social impact on our lives (Turner, 1985: B7). By October 1988, over 75,000 cases of AIDS had been diagnosed in the United States; of these, 42,000 have died. New AIDS cases for the first nine months of 1988 numbered 23,000, up by nearly 10,000 compared with the same period for 1987 (Boffey, 1988). AIDS has an extremely long incubation period; individuals can have been infected with the virus for as much as seven years without contracting the disease itself. Therefore, even if the spread of the virus is completely halted, many more new cases of the disease will continue to appear for some time to come. The Centers for Disease Control (CDC) estimates that as many as 1.5 million Americans may be infected with the AIDS virus who have not yet developed symptoms of the disease itself. (At the same time, everyone admits this figure is extremely rough and could be wildly off the mark. Moreover, no one knows what proportion of those who carry the virus will eventually fall victim to the disease itself; it could be one in 10, half, or the majority.) The World Health Organization estimates 5 to 10 million people worldwide are infected with the AIDS virus, and between 500,000 and 3 million new cases will appear between 1988 and 1993. In the United States, the actual number of new cases will not begin to plateau or decline until the early 1990s.

In Africa, thought to be the origin of the disease, the vast majority of AIDS cases are heterosexuals, and half are women. In contrast, in Europe, North America, Australia, and New Zealand, the majority of AIDS cases are homosexual men; because of this, in the early years of the disease in this country, it was termed the "gay plague." There is still a strong identification in the mind of the public between homosexuality and the disease, in spite of the fact that a quarter to a third of all AIDS victims are not homosexual. Actually, the virus has ceased to spread among homosexuals, although tens of thousands (possibly hundreds of thousands) more male homosexuals will contract the disease in the future. New infections have occurred among gay men at the rate of only 1 percent a year for the late 1980s; in contrast, among intravenous drug users, new infections have occurred at the rate of 7 to 8 percent a year. It is possible that a quarter of all American gays are infected with the AIDS virus and, further, that a substantial proportion of them will eventually die of the disease unless a cure is found. Thus, in spite of the halt in the spread of the AIDS virus among male homosexuals, AIDS could become a holocaust among gays.

Experts at the Centers for Disease Control (CDC), putting together data from dozens of separate studies, have estimated the number of infected individuals at between 945,000 and 1.4 million (see Table 8.1), of whom only 75,000 have actually contracted the disease itself.

It must be emphasized that AIDS is an extremely frightening disease; it is always fatal, it is extremely recent, the number of cases is growing rapidly, and the total number of victims may reach staggering totals. Taken individually, these facts ought to frighten anyone; and taken as a whole, they are over-

TABLE 8.1 CDC Estimates of Proportions and Numbers Infected with AIDS Virus

	Proportion Infected with AIDS Virus	Estimated Number Infected
Homosexual men	20–25 percent	500,000–625,000
Bisexuals	5 percent	125,000–375,000
IV drug users	20 percent	235,000
Hemophiliacs	63 percent	10,000
Heterosexuals*	.021 percent	30,000
Others**	unknown	45,000–127,000
Total		945,000–1.4 million

*Heterosexuals without specific identified risks

**Includes heterosexual partners of people at high risk, transfusion recipients, and individuals born in Haiti and Central Africa

SOURCE: Boffey, 1988: 18, based on data supplied by the Centers for Disease Control

whelming. On the other hand, there are much less frightening features of AIDS as well, the most important is that it is extremely *difficult* to contract the disease. The AIDS virus lives outside the body for only a short period of time, and it is not very communicable. Someone can't get AIDS by being bitten by a mosquito or from a toilet seat, or being in the same room as, shaking hands with, touching or hugging, kissing, drinking out of the same glass, being sneezed on, swimming in the same pool, or eating food prepared by an infected person. As far as experts are able to tell, the only way someone can contract the AIDS virus is through an exchange of bodily fluids with a carrier. Practically speaking, this means in only one of four ways: (1) receiving contaminated blood through a transfusion; (2) injecting oneself with a needle previously contaminated by a carrier; (3) having sex, especially anal sex, with someone carrying the virus; and (4) being born to an AIDS-contaminated mother. A small number of health workers, including one physician, have become infected by being stuck with an AIDS-contaminated needle. As we saw in Chapter 7, vaginal intercourse is an extremely *inefficient* means of spreading AIDS; experts estimate that someone who engages in a single act of intercourse with an infected person has between 1 in 1,000 and 1 in 100,000 chance of catching the virus. Said one science writer, the chance of picking up the AIDS virus from a partner in a singles bar "is about the same as the chance of winning the jackpot in a state lottery" (Langone, 1988). The likelihood that a non-drug-using heterosexual who is not a hemophiliac and has only non-drug-using heterosexual partners who are not hemophiliacs, will get AIDS over a lifetime is less than the chance of being struck by lightning; such a person is 200 times more likely to die in an automobile accident than get AIDS, and 1,000 times more likely to be murdered (Langone, 1985: 31).[3]

Given these facts, we would have to conclude there is something of a contemporary AIDS *panic* among heterosexuals. There is far less threat from AIDS to them personally than most people believe. To put it another way, Americans fear AIDS more than they fear many other more prodigious causes of disease and death.

In a Gallup Poll conducted in 1987, an overwhelming majority (87 percent) said contracting AIDS is "likely" for people who have "several sexual partners"; a clear majority of those questioned (59 percent) said it is likely for married people who "have an occasional affair"; and a bare majority (51 percent) said it is likely *for the population at large!* Less than 1 in 10 (9 percent) believed AIDS is likely for "couples who are entirely faithful" (Gallup, 1988: 292–309).

In the same poll, a substantial minority of Americans questioned believed it is possible to contract AIDS from insect bites (30 percent), donating blood (29 percent), eating food prepared or handled by someone with AIDS (26 percent), from a drinking glass (26 percent), being coughed or sneezed upon (25 percent), from toilet seats (18 percent), working alongside or in close proximity to someone with AIDS (11 percent), and from a friendly kiss on the cheek (8 percent). Although nearly all (97 percent) said one could get AIDS from sharing a hypodermic needle and having "intimate sexual contact" with someone of the same sex (95 percent), almost the same proportion (88 percent) said the same for sexual contact with someone of the opposite gender (Gallup, 1988: 274–289).

[3]It should be said that not all experts agree with this assessment—although nearly all do. Three sex experts (they are not epidemiologists and have no expertise in

this highly technical area), Masters, Johnson, and Kolodny (1988a, 1988b) claim the infected population is over two times the Centers for Disease Control (CDC) estimate and argue, generalizing from a single unrepresentative sample, that the AIDS virus is "now running rampant in the heterosexual community"; their estimate of the number of non-drug-using heterosexuals who are AIDS virus carriers is nearly seven times the CDC's estimate—or 200,000. It should also be added that the Masters-Johnson-Kolodny estimates wildly exceed those of the vast majority of experts in the field (Eckholm, 1988; Monmaney, 1988), but they do point out that very little is known for certain in this new and controversial area.

In addition to much of the public's substantially overblown conception of the likelihood of contracting AIDS, Americans are also highly likely to *stigmatize* AIDS victims. Over three-quarters of the respondents of the 1987 Gallup Poll said AIDS sufferers should be treated with "compassion" (78 percent), nearly half (48 percent) said they should be allowed to live in the community "normally," and only a minority (33 percent) said employers have the right to dismiss an employee because that person has AIDS; but a substantial proportion displayed more punitive and condemnatory attitudes toward AIDS victims. Over half (51 percent) agreed with the statement, "In general, it's people's own fault if they get AIDS." Nearly half (42 percent) said, "I sometimes think AIDS is a punishment for the decline in moral standards." And a whopping 6 in 10 (60 percent) said, "People with the AIDS virus should be made to carry a card to this effect" (Gallup, 1988: 211, 264). A substantial minority (43 percent) said they plan not to associate with people they "suspect might have AIDS." This figure was exactly 50 percent for males; and for the youngest age group, 18 to 29, it was a staggering 60 percent (Gallup, 1988: 168, 169).

It should come as no surprise that the negative sentiments held by much of the American public toward AIDS sufferers, which emerge in these polls and interview studies, have also expressed themselves in numerous discriminatory and even hostile incidents. In New York City, a physician who treats AIDS patients was evicted from his office by the building's co-op board. Said the doctor, "People in the building didn't like AIDS patients walking through the lobby." In New Orleans, a writer was fired from his editing job after publishing an article discussing his own suspected case of AIDS. "They just walked in and said, 'Get the hell out,'" he recalls. In Indiana, Ryan White, age 13, a hemophiliac and an AIDS patient, was not allowed to attend the seventh grade; school officials, fearing contamination of the other pupils, did not want the youngster in class. Said the superintendent, "What are you going to do about someone chewing

pencils or sneezing or swimming in the pool?"

"AIDS victims are treated like lepers even by some in the medical community. Ambulance workers in several cities have refused to transport desperately ill patients to hospitals. Hospital orderlies are reluctant to clean their rooms. Nurses are wary. . . . In St. Louis and New York, undertakers have refused to embalm the remains of patients." Even in the face of the horror of their medical problems, many AIDS sufferers say the most painful aspect of their condition is the stigma, rejection, and social isolation they experience (Wallis et al., 1985: 45).

As we saw in the Gallup polls, negative feeling toward homosexuals has increased since the advent of AIDS. One "openly homosexual faculty member" at a conservative, religiously affiliated university (Southern Methodist) attended a public debate held by the SMU Student Senate on the question of whether the Gay/Lesbian Student Support Organization should be recognized. "In the glare of television cameras, homosexuals (including, presumably, the dozens of us present, both students and faculty) were compared to rapists, thieves and robbers. We were portrayed as sinners and liars. The group would serve as a student-faculty sex club, a vehicle for orgies and recruitment." Worst of all, said a speaker, homosexuals were "disease-carrying, sexual deviants"; because of AIDS, "the health—the very lives—of every person on campus would be at risk." In the midst of the debate, when the point on AIDS was raised, one young man shouted out, "Now we can shoot you" (Beauchamp, 1983).

Until the late 1960s, homosexual behavior tended to be furtive and clandestine. There were few openly gay people, and meeting other homosexuals for sexual contact was, for most, a proposition fraught with guilt and fear. Gay bars existed, to be sure, especially in large cities, but they were subject to periodic busts—and hence, public exposure. Then, one summer night in 1969, this changed dramatically. The police raided the Stonewall Inn, a bar in Manhattan's Greenwich Village. In the past, gays would have passively accepted arrest, but on this particular night, the clientele of this particular bar resisted, which touched off a riot; and the riot, in turn, some say, "gave birth to a social cause and sexual style." One outcome of the Stonewall riot was an active, open gay civil rights movement; another was a more open sexual style among gay men. Homosexual promiscuity became more acceptable, less furtive, more militant. "When liberation came along," said one homosexual spokesman, "there was a proliferation of what we already had, more bars, bigger bars. What gay men wanted was easy anonymous sex with no attachments." Throughout the 1970s, "extreme sexual activity" was regarded as legitimate by a certain segment of the male homosexual community (Norman, 1983: B8).

AIDS has completely transformed the social and sexual life of male homosexuals. As a result, promiscuous sex is no longer "in" in the gay community; the proportion of homosexual men who engage in casual pickups has declined precipitously. Steam baths, once the locus of an enormous volume of casual, anonymous sex, have either been closed by local health departments or have gone out of business due to lack of patronage. Most of the notorious sadomasochistic bars featuring on-the-premises, back-room sex—the Mine Shaft and the Anvil in Manhattan were examples—have been closed, have gone out of business, or have closed their back rooms. One study conducted in San Francisco by representatives of Atlanta's Centers for Disease Control showed that, in the four months preceding the interview, the average number of "nonsteady" sex partners among gay males—that is, those with whom the individual had sexual contact just once or twice and not again—dropped from 16 in 1978 to 3 in 1984 to only 1 in 1985. Between 1978 and 1985, 90 percent of this sample reduced the number of their nonsteady sex partners. The exposure risk from receptive oral sexual contact dropped by 68 percent, and the exposure risk from receptive anal-genital contact dropped by 96 percent (Doll et al., 1987).

Clearly, promiscuous sex and "at-risk" sexual behavior have declined sharply and significantly among gay males in recent years. Said a gay activist, the majority of gays are "no longer willing to play Russian roulette. Safer sex and monogamous relationships have taken root" (Clark et al., 1985). Psychologist Stephen Morin reported one-fifth as many homosexual men are engaging in sex with multiple partners in 1985 as compared with 1983 (Gelman et al., 1985: 29). In a survey of 500 gay men living in San Francisco in 1985, 81 percent reported they were monogamous or celibate (just a year before, the comparable figure was 69 percent); the proportion saying they had had more than one sexual partner during the previous month declined from 49 percent in the 1984 survey to 36 percent in 1985 (Anonymous, 1985). Commenting on the drastic change AIDS has had on the sex lives of gay men, one homosexual spokesperson said: "The party's over" (Clark et al., 1985).

ACCOUNT: ADOPTING A HOMOSEXUAL IDENTITY

The contributor of this account is a 35-year-old male social scientist.

The term "coming out" has many meanings. As used here, the word refers to the decision to label oneself as homosexual. I shall describe below how I came to see myself as "being" homosexual in the sense of an identity. For me (and for many other homosexuals), coming out was confusing and difficult for a number of reasons.

First, I found it difficult to identify my feelings as homosexual due to my involvement with sports. I was a very athletic and sports-minded child. I boxed; played football, basketball, and baseball; ran cross-country and track; skied, swam, and bowled; hunted, fished, and water skied. I was also active in scouting. I was an Eagle scout and earned the bronze, silver, and gold palms. Since I had been taught that "queers" were girlish, incompetent at sports, and unable to rough it in the wilderness, I found it nearly impossible to view my emerging sexual interests as homosexual.

Another reason I found it hard to see myself as gay had to do with my experiences with women. I liked women very much. I enjoyed their company and like many adolescents I dated frequently. By the time I was 16, my sexual experiences with women had included petting (above and below the waist, clothed and unclothed), intercourse, and oral sex both ways. Inaccurate stereotypes held by certain segments of Anglo-American society led me to believe that gay males hated women and were repulsed by the idea of sexual contact with them. It never entered my mind that someone could desire men sexually without disliking women. So I reasoned I could not be homosexual because I liked women, was not repulsed by them sexually, and had never had a homosexual experience. One aspect of sex with women, however, bothered me quite a bit. Although I enjoyed very much the physical release of orgasm during lovemaking with them, I never felt totally involved with them in an emotional sense. Instead, I felt distanced, removed, and detached from the lovemaking experience, as if I were viewing it from a great distance through the lens of a telescope. This sense of alienation led me to conclude that I was sexually different, but not homosexual.

Inaccurate knowledge about homosexuality and homosexuals also prevented me from labeling myself as homosexual. I thought that all male homosexuals were of two types: the masculine homosexual, who spent most of his time preying on young boys foolish enough to wander unescorted into public toilets, or the effeminate homosexual, who dressed like a woman and pranced the streets, shrieking and simpering, limp wrists aflutter. To make matters worse, I also thought that homosexuals were mentally ill, unhappy, suicidal, insane, or turned on by young boys. I was unable to conceive of myself as homosexual. As far as I could tell, there existed no points of similarity between myself and homosexual males. Although I knew I was sexually attracted to other men, I wrote such feelings off as reflecting a phase of development I would soon outgrow or bisexual tendencies. I thought that I was the only person in the world who felt this way. In short, I felt very much alone with a very terrible secret.

I decided that I was homosexual and defined myself as such once I began to meet homosexual males through mutual heterosexual friends. Initially, my mind was blown. I could not believe my eyes, or my other senses, for that matter. I mean, here I was meeting good-looking, masculine-acting and successful gay males; men who

bore scant resemblance to the negative stereotypes I had assimilated and internalized while growing up. More important, these men were decent people—thoughtful, kind, funny, intelligent, and accepting.

Sex was different too. Not so much physically, but emotionally. During lovemaking with other men, I was not plagued by the sense of detachment that had marred my heterosexual encounters. Instead, I felt vitally involved and integrated on a number of levels. In addition, I had always worried that if I were gay I would never find anyone to love and grow with over the years. Accordingly, I was shocked and delighted to learn that most homosexual males are not just interested in sex; that many desire and enter into love affairs with other men, with some relationships lasting a protracted duration.

Positive social encounters of this sort forced me to revise my attitudes and opinions radically regarding homosexuality and homosexuals. I realized that homosexuality did not preclude the possibility of being happy, well adjusted, masculine, and successful. For me, this realization dramatically marked the outset of a new way of life. Exposure to gay institutions and the opportunity to assimilate gay culture left me convinced that I had made the right choice in opting for a homosexual life-style. Would I return to heterosexuality if given the opportunity? Not a chance! (From the author's files.)

ACCOUNT: HOMOSEXUALITY

The author of this account is an office administrator in her late twenties.

When I was growing up, I regarded homosexuality as repulsive. The thought of two females or two males together sexually just didn't make any sense to me. For starters, the parts don't fit! I was under the impression that it was unnatural for two people of the same gender to be together sexually. Even science taught us that opposites attract and likes repel. But as I grew a little older, homosexuality seemed less and less unnatural to me. When I was in junior high school, it no longer seemed repulsive to me, but I still never thought I would be involved in it one day. I could accept the fact that other people chose to live their lives that way. They were happy, and that's what was important. I just never imagined that it could make me happy.

Actually, I grew up around homosexuality. I was always interested in sports and loved to play on teams. Starting in the seventh grade, I played in a summer softball league. Many of the players in this league were homosexuals. So what? I was there to play softball and as long as they kept their preference to themselves, I didn't care what they did. I found out that even some of my friends were involved in homosexuality. It bothered me at first to find this out, but I got over it. I feel that if I had not grown up around homosexuality, I never would have experienced the homosexual feelings I had.

Another big influence for me was my strong feelings for friendships. I liked to get very close to my friends. When I was a senior in high school, I met Sally. We didn't become really close until my first year in college, though. Sally was a lot of fun to be around. We seemed to be interested in the same things. We were both involved in sports, so we often ran into one another at the gym. We both liked to roller skate, and so we ended up going skating together twice a week. We were great buddies. Also, Sally is a very caring person and would do just about anything for someone. She is an especially good person to talk to. She's a good listener and she always seems to know the right thing to say. I always felt comfortable around her. It was no wonder when I did experience homosexual feelings in myself, they were for Sally.

I had been involved in a relationship with a man for over two years, and it was time for it to end. I just wasn't happy with him any more. I had become too dependent, and thought that if I ever did let go, I would be all alone. This thought made me afraid. I needed someone to talk to, and Sally was there. She listened, commented, and above all, she helped me see that I wouldn't be alone if I did let go of this relationship. The next night, she came by again and we talked some more. This time, when she left, she gave me a big hug. She said that I looked like I needed it. She made me feel very comfortable.

Right after she left, I saw my boyfriend. He told me he never wanted to see me again. So when I left, I called Sally. I told her what happened, and she came over right away and picked me up. We went to the beach and sat there for hours. She held me in her arms the whole time we were there. I felt very secure and wished we didn't have to leave. My feelings for her grew, but I still wasn't sure what to do about them.

We spent a great deal of time together. All I could think about was Sally. My only problem was whether or not to let her know how I felt about her. We sat on the beach at night and talked. I wanted to tell her exactly how I felt, but I was just too afraid. Even though she held me close that night, I couldn't be sure if there was anything else behind it, or if she just knew I needed someone to be close to, and so she comforted me. Everything up until this point had happened very naturally between us, so I decided just to continue to be natural with her. I couldn't hide how I felt any longer. The night before her birthday, we took a walk on the beach. I asked her what time it was. It was a few minutes past midnight, the day of her birthday. I looked at her, wished her a happy birthday, and then I kissed her. I realized that she was also attracted to me. I told her that I loved her, and we let nature take its course. I was overwhelmed when she told me that she loved me, too. It all seemed very natural. The two of us just came together and we've been together ever since.

The first decision I had to make was whether or not to be open to others about our relationship. At first, I didn't want anybody to know or even to see us together. It would be just between Sally and me. I told myself that I would never go into a gay bar because people who know us would see us there. And for the first couple of months, we did keep it to ourselves. Eventually, some other people did find out, but it wasn't a problem because they were homosexuals, too. We all ended up becoming good friends. This was nice because we could hang out together and more or less be ourselves. We didn't have to hide our feelings. It doesn't seem fair that homosexuals have to keep their feelings inside when they are in public. We are two people who are very much in love with one another, but we can't show it unless we are alone or among homosexuals. That's the main reason why I like to go to gay bars now. It is the one place where we can openly show our affection for one another. The first time I went into one, though, I felt very uncomfortable. Even though I was with Sally, I was worried about who I might know there. Once I was relaxed, though, I began to feel great. Now I look forward to going out to gay bars. I don't care if I do know anybody there, or if anyone sees me there.

There's a common belief about homosexuality I can't agree with. This is the belief that homosexuals only like people of the same gender. When people began finding out I was seeing Sally, their first reaction was, "How could you like girls that way?" Well, I don't "like" girls that way. I fell in love with Sally, a person—and not her gender. With me, I fall in love with the person first, and only then do I consider their gender. When someone is called gay, it gives me the impression that the person is only interested in people of the same gender and thinks of heterosexual relations as repulsive. I don't like to be referred to as gay. I prefer to be considered as a homosexual *right now.* I am sexually attracted to and romantically involved with a person of the same gender now—Sally. The only unanswered question in my mind now is whether or not I will always be a homosexual. I don't know for sure if my relationship with Sally is going to last. I do know that if it doesn't work out, the next person I fall in love with could very well be a man. It could also be another woman. I don't know now, and I won't know until it happens. It all depends on who—not what—I fall in love with.

I think the high point of homosexuality for me is the equality in the relationship. There is a certain degree of equality that is not found in the majority of heterosexual relationships. No one partner is expected to call the other up first, to pay for everything, to drive the car, or to pick the other one up. In a homosexual relationship, all this is shared. In most marriages, the man works full-time while the woman stays home to cook and clean. In a homosexual relationship, both parties usually work, and everything is split fifty-fifty. This equality even applies to making love. When a man and a woman make love, the man usually plays the active role and the female, the passive one. I'm not saying that in a heterosexual relationship, equality in these things doesn't exist. I'm simply saying that it just doesn't happen as much as it does in homosexual relations. I really like the sense of equality that Sally and I have. We are equals in the relationship. This makes it more of a sharing experience.

I've never been as happy as I am now, and I'm happy because of whom I'm with. I love everything about Sally. She is always there when I need her and she's always ready to help me out. I do not feel I'm missing out on anything because I'm not with a man. The only part that makes me unhappy is that homosexuality is not accepted by society. I sometimes wish I could tell my family how I feel about Sally. I know they wouldn't accept it, but I do want them to share in my happiness.

A major question in my mind right now is whether or not I'll ever get married. I think I wonder about it so much because of my parents and because of society's expectations. Ever since I was little, I was always told that you grow up, you meet someone nice, and you get married and start a family. I don't know what's going to happen, but right now I don't see marriage in my future. I'm happy with Sally, so why should I be looking any further for a partner? Sally and I have many common interests and we enjoy being together. We are two very compatible people. There is a high degree of giving and sharing. We understand and trust one another very much. I am happy with Sally; in fact, I couldn't be happier. My relationship with Sally has really made a difference in my life. We are very good together, but we have both kept our identities. I can always be myself, and she can always be herself. We are best friends, something that is not very common in most heterosexual couples. I like having the person I'm in love with as my best friend. I hope that sometime in the future, Sally and I will eventually live together. I really think we could make it work.

Sometimes I wish I knew where my life was going. I often wonder about marriage and having children; but at this point, I really don't have much to say about either one. I only wish society could accept homosexuals. Why can't society simply accept it when two people of the same gender fall in love? My feeling is that if two people are happy together, no one should care who they are. Sally and I are happier than most heterosexual couples. The feelings we share are not any different from those that are shared in a heterosexual relationship. Love is love, and there should not be any restrictions on who can share it and who can't. Why should we have to hide our beautiful relationship from others? Is that fair?

CHAPTER
9

Violent Behavior

We all know what violence is, and we don't like it: true or false? On the surface, it might seem that defining violence would generate less controversy than is true of any other form of deviance. We might assume that what is violence is obvious and nonideological: Everyone knows what it is and nobody likes it. This is at best a half-truth; like most other half-truths, it is less than half useful. It is probably true that we would get a fairly high level of agreement concerning what constitutes violence if we were to show films of certain behavior and ask an audience to rate just how much violence takes place on the screen. Inflicting a stab wound or throwing a punch at someone's jaw are not easily classified as friendly acts. But notice: The behavior that is evaluated in this hypothetical example would be stripped of its social context. If we were to ask the members of that same audience to write down the first half-dozen acts of violence that come to mind, we

would realize just how powerfully ideological forces shape our vision of what's violence and what isn't. It isn't simply that the latter effort would yield more variation than the former. It is that people's examples will never quite match their definition.

Are civil disturbances, riots, revolutions, or uprisings violent? If we approve of the goal or the politics of their participants, we are not as likely to call them violent than is true of collective uprisings we disapprove of, even if the death toll is the same in both cases. We disapprove of *certain* acts that kill or harm people or destroy property, and we call them violent; other acts that produce the same damage and loss of life, but which we approve of, we do not label as violent. In short, violence has a *political* character. It is *"an ambiguous term whose meaning is established through political processes.* The kinds of acts that become classified as violent, and, equally important, those that do not become so classified, vary according to who provides the definition" (Skolnick et al., 1969: 4). This might seem extremely peculiar; violence is a hard, concrete fact—how can it "vary" at all?

For example, consider the behavior some observers have called *covert, institutional* violence. Racism, sexism, and the indignities of social class would be examples of this type of violence: The denial of a job to a qualified woman because of her sex, the refusal to rent an apartment to a black family simply because they are black, the unwillingness of the government to institute policies that would result in a more equitable distribution of income are examples of "institutional" violence. These actions would appear on no more than a very few people's lists of what constitutes violence. And yet, these acts do constitute harm one person does to another. Violence, one sociologist explains, means a person is violated in some way. There is harm done to that person's body, dignity, autonomy, freedom.

Seen in this way, a person can be violated in many ways; physical force is only one of them. . . . We must realize that people's lives are violated by the very normal and everyday workings of institutions. We do not see such events and situations as violent . . . but they kill, maim, and destroy many more lives than do violent individuals. . . . A person may be violated by a system that denies him a decent job, or consigns him to a slum, or causes brain damage by near-starvation during childhood, or manipulates him through the mass media. . . . Surely this is violence; it is caused by the normal, quiet workings of institutions run by respectable members of the community. Many . . . suffer from the institutional workings of a profit-oriented society and economy; poor health, dead-end jobs, slum housing, hunger . . . , are daily realities. . . . This is surely much worse violence than any committed by the Hell's Angels or street gangs. . . . Violence is committed daily by the government, very often by lack of action. The same system that enriches businessman farmers with billions of dollars through farm subsidies cannot be bothered to appropriate a few millions to deal with lead poisoning in the slums. . . . Similar actions of violence are committed daily by the government and corporations . . . , but we do not see the destruction inherent in these actions. Instead, we get fasci-

nated, angry, and misled by the violence of the poor and the powerless (Liazos, 1972: 111, 112).

In contrast to this view, which could be called the *radical* view, the view that aims to underplay "street" violence and emphasize the "covert, institutional" forms of violence, we have what might be called the *conventional* view of violence: how most people view it. Both are important for our purposes, the radical to remind us definitions that many people lay down of a phenomenon don't always match up with exactly what they actually *see* when they point out examples of violence and the conventional to keep us in touch with how most people categorize behavior as deviant. The more objectionable and deviant a given form of behavior is regarded, the more that violence is going to be perceived in it.

As students of deviant behavior, we must pay close attention to the manner in which behavior is seen and classified by the members of a society. What is or is not regarded as an act of violence—and, consequently, classified as an act of deviance—is not solely dependent on the damage inflicted by that act. Rather, what leads observers to think of an act as an instance of violence depends on what they see as legitimate or illegitimate, justified or unjustified, excusable or inexcusable actions taken against another person or other persons. Part of the task of this chapter is to explore on what basis these judgments are made.

VIOLENCE: A CROSS-CULTURAL PERSPECTIVE

Since the late 1960s, some of the once-moribund biological theories claiming that human behavior is genetically dictated have undergone a renaissance. This has been particularly true of explanations for violence, aggression, and homicide. Humans killing one another or aggressing against one another, it is claimed, is the manifestation of an ineradicable drive to inflict harm on others. It is a *natural* drive, an instinct, similar in strength to the need for food, water, and sex. The school of thought whose members propound this theory is called *ethology;* it is associated with its founder Konrad Lorenz, author of *On Aggression* (1967). Robert Ardrey, a popularizer of the school, sees no essential distinction between humans and animals: He posits hostility, aggression, and violence as a basic, essential component of all animal species. "Enmity is the innate response of an organism to any and all members of its own species," Ardrey writes, in a sweeping, gloomy overview of what it means to be alive (1966: 272). "Man is a predator whose natural instinct is to kill," he declares (1961: 316). Ethology spawned the contemporary school of *sociobiology* (Wilson, 1975, 1978, 1984), whose adherents believe humans are "genetically programmed" to kill and have a "natural penchant for violence" (Van den Berghe, 1978: 175).

There are a number of serious problems with this position. The first is that it confuses many different types of behavior, lumping them all together under the same rubric as "violent" and "aggressive" behavior. As one psychiatrist pointed out, what ethologists call "attack behavior" can be observed "in organisms as varied as insect, bird, carnivore, ape, and man."

In the first, it may be triggered by trace chemicals; in the second, by territorial defense, but only during the breeding season; in the third, by prey, but only if the appropriate internal state of arousal is present; in the fourth, by the appearance of a predator, if escape routes are unavailable and if the troop is threatened; and in man, by a mere verbal slur, if the context and prior individual experience indicate attack as the socially appropriate response. The mere observation in divergent species of similar behavioral outcomes that fit the generic label "attack" justifies no conclusion about an underlying aggressive instinct, without detailed study of the conditions evoking, and the mechanisms governing, the behavior of each. Such "explanations" reify a descriptive label that has been indiscriminately applied to markedly different levels of behavioral organization, as though naming were the same as explaining (Eisenberg, 1972: 125).

There is another reason why the ethologists' and the sociobiologists' view that vio-

lence is innate and universal must be rejected: The incidence of physically aggressive behavior varies wildly from one society to another and, within the same society, from one group and area to another. There are peasant and tribal societies in which violence is practically if not literally unknown. In Margaret Mead's classic study, *Sex and Temperament in Three Primitive Societies,* the Arapesh are described as cooperative, unaggressive, responsive to the needs of others, mild-mannered, passive, nurturant, contented, and secure. Violence is simply not known among the Arapesh. On the other hand, Mead also describes the Mundugumor, a nearby tribe, as ruthless, aggressive, undisciplined, insecure, disgruntled, hostile, and very violent. How can we account for these differences with an explanation that invokes some universal, innate characteristic to aggress against one's fellow humans? The Tasaday,[1] a tiny isolated band living in caves deep in the Philippine rain forest, are never angry, hostile, or aggressive with one another. There is no fighting, no punishment of children, and virtually no conflict or even disagreement among themselves. The Tasaday do not even have words or concepts for what we would call "weapons," "war," "murder," "enemies," or "fighting" (Nance, 1975: 19–20, 129, 130, 444). However, it is also true that their contact with any other tribe or band has been, until the 1970s, practically nil. Two other peoples who exhibit practically no hostility or violence toward one another are the Lepcha of Sikkim (Gorer, 1967) and the pygmies of the Ituri rain forest in Central Africa (Turnbull, 1961).

Societies in which gentleness and nonvio-

---

[1]Two anthropologists, Jerome Bailen and Zeus Salazar, claim the Tasaday are a hoax. They contend Philippine Minister for Tribal Minorities Manuel Elizade, Jr., convinced a group of Philippinos to wear leaves, make stone tools, and pose as cave dwellers and pretend to be a Stone Age tribe—the Tasaday (Mydans, 1988). Molony (1988) reviews both sides of the controversy and suggests, though the Tasaday were encouraged to display their most primitive characteristics to outsiders, "There is simply no getting around the linguistic evidence of their authenticity." Whoever the Tasaday are, they are a peaceful people.

lence are the rule provide two object lessons for any observer of violence and its relation to human behavior. The first is that violence cannot be innate or instinctual because it is not universal; peoples everywhere are not uniformly or necessarily violent. And the second is that the rate, incidence, and occurrence of violence the world over vary enormously; violent behavior is a variable, not a constant. It is present in various societies *in degrees*. These basic and hard facts force us to look at violence as culturally learned and maintained, and not inborn.

It must also be said that different societies designate as appropriate targets of violence quite different groups of individuals. Violence, including its most extreme form, homicide, taking place among members of tribal societies acquires a starkly different coloration from that which obtains in a unified nation-state with a formally administered, bureaucratically controlled legal system. The issue is just *who* could be killed with impunity. Some peoples are peaceful regardless of who they come into contact with. However, many others regard people who are not members of their tribe as not fully human. Among some societies (but not others) this meant they could be robbed, raped, or killed with absolutely no pangs of conscience whatsoever. One anthropologist writes, with perhaps a bit of exaggeration, "For most of humanity, the tribe is the unit within which killing is considered murder, and outside of which killing may be a proof of manhood and bravery, a pleasure and a duty. . . . Man, as a species, has no inhibitions against killing his fellow men who did not belong to the same pack, however the pack may be defined, and often gets intense pleasure and a sense of pride from doing so" (Gorer, 1966). For instance, the Kaingang of Brazil never kill one another; in 200 years of oral history only one instance of an intratribal homicide took place. On the other hand, their violence against other tribes, and that of those tribes against them, has decimated their numbers to nearly total obliteration (Henry, 1941).

With the institutionalization of the nation-state, the willful killing of all fellow citizens came to be defined as off-limits, illegitimate—illegal. Permissible killing was confined to members of other nation-states, and only in the course of an activity their political leaders declared and defined as "warfare."

If it were true that the will to commit violence is caused by a strong and more or less unmodifiable instinct, then we would expect a fairly high and fairly standard level of violence from individual to individual and a fairly standard rate of violence from one society, nation, and period of history to another. Instead, what we see is immense variation for all of these comparisons. Taking murder as the ultimate form of violence, some individuals murder dozens of people, while nearly all the rest of us murder no one. The variation in the murder rate from one country to another is as much as a hundred times. Clearly, there are sizable fluctuations from one year, decade, or period of history to another. It is difficult to understand how an instinct could produce this much variation.

FAMILY VIOLENCE

A nation whose members fear assaults from strangers on city streets may be surprised to learn that violence within the home at the hands of family members is far more common. Relative to their numbers in the population, violence inflicted by family members is hundreds of thousands of times more common than violence inflicted by strangers. In fact, even in absolute terms, a person is more likely to be assaulted by a family member than by a stranger. In the words of two experts on family violence, "The family is society's most violent institution, with the two exceptions of the police and the military" (Gelles and Straus, 1988).

If you punch or hit a stranger with an object and inflict severe bodily injury on that person, this is called *assault*. It is a serious crime, and you will be arrested for doing it. If you do the same thing to your child or spouse, the chances are, it will be ignored by the police and the courts. It is a peculiar fact that violence among family members, when it does not result in death, is lightly regarded by the legal system as well as by the public. If a wife appears before the police bruised, battered, and bleeding, the typical response will be, "It's not a Police Department thing. . . . It's really a family thing. You'll have to go to Family Court. . . . There's nothing I can do" (Maitland, 1976). Violence within the family is not generally regarded as a crime at all—unless it results in death—and is routinely treated with great leniency. One attorney who specializes in marital cases, Emily Jane Goodman, puts it this way: "In essence, nothing is done about this type of crime. . . . A man can assault his wife with relative impunity and walk down the street and assault a stranger and be arrested. It is the only crime in which marital status dictates how it is treated" (Maitland, 1976).

The same holds for the public's attitudes. In a study of responses by a sample to a list of offenses whose "seriousness" was rated, it was found that violent acts among intimates were less harshly evaluated than when they took place among strangers. Beating up a spouse ranked 91 in seriousness out of a total of 140 offenses; beating up a stranger ranked 64. The forcible rape of a stranger in a park was ranked 13; the forcible rape of one's former spouse was ranked 62 in seriousness (Rossi et al., 1974). However, again, when the violence resulted in death, intimacy did not soften the judgment of the seriousness of the act. The same holds for violence directed at children by parents; the "battered child" syndrome is common and yet politely ignored by authorities and lightly regarded by the public (Van Stolk, 1972). A study of 300 homicides in Houston found that "the severity of the penalty for killers correlates inversely with the degree of intimacy between killer and victim." Of all killers of relatives, 61 percent "escaped any form of legal penalty," this was true of 53 percent of killers of friends and associates and 36 percent of killers of strangers (Lundsgaarde, 1977: 16). Although this has been changing in recent years, as a general rule, the closer the relationship between victim and attacker, the greater the public toler-

ance for violence. We will explore this seeming anomaly.

Under what circumstances is family violence regarded as deviant and illegal? And what factors are related to its incidence? The three most serious and most common types of family violence are *wife beating, child battering,* and *incest.* Let's look at each in turn.

Wife Beating

Although a national survey found that violence inflicted on husbands by wives is as common as violence inflicted on wives by husbands (Straus et al., 1980: 36–38; Dutton, 1988: 190), I will concentrate here on the latter. This is not because of a double standard that dictates the injury of a woman is more serious than that of a man. Rather, there is evidence that shows the beating of husbands by wives is less serious than is that of the wives by husbands. In this same national survey, it was found (1) husbands have higher rates of the *most dangerous* and *injurious* forms of violence; (2) abuse by a husband usually does more damage than abuse by a wife— partly because the husband is usually larger, stronger, and better trained in violence; (3) husband violence is more likely to be *repeated;* (4) a higher proportion of the wife's violence against the husband is in self-defense; (5) a fairly high proportion of the violence inflicted on women (roughly one-quarter) takes place when they are pregnant; and (6) women are more likely to be economically dependent on men and to have fewer alternatives to putting up with the beating (Straus et al., 1980: 43–44; Gelles, 1987). Because of these factors, I will concentrate on wife beating by husbands.

Asking a nationally representative sample of Americans about various violent acts couples inflict on one another turned up the following findings. About 7 percent said they had thrown something at their spouse in the past year; 16 percent said this had happened at least once during their marriage. Seven percent said they had slapped their spouse last year; 18 percent said this happened at least once. Thirteen percent shoved, pushed, or grabbed their spouse during the previous year; 24 percent said this happened once during their marriage. During the past year, 1.5 percent said they had beaten up their spouse; 5 percent said this ever happened. And one-half of 1 percent said they *had used a knife or a gun* on their spouse; 4 percent said this happened at least once during the course of their marriage (Straus et al., 1980: 33–34). This places the total at close to *2 million* Americans who had at some time faced a husband or wife wielding a knife or a gun and slightly more than this figure who had been beaten up by his or her spouse. The researchers who conducted this survey state that these figures probably *underestimate* the amount of violence that takes place in the American family, partly because of shame or guilt, or faulty recall, or because these families are all intact; other research shows couples that have separated or divorced have higher rates of violence than do those that are intact. The authors estimate the rate of violence for American families is probably roughly *double* what these figures reveal (1980: 35–36).

In short, the marriage license seems to be some sort of a "hitting license." Violence seems to be "built into the very structure of the society and the family itself" (Straus et al., 1980: 44). There is an unacknowledged norm that hitting is acceptable. Overall, about a third of all American couples experience a violent incident every year, and two-thirds do so at least once in the marriage. One-eighth of all couples admitted at some time during the marriage there had been an act of violence that could have caused serious injury to the spouse—an act that qualifies as the crime of assault. Translating these figures into rates of assault, this works out to a national rate for 6,100 per 100,000 in the population per year for these couples—while the assault rate recorded by the police is only 280 per 100,000 in the population per year. In other words, if serious family violence were recorded as assault, the rate of assault as a crime in the United States *would increase by over 20 times* (1980: 48, 49).

Why does this level of family violence exist? More specifically, what factors are related to wife beating by husbands? What fac-

tors are related to the chance that husbands will slap or punch their wives or strike them with an object? What kind of man beats his wife? There are at least two distinctly different types of factors clearly related to the incidence of wife beating: those that all American couples have in common and those that distinguish some couples from others.

The factors all American couples have in common relate to the structural and cultural institution of *patriarchy*. This is the view that the man should automatically exert power and authority over the woman, that the home "belongs" to the man, and that the woman must endure whatever abuse or punishment inflicted on her by her husband. It is difficult to argue with the fact that the sexist character of American society contributes to wife beating (Gelles, 1979: 18–19). Where the man is the sole financial support of the family, he is more likely to think he has a right to do whatever he wants to whomever lives in the household he supports. Culturally, this view has an ancient history. Historically, wives have been seen as the property of men. The term "rule of thumb" stems from English common law that regarded it as the husband's right to beat his wife with a stick no bigger around than the circumference of his thumb.

But the simple fact is that not all couples accept patriarchy or sexism as valid. This is a question of degree, not an absolute rule. While living in a society with sexist institutions encourages wife beating generally, many husbands do not beat their wives. What distinguishes those who do from those who do not? *Unemployment* dramatically increases the likelihood of violence in the home. Unemployed men are two times as likely to use severe violence on their wives as are men who are employed full time. And men who are employed only part time are three times as likely to be wife beaters as are the men who are employed full time (Straus et al., 1980: 150).

Poverty is also related to wife beating. It is erroneous to assume family violence is exclusively or even primarily a lower-class phenomenon. However, wife beating is statistically more common in the poorest homes

(O'Brien, 1975). Husbands living in families who earned in the lowest income bracket are about six times as likely to beat their wives as are husbands who lived in families who earned in the most affluent income category (Straus et al., 1980: 148). Poverty is associated with feelings of failure and powerlessness in a wide range of areas of life, and the husband's frustrations are often translated into violence against the wife. Ultimately, then, wife beating can be traced to the unequal distribution of wealth in American society and to an economic structure that severely restricts access to achievement and success.

Stress, too, is related to violence against the wife. As stress within the family increases, so does wife beating. The greater the number of extremely stressful events in a couple's life (in the study cited, 18 were mentioned—such as trouble with a boss, the death of a loved one, sickness), the greater the likelihood that the husband beats the wife (Straus et al., 1980: 183–185; Linsky and Straus, 1986).

And last, wife beating is much more common in homes where power is concentrated in the hands of the husband; the least amount of wife beating occurs where the household is democratic with respect to power and authority. Violence is a means of asserting or legitimating a dominant position. The greater the sharing of decisions, the lower the likelihood of violence against wives (Straus et al., 1980: 193–196).

One commonsensical question many observers are led to ask with regard to wife beating is Why does the wife put up with it? There is a hint of "blaming the victim" reasoning in this question—it's her fault, or there must be something wrong with her to stay in such a relationship. Some might even assume the woman must subconsciously wish to be beaten. An Ann Landers column states: "According to the experts, a man who gets his jollies beating up women can always find someone who will tolerate it and they are both sick" (quoted in Langley and Levy, 1977: 123). Actually, experts today reject the idea that either the husband or the wife in a wife beating case is sick; the contemporary position accepts the view that the wife does not wish to be beaten, either consciously or subconsciously, but is by and large a victim of circumstance (Dutton, 1988: 190; Martin, (1976). Nonetheless, the question: Why does she stay?, must still be answered. After all, some wives leave abusive husbands, and some do not. Another crucial question is: Why do some wives react to violence with violence, while some do not? (Browne, 1987).

As with the issue of what factors lead husbands to beat wives, the question of what leads wives to stay with husbands who beat them may be answered by examining two different sets of factors. The first set is made up of those that all couples in the same society have in common; the second consists of those that distinguish couples from one another. In the first set, we must include the sexism that prevails in American society. In the second set, we must include, at the very least, degree of violence and the resources a wife commands.

In a sexist and patriarchal society, women are socialized into thinking of themselves as powerless and dependent—a state psychologists term "learned helplessness" (Walker, 1979: 42–54). The "very fact of being a woman, more specifically a married woman, automatically creates a situation of powerlessness" (1979: 51). Women are taught they have value only in relation to how men, or a specific man, responds to them. They are trained to be passive. These cultural values, the laws pertaining to marriage, economic realities, attitudes of the community, the unwillingness of the police or the courts to do much about wife abuse, "all these teach women that they have no direct control over the circumstances of their lives" (1979: 52). For the most part, the social, cultural, and economic institutions in this society conspire to convey a message to the wife that she had best endure the physical abuse to which she is subjected by her husband.

And yet, many—perhaps most—women who are married to a violent man will seek outside assistance or, in the long run, terminate the relationship rather than put up with severe, prolonged abuse. What distinguishes those who leave from those who stay?

Degree of violence is one distinguishing factor. As a general rule, the more severe and the more extended the violence is, the greater the likelihood of seeking outside assistance or intervention from a relevant agency and the greater the likelihood of separation or divorce. One study (Gelles, 1976, 1987) coded the severity of violence on a 10-point scale and found that the "mean violence severity" inflicted on wives that did not seek intervention was 2.1, whereas it was over twice as high, 4.6, for wives who did go outside the home to secure assistance from a relevant agency; this figure was 5.1 for wives who divorced or were separated from their husbands. Only 42 percent of the women who had been struck once in the marriage sought outside intervention, whereas 83 percent of those who had been struck at least once a week obtained a divorce or separation, called the police, or went to a social service agency.

Second, the fewer the resources at the woman's command and the more "entrapped" she is in the marriage, the more reluctant she will be to seek outside intervention or to leave her husband. The greater her education, the greater the likelihood she will seek the help of an agency or leave her husband. Her employment is also related here: Women who are employed, who are not economically dependent on their husbands, and who are able to support themselves and their children are much less willing to submit passively to their husband's physical abuse and are much more likely to seek outside help or leave him. This suggests that full employment for wives would increase their options, decrease their dependence, and assist many who are in bad marriages to terminate them.

Prior to the late 1970s to the early 1980s, nearly every police jurisdiction in the country routinely ignored complaints of wife beating, regarding it a family rather than a criminal matter. In 1981, the Minneapolis Police Department began an experiment to determine which of three responses to complaints of domestic assaults was most effective in reducing their incidence: advice, ordering the suspect to leave the premises for eight hours, or arrest. The experiment clearly demonstrated the superior deterrent effect of arrest; within a six-month period, 37 percent of the advised suspects, 33 percent of the suspects ordered off the premises, but only 19 percent of the arrested suspects committed another assault or other crime against the woman who made the original complaint (Sherman and Berk, 1984). The results of this experiment, it should be said, were surprising even to experienced police officers, who typically see such arrests as futile and bothersome. In fact, simply calling the police, even if they do not make an arrest, has something of a deterrent effect. A nationwide study that compared women who called the police after being assaulted by their spouses with those who did not revealed that far fewer callers (15 percent) were reassaulted within six months than were those who did not call (41 percent). Clearly, calling the police reduces the woman's chances of being revictimized (Langan and Innes, 1986). As a result of the findings of these and other such studies, for the police in some jurisdictions, "domestic violence is no longer low priority" (Nix, 1986). Said Police Commissioner Benjamin Ward of the New York City Police Department, "We have made enforcing the law against batterers a top priority. . . . I know that one of the most effective methods of dealing with domestic violence is to arrest the batterers. Every arrest sends a clear message that violence in the home is just as criminal as violence in the streets" (Bohlen, 1988). Arrests in domestic violence cases in New York City have quadrupled between 1984 and 1988. Statistics in Suffolk County, a suburb of New York City, are an indication of the recency of the policy of arresting batterers. In all of 1987, the police made a total of only 126 arrests for domestic violence; between March 28 and November 11, 1988, they made over 1,000 arrests on the same charge (Brasley, 1988). It may, however, take decades for this policy to be effected in jurisdictions all over the country.

Child Battering

Imagine a 5-year-old boy being approached by a grown man, a stranger, on the street of a small town in the United States. The man asks the boy to go inside a local store and purchase a pack of cigarettes for him. The boy refuses; the man slaps the boy across the face. The boy begins to cry; his crying appears to infuriate the man, and the man's blows, now inflicted with his fist, increase in severity and swiftness, until the boy lies unconscious on the sidewalk. A crowd gathers and restrains the man from leaving the scene; a police officer is summoned and the man is arrested and charged with aggravated assault. For weeks following the incident, the residents of the town talk about what happened with indignant, righteous anger. Everyone agrees the man is a "maniac," a "pervert," an archcriminal, a "menace to society"; they believe, down to every last man and woman, the boy's attacker deserves a very long prison sentence.

Yet, in the very same town half a dozen respectable couples routinely do the same thing to their own children. This form of physical abuse rarely comes to public attention; when it does, those who know about it keep it a secret. Incidents of parental child abuse in this town never result in criminal charges against the perpetrators, even though pediatricians and social workers in the local hospital know about these cases. No one is ever arrested; everyone is considered respectable, conventional, and law-abiding by the members of the community.

The moral of the story is that we may beat or otherwise physically abuse our own children almost with impunity—but not the children of others. It is almost as if children were property. Children, especially if they are young and small, are relatively powerless to resist the punishment inflicted upon them by their parents, no matter how senseless it might seem. Parental punishment has to approach being life threatening before authorities will act and the community will consider it an instance of wrongdoing—as an example of deviant behavior.

Extreme physical cruelty to children in the form of murder, life-threatening beatings, and maiming is certainly far less frequent today than it was centuries ago. If any parents were to subject their children to the extreme brutality of the *average* family of the past, they would be thought of as child abusers and would probably lose custody of the children in their care. So the definition of what is considered appropriate punishment and physical treatment has shifted over the years. *Extreme* physical cruelty and violence against children is certainly the exception, but it is far from uncommon. Children are more likely to die violently at the hands of their parents than at the hands of everyone else combined.

There is something of a continuum or an *unbroken spectrum* from the routine physical punishment most children receive, without injury, to full-blown cases of the actual murder of infants. There is, in other words, a great deal of "soft-core abuse" (Van Stolk, 1972: 91) in our society. Child battering grows out of a larger cultural matrix—it is not an isolated, random event practiced by a few scattered psychopathic parents. The greater the general level of physical punishment that is accepted and encouraged by parents toward children in a society, the more physical abuse of children there will be, the more injuries children will suffer as a result of punishment, and the greater the number of children that will be killed by their parents. Inflicting permanent injury upon children is simply the extreme outcome of widely practiced and accepted norms dictating that parents have the right to punish their children physically. Where force is used as a legitimate solution to problems, and where parental respect and punitive discipline is demanded, child abuse will be common.

The use of physical violence against children has much more cultural approval than does violence between spouses. When asked if "a couple slapping each other" was *normal,* 28 percent of the husbands in a study said yes, and 23 percent of the wives agreed; 15

percent of the husbands said it was *good,* and 9 percent of the wives agreed; and 8 percent of the husbands said it was *necessary,* and 4 percent of the wives did so, too. Yet when this same sample was asked about parents "slapping or spanking a 12-year-old child," 77 percent said that it was normal, 71 percent said good, and 70 percent said necessary (Straus et al., 1980: 47, 55). In other words, hitting children is considered normative; it is believed to be acceptable behavior.

It is, in addition, widely practiced. This same survey demonstrated an extraordinarily high rate of violence against children by their parents: 58 percent of all children were spanked or slapped by their parents last year, and 71 percent were at least once in their lives; 41 percent were pushed or shoved last year, 46 percent were ever; 13 percent were hit with an object at least once during the previous year, 20 percent ever were; 5 percent were struck by a thrown object last year, 9 percent were at least once in their lives; 3 percent were kicked, bitten or punched last year, 8 percent ever were; 1 percent were beaten up, and 4 percent were at least once. A small 1 out of 1,000 were threatened with a gun or a knife by their parents last year, and 3 percent were at least once in their lives (Straus et al., 1980: 61). Taking only the most violent of these acts, between 1.4 million and 1.9 million children were vulnerable to physical injury from their parents during the last year.

Mothers are slightly more likely to use violence against children than are fathers and to use more severe and abusive forms of violence (Straus et al., 1980: 65). They are with the children more, in a wider range of circumstances. In addition, mothers are more likely to believe that the inability of children to live up to their expectations reflects more on their competence as a parent. And last, children disrupt and frustrate the mother's life and aspirations more than the father's, since, in a sexist society, taking care of children is regarded as "the mother's responsibility." In addition, sons are slightly but significantly more likely to be the target of the more extreme forms of violence than are daughters. It is not clear this is because sons are considered more "unruly," because more is demanded of their behavior, or because they are more capable of enduring physical punishment.

What sorts of factors are related to child abuse? Which parents batter their children? One factor that is strongly related to extreme physical violence against children by parents is *authoritarianism:* The more authoritarian the parent, the greater the likelihood that he or she will abuse children. Authoritarianism is the belief that some people are meant to tell others what to do, that there is only one correct way of doing everything, that compliance must be automatic and unquestioning, and that authority in the home should never be challenged. Physical punishment is viewed as serving authority—to many parents, a "regrettable but nevertheless *correct* way of dealing with children" (Van Stolk, 1972: 32). Two boys, ages 5 and 16 *months,* were brought into the Colorado General Hospital with multiple bruises, lacerations, and fractures. Their father, who had injured them, told the examining physicians: "Children have to be taught respect for authority and be taught obedience. I would rather have my children grow up afraid of me and respecting me than loving me and spoiled" (1972: 22). The child's behavior becomes an occasion for punishment, and the inevitable crying that follows is interpreted as an insult to the authority of the parent. Abusive parents typically respond to it with rage and a self-righteous fury.

Probably the single factor that is most firmly established in the research literature on child abuse is *being abused as a child.* Parents who batter their children were socialized into parental violence when they grew up, in an unwitting, unintended fashion. Battered children learn, as a result of receiving violence at the hands of their parents, that those who love you are also the ones who hit you; a link is forged between love and intimacy, on the one hand, and violence, on the other. Hitting children establishes the moral correctness of hitting members of the family; children learn that it's okay to hit (Straus et al., 1980: 102–104). It has also been argued that abused children are far more likely to become murderers, violent delinquents, and spouse beaters than are children who grow up in a nonabusive family (Straus et al., 1980: 74).

And last, precisely the same factors that are associated with spouse abuse are also related to child battering: poverty, unemployment, and stress within the family (1980: 144–151, 183). This does not mean that affluent parents are never abusive—only that they are less likely to be. Poverty and unemployment are causally related to stress, anxiety, and a powerful sense of failure, which often translate into rage toward children, who become targets of their parents' frustrations.

Incest

It might seem surprising to include incest as a type of family violence. It might appear at first glance that it is a distinctly nonviolent form of behavior—deviant in most quarters, to be sure, but nonviolent nonetheless. Moreover, incest has been described as "the last taboo"—the last remaining activity that will eventually be tolerated with the encroachment of sexual freedom. In fact, contemporary thinking does *not* view its tolerance or its enactment as an aspect of sexual freedom. The taboos on it are not the same sort of taboos that automatically condemn homosexuality, premarital sex, and consensual adultery. It is now recognized that incest, for the most part, grows out of sexual *repression*—not sexual freedom.

To grasp this point, it becomes necessary to distinguish between incest that is initiated by a considerably older relative against a considerably younger one from those cases of incest that take place between age equals. Children have been taught to respect and obey their parents; obedience *by* the daughter is especially stressed more so than by the son and particularly obedience *to* the father more so than to the mother. In addition, children look to parents for moral guidance (Forward and Buck, 1978: 21). This makes it inconceivable that *any* sexual act initiated by the father could be willingly complied with by the daughter. Any passive acceptance by

her of her father's sexual advances must necessarily be regarded as an outcome of coercion, intimidation, and fear, not free choice. Moreover, given the great disparity between the physical size, authority, and knowledge and sophistication of adults versus children, it is simply not possible for a child to consent to a sexual relationship with an adult (Finkelhor, 1979: 52). Since one study found that the average age of female sexual victims was 10.2 (1979: 60), it is clear that father-daughter incest typically entails adult-child experiences. Consequently, coercion and intimidation, not free choice, characteristically dominates in cases of father-daughter incest. Since freedom, not coercion, is the main ingredient of sexual liberation, incest cannot be a case of liberation.

The distinction between incest that takes place between age equals and that which is initiated by a considerably older relative against a younger one emphasizes that incest per se must be distinguished from *sexual victimization*. By its very nature, sex between children and adults constitutes victimization. In addition, one study (Finkelhor, 1979: 56) included sex between a child and an adolescent 5 or more years older and sex between a young adolescent and an adult partner 10 or more years older.[2] Not all these cases constitute incest, though for the girls, 43 percent were with a family member; for the boys, this was 17 percent. Likewise, not all cases of incest entailed sexual victimization—two 5-year-old cousins playing "doctor," for instance. In this same study 23 percent of the boys and 28 percent of the girls had at least one incestuous experi-

[2]It should be pointed out that very few cases of adult-child sexual victimization—including father-daughter incest—involve literal intercourse. In one study (Finkelhor, 1979: 62), 4 percent of the cases of adult-child sexual encounters entailed intercourse. In another (Russell, 1986: 99), 9 percent of all the cases of "incestuous abuse" entailed genital intercourse. Most involved genital fondling, exhibitionism, or, more rarely, oral sex. The explanation offered was that the vaginas of preadolescent girls are far too small to accommodate the penis of an adult male; intercourse would result in severe medical trauma—and, consequently, hospital care, and inevitably, the attention of authorities.

ence—of which only 10 percent crossed generational lines (1979: 87). Consequently, sexual victimization and incest must be thought of as overlapping but distinct phenomena.

The exploitative, victimizing nature of adult-child sexual contacts can be seen in a contrast between father-daughter and mother-son incest. The simple fact is women generally, and mothers specifically, hardly ever initiate overtly sexual actions with children, male or female. The cases of mother-son incest that take place are so rare as to constitute an anomaly, a sociological and psychiatric curiosity. In fact, little boys are more likely to be sexually victimized by their fathers and stepfathers than by their mothers and stepmothers. Why? The overwhelming predominance of male cross-generational incest and sexual victimization over female (by roughly 30 times) is explained by the institution of patriarchy, some observers argue (Herman and Hirschman, 1977; Herman, 1981; Janeway, 1981). It is because men are dominant in this society and feel entitled to use children for their sexual satisfaction and pleasure that incest takes place. It is ingrained in males that their will should be unopposed, that others exist to service and please them, that others exist only for their private purposes. Historically, the father has had more or less uncontested power to do with his daughter as he wishes.

As long as fathers dominate their families, they will have the power to make sexual use of their children. Most fathers will choose not to exert this power; but as long as the perogative is implicitly granted to all men, some men will use it. . . . As long as fathers rule but do not nurture, as long as mothers nurture but do not rule, the conditions favoring the development of father-daughter incest will prevail (Herman, 1981: 202, 206).

Although brother-sister incest does not contain the same element of disparity in authority and physical size that father-daughter incest does, nonetheless, a very high proportion of brother-sister incest cases entails a brother who is five or more years older than his sister; in one study, nearly a third of the cases of sibling incest actually entailed coercion (Finkelhor, 1979: 90). In another study (Russell, 1986: 276), the average age disparity between brothers and sisters was seven years—17.9 for the brother and 10.7 for the sister. The age discrepancy, the degree of coercion, and the impact of brother-sister incest (in this study, almost half of the females in brother-sister incest cases never married) led Russell to write "the notion that brother-sister incest is usually a harmless, mutual interaction is seriously wrong" (1986: 289).

Who is the victim of incest? What forms of incest are most common? One study of the sexual victimization of children by adults and adolescents (which included incest) found that 19 percent of the women and 9 percent of the men surveyed had been sexually victimized as children (Finkelhor, 1979: 53, 58). Of the 151 women in this study who reported an incestuous experience, 5 were with a father and 2 with a stepfather; of the 60 men in the study who had at least one incestuous experience, none was with a mother, father, or stepfather. For the girls, incest with a brother was most common (72 out of 151) and a male cousin (48) next most common. With the boys, incest with a female cousin (33 out of 60) was most common, a sister next (16), and a homosexual relation with a brother close behind (15). In this study, then, girls were twice as likely to be victimized by an older sexual aggressor as boys. And father-daughter incest constituted only 3 percent of all the cases of the incest the women had experienced. This made up 1 percent of all the women in the sample. Brother-sister incest appears to be extremely common; it made up half of all the cases of incest and 94 percent of all incest that took place within the nuclear family (1979: 87). Far more cases of father-daughter incest come to the attention of authorities, which indicates they may be far more traumatic for the family than are cases of brother-sister incest.

Another study of incest, focusing specifically on incestuous abuse, tells quite a different story. Defining incestuous abuse as an attempted or completed physical act of a sexual nature, perpetrated by a relative five or more years older, that took place before the victim was 18, or an *unwanted* act initiated by a relative less than five years older, Russell found that *uncles* made up the largest category of incestuous abuse perpetrators (25 percent), with fathers next most common (24 percent—of whom 14 percent were biological fathers, 8 percent stepfathers, and 1 percent adoptive fathers)—male cousins were next (16 percent), and brothers (13 percent) were fourth (Russell, 1986: 217). It is possible that the difference between the Finkelhor and the Russell studies is the delineation of their respective areas of inquiry: Finkelhor was interested in incest, in sexual abuse, and in the overlap between the two, whereas Russell focused specifically on *abusive* incest. Not all cases of brother-sister incest were abusive, whereas *all* father-daughter cases, by definition, were. Thus, their tallies of the respective contribution made by each category of relatives were likely to be quite discrepant.

Perhaps the most dramatic axis of difference in the occurrence of incest is between fathers and stepfathers. In Russell's study, stepfathers were *seven times* as likely to sexually abuse their stepdaughters as biological fathers were to abuse their daughters (17 percent versus 2 percent). *One-sixth* of all the women in her sample who had a stepfather as a "principle figure" in childhood was sexually abused by him by the age of 14 (Russell, 1986: 234). Moreover, they were significantly more likely to also have been abused by other relatives than was true of the girls who grew up exclusively with their fathers. In addition, of those fathers and stepfathers who did abuse their daughters, stepfathers were over three times as likely to abuse their stepdaughters 20 or more times (41 percent) as biological fathers (12 percent), and just a bit more than one-third more likely to have done so only once (18 versus 48 percent). So pronounced was this tendency for stepfathers to sexually victimize their stepdaughters that Russell suggests divorced mothers "be more careful in their evaluation" of potential husbands. More generally, she suggests that strengthening the mother-daughter bond will help to protect daughters from abuse by male relatives (1986: 269).

Russell, who terms father-daughter incest "the supreme betrayal," states the case bluntly: *"Not a single case of father-daughter incest was reported to be positive in its entirety"* (1986: 44). In her study, the women who were victims of father-daughter sexual abuse were twice as likely to report being "extremely upset" by the experience as was true of the combined other categories of victims of abusive incest (1986: 231); it was the most traumatic form of incestuous abuse. Twice as many such victims report "great long-term effects" than was true of the sample as a whole. Moreover, fathers (mainly stepfathers) were more likely to impose vaginal intercourse on their victims than were all other incest perpetrators—18 versus 6 percent (Russell, 1986: 231); to have abused her a greater number of times—38 versus 12 percent 11 or more times (again, this was mainly stepfathers); and they were far more likely to have used physical force (1986: 232). Moreover, they were nearly a decade older than the combined average age of all other categories of abusers. And in 86 percent of all father abusers, they were the principal economic providers of the family, making their power all the more entrenched. In all, empirical studies of father-daughter incest paint a grim picture indeed.

Regarding sex between a child and an adult—or a child and a much older child or adolescent—as victimization is not simply a definitional exercise. Actual victimization is reflected in the psychological impact of these experiences. In one study, *not one* of the females who had such an experience said that they were glad it happened; only 7 percent said that the experience was mainly positive (Finkelhor, 1979: 66). Computing the degree of trauma from the experience with a scale running from 1 (positive) to 5 (negative), it was found that there was a strong association between the degree of trauma experienced and the age of the sexual victimizer—the larger the age difference, the greater the trauma. When this age difference was 10 or more years, the trauma score was 4.2. And of the various incestuous experiences the female had, incest with the father had the *highest* trauma score—4.8 (1979: 99,

102). Incest with a brother or a male cousin was coded as mostly neutral. (Interestingly, the incestuous experiences of these women when they were girls with their sisters and female cousins were more positive than they were with their brothers and male cousins.)

The strong association between trauma resulting from incest and generational differences is verified by a study conducted by Warren Farrell (reported in Janeway, 1981: 64, 78). Of all fathers reporting incestuous experiences with their daughters, 18 out of 24 said that they were positive and 5 said negative. Of the 34 women who had incestuous experiences with their fathers, 28 said that they were mainly negative. Forty-seven out of the 51 males who reported incest with their sisters said they were positive, whereas 9 of the females who had experienced brother-sister incest said it was positive, 10 said mixed, and 15 said negative. In cousin incest, the women showed a very strong positive reaction. In short, incest between fathers and daughters is *almost always* a very negative, traumatic experience for the daughters. Given the factors just discussed, it is difficult to envision how this could be otherwise.

The destructiveness of father-daughter incest is revealed by its dynamics. In addition to an authoritarian, domineering father, a combination of factors relating to the wife and mother is causally connected here: If the mother is ill, an alcoholic, or incapacitated in some way or if she and her daughter are significantly estranged, the likelihood of incest increases significantly (Finkelhor, 1979: 124–127; Herman and Hirschman, 1977; Herman, 1981). This incapacity often results in the oldest daughter stepping in and assuming the mother's household duties and becoming a kind of "surrogate wife." One observer argues that such "distortions of family role" betray the daughter's trust and prevent her movement toward growth, maturity, independence, and autonomy (Janeway, 1981: 81). Father-daughter incest is not only generated out of malfunctioning family relations, as well as a sexist, patriarchal culture, but, in addition, this critic observes, it also has devastating consequences for the daughter. Some of the costs of incest include the following:

First, there is the cost of "the experience of exploitation of seduction by a powerful person to whom affection is owed. Will affection always be tainted, afterward, by the expectation of exploitation? Will this experience teach the clever use of counterexploitation, of manipulation, of blackmail?"

The second cost entails entering into a terrible and destructive secret with the father. Even though the vast majority of girls who are forced to endure incest with their fathers find the experience repellent, they are typically intimidated into a pact of secrecy. This creates tension and tends to be destructive of relations among all members of the family.

Third, the girl usually enters into a kind of unholy alliance with the father against the mother, which results in "the sacrifice of female connections to one another in patriarchical loyalties to the male. Incest often culminates in cultivating competition between female generations or between sisters, one of whom may see herself as the loved and favored one" (Janeway, 1981: 81).

And fourth, there is the cost of the "establishment of the girl's perception of herself as a sexual being, instead of a complete person who can enjoy and control sex as she wishes, and can also enter into other sorts of relationships as she chooses: nonsexual relationships of friendship with either sex, of shared work, of continuing, cross-generational respect" (Janeway, 1981: 81).

In short, it is difficult to see adult-child sexual victimization generally, and father-daughter incest specifically, as anything but a form of violence against the child. In many cases, its impact is even more devastating than actual physical violence, such as being beaten. A significant part of this devastation stems from feelings of guilt. The girl often—even typically—feels that, somehow, she *provoked* her father's attention. Even more traumatic than simply being physically assaulted by a complete stranger for no reason at all is passively acquiescing to an act that is a mockery of love and affection with a powerful and loved figure. The girl is made to feel *responsible* for the incest; most victims later report that this was one of its most troubling aspects. A simple act of assault can be externalized; the attacker can be labeled a monster. But an act in which the victim is made to feel responsible—however wrong this perception may be—and in which there is some degree of technical complicity is far more psychologically damaging. The true mark of an oppressive institution can be found in the cooperation the victim extends to his or her oppression.

HOMICIDE

One warm August morning just before dawn in an affluent suburb of Johannesburg, South Africa, Wally Dowling, recently bankrupt and deeply entangled in a costly business fraud, crept into his two sons' bedroom and killed them both with a crossbow. He shot a third arrow into his wife, Joanne, and set the house on fire. As his final act, he shot himself in the head with a handgun. Dowling was described by his best friend as "a very stable, very quiet man who adored his wife and kids" (Walt, 1987).

Percy West, age 15, showed an imitation gold ring to an older teenager, who promptly attempted to steal it; in the ensuing fight, Percy broke his hand. He then told his brother Carl, age 21, about the fight, who sought out the teenager, found him, and had a fight with him. Neither was badly hurt. Four nights later, the two bumped into one another and, once again, began fighting. Shortly thereafter, West, who was unarmed, was shot twice in the face with a .22 caliber handgun; he died in a hospital 48 hours later. A suspect was arrested and charged with murder (Verhovek, 1988).

On a Wednesday morning at 4:15, police officers found a comatose light-skinned black or Hispanic male, age 25 to 30, lying in a sizable pool of blood in the marshy area near John F. Kennedy International Airport; he had bullet wounds in his chest and head. An hour later, he died. The police said that he was shot in front of an air cargo warehouse. The man had no identification, no

wallet, and no jewelry; there was no suspect in the crime. Said a man who worked nearby, "Who in their right mind would be around here at 4 A.M.?" (Verhovek, 1988).

It was Saturday night, and Karen Toshima, 27, a graphic artist, was strolling with her dinner companion through Westwood Village, a pleasant, affluent neighborhood of Los Angeles. Suddenly, a shot rang out, and Ms. Toshima was struck in the head by a bullet; she slumped to the sidewalk, mortally wounded. She was caught at random in the crossfire during a youth gang shootout (Reinhold, 1988).

Jim Collums, called "J.K." by his friends and relatives, lay in a nursing home, a victim of Alzheimer's disease. Unable to speak or care for himself, kept alive by means of tubes, J.K. lay near death for over six months. The disease was irreversible, and his brain was progressively deteriorating. On November 16, 1981, his brother, Woodrow, walked into the nursing home and pumped five bullets into J.K.'s body. Two minutes later, J.K.'s pulse stopped; he was dead. Woodrow placed his gun, a .38 caliber revolver, on J.K.'s feeding tray and waited to be arrested. Interviewed by the news media later that day, Woodrow explained that he wanted to put his brother out of his misery. "He's suffered long enough," he said. Although he did shoot his brother, he maintained he did not murder him, "because I feel like he's been dead since he's been in this condition." J.K.'s widow, Helen agreed; when asked if she blamed Woodrow for what he did, she replied, "Oh, no! God, no, no!" The general consensus was that Collums had committed a "mercy killing" (Stevens, 1981).

All these acts have at least one element in common: They are all instances of homicide.

Most of us have a stereotype of what a typical killing looks like, what the typical killer looks like. Our dread of the act and of the actor is deep-seated and intense. Few activities can generate as much horror in us as taking another person's life. It would seem that homicide is a form of deviance par excellence.

In fact, matters are not quite so simple. Actually, the term "homicide" refers broadly to the killing of one human being by another—any killing. Whether it is a criminal act, or an instance of murder, or is seen as something else—an act of heroism, of negligence, as excusable, as an accident, or whatever—is for people to make social and legal judgments about.

Forms of Homicide

There are basically two forms of homicide, criminal and noncriminal. And within each of these broad categories there are subtypes. Each legal jurisdiction, each state, and each nation have a somewhat different classification of homicide. And in each individual case, extenuating circumstances render an act an instance of one or another category, according to who did it, to whom, how, why, when, where, and so on. In other words, a very hard, basic, seemingly indisputable act—the taking of a human life—is judged very differently, is subjectively evaluated, and is put into vastly different categories according to how it is seen by people surrounding the killer and the victim.

Another matter to keep in mind is that a killer may be convicted by a court on a charge that bears little relationship to the original act, but is the outcome of various factors that relate to convenience. One person may have intentionally caused the death of another (murder), but after the case winds its way through the maze of the courts, the charge may have been reduced to manslaughter—an unintentional, though criminal, act of homicide. In New York City (as well as elsewhere) something like 8 out of 10 homicide cases result in "plea bargaining," or the exchange of a lighter sentence and charge for certain conviction (Raab, 1975b).

Two basic forms of *non*criminal homicide are *excusable* and *justifiable* homicide. Excusable homicide is an accident. If someone jumps in front of your car and you run him over, killing him, that's excusable homicide. Killing someone in a hunting accident would typically be ruled a case of excusable homicide. Justifiable homicide is a killing that results from the dictates of some legal demand, such as a policeman shooting a

fleeing felon, or an execution. *Self-defense* is also a form of noncriminal homicide. It may be excusable, justifiable, or some other form of homicide, depending on how it is perceived by the appropriate authorities. Although the death of a human being is almost always an indisputable fact, exactly how the killing is perceived and classified is highly variable and subject to endless debate. So one thing we should keep in mind is just *how* homicides are categorized and *why*. Is a "mercy killing" criminal or noncriminal? The Collums case was regarded as noncriminal by a Texas court. How much force constitutes "reasonable" force necessary to subdue a suspect? The police kill roughly five times as many civilians as civilians kill police officers; these killings are rarely judged to be criminal in nature. Is the killing of civilians in warfare by enemy soldiers justifiable or criminally prosecutable? These and similar questions engage the courts and the public in heated and protracted dispute.

How *criminal* homicide is further classified varies from one jurisdiction to another. In New York State there are three basic forms of criminal homicide. The first is *murder*. This is defined as intentionally causing the death of another, or killing someone in the course of committing a felony, like a burglary or a robbery, or demonstrating a "depraved indifference for human life," by wantonly and recklessly endangering the lives of others, such as firing a gun into a crowd. There are two degrees of *manslaughter*. The first is "voluntary," or first-degree, manslaughter, in which a death resulted from an act that reasonably could have been expected to result in another's death, or at least where one person had the "intent to cause severe injury" to another. And the second is "involuntary," or second-degree, manslaughter, where the act was less directly related to the death. In addition, there is another charge of criminal homicide— "criminally negligent homicide." This usually refers to "the reckless or negligent operation of a motor vehicle."

A basic question we have to ask here is *What sorts of killings qualify as criminal?* When does a homicide—simply the killing of one person by another—become seen as an instance of murder or manslaughter? When we read that there were roughly 20,000 criminal homicides in the United States each year in the 1980s, we should ask ourselves, *Which* killings of one human being by another were put into this figure? And which ones were *excluded?* Some Catholics and fundamentalist Christians believe abortion is murder. Most Americans do not agree. If all abortions were classified as murder, the murder rate would skyrocket, not because people killing one another has increased, but because the classification scheme and the perception of what constitutes murder have changed. An absolute pacifist would see all killings, including those that take place in warfare, as murder. If killings in warfare were, in fact, classified and recorded as murder, the incidence of murder—and any explanation for why murder occurs—would have to be drastically revised. One of the more common sources of death inflicted by one human being upon another is often not classified as criminal homicide; many cases will be ignored by the criminal courts altogether. This is what is called the "battered child syndrome" (Chase, 1975). Some observers feel that many automobile fatalities are, from a psychoanalytic point of view, unconscious and repressed homicides. As to whether this is true or not, or can even be determined with any precision, can probably never be known. But this point should be clear: *The taking of human life is tolerated under certain circumstances. Some* killings are not seen as murder, as criminal, or as deviant. They are permitted for a variety of reasons. Human life is not an absolute value in this society (and probably not in any other either). What is evaluated as murder, or as criminal homicide, or as a deviant form of killing, is the result of a socially and culturally based judgment.

Some Myths about Murder

There are several clear-cut, sharply etched popular stereotypes of what the typical murder looks like and who the typical murderer is. (From now on, I will refer to all criminal homicide as "murder" or "homicide," out of convenience.) All phenomena have a certain size and shape in the public imagination. Murder occupies a large space and tends to take on a certain form. There are at least four widespread images of murder. The first would be the *murder mystery* murder: premeditated, calculated, executed in cold blood, a "whodunnit" murder. The second image would be that which occurs as a consequence of a felony, like a rape, a burglary, a robbery, where the felon panics, or intentionally kills after getting what was wanted. A third stereotype is that of the psychotic killer who goes berserk, slaughtering a dozen people on a spree. And fourth is the gangland slaying—the planned execution of a professional criminal who took the wrong move with the wrong person.

The first thing that we should notice about murder is that it occurs far less than do many other causes of death that rarely impose themselves upon our minds. Our "mental map" of murder is far more expansive than the actual incidence of it would warrant. It ranks high in subjective importance and emotional impact. It is prominent in the news, prominent in our conversations, it captures our imagination, it ranks high in the concerns of citizens. Automobile fatalities are two to three times as frequent. As many people die as a result of accidental drownings as die violently at the hands of others. There are more suicides than murders. And yet, these sources of death do not grip us quite so forcefully as murder does.

Points two and three about murder, contradicting its dominant stereotypes, are that the typical murder takes place between intimates, not strangers, and it is usually unplanned. It is true that murder between strangers is more common in large urban areas than in smaller communities, and it is also true that deliberate, premeditated murders may be on the increase (Raab, 1976a), but it is still true that criminal homicide usually takes place between people who are well known to one another and is typically spontaneous, arising out of the seeming demands of an immediate situation. And a fourth myth about murder is that it frequently occurs between individuals of different races. The fact is that criminal homicide is overwhelmingly *intra*racial—that is, it tends to take place between people who share racial characteristics.

Let's examine the reality of murder.

Relationship

In a study of homicide in Detroit, where the relationship between killer and victim was known, only a quarter of all murders (27 percent) took place between strangers (Wilt, 1974; Daly and Wilson, 1988: 19). Every year, the Federal Bureau of Investigation (FBI) collects data on crime in the United States based on information sent to them by nearly all police departments in the country (see *"Uniform Crime Reports,"* pages 237–238). Included in its tabulation are the relationships between victim and killer. Only 13 percent of all murders (where there is only one victim and one killer) in the United States in 1987 took place between complete strangers; in an additional 30 percent of the cases, the FBI did not know the relationship between killer and killed—and most likely, a majority of these were strangers to one another.

In 1987, family members killed one another in the following proportions. Not quite 1 in 12 criminal homicides (7.7 percent) took place between husband and wife—2.7 entailed a wife killing her husband, and 5.2 percent, a husband killing his wife. In 1.5 percent of the cases, a child killed a parent; 3 percent of the time, a parent killed a child—1.3 percent were daughters, and 1.7 percent were sons. In 1.3 percent of the cases, a sibling was killed: 1.1 percent of the time, a brother, and .3 percent of the time, a sister. Other family members made up 2.7 percent of the FBI's murder cases. In all, family members contributed 16.5 percent of all cases of criminal homicide in the United States in 1987, a substantial contribution if we realize we have only a small handful of family members, and an even more substantial contribution if we realize members of our own family are supposed to love, not kill us.

In addition to the contribution family members make, lovers made up 3.7 percent of the total number of criminal homicides— 1.4 percent entailed a girlfriend killing a boyfriend, and 2.3 percent involved a boyfriend killing a girlfriend. The FBI classified 5.3 percent of all criminal homicides as killings between friends, 30 percent were between acquaintances, and 1.4 were between neighbors. Clearly, intimacy is closely related to murder. In fact, it could be said the more intimate you are with someone, the greater the chance you will kill or be killed by that person. This relationship is one of the most thoroughly documented in the entire social science literature (Goldstein, 1986: 80–82; Daly and Wilson, 1988: 17ff; Barlow, 1987: 135–136).

Why are intimates so likely to kill one another? We could probably come up with many elaborate explanations for this strong relationship, as psychoanalysts have over the years—that there is an element of hate in all love; that we are really killing ourselves when we kill a loved one—but the most fundamental if obvious explanation is that we are *with* family members more than with any other category of individuals. We also are highly likely to engage in a wide range of activities with family members—have breakfast with them, talk to them, make purchases with them, drive in cars with them, in short, do all sorts of things with them. We just don't interact with strangers that much and, consequently, we don't do too many things with them—including kill them. "Perhaps the most powerful if crude answer" to the question of why we kill and are killed by intimates "is that they are *there*. . . . We are all within easy striking distance of our friends and spouses, for a goodly part of the time" (Goode, 1973: 148).

We should not, however, fall into the trap of thinking, because members of our family are substantially more likely to kill us than strangers, based on their numbers in the population, that the home is an extremely unsafe place to be from the standpoint of being murdered. Although most people are murdered in the home, they also spend most of their time there; that does not mean the home is an unsafe place to be. Three legal scholars make just this error; writing about our physical safety, they say: "A person is safer in Central Park at three o'clock in the morning than in his or her bedroom" (Zimring et al., 1983: 910). Here, the researchers have confused *frequency relative to other forms of homicide* with *frequency relative to total amount of time spent with the family*. On an hour-by-hour basis, being with the family is a very *safe* place to be, whereas Central Park at 3 A.M. is most decidedly *not* a safe place to be. Wrestling sharks is more dangerous, on an event-by-event basis, than driving a car, although far more people are killed as a result of driving cars than as a consequence of wrestling sharks.

Perhaps as important an explanation of why intimates are highly likely to be involved in homicides is that *intimacy means emotion*. And emotions are volatile and easily ignited. The greater the emotion, the greater the chances of hostility—*in addition to* love. We "are violent toward our intimates—friends, lovers, spouses—because few others can anger us so much. As they are a main source of our pleasure, they are equally a main source of frustration and hurt" (Goode, 1973: 148–149).

Race

An extension of the "intimacy" dynamic between victims and slayers is the fact that murders are overwhelmingly intraracial—whites tend to kill whites, and blacks tend to kill blacks. When a white person is killed, his or her slayer is usually white; when a black person is killed, his or her slayer is almost always black. And when a white person kills, he or she usually kills a white person; when a black person kills, again, he or she is highly likely to kill a black person. It is true the interracial factor is greater in cities than in smaller communities; it is also possible the contribution interracial killings make to all killings may be rising. But even today, and even in the country's largest cities, intraracial killings are the rule. It makes sense: People who know one another and are close to one another stand a higher likelihood of killing one another than people who are

more socially distant. And people tend to be more intimate with members of their own race than with members of another race. Consequently, people of the same race tend to kill one another with greater frequency than people of a different race do. People of the same race also interact more with one another; they spend more time with one another; they are emotionally important to one another; they tend to marry one another; and so on.

In the FBI's annual statistics on murder for 1987, in cases where there was only one killer and one victim, the race of both was known, and the police apprehended the suspect, 52 percent of all murder victims were white, 46 percent were black, and 2 percent were other races. And, excluding other races, 89 percent of all white victims were killed by a white assailant, and 94 percent of all black victims were killed by a black assailant (see Tables 9.1 and 9.2). When the Hispanic ethnicity was considered, the same pattern prevailed: In 1986, 82 percent of the Hispanic victims of a murder were killed by a Hispanic. (The FBI categorizes Hispanics as white.) Overwhelmingly, when someone is murdered, he or she is killed by someone of his or her own race. The same applies even in killings that entailed a single victim and multiple offenders (which made up 12 percent of all murders recorded that year); in the FBI's 1981 figures, 87 percent of the multiple killers of a black victim were also black, and 73 percent of all the multiple killers of a white murder victim were also white. As with

TABLE 9.1 Race of Victim and Killer (1987)*

		Killer		
		Percentage White	Percentage Black	Total
Victim	White	89	11	5,176
	Black	6	94	4,695

*Excludes whites and blacks who killed, or were killed by, members of other races. As a result, the total numbers for tables do not correspond precisely.

SOURCE: Adapted from Federal Bureau of Investigation, 1988: 9.

TABLE 9.2 Race of Killer and Victim (1987)*

		Victim		
		Percentage White	Percentage Black	Total
Killer	White	94	6	4,890
	Black	11	89	4,981

*Excludes whites and blacks who killed, or were killed by, members of other races. As a result, the total numbers for tables do not correspond precisely.

SOURCE: Adapted from Federal Bureau of Investigation, 1988: 9.

intimacy, the intraracial character of murder is one of the more thoroughly confirmed findings in the social science literature.

Socioeconomic Status

It is also true that criminal homicides are not committed equally frequently by members of all social class or racial groups. Murder is very strongly related to social class. The acts American society and law call murder are far more likely to be committed by the poor and the powerless, the uneducated, the unemployed, and the underemployed. No matter how much we tinker with the definition of what murder is (remember, excepting wars, accidents, abortions, indirect killings, auto fatalities, and so on), even after we have taken account of the inadequacies of officially recorded criminal statistics, and no matter how we define social class, the same ineradicable fact remains: The lower the social class, the higher the likelihood of committing murder; and the higher the social class, the lower the chance of committing murder. It is simultaneously true that the powerful in any society start wars and are responsible for far more deaths than common murderers. Executives, powerful and affluent all, manufacture unsafe products that kill people; likewise, they refuse to provide much adequate protection for their workers, resulting in a calculated, preventable number of deaths. Politicians fail to pass legislation that could save lives. Were the entire economic structure to be radically revamped to ensure a more equitable economic distribution, I have no doubt the rate of ordinary "street" violence would drop, and that includes homicide (Braithwaite and Braithwaite, 1980). So both directly and indirectly members of the upper socioeconomic echelon are responsible for far more deaths than working- and lower-class people are. But after these qualifications are registered, we are still left with the far greater rate of "ordinary" murder at the bottom of the class structure.

In 1973 the *New York Times* computed a precinct-by-precinct homicide rate for New York City for 1972, along with the median family income for each police precinct (Burnham, 1973a). Of the 37 precincts with a median family income *under* $10,000, two-thirds (68 percent) had a homicide rate of 25 or higher per 100,000 population for 1972. Of the 34 precincts with a median family income of $10,000 or *over,* only 3 (or 9 percent) had a homicide rate this high. The city's highest homicide rate was achieved by Manhattan's twenty-eighth precinct in Central Harlem, with 203 per 100,000 population; its median income was $5,648, ranking sixth from the bottom, out of 71 precincts. The wealthiest, Manhattan's nineteenth precinct, the so-called silk stocking district, earned an average of $20,865 and ranked 57 in its homicide rate, which was 4 per 100,000, or *one-fiftieth* as high as that of Central Harlem,[3] Certainly there is far more to the homicide picture than income, but it cannot be doubted that the economic factor is massively evident in killing and being killed at the hands of others.

It is not sheer poverty or material want, by itself, that influences the frequency with which people murder one another, however. The residents of Central Harlem are wealth-

[3]It should be kept in mind that when a killing takes place in a precinct, it is not necessarily committed by a resident of that precinct. However, when people do cross precinct lines, it tends to be a resident of a less affluent precinct killing in a more affluent precinct. This would *increase* the differences in the homicide rate, not decrease them.

ier by far in absolute terms than are the peasants of Spain or the Lepchas of Sikkim; white southerners (with an extremely high homicide rate) are more affluent, many times over, than are the citizens of Haiti or the People's Republic of China. It is probably true that homicide is more frequent among the least affluent *within* a given society or nation (though this isn't a universal rule). The nobility in peasant societies until the past few centuries in Europe and the kingdoms of Africa were far more murderous and homicidal than were the settled peasants living within their realm. Lower- or working-class members of a number of societies around the world are more likely to be participants of what has come to be called the "subculture of violence" (Wolfgang and Ferracuti, 1967), a social animal I will discuss momentarily.

Gender

The matter of gender and homicide is much more complicated than race. There were 10,182 murders in the United States in 1987 with one killer and one victim where the gender of the killer (and the victim) were known. Of these, not quite three-quarters (73 percent) of the victims were male, and just over a quarter (27 percent) were female. Although people of the same race tend to kill and be killed by one another, this is not quite the same with gender. When a man *is killed,* he tends to have been killed by a man: 84 percent of all male victims of a criminal homicide are slain by another man (see Table 9.3). And when a man *kills,* his victim is usually a man; 71 percent of the victims of male slayers are also men (see Table 9.4). However, when women kill or are killed, the situation is drastically different: When a women *is killed,* she is usually killed by a man, not a woman: 91 percent of the killers of female victims are men. At the same time, when a woman *kills,* she usually kills a man: 83 percent of the time that a woman is the killer, a man is her victim. In other words, men victims loom much larger than women victims in the fewer killings that women do, and men loom much larger as the killers of the fewer women who die of a homicide. To put matters another way, roughly one-third of all criminal homicides (36 percent) are *inter*gender killings, and two-thirds (64 percent) are *intra*gender. Of the third that are intergender, about two-thirds (68 percent) entail a man killing a woman, and one-third (32 percent) entail a woman killing a man.

Why do men kill men, and women also kill men? There are at least two reasons for this pattern. First, men are much more likely to kill their friends and companions, while women are more likely to kill their lovers or husbands (and their children). In our sexist society, men tend to be extremely concerned about the evaluations made of them by their peers; they tend to take the opinions of women less seriously. Women, too, are extremely involved in the judgments made by the men in their lives closest to them; the opinions of other women are less likely to matter to them. When women achieve fuller social and economic equality, it is possible an ironic consequence will take place. The more equal the position and role of women

TABLE 9.3 Gender of Victim and Killer (1987)

		Killer		
		Percentage Male	Percentage Female	Total
Victim	Male	84	16	7,394
	Female	91	9	2,730

SOURCE: Adapted from Federal Bureau of Investigation, 1988: 9.

TABLE 9.4 Gender of Killer and Victim (1987)

		Victim		
		Percentage Male	Percentage Female	Total
Killer	Male	71	29	8,702
	Female	83	17	1,422

SOURCE: Adapted from Federal Bureau of Investigation, 1988: 9.

in society, the greater the likelihood women will kill one another, and the more closely female-female killings will approximate male-male killings. The lopsidedness of the sex ratios in homicide in our society is a reflection of the sexist treatment of women. Women kill men in part because they loom large in their consciousness; men kill men because they care very much about what they think and how they feel about them. When women begin to care as much about how other women feel about them as they do about how men feel, they will begin killing one another in large numbers. Of course, it is also possible that in a more equalitarian society, one in which women have more power, more influence, and more impact on cultural values and norms, there will be less killing generally.

A second reason women tend to kill men, when they commit murder, is that a substantial proportion of them are defending themselves against physical abuse. Battered women kill men rather than women, because it is men who are abusing them, and murder seems like the only means of escaping that abuse (Browne, 1987; Gillespie, 1989). If a woman kills a man who is beating her, we might make the assumptions that it is self-defense, not murder, and that a jury would automatically acquit such a woman. These assumptions would fall into what one expert (Ewing, 1987) calls a "media myth." Among the 100 cases he examined of women who killed their batterers "nine pleaded guilty to homicide charges, three entered pleas of not guilty by reason of insanity, and three had the charges against them dropped before trial. The remaining 85 women all went to trial claiming self-defense. Sixty-three were convicted of various forms of criminal homicide. Twelve of these women were sentenced to life in prison. The others received sentences ranging from four years probation (with periodic incarceration) to 25 years in prison. Seventeen women received prison sentences potentially in excess of ten years" (Ewing, 1987: 3).

Why are so many battered women who kill their batterers convicted and imprisoned in spite of the strength of the evidence supporting their abuse? All these women had been beaten not once, but numerous times, and often seriously; all had been subjected to severe psychological abuse and humiliation as well. In a substantial proportion of these cases (41), these women's husbands threatened to kill them, and many had contacted the police repeatedly. The problem with a self-defense plea was that in a majority of these cases (about two-thirds), the women did not kill their husbands during an incident of physical abuse, but some time *after* one; only a third killed their batterers while they were attacking them. In at least 18 cases, "the killing took place while the batterer was asleep or nearly asleep" (Ewing, 1987: 5). Thus, the majority of women who kill their husbands are nearly always arrested for murder or manslaughter, are usually charged with one of these crimes, and are usually convicted of one of them. Though this practice seems unjust (and I am persuaded by Ewing's argument that it is), the killings by these women appear as criminal homicides on official tabulations (see also Browne, 1987; Gillespie, 1989).

The "Subculture of Violence" Theory

It is the thesis of many criminologists today that an extremely high proportion of the homicides are committed by men who share in the "subculture of violence" (Wolfgang and Ferracuti, 1967). Among some segments of many societies of the world, group norms call for, and even demand, violence in face-to-face situations in which one's honor, manhood, and dignity have been challenged. It would be considered shameful for many men to ignore an insult, to let a demeaning comment go by without an appropriate response, to allow another man to question one's masculinity, courage, status. This is especially true if one is in the company of others that one is close to. Certain situations, then, come to be defined as requiring an aggressive and, eventually, a violent response. A male is expected to defend his *machismo:* not only is a ready resort to violence *not* seen as illicit, a restraint from using violence under these circumstances would generate guilt feelings, would be experienced as frustrating and ego-deflating, even degrading. But notice: The subculture of violence thesis does not argue that these men positively value violence in and of itself, under any and all conditions. Certain situations—in fact, *most* situations—are not regarded as legitimate arenas within which one may aggress against another. And certain people are not considered legitimate targets of one's aggression. Where it is crucial to establish and maintain an image of masculinity in the eyes of other men, where one's masculinity is felt to be continually under attack, and where aggression and masculinity are closely linked, the quick resort to violent acts will be relatively common. Where men are more secure in their manhood, and where virility does not have to be demonstrated by physically aggressive acts, violence—and homicide—will be far less widespread. But where physical confrontation and combat are seen as the key to manhood, much ordinary masculine aggression will escalate into killing.

The subculture of violence thesis requires that *both* parties—the killer and his victim—accept the legitimacy of violence as a demonstration of their manhood for this ethos to have a significant impact on the incidence of homicide. There is, in most violent killings, a personal interplay, a truly interactional dynamic. It is out of this basic framework that the idea of the *victim-precipitated* homicide developed. In an early theoretical work on criminology, Hans von Hentig discussed the "duet frame of crime" (1948). A later study verified this insight. Piecing together police and coroner's reports, sociologist Marvin Wolfgang (1958) concluded that about 26 percent of the criminal homicides he investigated could be classified as victim precipitated. By that he meant those killings "in which the victim is a direct, positive precipitator in the crime. The role of the victim is characterized by his having been the first in the homicide drama to use physical force directed against his subsequent slayer. The victim-precipitated cases are those in which the victim was the first to show and use a deadly weapon, to strike a blow in an altercation—in short, the first to commence the interplay

or resort to physical violence" (Wolfgang, 1958: 252). The killing escalated from, or began with, the victim. As it turns out, it was blind luck as to who was the slayer and who the victim. Often the difference between victim and slayer was a matter of strength, a superior weapon, or skill in using that weapon.[4]

Often homicide escalates from a fight. The line between what is legally classified as "aggravated assault" and homicide is simply whether the victim died or not. Assault and homicide are often the same crime with a different outcome. One criminologist says that "aggravated assault is really a first cousin of murder" (Reckless, 1973: 186). It is the fate of the victim rather than the behavior of the assailant that distinguishes them. Generally, with some small exaggeration, homicide is an act of assault in which the victim died. In fact, one shift that has taken place over the past generation or so is that many assault victims who would have died in the past now live because of improved medical care and the speed with which they are rushed to a hospital. Much the same acts that were committed then, result in a completely different outcome because of a change that has nothing to do with the incidence of violent behavior. The desire to retaliate in a fight, to humiliate another, to defeat him, to assert oneself, to punish an antagonist, rarely includes the determination to annihilate him completely. Not only do assaults and homicides look remarkably similar, but

[4]In a study conducted by the New York Police Department in 1977 of the 1,622 homicide victims killed in that city in 1976, it was discovered that over half (53.5 percent) of the *victims* had prior arrest records. This was true of three-quarters (77 percent) of the suspected arrestees. Almost the same number of the victims (35) as suspects (40) had been arrested previously for the charge of murder. Almost half of the victims were found with "detectable levels of alcohol, narcotics, or both in their blood at the time of death." In addition, about four-fifths of the victims (82 percent) were male; 90 percent of the suspects were male. In over three-quarters of the cases (79 percent) the victim and the arrested suspect were of the same race. Nearly half (48 percent) of the victims were black; 30 percent were Hispanic. More than half of the victims were killed by friends or acquaintances in an argument or dispute. (Buder, 1977)

also the killer and the killed look remarkably alike. They both have extremely high rates of prior arrest, usually for assault. Both victim and slayer, in about half of the cases, were drinking prior to the killing. And they both, characteristically, share in the subculture of violence.

It must be stressed that for some, the threat to their masculinity is seen as a legitimate spur to a violent response. Yet this explanation only covers a certain proportion of all violent killings; exactly what proportion cannot be known for certainty. But almost as important is the fact that *almost any one of us* could, conceivably, act in a lethally violent fashion toward another person. (This is a theme stressed in a number of films of the violent 1970s, such as Sam Peckinpah's *Straw Dogs* and James Dickey's *Deliverance.*) Frightening as it seems, most of us would kill under the right conditions; the reason why we do not is that we never encounter those conditions. Just what each of us finds as an occasion for violent and, eventually, a homicidal reaction will vary a great deal. Encountering an unfaithful spouse *in flagrante delicto* will touch off homicide in one person, an amused laugh and a shrug of the shoulders in another, and the impulse to disrobe and join the party in a third. Political matters leave most of us cold; others will, and do, kill for them. In 1975, a woman, Joan Little, killed a man who had raped her; another woman, Inez Garcia, killed a man who helped another rape her. On the other hand, some women do not consider murder an appropriate response to rape. Both cases touched off a great deal of controversy; commentators asked, "Is murder a just response to rape?" (Gordon, 1976), with advocates on both sides of the issue.

In earlier times, differences in religion prompted mass slaughter. Even in the 1980s—in Lebanon, in Northern Ireland, in and around Israel—religion and homicide are linked, though on a far smaller scale than in the past. It happens that in contemporary America (and in some other places as well) threats to the manhood of millions of males provide the most common stimulus to killing others. But if the masculinity of most college professors, let's say, were to be either verbally or behaviorally challenged, threatened, or attacked in some way, even in public, they would respond, in all likelihood, by just walking away. Aggression would in most cases not be met with further aggression. But each one of us will have his or her own private—and different—reasons for greeting some action with deadly violence.

In many nations around the world and in some ethnic groups in the United States, matters of family honor rank high among the reasons for generating the homicidal impulse. In rural Sardinia and Sicily, there are some families among whom practically all the adult males have been killed in feuds and vendettas originating decades ago over matters that, to outsiders, would appear trivial—a slap, an insult, the failure to repay a loan, a stolen sheep, boundary disputes, a broken promise. It is not uncommon, even today, in the remote regions of these provinces of Italy for a godfather to give a shotgun as a baptismal gift to a male child. Local custom and the code of honor are rigidly enforced. Mainland Italian law is seen as remote, optional, secondary, nonbinding, and even, at times, meddlesome. Murders do not occur because the killer acts in opposition to the dictates of his community. Exactly the opposite is true: He would be an outcast if he did *not* kill under certain circumstances. Custom *demands* murder when it can cleanse the family name. Sicilian and Sardinian killers tend to have no guilt feelings about their offense, they are not rejected by their families—indeed, are supported by them—are "devoid of psychopathologies," and seem to be conventional and "normal" within the confines of their community's definition (Ferracuti et al., 1973). Far from being the psychoanalytic monster with a weak superego that some psychiatrists make him out to be, the subcultural killer seems to be, if anything, far *more* powerfully bound in by his conscience than any other category of criminal. Where the culture or the subculture demand it, the murderer suffers not from being "abnormal," but from being *super-normal!*

Several qualifications to the subculture of

violence thesis are in order. It does not claim violence is legitimately directed to others under any and all circumstances. Participants in this subculture consider a violent response legitimate *only under specific circumstances;* they generally turn out to be those perceived as threats to one's manhood and honor. Second, one participates in this subculture *to differential degrees.* That is to say, although it is possible that we all would be violent under what we see as the "appropriate" circumstances, the *range* of circumstances is different for each of us. Some of us consider a *wide* range of circumstances appropriate for us to respond with violence; others see only a very narrow range as such. The crucial factor, then, is how frequently we encounter these circumstances. A third qualification is also in order: We must be very careful about how we use the word "subculture." It is legitimate when we compare Sardinia and Sicily with mainland Italy and when we compare the American South with the North. In these cases people learn how, why, and when to be violent in much the same way they learn to drive a car or to speak English. However, when we are talking about class and racial differences within the same nation and region, we run into a somewhat different phenomenon. Our society, for example, disvalues people who work with their hands; more strongly, it stigmatizes being unemployed. Being at the bottom of the heap is *already* ego-deflating. Even before anyone interacts with anyone else, one's manhood is called into question by being a socially and culturally disvalued human being. Being placed at the bottom of the heap, being poor, being materially insecure, by themselves, will generate frustration and anger. And often, one will strike out not at the agents that are responsible for one's position in life, but at those who are close at hand. If professors, say, or business executives, were to be unemployed for long periods of time, on the edge of economic disaster with no hope of improvement, the chances are their feelings of security and complacency, and their low likelihood of committing violent acts, would dissipate; they would see many more occasions as legit-

imate for the expression of their violence. This is not something they have learned directly; it is not "subcultural" in this sense. Rather, it is something that is a response to one's *immediate life situation.* And this is not a stable factor in one's life; it is dependent on what one's life is like.

The Murder Weapon

The massive increase, however, in the use of firearms in the past generation or two may drastically alter the victim-slayer relationship. Wolfgang's (1958) data were gathered in 1948 and 1952. In only 33 percent of the homicide cases in his sample was a gun the murder weapon. Today, the picture is quite different. According to the 1987 edition of the FBI's *Uniform Crime Reports,* nearly 6 out of 10 (59 percent) of the victims of criminal homicide in the United States died as a result of being shot by a gun (see Table 9.5). Where guns are involved, it is difficult to imagine one or both participants being unaware that a homicide was highly likely. The role of guns in altercations and, subsequently, in homicides, does not invalidate the victim-precipitation theory, but it does demand reworking it. Although killings by strangers, particularly murders committed during a felony, such as robbery or burglary,

TABLE 9.5 The Murder Weapon (1987)

	Percent	Number
Firearm	59	10,556
Cutting or stabbing instrument	20	3,619
Hands, feet, fists, etc.	7	1,162
Blunt instrument	6	1,039
Strangulation	2	357
Fire	1	199
Asphyxiation	1	115
Drowning	*	51
Poison	*	34
Narcotics	*	24
Explosives	*	12
Other	4	691
Total	100	17,859

*Less than .5 percent

SOURCE: Federal Bureau of Investigation, 1988: 10.

are increasing, they are still a minority of all murders; but the larger that they loom in the homicide picture, the less applicable is the current theory of victim participation.

Uniform Crime Reports

FBI data on criminal homicide are probably the only reasonably accurate and valid official criminal statistics available. (The victimization surveys conducted periodically by the U.S. Justice Department are quite good, but they are not "official" criminal statistics.) There were 20,096 cases of "murder and nonnegligent manslaughter" in the United States in 1987, producing a murder rate of 8.3 per 100,000 population; this represents a 2.5 percent decline in absolute number from 1986, and a 3.5 percent decline in the murder rate. Murder and nonnegligent manslaughter are defined as "the willful (nonnegligent) killing of one human being by another." The total number of killings recorded by the FBI is based solely on charges made by the police—not as determined by a medical examiner, coroner, court, jury, "or other judicial body" (Federal Bureau of Investigation, 1988: 7).

Murder is correlated with a number of variables, two of which are *size of community* and *region of the country*. Murder is far more frequent, per 100,000 population, in large cities than in small communities; and it is far more common in certain parts of the country than in others. The South has an extremely high rate of criminal homicide; in New England and the more westerly parts of the Midwest, the rate is extremely low. The rates of criminal homicide are far higher in large cities than in smaller ones and in rural areas (although rural areas have slightly higher rates of murder than very small cities do). Four of the states at or above the national average (Texas, New York, California, and Illinois) contain the nation's four largest cities—New York, Los Angeles, Chicago, and Houston. Only two of the states among those with the 15 lowest rates of murder (Massachusetts and Wisconsin) have a city with a population of 500,000 or more, and not one

has a city above 1 million people. Tables 9.6 and 9.7 demonstrate the likelihood of murder per 100,000 population and the extremely close relationship between community size and murder rate. The murder rate in large cities is seven times as high as it is in small ones, and it is nearly five times as great as in rural areas. Clearly, there is something about big-city life that generates a higher level of violence—more anonymity, a weaker sense of community, weaker social control, more social and economic inequality.

It is possible city life also contributes more than its share of murders because of the drug trade, and in recent years, because of the rise of cocaine, especially crack-related murders. Although the role of the drug trade in murder has been exaggerated by the media, several states known for rises in crack use between 1986 and 1987 also rose in state

TABLE 9.6 Homicide Rate by State (1987) (Murders per 100,000 Population)

Michigan	12.2	Indiana	5.6
Georgia	11.8	Oregon	5.6
Texas	11.7	Washington	5.6
Florida	11.4	Pennsylvania	5.4
New York	11.3	Delaware	5.1
Louisiana	11.1	Connecticut	4.9
California	10.6	West Virginia	4.8
Mississippi	10.2	Hawaii	4.8
Alaska	10.1	New Jersey	4.6
New Mexico	10.1	Kansas	4.4
Maryland	9.6	Montana	4.1
Alabama	9.3	Rhode Island	3.5
South Carolina	9.3	Wisconsin	3.5
Tennessee	9.1	Nebraska	3.5
Nevada	8.4	Utah	3.3
Missouri	8.3	Idaho	3.1
Illinois	8.3	New Hampshire	3.0
National average	8.3	Massachusetts	3.0
North Carolina	8.1	Vermont	2.7
Arkansas	7.6	Minnesota	2.6
Arizona	7.5	Maine	2.5
Kentucky	7.5	Iowa	2.1
Oklahoma	7.5	Wyoming	2.0
Virginia	7.4	South Dakota	1.8
Colorado	5.8	North Dakota	1.5
Ohio	5.8		

SOURCE: Adapted from Federal Bureau of Investigation, 1988: 44–51.

TABLE 9.7 Size of Community* and Murder
Rate (1986)

Size of Community	Murder Rate (per 100,000)
1,000,000 or more	24.5
500,000–999,999	19.5
250,000–499,999	15.1
100,000–249,999	10.4
50,000–99,999	6.4
25,000–49,999	5.1
10,000–24,999	3.9
Under 10,000	3.3
Rural counties	5.7

*Suburban areas and counties not included.
SOURCE: Adapted from Federal Bureau of Investigation, 1988:146–147.

rankings in criminal homicide: New York, from tenth to fifth; Michigan, from sixth to first; Maryland, from fifteenth to eleventh. Florida and California remained at fourth and seventh places, respectively. The role of drugs, especially drug selling, cannot be dismissed as a source of murder; it actually influences the overall murder rate in some cities, such as Los Angeles and Miami where police estimate that half of all murders are drug-related (Wilkerson, 1987).

Rates of criminal homicide vary, likewise, by region. While the murder rate for the nation as a whole was 8.3 per 100,000 in the population for 1987, for the South, it was 10; for the West, 8.5; for the Midwest, 6.7; and for the Northeast, 6.9. Of the 17 states at or above the national average, 10 are Southern or border states; a majority of the states with the 12 highest rates of murder are Southern states. In contrast, all of the New England states are below the national average—indeed, all except Connecticut are among the 15 states with the nation's lowest murder rates. And of the states in the western Midwest, only Kansas is not in the bottom 15, and 2—North and South Dakota—have the nation's lowest rates of criminal homicide. As can be seen from Table 9.6, the chances of being murdered are about eight times higher in Michigan (12.2) than they are in North Dakota (1.5).

International Comparisons

International comparisons of criminal behavior are difficult to make, even for murder, for which the data are better than for any other category of crime. First, most countries do not keep accurate or complete crime statistics. Second, many killings take place during demonstrations, riots, executions, civil war, and other political actions, which are difficult to classify. On one side of a border, a bomb that explodes on a bus may be regarded as an act of heroism; on the other, it will be seen as murder. Does it make any sense, for instance, to classify the killings that have taken place during Lebanon's bloody civil war as murder? When the South African police shoot into a crowd of demonstrators, is it murder? Many of us would answer yes. Or is it simply a question of the police doing their job, as many white South Africans would argue? Or the hundreds of thousands, possibly millions, of deaths that occurred during the Khmer Rouge regime in Kampuchea? Are these murder or political executions? In the context of numerous regimes around the world, the concept of murder seems almost irrelevant. As the Captain Willard, a character in the film *Apocalypse Now*, says with reference to the war in Vietnam, "Charging a man with murder in this place is like handing out speeding tickets at the Indy 500." A third problem with making international comparisons of murder rates is that the categories are different—even for classifying homicides. In Italy, Spain, Australia, and Syria, attempted murder is included with murder itself, which artificially inflates the apparent murder rate of those countries.

In spite of the problems any researcher of murder faces, one attempt was made to obtain international data on the subject (Archer and Gartner, 1984). Unfortunately, when the book was published, most of their data were already more than a decade old, having been collected in the late 1960s or early 1970s. Some tentative international generalizations about murder can be made, however.

Mainly, the generalizations we make

about murder from the *Uniform Crime Reports* (FBI: 1988) also apply internationally: Intimates are more likely to kill one another than strangers, at least, on a per population basis; murder tends to be intraracial rather than interracial; men tend to kill men; women tend to kill men; men tend to be killed by men; women tend to be killed by men; murder tends to be committed more often at the bottom of the class structure than at the top (again, with the necessary political qualifications); gun possession increases the likelihood of a murder taking place; murder is more common in cities than in less densely populated areas; and regional variations in criminal homicide tend to be substantial. However, in addition to what we know about murder in the United States, we can also examine differences worldwide in rates of criminal homicide. (I will follow Archer and Gartner (1984) here; although their data are quite old, several valid generalizations can still be made.)

First, Western Europe, Canada, Australia, and New Zealand typically have extremely low rates of criminal homicide compared to the United States. For 1972, the rate in England and Wales was .51 per 100,000, compared to 9.07 for the United States in 1973. Finland was .30 (1970); France, .35 (1971); the Netherlands, .55 (1972); Sweden, 2.43 (1971); Norway, .23 (1970); and so on. In 1971, Iceland, a country of about 200,000 people, had one murder; in 1972, New Zealand, with a population of 3 million, had two. Since the early 1970s, the murder rate of nearly all Western societies has grown, but even today, it is still about one-fifth to one-tenth that of the United States.

Second, the murder rate of those Third World countries in which a substantial proportion of the population has been uprooted from its traditional communities and now lives in large urban areas is generally extremely high, often even higher than that of the United States. In 1972, Thailand's murder rate was 13.65; Zambia's was 10.17 for 1970; Mexico's, 11.05 (1972); Peru's, 18.20 (1970); and Uganda's, 25.08 (1970). When traditional values no longer have the relevancy they once had, when traditional authorities no longer have the power they once had, when the norms, laws, and rules that held sway in one place are no longer meaningful in another, when relatives and community figures no longer observe one's every move, and when much of one's social contact is with strangers, much of the conflict that used to be smoothed over by members of the community in which one lived one's entire lifetime is now free to escalate into violence, even lethal violence. South Africa is a good example. In 1971, South Africa's criminal homicide rate was 16.56, not quite double that of the United States for 1973 (9.07). But the discrepancy between its *urban* homicide rate and that of the United States is even greater. Witwatersrand, for instance, had a criminal homicide rate for 1986 of 80.7 (Walt, 1987), considerably above America's most dangerous cities—62.85 for Detroit, 48.14 for Atlanta, 37.30 for New Orleans, 36.17 for Washington, D.C., 35.63 for St. Louis—and over three times higher than our only moderately dangerous cities, such as New York (22.95), Los Angeles (24.27), and Chicago (22.89). (Here, I used 1987 figures for U.S. cities (see Table 9.8) rather than 1986 figures for Metropolitan Statistical Areas, as Walt seems to have done.) There can be no doubt that the destruction of traditional cultures is a major factor.

Third, it is likely that substantial economic discrepancies play a role as well. At least, the correlations are quite clear: In countries where income is more equitably distributed (Western Europe and the socialist nations, such as China and the Soviet Union), the murder rate is comparatively low; in countries where income is significantly less equitably distributed (the United States), it is significantly higher; and it is the highest in countries with the least equitable income distributions (such as South Africa and many Third World countries, like Peru and Brazil). Of course, there are other factors at work. Nonetheless, there seems to be little doubt that a substantial redistribution of a nation's income would result in a lower

TABLE 9.8 Murder Rate (per 100,000) in U.S. Cities above a Population of 350,000 (1987)

Detroit, Mich.	62.85	Denver, Colo.	15.50
Atlanta, Ga.	48.14	Milwaukee, Wisc.	15.13
New Orleans, La.	37.30	Long Beach, Calif.	15.26
Washington, D.C.	36.17	Columbus, Ohio	14.97
St. Louis, Mo.	35.63	Charlotte, N.C.	14.58
Miami, Fla.	33.24	San Francisco, Calif.	13.41
Dallas, Tex.	31.98	Boston, Mass.	13.20
Ft. Worth, Tex.	31.22	Albuquerque, N.M.	12.91
Oakland, Calif.	31.15	Indianapolis, Ind.	11.91
Baltimore, Md.	29.55	Phoenix, Ariz.	11.89
Kansas City, Mo.	29.48	Seattle, Wash.	10.92
Cleveland, Ohio	26.45	Oklahoma City, Okla.	10.87
Los Angeles, Calif.	24.27	Minneapolis, Minn.	10.57
Jacksonville, Fla.	23.34	Las Vegas, Nev.	9.76
New York, N.Y.	22.95	Pittsburgh, Penn.	9.51
Chicago, Ill.	22.89	Tulsa, Okla.	9.46
Memphis, Tenn.	21.68	San Diego, Calif.	9.22
Philadelphia, Penn.	20.49	Austin, Tex.	8.31
Nashville, Tenn.	20.32	Omaha, Neb.	7.47
San Antonio, Tex.	18.91	El Paso, Tex.	5.05
Cincinnati, Ohio	18.57	Honolulu, Hawaii	4.32
Houston, Tex.	18.56	San Jose, Calif.	3.29
Portland, Ore.	16.89		

SOURCE: Adapted from Federal Bureau of Investigation, 1988: 63–109.

rate of criminal homicide (Braithwaite and Braithwaite, 1980).

And fourth, countries that experience political upheaval and civil war typically have high rates of criminal homicide (even if political killings are not officially recorded as murder). For 1966, Ethiopia's rate of criminal homicide was 25.7; in 1968, El Salvador's was 24.16; for 1973, Northern Ireland's was 12.93. And in 1967, Colombia's was at, perhaps, a record high of 56.97. Of course, rates of criminal homicide grow and recede yearly, but one of the factors that accounts for such changes is the degree of political upheaval occurring. If officially sanctioned killings take place (for instance, soldiers murdering innocent civilians), it is unlikely they will be recorded as murder. Still, if the tally of criminal homicide is even remotely complete and accurate, it will be found to reflect or be strongly influenced by extreme political turmoil.

In short, although making international comparisons of murder and criminal homicide rates can be a difficult, tricky business, it can be done, and it often yields important generalizations (Archer and Gartner, 1984).

Guns, Murder, and Gun Control

Clearly, guns play a major role in murder. In the United States, as we saw, nearly 6 out of 10 criminal homicides are caused by guns. Internationally, although there are exceptions, the countries with high rates of gun ownership are generally the countries with a high murder rate; those with low rates of gun ownership are also those with a low murder rate. Can there be any doubt that guns—both directly and indirectly—cause murder—that is, cause people to die?

Recently, a comparison was made of guns and murder in the cities of Seattle, Washington, and Vancouver, British Columbia, by a team of medical and public health figures (Sloan et al., 1988). Seattle and Vancouver are located in the same geographic area only 140 miles apart; their residents watch the same television shows, have similar rates of poverty and unemployment, and earn the same median wage (household income just over $16,000). Their racial composition does differ somewhat: Although their proportion of whites is about the same—slightly more than three-quarters—Seattle has more blacks (9.5 percent) and Hispanics (2.6 percent), and Vancouver has more Asians (22.1 percent). For a large American city, Seattle's crime rate is very low; for a large Canadian city, Vancouver's is very high—as a result, their crime rate is remarkably similar for most crimes. Their robbery rates are very similar; their burglary rates are almost identical; for assault with a weapon other than a gun, their rates are nearly the same; and for homicide, again, with a weapon other than a gun, their rates are very similar. In other words, the populations of the two cities are remarkably alike in criminal activity and several measures of "aggressiveness."

One way these two cities do differ is in their regulation and control of guns. In Seattle, a citizen may acquire a concealed weapons permit to carry a handgun on the street for self-defense; no permit is required for keeping a gun in the home. Registration of handguns is not mandatory for private sales. In Vancouver, in contrast, permits are issued for handguns solely for sporting and collecting purposes; they may be discharged only on a firing range. Self-defense in the home or street is not legally recognized as a reason for the possession of a handgun. Seattle's gun ownership is over three times as high as Vancouver's: Roughly 4 out of 10 households in Seattle have at least one gun; in Vancouver, it is only 1 out of 8 (Sloan et al., 1988: 1258).

Not surprisingly, crimes involving guns are far more common in Seattle than in Vancouver. Between 1980 and 1983, Seattle's rate of aggravated assault—one person intentionally hurting another badly with a gun—was 87.9 per 100,000; Vancouver's was *one-eighth* as high, 11.4. In Seattle between 1980 and 1986, the homicide rate involving guns was 4.8; in Vancouver, it was *one-fifth* as high, 1.0. Sloan and his colleagues conclude from their study's findings that "the modest restriction of citizens' access to firearms (especially handguns) is associated with lower rates of homicide." It is probable, they say, that "a more restrictive approach to handgun control may decrease national homicide rates" (1988: 1261), an assertion echoed by an editorial in the *New York Times* (November 18, 1988) in response to the study.

The National Rifle Association (NRA) has a motto, emblazoned on millions of bumper stickers: "Guns don't kill people; people kill people." This is not quite true: It is people *with* guns who kill people. The NRA claims that if killers are sufficiently motivated to kill someone, they will find a weapon that will do the job. In reality, most people who kill are not "sufficiently motivated" to kill; they tend to strike out at an opponent with whatever weapon is at hand. If it is a gun, they will use a gun; if it is a knife, they will use that. And a knife is not a very effective killing instrument, while a gun is. To put the matter another way, when two combatants square off against one another with knives, the chance that one or both will die is far, far lower than is true if they square off against one another with guns. That all households in the country have knives and only one out of five homicides is caused by a knife show it is not the motivation to kill that is the main determinant of homicide. That guns are far less often owned, and are far more likely to be involved in killings than is true of knives, shows it is *the opportunity to use an effective killing instrument in the heat of battle* that determines whether most killings take place.

On the other hand—and here the NRA is right—it is probably next to impossible to control gun ownership; that is, to control it to the point where such control will make a difference in the murder rate. Rigorous control, or the lack of it, will make a difference in one or another specific individual dying or not dying, but it will not bring down our high rate of criminal homicide. Guns are already widely distributed in the United States (although, clearly, less so than knives!), and here, as opposed to elsewhere, a substantial proportion of our citizenry feel it is their right to own guns. It has been estimated there are 100 to 120 million guns in the United States today (Wright et al., 1983: 320, 321), close to one gun per household. Even if a total and effective embargo prohibited all gun manufacture and importation, and it remained in effect for a century, the guns now in circulation in America would be sufficient to provide potential killers with enough weapons to murder at very close to the current rate. Each year, there are 1 million gun-related crimes; less than 1 percent of all the guns in circulation are involved in a gun-related crime annually. This means that 100 guns would have to be confiscated to prevent one gun-related crime—not a very feasible endeavor, or one terribly effi-

cient in the deployment of law enforcement personnel. In addition, there are 20,000 murders in the United States each year, of which some 12,000 are caused by guns; so roughly a thousand guns would have to be confiscated to prevent a single murder (Wright et al., 1983: 320). Again, the logistical and legal problems such an endeavor would entail is far beyond the capacity of a nation with a strong tradition of civil liberties and due process. In short, gun control, although it may prevent individual, scattered murders from taking place, is not likely to make much of a dent in the murder rate overall (Wright et al., 1983; Wright and Rossi, 1986).

Middle-Class Murder

As we all know, murder is overwhelmingly "a crime of class" (Edmiston, 1970); that is, it is nearly always committed by lower- and working-class individuals. An extremely low proportion of people with middle-, upper-middle-, or upper-class jobs, incomes, or educations ever murder anyone. We've already explored some of the reasons for it—certainly anger, status and economic frustration, poor impulse control, and a hazy thought for the future figure into the causes for this relationship. Middle-class murder, however rarely it occurs, does take place. And yet, it has almost never been studied. A fascinating question might be how the fewer middle-class murders that do occur differ from the many more numerous lower-class murders. It is possible they differ only in number, not in kind; or it is also possible they differ both in number and in type of murder—that is, how it is committed, why, by whom, and so on.

One study (Green and Wakefield, 1979) examined 119 cases of criminal homicide reported in the New York Times (1955 to 1975) where the killer "met the criterion" of middle- or upper-class status; there were 121 offenders and 191 victims. Although the sample is not ideal, it is adequate for rough purposes of comparison. Since most murders (roughly 95 percent) are committed by working- and lower-class individuals, comparing the murders in this

sample with murders in general (for instance, those reported in the FBI's Uniform Crime Reports) will yield, in effect, a comparison between middle- and upper-class murders with lower- and working-class murders.

In this study, middle-class murderers were significantly older—an average of 14 years older than lower-class murderers. Half of all lower-class murderers were under 30, while under a quarter of the middle-class murderers were this young. Murders by these two categories of offenders are similar in some respects, however. Middle- and upper-status murders were, like lower-class murders, overwhelmingly intraracial, and they both were largely committed by males (about 80 percent of the time). However, while over 60 percent of all murders entail a man killing another man, in only a quarter of all the middle-class murders was this true. In fact, 58 percent of all middle-class killings involved a man killing a woman, while in only 20 percent of lower-class killings is this true. Middle-class murderers were three times as likely to kill a member of their own families (roughly three-quarters of the time) as was true of lower-class murders (about 16 percent of the time).

The motives for killing also contrast sharply. Trivial altercations, primarily, and robbery, secondarily, figure dominantly in the lower-class murders. In roughly a quarter of middle-class murders, factors such as property, inheritance, and insurance loomed extremely large; the average sum involved in the murders with such motivations was a shade over $330,000. Ironically, the middle-class murders correspond much more closely to the stereotypical, popularly conceived "whodunnit" murder than the far more common lower-class murders. Robbery and trivial altercations hardly figured at all in middle-class murder, although domestic quarrels did seem to be as common as in lower-class households. Interestingly, in well over a quarter of all middle-class murders, a homicide was followed by a suicide (in contrast with only 5 percent of all lower-class persons), indicating a far stronger sense of guilt. This statistic would seem to support Wolfgang's subculture of violence thesis: Where norms call for violent retaliation, guilt for killing is minimal; where they do not do so, guilt is stronger. Hardly any of the middle-class murderers in this study corresponded to the model spelled out in Wolfgang's notion of the subculture of violence.

The two categories of murder do not differ strikingly in their use of guns (on the order of 6 out of 10 of all murder weapons); however, knives and fists very rarely figured in middle-class murders, while they make up nearly 3 out of 10 of all lower-class murder weapons. In contrast, more exotic instruments of death, such as poison and hypodermic injection of a lethal drug, were more prominent in middle- than in lower-class murders.

The results of this study "underscore the necessity of broadening the theoretical base for the explanation of homicide in a way that reflects the full range of personal, situational, motivational, and interactional factors associated with this most seriously regarded form of criminal behavior" (Green and Wakefield, 1979: 181).

ACCOUNT: INCEST

The contributor of this account is a schoolteacher in her early thirties. She has a child and is divorced. The details of her experiences are considerably more extreme than those of the typical incest victim (if such an individual can be said to exist), but some of the more general features of this account are characteristic.

The first I recall of a long history of sexual abuses inflicted upon me by my father took place even before I entered kindergarten. My father was a strong, huskily built ex-boxer who engendered fear in everyone who knew him. He would come into my bedroom while I was asleep, pull off the covers, and raise my nightclothes, exposing my buttocks (he would turn me over onto my stomach if necessary) and, while I was lying in bed, would train a flashlight on me, and then proceed to the bathroom just across the hall, where he would disrobe and turn on the water, wash his hands, open a jar of petroleum jelly and "massage" himself. At the time I thought he was softening his aching hands; it wasn't until I was a married woman that I realized that it was not his hands he was caring for with such regularity and devotion!

At the time, I only knew I didn't like the part I was expected to play in the ritual and I tried several ploys in an attempt to abort my participation in these nightly ordeals. Feigning sleep, I would try to remain in position on my back with my nightie wrapped tightly around me so as to make myself as inaccessible as possible. I lay awake in fear of both his arrival and the possibility of sleeping through it. I tried to move into a nonrevealing position "in my sleep." When he would try to reposition me, I would pretend to wake up. But he just scolded me for not being asleep at such a late hour, ordered me to lie still and go back to sleep immediately, while warning me not to let him find me awake upon his return the following night under pain of a severe beating. He would then wait 5 or 10 minutes and start the entire procedure all over again. My only recourses were to beg my mother to let me sleep with my underwear on or to sneak panties on if she said no, to request pajamas instead of a nightgown, and to be as uncooperative as I could while feigning a very restless "sleep." Unfortunately, my father was able to overcome all the obstacles I set in his path.

Very early in my life, I sensed there was something wrong and indecent with some of the ways my father treated me. When I was 6 or 7, he would arrive home late from work and under the guise of warming either his or my feet, would climb into bed with me clad only in his undershorts. (I couldn't understand why he would wake me from a sound sleep in order to warm feet that didn't seem cold to me.) He would then move his entire body back and forth over me rapidly and heavily. He explained away my objections by going into a complicated theory on "friction" and the "transfer of body warmth." Although I was too afraid and ashamed to say so, I always thought it repulsive, especially since one particular part of his anatomy seemed to be getting more friction and warmth than any other. I became so upset by these recurring incidents that I eventually developed into quite an insomniac, fearful worse things would happen to me if he thought I slept through these attacks, leaving him free to act at will in any manner that might suit his perverted fancy.

I have a sister two or three years younger than I, as well as two even younger brothers. Almost everything he did to me he also did to my sister. My father loved to give us baths, enemas, rubdowns (always in a position that would expose us, even if the ache or pain were way down in a knee or a toe), to play blind man's bluff (so as to have an excuse for groping us with his hands), to teach us acrobatic "tricks" that involved his grabbing us by the crotch, to play doctor to any ailment of a private nature (he once conducted a 45-minute "operation" on me to remove a blackhead on my buttock). We were forbidden to lock the bathroom door, through which he often marched unannounced. He cut out a hole in a strategic spot in the bathroom ceiling so that we could be easily observed using any of the fixtures from his room in the attic. (He passed it off as a vent by covering it with a grill.) One hot day when I was almost old enough to need a bra, he saw me perspiring and suggested that I remove my halter top. When I objected for reasons of modesty, he ordered me into the house and demanded that I bare my chest. He then cupped and fondled my breasts and compared my size to his, reasoning that if he were not ashamed to appear barechested in public, then I, who measured no larger than he, should not be embarrassed either. I was at a severe disadvantage, since I was so young and overly protected, religious, and innocent, trying to match wits with my father, who was an authority figure and so much older, but somehow I managed not to submit. One for me! However, later that same day, we observed a boy climbing a picket fence, and my father insisted on demonstrating the injury I would sustain if I fell while climbing such a fence by forcefully and repeat-

edly plunging his finger into my rectum. I lost that round!

One day when I had just turned 12, my father returned home unexpectedly to find me and my sister on the front porch (we weren't allowed to be there) talking with the boy next door. We were looking at a slightly suggestive article in the local newspaper, which we were not permitted to read. My sister and I were marched into separate rooms and questioned as to what we were doing. Incredibly, my father concluded, or at least claimed to—possibly this was just an excuse—that we had an intimate and thorough knowledge of every aspect of sex. He imagined our sex lives to be very active, including such practices as masturbation, oral sex (homo-, hetero-, and incestual), anal sex, fornication, and so on. To this day I do not know whether he was really so demented as to believe his charges, or if they were just a part of a fiendishly devised but brilliant plan to put him into the position of having to "save us from ourselves."

He began by confronting us separately and calmly explaining to us that he *knew* that we had been masturbating, so we might as well admit it and let him help us. (I never heard of the word, let alone practiced it.) When I denied the charge, he tried to appear sympathetic as he explained that he understood how compelling these urges were, that it was only normal to react by gratifying ourselves in an immoral way. He insisted he had seen us "playing with ourselves" on many occasions. (A lie? Hallucination? Sickness—or sadism? Most likely a projection on his part!) He offered to pray with me for the strength to resist the next temptation. When I still maintained I had never performed such an act, he became increasingly annoyed, then agitated, then furious. He warned that the next time he questioned me, I had better make a clean breast of it, *or else!* So it happened that after being knocked silly as the result of repeated denials, I saw that the only way to stop this madman was to stage a mock "confession."

I agreed that he was right. He demanded an apology for lying to him so doggedly. I apologized. He demanded to be told about all the details. I simply repeated the things of which he had accused me. He advanced to his next ploy. He would try a new method to attempt to wean me away from this evil practice. Whenever I had an "urge," I was to refrain from touching myself and instead, notify him. He would make the great sacrifice of offering his leg for me to straddle and placate myself upon. This, he insisted, was an act of the greatest love and concern. Of course, I never volunteered to participate in this scheme—much to his displeasure. My urges couldn't have suddenly ceased, he reasoned. Therefore, I had to be lying again. More beatings, more denials. After days of virtual imprisonment in my room and constant beatings, I didn't see how I had any choice but to readmit my supposed guilt. At least once a day I had to "confess" to an overpowering urge to "play with myself" and ask for his help. I was instructed to put my arms around his neck, kiss him, and wiggle my hips, which he "caressed" as I utilized his all-too-willing leg to "relieve" myself. At first we were clothed, later, unclothed. (Even now I find myself clenching my fists and grinding my teeth whenever I think about it.)

In time, he decided this ritual was not enough; he believed I was still compelled to masturbate on the sly. He claimed to have consulted a psychiatrist about his promiscuous daughter who, he accused, was carrying on with everyone she knew (sister and brothers, aunts, uncles, and cousins, as well as classmates of both sexes). The psychiatrist supposedly recommended that my father offer the *full* use of *his* body to convert my interest to that of the opposite sex exclusively, and to men, not to children. According to the psychiatrist's explanation, he reported, the responsibility fell to him to make my sex life with him as varied and as exciting as possible so as to divert my attentions to a "normal" relationship. Whenever I or my siblings denied having abused each other, he beat us with a belt, and later, a special heavy-duty whip he had constructed out of the inner tube of an auto tire. If we desired relief from being beaten, he insisted, all we had to do was to *tell the truth*. In an attempt to elicit from us his version of the "truth," namely detailed accounts of the incestuous sexual encounters he imagined taking place among us, he beat my sister and my brothers unmercifully, and I could hear each one scream while isolated in the next room. All the while, my mother busied herself preparing a "healthful" evening meal, ignoring our screams, not even showing any curiosity. What could she have imagined our crime to have been that we might have deserved such severe beatings? She never asked.

During this time, I lived the life of a prisoner, only worse. I had been accused, tried, and convicted—and yet, I was retried for the same offenses at least once daily for months. Finally, after I had once again denied any sexual activity with my sister, to my horror and amazement, she stood there at my father's behest, attesting almost verbatim to the scenes of debauchery, which my father had depicted to me in his accusations. When my sister, a "star witness," was dismissed from the "courtroom," my father asked if I was ready to "confess" in the face of this "proof" or if I required the testimony of yet another witness. Knowing my sister not to be a tower of strength or a paragon of truth, and refusing to believe even a demented fiend like my father would involve my innocent little brothers (then aged 5 and 7) in a mess like this, I had him call in my 7-year-old brother. I was utterly astonished to hear that poor terrified little child accuse me of fondling his penis with my mouth and my hands while bathing him. Upon his departure, my father asked if I was ready for him to commence administering "the worst beating of my life" for repeatedly lying in the face of all this "evidence" or if I wished him to call in the youngest, my 5-year-old brother. I knew I couldn't stand to hear that little child uttering those foul accusations, so I decided not to gamble again and to just get the whole thing over with. I survived the bloody beating, but distinctly recall wishing I hadn't.

Now the real ordeal was just beginning. My father had me right where he wanted me—at his total mercy. I had been found guilty of being a total pervert. Since he claimed he had no idea where my hands and mouth had been, I was assumed to be filthy and disease-ridden, and therefore not permitted to use the family dishes. I was assigned my own plate, glass, and flatware, which had to be washed separately by me in boiling water after the "clean" family dishes had been washed. More importantly, I needed more "help" with my "problem." My father escalated his atrocities on me to the point of total nakedness, lying prone on the bed at least once daily. He complained that I lay there cold, like a dead fish, registering no pleasure. He counseled me to "relax and enjoy," and even to request such activities as nipple sucking and cunnilingus. He once bragged to me that he had such enormous self-control that even if I lay on the bed with my legs wide open begging for penetration, he would resist my pleas. He demanded that I writhe and moan and sigh to excite him. I refused. He responded that he couldn't become excited in the face of my lack of participation and demanded that I take a more active role. I understand now that he had me simulating orgasm as a sign that I appreciated such "favors" from him. I was also forced to duplicate every act he performed on me. (These activities were always to the exclusion of actual intercourse.) I reproached him for claiming he was doing all this to prove he loved me, while he was actually torturing me. I asked him, "How, if you love me, can you persist when so often you can see that I'm sobbing in bed?" He replied that he thought they were really tears of ecstasy!

I doubt someone so intelligent and observant as my father could truly have been so out of touch with reality as his absurd comment would suggest. And yet he must have convinced himself on some level that it was true in order to have been able to rationalize his continued torment of me for years thereafter until, at age 18, I was finally able to flee the living hell he called his paradise. However, it is clear to me now that to some greater or lesser degree, my father was a very disturbed man. And so, after working through years and layers of hatred, pain, rage, and the almost debilitating emotional trauma of discovering at a very tender age that neither of my parents was capable of providing the love and security I so desperately needed, I have finally come to a place where the anger has diminished and usually simmers beneath a surface of a more enlightened and objective perspective on my childhood relationship with the demented tyrant who was responsible for so much suffering in my family. The persecuting monster I perceived as a fearful child has become, in my grown-up eyes, what he always had been: merely a man with his own sad story of a tormented youth, a victim badly in need of help.

It is somewhat comforting to see there is some help available today for both the abused and, just as importantly, the abuser. Sadly, though, my father has, to date, refused any such help, never admitting the need or the deeds that took place, and thus not allowing for any repairs to our relationship. So there is no contact between us and has not been since my departure at age 18. I am presently involved, on several levels, in helping to offer solace, solutions, information, and donations to victims of this problem and finding it very rewarding and therapeutic. (From the author's files.)

CHAPTER
10

Forcible Rape

Considering the gravity of rape as a social problem by almost any conceivable measure, relatively little has been written on the subject until fairly recently. Until the 1960s, most of the writings on rape by supposed experts were penned by psychoanalysts, who insisted women yearned to be raped; those who were "got what they really wanted." During that decade, sociologists began to make a contribution to the subject. Most were men, however, and many simply recast the psychoanalytic approach into sociological terms. It was not until the 1970s that feminists received widespread notice with their persuasive arguments. Susan Griffin (1971), Diana Russell (1975), Susan Brownmiller (1975), and dozens of other feminist critics, analysts, and observers have sharpened the vision of all of us on the subject of rape so that, we hope, a more adequate view will emerge in the future. The sociological study of deviance is gradually being informed by

the feminist perspective in all deviant behavior that involves men and women. (For a sampling of feminist writings on deviance, see Millman, 1975; Smart, 1976; Smart and Smart, 1978; Leonard, 1982; Schur, 1984; Naffine, 1987.)

The reader will notice that rape is discussed in a chapter on violence, not in one on sexual behavior. Regarding rape primarily as a violent rather than a sexual act has been common practice in sociology for over a decade. Rape is an assault; it employs force, violence, or the threat of violence. Men who assault women are not moved to act because of sexual motives or an unusually strong sexual urge. Most have sexual access to women; indeed, many are married. Their primary aim is to hurt, humiliate, punish, or subdue women, not to have sex with them; sex for these men is merely an instrument, not a goal. This is not to say that sex is not involved in any way—after all, there is a difference between beating a woman up and sexually assaulting her. If there were no difference, acts of rape would be classified as assault, not rape. There is, to be technical, genital contact, or an effort to effect genital contact, in rape, while there is no such element in assault by itself. Rather than seeing rape as primarily a sexual act, it is more fruitful to see it as a *pseudosexual* act—one that is motivated more by hostility and the urge to exercise power than by passion (Groth, 1979: 2). This is not to say that for some men, the sexual motive is absent; indeed, for some, rape is a "sexual adventure" like "riding the bull at Gilley's" (Scully and Marolla, 1985). Legally, rape entails the use of force, violence, or the threat of violence (we'll have to qualify this shortly); and thus it is, by definition and by its very nature, a violent act.

The Federal Bureau of Investigation (FBI, 1988: 13) defines rape as the "carnal knowledge of a female forcibly and against her will." The FBI also includes attempted rape in its classification; in its yearly tally of rapes in the United States, about four-fifths are "completed" rapes, while one-fifth are rape attempts (1988: 14). As we might expect, the total rapes tabulated by the FBI represents only a small fraction of those that actually occur. (We'll see why so few rapes are reported to the police very shortly.)

It should be emphasized that the FBI follows current ideology and law in excluding *statutory* rapes from its definition of rape. I am often asked by students, when discussing the subject of forcible rape, "Isn't that redundant? Aren't *all* rapes forcible?" The answer is yes and no; most instances of statutory rape would not be regarded as forcible. Originally, the law assumed that below a certain age, which varies in different jurisdictions, a woman should be considered incompetent to consent to sexual intercourse. Thus, by definition, *any* intercourse with her constitutes rape. In practice, however, law enforcement treats, and the courts prosecute, perpetrators of statutory and forcible rape in an entirely different fashion. The statutory rape category confuses two distinctly different phenomena—the first, rape

in legal name only, and the second, essentially no different from forcible rape. If the offender is 18 and the young woman who consents to have intercourse with him is 17, in the strict legal sense, this would be a case of statutory rape in a number of states—but it would *not* be so regarded by the police, by the courts, by the general public, or even by a majority of feminists. Most of us would feel this case should not be regarded as statutory rape at all. On the other hand, if the female is below a certain age, the question of her consent becomes irrelevant, and we *would* see intercourse with her by an adult male a rape—indeed, as *forcible* rape. For instance, in New York State, intercourse with a girl who is less than 11 years old is first-degree rape, and is a Class B felony. Nearly everyone would agree that a 10-year-old girl is not competent to grant sexual consent; consequently, any intercourse with her by an adult is automatically a rape—consent or no consent. Thus, there are both parallels and differences between statutory and forcible rape.

We should keep in mind that the FBI's definition of rape includes the phrase "against her will." There have been instances of men raping women without using force: Either trickery was involved, or the woman, although an adult, was not capable of granting consent. There are, then, cases of intercourse with a woman "against her will," although, technically, force was not used. Consensual sex with a mentally retarded or an insane woman is regarded as rape because she, like the 10-year-old girl, is considered incompetent to decide to consent to intercourse. Having sex with a sleeping woman qualifies as rape. The same applies, in principle (although rarely in real life), to having intercourse with a woman who is under the influence of alcohol or drugs. Likewise, certain kinds of deception may qualify as rape. Men have been convicted of rape after crawling into bed with a woman in the dark, pretending to be her husband. Thus, the determining element here is not the force itself, but that intercourse is not desired by the woman, that the act is *against her will;* force is simply an important criterion of whether sexual contact was desired by the woman or not. What counts is that she does not desire the sexual contact, and, if she is conscious or legally capable of granting or refusing sexual access, makes this sufficiently clear to the man.

One last definitional issue: The law in most jurisdictions recognizes only rape *by* a man *of* a woman. There are, of course, other kinds of rape. In prison, the rape of men by men is extremely common (Wooden and Parker, 1982); to the law, this would be assault or sodomy—not rape. In addition, in principle, it is possible for a woman to rape a man, or even another woman. (In 1987, for example, New York State amended its statutes to include the rape of a man by a woman.) Most of us, however, correctly recognize the extreme rarity of such acts. Since men tend to be larger and stronger than women, as well as better trained in the use of weapons, including their own hands and feet, and socialized to be more aggressive, even violent, while women, traditionally, are more likely to have been taught to be passive in the face of male aggression, rape (at least, outside of prison) is *almost always* an act of violence perpetrated *by* a man *against* a woman.

DEFINING RAPE BY AUDIENCES

Even if we settled the above definitional issues and problems, we would still have a great deal of controversy concerning what is and is not rape. Two individuals could watch a film or a videotape of an enactment, or hear a description of exactly the same behavior, and one would regard it as an instance of rape and the other wouldn't. Social, cultural, group, and individual conceptions vary as to just what constitutes rape. Rape,

---

Adolescent Males and Females Differ on Meaning of Sexual Behavior

A group of psychologists interviewed over 400 adolescents between the ages of 14 and 18, evenly matched for gender, living in the Los Angeles area about their expectations of appropriate heterosexual behavior in various dating situations. They found males and females had drastically different expectations and definitions of acceptable behavior. In fact, they discovered, boys were more likely to interpret certain actions as *consensual* than girls, while girls were more likely to see certain actions as *coercive*. The signals each perceived for sexual relations to proceed or escalate, and the circumstances that legitimated the use of force for intercourse, were markedly different for boys and girls. Males tended to read or interpret a wider range of circumstances as indicating that a girl wanted to have sex with them than the females did. For instance, to the boys, "going to a guy's house alone" was significantly more likely to mean the girl "wants to have sex" than was true for the girls.

When asked "under what circumstances" it was "okay for a guy to hold a girl down and force her to have sexual intercourse" 82 percent of both the males and the females said there were never any such circumstances. However, when the researchers asked about nine specific, concrete circumstances, the percent saying that it was not okay averaged 75 percent for the girls and only 56 percent for the boys—nearly a 20 percentage point difference. For instance, while 73 percent of the females said force was not okay when a girl led a guy on, only 46 percent of the males agreed.

The divergent expectations males and females had of the meaning of heterosexual interaction, and the greater the male attribution of "sexiness" to a wider range of social circumstances, the authors argued, set the stage for acquaintance rape (Giarruso et al., 1979; Zellman et al., 1979; Goodchilds et al., 1979; Goodchilds and Zellman, 1984).

in short, is *partly* a matter of definition. Some might claim that introducing the subjective dimension into rape denies its objective reality and suggests the possibility that if someone thinks an instance of sexual aggression isn't rape, then it isn't "really" rape. Nothing could be further from the truth. In fact, one of the more frightening features of rape is the discrepancy between the objective definition of the phenomenon and subjective judgments of its reality by audiences and individuals. According to the objective definition, hundreds of thousands of women are raped each year in the United States and yet, subjectively, they are not *regarded* as victims of rape. What we have here is a striking contradiction between how the law defines rape ("the carnal knowledge of a female forcibly and against her will") and how most people judge concrete cases *that actually qualify as rape.* As a result, it is absolutely necessary to examine *how rape is seen, defined, and judged by audiences.*

To understand rape and the judgments as to what constitutes rape, it is necessary to recognize there is a *spectrum* or *continuum* of judgments. At one end, we have judgments that are extremely *exclusive*—that is, which are very narrow, very strict—which judge few acts of sexual aggression by men against women as rape. At the other end, we have judgments that are very *inclusive*—that is, which are extremely broad—which include many acts as rape.

Perhaps the most extreme and exclusive view would be held by many rapists, who believe, in effect, that rape does not exist, that nearly all charges of rape are false. One convicted rapist expressed this view when he denied the existence of rape on the grounds that "if a woman don't want to be raped, you are not going to rape her." Said another, rape is when a woman says, "No, you're not going to get it and you're going to have to kill me to get it, or you're going to have to beat me senseless to where I can't fight you" (Williams and Nielsen, 1979: 131). An extremely minuscule number of acts of intercourse against a woman's will would qualify as rape by this extremely narrow definition, which sees men as having a nearly unlimited

right of legitimate sexual access to women, regardless of their resistance, and women as having no rights at all—only the choice between death or unconsciousness on the one hand, and being assaulted on the other. In one study of convicted, incarcerated rapists (Scully and Marolla, 1984), nearly a third said they had sex with their victims, but denied it was rape. "As long as the victim survived without major physical injury," these men believed, "a rape had not taken place" (1984: 535). Said one rapist, who pulled a knife on his victim, then hit her "as hard as I would a man": "I shouldn't have all this time [length of sentence] for going to bed with a broad" (1984: 537). In addition, nearly a third of these men, actually convicted for the crime of rape, denied they had even had any sexual or any other contact with the victim.

At the other end of the spectrum, equally as extreme, is the completely *inclusive* definition held by some radical feminist separatists, who believe *all* intercourse between men and women, however consensual it may appear on the surface, represents an assault, an act of aggression, an invasion, a violation—in a word, rape. Men exercise power over women—*every* man has power over *every* woman—and, consequently, no relationship between any man and any women can be freely chosen by the woman. Consequently, *all* heterosexual sex is coerced—that is, not freely chosen by the woman—and, hence, qualifies as rape. In a patriarchical society, women are brainwashed to think they want male companionship and all that goes with it, sex included. In contrast, in a truly equalitarian society, no woman would want to have sex with any man. (It should be recognized that *most* feminists do not endorse this view.)

Both the extremely exclusive view, held by some rapists, and the extremely inclusive view, held by some radical feminist separatists, represent minority views; very few Americans would agree with them. Between these two extremes are the *moderately exclusive* and the *moderately inclusive* views, which encompass the overwhelming majority of the American population.

The moderately exclusive view tends to be held by sexual and sex-role *traditionalists* and *conservatives*. Individuals who hold the moderately exclusive view believe a woman's place is in the home, that she must have a man to protect her from the advances of other men. If she puts herself in vulnerable situations, like going to bars, acting flirtatious or seductive, being alone in a man's apartment, allowing him in hers, wearing provocative clothing, dating a number of men, hitchhiking or walking on the street alone at night, or even remaining single too long, well, maybe she provoked men's sexually aggressive behavior, maybe she is *responsible* for men forcing intercourse upon her. In fact, maybe she really wanted it all along—maybe it wasn't force after all. These people do not see acts of coerced intercourse as rape because they feel a woman does not, or should not, have complete freedom, especially sexual freedom, to do what she wants. This view is summed up in the saying, "Nice girls don't get raped"; that is, if they didn't do all these sexually provocative things, they wouldn't have brought on men's attention in the first place. The corrollary is if a woman is raped, maybe she wasn't so nice after all. It is possible that some version of this view is held by a majority of the public; most Americans are moderately exclusionist in their judgment of rape. Most Americans, to a degree and under certain circumstances, will blame the woman for a sexual attack against her. They restrict their notion of what rape is to a relatively narrow set of acts, as we'll see.

The moderately inclusionist view tends to be held by sexual and sex-role *liberals* and *nontraditionalists*. They believe a woman has the right of sexual self-determination, the right to choose when and where she wants to be; thus, she is not responsible for an attack against her. If a woman makes it clear she is not interested in a man's sexual advances, and he persists, then he is forcing himself on her; she has been coerced, against her will—an act of rape. Moderate inclusionists feel a woman should not have to be protected by a man to live a life free of assault; she has the same rights to the streets as a man; and she has the right of control over her own body, whom she chooses to go to bed with, and whom she refuses to bed down with. Men have no right to force her to do anything sexual, and if they do, it's rape. Men do *not* have the right to pin a woman's shoulders down, twist her arm, force her legs open, physically restrain her, jam an elbow into her windpipe—or do anything to physically overpower or coerce her—in order to have intercourse with her. If they do, it's rape. The moderately inclusivist view is probably held by a minority, although a substantial minority, of the American public.

The absolutely central importance of subjective judgments of rape becomes clear when we examine how they operate with three important audiences: *the general public, the criminal justice system,* and *victims of rape.*

One study (Klemmack and Klemmack, 1976) distributed questionnaires to and conducted interviews with 208 randomly selected women residing in an Alabama city. The respondents were presented with seven situations and were asked to state whether they believed rape had occurred. Each entailed forced intercourse; therefore, legally, each represented a rape case. Yet only *54 percent* of their responses indicated that they believed rape had occurred. Even in a case in which a woman was accosted in a parking lot, beaten, dragged away, and sexually assaulted, only 92 percent agreed it was rape. (One is tempted to ask, if that isn't a case of rape, *what is?*)

There are at least two sets of factors that influence someone's decision to see acts of sexual aggression by a man against a woman as rape. The first set of factors has to do with the *respondents*—that is, the characteristics of the individuals who make the judgment of rape—and the second set has to do with the nature of the *act*—more specifically, the *relationship* between the aggressor and the victim.

In this study (Klemmack and Klemmack, 1976), the higher the education of the respondent, the greater the tendency to judge that a rape had occurred. Respondents who were highly educated were more likely to judge an act of sexual assault or aggression as an instance of rape; those who were less well-educated were less likely to do so. Second, women who held a paying job outside the home were more likely to make this judgment than women who did not work for a living. Third, respondents who were tolerant and accepting of sex before marriage also classified more acts of forced intercourse as rape than did the respondents who did not approve of sex before marriage. And last, respondents who held a conservative, conventional, traditional view of women's roles were less likely to see rape in these actions. Women who believed "a woman's place is in the home" also believed that if a woman is assaulted it might have been her fault, because she shouldn't have been where she was in the first place; consequently, they often feel the assault against her wasn't really a case of rape. These respondents seem to be saying a woman has no right to place herself in a vulnerable position; if she does, she brings sexually aggressive actions on herself. The respondents who did not see these actions as rape—all of which, remember, are legal instances of rape—refused to see women as free and independent with rights and privileges to go where they wished and to do what they wanted. In contrast, the respondents who believed women have the right to sexual, economic, and physical equality, independence, and freedom were far less likely to blame the woman for sexual aggression directed against her by a man; were significantly more likely to blame the man for his actions; and were much more likely to define such acts as instances of rape.

The second set of factors that influenced a respondent's likelihood of classifying an act as rape is related to the relationship between the victim and her attacker. The more intimacy that exists the lower the likelihood that a given action will be categorized as rape by observers. "If any relationship is known to exist between the victim and the accused, no matter how casual, the proportion of those who consider the event rape drops to less than 50 percent" (Klemmack and Klemmack, 1976: 144). This holds especially for a woman who once had a sexual relationship with her attacker: If a former husband or lover attacks a woman and has intercourse

with her against her will, only a small proportion of observers will regard that act as a legitimate instance of rape. It is almost as if they are saying once a woman has granted sexual access to a man willingly, she has no right to refuse him that access in the future; according to a high proportion of observers, any act of sexual aggression or assault by him against her is not a serious matter. In dealing with the issue of rape, the student is forced to grapple with difficult issues such as these.

Judgments made by the criminal justice system—by the police, prosecutors, and the courts—reflect the same discrepancy between what rape is legally (or objectively) and what rape is subjectively. Each year in the United States, hundreds of thousands of women are victims of coerced intercourse— are raped, according to the legal definition—who are not *regarded* as having been raped by the criminal justice system. Sexual violence inflicted against women is tolerated by the criminal justice system under certain circumstances. To understand how this happens, it is necessary to grasp the distinction between two kinds of rape—*simple* and *aggravated* rape. These categories correspond roughly, but not perfectly, with acquaintance and stranger rape (Estrich, 1987: 4ff).

Simple rape is forced sexual intercourse in which there is little overt, clear-cut violence (that is, there is no weapon, and no beating), there is a single assailant, and he has some relationship with the victim. Aggravated rape is defined by violence (a weapon or a beating), or multiple assailants, or no prior relationship between victim and assailant. The American criminal justice system is schizophrenic about rape. Even though, by law, there is only one kind of rape, the way sexual violence by men against women is prosecuted, or not prosecuted, makes us realize that, in fact, there seem to be *two* kinds of rape: simple and aggravated rape, as spelled out above.

If our definition of rape is limited to aggravated cases, then rape "is a relatively rare event, is reported to the police more than most crimes, and is addressed aggressively by the police." On the other hand, if the cases of simple rape are considered, "then rape emerges as a far more common, vastly underreported, and dramatically ignored problem" (Estrich, 1987: 10).

Almost no one "has any difficulty recognizing the classic, traditional rape—the stranger with a gun at the throat of his victim forcing intercourse on pain of death—as just that" (Estrich, 1987: 13). In such cases, victims usually report the crime to the police, who record it as a crime and undertake an investigation to discover the perpetrator. If the perpetrator is caught and the evidence against him is good, he will be indicted and prosecuted. Chances are, he will be convicted as well; although, given our system of plea bargaining, probably of a lesser charge than first-degree rape. Moreover, the chances are fairly good, at least compared with comparable felonies, that he will serve some jail or prison time for the conviction.

On the other hand, when the case is one of simple rape—say, when a man has forced himself on a woman he knows, especially in a dating situation; when he is in her apartment, or she in his, willingly; and when there is no violence and no weapon—the criminal justice outcome is almost always very different. Women who are victims of such attacks rarely report them to the police; if they do, the police are not likely to pursue the case, or even to record it officially as a rape. Even if the suspect, by some accident, is arrested, he is extremely unlikely to be indicted; if he is, the case is unlikely to go to trial. If it does, he is almost certain not to be convicted; if he is, he will not go to jail or prison. In a classic experiment of juries, Kalven and Zeisel (1966) found juries were four times as likely to convict in cases of aggravated rape as in cases of simple rape. In New York, 24 percent of the rape complaints in acquaintance cases were "unfounded" by the police, that is, judged to be without merit, while this was true of only 5 percent of all stranger cases (Chappell and Singer, 1977). A study of decisions made of cases brought to the district attorney's office revealed only 7 percent of the acquaintance cases led to indictments, while this was true of 33 percent of all stranger cases (Estrich, 1987: 18, 114).

Clearly, a number of factors go into the making of these decisions by the criminal justice system; still, acquaintance is one such major factor. It influences the determination of whether or not a crime has taken place—indeed, whether a woman has been raped or not. Notice that the criteria used to pursue, or fail to pursue, a case are completely *extra-legal;* that is, *they have nothing to do with whether a rape in the legal or the objective sense took place.* They are used to make judgments about whether an act qualifies as a case of rape, *even though the act being described qualifies objectively.* Again, what we see is a huge discrepancy between the objective definition of rape and the subjective judgment of its reality in specific cases.

The crucial importance of this subjective dimension becomes even clearer when we look at definitions of rape *used by the victims themselves.* The *majority* of women who are victims of forced intercourse *do not see themselves as having been raped!* Anytime a man coerces, forces, or threatens violence against a woman to have intercourse with her, it is rape. But most women who are so coerced, forced, or threatened do not define themselves as the victims of rape. One study asked a sample of 595 undergraduates at a large Eastern university several questions about rape and forced intercourse. One question read: "Have you ever been forced to have sexual intercourse when you did not want to because some degree of physical force was used (e.g., twisting your arm, holding you down, etc.)?" Sixteen percent answered this question in the affirmative. But when they were asked, "Have you ever been raped?" only *2 percent* of the respondents said yes. (In addition, not all of those who said yes to the second question also said yes to the first.) In other words, only about one out of seven (15 percent) of the women who had been forced to have intercourse saw themselves as having been raped; for most of them, there was a failure to perceive forced sex as rape. "There seems to be a tremendous confusion among these victims regarding their experiences and their legal rights. They were legally raped but they do not understand this behavior to be rape, or they are not willing to define it as such" (Parrot and Allen, 1984: 18). Clearly, here again, the patriarchical values of our society excuse the violence and force men use against women as justified or acceptable. So ingrained are these values that they are held, to a degree, even by the very women who have been the victims of that violence or force.

BLAMING THE VICTIM

Many men are genuinely astonished when they are accused of raping a woman they just had intercourse with. These men feel that their behavior constituted an appropriate response to their interactions with the woman. They do not believe what they did should be regarded as wrong by anyone. They feel they are taking what is rightfully theirs. They feel they have managed to maneuver the woman into a situation in which sexual aggression was inevitable. In one interview study of inmates of a prison who were convicted of the crime of rape, a majority felt *all* accusations of rape are false (Williams and Nielson, 1979: 131). These men, the authors state, did not recognize a woman's need to control her body and her choice of sex partners. Her resistance was not taken seriously, they felt, because she did not have the same rights as a man.

For instance, many men feel a woman who allows herself to be picked up while she is hitchhiking has made herself available for sexual intercourse. Her resistance, they feel, is irrelevant; if raped, they would say "she got what she deserved." There are men who feel if a woman has willingly consented to come to their apartment, that indicates she has consented to have intercourse. Her resistance, they would maintain, is for display, to convince the man, vainly, they are respectable. Two feminist authors comment on this attitude: "Rape does not apply to a woman who falls outside the limits of respectability; she is just a free lay" (Medea and Thompson, 1974: 45). These men do not "see" that an instance of rape has taken place because they do not draw a sharp line between rape and consensual intercourse. To them, the fact that they managed to have sex with a woman at all is what counts: They have "scored," resistance or no resistance. To them, women are objects to be used in pursuit of their own private sexual gratification. The will and desire of the woman is relevant only insofar as they permit them to manipulate her into a situation in which exploitation and abuse are facilitated.

The fact is that *rape grows out of masculine contempt for women.* Many men feel sexual aggression against certain women is justified because they see them as objects of exploitation. These men do not consider what they do as rape because, for them, the mistreatment of women is routine and deeply ingrained. Perhaps more than any other single fact, knowing rape is interpreted differently by different observers, and differently by men and women, reveals and emphasizes the sexism that is firmly entrenched in our society.

The majority of rapists, according to a study by the Institute for Sex Research, "may be succinctly described as . . . men who take what they want, whether money, material, or women"; their sex offenses are a by-product of their general inclination to seek a goal without being particularly concerned about how they secured it. The notion that a man should be able to grab what he wants, that it is up to the woman to realize this and not put herself in a vulnerable situation, is present in the mind of many members of our society. Even some women believe in this view. Said one rape victim, "I thought women couldn't be raped" (Russell, 1975: 19). Their view is "It can't happen to me—I'm a *good* girl!" This view places the primary burden of responsibility on the woman and excuses man for his natural, normal passion. This sexist attitude is most decidedly reflected in our (male-dominated) system of justice. Judges will typically refuse to convict a man of rape if they feel there is any complicity on the woman's part—and complicity is defined in extremely broad terms. This orientation has been called *blaming the victim* (Ryan, 1976).

A considerable quantity of work on rape has examined the role of the victim. We saw in the discussion of homicide that in a significant number of the cases of murder—perhaps as many as a quarter—victim precipitation was deemed to be a determining factor in the commission of the act. Some theorists and researchers have suggested that rape, too, might be victim precipitated (Mendelsohn, 1963). In a study of 646 cases of rape reported to the Philadelphia police, one sociologist claims about one in five (19 percent) were victim precipitated (Amir, 1971b: 259–276). This was defined as "those rape situations in which the victim actually, or so it was deemed, agreed to sexual relations but retracted before the actual act or did not react strongly enough when the suggestion was made to the offender" (1971b: 266). In a later study of hitchhiking rapes, this same researcher sees *all* cases of rape that take place while the woman is hitchhiking as victim precipitated—"in which the victim's behavior contributes to her victimization." "Subconsciously," this report states, "many of those who hitchhike may be reacting to the thrill gained from deliberately challenging a potential dangerous situation" (Nelson and Amir, 1975: 48).

The notion of the victim's "participation" in her own rape has been couched within an ideological framework. This is partly appropriate (because such a view does have ideological implications and consequences), but also partly inappropriate. Feminists correctly point out that the woman "provoking" a man into raping her is a male-centered notion. Few criminologists would claim that the victim of a robbery "provoked" the robber into committing the crime (Brownmiller, 1975: 383–384). They also rightly argue that current definitions as to what constitutes victim "precipitation" are overly broad. Brownmiller (1975: 355) takes Amir (1971b) to task for adhering to a concept of victim precipitation that is "generous to the rapists." On the other hand, as Amir stresses, rape is not "a wholly and genuinely random affair." Feminists acknowledge this fact by issuing survival handbooks on "how to avoid entrap-ment" (Medea and Thompson, 1974) that inform women "what they must do to protect themselves" (Connell and Wilson, 1974). Consequently, it is possible to discuss factors relating to the woman—who she is, what she does—that make rape more or less likely, without making the claim she "provoked" her own rape. Factors statistically related to rape need not—and should not—be considered precipitation. Some women stand greater or lesser likelihoods of being raped, just as there are differing statistical chances for some men and women to be robbed.

In fact, I believe the entire concept of victim precipitation in regard to rape is completely meaningless. It is not that I believe its role has been exaggerated—for instance, that I feel that Amir's 19 percent figure is somewhat inflated. It is that it is a worthless, misleading, and sexist notion to begin with. It should be discarded altogether from the sociological lexicon.

Recall what Amir's definition of victim precipitation was in rape: The victim agreed to have intercourse, *or so it seemed to the rapist,* and then changed her mind or did not put up a sufficient show of resistance. This notion is based on a number of ideological and highly questionable assumptions. The first is that the woman does not have a right to change her mind about intercourse. Once she has indicated any interest at all, she bears a contractual obligation to complete the act. It further assumes the man's desires are overwhelming and uncontrollable; once he has the prospect of a sexual conquest dangled before his eyes and penis, a mechanism is triggered that makes intercourse—if necessary, by force—inevitable. This, too, is specious: The man is highly capable of controlling his lust. Further, by indicating it is the *man's* definition of the situation that counts and not the woman's, the notion of victim precipitation reserves what might seem to be a reasonable source for defining when a rape has taken place: the victim herself. Rape is, after all, the violation of the life, the body space, and the autonomy of a woman. According to the male-centered notion of precipitation, the woman is *responsi-*

ble for displaying a sufficient level of resistance, but *it is the man who defines what that level is.* Thus, the concept of victim precipitation in rape is based on an unresolvable contradiction.

Rape is one of the very few forms of deviance where the victim is stigmatized almost as much as—and in some cases, even more than—the perpetrator. *She* is often tainted with the stigma of the crime perpetrated *against her.* A woman who was raped states, "After that, it was all downhill. None of the girls were allowed to have me in their homes, and the boys used to stare at me on the street when I walked to school. I was left with a reputation that followed me throughout high school" (Brownmiller, 1975: 364).

If a woman reports the offense to the police, her experience is typically humiliating. Her story is often disbelieved and at times she is ridiculed. "I went to the police station and said, 'I want to report a rape.' They said, 'Whose?' and I said, 'Mine.' The cop looked at me and said, 'Aw, who'd want to rape you?'" (Brownmiller, 1975: 364). "I'm on the floor, completely paranoid and crying" when the police arrived, another woman explains. "They took me back to what they call the scene. Eventually they said the guy was my boyfriend"—the man was in fact a complete stranger to this woman; he followed her out of a bus station—"and that everything was okay between us until he took my money. At that moment if I had a gun I could have killed them all, I was angry enough. After the questioning I left my number and name and address so as they could reach me. Nothing was ever done about it. Some time later, when I was back in school, I tried to contact them. They hung up on me" (1975: 367).

Even if the woman manages to have her report believed and the police take it seriously enough to investigate the case, and if, through a stroke of improbable luck, the rapist is arrested and brought to trial, another humiliation awaits her: the trial. "They trotted out my whole past life," one woman explained, "it looked like I was the one who was on trial" (Brownmiller, 1975: 372). "I don't understand it," another states.

"It was like I was the defendant and *he* was the plaintiff. I wasn't on trial. I don't see where I did anything wrong" (1975: 373).

In a highly publicized trial in San Francisco, one Jerry Plotkin was accused of forcing a woman at gunpoint to come with him to his apartment where she was raped by him and three other men. Plotkin's lawyer argued that the plaintiff, a young mother, was a sexual libertine. She was asked if she was "familiar with liquor," if she had worked as a cocktail waitress, if she had been fired from a job "after it was discovered that" she had had "sexual intercourse in the office" ("That is a lie," the woman replied), whether she was living with a married man, whether her children "have a sex game in which one gets on top of another" ("That is a lie!" the woman answered again). Finally the woman burst out in the courtroom: "Am I on trial? . . . I did not commit a crime. I am a human being" (Griffin, 1971). The woman who is raped is called upon to prove *her* innocence. (Plotkin was acquitted, by the way.)

SOME MYTHS AND TRUTHS

Rape is one of the most difficult of all human activities to study because most of the time it isn't reported, even in cases that are clear-cut, in the sense that if they were observed and objectively considered, nearly everyone would consider them cases of rape. A much larger number of cases would fall into a gray area in between where many observers would call them rape and others would consider compliance in some degree to have occurred. So two basic questions anyone has to answer who wishes to understand the nature of rape are (1) What are the characteristics of officially *known* cases of rape? and (2) How would we go about finding out how *hidden* cases of rape differ from those that are known?

Our society harbors what might be called a "schizophrenia" with regard to rape. On the one hand, many believe that "nice girls and women don't get raped," that the woman, in most cases, "provoked" the attack. On the other hand, another dominant belief is maintained, one that is equally as unrealistic—and yet, it is totally contradictory and usually believed by the very same people who believe the first myth: that rape is a rare, unusual, isolated act perpetrated by deranged, psychopathic men on women who are total strangers to them. Violence, according to this view, is a standard fixture of rapes; murder is a frequent accompaniment. Perhaps the model for this image would be the case of the Boston Strangler, who, according to his own estimate sexually molested some 2,000 women and murdered 12. It seems that to view a woman as a rape victim, we have to construct her in our mind as totally innocent and totally victimized by an insane and perverted monster. Actually, the rape-murder is extremely rare, contributing considerably less than one-tenth of 1 percent of all instances of rape. Of course, *any* case of murder—or rape—is too many, but as a feature in the rape picture, murder is insignificant.

Knowing that most cases of forced intercourse by men against women *are not even regarded as rape by the victims of such acts themselves* points to the extreme difficulty of estimating how frequently rape takes place in the general population. On the one hand, we have some idea of how common the classic or aggravated rapes are from victimization data; on the other hand, the far more numerous cases of simple rape are not only very unlikely to be reported, victims don't even tell an interviewer about it because they don't regard themselves as having been raped. Numerous researchers (for instance, Johnson, 1980; Gollin, 1980; Koss and Oros, 1982; Russell, 1982a; Russell and Howell, 1983) have attempted to estimate the incidence of rape in the general population, and all admit that it is a difficult, tricky issue.

The image of the lone, mad, rare, and violent stalker of women as the typical rapist is fallacious for a number of reasons. First, rape is a more frequent act than official records indicate. Imagine three circles (see Figure 10.1). The outer circle (Figure 10.1a) represents all cases that would qualify in the legal sense—that is, cases of forced intercourse. We've already seen that an extremely

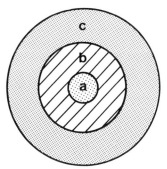

FIGURE 10.1   Actual Rape versus Judgments of Rape. (c) All cases of actual rape, that is, forced intercourse—which therefore qualify as rape in the legal sense. (b) All cases of forced intercourse which are judged by the woman to have been instances of rape. (a) All cases of forced intercourse which are judged by the woman to have been instances of rape which are reported to the police.

high proportion of cases of forced intercourse *are not even regarded as rape by the victims themselves* (Parrot and Allen, 1984); consequently, this outer circle is extremely large. A much smaller inner circle (Figure 10.1b) represents cases in which the women who had intercourse forced upon them judge that they have, indeed, been raped. The smallest circle (Figure 10.1c) represents those cases where these women not only have been raped but they also report the incident to the police. The comparative size of the two inner circles would be determined by the proportion of women who have been raped and who define the incident as rape and report it to the police.

The FBI tallied a total of 91,111 rapes in the United States in 1987. Of these, 81 percent were defined as "rapes by force," and the remainder were called rape attempts or "assaults to commit forcible rape," where, technically, no genital penetration took place. This figure gives us a reported rape rate for the United States in 1987 of 37.4 per 100,000 population. (Clearly, a more meaningful population base would include only women, not the entire population; hence, the rate of reported rape should be at least twice as high.) This figure represents an increase of 15 percent for the total number, and an increase of 11 percent for the rate, since 1983. Focusing only on cases where the woman judges herself to have been raped, what proportion of the total number of women who were raped in 1987 reported that fact to the police? In other words, how large is the inner circle relative to the one surrounding it?

In 1987, a survey focusing on victimization was conducted on a sample of U.S. households; individuals were asked which crimes they had been a victim of during the previous year, including rape (Shim and De-Berry, 1988). The survey tallied a rate of rape for the United States as a whole at 70 per 100,000, roughly twice the rate for reported rapes. Moreover, the proportion of women who had been raped who said they had reported the incident to the police was just over half, 53 percent, which brings us amazingly close to the FBI figures. Of course, it is also likely a substantial proportion of women who were raped will not admit that to an interviewer in a victimization survey, which would certainly increase the size of the middle circle relative to the inner one. Still, such a survey does bring us closer to the "actual" number and rate than police figures do.

The rise in officially reported rapes from 17,000 in 1960 to 91,000 in 1987 may or may not represent a rise in the actual incidence of rape. The rise may be mostly due to a greater willingness of women to report rape than was true in the past, which is another way of saying there is a growing refusal by women to be passive victims of male aggression. Many more women are willing to subject themselves to the humiliation that reporting rape to the police entails. Perhaps women's definition of what rape is has changed. They may be less likely to accept masculine sexual aggression as routine and "natural." This makes rape reporting more common because more male sexual behavior is seen and experienced *as* rape. The greater the pride and self-confidence that exists among women, the greater the likelihood that male sexual aggression against them will be both mentally and officially recorded as rape. The lower this sentiment is—the more hidden from view rape is—the greater the likelihood that women will walk away from masculine aggression and think: "Was I raped? I'm not sure. Maybe I did provoke it," and the less likely that they will report it to the police. But it may also be true male sexual aggression itself is also increasing; no one knows for sure.

Not only do police figures give us an extremely misleading view of the *extent* of rape, but they also present a biased view of the *nature* of the rapes that take place. Although it is difficult to avoid using data on rapes known to the police—for this is almost the only information we have—scattered studies based on interviews yield a very different picture. Pauline Bart (1975) demonstrates that there are systematic differences between the kinds of rapes that are reported to the police and those that are never reported. She found, in her analysis of 1,000 questionnaires distributed at women's centers (not a true cross section of rape victims, remember) that about 70 percent of her victims of rape did not report the offense to the police. As important, the 30 percent representing the cases that were reported were quite different from the unreported, hidden 70 percent. For one thing, the *older* the woman, the greater the likelihood of reporting the rape; the younger the woman at the time that the rape occurred, the lower the likelihood that she reported it. (This relationship probably breaks down below a certain age, however.) This means the typical rape victim may be significantly *younger* than the official data show. The average victim's age computed from official police information is roughly 19; an accurate knowledge of unreported cases might shave a year or two off this age.

Second, rapes occurring *recently* (in the past four years) were far more likely to have been reported than rapes that took place in the more distant past. This suggests the strong increases that have taken place in the frequency of rape in the past few years are partly a function of the greater willingness of female victims of rape to report the offense.

The greater the knowledge of her attacker, the *lower* the likelihood that the victim will report the incident (Bart, 1975). Stranger rapes are far more likely to be reported to the police than are rapes by friends, relatives, and even acquaintances. This means that rapes known to the police are biased in the direction of, and tend to *overstate,* stranger rapes.

And last, Bart's study indicates that highly educated women with professional occupations tend to report cases of rape far more than women who are less well educated and who have less than professional occupations. This leads us to suspect that the current picture of rape as taking place more frequently between men and women in the working classes is probably *even more* lopsided in that direction than we realize. The overrepresentation of working-class women who are raped and whose cases are known to the police might actually turn out to be an *under-enumeration.* Working-class rapes may be more common than the official data record them to be.

A stimulus to the change in reporting rape by women in the past few years is in part attributable to the institution of female-administered police rape squads in large cities to whom rape victims can report their cases. As I said earlier, in the past women who have reported the offense to the police have often been met with a disbelieving, unfriendly, and at times even contemptuous response. However, police*women,* they say, tend to be far more sympathetic. The difference is so basic as to extend to whether the police believe the woman's story or not. To be officially recorded as a rape, a case has to be "founded"—that is, believed by the police. One study conducted a number of years ago estimated that roughly 50 percent of all rape cases were unfounded—that is, the police did not believe the woman's report that she was, in fact, raped (King, 1968). The FBI's *Uniform Crime Reports* estimates that 15 percent of reported cases are (or become) "unfounded." And yet, when New York City instituted a special sex crimes analysis unit consisting of policewomen, cases deemed by them to be "false charges"—that were "unfounded"—*dropped to 2 percent,* "a figure that

corresponds to the rate of false reports for other violent crimes" (Brownmiller, 1975: 387). Clearly, women police officers are far more likely to believe the word of another woman; men are less likely to do so. This phenomenon of "unfounded" cases that come to the attention of the police—that are reported but not recorded—actually lowers the official percentage of rapes taking place between intimates. (Remember, if a rape case is unfounded, this does not mean that it did not occur, only that the police did not see it as a legitimate instance of rape.) In addition, if a woman has had consensual intercourse with a man previously and refuses to do so on a later occasion, the police will look with disfavor upon her accusation of rape and will, in all probability, consider the case unfounded. The greater the degree of intimacy between victim and rapist, the greater the likelihood the case will be considered unfounded by the police. In an unpublished study of rape cases in Memphis, Brenda Brown writes, "The closeness of the relationship was a frequently used reason for categorizing cases as unfounded." Knowing their cases are likely to be dismissed out of hand, women who have been raped by an intimate will be far less likely to report their experiences to the police. (For an excellent study of how rape is handled by the criminal justice system, see LaFree, 1989.)

MARITAL RAPE

The most extreme form of rape between intimates is, of course, marital rape (Russell, 1982b). In 30 states of the United States, a man cannot be legally arrested or prosecuted for raping his wife; in fact, sexual assault is perfectly legal in those states. One book on marital rape is entitled *License to Rape* (Finkelhor and Yllo, 1985) because that is exactly what husbands have in a majority of our states. A husband can force his wife to submit to him sexually at knifepoint; he can attack her in a dark alley; he can do practically anything to her in the way of forced intercourse, and the law cannot touch him. (Of course, if he beats her up or injures her with a weapon, he could be arrested for assault, legally at any rate, which shows us that rape and assault by itself are not exactly the same—that is, rape is not *solely* and *exclusively* a crime of violence.) It is still felt in some quarters that the marital contract obliges the wife to have sex with her husband under any circumstances, whenever he wants. This view, not to repeat this point too often, fails to recognize that forced intercourse is not simply a sexual act—it is a case of violence against the wife.

In one study, 1 wife in 10 had been sexually assaulted at least once by her husband (Finkelhor and Yllo, 1985: 6–7); in another study, the figure was 14 percent, or about 1 in 7 (Russell, 1982b: 57ff). What social factors are related to marital rape? Among women who were separated or divorced, as we might expect, the figure was considerably higher—about a quarter of all wives. Clearly, marital rape is both cause and consequence of poor marital relations. In one study, women who did not finish high school (a measure of socioeconomic status) were four times as likely to have been raped by their husbands as women who did finish high school (Finkelhor and Yllo, 1985: 8–9). Of course, marital rape is far from *limited* to the less well educated and members of the lower class; it can be found in all classes. Even women with a graduate degree or professional education were hardly immune; in fact, 1 out of 14 of all women with an advanced degree had been raped by their husbands (1985: 9). In addition, women who had been sexually victimized as children were roughly three times as likely to have been raped by their husbands as women who had not been molested.

Most people do not see forced sex in the marital context as "real" rape (Finkelhor and Yllo, 1985: 13). To most Americans, it represents, in all probability, a marital spat, which the husband wins. Even when marital rape is depicted in the media, it is glossed over with a patina of social acceptability. Probably the most famous scene of forced intercourse is in the film *Gone With the Wind*, in which Rhett Butler (played by Clark Gable) carries a struggling Scarlett O'Hara (played by Vivian Leigh) upstairs to a fourposter bed—and the fadeout leaves the rest of the viewer's imagination. The next morning, Scarlett is happy, glowing, and chirping, which seems to say a little rape can make a marriage happier. (In the film, the reconciliation was temporary, however.) Matters have not changed very much since *Gone With the Wind* premiered in 1939; recently, a character in a popular soap opera rapes his wife and, again, it is portrayed in a positive light. In the film, *Blume in Love*, the character Blume (played by George Segal) rapes his estranged wife (Susan Anspach) to show that he loves her; it works—she becomes pregnant and they get back together.

The fact that in real life marital rape is often (although not always) accompanied by other physical abuse, including battering, shows us that the commonly held stereotype of marital rape as largely trivial is erroneous. Although wife beating and marital rape are not the same and should not be confused (Russell, 1982b), one often accompanies the other. Even if overt, concrete violence does not accompany marital rape, no woman should have to submit to forced sex, even if the assailant is her husband. My guess is that, sometime before the end of this century, most of the 30 states that do not now criminalize marital rape will do so.

MEN WHO RAPE

There are two basic perspectives toward the etiology or cause of rape—the *psychological* and the *cultural* approaches. A third approach, held by the radical feminists, that rape is universal, that men rape because they are men, because they have a penis, and because "all men are rapists," is not taken very seriously nowadays. (See the critique of this approach in Schwendinger and Schwendinger, 1983: 77–88.)

The psychological approach emphasizes the *difference* between rapists and nonrapists; it argues that some men rape because their personalities are different from those who do not. Rapists tend to be more violent, have less control over their impulses, have a greater need to exercise control and power over others, and to feel and express a great deal of anger and hostility toward women. In its most extreme form, the psychological approach takes a *psychopathological* position; it holds that rapists are severely disordered—sick, pathological, abnormal, mentally ill. The psychopathological approach basically sees rape as alien to the society in which it takes place, and rapists as enacting behavior that is contrary to the central values of the culture of which they are a part. They are acting out the dictates of a relatively rare mental illness, which distinguishes them from more typical representatives of their society. (For a moderate and sophisticated version of the psychopathological approach, see Groth, 1979.)

The cultural model argues that rape is "normal," not abnormal, and is caused by the dominant, mainstream values of the society in which it takes place. Far from representing an alien phenomenon, rape is a consequence of the very norms and values the culture holds dear. These values include sexism, patriarchy, misogyny (a hatred of women), and the valuation of aggression and violence generally. Rape, in fact, is simply an exaggerated form of routine, conventional relations between the sexes. It grows out of the very fabric of our civilization; it is not something a few abnormal men do, out there somewhere. The nature and character of the relations that prevail between the sexes in a society determine the form and the incidence of rape in it. In some societies, rape is almost unknown; the men are gentle and caring, respect women, do not inflict violence on them, and simply do not force women to submit sexually to them against their will. These men would find rape an incomprehensible act. In other societies—and here we would have to count our own— women are too often brutalized by men, and rape is fairly common. In such societies, male aggression and dominance are deeply felt cultural values. (Some version of the cultural approach can be found in Bart and O'Brien, 1985: 92–103; Beneke, 1982; Griffin, 1971, 1986; and Schwendinger and Schwendinger, 1983.)

It should be clear that neither the cultural nor the psychological approach by itself can account for the phenomenon or incidence of rape. The cultural approach fails as a complete explanation because it cannot account for the fact that some men rape and most do not. If taken to its logical extreme, this theory would predict that, in a "rape-positive" culture, all men are rapists, an obvious absurdity. On the other hand, the psychological approach cannot account for the fact that there are significant differences among societies, cultures, and subcultures in their rates of rape. Moreover, the rate of rape in our society, as much recent research indicates, is far higher than the psychological theory would predict. And where the rate of rape is extremely high, it is entirely likely the cultural dimension must be called into play. Given the difficulties that adopting an exclusively psychological *or* an exclusively cultural approach entails, some synthesis between the two is necessary.

In many ways, rape is the polar extreme of a number of basic American values. Although most of us regard the rapist as a deviant, in fact, the kinds of violent sexual attacks upon women that are perceived by the law and by members of our society *as* rape are simply the end product of much that many of us value in somewhat diluted form. We expect the man to take the initiative and to be somewhat aggressive in matters both sexual and nonsexual. Many of us believe the woman is indecisive in making up her mind—and often needs the assistance of a man to "help" her along. To many men, "no" means "maybe" or "later" or even "yes." Female autonomy and independence are disvalued, frowned upon, discouraged— or even punished. Many men feel women have no right to be in certain places at certain times; their adventurousness, these men will say, makes them deserving of rape. A double standard of morality is encouraged. An inevitable corollary is that there are "good" women (who are never raped) and "bad" women (who are legitimate targets of male sexual aggression). A society that discourages women from seeking their own destiny, from wanting to have some of the power and privileges men enjoy, will be one that will excuse certain forms of rape as justified or as provoked by the woman. "The propagandists for male supremacy broadcast that it is women who cause rape by being unchaste or in the wrong place at the wrong time—in essence, by behaving as though they were free" (Griffin, 1971: 33).

Just as rape is almost unknown in many societies of the world, it is encouraged by some of our most honored values. Men learn that women are creatures apart, that they are inferior, that they have a definite place, are exploitable, and, if they step out of line, deserve to be punished. Rape is, without a doubt, *learned* behavior; it does not come naturally. And, moreover, it is learned both directly and indirectly—indirectly from the values and the way in which women are treated (and extrapolated from there), and directly, from within a group context. Other men often encourage the practice of rape. One of the most surprising statistics to be revealed about rape is the prevalence of *group* rapes.

Rape is also characteristically not a solitary act, but an expression of attitudes that groups of men have toward women, toward relations between the sexes, and toward human relations in general. In Amir's study of rape cases known to the police, 57 percent were a single man raping a single woman; 16 percent involved two rapists attacking one victim; and 27 percent involved more than two offenders raping a single victim. Put another way, of all *offenders*, 29 percent raped a woman alone; 16 percent were involved in "pair" rapes; and 55 percent were participants in a group rape (Amir, 1971b: 200). In a sense, there are *subcultures* of rapists. The greater the number of men involved in the attack, the greater the planning: 58 percent of the single rapes were planned, 83 percent of the pair rapes were planned, and 90 percent of the gang rapes were planned. Planning is an indication of the togetherness and camaraderie men share in directing their attack against women.

Saying rape has a cultural component and sexual assault is an exaggeration of conventional American values and behavior is not to say there is no difference between conventional and deviant sexual aggression, or that "all men are rapists," or that there are no detectable differences between men who rape and those who do not. Just as violence is a cultural value for some Americans, not all men are violent to the point of homicide or even assault. Just as in a sexist society, women are encouraged to barter sex for favors from men, very few women are mercenary about sex to the point of prostitution. Cultural values are adapted, shaped, transformed, or ignored by each individual living in a society. In American society, clearly, there is a continuum from men who are the most sexually aggressive to those who are the least. To say all American men are equally sexually aggressive would be to make a crude, simplistic, and erroneous statement.

One research team (Abel et al., 1978, 1980) compared the sexual arousal of a group of men who had been incarcerated for the crime of rape with a group of nonrapists. These experimental subjects listened to audiotapes of three scenes—a description of mutually consenting sexual intercourse, one of rape, and one that entailed a physical assault that was devoid of sexual content. By means of a small device, the men's erections were measured. By comparing the percentage of full erections under the rape description with that of the mutually consenting intercourse description, the researchers computed a "rape index." They hypothesized rapists would be more aroused by the rape description than by the mutual consent description, and with nonrapists, this would be the reverse. This is precisely what these researchers found. The men who had been convicted of rape were consistently more sexually aroused by the description of forced sexual intercourse. The matched nonrapist controls were either minimally aroused by the rape scene or were not aroused at all; they were, in contrast, highly aroused by the description of consenting sex. Moreover, the *more* aroused the rapists were by the rape scene, in comparison with the consenting scene, the greater the likelihood that they injured their victims when they raped them. *Sadistic* rapists were those who were over four times as aroused by the rape depiction as the consenting one; they were also highly likely to be aroused by the scene depicting a nonsexual assault on a woman (Abel et al., 1978).

Another researcher, Neil Malamuth, a psychologist (1981), took this issue a step further. Using a scale of one (not at all likely) to five (very likely), he asked a sample of male undergraduates whether they would rape a woman if they knew they would not be caught. Over a third of Malamuth's sample (35 percent) said there was some likelihood—that is, they were categorized as twos through fives—while the remainder of the sample (65 percent) said there was no likelihood at all they would rape a woman even if they would not be caught. (The proportion saying there was at least some likelihood rose to just over 50 percent if the wording of the question was changed from *raping* a woman to *forcing her to have intercourse,* which, as we've already seen, has fewer negative connotations for most people.)

Malamuth was interested in whether it was possible to measure individuals along a scale of rape "proclivity"—that is, the likelihood that they would actually rape a woman—and whether simply asking men would accurately and validly tap into this dimension. (Clearly, men could lie in their answers to such a direct question; thus, we may simply be measuring the tendency to tell the truth rather than the tendency to rape!) What Malamuth found was that the tendency to give a "likely" response to the question is part of a whole cluster of dimensions and measures that, indeed, reflect the tendency to rape. He compared respondents in his college sample who were ones, on the one hand, and the twos through fives, on the other, with a third group of individuals—convicted rapists. Clearly, men who are in prison for the crime of rape have (in all likelihood) actually *engaged* in the behavior that is being *predicted* for the others. If the twos through fives are more similar to the ones in a number of crucial respects, then asking men directly as to their likelihood of raping a woman will not turn out to be particularly revealing. On the other hand, if the twos through fives are more similar to the con-

victed rapists, then the chances are we have a strong clue as to their respective rape "proclivities."

What Malamuth found was, in all important respects, the college men who said there was some likelihood they would rape a woman (the twos through fives) were significantly more similar to the convicted rapists than they were to the college men who said there was no likelihood (the ones). The twos through fives, like the convicted rapists and unlike the ones, were more likely to believe in rape myths—that is, that women yearn to be raped, that if a woman is raped, she was "asking for it," that women enjoy being raped, and so on. They also, like the rapists and unlike the ones, were more likely to state they personally have used force against women in the past to have intercourse with them and may do so again in the future. And they, like the rapists and unlike the ones, were highly aroused sexually by listening to tapes depicting a woman being raped and hating it. Although it is easy to lie on a questionnaire, it is much harder to fake having an erection in a study on sexual arousal. Malamuth states his findings suggest the answers men give to a direct question asking about their likelihood of raping a woman provide a good indicator of their propensity or proclivity to rape (1981: 153).

Although rape is *technically* a sexual act in the narrow sense that there is some sort of genital contact and/or arousal, it is *not* a sexual act in the sense that sexual satisfaction is primarily sought—or even sought at all—by the attacker. Rather, rape is a *pseudosexual* act; "the motives underlying such assaults have more to do with issues of anger and power than with pleasure and desire" (Groth, 1979: 84). Rapists can be studied in terms of the *motive* for their assaults. Of course, in all rapes, there are multiple motives, and not simply one. However, in most cases, one motive seems to stand out more prominently than others do. Groth (1979), in a psychological study of both prosecuted and unprosecuted (but detected) rapists finds three fairly distinct types of rapes, based on the motives of the attacker.

Anger rapes, in Groth's view, entail cases

where the assault is "a means of expressing and discharging feelings of pent-up anger and rage." Far more force is used than would be necessary simply to achieve penetration. "Instead, this type of offender *attacks* his victim, grabbing her, striking her, knocking her to the ground, beating her, tearing her clothes. . . . His aim is to hurt and debase the victim." Why not simply assault the victim without raping her? Such a man "considers rape the ultimate offense he can commit against a woman. Sex becomes his weapon, and rape constitutes the ultimate expression of his anger" (1979: 13–14). Typically, the rapist achieves little or no sexual satisfaction in the act and often feels disgust rather than pleasure.

The anger rape shades over into what Groth calls the *power rape.* In these assaults, the offender does not want to harm his victim physically, but to *possess her* sexually. Forced intercourse expresses "mastery, strength, control, authority, identity, and capability. . . . His goal is sexual conquest, and he uses only the amount of force necessary to accomplish this objective. His aim is to capture and control his victim. . . . Physical aggression is used to overpower and subdue the victim, and its use is directed toward achieving sexual submission" (1979: 25–26). The rape constitutes a test of the rapist's manhood. The rape experience for this type of offender "is a mixture of excitement, anxiety, anticipated pleasure, and fear." This type of rapist needs to believe his victim enjoyed the act, is attracted to him, and desires to repeat the experience. Depending on his capacity for self-delusion, some retain this belief, even after witnessing his victim's trauma, while others feel the act did not live up to their expectations and seek out another, possibly ideal, victim whose responses will correspond with these fantasies and motives (1979: 25–30).

The *sadistic rape* goes considerably beyond a simple expression of anger; here, violence becomes eroticized. The intent of the sadistic rapist is to torture his victim. "His instrument is sex, and his motive is punishment and destruction." Struggling with his victim is sexually arousing for this man, and often,

it results in an escalation of the violence against her. This type of rapist, unlike the others, will break his victim's bones, cut her skin, burn her with lighted cigarettes, or, in a few cases, actually kill her. "This offender finds the intentional maltreatment of his victim intensely gratifying and takes pleasure in her torment, anguish, distress, helplessness, and suffering. The assault usually involves bondage and torture and frequently has a bizarre or ritualistic quality to it" (Groth, 1979: 44).

Groth estimates that the majority of all reported rapes (55 percent) are primarily power rapes, a smaller proportion (40 percent) are anger rapes, and only a tiny minority (5 percent) are sadistic rapes (1979: 58). In speculating about the difference between reported and unreported rapes, he argues that anger rapes are far more likely to be reported than are power rapes, and so this discrepancy would undoubtedly grow if all cases could be considered, both reported and unreported. This analysis suggests it is fruitful to examine differences between rapes and rapists in addition to looking at their similarities. This approach has both practical and theoretical payoffs. For instance, the question of whether a potential rape victim would be harmed more by vigorously struggling against and fighting her attacker or by yielding cannot be answered without reference to the rapist. In the overwhelming majority of all cases, her struggle will not result in greater harm and may result in escape; in a very small proportion of all cases (that is, when she encounters a sadistic rapist), her attacker will harm her more—if that can be imagined—as a result of her struggle.

Are rapists different from the majority of the male population who does not rape? The available studies (Abel et al., 1978, 1980; Groth, 1979) suggest most emphatically that they are marked off by significant and striking differences. However, this should not be taken as a refutation of the "cultural" view that sees rape as the exaggeration of basic positively valued attitudes and behavior among most men. Rape represents the *end point* of a continuum of valuing the domination and exploitation of women, which exists *in a more watered-down version* in the general society. Rape is perhaps *the most extreme* version of an act of men dominating and exploiting women. Only a minority of men resort to this extreme; most do it in more subtle and socially approved ways.

Moreover, sexual aggression by men against women is extremely common in our society—once again, in a more watered-down version than rape itself. The man is expected to take the initiative, to "make the first move," and the woman, if she is willing, to comply by being passive; there is an element of sexual aggression in this pattern. If she resists, the man is expected to overcome her resistance with flattery, cajolery, seduction, and even some physical forcefulness; here, too, sexual aggression manifests itself. A high proportion of sexual acts entail a woman giving in to the man's insistent demands, not because she wants to have sex with him but because she wants to be with him, or to please him, and sex may be the price simply because resisting would be futile.

In other words, the most sexually aggressive acts that would *not* be categorized as rape by most observers bear some strong similarities to many clear-cut cases of rape, especially those where the least amount of violence is involved (Groth's *power* rapes). A more or less unbroken spectrum can be detected from completely mutual, equalitarian, consenting sexual encounters through those that are consenting but where the man takes the initiative and the woman follows; through those where the woman is reluctant and passive, but willing; through those where she does not desire intercourse but her resistance is feeble; through those where her resistance is strong and unambiguous and the man rapes her, using force instrumentally (power rapes); through those where force and even violence are used to express anger (anger rapes); to those where violence is used to degrade, humiliate, and torture the victim (sadistic rapes). Although it is possible to differentiate most acts from one another by the woman's degree of compliance and the man's degree of force or violence, nonetheless conventional sexual aggression *shades over into* deviant sexuality—culminating in the various forms of rape.

And, as with most forms of deviant behavior, the more deviant the act (that is, the farther it is from conventional norms and the more outrage it generates in the conventional members of society), the rarer it is. The type of rape that is most similar to conventional sexual expression (the power rape) is most common, while the type that is most deviant and least similar to conventional sex (the sadistic rape) is by far the rarest. What the research on rape indicates, then, is *neither* that rapists are totally unlike nonrapists *nor* that "all men are rapists," but that a *synthesis* of the cultural and the psychological perspectives is necessary. Although aggression by men against women is a basic American value, not all men adopt it in the fashion rapists do: Only a minority take it to that extreme. Thus, there are similarities *and* differences between rapists and nonrapists—both of which must be examined. Only a well-rounded and accurate view of the phenomenon can be useful in addressing the problem and make a dent in its incidence.

ACCOUNT: ACQUAINTANCE RAPE

This account was contributed by a 21-year-old college student. She describes being raped by her date.

In the middle of one of my classes, someone I had met recently named Ed flew a paper airplane at me asking if I'd like to go to dinner with him. I thought it was a cute gesture, but refused the date after class, since I had to study. Ed asked me out about five times during the next two weeks, but each time I would say no. The older women in the class had been observing his persistence, and one of them finally said to me: "He seems like such a nice boy. Why don't you go out on a date with him? If you don't have a good time, don't go out with him again. No harm done." That Thursday night I agreed to go out with him and gave him my number.

That Saturday night Ed came to pick me up in my dorm room. I was quite excited and even glad I had decided to go out with him. All my roommates and friends loved him. Ed was 6 feet 4 inches tall, muscular, had light brown hair and deep blue eyes, and a great personality. He was very clean-cut and very conservative looking; he looked like Mr. All-American. Boy, would my Mom and Dad have been glad to meet him.

The evening progressed well. We went to dinner at a local restaurant; I was amazed at how easily Ed could converse with me; I seemed to know his whole life story by the end of the evening. After dinner, Ed decided to show me some parts of the area I was unfamiliar with, and we eventually ended up at some lover's lane overlooking the water. After some hugging and kissing, I asked Ed to bring me back to my room. He decided I didn't really want to, and it took a half-hour of persuasion before Ed drove me to my room. It was a typical male-female first-date situation, I thought. I guess I could not blame him for at least trying. Besides, I really liked Ed. He seemed to be everything I would want a boyfriend to be: good looking, intelligent, hard-working, responsible, and witty.

For two weeks after that, he called me every day, and we sat next to one another in class. All my girlfriends loved Ed, and their approval made me like him even more. A vacation came up soon after that; instead of staying home the whole week, I returned to the campus early. I was the only person in my room, and there were only two other students, both guys, staying in my hall.

Saturday afternoon I called Ed and spoke to his mother. She seemed like an extremely pleasant woman. No wonder Ed had such good manners. That night, Ed showed up at my room with a rose and a bottle of wine. We went to the movies and had dinner. When we got back, it was one in the morning, and the hall was dark and quiet. The two guys on my hall were out, but it never occurred to me to be worried. I had come to like Ed and I trusted him as much as any other friend of mine.

We took our shoes off and watched television for a while; Ed asked if I'd like to smoke some pot. I rarely ever did, but we were having a good time, I was mellow, so I figured, why not? We shared a joint, and then Ed smoked another whole joint himself. I wasn't affected by it at all, but he said that he felt pretty good. We sat on the bed and continued to watch television. We hugged and kissed, and I felt really comfortable in Ed's arms; I was happy with the thought that I had found someone who could make me feel so secure. Then, when Ed started to unbutton my shirt, I became annoyed and asked him to please stop. He seemed perplexed and could not understand why I was stopping him. I didn't feel I had done anything to lead him on. It isn't as if I had never been intimate with a man before. I didn't consider myself a tease. In fact, I was very reserved with Ed because I knew he would jump at the first positive indication I gave him. He began a discussion on making love with someone you care about—even if it was only the first date. I told him I didn't care if I went out with someone for six months. If I wasn't ready, I would not sleep with him. Then Ed said he had heard stories to the effect that all resident students who lived in dorms "slept around." (Ed was a commuter.) When I told him I was not one of "those" females, he seemed amazed and even upset. I think he took the rejection personally. The situation probably seemed perfect for him: alone after a date with a girl who liked him, whom he also liked.

I went to the bathroom. When I came back, Ed was lying on the bed; he apologized, and then started to undo my blouse again, this time with more force. I couldn't believe what was happening; before I knew it, I was lying on my bed with him with no clothes on. I begged him to leave me alone and began crying. He refused to stop kissing and caressing me. I tried to push him away, but it was impossible—he weighed well over 200 pounds. At this point he was oblivious to anything I did or said; he was in his own world. I knew even if I screamed, no one would hear me. I was afraid if I struggled, he would beat me up. Finally, I relaxed and just let him do what he wanted, begging him to please be careful—I did not want to get pregnant.

When it was over, I became hysterical. All I could think of was that I had become pregnant on top of this nightmare. I was uncontrollably hysterical, and he *still* could not understand why. He had the nerve to ask me if it felt good and told me he would call the next day. He wanted to stay, but I threw him out. After he left, I was physically ill. I threw up twice and couldn't get to sleep at all that night. I wanted to talk to someone, but there wasn't anybody. What could I do—call my mother at 3 A.M. and say, "Mom, I was just raped"? What could she do anyway? What could anyone do? I was not going to subject myself to being interrogated by police officers. I didn't have bruises on my body. No one would believe that Ed could hurt anyone. I felt alone and devastated. I had never felt this way before in my life.

The next day Ed sent me a dozen red long-stemmed roses so I would forgive him for upsetting me so much the night before. I couldn't believe it. I almost threw the flowers at the woman who delivered them, but instead, I put them on my desk and cried on them. It was now Sunday, and everyone was returning from the vacation. My roommate saw the roses, put them in water, and paraded them around. All I heard for the rest of the night was how wonderful Ed was and how lucky I was. One of my suitemates said, "Don't let him go, he's such a good catch." I told her she shouldn't be so sure—he wasn't all he was cracked up to be. They thought I was just being fickle. It twisted my insides that they were telling me how wonderful Ed was when I knew what he had done.

When my best friend returned to school and saw me, she immediately knew there was something wrong. One night, a few days later, I poured the whole story out to her. She was very concerned, and it made me feel good to be able to tell someone about the incident. We sat together and both cried. If it had not been for her, I probably never would have told her, because I knew she wouldn't look down on me because of what happened. She agreed with me that the best thing to do was nothing.

The thought of Ed terrified me. He called a few times, and I told him to leave me alone. I stopped going to the class we were in. The next time I went to that class was at the final, and we were scheduled to take it in different rooms. I had no desire to see him or any other guy—ever. To this day, I am wary of any guy I become involved with. I don't even want to be alone in a room with a guy. I don't trust people as much as I used to. It saddens me that I have become this way, but I have to protect myself.

I often have nightmares about that night. I think the fact that I was two years older than he was had something to do with what happened. I think he imagined I was very worldly and sophisticated. He knew I went out with a boyfriend for two years before then, and someone else for three years before him, and he just assumed I would want or need to sleep with him. Sometimes I think he wanted to show me his masculinity. (Just the day before, I had teased him about the gay guys he worked with.) Whatever his reason, I will never understand him, nor will I forgive him. He has slashed a deep scar in my mind that will never heal. No one has ever made me feel so dirty, cheap, humiliated, or suicidal.

I did not report Ed for several reasons. I have heard about the many rapes that take place on the campus, and how nothing ever gets done about them. I did not want this to be publicized if nothing could come of it anyway. I also felt no one would believe me. Ed maintained a good impression. Chances are, people would assume it was just another case of a girl with a crush on him who changed her mind after things got rough. I was also angry with myself for getting into a situation like that. If I had reported it, the police—and just about everyone else, too—would want to know why I had let him in my room in the first place. I really never imagined such a thing could ever happen to me. The thought never entered my mind not to trust Ed. Imagine—I felt safer with him in my room than alone, in that empty dormitory. In spite of my anger and grief, I was still afraid of getting Ed in trouble. How could I even think of protecting someone who hurt me so badly? The fact that I might have been responsible for his imprisonment actually scared me. There are many things about what happened that I will never fully understand. (From the author's files).

ACCOUNT: STRANGER RAPE

This account was contributed by a woman in her early thirties; she is married and is raising a young son. She manages a small dress store. This account is quite a bit more violent and gruesome than the previous one. However, both involve force and, therefore, violence; both are instances of rape.

I was half-walking, half-jogging down a road lined with a few houses and wooded lots. My car was parked at the side of the road near the intersection of this road and a main street where a few small stores, a post office, and a bar were located. It was dusk. I was very deep in my own thoughts as I made my way down the road. Passing one of the wooded lots, I realized someone was near me in the woods. I immediately sensed danger, and turned back and began running toward my car. As I ran I could hear twigs and branches break in the woods. In a panic, running, I let out a scream. A few feet ahead of me, a huge man, at least 6 feet 5 inches tall, came crashing out of the woods, laughing crazily, and panting. I stopped and began running in the opposite direction, toward a house. I ran smack into another man who had also been hiding in the woods. He wasn't as big as the first man, but he also towered over me. Before I had time to react, the bigger man grabbed me from behind, locking my arms in a bear hug. He held me so hard I thought my ribs would break.

I was lifted and forced back into the woods,

thrown on the ground, and punched twice in the face. I kicked at the men and tried to crawl away, but the smaller of the two men jumped on top of me, grabbed my hair in both hands, and slammed my head on the ground several times. I screamed, "All right! All right!" and he stopped. I looked at my attacker and cried out, "Oh, please, God, help me." The one holding me laughed at me and whispered, "Sweet thing, God isn't on this road, not for you, not tonight." I begged him, "Just don't hurt me, please don't hurt me." He slapped me hard across my face with the back of his hand and screamed at me, "Shut up, you filthy cunt!"

He reached down and ripped my blouse and bra right off my body, throwing them at the bigger one who stood watching. He then put his hands around my neck and ordered the big one to pin me down. The big one knelt near my head and wrapped my bra around my neck, just to the point of strangulation. The smaller one ripped my pants off, and then raped me as the other one held the bra tight around my neck. It only lasted a minute or two. After he withdrew, he bit my breasts as hard as he could, drawing blood. I screamed out from the pain and was ordered to keep quiet. The face of the man who bit me was covered with blood.

The big man then asked the other one to hold me; he undid his pants. The smaller one pulled my arms over my head and stood on my hands. If I moved, he would crush my hands under his boots. I was then raped a second time. Then the smaller one yelled, "Let's cut off her tits!" He laughed like a sadistic child who had just thought up a new game to play. The big one replied, "Well, that's good idea, Bub. Why don't you go back to the truck and get that big Bowie knife." The smaller one got off my hands and ran through the woods to get the knife. "Please, please," I begged the bigger man. He got off me and pulled me to my feet. "Listen woman," he said, "if you want to see the morning sun, you better run like hell, cuz if Bub comes back with that knife, he's gonna chop you up so your own momma won't know you. Now get on, girl—get on!"

I ran through the woods, back to my car as fast as I have ever run in my life. I locked my doors and drove to the first gas station I could find. The attendant called the police, and they took me to the hospital. I was tested for smears and treated for my wounds. The police were actually very compassionate and understanding. I wasn't the first victim of these two sick men. The police felt frustrated at their inability to find them. For me, it was over. I just wanted to go home and be left alone to lick my wounds. (From the author's files.)

CHAPTER
11

Property Crimes

Two major types of crimes are *crimes against the person,* also called crimes of violence, and *property crimes.* We've looked at violent crimes, but far, far more common are property crimes, crimes where something of value is taken away from its owner by the perpetrator. Just about all of us steal at some time in our lives; rip-offs of one kind or another seem to be the American way. Larceny, it can be said, is "in the American heart" (McCaghy, 1985: 158). This doesn't mean that every act of stealing is exactly like every other. Or that the people who steal can be lumped together and studied as a homogeneous category. Some thefts involve direct, face-to-face confrontation, while others entail stealth. Some involve force, violence, or the threat of violence; others are completely nonviolent. Some acts of thievery are done with a pen and not a weapon: These are what is known as *white collar crimes* and will be discussed in Chapter 12. With many

white-collar crimes, even the victim may not be aware thievery has taken place, so subtle, indirect, complex, and diffuse are its effects. Some acts of theft are highly visible and are known about as they occur. Others can be detected only by the expert, such as an accountant or a banker. Some acts of theft result in a high likelihood of detection, apprehension, arrest, and prosecution. Others are technically against the law, but are only superficially and cursorily dealt with by agents of law enforcement. And shifting our gaze from the act to the perpetrator, even though most of us steal a little, once in a while, and from few parties, most of us do not make a habit of stealing. On the other hand, some, a minority, steal regularly, routinely; some, in fact, earn a *livelihood* through stealing; that is, they make a *career* of theft.

Basically, there are two major types of theft; and within each of these two types, there are a number of subtypes. The first is theft through the adjustment of *records*—that is, theft with a pen, white-collar thievery. The second type is the physical removal of money, property, or anything of value, from the possession, and against the wishes, of the original legal owner into the hands of the perpetrator. Both main types occur in a large number and wide range of varieties. And one special type, embezzlement, involves *both* the doctoring of written records *and* the physical removal of cash from its legitimate location into the embezzler's possession.

There are many ways of dividing the realm of theft, or the physical removal of things of value from the possession of their rightful owner. First, there is the ordinary, "conventional" *street crime,* of which robbery, burglary, motor vehicle theft, and larceny-theft are major representatives. Second, there is the *organized rip-off:* the theft of a large quantity of goods by a ring of criminals. Often, the actual perpetrators have been hired by higher-ups to do the job. Hijacking is usually just such an organized theft. Third, there is *shoplifting:* the petty (and not-so-petty) thievery of merchandise from stores by customers and would-be customers. And fourth, there is *pilferage:* the inside job conducted by employees of a company who steal things of value from his or her place of employment.

Illegal behavior varies enormously in regard to the likelihood that law enforcement will regard it *as* criminal. Crimes vary in visibility, in seriousness, and in whether their perpetrators will be caught and prosecuted. It is only for "street" property crimes that the likelihood is high that the perpetrator will be caught. Consequently, the population that is studied that supposedly represents thieves and robbers is made up primarily of those who engage in a narrow and skewed type of stealing. So when we ask: Why do people steal?, and base our answer on those who are available for study, we are biasing our answer in the direction of a particular kind of thief. We are talking only about a certain segment; to get a more accurate answer, we have to shift our attention to include the fact that *these people are not well connected.* They tend to steal in such a way that they are likely to get caught. So our answer has to include the explanation as to why they are not well connected and why they enact behavior with a high likelihood of apprehension and prosecution.

If just about all of us steal, likewise, *we are all stolen from.* The difference is that most of us steal only occasionally. Very few of us steal a great deal, often, from many parties. The thief, whether in a white collar or behind the muzzle of a .38, is simply an exaggerated version of the rest of us not-altogether-honest folk. We steal because we do not care about the deprivations we cause our fellow citizens. We steal because the collective conscience has broken down. We steal because the social community has become a fiction. Theft is common among us because we want certain things, and it doesn't matter as much just how we get them. We steal because we are successful at convincing ourselves "it really isn't so bad," that "no one will miss it," or that "it's covered by insurance," or "I need it more than they do," or "they're bigger thieves than I am." Basically, we steal because those from whom we steal have become impersonal, faceless, almost nonhuman to us.

This isn't true everywhere. In societies in which a strong sense of collective identity prevails—some tribes of Africa, the People's Republic of China, probably Iceland—theft is uncommon. Where we care as deeply about the well-being of our fellow man and woman as we do about our own, we tend to be markedly unwilling to rip them off. Nor has this impulse to steal from one another always prevailed in American society. It varies directly with impersonality; we have become, indeed, "a nation of strangers." Alex Haley, author of *Roots,* which traces his ancestry back to Africa, comments in a *Playboy* interview (January 1977) on this society's transition from a communal to an individualistic nation and its attendant impact on the incidence of theft; he contrasts his early childhood in Henning, Tennessee, to contemporary life in Los Angeles. Since he grew up in Henning, Haley explains, the American family has diminished in size and has been geographically separated. As families have moved from the country to the city, from family units with three generations under the same roof, to singles and couples living with and for themselves, from grandparents passing on family traditions to their grandchildren to parents leaving their children in the care of babysitters, we have also moved from leaving doors unlocked to triple-locking all doors and windows. Somewhere along the way, Haley wistfully adds, *a sense of community* has been lost.

Homicides occur for the most part because we care about how others regard us, how we appear in their eyes. But theft is a quite different type of crime. The choice is not simply honor in the face of dishonor, which is usually the way that killers see their dilemma: kill or be dishonored. Rather, it is between goods and services and all they will bring, as opposed to doing without them. The honor we seek—and the dishonor we seek to avoid—in killing another is specifically one that is bestowed upon intimates. Yet because we live in a materialistic society the honor that goods and services bestow travel everywhere. "Money talks" and so does all that it will buy. Money is uniquely *impersonal*. And where impersonal commodities are valued almost above any other value, the stage is set for a *predatory* or a "rip-off" society.

Definitions of Property Crimes

Robbery "is the taking or attempting to take anything of value from the care, custody, or control of a person or persons by force or threat of force of violence and/or by putting the victim in fear." In 1987, between a third and half of all robberies in the United States that were reported to the police (44 percent) were "strong-arm" (weaponless) robberies; that is, no weapon was used aside from the strength or apparent strength of the perpetrator. In a third of all cases (33 percent), a firearm was used; in 13 percent of all robberies, a knife or some other cutting instrument was used; and in the remaining 10 percent, some other weapon was used.

Burglary is "the unlawful entry of a structure to commit a felony or theft. The use of force to gain entry is not required to classify an offense as burglary." In 7 out of 10 cases (70 percent) of reported burglary in the United States in 1987, forcible entry was involved; in a fifth (21 percent), the act entailed simple "unlawful entry" without forcible entry; the rest were merely burglary attempts.

Larceny-theft "is the unlawful taking, carrying, leading, or riding away of property from the possession or constructive possession of another." In the United States in 1987, 1 percent of all larceny-thefts reported to the police were purse-snatchings; 1 percent were pocket-pick-

ings; 1 percent were made up of thefts from coin machines; 6 percent were thefts of bicycles; 15 percent were shopliftings; 15 percent were thefts "from buildings"; 17 percent were thefts of motor vehicle accessories; 21 percent were thefts from motor vehicles; and the remaining 23 percent included "all other" types of theft. In order to qualify as a larceny-theft, no force, violence, or fraud must occur, and a burglary must not be involved. This crime category does not include embezzlement, "con" games, forgery, or passing or attempting to pass worthless checks. Motor vehicle theft is also excluded from this offense inasmuch as it is classified as a separate crime. Clearly, larceny-theft is a grab-bag, miscellaneous category.

Motor vehicle theft is "the theft or attempted theft of a motor vehicle," including "the stealing of automobiles, trucks, buses, motorcycles, motorscooters, snowmobiles, etc." This definition "excludes the taking of a motor vehicle for temporary use by those persons having lawful access." In the United States in 1987, roughly three-quarters of all motor vehicle thefts were of automobiles; 15 percent were thefts of trucks or busses; and the remainder were of other types of vehicles.

SOURCE: FBI, 1988: 16, 24, 28, 33.

STUDYING CRIMINAL BEHAVIOR

How do we know what we know about criminal behavior, including property crimes? How do we find out how often crime is committed, who commits it, and who its victims are? Criminologists use three principal methods to study criminal behavior. The first is *official police reports,* of which the *Uniform Crime Reports,* tabulated by the Federal Bureau of Investigation (FBI), is the standard source. The second is *victimization surveys,* of which the National Crime Surveys (NCR) are most often used. And the third method of studying crime is conducting *self-report surveys* or studies, which ask people directly if they have engaged in certain types of crimes (O'Brien, 1985).

Each year, nearly all of the more than 16,000 city, county, and state law enforcement agencies in the country tabulate the crimes and arrests that take place in their jurisdictions and send the results to the Federal Bureau of Investigation in Washington. The FBI combines and tallies these figures and publishes the results in a volume entitled the *Uniform Crime Reports, Crime in the United States.* Clearly, there are serious problems with using the *Uniform Crime Report's* figures as an accurate reflection of the amount of crime occurring in the United States. Probably the most serious of these problems is that of *underreporting.* Not all people who are victims of a crime report that fact to the police; in fact, overall, only slightly more than a third (37 percent) do so (Shim and DeBerry, 1988: 5). At the same time, violent crimes are more likely to be reported than property crimes, and more serious offenses are more likely to be reported than less serious ones. For instance, although only a quarter of all thefts (28 percent) were reported to the police, over half (56 percent) of all robberies—which entail force, violence, or the threat of violence—were reported (1988: 5). Motor vehicle theft is typically reported (73 percent), mainly for insurance purposes. Criminal homicide or murder, as we saw in Chapter 10, is almost always reported. Even though the victim can't complain (in the case of murder, the

victim is dead!) the police usually find the body and usually surmise that a murder did, in fact, take place. Of all crimes, the police statistics on murder are by far the most accurate. For crimes where there is no clear-cut victim and no complainant, such as drug possession and sale, official police statistics are virtually worthless as a reflection of their frequency.

Table 11.1 shows the total number of property crimes reported to the police by victims in the United States for 1987. As I said, these figures represent a serious underestimation of these crimes, especially so for larceny-theft, less for burglary and robbery, and even less for motor vehicle theft. These are "official" police statistics on crime, although, clearly, official crime statistics are not necessarily the most accurate.

More reliable than the FBI's *Uniform Crime Reports* are the results of *victimization surveys* conducted by the National Crime Surveys. Almost every year, nationally representative samples of some 60,000 households are questioned about crimes suffered during the previous 12 months. For nearly all crimes, the likelihood that someone will report a crime to a survey interviewer is much greater than the chance they will report it to the police. As a general rule—which varies from one type of crime to another—victimization surveys uncover crime frequency figures roughly twice as high as those that appear in official police statistics. For instance, the *Uniform Crime Reports* tabulated roughly half a million robberies in the United States in 1987; the National Crime Survey's tally of robberies (see Table 11.2), reported by the Bureau of Justice Statistics, was about a mil-

TABLE 11.1 Property Crimes in the United States (1987)

Crime	Total Number	Rate/100,000
Robbery	517,704	212.7
Burglary	3,236,184	1,329.6
Larceny-theft	7,499,851	3,081.3
Motor vehicle theft	1,288,674	529.4

SOURCE: Federal Bureau of Investigation, 1988: 16–35.

TABLE 11.2 Property Crimes, National Crime Survey (1987)

Crime	Total Number	Rate/ 100,000*	Percent Reported
Robbery	1,030,000	520	56
Burglary	5,623,000	6,130	52
Theft**	13,235,000	6,750	28
Vehicle†	1,479,000	1,610	73

*Rates for National Crime Surveys, unlike the *Uniform Crime Reports*, are based on the *relevant* population, not on the *total* population. Burglaries, for instance, are based on households, and theft is based on the total number of individuals age 12 and older in the population.

†Refers to motor vehicle theft, including attempts as well as completed thefts

**Includes personal crimes of theft, such as purse snatching and pocket picking

SOURCE: Shim and DeBerry, 1984: 2.

lion—about twice as high. For burglaries, the totals were close to that same 2-to-1 ratio—3.2 million for the *Uniform Crime Reports,* and 5.6 million for the National Crime Survey (FBI, 1988: 17, 24; Shim and DeBerry, 1988: 2–3). Even though there are some methodological problems with victimization surveys (O'Brien, 1985: 49–56), nearly all criminologists agree that, as a measure of criminal activity, they are more accurate and valid than are official police statistics.

Self-report surveys are a third method of studying crime. Here, samples of respondents are asked about crimes, offenses, or delinquent acts they themselves may have committed. Most people would say, commonsensically, that hardly anyone would tell the truth when asked about having committed crimes for which they could be arrested. But here, as in so many cases, common sense is dead wrong. Surprisingly, most people are quite willing to admit their own participation in criminal activity. They tend to tell the truth to the best of their ability, as long as they are certain there will be no harmful personal consequences in telling the truth. People admit to many more crimes than the police record in their official statistics; whenever a researcher checks what people say they did against the objective evidence of

the same offense, the respondent is telling the truth in an extremely high proportion of the cases. (See, for example, Inciardi, 1986: 121; Johnson et al., 1985: 208–209.) However, unlike the *Uniform Crime Reports* and the National Crime Surveys, self-report surveys have not been standardized, are not part of a single, ongoing research effort, and cannot be used to determine frequency, incidence, or rates of criminal behavior. What self-report surveys are good for is establishing correlations between criminal behavior and various sociological characteristics and determining the causes of criminal behavior. What they are *not* good for is determining how often certain crimes are committed in the United States (O'Brien, 1985: 65ff).

THE SEVERITY OF CRIME

How serious is murder? Or robbery? Rape? Burglary? Common theft?

A sample of 60,000 Americans was asked to rank dozens of crimes in terms of seriousness. Table 11.3 gives the seriousness score of some representative property crimes and crimes of violence. In this survey, an offense that is given a seriousness score of 20 is regarded as twice as serious as one with a score of 10, which, in turn, is seen as twice as serious as one with a score of 5. Notice, this is a study of the *subjective* seriousness of crimes, not their *objective* seriousness—that is, it is how seriously crimes are *regarded* by the public. (The two dimensions may overlap, of course.) What does this survey tell us about the seriousness of crime?

First, we notice that *crimes of violence are rated as significantly more serious than property crimes.* People rate crimes in which victims are killed or injured as vastly more serious than crimes in which victims merely lose money or property. The 9 crimes in Table 11.3 with the highest severity score are all crimes of violence, and the 11 crimes with the lowest scores are all strictly property crimes.

Second, robbery or the theft of money or property, which involves victim confronta-

Whenever someone is arrested for a given reported crime, the police classify that crime as having been "cleared by arrest," regardless of whether or not the person arrested is convicted of the crime. In most cases, the assumption that the actual perpetrator has been caught when someone is arrested is justified, although in some cases, a false arrest did take place.

As we might expect, the arrest rate is highly variable according to the type of crime committed. For crimes of violence, the arrest or "clearance rate" is fairly high. In 1987, it was 70 percent for murder, higher than for any other type of crime. (Still, we might wonder why only 7 out of 10 of all murderers are arrested—Why isn't this figure higher?) Contrary to what some feminists claim, over half of all rapes that are reported to the police (53 percent) result in arrest. (Of course, remember the qualification I made in Chapter 10 about the distinction between simple and aggravated rape. The category of rape that is more likely to be prosecuted—that is, aggravated rape—is also the category that is more likely to be reported to the police.) How do property crimes compare with these figures on violent crime?

Not very well. Robbery, which is both a property crime and a crime of violence, had a clearance rate of just over a quarter (27 percent) in 1987. Since only a bit more than half of all robberies are reported to the police, the police really solve only one robbery case out of eight. The clearance rate for larceny-theft was one-fifth of all cases reported to the police (20 percent); again, if we are being realistic, since roughly a quarter of all larceny-thefts are reported to the police, these cases have an arrest or clearance rate of only 1 in 20! Only a seventh of all motor vehicle thefts (15 percent) were cleared by arrest, approximately an accurate figure, since some three-quarters of all motor vehicle thefts are reported to the police. The figure for burglary was a bit lower than for motor vehicle theft (14 percent); again, since burglary is reported about half the time, perhaps 7 percent of all burglaries result in the arrest of a suspect. Since all property crimes are crimes of stealth in which the perpetrator is not usually known to the victim, detection and arrest are obviously very problematic. Robbery, the only property crime that is also a crime of violence, entails confrontation between the victim and the perpetrator, and so, in principle, the victim should be able to identify the offender. The problem is that robbery not only takes place between strangers, it is also, overwhelmingly, a big-city crime and, therefore, typically one in which the offender remains anonymous to both the victim and law enforcement.

SOURCE: Federal Bureau of Investigation, 1988: 12, 14, 20, 25, 32, 35.

tion where force, violence, or the threat of violence is used, is regarded as more serious than stealing that involves no such element. Even though, technically, violence and physical harm may not have occurred, the very *threat* of, or *potential* for, violence in a given act of robbery causes most people to regard such acts as more serious than where no such threat or potential exists. Robbing a victim of $10 at gunpoint is seen as more serious (9.4) than picking someone's pocket (3.3). Nonviolent crimes in which property is stolen—that is, those entailing no force, no violence, and no threat of violence—are seen as much less serious than violent property crimes.

Third, offenses that took place when no one was present were ranked as less serious than those where individuals—potential victims—were actually present. Stealing $1000 worth of merchandise from a department store counter was ranked as more serious (7.6) than breaking into a department store and stealing merchandise worth the same amount of money (7.3). At first, this ranking doesn't make much sense, since one involves committing burglary and the other, mere theft. When we realize the first act takes

TABLE 11.3 How People Rank the Severity of Crime

Severity Score	Offense
72.1	A person plants a bomb in a public building. The bomb explodes and 20 people are killed.
52.8	A man forcibly rapes a woman. As a result of physical injuries, she dies.
43.2	A person robs a victim at gunpoint. The victim struggles and is shot to death.
35.7	A person stabs a victim to death.
30.0	A man forcibly rapes a woman. Her physical injuries require hospitalization.
25.8	A man forcibly rapes a woman. No other physical injury occurs.
24.8	A person intentionally shoots a victim with a gun. The victim requires hospitalization.
21.0	A person robs a victim of $1000 at gunpoint. The victim is wounded and requires hospitalization.
18.0	A person stabs a victim with a knife. The victim requires hospitalization.
17.7	A person, armed with a gun, robs a bank of $100,000 during business hours. No one is physically hurt.
16.8	A person, using force, robs a victim of $1000. The victim is hurt and requires hospitalization.
15.5	A person breaks into a bank at night and steals $100,000.
11.9	A person intentionally injures a victim. The victim is treated by a doctor and hospitalized.
10.9	A person steals property worth $10,000 from outside a building.
10.3	A person threatens to harm a victim unless the victim gives him money. The victim gives him $1000 and is not harmed.
9.7	A person breaks into a department store, forces open a safe, and steals $1000.
9.7	A person robs a victim of $1000 at gunpoint. No physical harm occurs.
9.7	A person breaks into a display case in a store and steals $1000 worth of merchandise.
9.7	A person breaks into a home and steals $1000 worth of merchandise.
9.4	A person robs a victim of $10 at gunpoint. No physical harm occurs.
8.5	A person intentionally injures a victim. The victim is treated by a doctor but is not hospitalized.
8.0	A person steals an unlocked car and sells it.
8.0	A person, using force, robs a victim of $1000. No physical harm occurs.
7.6	A person steals $1000 of merchandise from a department store counter.
7.3	A person beats a victim with his fists. The victim is hurt but does not require medical treatment.
7.3	A person breaks into a department store and steals merchandise worth $1000.
6.9	A person steals property worth $1000 from outside a building.
6.6	A person does not have a weapon. He threatens to harm a victim unless the victim gives him money. The victim gives him $10 and is not harmed.
6.6	A person steals $1000 of merchandise from an unlocked car.
4.9	A person snatches a handbag containing $10 from a victim on the street.
4.4	A person steals an unlocked car and later abandons it undamaged.
4.4	A person picks a victim's pocket of $100.
3.6	A person steals property worth $100 from outside a building.
3.3	A person breaks into a department store, forces open a cash register, and steals $10.
3.3	A person picks a victim's pocket of $10.
2.2	A person steals $10 worth of merchandise from a department store counter.
1.7	A person steals property worth $10 from outside a building.

SOURCE: Klaus and Kalish, 1984.

place in the presence of others, while the second takes place where the perpetrator is completely alone, the ranking becomes understandable.

Fourth, consequences are important in the public's rating of the seriousness of an offense. Two offenders may have engaged in precisely the same action, but if, by happenstance, the action of one results in more damage, the public will see it in a more serious light. For instance, the public gave the offense, "A person attempts to kill a victim with a gun. The gun misfires and the victim escapes unharmed," a score of 16.4—considerably lower than any of the other offenses entailing a firearm.

Fifth, a weapon, and more specifically, the *type* of weapon used, weighs significantly in the public's consideration of seriousness. Crimes entailing the use of a gun are ranked as more serious than those in which a knife is used; which, in turn, are ranked as more serious than those in which a lead pipe was used; which, again, were ranked as more serious than those in which no weapon was involved. The use of a weapon, and a potentially more lethal weapon, indicates to the public that the perpetrator is more committed in his intention to commit a serious crime and less concerned about the consequences of his action. The fact that victims are more likely to be injured in weaponless robberies (although those who are injured with weapons are more seriously injured) is irrelevant in the public's evaluation of seriousness.

Sixth, the *amount* of money stolen plays a significant role in the public's judgment of seriousness. For instance, a person stealing $10,000 worth of property from outside a building is given a seriousness score of 10.9; a person stealing $100 from outside a building is scored only 3.6; and a person stealing only $10 worth of property is scored 1.7. Breaking into a home and stealing $1000 is rated as more serious (9.7) than breaking into a home and stealing $100 (3.1). Although this generalization appeals to common sense, it did not appear to be supported in an earlier survey of the seriousness of crimes (Rossi et al., 1974); moreover, the relationship between the amount of money or property taken and seriousness—other things being equal, of course—is not perfect.

And *seventh,* the more that the perpetrator has to do to commit a given offense, the more seriously the act is regarded by the public—again, other things being more or less equal. Breaking into a display case and stealing $1000 (9.7) is seen as a more serious offense than stealing merchandise worth the same amount of money from a store counter (7.6). Stealing a locked car is seen as more serious than stealing an unlocked car. A person breaking into a home and stealing merchandise worth $1000 is regarded as more serious (9.7) than someone stealing property worth $1000 from outside a building (6.9). The crime is seen as less serious when the perpetrator acts on an existing opportunity than when the perpetrator has to make a much more active effort (Klaus and Kalish, 1984).

MOTIVES FOR STEALING

The street thieves tabulated in the pages of the *Uniform Crime Reports* run the gamut from the rankest amateur who steals from time to time to buy things he sees others enjoying, to the professional who earns a comfortable livelihood exclusively from stealing. For both, stealing tends to be a *rational* activity: It is a means to an end that most of us seek, though in a somewhat different fashion. Whatever other benefits are derived from stealing ("kicks," fun, excitement, and so on) they are secondary to the monetary benefits. A nation with high rates of theft, as Merton's anomie theory argues (Merton, 1938, 1957), is one that:

1. Emphasizes material values;
2. Manifests great material differences between rich and poor;
3. Prominently displays the possessions of the affluent;
4. Portrays the possessions of the affluent as attainable for everyone;
5. De-emphasizes the means of attaining these possessions;
6. Makes it difficult, if not impossible, for a large number of the members of that nation to attain these possessions legally.[1]

It is these features that almost guarantee that a given society or nation will have high rates of theft. They make for the "rip-off" society.

Among the tugs and pulls inducing people to attempt thievery as a means of earning money, certainly two stand out as most prominent. The first would be the

[1] I find Merton's argument on social structure and anomie convincing for illegal money-making activities, including stealing. I do not regard it at all persuasive for most other forms of deviance, such as sexual deviance, alcoholism, and drug use.

choice between poverty and cash. In a nation with high unemployment rates in many neighborhoods, with a black unemployment rate twice that of whites, and with an unemployment rate for teenagers over three times that for adults, many people are induced to steal because they literally have no other means of earning money at all. Even holding a job doesn't guarantee many of us enough cash to move in the world with much dignity or comfort. Poverty has to be counted as a major inducement to thievery. We have a great deal of theft in this society because the economy does not guarantee enough people a decent livelihood. But remember, it is not poverty alone that does it; theft tends to be rare in the nations of the world in which people are *the most* impoverished, partly because the rule of the rich is far more tyrannical than is true here and partly because the poor do not dream that they could, through acts of theft, acquire what the rich have.

The second factor that induces people to steal is that most jobs, even if one is able to work at one, are not very interesting. In fact, most are boring, alienating, even demeaning. So the choice, for some, isn't simply between poverty and cash, but between working at a regular job that one despises and doing something that is illegal but is perhaps less humiliating, or at least that doesn't consume 8 or 10 hours a day. Stealing from others involves being one's own boss, choosing one's working hours, and doing the jobs one decides to do. It is difficult to imagine inducements more persuasive than these.

Let's listen to what a professional armed robber has to say about what led him to pick up a revolver and earn a livelihood using it.

I've never had any trouble getting a job. Anybody can work, but of course I don't dig working. I mean, not that type of manual work. And then when we got together and talked it over and decided that in order to get the amount of money we wanted in the shortest time, that crime was the way to get it. And crime, we feel, is just like any other business. In other words, there's setbacks in crime and there's deficits, just like you run a business and there's a chance that you might burn down or you might go bankrupt or your employee might have embezzled everything you got

without the insurance to cover it, and it's the same way with crime. Of course the penalty for going bankrupt in crime is much stiffer, but at the same time your material gain is much more than it is in a regular business. (Jackson, 1974: 44–45)

A journalist, James Willwerth, talked to, followed around, and hung out with a young man, Jones, who made a living out of mugging people on the street, usually with a knife, sometimes with a gun, occasionally with his fists. Willwerth wrote a "portrait of a mugger" from the information he gathered:

Jones is a violent man; he knows the streets may kill him. He looks over his shoulder every moment of his life. He hates the tension of this, while knowing it comes with the life he chooses to lead. For the streets allow him to run away from himself, and from the demands and limitations of ghetto life. The alternative is a job; years of dreary work and grinding semi-poverty. The people uptown have good-paying jobs, houses and cars and good clothes. It doesn't happen to anyone in Jones's neighborhood. The way to get over is to stay in the street. If you stay alive, you can be *anything*—sooner or later the "big sting" comes your way and you can have all the women, clothes, cars, and penthouses you need, right? In the meantime, keep moving.... When Jones works regularly [at mugging], he says he makes more than a hundred dollars a day.... It is tax free.... So he has the equivalent of a $25,000 job.... "Fear is just another emotion" [Jones explains]. "You are taught from birth you will be punished if you do something wrong. Dig it: pulling a rip is against the law, and you are taught fear of the law. But then you say, if this can help *me,* it's right.... I won't lie to you. What I do is wrong.... *But man, it gives me life."* (Willwerth, 1976: 23, 32, 46)

FACTORS IN PROPERTY CRIME

Socioeconomic status (SES), including social class, income, education, and occupation, are very strongly correlated with the property crimes under discussion. In fact, this relationship is so strong and well documented (Braithwaite, 1981; Clelland and Carter, 1980; Elliott and Huizinga, 1983) that it

A Mugger's Tale

A "mugging" is a term used by the public to refer to a mixed collection of crimes. Some muggings are robberies: the use of violence or the threat of violence to steal. Some are larceny-theft: stealing without the use of violence, such as purse-snatching. Most take place on the street, but some entail pushing in the half-open front door of an apartment and stealing some of its contents while the frightened resident is inside. (This is called a "crib job.") All entail at least one victim and at least one assailant.

Harvel Wilder, a 20-year-old convict, spent the last five years of his life earning a living by mugging people, earning hundreds of dollars a night. He prowled the streets of Manhattan looking for "people who had money." "There was about four of us . . . and we'd snatch six or seven people till we felt we had enough—till we was satisfied." He explains that in five years of almost daily and nightly mugging, 11 arrests, and 5 convictions, he served a total of one year in jail. Six of his cases were dismissed, even though, several times, he had been caught in the act.

After a victim resisted a strong-arm robbery, Mr. Wilder purchased a .25 caliber handgun; after seeing the movie *Magnum Force,* he got a magnum pistol. Whenever he pointed the huge weapon at a victim, he explains, "They was scared. . . . You see, you don't want nobody to fight back." He never put bullets in the gun, however; he wanted to scare his victims, not kill them.

Harvel Wilder explains his method of opera-

tion in the following words. "I'd wake up in the morning and I'd already have money in my pocket. . . . And I'd go outside, see the fellows, get high. And all of a sudden one of us would say 'Let's go get some money.' And we'd decide we wanted to do a store or we going to rob some, and I'd go home and get my pistol."

An average night's take was $800, split four ways. "I bought clothes, TV, a whole stereo system," he said, "anything I thought I needed. I always had a new pair of sneakers." Much of the money went to set up an apartment with his girlfriend. "I was crazy about furniture," he explained. "Couches, big chairs, love chairs." He never accumulated enough to purchase a car. The car he fantasized having was "the best there was, the best they got." His two biggest ambitions were to buy a dream house and to rob an armored car. He didn't have enough money for the first of these, and his friends "just didn't have the heart" for the second.

Mr. Wilder never tried to get a job. "I just always knew I couldn't make the kind of money I could make robbing by working. . . . I always wanted to have money—to do whatever popped in my head." To attain that end, he would rob. "You get a nice block that ain't too crowded and just snatch the first person you see," he explained.

He intends to go straight after being released from prison. "I'm going in the Army, get married, and—I don't know, just live like you're suppose to" (Basler, 1980).

---

seems futile to deny it, as some observers have (Tittle and Villemez, 1977; Tittle, et al., 1978). The discussion in Chapter 3 deals in some detail with this controversy and its clear-cut resolution. Overwhelmingly, the poor are much more likely to steal in conventional ways—that is, in the ways discussed in this chapter—than the affluent. (The affluent steal in different ways, of course, as we'll see in Chapter 12 on white-collar crime.) Although members of the mid-

dle class do engage in conventional property crimes, they are less likely to do so than members of the lower and working classes; moreover, they are strikingly less likely to engage in *serious* property crimes, especially robbery.

As we have seen, it is less the factor of a society's absolute poverty level that influences the rate of property crimes than its *income distribution.* With all due deference to the differing definitions of the crimes we've been discussing that prevail worldwide, an international comparison of crime rates bears this out. (For one such comparison, see Kalish, 1988.) In socialist countries such as the Soviet Union and the Eastern bloc nations, which have fairly equitable income distributions, the rates of the property crimes I've been discussing, all observers agree, are extremely low (though other property crimes that are more or less unique to socialist regimes, such as "profiteering," are infinitely more common than in capitalist societies). Likewise, in capitalist societies with fairly equitable income distribution, such as Sweden, Denmark, Norway, and the Netherlands, property crimes are comparatively uncommon. On the other hand, property crimes are much more frequent in the United States, with its far less equitable income distribution, and may be even more common in many extremely poor Third World countries, such as Brazil, Jamaica, Colombia, and Nigeria.

One factor that tempers this relationship is that one necessary ingredient of property crime is *the existence of property in the first place.* It makes sense that, in a society in which privately owned goods are extremely scarce, there is little in the way of goods to steal. Ironically, it could be that one major cause of property crime is *affluence:* The greater the abundance of material goods the members of a society have, the more there is to steal, and thus, the higher the rate of property crime (Gould, 1969). Few crimes demonstrate this principle better than motor vehicle theft. Where there are many cars, there are many cars to steal, and thus, auto theft will be more common; in societies with few cars, few cars will be stolen. (This leads us to a methodological problem: Should the rate of motor vehicle theft be calculated on the basis of the entire population, or on the basis of the total number of cars? If it is calculated on the basis of the entire population, China, a society with few cars and many people, will have a minuscule rate of motor vehicle theft by virtue of this fact alone.) Of course, this argument cannot be pushed too far since the rates of property crime in nations in which material want is practically nonexistent (for example, Kuwait, Brunei, the United Arab Emirates, and Switzerland) are undoubtedly extremely low, while those of the poorer nations of the Third World are far, far higher.

In addition to the role of socioeconomic status (SES) in the *commission* of property crime, we might also investigate the role of SES in property crime *victimization.* If it is the members of the lower and working classes who are more likely to commit property crimes, is this also true for the victims of these crimes? As we saw for violent crimes, especially murder, as a general rule, victims are likely to have the same social class characteristics as perpetrators; is this also true for property crime? The answer is yes and no; it depends on the crime. As we can see from Table 11.4, the relationship between household income (one measure of SES) and the likelihood of being a victim of property

TABLE 11.4 Percent of Households Victimized by Specific Crimes by Household Income (1987)

Crime	Household Income			
	Under $7500	*$7500–$10,000*	*$15,000–$24,000*	*$25,000 and over*
Robbery	1.6	1.1	.8	.7
Burglary	7.3	5.6	4.7	4.8
Personal theft	8.6	8.8	10.8	14.0
Household*	8.2	7.8	8.3	8.2
Vehicle**	1.0	1.3	1.5	1.8

*Household theft

**Motor vehicle theft

SOURCE: Rand, 1988.

theft varies enormously according to the crime in question. Income has a positive relationship with victimization for some property crimes; that is, the *higher* the income, the greater the likelihood of victimization. On the other hand, there is a negative relationship with some other crimes; that is, the *lower* the income, the greater the criminal victimization.

In this survey, members of poor households were twice as likely to have been victims of robbery than members of more affluent households; for burglary, this was one-and-one-half times. For personal theft (such as purse snatching and pocket picking), it was the opposite: Members of more affluent households were nearly twice as likely to have been victimized than members of poor households. For household theft, however—that is, having things stolen directly from one's apartment or house—no relationship existed: Poor and more affluent households were just as likely to have been victims of this particular type of crime.

Although these relationships might seem contradictory, they become understandable when the relationship of particular types of crime to income and socioeconomic status is made clear. Robbery is partly a crime of violence; consequently, it is likely to be more common in poorer neighborhoods and communities where the rate of violence is high. And, as we saw in Chapter 10, violence is negatively correlated with SES, including income; that is, the lower the SES, the higher the rate of violent acts. The relationship of income to personal and motor vehicle theft is, for the most part, due to the fact that members of affluent households simply have more to steal. Clearly, households whose members own more cars are more likely to be victims of auto theft than households whose members own few cars.

The seemingly contradictory relationship between income and criminal victimization reveals that property criminals are moved by at least two contradictory impulses: *propinquity*, or their physical and social nearness to potential victims, and the *affluence* of potential victims. It is easier to steal from people living in neighborhoods one is familiar with than from those who live in unfamiliar neighborhoods. But it also makes more sense to steal from individuals who have money or valuable goods than from those who do not. Thieves who steal vehicles and thieves who steal personal items from others on the street (chain-snatchers, pickpockets, purse-snatchers) are clearly attracted more by affluence than by propinquity, while robbers and burglars seem to be moved more by propinquity than by affluence.

Age is an excellent predictor of property crime—indeed, of crime in general. The age distribution of crime "represents one of the brute facts of criminology"; it is seen by many criminologists as "invariant across social and cultural conditions" (Hirschi and Gottfredson, 1983: 552, 554). The rate of property crimes rises very sharply after the age of 10 or so, reaches a peak in the middle-to-late adolescent years, and declines fairly steeply throughout the twenties and thirties. Since the Industrial Revolution, this relationship has held pretty much everywhere and at all times and has not diminished with the introduction of any other explanatory factors. The explanation of exactly what it is that causes this relationship is hotly debated by the experts (Greenberg, 1979, 1985, 1988; Hirshi and Gottfredson, 1983, 1985; Gove, 1985). Is it the social position of adolescents—for instance, that they earn less money than adults—that causes this relationship or that they are less closely supervised by, or less responsible to, representatives of conventional institutions? Or is it the condition of adolescence itself that causes it—for instance, physical, physiological, or maturational characteristics? No clear-cut answer has been provided by researchers, and it is likely this issue will be debated for some time.

Sex or *gender* is also powerfully related to crime. As we know, arrest figures are not perfect reflections of the crime rate; perpetrators who are caught may be significantly different from those who are not. Still, characteristics of arrestees do provide at least a glimpse of the characteristics of offenders generally. In 1987, 9 out of 10 arrested robbers (92 percent), burglars (92 percent), and motor vehicle thieves (90 percent) were male. Only for larceny-theft (which includes shoplifting) were a sizable proportion of all arrestees female—31 percent (FBI, 1988: 20, 27, 32, 35). Clearly, being male has a great deal to do with committing property crimes, as it does with committing crimes generally. So much is this the case that two criminologists flatly state: "If you were asked to use a single trait to predict which children ... would become criminals, you would make fewer mistakes if you chose sex status as the trait and predicted criminality for [all] the males and noncriminality for [all] the females. The prediction would be wrong in many cases.... But you would be wrong in more cases if you used any other single trait, such as age, race, family background, or personality characteristic" (Sutherland and Cressey, 1978: 130).

Again: Is it the social position of men and women that causes this relationship, or is it some invariant property of men and women, such as size, strength, or physiology? Once again, the literature offers no clear-cut answer (Gove, 1985; Balkan and Berger, 1979; Bowker, 1980), although the evidence for the relationship itself is overwhelming.

ROBBERY

Most people use the term "robbery" very loosely. They say, for example, "My apartment was robbed yesterday." In fact, to criminologists, robbery has a very specific meaning. Robbery entails *victim confrontation;* it is a theft involving force, violence, or the threat of violence. As we saw, just over half a million robberies (517,704) were reported to the police in the United States in 1987 (Table 11.1). According to the FBI, the number of robberies has declined throughout the 1980s; in 1981, the figure was 574,134. There is some controversy over whether robbery is a property crime or a crime of violence. Clearly, it has some features of both. In fact, it is the one crime that is *both* a property crime, since the perpetrator takes goods away from the victim, *and* a crime of violence, since the perpetrator uses force, vio-

lence, or the threat of violence. As we saw, a third of all robberies in the United States entailed the use of firearms, 1 out of 8 involved a knife, and more than 4 out of 10 were strong-arm or weaponless robberies.

Because of the confrontational nature of the offense and because both robber and victim might be injured during the offense, robberies are much less common than other property offenses. Few perpetrators have the daring and recklessness to face a victim and demand cash or other property; most prefer stealth and anonymity. Compare the roughly 500,000 robberies that take place in the United States each year (and we'd have to double that figure to get an accurate estimate, since only half of all robberies are reported to the police) with the 3.2 million burglaries and the 7.5 million larcenies reported in 1987 (and, again, we'd have to double the burglary figure and quadruple the larceny figure to get roughly the right number of offenses). Thus, the two less serious forms of stealing, burglary and larceny, are about 20 times as common as the more serious one, robbery. Actually, most offenders simply do not want to engage in robbery. It is a dangerous, high-risk activity.

According to the FBI, more than half of all robberies reported in 1987 (54 percent) took place on the street or on a highway; 1 in 10 occurred in a residence; 1 in 8 (13 percent) was a robbery of a "commercial house"; 3 percent, of a gas or service station; 6 percent, of a convenience store; and only 1 percent of all reported robberies were of banks (1988: 18). The total financial take in 1987 for all robberies reported to the police was $327 million—not much of a haul for such a well-publicized crime. Cash or property worth only $631 per incident was taken, although bank robbers ($3013 per incident) did better than robbers of convenience stores ($292 per incident).

As I said before, the clearance or arrest rate for robbery was 27 percent in 1987. Although this might seem low, consider that, if a hypothetical typical robber steals only $631 per offense and is arrested 25 percent of the time, he will earn only $2500 before being arrested. Stated this way, robbery doesn't seem like a very promising way to make a living. Of course, the FBI's statistics include a great many young, inept, unprofessional robbers who do not plan their jobs and who are very likely to get caught, and relatively few older, professional robbers who plan their jobs carefully. Robbery may very well be a lucrative career for a small professional elite.

Robbery is overwhelmingly a big-city offense (see Table 11.5). The likelihood of being a victim of a robbery in a big city is *stupendously* greater than in a rural area. The robbery rate for rural areas was 14.0 per 100,000; in cities with a population of 1 million or more, this figure was 889.7—over *63 times as great.* Moreover, the robbery rate for every category increased as community size increased; mid-size cities were also in-between with respect to their robbery rates. There probably is no crime that increases so sharply with community size as does robbery. The reason should be obvious: Since robbery is a crime that entails victim confrontation, the victim generally sees the perpetrator. In a smaller community, the likelihood of identification is vastly greater than in a larger one. What big cities offer to the robber is *anonymity.* The two other offenses, both crimes of violence, that entail victim confrontation—rape and assault—also increase with city size, but not nearly so sharply. Assault is usually a crime that takes place between intimates, and it is almost never planned; thus, anonymity rarely fig-

ures into the perpetrator's calculations as to when, where, and with whom to commit the offense. And rapists rely on the victim not to report the offense to the police, an assumption valid to some degree for acquaintance rapes but increasingly less so for stranger rapes. Clearly, anyone who wants to understand robbery must understand big-city life.

In most cases, then, the robbery victim is confronted by a stranger. In a victimization survey of robbery victims (Harlow, 1987), this was true in just under 7 out of 10 cases of robbery by a single offender (69 percent) and just over 8 out of 10 cases involving multiple offenders (82 percent). For single offenders, not quite 1 in 10 (9 percent) was a casual acquaintance, just under 1 in 8 (12 percent) was well known to the victim, but was not a relative; 4 percent of all single offenders entailed one *spouse* robbing another (usually a husband robbing a wife), and 2 percent entailed other relatives robbing one another.

The seemingly high percentage of acquaintances and relatives—including spouses—among the victims and perpetrators of robbery might seem to contradict our point about the crime being one in which anonymity is an essential ingredient. What these statistics show us, however, is that robbery is not a completely homogeneous category. In fact, the robberies between relatives and acquaintances are less likely to be reported to the police than robberies between strangers, because they often represent disputes between parties over the ownership of a given article of property. For instance, two friends may have made a $10 bet, which the loser refuses to honor; to force the loser to pay up, the winner may simply take what he sees as rightfully his—by force. Or a separated couple may have an argument about who owns a stereo or a television; one night, the husband may come to the wife's apartment and take the item—again, by force. Such offenses will be reported to an interviewer in a victimization survey, but not to the police. Because these offenses are not uncommon—although, nonetheless, in the minority—requires us to modify our general point about robbery and anonymity. The original

TABLE 11.5 Robbery Rate in the United States by Size of Community (1987)

Size of Community	Robbery Rate/100,000
1,000,000 or more	889.7
500,000–999,999	572.9
250,000–499,999	494.5
100,000–249,999	302.7
50,000–99,999	193.0
25,000–49,999	128.9
10,000–24,999	73.9
Under 10,000	41.6
Rural	14.0

SOURCE: Adapted from Federal Bureau of Investigation, 1988: 140–141.

point still holds, however: Robbery tends to be a crime between strangers, in which the offender is not known to the victim; as a consequence, it is a crime much more likely to take place in a large city than in a smaller community.

As we've already seen, lower-income individuals are more likely to be robbed than are the more affluent. In a summary of a number of victimization surveys (Harlow, 1987), members of families earning less than $7500 annually were over twice as likely to have been victims of a robbery during the previous year (a rate of 1,080 robberies per 100,000 population) than were members of families earning $25,000 and above (470 per 100,000). Blacks were also more likely to have been victimized by robbery than whites—1,420 versus 590 per 100,000 per year. As we might expect, males were significantly more likely to be targets of robbery than females—roughly twice as likely (1987: 3). And the young were more likely to be robbed than the old—roughly 1,100 per 100,000 for all age categories between 12 and 24, but only 400 for 50- to 64-year-olds, and 330 for those over the age of 65 (1987: 3).

One of the reasons why robbery is so important to criminologists is that, typically, it is a much more serious crime than the other property offenses; that is, it is a far better predictor of an offender's overall rate of involvement in crime. Given its relative rarity and the strong inhibitions most people have against forcing, or attempting to force, someone to hand over money or property, it tells us a great deal about someone who overcomes those inhibitions and does the deed. Someone who robs is highly likely, statistically, to have previously engaged in a number of other types of offenses, whereas someone who engages in larceny-theft, for example, or even burglary, is significantly less likely to have engaged in other offenses. In other words, robbery is a very potent *indicator* or measure of someone's involvement in criminal behavior; it is a fairly good *predictor* of future criminal activity.

Although robbery is technically a property crime *and* a crime of violence, the violence is more often potential than actual;

usually the robber threatens his victims with harm rather than actually harming them. However, victims are harmed a fair proportion of the time. In a summary of a number of victimization surveys, victims were injured in 33 percent of all robberies and required medical care in 15 percent; 2 percent of all robbery victims were hospitalized at least overnight (Harlow, 1987: 7). The likelihood of being injured, however, varies with the nature of the weapon. As a general rule, gun robberies are the *least* likely to result in injury, and strong-arm or weaponless robberies are *most* likely to result in injury. Though the victim is extremely unlikely to be killed in a robbery, it is also true that, if the perpetrator does use a gun, death is more likely than for any other type of weapon used (Wright, et al., 1983: 208; Conklin, 1972; Cook and Nagin, 1979). The use of a weapon, and the occurrence of injury strongly influence whether a robbery will be reported to the police. In one victimization study, 45 percent of all strong-arm robberies, 54 percent of robberies in which a knife was used, and 73 percent of those in which a gun was used were reported to the police. Only 49 percent of noninjury, 61 percent of minor injury, and 76 percent of serious injury robberies were reported (Harlow, 1987: 9).

Who is the robber? The statistics on arrest compiled in the FBI's *Uniform Crime Reports* paint the following portrait of the robber. We already know he is overwhelmingly male—92 percent, according to the *UCR*. Over 6 in 10 of all arrested robbers (63 percent) are black; only a third (36 percent) are white. And he is young: 6 in 10 are 24 or younger. The problem with these statistics is, of course, that they represent *arrested* robbers, not robbers in general, and we suspect that robbers who aren't caught may differ in important respects from those who are.

One way of verifying this is to compare the FBI's arrest figures with the *perceived offender characteristics* supplied by robbery victims in the victimization surveys of the National Crime Surveys. The two sources of data generally agree with one another, although there are some relatively minor inconsistencies. In 9 out of 10 robbery victimizations (89 percent), the offenders were male; in 5 percent of all cases, they were female; and in 4 percent, the offender was robbed by both male and female offenders—that is, at least one male and at least one female committed the crime. In half of all robbery victimizations, the offenders were identified as black (51 percent); in a third, they were white (36 percent); in 4 percent, members of some other race were involved; and in 4 percent, the offenders formed a "salt-and-pepper" team of mixed-race offenders. In 4 out of 10 of all cases of robbery (41 percent), offenders were identified as 20 years old or younger; in another 4 out of 10, they were identified as 21 or older; and in not quite 1 in 10, they were of mixed ages (Harlow, 1987: 2).

The portrait we get of the robber, then, from the FBI's arrest figures and victimization surveys, is that he is overwhelmingly male, predominantly black, and young.

Clearly, any explanation of robbery focusing on the offender must make use of at least two factors: *daring* and *poverty*. Robbery is not a crime for the fainthearted; it entails a great deal of risk, both to the victim and to the perpetrator. Robbers, therefore, tend to be confident that they won't be caught and won't be injured. Such (often unrealistic) confidence is more characteristic of males than females and more characteristic of the young than the old. Therefore, the robber's gender and age characteristics are fairly predictable.

The race of robbery offenders is probably largely a function of a combination of the economic position of blacks in the United States and the fact that a high proportion of blacks live in large cities. Black family income is between 55 and 60 percent of that of whites, and black unemployment is twice as high. Moreover, many scholars believe, although a certain proportion of blacks earn incomes that increasingly approximate those of whites, a substantial proportion of the black population is seemingly permanently stuck in the "underclass" (Wilson, 1987; Auletta, 1982); it is out of the black underclass that most robbers emerge. Added to the economic picture is the demographic

factor: blacks are much more urban than whites. Nearly 3 out of 10 whites (29 percent) live in a rural area; Blacks are half as likely to live in rural areas as whites—only 15 percent do so. At the other end of the scale, a quarter of all whites in the United States live in central cities (25 percent); for blacks, this is well over twice as high—57 percent (Bogue, 1985: 115). The combination of a lower-per-capita income and a far more urban residence makes it predictable that blacks will have a higher rate of robbery than whites. In addition, there is the factor of age; while only 30 percent of the white population is under the age of 20, 40 percent of the black population is. Since the black population is so much younger than the white population, this factor alone would tend to boost its robbery rate.

SHOPLIFTING

Technically, shoplifting falls under the FBI's classification scheme as a form of larceny-theft; however, it has many features that are distinct, and consequently, it should be discussed separately. What distinguishes the robber and other "street" criminals from the ordinary, run-of-the-mill shoplifter? Both steal, and yet we perceive them to be radically different species of social animal. (Read the shoplifting account at the end of the chapter; do you consider the young woman in the account to be a dangerous criminal or a deviant?) One of the ways in which they differ is the total volume of the cash or the value of the merchandise stolen: The robber steals far less than the shoplifter. The FBI estimates that roughly a third of a billion dollars was taken in acts of robbery in the United States in 1987. The National Coalition to Prevent Shoplifting estimates the yearly value of shoplifted goods at $26 billion, resulting in an increase in consumer prices of 5 to 7 percent (Reid, 1988: 266). This entails more money than any single category of "street crimes."

Perhaps the most significant fact about shoplifting is that most of us do not regard it as a "real" crime. The majority of shoplifters do not regard themselves as criminals, and they are not so regarded by their non-shoplifting peers. Shoplifters generally take low-value items. Although they may do it often, they do not make a career out of shoplifting and do not earn enough to support themselves at it; they have no connections with people who do steal for a living, and have no values, beliefs, or practices that contrast with the rest of the population, other than shoplifting itself. The kind of stealing that most retail store thieves engage in requires no skill. Shoplifters stem from all walks of life. They are teenagers, housewives, stable working-class men and women, professionals, white-collar workers, the elderly on small, fixed incomes—shoplifters can be just about anyone. Shoplifters are conventional people for the most part, and shoplifting borders on being conventional behavior. Stigma does not adhere to anyone who steals low-value items from stores, even regularly. "Everybody does it," we say to ourselves, and that's the end of the matter; we hold ourselves blameless. "Just don't get caught," we add.

Shoplifting belongs to that miscellaneous grab-bag category the FBI calls "larceny-theft." Stealing from stores is not merely widespread; it is routine. Commercial security—personnel and equipment to protect retail business establishments from theft—is one of the nation's fastest growth industries. "Inventory shrinkage" in large cities has been estimated at *8 percent* of sales (Barmash, 1973). In one study in New York City it was discovered that 1 out of 10 of 500 randomly selected and observed customers in a store took some item of value without paying for it (Hellman, 1970). Not only is shoplifting conventional behavior engaged in by respectable folk, unlike the 1940s—when the only major study of shoplifting was conducted (Cameron, 1964)—*shoplifting today has group support.* This is especially the case among teenagers. They join one another in shoplifting "expeditions," ripping off items of value from stores for amusement and personal gain. There is peer pressure from others to join in, should anyone express reluctance to do so. Moreover, the activity is an adjunct to other pleasurable activities—socializing, fantasizing, "hanging out," meeting members of the opposite sex. In this respect it is not unlike going to a movie, to the beach, or driving around in cars. Meeting other teenagers to go to stores and steal—particularly in large shopping centers like suburban malls—does not appear to represent a form of deviant behavior at all. This is, in fact, what is so fascinating about it. More than anything else, it manifests adherence to four basic values: (1) sociability, (2) conventionality, (3) materialism, and (4) hedonism. For the most part, when adults steal from stores, they do so far less in the company of others and probably derive less excitement from it, but all the other basic ingredients seem to be present. "It is ironic," one sociologist writes, "that good citizens should be part of the crime problem, but all that distinguishes them from criminals is the degree of violence used" (McCaghy, 1976: 165).

Shoplifters come in two basic varieties: the *booster* and the *snitch* (Cameron, 1964). Boosters steal primarily for the purpose of resale; snitches are amateurs and steal mainly for personal use of the items they take. Boosters steal as a means of earning a living or of augmenting what they already make. They take more expensive items, those that are more readily converted to cash; they are, obviously, more likely to steal repeatedly; and they tend to be more cautious when they steal. Representatives of stores make a clear distinction between amateurs and professionals: The greater the value of the item stolen, the greater the likelihood they will report the theft to the police. In one study, there were over three times as many referrals by store representatives to the police for the theft of valuable items as there were for the theft of less valuable ones (Hindelang, 1974). In over 6,000 cases of shoplifters apprehended in drug and grocery stores, only 13 percent of those who had taken small-value items were reported to the police, but 40 percent who had taken large-value items were so reported. An indication that shoplifting is rarely reported, and that reporting is closely related to the value of the item stolen, is that in the study referred to, the average value of the items stolen when offenders were caught but not necessarily reported to the police was $4.00, but the value of shoplifted items recorded in the *Uniform Crime Reports* was $28 during 1968, the year when the study was conducted. In addition, the *nature* of the goods stolen influenced the decision to report the theft—and the thief—to the police: Items that can be readily *resold* elicited reporting behavior to the police—especially meat, liquor, and cigarettes (Hindelang, 1974). Since boosters specialize in lifting resalable items, this action on the part of store representatives appears to be motivated not so much by the desire to punish thievery per se, but to sanction the habitual professional thief, the "booster."

Some controversy reigns with regard to the *characteristics* or reported versus nonreported shoplifters. In Cameron's classic study (1964), sex and race were intimately related to being referred to the police. Only 10 percent of the apprehended women were reported, but over a third (35 percent) of the men received this treatment. The disparity along racial lines was even more glaring; while only a tenth of all nonblacks were reported to the police (11 percent), this was true of well over half of all blacks (58 percent). Clearly, prejudice of a high order of magnitude was at work here. Recall that the "labeling" theory of reactions to deviance holds that contingencies, or characteristics not directly related to the offense, powerfully shape how conventionals sanction the offender. Cameron's study seems to bear out this general perspective.

On the other hand, Cameron's study was conducted between 1943 and 1949, a period when racial prejudice was considerably higher than it is today. (Blacks were not even permitted to try on clothes in Chicago department stores until the 1940s!) Consequently, her generalizations about the characteristics of the offender leading to reporting may not hold today. Moreover, as recent data show, women's participation in crime, particularly serious, professional crime is rising over time (Adler, 1975). Con-

sequently, they are being taken seriously as genuine thieves, rather than simply as housewives lifting a few extra household items on a whim. And the authors of the hippie-straight shoplifting study (Steffensmeier and Terry, 1973) acknowledge the possibility that their findings may apply specifically to when their study was conducted by typing an addendum to the reprint of their article that reads:

We should point out that the domestic situation which existed at the time the field experiment was being conducted may have affected our results. The experiment was run in the spring of 1971, a time of vigorous protest against the Vietnam War throughout the nation and in this university town in particular. Many ... members of the general public tended to interpret the protests as being instigated by hippies. ... This public identification of hippies with the war protests may have overly sensitized our subjects to the saliency of a hippie identity of appearance. Thus, the high reporting of hippie shoplifters in the present research may, in part at least, reflect the intensity of community feelings and the saliency of a hippie identity *at this particular time.*

On the other hand, another study tabulated data supplied by the stores themselves found that three basic social characteristics—race, sex, and age—were almost completely unrelated to the decision of store representatives to report the offense and the offender to the police. Almost exactly the same proportion of blacks (28 percent) as whites (25 percent) were reported; almost exactly the same percentage of males (26 percent) as females (25 percent) were reported; and almost exactly the same proportion of adolescents (21 percent) as middle-aged adults (24 percent) were reported. Only the *value* of the item stolen and the item's *resalability* influenced whether the crime was reported (Hindelang, 1974). This researcher concludes that "the characteristics of the offense, more than the characteristics of the offender, are associated with decisions to take official action" (1974: 592). Another study (Cohen and Stark, 1974) corroborated these findings, the one difference being that an unemployed shoplifter was always referred to the police and never released, whereas an employed shoplifter had a 50:50 chance of being released.

EMPLOYEE PILFERAGE

Even more "respectable" and conventional than shoplifting by the amateur is what is called *employee pilferage*. Although estimates of its size must of necessity be extremely rough, since what little information on it we have is very incomplete, criminologists agree on ballpark figures. Recall that retail stores lose more than $26 billion a year in customer theft, according to some estimates (Reid, 1988: 226). In all likelihood, employees steal even more from retail establishments than customers do. Probably at least as much is stolen internally from factories, trucking and construction companies, hospitals, schools, ships and docks, the armed services, and other governmental agencies. One criminologist opined that employee theft "is one of the most costly, if not *the* most costly, offense by individuals in the United States" in terms of monetary value (McCaghy, 1985: 210).

Such thefts are rarely considered a problem by the general public and upset only representatives of the corporations, organizations, and insurance companies affected. Compare the estimated tens of billions of dollars stolen from firms by employees with what is stolen from the public as a result of other property crimes—$327 million in robbery, $3.2 billion in burglary, $6 billion in motor vehicle theft, and $3 billion in larceny-theft—a total of $12.5 billion (FBI, 1988). Even if we double this figure to account for unreported crime—which is overly generous, because more lucrative property crimes are more likely to be reported than less lucrative ones—it becomes clear that employee pilferage probably accounts for at least twice as much theft in monetary value as street crime. And yet, employee pilferage attracts relatively little attention from sociologists and criminologists. Criminological studies on ordinary money-making street crimes probably outnumber those on employee pilferage by a ratio of more than 20 to 1. Employees rationalize and justify their participation in theft by saying: "It's a corporation—it's not like taking from one person"; "The company doesn't mind, they've got plenty, they're not losing anything on what I take"; "Everyone's doing it"; "The insurance company pays for it" (Barlow, 1987: 257). And the public feels considerably more threat from street crime than from employee pilferage. In fact, perpetrators of the latter crime actually *are* the general public; why should they feel threatened?

Shoplifting and employee pilferage are instances in which the organization and, ultimately, the general public are the victims. Analyses of employee theft hold that it *boosts morale*, it compensates the worker for low wages, and it acts as an *unofficial reward system* (McCaghy, 1976: 181). It is, some observers believe, a system of "controlled larceny" (Zeitlin, 1971). Employers typically know of this thievery and are aware of its impact on employee morale. It compensates for low wages and alienating, boring jobs. It is, therefore, not only tolerated by employers, but also it may be considered a worthwhile price to pay for a valuable device to control and pacify their employees. By tolerating theft, employers can continue paying low wages and do not have to worry so much about their workers hating their jobs. Employee theft, in fact, supports the status quo and serves to retard meaningful change on the job. The ultimate victim of this thievery is not the organization from which items are stolen, of course, but the public. Losses are recovered by a rise in prices, or a lowering of quality of goods, or a curtailment of services. Radical manifestoes written in the late 1960s and early 1970s—like Abbie Hoffman's *Steal This Book*—that urged stealing as a revolutionary act failed to point out the business community loses considerably less than the consumer does from theft. In an economy controlled by capitalists, steps are taken to ensure that the business community does not suffer significantly from criminal behavior. In fact, some crimes may actually *profit* the business community.

ACCOUNT: SHOPLIFTING

The contributor of this account is a 20-year-old college student.

It all began the day before Christmas as I was doing my holiday shopping in New York. I went into a few stores and purchased some gifts, when I noticed that my bag was open. I searched frantically for my wallet—only to find that it was gone. I had been robbed! I went out onto the street and looked at all of the faces around me trying to figure out who had stolen my wallet. I was so angry that I wanted to scream out, *"Who stole my wallet,"* but I didn't because I was afraid. Then I remembered that the $80 I had saved for holiday shopping was in that wallet. All my money was now gone, and I wouldn't be able to give my family or friends any gifts. I stood there feeling hurt and scared. Soon I began to get cold, and so I wandered into a department store. I noticed a beautiful sweater that would have looked terrific on my boyfriend. I really wanted to give him something for Christmas, but without any money, I wouldn't be able to. In an instant, I realized that if someone stole from me, why can't I steal, too?

That's when it began. I got a shopping bag from a cashier and put my gloves, hat, and scarf into the shopping bag so it didn't look so empty. I looked around. When I felt that no one was looking, I casually slipped the sweater into the shopping bag. I thought to myself, this isn't so hard, and I felt satisfied. But then I became aware of the fact that the sweater cost $20, but the thief who stole my wallet took $80. This just didn't seem very fair. I felt I had to take something else to compensate for the rest of the money that was taken. So I picked up a shirt and slowly slipped it into my bag. I thought to myself, "I did it again." I had stolen $35 worth of merchandise—not enough to get even, but enough to feel satisfied for the time being. Then I rushed out of the store.

Outside I felt relieved. I felt a sense of accomplishment, as if I had done something wonderful, like getting an "A" on an exam or being praised for something I had done. But how could I feel this way? I had done something wrong, something illegal—a sin. Then I realized I didn't care. Anyone in my position would have done the same thing. I felt that I had found revenge on society for stealing my money, for taking what was rightfully mine. I had done the same thing they had done to me; it was "an eye for an eye, a tooth for a tooth." How could anyone condemn me—I was only getting even. After I reached $80, I would stop. Then I would be even.

As time went on, I didn't really feel that I had gotten even. I had stolen $35 worth of merchandise, and they took $80 from me. Therefore, I still had $45 to go. As time went on, I felt less and less guilty. I even started to feel proud of the fact that I had gotten away with it; I had tricked society. It now seemed much easier to steal than to pay for something I wanted. The next time, I stole a bottle of expensive perfume for my Mom by slipping it under my sweater. It seemed so much easier this time, so natural. The more I stole the more I enjoyed the excitement. The idea of getting caught both scared and fascinated me. My heart beat rapidly, my palms would sweat; when I did it, I could think only about getting out of the store as soon as possible. The moment I left the store, I felt relieved and totally relaxed. A sense of total satisfaction came over me. It was like an emotional high.

At some point, I realized that I had reached the $80. I had gotten even with society and had reached my goal. But I still didn't feel the sense of relief I needed. I vowed that I would stop stealing, but whenever I saw something I wanted I thought, why not take it? It takes so long to make money, and so little time to spend it. I found that I enjoyed stealing and felt that I wasn't going to stop. This all changed when my brother caught me stealing. We went shopping, and he wanted to purchase a pair of sunglasses. I told him I would get them for him as a present. I went over to the counter and slipped them into my bag, looking around to see if anyone was looking. I thought, great—I did it again. Then I casually walked out of the store. Later, in the car on the way home, my brother said that he saw me stealing the sunglasses. He said that he was ashamed of me and couldn't understand why I had to steal when I could always get money from home. I felt disgusted with myself. I hated myself for making my brother feel ashamed of me. I told him that I would promise never to do it again if he would never repeat this incident to anyone. He agreed.

Afterward, I felt as if someone lifted a huge burden from my shoulders. I have never lied to my brother, and I wasn't going to stop now. I never want to see that hurt look in my brother's face again. It has been a year since I shoplifted anything, and I'm glad that I haven't. I now feel better about myself. However, that exciting thrill of taking something is gone. I can never feel that way again. I still have some trouble when I see something I really want and can't afford; I still say to myself, why not take it? But I feel that I can fight that desire. I feel much better about myself and my life now than I did when I was stealing. (From the author's files.)

CHAPTER
12

White-Collar Crime

Henry N. Pontell, Stephen M. Rosoff, and Erich Goode

Devoting an entire chapter of a book on social deviance to "white-collar crime" may in itself appear deviant. Business frauds, false advertising by corporations, and illegal chemical dumping may seem out of place in an area of study that has traditionally focused on the behaviors of drug addicts, street criminals, prostitutes, homosexuals, and the mentally ill. Perpetrators of white-collar crimes are "respectable" persons. Moreover, their illegal acts seem less offensive than street crime. How can such behaviors be regarded as deviant? There are several factors that mask the potentially deviant status of white-collar crime. First, there is more disagreement on the part of different audiences about whether such acts ought to be condemned than for any other type of behavior. And second, white-collar crime is more routinely concealed from the general public than most deviant behavior is, which makes it difficult to determine who engaged

in a specific instance of it—or even if it ever took place at all.

The term "white-collar crime" was coined by Edwin H. Sutherland in his presidential address to the American Sociological Society in 1939. It almost immediately sent shock waves through the criminological community.

Sutherland's talk was entitled "The White-Collar Criminal," and it altered the study of crime throughout the world in fundamental ways by focusing attention upon a form of lawbreaking that had previously been ignored by criminological scholars. Sutherland's targets were several: First, he ridiculed theories of crime which blamed such factors as poverty, broken homes, and Freudian fixations for illegal behavior, noting that healthy upbringings and intact psyches had not served to deter monstrous amounts of lawbreaking by persons in positions of power. Thereafter, Sutherland documented in detail derelictions by corporations, concluding that their "rap sheets" resembled, at least in length and frequency, those of many professional predators, such as con men and bank robbers, persons who by choice prey upon the public. He focused on such representative corporate offenses as antitrust violations, false advertising, theft of trade secrets, and bribery in order to obtain special privileges.

Sutherland insisted that the white-collar behaviors he detailed were criminal, not civil, offenses, and that the persons who committed them ought to receive the same kind of scorn and punishment that attends other kinds of property and personal crime. He regarded white-collar crime as in many instances more consequential than run-of-the-mill street offenses, insisting that it was more apt to tear at the core of a social system and render citizens cynical and selfish (Geis and Goff, in Sutherland, 1983: ix-x).

The term "white-collar crime" is now recognized throughout the world. It has broadened the scope of the study of deviance, which is no longer seen as behavior that can be engaged in solely by disenfranchised groups in society. Although the number of researchers who have worked in the area of white-collar crime has been modest and the impact of their studies on mainstream deviance theory less than profound, white-collar crime research has the potential for substantially impacting on public opinion and social policy.

Sutherland maintained that corporate crimes are not merely technical violations, but represent deliberate acts. He likened white-collar crime to professional theft and noted points of similarity and difference. Both groups, he claimed, show "persistence of behaviors" over time. That is, a large proportion of violators are repeaters. Also, in both kinds of crime the behavior is more widespread than indicated by official reports and convictions. Another similarity noted by Sutherland was that violators generally do not lose status among their immediate associates. While a few may think less of the violator, others may admire the person ("how clever, how shrewd!"). Both thieves and businesspeople often express contempt for the law and for government regulations that impede business practices. Both kinds

of crime can also be organized as well as deliberate in nature. Sutherland cites two major differences between the thief and the white-collar criminal: their self-conceptions and the public's perception of them. White-collar criminals do not take pride in their status as criminals, unlike professional thieves. Also, the public is not apt to label legitimate business persons as criminals as readily as they might other members of society.

Crimes committed by the affluent and powerful on behalf of a corporation, organization, or agency have been called "upperworld" crimes (Geis, 1981). They are important to the study of deviance for a number of reasons. To begin with, they challenge traditional criminological theories about the causation of criminal activity. If it is true that corporate executives routinely engage in illegal activities, then it is no longer possible to argue that only poverty causes crime; this "fails utterly to account for the widespread lawbreaking by persons who are extraordinarily affluent" (1981: 179). Such crime also reveals the distribution of power in a society. As we will discuss, some groups and individuals have more power to shape the content of legal statutes so that their own dangerous or harmful activities are never defined as crimes. Moreover, even when such acts are defined as crimes, the laws against them may not be enforced. White-collar crime thus reveals a "double standard" of sorts; the crimes of the poor tend to be vigorously enforced, while the crimes of the powerful receive less attention. For the student of deviance, this is especially revealing, because it shows that acts are not necessarily stigmatized as a result of their impact alone. Who engages in them also influences the stigmatization process. Due to their higher status, those who engage in white-collar crime can be particularly adept at negotiating their criminal labels. This may take the form of escaping detection altogether, impeding the location of responsibility for criminal behavior within an organization, preventing effective investigation and prosecution, garnering support from groups in the community, and swaying judges and juries with their appearance and social and educational backgrounds.

Most experts agree that considerably more is stolen from the public as a result of white-collar and corporate crimes than by common street crimes. Price-fixing by corporate executives, where a higher price is ultimately paid for goods distributed by the companies, can lead to enormous profits criminally obtained. A medical clinic that intentionally overtreats patients and/or submits inflated bills to a state Medicaid system can reap great sums of money from public funds. A hazardous waste disposal company can increase its profit margin by violating laws regarding the disposal of dangerous chemicals. These corporate actions are not only considered deviant by most people, but are not infrequently labeled as criminal acts.

What makes something a "white-collar crime?" Sutherland's conceptualization of white-collar crime was not at the time, nor is now completely satisfactory. Shortly after it was introduced, sociologist-lawyer Paul Tappan (1947) dubbed it "loose, doctrinaire, and invective." He claimed that it simply referred to "occupational behavior to which some particular criminologist takes exception. It may easily be a term of propaganda." While it is true that Sutherland often failed to distinguish between actions that violated civil versus criminal codes, his "confusion" was not altogether capricious or without foundation. To the extent that business executives wield influence in the making and the administration of law, they will make sure that unethical and damaging corporate activities will remain in the civil sphere, rather than being regarded as crimes. This is a conceptual problem that has dogged research on white-collar crimes.

Part of the controversy lies with the fact that white-collar crime is not a legally defined category of offenses. Rather, it is a catch-all grouping that is used by sociologists, criminologists, law enforcement officials, and others for their own purposes in referring to the activities of individual offenders or organizations that do not fit a traditional picture or explanation of crime. In this sense, white-collar crime is more a "social construct" than a specific group of legally defined offenses.

Part of the confusion in regard to an exact definition of white-collar crime also arises because of a failure to separate the criminal's social class position from the criminal behavior itself. Sutherland's original definition of the term was "a crime committed by a person of respectability and high social status in the course of his occupation"(1949: 9) At first glance this seems to be a reasonable definition. On closer inspection, however, it raises some interesting questions. How much "status" is necessary before an act can be labeled a white-collar crime? Must the act involve crime on behalf of a company, or for the individual's own gain, or both? Exactly what should go into a definition of "respectability?" These are questions that have yet to be resolved, nor are they likely to ever be resolved, in research on white-collar crime.

While the exact definition of white-collar crime has yet to be offered, there are characteristics that such acts usually share. White-collar crime can affect identifiable victims, but is usually characterized by what has been described as *diffuse victimization*. This means that a specific person or group does not typically exist to report a white-collar crime. Rather, the "victim" is more likely to be a government, the public, or a community. Moreover, in some instances where identifiable victims do exist, they may never know that they had in fact been victimized. In other cases, when persons become aware that they have been victimized, they may come to know this only long after the fact. In the case of price-fixing, consumers as a whole would be victimized, or in the case of fixing bids for a contract with the government, the government would be the victim. In the case of medical fraud against Medicaid, the government sponsored medical program would be the victim and taxpayers whose dollars support the program would be indirectly victimized. If Medicaid patients were intentionally exposed to extra medical tests, or were in fact harmed by a needless medical treatment (unnecessary surgery, for example), then they most assuredly would also have been victimized, although they might never have realized it at the time. In the case of illegal chemical dumping, the victims might be much harder to identify as a group, depending on the scope of contamination, and what effects—both long and short term—such contamination would have on those who come into contact with it.

Secondly, the victimization is not apt to be reported. Unlike common crimes, which typically come to the attention of authorities through complaints of victims, white-collar crimes are usually discovered through investigations. This makes it extremely difficult to enforce laws against white-collar crime, given that the resources of the criminal justice system are already stretched thin searching out and punishing street crimes.

Officials sometimes become aware of white-collar crime through serendipitous or lucky events. The Watergate scandal, for example, which involved the highest offices of government, would probably never have come to light had it not been for a wary hotel custodian who happened to notice tape on the open door of the Democratic Campaign Headquarters, left there by the inept burglars ("plumbers") working for the Nixon reelection campaign. In other instances, a disgruntled worker may give authorities information on their employers' misdeeds, or a routine business audit might uncover an instance of malfeasance. Detecting white-collar crime is often a matter of happenstance or accident.

The fact that most white-collar crime does not typically come to public attention also means that it is likely to be severely underestimated by official accounts of its occurrence. It is almost certain that the unknown amount of white-collar crime is far greater than the amount of unreported common crimes. Finally, the fact that it is not apt to be reported by a victim means that what we know about the frequency and types of white collar crime depends largely upon authorities going out and looking for it. Police do not typically "react" to white-collar crimes, as much as they "proactively" uncover it.

Special investigations and undercover work are frequently used by police to discover instances of white-collar crime.

Another characteristic of white-collar crime is that it is generally well concealed within ordinary occupational routines; that is, it is performed in conjunction with a person's usual work tasks. As we will discuss in more detail, this characteristic of white-collar crime makes it extraordinarily difficult to discover, investigate, and prosecute. Even when such acts are uncovered, finding specific legal evidence of wrongdoing can be very complicated. Sometimes this difficulty in proving that a crime took place prevents the prosecution and subsequent labeling of such acts as "crimes."

There are relatively few crimes that can be committed only by those in white-collar positions during the course of their occupations. Most common crimes can be committed by anyone. Neither the structure of the behavior nor the social class of the person alone is adequate for defining white-collar offenses. "Crimes of deception" or "abuses of trust," another characterization present in the literature, also falls short of realizing the full nature of white-collar crime, as such acts do not require particularly high social status. They can involve carnival frauds, lower-status individuals who forge checks, and low-paid bank tellers who embezzle small amounts of money. Without the inclusion of social class as an ingredient in white-collar crime, the concept would be indistinguishable from a range of nonviolent criminal acts, and would be unamenable to critical analysis.

In order to avoid these problems, some commentators have noted that the classification of an act as a white-collar crime "should depend on use of the perquisites or routines of a white-collar occupational status in constructing a crime. A bank president who unlawfully borrows money from his own bank would be committing a white-collar crime, but not an unemployed individual who obtains a bank loan by falsifying his job status" (Katz, 1979: 434). But the question of how much status and power a person must have in order to commit a white-collar crime is not readily answerable. Most research considers professionals (doctors, lawyers, accountants, for example), managers and executives in both public and private organizations, political officeholders, and owners of substantial amounts of wealth as those persons most able to commit white-collar crime. These individuals generally occupy positions of high status, trust, and power that can be used to perpetrate acts of deviance.

Although each white-collar crime has certain characteristics unique to itself, there are certain features all share.

In the purest "white-collar" crimes, white-collar social class position is used (1) to diffuse criminal intent into ordinary occupational routines so that it escapes unambiguous expression in any discrete behavior; (2) to accomplish the crime without incidents of effect that furnish presumptive evidence of its occurrence before the criminal has been identified; and (3) to cover up culpable knowledge of participants through concerted action that allows each to claim ignorance. (Katz, 1979: 435)

This definition of pure white-collar crime allows for an understanding of how positions of power can be effectively used to

Insider Trading: White-Collar Crime on Wall Street

Insider trading has recently been revealed to be a rampant practice among major stock traders. This practice is illegal, and involves the use of "inside" information not available to the public to buy stock in a company before it increases in value. The stock is then sold after the increase, netting a hefty profit for the trader. With the increase in company takeovers, it is presumed that this practice is becoming more widespread. This is because a company's stock will go up suddenly if there are rumors of a takeover. In December 1985 for example, RCA Corporation's stock rose 33 percent in the four days preceding the public announcement that it had agreed to be acquired by the General Electric Company. This rise in stock price is known on Wall Street as a "pre-announcement run-up." Federal regulators from the Securities and Exchange Commission have another name for the phenomenon: insider trading. The practice undermines a principle that securities-market regulation was intended to protect: that all investors be given equal and timely access to relevant corporate news so that those persons who have knowledge of changes that will affect stock prices will not have an unfair advantage. Not all stock trading by those with inside information is illegal, but the dividing line is not clear. To show that it is, regulators must prove that the person took advantage of undisclosed information related to the stock price such as a takeover bid, or a new development in the company. They must also show that the insider intended to trade the stock in a manner that took advantage of such information. In the case of Ivan Boesky, one of Wall Street's richest and most successful speculators, they did precisely that and produced the biggest insider trading case in history. Boesky agreed to pay $100 million to settle the case which included both civil and criminal penalties. He will also be barred for life from stock trading in the United States after a 16-month "transition period" in which he will dispose of his stock holdings in an orderly manner and return money to investors under the watchful eye of a court-appointed supervisor. Other prominent stock brokers have also been caught and punished for trading illegally, which clearly illustrates that such practices are common on Wall Street. While deviant and illegal behaviors for economic gain may come as no surprise given the generally profit-hungry atmosphere of Wall Street, the insider trading cases show that a pen can yield much more ill-gotten cash than a gun, and that more white-collar crime exists at the very foundation of our entire economic system than we might ever be able to accurately measure.

commit deviant acts by providing a protective context in which detection of such deviance is difficult, if not sometimes impossible. For example, individuals may have a great deal of autonomy in their jobs, which allows them to commit deviant acts as part of their ordinary work without anyone ever knowing about it. A doctor who sends bogus bills to an insurance company may never be caught if the bills are only slightly altered. The doctor submits his bills as part of his "ordinary occupational routine." Even if the doctor were questioned about such bills, there may be no evidence that a crime was committed (that the doctor "intentionally" sent in phony bills). The aberration could be claimed to have been an "honest mistake" in filling out forms, or a "clerical error" on the part of a bookkeeper. There may also be no "culpable knowledge" of other participants

to cover up, as the doctor may be the only one to know about the scam. The "ideal" white-collar crime is one which is carried out with almost no chance that it will ever be discovered as such. Those occupying positions of autonomy and power that provide a "protective cloak" can accomplish this most readily.

White-collar crime, like any other form of deviance, should be thought of as occurring on a continuum, or in this case, two continuums. That is, if a deviant act is performed by a person of extremely high status (a physician, for example), and the act is also well embedded or almost hidden in ordinary occupational routines so that it is extraordinarily difficult to detect, then the deviance might be considered as what Katz (1979) has termed "pure white-collar crime." In other words, when deviant acts are performed by

---

White-Collar Crime Wave?

Corporate illegality usually escapes major media attention—until its tawdry existence is rediscovered in shocking headlines. Some prominent examples from one month in 1985: Paul Thayer, former chair of LTV, is sentenced to four years in jail for perjuring himself to a federal commission over insider trading activities. Executives at E. F. Hutton confess to engaging in a multibillion dollar check-kiting scheme. General Electric admits it has defrauded the Pentagon by passing on bogus costs. The First National Bank of Boston admits to violating the Bank Secrecy Act because it failed to report $1.22 billion in large cash transactions, some of which, according to the Justice Department, involved laundering drug money. Cartier is accused of tax fraud by the New York Attorney General's Office, and General Dynamics is charged with contractor fraud by the House Oversight and Investigations Subcommittee.

While the suffering exacted by violent crime should not be deprecated, it is also true that the loss of lives and dollars from unsafe products, pollution, and price fixing greatly exceeds that from all the Saturday night specials in America.

Moreover, unlawful business behavior is extensive as well as expensive. Four-fifths of the respondents to a 1961 reader survey by the *Harvard Business Review* thought that certain practices in their industry were unethical. Two decades later, 4 in 10 businessmen and -women told a Gallup Poll that a superior had requested that they do something unethical; one in ten said they were asked to engage in unlawful conduct. A survey conducted in 1982 by the *U.S. News & World Report* concluded, "Of America's 500 largest corporations, 115 have been convicted in the last decade of at least one major crime or have paid civil penalties for serious misbehavior. Among the 25 biggest firms the rate of documented misbehavior has been even higher."

Those statistics indicate that the recent headlines are less spectacular aberrations than revealing examples. The cost of such corporate malfeasance is a "tax" of several billion dollars a year which cheats consumers, and undermines the integrity of our business system.

SOURCE: Green and Berry, 1985: 689–705

---

persons of very high status and the acts are very much a part of, or very well concealed in their ordinary occupational routines, it is more "white-collar" than acts that are less marked by these dimensions.

White-collar offenses represent a general subset of "uncommon crimes." The case of Jeffrey MacDonald, an army physician convicted of slaughtering his wife and two children with a knife and a stick, is certainly an uncommon crime because of the combination of his status and the extreme violence involved in the killings. It can hardly be considered as "white-collar" crime, however, because it did not involve actions taken in the course of occupational routines.

ORGANIZATIONAL DEVIANCE

It has not been until fairly recently that sociologists and criminologists have seriously considered the organizational dimension to deviant behavior. In fact, it could be said that concern over the exact nature of individual white-collar offenses has resulted in a neglect of deviance by organizations themselves. Organizations present new settings and opportunities for forms of deviance that are different from those of individuals. Large corporations, for example, generate a sizable number of arrangements and transactions both in their own offices and with other individuals and organizations. Within such a context the opportunities are largely increased for deviance to take place.

What is it that distinguishes organizational from individual deviance? One popular definition of organizational deviance has been offered by Ermann and Lundman who state:

First, the action must be contrary to norms maintained by others outside the organization. That is, an act can be deviant if it is defined as deviant by other persons or organizations. These other persons and organizations constitute the normative environment of the organization. . . . The second requirement for an action to be considered organizational deviance is that the action must be supported by the internal operating norms of the organization. These internal norms often contra-

dict the publicly stated goals of the organization. For instance, the stated goals of labor-union pension funds are to serve contributors, but the actual internal norms often appear to favor fund management at the expense of contributors. Similarly, the goals of police organizations include the protection of the interests of the public at large, yet internal operating norms often appear to emphasize maintenance of the organization instead (1978: 7-8).

In addition to these general conditions, there are several others which must be satisfied. New members of the organization must be socialized to accept the justifications for behavior that are contrary to norms outside the confines of the organization. Also, if a person's deviance is to be considered "organizational" rather than individual, the behavior must be supported by others in the organization. This support can be active or passive. That is, others may engage in it also, or merely tolerate it if they become aware of it. Finally, organizational deviance is supported by the dominant administration of the organization. This group is seen as having absolute authority in the organization and is ultimately responsible for its activities. Without their support, either direct, or implied, an activity cannot be considered as "organizational deviance."

The study of organizational deviance is enlightening for a number of reasons. First, it demonstrates that legitimate organizations can be considered deviant. Even though individuals within the organization might decide on committing deviant or illegal acts, the organization can be labeled deviant when the acts benefit the organization (not the individuals directly) and when such activities are organizational in nature, or emanate from organizational goals. There is a distinction between individual deviant acts that are performed on behalf of organizations, which could be considered as deviance by organizations (for example, price-fixing, or stealing trade secrets), and individual deviance within organizations (for example, sexual exploitation), which are not tied to organizational activities and goals.

How do organizations become deviant? There are two main ways: First, an organiza-

Corporate Malpractice in the Health Field

In the early 1970s a new intrauterine contraceptive device was introduced in this country which had disastrous effects on women who used it. The Dalkon Shield was put into production without adequate testing, promoted through misleading advertising, and marketed even after warnings of its potentially dangerous health effects. The device was developed by a medical professor at Johns Hopkins, who sold it to the A. H. Robbins Company, one of the largest pharmaceutical companies in the United States, after conducting only limited research on the new product. The researcher, who published his tests in a prestigious medical journal, earned hundreds of thousands of dollars on the sale of the device. Doctors who recommended this new contraceptive soon found cases of septic abortion and patients suffering from pelvic inflammatory disease, massive bleeding, and incessant cramps. One military doctor remarked that he was "revolted by the gap between the glossy advertising claims and the occurrence of serious and even fatal complications." No one knows how many women have died from using the device because it was sold world-wide. As of January 1976, 17 American women had died from complications related to the use of the Dalkon Shield.

Many doctors who were interviewed about the Dalkon controversy either avoided comments or seemed to consider it "business as usual." While it might have been highly unethical for the researcher to report favorable results for his product, at the same time hiding his financial interest, no law was broken by his doing so. This conflict of interest is fairly common in the medical field. Many researchers are paid by drug companies to test new products, but do not mention this fact when they write up their results.

As of 1984, more than 11,000 lawsuits have been filed against A. H. Robbins Company, resulting in payments of $245 million to more than 7,600 women (Dowie and Johnston, 1985).

tion can adopt goals that deviate from societal norms. These goals may not be the ones espoused publicly by the organization, but informal goals created by powerful groups and individuals within the organization. Such deviant goals may arise through conflicting demands on the organization's activities. A second source of deviance in organizations arises where deviant means are used to attain legitimate organizational goals. This can occur when dominant groups in the organization decide to use illegitimate means to attain organizational goals because of externally generated pressures for performance. Such pressures may arise from competitors, market conditions, the government, stockholders, or the public. As it becomes more difficult to achieve organizational goals through legitimate means, the more likely it is that illegitimate means will be employed.

In a major study of corporate crime, Clinard and Yeager (1980) examined the question of how pressures on corporations produce violations of the law. They found that there is a conflict of corporate norms with the legal and ethical norms present in wider society. A corporation may put more emphasis on profits than on ethics, and in so doing ignore its responsibilities to the community, the consumer, or the larger society. The desire for expansion, security, maintenance of the corporation, fear of failure, and group loyalty in the corporate ranks can also lead to illegal conduct. There is also pressure by superiors for "performance" from those who serve the organization. The ethical tone or climate of an organization is often established by superiors. They set an example, as well as select others to serve under them. Sometimes they are corrupt, and corruption is tolerated in the organization from within. Sometimes illegality is due to the normative structure of a particular industry. That is, sometimes an entire market structure exists which encourages companies to violate the law.

A clear example of a market structure that encourages crimes by businesses occurs in the used car industry. Used car dealers have a reputation in the public mind for dishonesty. They are, in fact, more or less routinely dishonest, but probably not any more so than managers of many other businesses. By "dishonest" it is meant that they systematically and continually engage in white-collar crimes. This is known and accepted within the industry; indeed, business could not proceed in any other way. It would be erroneous to point to any "special qualities" of men and women who become used car dealers. Instead, we should look at the criminogenic market structure of the used car business. Used car dealers could not stay in business without violating the law; illegality is built into the transactions that are necessary to keep a dealer afloat (Farberman, 1975). One such transaction is the "short-sale."

A "short-sale" begins to develop when a retail customer observes the sales manager compute and add onto the selling price of the car the sales tax—a hefty 8 percent. Often, the customer expresses some resentment at the tax bite and asks if there is any way to eliminate or reduce it. The sales manager responds in a sympathetic fashion and allies himself with the customer in a scheme to "cut down on the Governor's share of the deal" by suggesting that the customer might make out a check for less than the actual selling price for the car. In turn, the manager will make out a bill of sale for the lesser amount. The customer will pay the difference between the recorded selling price and the actual selling price in cash (Farberman, 1975: 442).

While the transaction above benefits the customer directly, it is of far greater benefit to the dealer. A dealer makes "many" such transactions; the customer only makes one. Consequently, the dealer finds himself accumulating large sums of untaxed money. "Stealing money off the top" has a specific purpose; it isn't just to avoid paying taxes. The dealer, to stay in business, needs a large volume of cars coming in so that they can be sold. Trade-ins and sales by individual customers are insufficient; he must have a supply from agencies that will offer him a large number of cars. And one of the most convenient of such sources is the used car agents of new car dealers. The agent knows that the used car dealer is dependent upon him; consequently, he demands a "kickback," or a bribe, for every used car sold to the dealer. This transaction cannot be conducted with a checkbook, for that would entail a written record of an illegal transaction. Nor does it make any sense to the dealer to pay out money on which he has to pay taxes. Kickbacks, therefore, come from the untaxed, unrecorded cash earned on the short sales. Just as an illegal kickback necessitates the short sale, the "legal" pricing structure of the automobile industry necessitates these illegal practices. New car agencies set an extremely low profit margin for franchises who must, consequently, turn over a high volume of cars to stay in business. The new car agencies are motivated to move their inventory quickly and to engage in collusive practices with the used car dealers who have a great need of the used cars that make their way into their lots (Farberman, 1975).

Such a criminogenic market structure can encourage—even demand—illegal practices. As new businesses come into existence, they will have to engage in similar practices in order to survive. A major finding by Clinard and Yeager (1980) demonstrates this point; corporations located in the same industry have similar rates of recidivism.

One of the most famous of all white-collar crime cases is the "Great Electrical Conspiracy." This case is important to the study of white-collar crime in two ways. First, it revealed in great detail how large, respected corporations cheated consumers as well as a municipal government. Second, the research work that analyzed the case, written by Gilbert Geis almost three decades after Sutherland's initial publication introducing the white-collar crime concept, was largely responsible for a reawakening interest among criminologists in the topic of white-collar crime.

Starting at about the end of World War II

Car or Coffin? The Case of the Ford Pinto

One major investigation into corporate misconduct documented how the Ford Motor Company manufactured the Pinto despite internal tests that revealed a serious and potentially lethal flaw in the car's gas tank design. Perhaps most disturbing in this case was the use of a "cost-benefit analysis" in which Ford weighed the cost of a gas tank modification at $11 per vehicle, against the probable cost to the company of potential fire deaths resulting from the flawed original design ($200,000 per death). This provides a glaring example of a corporation putting a specific price tag on human life. The extensive investigation uncovered the following:

Fighting strong competition from Volkswagen for the lucrative small car market, the Ford Motor Company rushed the Pinto into production (under the direction of former president Lee Iacocca) in much less than the usual time.

Ford engineers discovered in pre-production crash tests that rear end collisions would rupture the Pinto's fuel system extremely easily. Because assembly-line machinery was already tooled when engineers found this defect, top Ford officials decided to manufacture the car anyway—exploding gas tank and all—even though Ford owned the patent on a much safer gas tank.

For more than eight years afterward, Ford successfully lobbied, with extraordinary vigor and some blatant lies, against a key government safety standard that would have forced the company to change the Pinto's fire-prone gas tank. Ford waited eight years because its internal "cost-benefit analysis," which places a dollar value on human life, said it wasn't profitable to make the changes sooner.

By conservative estimates Pinto crashes have caused 500 burn deaths to people who would not have sustained serious injuries if the car had not caught fire. The figure could be as high as 900. Ford has paid millions to settle damage suits out of court. The Pinto case was the first in which a corporation was indicted and prosecuted for homicide. After a ten-week trial a jury found the "defendant" not guilty on three charges of reckless homicide (Dowie, 1985).

---

and continuing throughout the 1950s, all the corporations manufacturing and selling heavy electrical equipment were involved in an illegal price-fixing scheme. They ran from the biggest giants in the field, such as General Electric and Westinghouse, to small and less well-known manufacturers. Actually, not just 1 but some 20 separate conspiracies were operating simultaneously, since most of the electrical manufacturing companies were decentralized into semiautonomous departments. Prices were fixed on equipment like circuit breakers, huge transformers, turbine generators, switch gears, and insulators. Most of the equipment was not sold to the public, but to organized bodies like city governments, power and light companies, and federal agencies. Executives would hold secret meetings, agree on prices, and arbitrarily divide up the market.

In so doing they violated the Sherman Anti-Trust Act. They had formed a cartel and were guilty of collusion, conspiracy, price-fixing, and bid-rigging. They submitted price bids to their customers in sealed envelopes, but it was all a hoax. There was no competition; the prices had been agreed upon in advance by the offending companies. Each took turns in submitting the winning bid. As is apt to happen, someone got his signals crossed. In the fall of 1959, representatives of the Tennessee Valley Authority complained to the Department of Justice that they had received identical bids from several supposed competitors. The Justice Department decided to investigate the case. The investigation provided the evidence necessary for criminal prosecutions.

The Sherman Act was designed to discourage the formation of monopolies because they represented "restraints of trade." The act was established to protect the ideal of a "free market system." A truly competitive market could be bad for business, as competitors would have to cut profit margins to attract customers away from competing companies. By regulating the market through working arrangements with one's competitors, a company would have a more comfortable arrangement and reap bigger profits while sharing the market. Some electrical manufacturing executives did just this because they felt that profits were not high enough. In the words of one, "The market was getting in chaotic condition." Conspiring with other manufacturers, said the president of one electrical company, "is the only way a business can be run. It is free enterprise," he said, with no apparent irony intended. True competition, these executives felt, would narrow profits and put some manufacturers out of business. Bid-rigging kept marginal companies in business and prevented a monopolistic market, or so, at any rate, went their explanations for their criminal activities. Getting together with their competitors" became a way of life for them.

The prevailing estimate as to how much money was involved in these transactions is roughly $1.7 billion in sales annually, for about 10 to 12 years. The amount of money unnecessarily paid as a result of their price rigging runs into millions of dollars, and perhaps as high as a billion dollars. This was money that was ultimately stolen form the public pocket. It represented money that all consumers and taxpayers paid over and above what they would have paid had more honest business practices prevailed. It represents real money, just as would money obtained through a bank robbery (in fact, hundreds or thousands of robberies). Whenever a municipal government was overcharged $250,000 for a turbine, its taxpayers had to make up the difference. Whenever a power and light company bought a generator for 10 percent more than it was really worth, its customers paid correspondingly more for the energy they consumed. As in other forms of white-collar crime, the fact that each individual consumer lost a relatively small amount made the practice seem less evil.

It was also found that the conspirators were not much different than other criminals in the techniques they employed. They were secretive about their activities and optimistic that they wouldn't be caught. They minimized telephone calls to and from their offices, using public telephones most of the time, used plain envelopes for correspondence, and had fake names and special codes to identify business transactions. Also, as in the case of common criminals, they tended to rationalize their behaviors. A number said that their actions, while "technically illegal," served to stabilize prices. They shifted blame to the market structure rather than to themselves. The reactions of the judiciary and the companies themselves also shed light on the nature of the offenses. One judge said of the defendants: "They were torn between conscience and an approved corporate policy, with the rewarding objective of promotion, comfortable security, and large salaries. They were the organization or company man, the conformist who goes along with his superiors and finds balm for his conscience in additional comforts and security of his place in the corporate set-up" (Geis, 1967: 147).

General Electric fired its offending executives, but Westinghouse did not for four reasons.

First, . . . the men involved had not sought personal aggrandizement—"While their actions cannot in any way be condoned, these men did not act for personal gain, but in the belief, misguided though it may have been, that they were furthering the company's interest"; second, "the punishment incurred by them already was harsh" and "no further penalties would serve any useful purpose"; third, "each of these individuals is in every sense a reputable citizen, a respected and valuable member of the community and of high moral character"; and fourth, there was virtually no likelihood that the individuals would repeat their offense (Geis, 1967: 146).

Eventually, 45 executives working for 29 corporations were indicted for criminal conspiracy. Almost all of the corporate defendants, in effect, admitted their guilt by entering pleas of nolo contendere (no contest). Seven of them received jail sentences—of 30 days. (Twenty-four were convicted but received suspended sentences.) The companies themselves were slapped with criminal fines totaling roughly $2 million, which was paid mostly by General Electric and Westinghouse. Considering the huge sums of money involved, the criminal penalties meted out seem insignificant. Geis estimated that the $400,000 fine levied against General Electric would be equivalent to a man earning an income of $175,000 a year receiving a $3 parking ticket (1967: 142).

The offenders did not see what they did as criminal. "Sure, collusion was illegal," explained one General Electric executive, "but it wasn't unethical.... Those competitor meetings were just attended by a group of distressed individuals who wanted to know where they were going." When a federal attorney asked a Westinghouse executive, "Did you know that these meetings with competitors were illegal?" the reply was "Illegal? Yes," he explained, "but not criminal. I assumed that criminal action meant damaging someone and we did not do that." An Allis-Chalmers officer was asked, "Why did you go to the meetings?" He answered, "I thought it was part of my duty to do so." Another added, "Meeting with competitors was just one of the many facets of responsibility that was delegated to me." So ingrained was the practice that, when convicted, these executives saw themselves as "scapegoats," sacrificial lambs. The whole industry—in fact, all of business, not just the manufacture of electrical equipment—made use of collusion, monopolistic control, informal "regulations" of the market. Why should we be the fall guys? they asked, outraged by their convictions. One executive, who had managed to garner a decent amount of support for his cause from the community, "got, frankly, madder than hell" when he found out that he would not be paid while he served his brief jail sentence—a sum of $11,000. "We did not fix prices," one president of a small company explained. "I am

telling you that all we did was recover costs." A sales manager of the ITE Circuit Breaker Company put it this way: "The spirit of such meetings only appeared to be correcting a horrible price level situation; there was not an attempt to actually damage customers." One executive who refused to go along with the arrangement was replaced; he was described as "getting us in trouble with competition."

At least three of the basic elements common to most forms of deviance are lacking in this case: The offenders did not see themselves as committing deviant acts, nor did they see themselves as deviants; second, the public did not view their actions as grossly reprehensible, nor did they feel that they were, in fact, deviants; and third, the formal agents of social control, in this case the judges, did not penalize them severely for their actions, at least in proportion to their magnitude. The executives received a large volume of supportive letters, telegrams, and phone calls; their thrust was "you didn't do anything wrong, and your conviction is grossly unfair." A defending lawyer claimed that the judge "did not understand what it would do to his client, this fine man, to be put behind bars with common criminals." A judge suspended the sentence of another executive by saying that he didn't think that this was the type of offense that probation lent itself to or was designed for. And Westinghouse's defense of its convicted executives certainly summarizes a widespread feeling concerning the respectability of the actions of these executives.

As a final note, it should be pointed out that the heavy electrical equipment conspiracy cases received only sparse newspaper coverage. A bank robbery, even when it involves little or no violence, generally makes headlines if it involves a substantial sum of money. The Great Electrical Conspiracy involved sums of more than $1 billion, a massive effort at prosecution on the part of the federal government, and prison sentences for corporate executives. Yet the newspaper industry did not consider these events particularly newsworthy. Stories tended to emphasize the individual executives, divorced from any organizational or industry context. Their acts were considered isolated and idiosyncratic, rather than tied directly to company and industry-wide practices. This seems typical of white-collar cases, although major cases today often make front page news, if only for a brief time during the course of the investigation and final disposition.

If nothing else, the electrical equipment cases show strong support for Sutherland's contentions concerning white-collar crime, especially those tied to his theory of differential association: that criminal behavior is learned from associates. The research on these cases also led others (albeit slowly) into the study of white-collar crime as a fertile area for scientific inquiry. While data are not as readily available for examining white-collar crime as may exist for researching other forms of deviance, the electrical equipment conspiracy cases demonstrated that some data were available and could be used to describe and understand the transgressions of powerful individuals and organizations.

OCCUPATIONAL AND PROFESSIONAL WHITE-COLLAR CRIME

Although the white-collar crime designation is usually applied to illegal money-making activities conducted at the corporate or organizational level, the basic definition can be logically extended to include certain crimes committed by members of the various professions. Lanza-Kaduce (1980: 333–334) defines professional deviance as those actions of professionals performed in the course of practicing their occupations that violate norms governing professional activities. Like the business executive, the professional is typically a well-regarded member of the community, characterized by both upper-middle-class status and a prestigious means of generating a considerably higher than average income. Despite this important similarity, however, professional or occupational crime differs from traditional white-collar crime in that it is committed for personal

gain rather than on behalf of an organization. If, as is often suggested, business crime has been inadequately examined, professional white-collar crime has been accorded even less attention. Yet, in a sense, it is a more insidious phenomenon for at least two reasons. First, since personal accountability is more easily diffused across a corporation or agency it is usually more difficult to place blame on a specific individual; in some instances there may in fact be no one responsible for deviance emanating from a faulty organizational structure. Second, and more importantly perhaps, is the fact that professionals by definition are largely self-regulating groups whose special position in society is marked by trust from others. When that trust is broken it raises many interesting issues regarding the roots of deviance and white-collar crime. We naturally expect that professionally trained persons deserve their high status and special privileges, but, at the same time, we also believe that they are least likely to violate the law. When professional persons engage in white-collar crime they rattle the very foundation of the stratification and reward system in society.

The two classic defining features of professions are that they require specialized training and entail client service. The most obvious examples would be law and medicine, but science, architecture, and public administration also qualify. Due to their diversity, it is difficult to generalize about deviance across professions. At the same time, several studies have investigated crimes within specific types of professions; from these studies, certain important common features do emerge.

Pharmaceutical Prescription Violation

One of the early systematic investigations of professional white-collar crime was conducted by Quinney (1963). The study considered how the social structure of one profession—that of retail pharmacist—might explain criminal behavior within that profession. The particular offense examined was the violation of laws and regulations governing the compounding and dispensing

The Story of an Embezzler

The story of David L. Miller illustrates the common unwillingness of businesses to seek prosecution of white-collar criminals—even when such persons steal millions of dollars from company funds. Miller, a middle-aged executive, has been a successful embezzler for over 20 years, stealing from six different employers. During his career, which has been fostered by companies who have not sought prosecution or told other prospective employers of his misdeeds, Miller has been released from employment after promising to repay stolen funds, or at least part of them. In most cases he accomplished this by embezzling from his new employer. Many executives fear that prosecuting (and thus publicizing) white-collar crimes, especially those committed by persons within their ranks, might raise serious questions about financial controls within the company, and thus may jeopardize their own jobs or give rise to shareholder suits. Experts claim that such inaction makes the problem worse, since the lack of punishment often leads to repeated embezzling. When confronted with information from his past, Miller said, "It was an illness. I didn't want to hurt anyone. I'm not a bad person." He claims that psychiatric counseling has now cured him. After embezzling $1.3 million, he was fired from his $130,000 a year job as chief financial officer of a cellular-phone company in Pittsburgh, and then hired by a former colleague of the company to run the Boston office of another corporation where he is now working (Burrough, 1986).

of prescriptions. Quinney found that prescription violation is strongly related to the violator's occupational orientation. Pharmacists oriented toward professional role expectations are more bound by both formal (i.e., legal) and informal (i.e., occupational) controls. Pharmacists more oriented toward a business role, stressing the merchandising aspects, are less bound by such controls and are primarily interested in monetary gain. For example, a sample of pharmacists in one city was interviewed in order to determine each individual's role orientation. It was found that 75 percent of those categorized as "business oriented" had been officially detected as prescription violators, while none of those categorized as "profession oriented" were known violators. In other words, "for each pharmacist, orientation to a particular role more than to another provides a perspective in which violation may seem appropriate" (Quinney, 1963: 184). This notion conforms closely to Glaser's (1956) concept of differential identification, whereby deviance may occur when one identifies strongly with real or imaginary persons from whose perspective the deviance seems acceptable.

Unnecessary Surgery

It is estimated that 85 percent of total surgical operations now performed in the United States are discretionary or elective; that is, they do not involve emergencies or life-prolonging circumstances (Bunker, 1976). Of these operations, it is believed that perhaps as many as 15 percent are performed unnecessarily, at an annual cost of almost $4 billion (Meier and Geis, 1979). For example, 90 percent of tonsillectomies are reportedly unneeded (Hiatt, 1975). D'Espo (1962) contends that at least 15 percent of all hysterectomies (surgical removal of the uterus) are performed in the absence of pathology. Lanza-Kaduce investigated this allegation and concluded that unnecessary surgery is indeed a regularly occurring phenomenon, attributable in part to differences in training and operating philosophies among doctors. He notes, "The proportion of operations of questionable necessity is sizable, and the cost of this professional misconduct in terms of mortality, morbidity, and money is substantial" (1980: 344).

Freidson (1970) offers a political explanation that focuses on economic factors and occupational self-interest as most responsible for unnecessary surgery. In fact, the highest surgery rates in the population have been reported among low-income patients with either private or governmental insurance coverage (Anderson and Feldman, 1956; Forum, 1977). In a 1984 case, a California ophthalmologist was convicted of performing unneeded cataract surgery on indigent patients in order to collect Medicaid fees of $584 per eye. In one shocking instance, he totally blinded a woman when he operated needlessly on her (Welkos, 1984).

Lanza-Kaduce (1980) concludes from his research that whether unnecessary surgery results from diagnostic incompetence or from greed, the most effective control mechanisms are those in which an offending physician is more likely to be detected, such as formal pathology reports and mandatory second opinions. This approach applies classical criminal deterrence theory to the area of professional deviance.

Medicaid Fraud

Medicaid is a government funded health benefit program designed to provide medical care for the needy. The fee-for-service structure of the program, in which a distant third-party insurer pays all charges, has created a new class of professional white-collar criminal. A number of providers have succumbed to the temptation to overcharge, bill for patients never seen, double-bill, prolong treatment, and perform other worthless services. Policing and enforcement within the program have been selective at best, and it is certain that a large "dark figure" (Biderman and Reiss, 1967) of unreported violations exists. The professional status of providers, notably physicians, makes it relatively easy to cover up offenses. Some government officials believe that as much as $40 billion is lost annually to fraudulent and abusive practices in the nation's health care programs. Uncovered violations are sometimes grossly arrogant in nature. Investigations have reported cases in which bills have been submitted for X-rays done without film, daily psychotherapy sessions totalling far more than 24 hours, and hysterectomies performed on male patients.

Why do doctors engage in Medicaid fraud? There are many reasons, most of which are tied to conflict and tension between the medical profession and the government. Physicians generally do not like the low reimbursement rates (sometimes as much as 50 percent below their normal and customary charges) and the red tape and paperwork associated with the Medicaid program. Some doctors cheat to "make back" what they feel they should be earning. In other instances doctors see the program as a "game" which, if played well, can provide a lucrative source of extra income. A study of Medicaid fraud, which included numerous interviews with convicted violators (Pontell et el., 1984a), quotes one physician as saying: "If you know how to play the game, you can stay out of trouble and you can milk the program." Researchers suggest that the behavior which enables a doctor to engage in fraud is probably at least partially learned from others in the profession, and that professional values may effectively neutralize the doctor's conflicts of conscience (Pontell et al., 1984b). Very few of the professional deviants interviewed displayed remorse for their wrongdoing, preferring instead to attack the program and its officials as the "causes" of their violations. A similar reaction was also manifested by sanctioned clinical psychologists in a study by Geis and his colleagues (1985b). This attitude, in which the professional keeps his or her positive self-identity intact in the face of rule-breaking behavior is akin to what Sykes and Matza (1957) describe as a form of deviance neutralization that is typically employed by criminals and involves the process of shifting blame to the accusers. Other studies (Pontell et al., 1982; Jesilow et al., 1985) suggest that occupational norms may support an attitude on the part of some professionals that they are "above the law."

A theoretically revealing finding of the Medicaid fraud studies concerns the excessively large proportion of psychiatrists convicted of program violations. While psychiatrists represent only about 8 percent of all

A Deadly Game of Medicaid Fraud:
The Story of Olga Romani

Olga Romani arrived in the United States from Cuba in 1960. She claims to have graduated from medical school at the University of Havana, and began practicing medicine in Miami in 1967 while she completed her state licensing requirements. In 1974 she received a sentence of five years probation after pleading guilty to charges of unlawful practice of medicine. The case arose after two women complained that her "acne treatments" had left them disfigured. In the five years since she began treating Medicaid patients in 1976, she had become the second largest provider of such services in the state of Florida, and was operating two medical clinics. According to official reports, she received $184,000 in state money in 1980. In March 1981 she was arrested on racketeering charges, which claimed that she had bilked Medicaid for more than $97,000 of treatments that were never performed. During her jury trial, the prosecutor asked a witness if he had ever been treated by Dr. Romani for acne, tonsillitis, viral fever, an ingrown toenail, depression, asthma, or diaper rash. The spectators and jurors laughed. The witness was a 19-year-old, 220-pound Florida A&M football player, Eddie James King. All of the above items were billed for after the young man had visited Dr. Romani twice "for a cold." Romani had billed the state for 51 visits, claiming payments of $1,885. Another of the ten witnesses testified that she had never even met Romani, despite the fact that Romani had used her Medicaid recipient number to bill the state for 165 visits, totaling $1638. The jury took only one hour to convict her on 24 counts of filing false claims and 24 more of receiving payments to which she was not entitled. A short time later, Romani showed

little emotion as a judge sentenced her to 20 years in prison for Medicaid fraud, saying, "This so-called white-collar crime is also stealing money allocated to the poor." A state attorney said that the money paid to Romani could have gone to treat more than 10,000 poor patients.

Unfortunately, the story does not end here. Shortly after she was sentenced, Romani became a prime suspect in the murder of her former partner, Dr. Gerardo DeMola, who was gunned down outside a Miami hospital a few weeks before her indictment on Medicaid fraud charges in 1981. Romani was suspected of paying $10,000 for a contract killing, fearing that her former partner might testify against her in the fraud case. During her murder trial, the prosecution produced a "hit list" which contained Dr. DeMola's name. Romani testified that the list was to be delivered to a santeria practitioner (santeria is a black Cuban religion similar to voodoo) who had requested that she furnish names of people she might be involved with in future legal disputes. She also claimed that she did not believe in santeria, but that her accountant had recommended that she try it to ease her mind. Romani was evasive during her questioning by prosecutors and proved not to be a credible witness. After returning verdicts of guilty on murder and conspiracy charges, a juror noted: "It was her. It was the way she testified." On February 3, 1983, Olga Romani was sentenced to life imprisonment with a 25-year mandatory sentence on the murder charge and another 30 years for conspiracy. The Florida judge also ordered that the new sentences run consecutively with the 20-year sentence she already had received on Medicaid fraud charges.

---

physicians (Harris, 1981), nearly 20 percent of the doctors suspended from Medicaid because of fraudulent practices have come from this single specialty (Geis et al., 1985a). In order to determine if psychiatrists are simply less honest than other physicians, or if they had been disproportionately targeted

for prosecution, researchers have examined the manner in which Medicaid fraud cases are investigated. Their conclusions illustrate some of the difficulties law enforcers encounter in white-collar crime cases.

Almost all doctors bill the Medicaid program for specific services rendered, including examinations, tests, X-rays, injections, and surgeries. The question of fraud centers primarily on whether the claimed services were actually carried out. Psychiatrists present one notable exception. Here, the bill includes not just a service, but a service rendered over a specific period of time. Most states compute their payment rates for psychiatrists in terms of 50-minute sessions. By clocking movement in and out of offices (sometimes through the use of a video camera in an unmarked van parked in the street outside the psychiatrist's office) or by verifying the times with patients themselves, investigators can readily determine if the actual time periods conform to those that have been billed. Psychiatrists, then, are especially easy enforcement targets. Unlike most other types of medical crime, investigators need not deal with complex legal and professional issues and enforcement problems; checking psychiatric bills requires little technical expertise beyond an ability to tell time. Thus, it is probable that this relative ease of apprehension, a rarity in white-collar crime, is responsible for the overrepresentation of fraud cases involving psychiatrists and not any significantly greater dishonesty on their part.

Conclusion

These three examples—prescription violaton, unnecessary surgery, and Medicaid fraud—obviously do not encompass the whole range of professional deviance. There are many other types of offenses involving professionals (for example, jury tampering by attorneys and corruption of public officials), although the health professions seem to be especially noteworthy, given their acknowledged status and power within society. Recognized medical offenses, in addition to those already described, include narcotics violations, fraudulent testimony in court cases, and fee-splitting, where physicians "kick back" part of their fees to other physicians who refer patients to them (Sutherland, 1949). As noted, however, several recurring threads appear to run through the examples cited. As we have seen, a state of

tension is apt to exist between the service and business aspects of the professions. Society expects its professionals to be honest and dedicated, and professionals expect to enjoy high socioeconomic status and power within society. These expectations are not necessarily incompatible, but conflicts clearly do arise. While it seems impossible to justify certain behaviors, such as knowingly performing needless surgery for monetary gain, professionals may well be able to rationalize other illegal behaviors, such as in the prescription and Medicaid examples, as appropriate responses to interference with what they feel they deserve in terms of remuneration.

Perhaps the most promising theoretical explanation of professional deviance focuses on the manner in which professionals are socialized and organized. In the case of physicians, an examination of the way in which medical students are trained (Becker et al., 1961) suggests that "idealism" invariably gives way to "cynicism" during medical education. Shoemaker reports a measurable incidence of cheating among pre-medical students—a practice which the stuents are generally able to justify. "Any advantage you can get, you take," explains one future doctor (1984: 94). Sutherland (1949) believed that professional behaviors are learned through association with fellow professionals. Within each profession—pharmacy, medicine, psychology, and so on—there is a strong demand for autonomy. The result is a "circle the wagons" mind set in reaction to outside regulation and to the external policing of deviant behavior.

Mumford (1983) observes that physicians engage in a "highly developed rhetoric" made up of myths and beliefs regarding their profession, which serve to sway the public in a direction favorable to maintaining professional dominance. Mumford's notion seems perfectly applicable to many other nonmedical professions as well. This rhetoric can also serve as an effective shield against the accusations of critics and law enforcers.

A focus on deviance perpetrated by professionals highlights a well-educated group of elite persons whose violations cannot in any reasonable way be attributed to the malaise created by poverty, inadequate socialization (though professional training might be deficient in the inculcation of adequate ethical standards) or similar "explanations" of more traditional kinds of crime. Professionals, as individual entrepreneurs, allow for an easier comprehension than do corporate executives of the importance of the person in the commission of white-collar crime.

POLITICAL AND GOVERNMENTAL CRIME

Another area of white-collar crime that cannot be ignored is occupational crime in government and politics. As one observer has noted: "While it would be comforting to believe that those we entrust with running our local, state, and federal governments are free of job-related criminality, the realities are such that there would be little substance to our comfort" (Barlow, 1978: 235)

Broadly speaking, political crime falls into two basic categories: (1) crimes committed by the government against its citizens—such as unlawful persecution and other violations of civil liberties; (2) crimes committed by corrupt officeholders or other renegade government officials to personally benefit themselves or to induce others to commit crimes—such as bribery. The first category involves organizational crimes and is roughly akin to the corporate crimes discussed earlier. Here, it is the government or one of its agencies that engages in illegal activities designed to perpetuate or increase political power or achieve some similar goal at the expense of citizens. The second category is more analogous to professional white-collar crime in that the offenders are individuals within the political system who abuse their powerful positions in order to bring about economic gain. Here, the emphasis is less on the promotion of some organizational goal or goals than it is on personal enrichment. We will examine each type of political crime in turn.

Eitzen and Timmer (1985) have identified several forms of "government lawlessness." The three which seem most applicable to our examination of white-collar crime are (1) the use of citizens as unwilling or unknowing guinea pigs; (2) abuse of power by government agencies; (3) secrecy, lying, and deception.

The use of citizens as unwilling or unknowing guinea pigs. The notion of illegal human experimentation usually conjures up images of the horrors of Nazi Germany. While it is clearly unfair to suggest any reasonable comparison between the Third Reich's disregard for human life and American policy in this area, it is unfortunately true that the United States does have a history of using unwilling and unknowing subjects in potentially dangerous medical experiments. One case, particularly notorious in its contempt for human subjects, is the infamous "bad blood" study conducted by the U. S. Public Health Service. Beginning in 1932, doctors in Macon County, Alabama, began observing 400 black males who had syphilis. The subjects were not told they had this serious venereal disease, but were told rather that they were suffering from a condition vaguely described as "bad blood." Proper diagnosis was withheld in order to assess the consequences of *not* treating syphilis. This inhuman experiment went on for *40 years*—in which time the subjects received no treatment, nor did their wives who invariably contracted syphilis, nor did their children who were subsequently born with congenital syphilis (Jones, 1981).

Another example of this type of government crime was a 1953 experiment conducted by the CIA, in which the hallucinogen LSD was slipped into the drinks of a group of naive subjects. One subject experienced such a severe psychotic reaction that he jumped to his death from a hotel window two days later. The CIA covered up the facts of this case for 22 years—even from the victim's family (Bowart, 1978). Similarly, the Freedom of Information Act has also revealed that the CIA formerly tested experimental knockout drugs and incapacitating substances on terminal cancer patients who had no idea they were being used as guinea pigs (Lee, 1982).

Abuse of power by government agencies.
Many incidences of government lawlessness have been perpetrated by such agencies as the FBI, the CIA, and the IRS under the guise of "national security." Illegal domestic surveillance is one prime example. Beginning with the "red scare" of the 1950s and peaking during the antiwar and civil rights protest of the late 1960s and early 1970s, it is now known that the government opened hundreds of thousands of first-class letters and collected secret dossiers on perhaps a half-million Americans. Moreover, many of these "targets" were harassed and persecuted for their political beliefs.

For example, the husband of an officer in ACTION, a St. Louis civil rights organization, received a handwritten note that said: "Look man, I guess your old lady doesn't get enough at home or she wouldn't be shucking and jiving with our black men in ACTION, you dig? Like all she wants to integrate is the bedroom and we black sisters ain't gonna take no second best from our men. So lay it on her man or get her the hell off Newstead [Street]." The couple soon separated, and the local FBI agent-in-charge wrote to headquarters: "This matrimonial stress and strain should cause her to function much less effectively in ACTION" (Eitzen and Timmer, 1985). Also, actress Jean Seberg, in 1970, helped raise money for the radical Black Panthers organization. According to documents released by the FBI in 1979, the FBI tried to discredit Seberg by planting the rumor that the father of her unborn baby was a prominent Black Panther leader. This false story led to a miscarriage, bouts with mental illness, and quite possibly her eventual suicide (Eitzen and Timmer, 1985).

Secrecy, lying, and deception. Government—even in our democracy—has frequently tried to withhold information from Congress, the courts, or the people. While some of this occurs in the name of "national security," when it takes the form of outright lying by government officials it can become an act of lawlessness. This has occurred in the cases of illegal intervention in the sovereignty of other countries—Guatemala in the 1950s, Cuba in the 1960s, and Cambodia in the 1970s. In the latter instance, the death certificates of Americans who died in Cambodia were falsified by our government to read that they had died elsewhere (Wise, 1973).

One of the most extreme examples of official secrecy and deception are those crimes known collectively as Watergate. In the words of David Wise:

Watergate revealed that under President Nixon a kind of totalitarianism had already come to America, creeping in, not like Carl Sandburg's fog, on little cat feet, but in button-down shirts, worn by handsome young advertising and public relations men carrying neat attache cases crammed with $100 bills. Men who were willing to perjure themselves to stay on the team, to serve their leader . . . men determined to preserve their own political power at any cost. It came in the form of the ladder against the bedroom window, miniature transmitters in the ceiling, wire-taps, burglaries, enemies lists, tax audits, and psychiatric profiles (1973: x–xi).

A partial list of Watergate-related crimes includes (from Eitzen and Timmer, 1985):

1. Burglars financed by the Commitee to Re-elect the President (CREEP) broke into and bugged the headquarters of the Democratic Party in the Watergate apartment complex. These burglars, after capture, were paid "hush money" and promised executive clemency to protect the White House.

2. Burglars also broke into the office of the psychiatrist of Daniel Ellsberg, the man who leaked the notorious "Pentagon Papers" to the press. While the case was still in trial, the White House reportedly offered the judge the directorship of the FBI.

3. President Nixon's personal attorney solicited money for an illegally formed campaign fund and offered an ambassadorship to one donor in return for a contribution.

4. The president ordered secret wiretaps of his own aides, several journalists, and even his brother. He also had secret microphones planted in his offices to record every conversation. When the president, under duress, did provide transcripts of the secret tapes, they were edited.

5. The director of the FBI destroyed vital legal evience at the suggestion of White House aides.

6. The attorney-general was involved in the planning of the Watergate break-in and even suggested at one meeting that CREEP employ prostitutes at the Democratic national convention as another means of gaining information.
7. CREEP employees participated in a "dirty tricks" campaign to discredit various potential Democratic challengers. These tricks included the publication and distribution of letters purporting to come from Senator Muskie claiming that Senator Jackson was a homosexual.
8. The White House requested tax audits of administration opponents.
9. Many high administration officials were convicted of perjury and obstruction of justice.

In 1987, another major example of government deception became the focus of national attention, with the Congressional investigation and public hearings regarding the "Iran-Contra Affair." As with Watergate, this scandal reflected a complex web of political intrigue—spawning in the White House basement and slowly reaching up to the very highest levels of the Executive Branch, including the Oval Office. At issue were a number of dramatic revelations and serious accusations:

The United States sold at least 200 tons of arms, including two missile systems, to the hostile nation of Iran in May 1985. The apparent goal of these sales was to obtain the release of American hostages held in Lebanon under the control of the Iranian leadership. President Reagan initially admitted that a "really minuscule" quantity of arms had been sold to Iran, but later conceded the full extent of the sale.

The United States authorized two additional indirect shipments of American arms from Israel to Iran in August and November of 1985. The CIA provided transportation for the November shipment, and the United States replaced the Israeli arms that were shipped. President Reagan initially denied knowledge of this arrangement to the Presidential Commission he had appointed to investigate the charges, but later retracted his denial. Again, this sale is believed to have violated American arms export laws.

Congress was told only after the story broke publicly in November 1986—nearly a year later—in violation of the Intelligence Oversight Act, which requires prior (or at least timely) notice of covert action.

Presidential aide, Oliver North, allegedly prepared a cover-up report indicating that the arms shipments were authorized. The report was then revised to suggest that U.S. officials believed only oil-drilling equipment was involved. This version was later changed again, when the Director of the CIA testified before Congress. As Watergate demonstrated, attempting to cover up illegal acts and lying to Congress are both crimes.

North was later fired for diverting profits from the Iranian arms sales to the *contras,* a rebel army attempting to overthrow the pro-Soviet government of Nicaragua. Additional allegations charged that North had used part of the profits to purchase personal items, such as snow tires. The misuse of government funds or the unauthorized diversion of profits from U.S. arms sales are also violations of the law.

While the so-called Iran-Contra Affair remains unresolved, at the time of this writing, in terms of the complicity or at least foreknowledge of the president and his top aides, it is clear that the lessons of Watergate have either been forgotten or were never learned by many government officials.

Bribery and Corruption

The second category of political crime involves personal corruption among government officials. Like other white-collar offenders, these criminals do not typically see themselves as criminals. Likewise, the penalties for such crimes have traditionally been rather lenient, considering the serious betrayal of public trust involved, as well as the considerable sums of money.

For example, in 1975 the Securities and Exchange Commission accused the Gulf Oil Corporation of funneling more than $10 million into a Bahamian subsidiary for use as illegal political contributions. Gulf's Washington lobbyist instructed the head of the Bahamian firm to disburse large amounts of cash to selected political candidates. Most prominent among those alleged to have received money from Gulf was the minority leader of the U.S. Senate, who was reportedly given $100,000. Congress chose not to investigate the matter when the senator decided to retire a few months later. Only one, far less powerful, member of Congress was indicted; and after pleading guilty, he was fined a mere $200 (Sobel, 1977).

Perhaps the best known (and most controversial) recent case of political bribery was Operation ABSCAM. ABSCAM ("Arab Scam") began in 1978, when the FBI undertook an investigation of racketeering and influence peddling among public officials. For the next year and a half, undercover agents approached persons suspected of political corruption and informed them that oil-rich Arab sheiks would offer money in exchange for various political favors. These bogus middlemen met with political figures in a number of locations around Washington, D.C., and paid out considerable sums in cash. The meetings and conversations were videotaped. Several public officials were indicted and convicted (Reid, 1982). Although this "sting" operation has been widely criticized for its use of entrapment tactics, the tapes did offer dramatic evidence of the potential for corruption in the U.S. Congress.

Political Reform

A number suggestions for reform can be offered in the area of political crime. Stressing the provision of stronger protections for individual civil rights, Coleman (1985) proposes a new federal law explicitly criminalizing any activities on the part of government agents that interferes with the freedom of expression. Although most such activities are already illegal, it is argued that such a law would still have an important symbolic value.

Regarding bribery and corruption, there is a need for change in the present system of campaign financing. The fact that most politicians have to rely on campaign contributions from well-endowed special interests is an invitation to corruption. One proposal calls for a system of federal and state financing of election campaigns, in which each qualifying candidate would be given the same amount of money to spend and would be permitted to spend only that amount (Coleman, 1985).

The creation of a permanent special prosecutor's office, similar to the temporary one created during Watergate, to deal with all forms of political crime represents another potential reform to existing arrangements. Coleman notes: "This office, equipped with its own investigative force, would have unrestricted access to all government records, files, and reports. The selection of the head of this office would best be left up to the Supreme Court or some prestigious nonpartisan group. With such a strong institutional base, the effort to control the government's abuse of power would seem to stand a much better chance of success than it has in the past" (1985: 249).

SERIOUSNESS OF WHITE-COLLAR CRIME

Conventional social science wisdom maintains that the average citizen regards white-collar crime rather indifferently. This idea has recently been challenged by a series of survey studies that report public ratings of the seriousness of white-collar offenses to be of similar magnitude as those for traditional street offenses (Rossi et al., 1974; Cullen et al., 1982; McCleary et al., 1981; Schrager and Short, Jr., 1980). Similarity in seriousness ratings are particularly pronounced when the white-collar offenses lead to physical, rather than to merely fiscal harm. In a study conducted in Illinois, Frank Cullen and his colleagues found that the offense of knowingly selling contaminated food that causes death was rated as more serious than forcible rape, aggravated assault, or selling secret documents to a foreign government. The same study also found that causing the death of an employee by neglecting to repair faulty machinery was deemed to be more serious than both child abuse and kidnapping for ransom. While there be some reservations about the precise meaning of such survey results where only rather brief descriptions of offenses are presented, it would appear that at least certain kinds of white-collar crime are seen as relatively serious offenses by the public.

Studies of law enforcement personnel have also shown similar findings regarding the seriousness of such offenses (Pontell et al., 1983, 1985). The nation's police chiefs regarded both traditional and white-collar crimes in much the same way as the public (Pontell et al., 1985). Another study found that federal investigators were apt to rate white-collar offenses more seriously than either police chiefs or the public, and perceived traditional offenses as less serious than these groups saw them. Such results may not seem surprising if one considers that federal investigators have much more experience in dealing with a variety of white-collar offenses than do the police or the public. They may therefore be more sensitive toward these crimes from first-hand experience with the harm they can cause. More importantly, perhaps, such studies also reveal that different groups hold varying opinions about the seriousness of crimes in general, and, in particular, about the social harm caused by white-collar crimes.

Dissensus about the seriousness of white-collar crime among different groups in society has generally been cited as one of the major reasons why it is not as vigorously labeled and punished as are street crimes. Although some dissensus is bound to exist, it is doubtful that this alone accounts for the rather low commitment to enforcing the law when it comes to white-collar crime. This apparent dilemma is considered in the following section.

ENFORCING LAWS AGAINST WHITE-COLLAR CRIME

Persons who can engage in white-collar crime are better able to manipulate the legal system itself, from the point of the drafting of specific legal statutes which may bear upon their occupational activities (for example, organized lobbying efforts by powerful

groups and professions), to the influencing of investigators, judges, juries, and the public through the respectable images they convey to these audiences. Conflict theorists have argued that it is in the interest of those in powerful positions to downplay the significance of white-collar crime. If it is true that powerful groups have the most influence in the passage and enforcement of laws, then it would be hard to imagine that they also would turn those laws to work against themselves.

Another reason for the relative inactivity in enforcing laws against white-collar crime has to do with the overall capacity of law enforcement personnel to respond to it. Enforcing laws against white-collar crime is extremely difficult and taxing, and often involves matters that are beyond the expertise of police officers. Investigations can go on for extended periods of time, with no certain results that will hold up in court. Even if evidence is obtained, an inexperienced prosecutor may not make the case well, especially when faced with a defense team that is likely to be paid handsomely to handle such cases. The current and past capacity of law enforcement is directed almost totally toward street crimes which are committed mostly by the poor. Relatively little attention is given to enforcement of laws against white-collar crime.

While limits to crime control are present for all offenses, they manifest themselves particularly clearly in the case of white-collar crime. In studying the behavior of prosecutors, Jack Katz (1980) has found that the capacity of the criminal justice system to investigate and prosecute white-collar crime is largely a function of practical resource limitations, given the overall role of the prosecutor's office in containing all types of crimes, as well as existing institutional arrangements for accomplishing this end. Resources and institutional arrangements are in turn affected by the laws governing the control of white-collar crime and the political setting in which such laws are enforced and resources distributed. Katz notes: "In a sense, the most serious crimes are those which attempt to make use of politically powerful or economically elite positions to frustrate detection and prosecution; white-collar crimes define the boundaries of the criminal justice system's capacities and the limits of moral integrity in the economy and polity" (1980: 175). This conceptualization also leads to another important point in understanding the inherent limitations of criminal justice in controlling white-collar crime. Given relatively fixed resources, the higher the demand for the control of common crime, the lower the remaining capacity of the criminal justice system to investigate and prosecute white-collar crimes. A federal prosecutor who has a lead on a $90 million drug case, for example, is not likely to shift limited resources away from it in order to investigate a complaint about a $5,000 Medicaid fraud. The prosecutor must select the larger, "more important" cases first. Which ones are "important" will be dictated by many considerations, many of which are likely to be directly political. The point is, that because of its limited capacity at any given time, the criminal justice system will accommodate the "most serious" cases (as determined by influential audiences in the immediate environment) first, lessening the potential for official processing of cases that remain; especially white-collar cases, which require proportionately greater amounts of resources for successful investigation, prosecution, and conviction (Pontell, 1984). This means that cases where strong evidence exists of white-collar crime will sometimes not be pursued by authorities because of limited resources. This does not mean that the deviance did not occur, but only that authorities were unwilling to officially label it as a "crime."

Enforcement of laws aimed at controlling white-collar crime has failed for a number of reasons (Coleman, 1985). For one thing, the laws designed to control white-collar crime are often vague and ineffectual. Ambiguously worded legal statutes favor the white-collar criminal, not only by allowing ways to circumvent their purposes, but by giving high-status individuals or large corporations a good chance to win their case in court, where such legislation can be openly challenged. Elite interests would appear to have the advantage of great financial resources and excellent legal representation for such matters. Even if statutes were worded more carefully, however, they might not be any more effective because of the methods white-collar criminals could employ to get around the specific meaning of the law. When formal penalties are meted out, they tend to be weak. In some instances, even the maximum penalties for offenses seem to be inadequate. In fact, criminal penalties are rarely pursued at all, as most white-collar and corporate illegality is handled through regulatory laws which impose fines and other sanctions on violators. Investigatory staffs of major enforcement agencies are notorious for lacking the number of persons necessary to deal with the cases that come to their attention.

White-collar criminals also have a distinct advantage in court, as they will appear as respectable citizens and gain sympathy more readily from judges and juries. Their status and legal resources give them a better chance of "beating the rap." In addition, if organizational crimes are involved, there is another advantage. In many cases where acts are committed on behalf of the organization, criminal intent will be very difficult to prove in court. Evidence will be difficult, if not impossible, to obtain in such cases; and when it is gathered, the exact location of responsibility for wrongdoing may be impossible to ascertain. The size and complexity of large corporations make the tracing of criminal responsibility to particular individuals extremely difficult to accomplish. Persons at top management levels can deny any knowledge of wrongdoing at lower levels of the corporation, and may even intentionally remain ignorant of the exact activities occurring there to avoid possible criminal prosecution.

There are distinct disadvantages to attempting to control and punish white-collar crime through "conventional" enforcement techniques. Even so, it is generally perceived that white-collar criminals may be among the most deterrable types of offenders. Chambliss (1967) has noted that in the case of white-collar crime, two major conditions are present that increase the likelihood of deterring such crimes. First, most white-collar criminals are not committed to crime as a way of life, which could make them more wary of legal threats. Second, their acts are rational, or "instrumental," rather than "expressive," or compulsive in nature. They may also be more amenable to changing their behavior if they know of the possible negative consequences for violating the law because they have much more to lose than do lower-class offenders. Even informal sanctions for them can result in the loss of income, status, respectability, and their families. It has also been suggested by Braithwaite and Geis (1982) that not only deterrence, but rehabilitation and incapacitation would be effective in dealing with white-collar crime. They argue that incapacitation could be achieved through the removal of professional licenses or preventing a company from producing certain goods, rather than by imprisonment. Rehabilitation would not take place in conventional ways either. As Braithwaite notes: "State imposed rearrangements of criminogenic organizational structures are easier to effect than state-imposed rearrangements of individual psyches" (1985: 16). For such responses to be effective in the vast majority of white-collar crimes, however, one must assume that criminal guilt can be proved—a matter extraordinarily difficult to accomplish. For this reason, other researchers have argued for the study of compliance systems, which involve the use of regulatory processes, rather than use of the criminal law for controlling white-collar crimes (DiMento, 1986).

Recent research suggests that another way to effectively control white-collar crime, especially corporate offenses, involves the use of adverse publicity. In a pathbreaking study of the impact of publicity on corporate crime involving major corporations, Fisse and Braithwaite found that "many of the companies introduced substantial reforms in the wake of their adverse publicity crisis" (1983: 227). Corporations may indeed be very sensitive to their depictions in the mass media, as stories affect not only their image

to stockholders, but to the consuming public as well. The researchers also found that the financial setbacks due to adverse publicity were only minor, and were due to legal costs in fighting allegations of wrongdoing and losses in short-term earnings. In all cases they studied, however, they found that adverse publicity about their cases led the corporations to make internal reforms to guard against the future occurrence of wrongdoing. Just as corporate advertising is important for establishing and maintaining a good reputation as well as corporate prestige, so is the avoidance of publicity that could destroy such an image. For this reason corporations seem to be particularly sensitive to negative media portrayals about offenses or alleged wrongdoing.

Recent studies of the sentencing of white-collar criminals have reached the rather surprising finding that white-collar offenders may not be treated more leniently by the courts. In one study, Hagan and his colleagues (1980) found that college-educated defendants were not sentenced more leniently than their less-educated counterparts. Of the cases they examined, however, only 4.7 percent involved college-educated persons convicted of white-collar crimes. Almost 75 percent of their cases were common crimes committed by those with less than a college education. Besides reflecting enforcement priorities, their data most likely do not mirror the true nature and degree of white-collar crime. It is possible that because so few white-collar offenders ever reach the stage of formal sentencing in the criminal justice process that those who do are not sentenced less severely. Another study conducted by Wheeler and his colleagues (1982) found that there was actually a positive relationship between socioeconomic status and sentence severity. In other words, the higher the status of defendants, the more likely it was that they received prison sentences. This appears to contradict Sutherland's (1949) notion about the advantages that a white-collar offender brings to bear on the criminal process. Of course, things may have changed since Sutherland's time as far as the perception of such offenders. Another explanation, mentioned by Wheeler and his associates, is that the effects of status may be involved earlier in the criminal process, where "the really big fish are siphoned off and only the losers—those without smarts or smart attorneys"—are sentenced to prison (Wheeler et al., 1982). The authors are not persuaded by this argument, however, and instead interpret their results as indicating that judges have cracked down on white-collar offenders. There are many remaining questions regarding the sentencing of white-collar offenders.

In a recent critique of these sentencing studies, Geis has noted: "It may be that for persons of notably high social status the evidence has to be overwhelming regarding their guilt before they will be prosecuted: That evidence may then trigger the tougher sentences. Judges also may take advantage of the opportunity in such cases to impose high penalties in order to try to frighten and deter others, who they regard as generally beyond the law's reach. . . . It is clear that the last word on white-collar crime sentencing has not yet been written. Studies are required which scrutinize official actions from the earliest stage of processing through the court proceeding, and which differentiate for particular offenses" (1984: 151).

CONCLUSION

Sutherland's intent in devising the concept and studying the phenomenon of white-collar crime was to reform criminology. White-collar crime fails to meet the stereotyped notion of a traditional crime, the classic crime of violence, crime in the streets. The profession of criminology had mentally and conceptually excluded from examination an entire universe of illegal actions. Even today, however, the overwhelming bulk of sociological work on crime deals with crimes of the poor, the powerless, the uneducated. Crimes committed by the more powerful do not find their way into the *Uniform Crime Reports* issued by the FBI. They attract relatively little sociological notice or study. The doings of the powerful—whether they be legal or illegal—tend to be immune from sociological study. The powerful have more resources to keep sociological scrutiny deflected from their activities. Otherwise a great deal of incriminating information could be gathered. No sociologists or criminologists are present when the directors of large corporations make major decisions. Criminologists do not have access to the secret files of corporate executives. The white-collar criminal is protected from outside scrutiny. The sociologist can gain access to the doings of drug dealers and junkies, prostitutes and pimps, burglars and armed robbers, convicts, even members of organized crime families, but not to those of upper-level corporate executives. It is by and large only as a result of accident that we discover the workings of white-collar criminal activity. Clearly it is to the advantage of the powerful to avoid close scrutiny. And they command the most formidable resources to make sure that precisely this takes place.

CHAPTER
13

Mental Disorder

We all know someone who seems odd, eccentric, who acts strangely, in a bizarre or totally inappropriate fashion. A stroll down many streets in the nation's largest cities will reveal men and women who look disheveled and who scream or mutter incomprehensible phrases at no one in particular. Some people are so fearful of lurking, unmentionable forces that they are literally incapable of walking out of their front door. Others are unable to hold a conversation that anyone else would regard as intelligible. Still others are so depressed they lie curled up in a fetal position for hours or days—or even weeks, or more—on end. Some make it a point to be abusive and offensive to practically everyone they know, insulting them, physically striking them, engaging in actions seemingly designed to shock, hurt, or outrage them at every opportunity. Individuals we may have read about hear voices from another planet commanding them to kill, to

become dictator of the world, or to deliver an urgent message to the residents of the Western hemisphere. And some people seem to wear a perpetual, peculiar smile and to exist in "their own little world."

We refer to such individuals in our everyday language. "He's whacko," we say. "She's out of her mind," "he's a nut," "she's completely cracked," "he's a weirdo," or "she's a sicko," we say, pointing to individuals who display what we regard as manifestations of a mind that's "not right." Experts refer to the phenomenon as *mental illness* or *mental disorder*.[1]

What is mental illness? In what ways can

---

[1]At this point, I do not want to distinguish between "mental illness" and "mental disorder"; I'll use the two terms more or less synonymously. The section on "Models of Mental Disorder" will clarify how the term "mental illness" is used in some quarters.

a mind be said to be "ill"? What is a mental "disorder"? How can a mind be said to be "disordered"? And is mental disorder an instance of deviant behavior? If so, in what specific ways?

WHAT IS MENTAL DISORDER?

Defining mental disorder or illness is not as easy or as straightforward a task as might appear at first. Even defining the deviant behavior we examined earlier that expressed itself in specific actions (such as homicide, homosexuality, and drug use) proved to be a thorny matter. Mental disorder presents much more formidable definitional problems because it cannot be pinned down to any single set or type of behavior, in most cases. Rather, mental disorder is a condition exhibiting itself in a wide range of behaviors. Consequently, no general definition of mental disorder can be completely satisfactory. However, tied to any such definition would have to be the twin notions of health and illness. Mental disorder is usually regarded as a pathological state, much like an illness, that is universally and intrinsically undesirable. In contrast, mental health represents adequate and optimal functioning.

Can we find a definition of mental disorder by beginning with defining mental health? Some observers have attempted to argue that mental health requires *a correct perception of reality*. Yet many cultures hold empirically incorrect notions of true and false (including our own); simply by being a member of a given society, one automatically learns things that are "incorrect" (Gallagher, 1980: 24). Does that mean that these individuals are mentally "disordered"? Another criterion that has been suggested for mental health is *one's adjustment to the social environment in which one lives*. Again, many social environments are unhealthy and destructive; can we say that adjustment to the political situation existing in Nazi Germany or to racism in many parts of the world represents mental health? Defining mental health generally and universally is perilous in part because it requires reference to a social con-

text—which may be regarded by many observers as unhealthy.

A number of attempts have been made to define the opposite side of the coin, mental disorder. The American Psychiatric Association's standard reference work, the *Diagnostic and Statistical Manual of Mental Disorders*, first issued in 1952 (referred to as *DSM-I*), and thoroughly revised in 1968 (*DSM-II*), and again in 1980 (*DSM-III*), then partially revised in 1987 (*DSM-III-R*), does not define mental disorder generally. Rather, *each specific disorder* spelled out is seen as a "clinically significant behavioral or psychological syndrome or pattern that occurs in a person and that is associated with present distress (a painful symptom) or disability (impairment in one or more important areas of functioning) or with a significantly increased risk of suffering death, pain, disability, or an important loss of freedom" (APA, 1987: xxii). Moreover, this pattern or syndrome cannot be a reasonable response to the stress of an immediate and particular situation, but a manifestation of an underlying "behavioral, psychological, or biological dysfunction" in the person. And lastly, mere deviance—that is, conflicts between the individual and the society in which he or she lives—do qualify as manifestations of a mental disorder unless they are a symptom of the dysfunctions described above.

Rather than offering a general definition of mental disorder, then, *DSM-III* and *DSM-III-R* spell out a taxonomy or classification of many types or categories of disorders. They include:

1. Developmental disorders (such as mental retardation and autism);
2. Organic disorders (such as senility and Alzheimer's disease);
3. Psychoactive substance-induced organic mental disorders (such as delirium tremens and hallucinations);
4. Psychoactive substance use disorders (such as alcoholism or drug dependence);
5. Schizophrenia;
6. Paranoia (an irrational and unrealistic belief that one is the target of persecution);

7. Mood disorders (such as depression and manic depression);

8. Anxiety disorders (such as phobias or an irrational fear of something specific);

9. Somatoform disorders (such as hypochondriasis or an unrealistic, irrational, and excessive belief that one is physically ill when one is perfectly healthy);

10. Disassociative disorders (having a multiple personality and feeling disassociated with or cut off from one's surroundings);

11. Sexual disorders (exhibitionism, fetishism, sexual sadism and masochism, voyeurism, and pedophilia, or the sexual love of children);

12. Impulse control disorders (such as kleptomania, a compulsive need to steal, and pyromania, the compulsion to set things on fire).

As we can see, *DSM-III-R* has a grab-bag, descriptive quality to it. It represents a listing and a description of a wide range of clinically agreed-upon disorders, but it has no internal logic, and it is atheoretical; that is, it sidesteps the issue of etiology or causality—what it is that generates these disorders or what generates mental disorder in general. Although not without their critics (Vaillant, 1984), *DSM-III* and *DSM-III-R* are regarded as substantial improvements over the predecessors and are accepted as standard reference works in the classification of mental disorders.

Most of us recognize there are *degrees* of mental disorder. This dimension is commonsensically captured in the distinction between neurosis and psychosis. Most people think of the neurosis as a less serious version of the psychosis. We tend to call someone whose behavior seems somewhat eccentric, excessive, compulsive, or unacceptable a "neurotic." Neuroses often entail anxiety that, from a "rational" point of view, is excessive, even needless. (This is why tranquilizers such as Valium are effective against such disorders, because they depress anxiety.) Other neuroses entail a compulsion—a ritualistic action that is repeated without apparent aim, for instance, washing away germs that no longer exist. To the man and woman in the street, neurotics cover a wide range of

unusual and annoying behavior. Someone who has to take six showers a day, is excessively tight with money, has an overwhelming fear of spiders, is compulsively neat and tidy, can't go outside without swallowing a Valium, feels the need to insult or demean others, or breaks out in a rash upon taking multiple-choice exams would probably be referred to as a neurotic by most of us. Nonetheless, neurotics can function in most areas of life; psychotics very rarely function in any area of life. Nonetheless, we tend to reserve the concept of the psychosis for those cases that are considerably more serious, and vastly less common, than the neurosis. The psychotic's condition, unlike the neurotic's, is almost always a barrier to academic and occupational achievement and social relationships, including marriage and the family. Although the outbreak of a psychosis is frequently grounds for institutionalization in a mental hospital, that of a neurosis almost never is. *DSM-III-R* does not mention psychosis or the psychotic and reserves the term "neurosis" only for a fairly narrow set of disorders, the anxiety disorders. Still, the neurosis-psychosis distinction tends to capture most laypeople's thinking about the dimensional quality of mental disorders.

There is no assumption among experts that mental disorders can be sharply and cleanly separated from the condition of mental health; mental disorder is not a "discrete entity with sharp boundaries (discontinuity) between it and other mental disorders, or between it and no mental disorder" (APA, 1987: xxii). In reality, experts argue, extreme or "textbook" cases can be detected by using diagnostic tools such as the *Diagnostic and Statistical Manual of Mental Disorders*. One observer criticizes "the idea that if it is difficult to make a distinction between two neighboring points on a hypothetical continuum, no valid distinctions can thereafter be made even at the extremes of the continuum. There are thus persons who would argue that the existence of several variations of gray precludes a distinction between black and white." This reasoning is invalid, it has been argued. "While I will agree that some patients in mental hospitals are saner than nonpatients, and that it is sometimes hard to distinguish between deep unhappiness and psychotic depression, I do *not* agree that the difficulty sometimes encountered in making the distinction between normal and abnormal necessarily invalidates all such distinctions" (Rimland, 1969: 716–717). In short, many feel "the fact that some distinctions are difficult to make, such as deciding whether sundown is day or night, does not mean that it is impossible to distinguish between noon and midnight" (Davison and Neale, 1986: 61).

Not all mental disorders are equally likely to result in treatment, hospitalization, or psychiatric intervention of any kind. Intervention typically takes place only when individuals are troublesome to others or present an immediate threat to their own lives—a theme we'll expand on shortly. Of all admissions to public mental hospitals, roughly one-third are diagnosed as schizophrenic; of all mental hospital residents at a given time, a shade less than half are diagnosed as schizophrenic (Cockerham, 1981: 142–143). Admittedly, psychiatrists tend to be free and easy with the schizophrenic diagnosis; yet, it seems clear that schizophrenia is the most common mental disorder that is widely felt to require serious treatment and hospitalization. (Many of the disorders listed in *DSM-III* and *DSM-III-R* are not regarded as grounds for treatment, such as dependence on tobacco—unless the individual seeks it out.) The key defining characteristic of schizophrenia is a "split" or a withdrawal from reality and the substitution of delusion and hallucination. Schizophrenia is frequently accompanied by distorted and incoherent language. Schizophrenics frequently believe themselves to be the victims of overwhelming powerful external forces over which they have no control, whose commands they must obey without question. For instance, they may hear voices commanding them to engage in behavior that others find bizarre, eccentric, disturbing, or dangerous.

There is growing agreement that genetic and hormonal factors play a major role in mental disorders generally and a number of specific disorders as well, such as manic-depression (Schmeck, 1987; Egeland et al., 1987); obsessive-compulsive disorders (Schmeck, 1988b); psychopathy, or the absence of a conscience (Goleman, 1987); and schizophrenia (Schmeck, 1988c). One international research team (Gurling at al., 1988) claims to have located an abnormally functioning gene or cluster of genes in common in their schizophrenic subjects that is absent in normal subjects. At the same time, experts warn, schizophrenia may be "a collection of distinct diseases" with diverse genetic roots, not under the control of any single genetic cluster. Mental illness generally, and schizophrenia specifically, may very well be the product of a combination of a genetic predisposition and environmental experiences; stressful events may "kindle" or "trigger" an outbreak in an individual who is biologically predisposed (Schmeck, 1988a; Weiner, 1975). Still, the exact etiology of schizophrenia remains unidentified. Most likely, the cause is exceedingly complex and "possibly involves some combination of genetic, biochemical, and sociocultural factors" (Cockerham, 1981: 147).

MODELS OF MENTAL DISORDER

In 1722, John Hu, a Chinese convert to Christianity, accompanied a Jesuit missionary to France; only two Chinese before him had ever visited that country. By European standards, Hu behaved oddly. During his first ride in a coach, he jumped from the moving vehicle, rushed over to some blackberry bushes, and gorged himself on the fruit. Acquiring a fine, coffee-colored suit, he promptly gave it to a beggar. And once, he marched through the streets of Paris, banging on a drum and waving a flag with the message "Men and women should be kept in their separate spheres" written on it in Chinese. After too many such incidents, the French authorities committed Hu to an insane asylum outside of Paris, where he remained for more than two years (Spence, 1988).

Hu's unfortunate encounter with European society serves to illuminate how the various perspectives toward mental illness examine the phenomenon. There are at least two major models of mental disorder in sociology: the *labeling* and the *medical* models, each with its "hard" and "soft" variants.

The labeling model would say that Hu was regarded by the French as mentally ill not because there was anything "sick" or pathological about his mind, but because what was regarded as inappropriate behavior in France was acceptable behavior in China. Definitions of mental disorder, the "soft" labeling model would argue, are culture-bound; what is called crazy in one society or social context may be seen as perfectly normal in another. Hu's behavior was regarded as a sign of mental illness simply because the French expected the man to act the way the French acted; when he acted quite differently, he was labeled crazy. The "hard" labeling or interactionist approach would take this argument a step further and argue that, to the extent Hu understood and took seriously the definition the French applied to him and his behavior, he probably *went* crazy as a result of being so labeled.

The positivistic or *medical* model would interpret Hu and his behavior quite differently. An observer holding the "soft" medical model toward mental disorder would argue that the understanding of mental illness prevailing in 1722 was still extremely primitive. It was well into the twentieth century before we realized, though mental disorder does indeed have a universal core, a great deal of behavior that is acceptable in one society may not be so regarded in another. Today, "soft" medical model theorists would say, psychiatrists would not make the same mistake. The diagnosis applied to Hu was, in all likelihood, due to ignorance and error by the medical establishment at that time.

A theorist adopting a "hard" positivistic or medical approach would argue that, since the rules for classifying people as mentally ill or normal are fairly universal, the chances are, Hu *really was crazy in the first place*. It didn't matter that he was only one of three Chinese who had ever been to France by that time; it didn't matter that the French were

unacquainted with the rules of proper Chinese conduct, or that Hu was unacquainted with the rules of proper French conduct. The behavior that caused the French to hospitalize Hu would have caused him to be regarded as mentally disordered everywhere, including China; culture had nothing to do with it. Labeling mental illness is uninteresting, nonproblematic, more or less straightforward, and unworthy of sociological investigation. What matters is the objective fact of someone's mental disorder, not how he or she is regarded by others. The labeling process that resulted in Hu's hospitalization was generated not by cultural differences between the French and the Chinese, but by the objective facts of his disorder.

The Medical Model

The most basic assumption of the medical model is that mental disorder is very much like a medical disease. This model assumes there are no essential differences between physical and mental illness; a disease of the mind can be likened to a disease of the body. The key to the medical model is that the bizarre, unusual, and inappropriate behavior exhibited by individuals who are mentally disordered are symptoms or manifestations of underlying internal pathology of some sort.

The "hard" or strict medical model argues that mental illness is always a manifestation of abnormal biophysical functioning—brain damage, a chemical imbalance, pathological genes, neurological malfunction, and so on. This school or model suggests environmental factors—such as stress, early childhood experiences, and so on—have little etiological significance; at most, they act as "triggering" mechanisms that exacerbate an already established predilection for mental illness. Consequently, any legitimate and effective form of therapy for psychic disorder must be physical in nature—such as drugs, or psychopharmacology, electroshock therapy (EST), and psychosurgery (prefrontal lobotomy).

The "hard" medical model seems to be gaining adherents in recent years, although some forms of strictly medical intervention are employed less now than in the past (such as psychosurgery). On the other hand, psychopharmacology is used much more frequently in treatment today than previously, as we'll see shortly.

The "soft" or less extreme medical model agrees that mental disorder is a disease in much the same way as physical diseases are. However, for this model, seeing mental disorder as a disease is taken as a metaphor rather than as a literal, concrete reality, as the adherents of the "hard" medical model believe. This means a mental illness need not have a pathological biophysical correspondence; a mentally ill person may have nothing physically wrong, yet still have a disordered mind. Mental illness, according to the "soft" medical model, is caused by a variety of factors, not the least of which are those that are psychological and social in nature and origin. The psychoanalytic school, founded by Sigmund Freud, is one major representative of this model.

Psychoanalysts believe early childhood experiences, particularly an inability to resolve the tension created by certain instinct-like drives at specific stages in one's life, lead to specific neuroses and psychoses. The psychoanalytic school has been declining in influence in psychiatry in recent years; one critic dubbed psychoanalytic theory "the most stupendous intellectual confidence trick of the 20th century" (Medawar, 1982). Other researchers argue that mental illness can be caused by a life of extremely *stressful* situations and experiences (Cockerham, 1981: 104–117).

The Labeling Model

An alternative to the medical model arose in the 1960s; it emerged from within psychiatry itself (Szasz, 1960, 1961; Laing, 1967), from psychology (Ullman and Krasner, 1969), and from sociology (Scheff, 1966; Goffman, 1961). It has come to be called the societal reaction or *labeling* model. As does the medical model, the labeling model has its "hard" and "soft" variants. The key to the labeling model is that mental disorder is a designation for a state of mind that presumably produces behavior that is an adaptation to the individual's social environment, behavior many others find troublesome, incomprehensible, or bizarre. Mental disorder can be studied, these researchers and theorists believe, without reference to disease, illness, or pathology. Mental disorder is not an objective condition, existing in a state of nature that the health practitioner has only to "discover," but a subjective judgment or inference made as a result of many factors, some of them having nothing to do with a patient's mental state. They argue that "the diagnosis, categorization, and labeling of mental illness are themselves profoundly social acts and that other social factors besides the behavior itself affect the informal and formal processes whereby persons are judged to have a mental pathology" (Akers, 1977: 312; 1985: 314).

One observer argued that mental patients suffer not from mental illness, but from *contingencies*. Whether someone becomes a patient in a mental hospital depends as much on the individual's social and economic status, the visibility of the offense committed, his or her proximity to a mental hospital, the available treatment facilities, and so on (Goffman, 1961: 134–135). In sum then, the labeling model argues that: (1) mental disorder is not a disease; (2) "being" mentally ill is the consequence of a judgment based on social values and not a condition of "having" an illness; and (3) this judgment is made as much on extrapsychiatric factors as on the individual's mental condition. To the adherents of the labeling model, the study of mental disorder is a truly sociological enterprise, since mental illness designations are based on sociological factors. The medical model, in contrast, sees no real place for the sociologist of mental disorder. Mental illness does vary by sociological factors or variables, according to the medical model, but this is because different social categories "get" mental illness at varying rates; it is not a consequence of social judgments being made. To the medical model, these judgments are made "objectively," independent of social characteristics.

The "hard" labeling model is associated with the name of Thomas Scheff; it represents research conducted over two decades ago and is largely summarized in a single volume (1966; revised, 1984). The medical model, in contrast, in both its "hard" and "soft" variants, is represented by some hundreds of thousands of publications and uncounted ongoing research projects. Among psychiatrists and other mental health experts, the "hard" labeling model is nearly entirely ignored; it is of consequence almost exclusively among sociologists and a small circle of psychologists.

Scheff distinguishes between *residual rule breaking* and mental illness. Residual rule breaking constitutes activities, feelings, or experiences that (1) entail a violation of social norms; (2) do not fall within a specific categorical realm (such as crime, drunkenness, sexual "perversion," and so on), for which society has no specific, explicit label; and (3) make up behavior that could lead to being labeled as mentally ill. In other words, by "acting weird" (residual rule breaking), one could be regarded by others as "crazy." With respect to residual rule breaking, Scheff argues, first, *it has many sources or causes*—temporary stress, deprivation of food or sleep, drug ingestion, and so on. Second, *many individuals engage in residual rule breaking;* however, *very few are categorized as crazy,* either informally, by others they know, or formally, by the psychiatric profession. There are more individuals in the general population, Scheff argues, who engage in residual rule breaking without being labeled than those who are designated as mentally ill. In other words, the rule breaking of most of us is unrecognized, ignored, or rationalized. Third, *most rule breaking is denied and is of transitory significance.* In other words, for the most part, if people don't make a big deal out of someone acting weird, eventually, the behavior will go away (1966: 40–51).

Yet there are some individuals who do have a *mentally ill "career."* That is, they continue to act "weird"; acting crazy does not go away. How are they different from the rest of us? Scheff's fourth point about labeling and mental illness is that *stereotyped imagery of mental disorder is learned in early childhood;* it is, fifth, *continually reaffirmed in ordinary social interaction.* In other words, we all learn and know what a crazy person is and does; it is part of our cultural tradition. Sixth, someone who is labeled as a mentally ill person—for whatever reason—*will be rewarded for playing that role* and, seventh, *punished if he or she attempts to return to normalcy or conventional behavior.* Eighth, in a crisis, when someone who engages in residual rule breaking is publicly labeled as a crazy person, *he or she is highly suggestible* and may accept the preferred role of being insane. In fact, Scheff argues, ninth, among residual rule breakers, *being labeled as mentally ill is the single most important cause of having a "career" in residual deviance.* In other words, if others (friends, relatives, the general public, psychiatrists, psychologists) call one crazy, one will continue to act crazy, and this label will intensify one's commitment to crazy behavior and a crazy role (1966: 64–93).

Gove (1975a, 1975b, 1979a, 1980, 1982a, 1982b) adopting the medical model, argues that the labeling theory of mental illness is empirically wrong in each and every particular. First, Gove's medical model argues, mental patients are unable to function in the real world not because they have been stigmatized, but because they are mentally ill; they have a debilitating disease that cripples their capacity to function normally. Second, the process by which psychiatric professionals single out someone as mentally ill is not significantly influenced by sociological or other extrapsychiatric variables, but is almost exclusively a result of the nature and seriousness of the illness itself. Labeling, the medical model argues, is neither capricious nor arbitrary. Individuals who are sick tend to be labeled as such; in turn, those who are well are extremely unlikely to be labeled as sick.

Third, with respect to *informal* (as opposed to professional) labeling, far from being eager to label someone as mentally ill, the general public is reluctant to do so, and moreover, does not hold particularly strong or particularly negative feelings about the mentally ill. This is true especially for intimates—spouses, children, parents, close friends—of the mentally ill, who avoid labeling until the disturbed individual's behavior becomes intolerable. And fourth, hospitalization and other treatment intervention, far from making the patient's condition worse, as the labeling approach claims, typically results in an amelioration of his or her symptoms. In short, a genuine healing process does seem to take place. Gove, the most outspoken and persistent of the critics of labeling theory of mental illness, claims these generalizations are so well founded empirically that he states flatly: "For all practical purposes, the labeling explanation of mental illness is of historical interest only" (1979a: 301).

Which model is right? Which one approximates empirical reality most closely? To begin, we need not be forced into the either-or, black-or-white position that Gove and the more extreme critics of labeling argue from. It is possible there is some middle ground here; labeling theory may be correct on some points, and its critics may be right with respect to some others (Cockerham, 1981: 70). In fact, what now seems clear is that a "soft" or *modified* labeling theory approach fits the facts of mental illness and mental illness labeling most faithfully (Link et al., 1989). The modified or soft labeling approach would accept certain aspects of the medical model without denying the importance of the labeling process.

First, mentally disordered individuals, while they do have difficulty in their everyday lives because of their psychiatric condition, also suffer serious debilitation and demoralization as a consequence of stigma and labeling. Everyone growing up in this society, including the disordered, is aware of the negative image of the mentally ill. Individuals who suffer from a mental disorder anticipate negative treatment from others, and these beliefs taint their interaction with "normals" and with mental health professionals (Thoits, 1985; Link, 1987; Link et al., 1989). Often, the expectations others have of

the disordered individuals' behavior will actually call forth the very behavior than confirms those expectations (Link and Cullen, 1989; Jones, 1986).

Second, although the nature and the seriousness of the illness are clearly related to labeling, the labeling process, both psychiatric and informal, is strongly influenced by extrapsychiatric factors. Two such factors are the emotional relationship and the cultural distance between the rule breaker and the potential labeler. One study (Simon and Zusman, 1983) looked at a legal case involving the victims of a flood who were suing a coal company that was responsible for creating the conditions that made it possible for the flood to ravage the community. The plaintiffs claimed "psychic damages" as one of the consequences of the flood; the defendants, representatives of the coal company, argued that the flood had no such impact on its victims. Two sets of psychiatrists, one set hired by the defense, and the other, by the plaintiffs, examined 42 flood victims. Not surprisingly, the defense's psychiatrists found little evidence of psychopathology, while the plaintiff's psychiatrists found considerable such evidence. If psychiatric diagnosis were the exact science the medical model argues it is, no such extreme discrepancies would be possible.

The strong or "hard" labeling position is clearly wrong, and the medical model clearly right when it come to the treatment outcome. Enough studies have been conducted on treatment outcomes to demonstrate that psychiatric intervention is more likely to be beneficial to the mental patient than harmful. Far from entrenching the mental patient more deeply in the mentally ill role, treatment tends to have some positive effects (Smith et al., 1980; Landman and Dawes, 1982). Some of these effects are not profound, and many do not persist over time; nonetheless, "it would be difficult for societal reaction theorists to argue that the effects of [psychiatric] labels are uniformly negative" (Link and Cullen, 1989). Not only does psychiatric intervention often move the patient out of, rather than more deeply into, disordered behavior, but also, undetected, untreated mentally disordered conditions often persist over long periods of time (Fischer et al., 1979), refuting "the labeling theory notion that symptoms are transient in the absence of labeling" (Link and Cullen, 1989).

In short, although it is difficult to deny the impact of the objective nature of mental disorder, at the same time, stigma, labeling, and societal reaction remain potent and crucial sociological factors to be taken into account in influencing the condition of the mentally disordered. Attempting to prove or disprove the labeling or the medical model *in toto* appears to be a silly and futile exercise. More refined and specific attempts to test these models will find that both have a great deal to offer (Link and Cullen, 1989).

The "soft" labeling model does not follow Scheff on the etiology of a mental illness career or on the consequences of labeling. Labeling theory is not and never was intended to be an "explanation" of deviance, in the sense of accounting for its origin (Becker, 1973: 178–179). Nor did it insist that the process of labeling always and inevitably results in an intensification of a commitment to deviance, the deviant role, or deviant behavior; this is an empirical question and must be studied in individual cases (Becker, 1963: 34–35; 1973: 179; Lemert, 1951: 63–64). However, regardless of the etiology of the behavior or the characteristic in question, and even independent of the consequences of labeling, the sociologist is obliged to study *the social organization of the labeling process*. That is, *what reactions do one's actions touch off in others?* In other words, to understand deviance, including mental illness, it is necessary to understand reactions to it. Regardless of its impact, it is a sociological phenomenon unto itself in need of study.

The importance of this line of thinking can be seen in several other forms of deviance. One critic of labeling theory insists the labeling process does not generate homosexual behavior or homosexual desires; consequently, he argues, the perspective is inadequate and must be discarded (Whitam, 1977). Aside from the fact that no one has ever asserted that labeling accounts for homosexuality, there remains the question of the social organization of the condemnation of homosexuality, an entirely separate question, one that the labeling perspective takes center stage in exploring. Likewise, many experts now believe biological factors are crucial in the etiology of obesity (Bennett and Gurin, 1982; Polivy and Herman, 1983; Kolata, 1989). Yet, independent of why people become fat is the matter of *the stigma of obesity* (Cahnman, 1968): the rejection and ostracism that fat people face at the hands of the general society. Etiology cannot be said to *subsume* societal reaction (Goode, 1981b: 79). Once a phenomenon such as acting crazy, engaging in homosexual behavior, or becoming obese arises, *What is made of it by others?* How do others react to it? What other factors influence or mitigate this judgment or reaction aside from the visible behavior or characteristic?

This concern was expressed decades ago by Edwin Lemert, who stated, "One of the more important sociological questions here is not what causes human beings to develop such symptoms as hallucinations and delusions, but, instead, what is it about their behavior which leads the community to reject them, segregate them, and otherwise treat them as . . . insane." Such a question leads to its corollary: investigating "the functions of such rejections and concomitant societal definitions in the dynamics of mental deviation itself" (1951: 387–388).

Thus, the "soft" labeling model is more likely to concern itself with the question of the dynamics of mental illness labeling than with the etiology of etiological issues. That is, What factors are related to being labeled as mentally ill? Is it a psychiatric condition alone? Or do extrapsychiatric factors play a role in this process? And how prominent is this role? The medical or psychiatric model would hold that psychiatric diagnoses (although not necessarily public labels) are an accurate reflection of the individual's "objective" condition.[2]

"Soft" labeling theorists insist this process of mental illness labeling is considerably less rational than the medical model holds, that factors other than severity of psychiatric symptoms influence the decision to admit and discharge patients. This process is guided by contingencies, they argue: A number of factors, forces, and variables influence how and why someone is labeled as mentally ill aside from the individual's "objective" psychiatric condition. There is, in other words, "a clear tendency for admission and discharge of mental patients to be related more to social than to psychiatric variables" (Krohn and Akers, 1977: 341).[3] It has been found that sociocultural factors, such as family desires and living arrangements, institutional resources and requirements, adequate patient resources outside the mental hospital, cultural conceptions, region of the country, and the danger the patient presents to others, can be determinants of psychiatric case outcomes (Townsend, 1978, 1980; Krohn and Akers, 1977). Other studies suggest voluntary versus involuntary patient status plays a role in discharge. It is also possible men are more successful pursuing petitions of incompetency against women than vice versa, and married petitioners are more successful against the unmarrieds.

One supporter of the medical model, Gove (1975a), argues that the mentally ill place their families "in an intolerable situation," often creating havoc in their lives. Indeed, it can be said that creating problems for others is a variable that influences mental illness labeling—but it is not, by itself, a psychiatric variable; it must be regarded as yet another labeling contingency. Holding psychiatric conditions constant, the greater the problems the mentally disordered individual creates for others, the greater the likelihood of being labeled as mentally ill and the greater the likelihood of being institutionalized and treated. It is possible for severely disordered individuals to create very little in the way of problems, trouble, or chaos in the lives of others; at the same time, mildly disordered individuals can create a great deal. Being "troublesome" is a factor that is likely to precipitate a disordered individual into the arms of the official psychiatric machinery, leading to mental illness labeling—yet it is a sociological, not a psychiatric, variable (Lemert, 1976: 245; Goffman, 1971: 356ff).

The influence of extrapsychiatric factors is in large part due to the vagueness of psychiatric diagnosis. Although more precise and reliable today than in the past, diagnoses of mental disorder are considerably less so than are strictly medical diagnoses. It is clear that agreement among psychiatrists as to patients' condition is high only when they present "classic" or "archetypical" symptoms of certain mental disorders. However, agreement is low among patients who present symptoms that are less clear-cut and more ambiguous. In fact, the majority of cases psychiatrists see are less classic and more ambiguous in their symptomology (Townsend, 1980: 270–272). A summary of the reliability of psychiatric diagnoses found it to be high only when the categories were extremely broad or the symptoms extreme and clear-cut; where the categories were specific and detailed or the symptoms less than clear-cut, disagreement between and among psychiatrists was high (Edgerton, 1969: 68–69). Two commentators conclude that "art far outweighs science" in psychiatric judgments (Stoller and Geertsma, 1963: 65). An

---

[2]The opposite point of view, that people are singled out randomly and capriciously with respect to mental condition and labeled as mentally ill, seems to be held by practically no one, in spite of some observers' claims. One critic (Gove, 1975a: 246) asserts, without documentation, that "a basic premise of labelling theory is that persons who are labelled do not differ markedly from each other in characteristics related to deviant behavior."

[3]But, again, these authors insist that "although psychiatric categories are vague and inconsistently diagnosed, the research does *not* show that individuals are randomly or capriciously singled out for assignment to or seek out the mental illness role" (1977: 357).

author of a textbook on psychiatric methodology states that expert judgments on mental disorder "are of a social, cultural, economic and sometimes legal nature" (Loftus, 1960: 13).

In one study (Kendall et al., 1971), videotapes of diagnostic interviews with patients were shown to a large number of psychiatrists in the United States and Great Britain. Those patients presenting "classic, textbook" symptoms generated almost unanimous agreement as to psychiatric condition. However, some patients manifesting less clear-cut symptoms touched off less than unanimity in diagnosis. One patient was deemed schizophrenic by 85 percent of the American psychiatrists, but only 7 percent of the British; another was judged to be schizophrenic by 69 percent of the Americans, but 2 percent of the British. Clearly, the American conception of schizophrenia is much broader than is the British. It is difficult to imagine such a disparity in the diagnosis of a strictly medical disease, such as cancer or tuberculosis.

Much the same labeling process can be found to take place if we examine mental disorder around the world. Cross-culturally, certain terms or labels are applied everywhere to individuals "who are thought to be conducting themselves in a manner that is inappropriate, abnormal, or unreasonable for persons in that culture who occupy a similar social position; that is, to persons who can provide no otherwise acceptable explanation for their conduct" (Edgerton, 1969: 50). Every culture has a label that indicates some version of mental disorder or illness. How are these labels applied? A summary of the available anthropological literature indicates two conclusions. First, the recognition and labeling of individuals "who are both severely and chronically psychotic" typically occurs with a high degree of consensus "because persons such as these are typically so dramatically, and enduringly, far beyond the pale of everyday rationality" (Edgerton, 1969: 51). And, second, most people who act strangely or "crazily" do not do so in an extreme and chronic fashion; consequently, be-

ing labeled, for these individuals, is a complex and problematic matter—influenced by a wide range of contingencies. As to whether someone is or is not regarded socially and publicly as psychotic is open to *negotiation* (Edgerton, 1969: 51, 65)—that is, decided in a give-and-take interaction between several parties on the basis of factors unrelated to objective psychiatric condition.

DEVIANCE AND MEDICALIZATION

Not only are certain *individuals* more likely to be declared as mentally ill both by the psychiatric profession and the general public, but, in addition, certain *activities* (and consequently those who practice them) are more likely to be seen as a sign of mental illness than others are, other things being equal. As a general rule, the more deviant an activity is, the greater the likelihood that it will be medicalized, especially in Western society. While there should be no a priori reason to anticipate an special relationship between the amount of public scorn directed at an activity and the degree of mental disorder that supposedly produces it, we do find each activity discussed in this book—from marijuana use to criminal homicide—explained in many quarters by invoking some form of psychic abnormality. In short, *deviant behavior becomes medicalized;* from the very fact of its deviance alone, it is likely to become a problem for the psychiatric and medical profession and to be designated as "sick" rather than merely "bad" (Conrad and Schneider; 1980: 17–18).

Not only is there a tendency within the profession toward a medical and psychiatric definition of deviance as illness, but this, in turn, necessitates a medical *solution* as well.

A woman rides a horse naked through the streets of Denver claiming to be Lady Godiva and after being apprehended by authorities, is taken to a psychiatric hospital and declared to be suffering from a mental illness. A well-known surgeon in a southwestern city performs a psychosurgical operation on a young man who is prone to violent outbursts. An Atlanta attorney, inclined to drinking sprees, is treated in a hospital clinic for his disease, alcoholism. A child in California brought to a pediatric clinic because of his disruptive behavior in school is labeled hyperactive and is prescribed . . . Ritalin for his disorder. A chronically overweight Chicago housewife receives a surgical intestinal bypass operation for her problem of obesity. Scientists at a New England medical center work on a million-dollar federal research grant to discover a heroin-blocking agent as a "cure" for heroin addiction. What do these situations have in common? In all instances medical solutions are being sought for a variety of deviant behaviors or conditions (Conrad and Schneider, 1980: 28).

Designating an activity as a manifestation of an illness makes a declaration of objectivity; the medical profession attempts to treat a condition because it is "sick," not simply because it is "bad." By assigning deviance to the twilight world of psychic pathology, its willful character has been neutralized. The labeled behavior has been removed from the arena of free will; its compulsive character effectively denies that it can be a viable alternative, freely chosen. An act reduced to both symptom and cause of pathology has had its claims to morality discredited. As a manifestation of an illness, it calls for "treatment," not serious debate.

Looking at all the actions of which society disapproves—"deviant" behavior—we notice that they share fundamental similarities. However, these similarities inhere not so much in the acts themselves as in the way that the members of a society respond to them. One of the more interesting of such responses is the tendency to impute psychological abnormality to the individuals who engage in them. It should be regarded as extremely significant that deviant behavior seems to have attracted explanations that activate a principle of psychological abnormality. The sociologist is forced to ask the question of what it is about American society that begets an explanation of mental disorder for drug users, alcoholics, prostitutes, homosexuals, violent men and men, as well as a host of other deviant groups and categories. The fact that each of these categories—and the activities associated with them—are condemned by the American culture society makes the nature of the process of constructing pathology interpretations of behavior at least as interesting as the "causes" of the behavior itself. (It is interesting that the least condemned of the behaviors discussed in this book, such as white-collar crime, are rarely explained by invoking a mental disorder.) In all these cases, adopting a medical approach to deviants and their behavior effectively neutralizes their moral legitimacy as well as the viability of their behavior. In this way, the constructors of such theories serve to mirror the basic values of American society (Goode, 1969: 90–91).

The medical model, in assuming the psychiatric profession simply diagnoses mental disorder in a neutral, objective, and reliable fashion, entirely misses out on an understanding of the relationship between a society's cultural values and the activities the psychiatric profession is likely to see as a manifestation of mental disorder. (The conflict perspective would also investigate a society's economic and political structure as factors in this process—factors that the medical model would also fail to investigate.) Labeling behavior is no less an extrapsychiatric process as labeling individuals. It is a process that the medical model, by its very nature, assumes is rational; in contrast, the labeling model (in both its "hard" and "soft" variants) sees it as "irrational"—that is, as *distinctly sociological.*

FAMILIES OF THE MENTALLY DISORDERED: LABELING BY INTIMATES

Deviant roles or labels very enormously according to how swiftly or slowly they are assigned to others and how skimpy or well documented the evidence must be for such an assignment to take place. Alcoholism and mental illness are similar in that they are roles or labels that are very slowly assigned to someone, and then only after a great and protracted effort at denial and the accumulation of many episodes that might point in these directions. Generally speaking, the more intimate the relationship between the potentially labeled individual and conventional others, the greater the effort to deny the condition and the greater the evidence necessary to pin a label on that individual. In short, "closeness permits one to see qualities other than the flaw" (Kreisman and Joy, 1974: 39). Still, some labels are slower to be attached than are others; perhaps of all such labels, alcoholism and mental illness require the most evidence by intimates and family members to be attached. In this sense, they might be called varieties of *conventional deviance.*

In contrast, homosexuality is swiftly assigned—to others, at any rate—and typically on skimpy evidence (Robins, 1975: 30). There is typically no overt behavior for non-deviant adults that can be labeled by anyone as homosexuality that is anything remotely like homosexuality, except homosexual behavior itself. (This is done in prisons, by street hustlers, and by bisexuals, but these scenes are already defined by conventional people as deviant.) Locker room camaraderie, homosociality, masculine competition, and *macho* efforts to demonstrate one's manhood are all kept within fairly narrow limits; they rarely resemble actual homosexual behavior to anyone except a psychoanalyst. But each individual act of same-gender sexual contact would typically be seen as a homosexual act by a nonparticipant, conventional outsider.

"Normals" typically refuse to assign a label of "mentally ill" to intimate deviant actors until their behavior has become blatantly public and onerously troublesome. Most of the people who would be regarded by a large proportion of clinicians and therapists as mentally ill are never professionally diagnosed as such. And most are also not so regarded by their peers and do not see themselves as ill. There is, in other words, a huge population of "hidden" psychotics in the population. But the more trouble a person causes others, the less power that person has and the more power the others have, the

more bizarre that person's behavior or ideas seem to others (that, within a certain cultural system), the greater the likelihood that intimate others will perceive their behavior as a manifestation of mental illness. The more visible a person's behavior is, the greater is this likelihood. The greater the harm done to others, the greater this likelihood is. The greater the departure from expected, normal social relations a person's interactions with others manifests, the greater the likelihood that person will eventually be seen as mentally ill. The greater the cost of the failure to fulfill one's social obligations, the higher the chances of this outcome, too. And the more that the individual's interpretations of reality depart from accepted cultural standards, the greater the chances of the imputation of psychosis. People do not cause trouble, nor do they exhibit a "strange" way of thinking or acting, simply because they are psychotic. People must be *experienced* as troublesome or *regarded* as strange by certain other people. What is experienced as trouble or as strange in one place is not so experienced, necessarily, elsewhere. There is certainly a central nucleus of behavior that would be felt as troublesome everywhere, thinking that would be seen as strange in just about any setting. But some variation in community tolerance covers most behavior that eventually would be regarded as clinically psychotic.

All phenomena have to be mentally conceptualized before they are understood. We see behavior around us all the time; it does not "make sense" until we sort it out with the assistance of some notions of how the world is ordered. Most of us do not "see" mental illness as such because we look at behavior, for the most part, in misleading stereotypes. And we do not "see" the psychosis of intimates for other reasons as well; we are genuinely motivated not to do so.

In a study of the wives of men who were eventually committed to a mental institution, the basic question was asked, "How were the disorders of illness interpreted and tolerated?" How did these men "come to be recognized by other family members as needing psychiatric help?" The concern was with "the factors which led to the reorganization of the wife's perceptions of her husband from a *well* man to a man who is mentally sick" (Yarrow et al., 1955: 12). The answer is that when and how "behavior becomes defined as problematic appears to be a highly individual matter." The subjective beginnings of this perception, these authors write, "are seldom localized in a single strange or disturbing reaction on the husband's part but rather in the piling up of behavior and feelings" (1955: 16). The husband's behavior must be, they say, *organized as a problem"* (emphasis added). The wife's initial reactions to her husband's strange and troublesome behavior float around in a sea of "fog and uneasiness." Eventually, she begins to "see" that something is wrong. Why? "In some instances, it is when the wife can no longer manage her husband. . . . ; in others, when she cannot explain his behavior." Her "level of tolerance for his behavior," they speculate, "is a function of her specific personality needs and vulnerabilities, her personal and family value systems and the social supports and prohibitions regarding the husband's symptomatic behavior" (1955: 18). In other words, being regarded as mentally ill is variable, and is not dependent solely upon one's "symptoms," but a host of accidental factors. If these factors are present, one's intimates will "see" one's mental illness; if they are absent, they may very well *not* regard one as mentally ill.

There are a number of factors that "make it difficult for the wife to recognize and accept"—in other words, to *regard*—"the husband's behavior in a mental-emotional-psychiatric framework. Many cross-currents seem to influence this process." One is the husband's behavior itself; it is, they write, a "fluctuating stimulus"; "He is not worried and complaining all of the time. His delusions and hallucinations may not persist. His hostility toward the wife may be followed by warm attentiveness. She has, then, the problem of deciding whether his 'strange' behavior is significant. The greater saliency of one or the other of his responses at any moment of time depends in some degree upon the behavior sequence which has occurred most

recently" (Yarrow et al., 1955: 21). The nature and quality of the relationship between husband and wife also impinge upon her judgment; their ability to communicate with one another also influences how she sees his behavior and what she thinks of it. In addition, it is *threatening* to the wife to look upon her husband as "crazy": It is possible for her to draw the conclusion that she is, somehow, *responsible* for it. In addition, she may visualize the next few years as the wife of a mental patient, and reject, suppress, and fight against the image, because it is too painful to consider. There are various coping mechanisms to deal with the anxiety stirred up by such a consideration. One is *normalization:* The husband's behavior "is explained, justified, or made acceptable by seeing it also in herself or by assuring herself that the particular behavior occurs again and again among persons who are not ill" (1955: 22). A second coping mechanism is to momentarily *attenuate* the seriousness of the behavior—to discount partly or underplay the degree of strangeness of it. She may also *balance* acceptable with unacceptable behavior, to see both "strange" *and* "normal" behavior and come up with the conclusion that her husband is not seriously disturbed. And a last line of defense is an outright *denial* that her husband could be emotionally ill (1955: 23).

Looking at the other side of the coin, three sociologists studying the *husband's* perceptions of their *wives'* disturbing, bizarre behavior conclude, "Becoming a mental patient is not a simple and direct outcome of 'mental illness.' . . . Persons who are, by clinical standards, grossly disturbed, severely impaired in their functioning, and even overtly psychotic may remain in the community for long periods without being 'recognized' as 'mentally ill.' . . . It is clear that becoming a patient is a socially structured event." There is a "monumental capacity of family members . . . to overlook, minimize, and explain away evidence of profound disturbance in an intimate." With regard to mental illness specifically, there is a "high tolerance for deviance" in many families. An informal judgment of a family member as mentally ill is suppressed in the minds of the others until the problems they encounter become "unmanageable" (Sampson et al., 1962).

The dynamics of this denial process are instructive because they contradict the "hard" labeling position, as Gove (1975a) points out. While Scheff correctly argues that most "residual rule-breaking" is denied (1966: 51), as we might expect from knowing the dynamics of mental illness labeling among intimates, he further assumes that *if* it is denied, ignored, or rationalized, *it will go away*. Here we have individuals who are *not* labeled by others—those others, in fact, *denying* the intimate's mental disorder—who nonetheless go on to manifest increasingly more serious symptoms. The condition seems to have arisen independent of labeling—by intimates, at any rate. Hospitalization took place in these studies in spite of the absence of labeling. Although Scheff denies the significance of these studies (1974a, 1974b), his argument remains unconvincing. The denial of mental illness by intimates shows us that labeling cannot possibly be a cause of disordered symptoms, nor does it appear to stabilize a labeled person's illness "career." The labeling process is certainly an aspect of the mental illness picture, but it does not seem to play the role that the "hard" labeling model insists it plays.

THE EPIDEMIOLOGY OF MENTAL ILLNESS

Epidemiology is the study of the distribution of diseases in the population. No disease is ever distributed evenly or randomly; it will nearly always be contracted by some social groups or categories at a higher rate than is true of other groups or categories. It is the job of the epidemiologist to find out, in a detailed, systematic, empirical fashion, just what the distribution patterns are for specific diseases. Two measures used by the epidemiologist are *incidence* and *prevalence*. Incidence refers to the number of new cases of a disease diagnosed during a given year. Prevalence refers to the number of cases at a given point in time; prevalence includes

everyone who has a given disease, regardless of whether that case is new or old.

An analogy can be made between physical disease and mental disorder: Epidemiologists attempt to study the rate of mental illness in the population at large, as well as among specific groups or categories in it, by examining data such as hospital admissions, clinical surveys, and so on. Each technique is an attempt to determine the "true" rate of mental disorder for the whole population or for groups within it. Unfortunately, there is enormous variation in the incidence and prevalence rates from one study to another; the figures vary by as much as 100 times (Dohrenwend and Dohrenwend, 1974: 423; Akers, 1977: 322, 323). Comparing the mental illness rates of different countries, each with its own definition of disorder, is even riskier still, indeed, practically impossible. Even within the same locale, definitions of mental disorder, and therefore its rate in the population, vary enormously. We have only to recall that one study claimed that 80 percent of the population of midtown Manhattan suffered from some form of mental impairment (Srole et al., 1962, 1978) to remind ourselves of the riskiness of determining rates of mental disorder in a population.

In spite of these and other problems in determining rates of psychic disorder in the population, a large number of studies have been conducted that have reached conclusions concerning the differential proneness of the groups or social categories in society to mental illness. It is clear that specific social processes are related to the development of mental disorder and that these processes are more characteristic of certain groups than others. How do the most important social categories fare with regard to mental health and disorder?

Gender: Men and Women

One team of researchers (Dohrenwend and Dohrenwend, 1976) found there is no consistent relationship between mental disorder and gender or sex. A crude, unidimensional, undifferentiated measure of mental disorder yields no differences between men and women. However, by specifying different *types* of mental disorders, differences do emerge. Women are significantly more likely to manifest depressive disorders and to score high in simple neuroticism. Men are more likely to suffer from alcohol and drug disorders and personality disorders, which are manifested in "irresponsible and antisocial behavior." Still, for both men and women, roughly half of all resident patients in state and county hospitals are diagnosed as schizophrenic; there appear to be no gender differences for this global diagnosis.

Over the past two decades, the sex ratio of patients in mental hospitals has been shifting: In the 1960s, there were slightly more female than male patients, and by the 1970s, there were slightly more males than females. Today, there are about 120 male resident patients in county and state mental hospitals for every 100 female patients. Among the youngest patients (under age 25) there are about 250 males for every 100 females; among the oldest (ages 65 and older), the ratio is about 75 males for every 100 females (Cockerham, 1981: 201). Gender seems to be a major contingency in admission and release: Men are not more mentally disordered than women, but the mental disorder of men is regarded as more disabling, threatening, and dangerous to society than is that of women (Gove, 1972; Rushing, 1979a, 1979b). Women are regarded as more cooperative and compliant and more readily influenced by the hospital staff and, therefore, more likely to be released (Doherty, 1978). Some researchers also feel that the social roles men and women and boys and girls are forced to play impacts on their mental health—or lack of it. Males are expected to be more aggressive, independent, and adventurous; consequently, the disorders they manifest ("antisocial" tendencies, especially toward violence) reflect that role expectation. Females are forced to be passive, dependent, and lacking in confidence; they, too, exhibit this tendency, in extreme form, in their own characteristic disorder, depression (Gove and Herb, 1974: 259).

It is hypothesized among many health experts that there is something of a "double standard" in the diagnosis, hospitalization, and release of mental patients with respect to gender (Cockerham, 1981: 213–215); Gallagher, 1980: 198–200). Psychiatrists and clinical psychologists seem to have a lower standard of mental health for women than for men. They are more likely to diagnose mental disorder for men, other things being equal; a woman's condition would have to be more severe to warrant hospitalization, and a man's less severe to warrant release. One hypothesis that has been put forth to explain this observed regularity is that in a sexist society, males are expected to perform in society to more exacting standards. Being a man in a very achievement-oriented society is incompatible with being mentally disordered; the penalties for stepping out of line are swift and strong. On the other hand, where women are relegated to an inferior and dependent role in society, their performance in that role is met with more indulgence and leeway. It is felt by both clinicians and the general public, male and female, that a mildly psychically impaired woman can perform in a less demanding role in an imperfect fashion and still "get by." Ironically, these sexist values result in a higher rate of mental illness labeling for men, supposedly the more powerful social category, and less for women, who are generally less powerful. As sex roles become more equalitarian, one would expect these gender disparities in diagnosis, hospitalization, and release to diminish and eventually disappear.

Marital Status

Another social dimension that has been studied extensively to determine its relationship with or impact on mental health and illness is *marital status*. Among men, a very consistent finding emerges from these many studies: Single, never-married men are strikingly more likely to score high on every available measure of mental disorder than are married men; separated and divorced men rank somewhere in between. Two hypotheses have been advanced to account for the observed relationship. The first is that men who marry and stay married are more stable, psychologically healthy, and conventional than are men who never marry—and therefore, they are less mentally disordered. The experience of marriage itself, these observers argue, has little or nothing to do with this regularity: It is only that the kind of man who marries is also the kind of man who exhibits comparatively few personality problems, while the man who does not marry is far more likely to exhibit them. Getting married entails a certain degree of social competence to attract a spouse; men with severe mental problems are not considered desirable partners and will be socially avoided by women (Rushing, 1979b). "The more symptomatic and/or ineffective an individual, the less likely he will find a marital partner . . . , and the more likely he will spend extended periods in the hospital" (Turner and Gartrell, 1978: 378). It is, in other words, "the inadequate man who is left over after the pairing has taken place" (Gallagher, 1980: 208).

A second hypothesis is that marriage confers a kind of immunity on a man: Married men have fewer mental problems than do bachelors because the experience of being married is conducive to a man's mental health, security, and well-being. "Marriage does not prevent economic and social problems from invading life," two researchers argue, "but it apparently can help people fend off the psychological assaults that such problems otherwise create" (Pearlin and Johnson, 1977: 714). Bachelors are less able than married men to form close emotional ties with others and are more socially isolated and, therefore, more psychologically vulnerable. Whether this is a question of social selection or differential experiences, the tendency for single men to exhibit strikingly more symptoms of mental disorder is well documented in the literature.

This generalization does not hold for women, however. Some studies show single women to have the same rates of mental disorder as married women (Warheit et al., 1976), while other studies show married

women to have *higher* rates of disorders (Gove, 1979b). In short, for women, marriage offers no special protection, as it does for men. It is even possible the opposite is the case: Some analysts argue that marriage is a stressful, anxiety-provoking, oppressive, exploitative institution, incompatible with the mental health of women (Bernard, 1983). Men have all the advantages in marriage, they feel, and thus profit from the experience; in contrast, women suffer as a result of being married because marriage is more demanding on women: It is frustrating, unsatisfying, and lacking in gratification for the women (Gove, 1972). The evidence seems to favor few differences between married and unmarried women in mental illness and health (Warheit et al., 1976), yet the remarkable difference in the impact of marriage between men and women should strike the observer forcefully. While it is probably a bit rash to state that, in terms of mental health, marriage is good for men and bad for women, the evidence does at least suggest it may be good for men and of considerably less consequence for women. In a less sexist society, marriage will become more equalitarian and, possibly, good for both sexes.

Socioeconomic Status

Of all sociological variables, social class or socioeconomic status (SES) is probably the most frequently studied. And the most commonly used indicators measuring socioeconomic status are income, occupational prestige, and education. The higher someone ranks on all three or any one of these dimensions, the higher is his or her socioeconomic status, or social "class," sociologists argue. Mental disorder is very closely related to socioeconomic status: The higher the SES, the lower the rate of mental disorder; and the lower the SES, the higher the rate of mental disorder. This holds true regardless of the specific measure or indicator of SES that is used—occupational prestige, income, or education. People at the bottom of the class ladder are far more likely to suffer from psychiatric distress, especially schizophrenia, than are those at the top. There are a few mental disorders that are more common at the top of the class structure, such as obsessive-compulsive neuroses, but the most serious illnesses, the psychoses, are most common toward the bottom of the class structure. In some 50 studies, conducted in countries on three continents, the relationship between mental illness and SES has been studied; almost without exception, "these studies have found a preponderance of schizophrenia at the lower social levels" (Gallagher, 1980: 257). This generalization has been verified empirically by studies stretching back more than half a century (Faris and Dunham, 1939; Hollingshead and Redlich, 1958; Srole et al., 1962).

Why should this strong inverse relationship between psychopathology and SES exist? Is it due solely to the fact that lower-status individuals are more likely to come to the attention of psychiatric authorities and are therefore more often recorded as mentally ill? Actually, this same relationship holds up regardless of how mental disorder is measured—clinical survey or commitment to a mental hospital. Moreover, upper- and middle-status individuals are more likely to cast their difficulties in living in a psychiatric framework and to seek out professional assistance to deal with such a problem. Lower-status individuals are less likely to attribute their problems to a psychiatric condition, are more likely to feel that some stigma adheres to consultation with a "shrink" or to being committed to a mental hospital, and are less likely to voluntarily seek out psychiatric assistance. Lower-status individuals are most likely to come to the attention of psychiatric authorities as a result of a referral by the police or a social worker; upper- and middle-status individuals are more likely to be referred by relatives or a private physician. A great deal of lower-status mental disorders, especially among men, manifests itself in the form of "antisocial" behavior—particularly violence—which is likely to attract the attention of agents of formal social control, the police. The explanation that the inverse relationship between SES and mental disorder is due solely to noticing the psychiatric condition of the members of the

lower classes more is not borne out by the evidence.

Some observers have argued that this strong inverse relationship between SES and mental disorder may be due to bias and the labeling process: Middle-class psychiatrists find lower-class behavior troublesome and are more likely to label it disordered than the behavior of middle-class individuals (Wilkinson, 1975). There is a built-in bias in psychiatric diagnosis against lower-class culture and individuals: Mental health is measured by a middle-class yardstick; lower-class values and behavior are automatically regarded as disordered by the psychiatric profession, made up, as it is, of individuals who are in the middle or at the top of the social class ladder. There is no doubt that this process influences the observed relationship. Nonetheless, it cannot be the whole story, because much of the behavior of the psychiatrically disordered is deemed undesirably by members of all social classes; characteristically, the lower-class individual comes to psychiatric attention by being reported by other lower-class individuals.

Stress has been cited as a major factor in the relationship between mental disorder and SES. Economic deprivation, poverty, occupational instability, and unemployment are strongly related to psychological impairment (Liem and Liem, 1978). As a result of having to deal with living an economically deprived existence and coping with this deprivation, the lower-class individual suffers a higher level of emotional stress and consequently is more vulnerable to a psychiatric breakdown (Kessler, 1979). The pressure of daily living under deprived conditions becomes overwhelming; problems that cannot be solved mount, become unmanageable and force the individual into a break with reality (Cockerham, 1981: 184–186). There is a great deal of evidence verifying the "social stress" hypothesis of mental illness.

A second hypothesis attempting to explain the strong inverse relationship between SES and mental disorder is the *social selection* or the *drift hypothesis*. This theory argues that social class is a *consequence* rather than a *cause* of mental illness. The mentally disordered are incapable of achieving a higher position on the socioeconomic hierarchy *because* they are mentally disordered (Dunham, 1965). Members of the lower class have drifted there because their mental illness prevents them from achieving a higher position. Their disorder retards their social mobility (Harkey et al., 1976). The social stress and the drift hypothesis are not necessarily contradictory or mutually exclusive; "class can determine illness in one case and illness can determine class in another" (Gallagher, 1980: 254). There is probably some validity to both the stress and the drift models.

CHEMICAL TREATMENT OF MENTAL DISORDERS

An important category of drugs is the "major" tranquilizers. "Major" tranquilizers are referred to as *antipsychotics* and are used in the treatment of psychosis. They do not produce a high or intoxication, are almost never used recreationally, and are not sold on the underground market. Nearly all use of the antipsychotics is legal, licit prescription use for the purpose of controlling mental illness, especially schizophrenia. The major tranquilizers are known technically as *phenothiazines* and include drugs that bear the brand names of Thorazine, Compazine, Stelazine, and Mellaril.

The impact of the phenothiazines can be measured by an examination of the changes in the number of the resident patients in public mental hospitals in the United States from the middle 1950s to today. In 1955, there were about 560,000 resident mental patients in hospitals. That year, the antipsychotic phenothiazine drugs were introduced to treat mental illness. The number of resident patients dropped every year after that; today there are a shade over 100,000 (Wines, 1988) resident patients. This dramatic change has not been due to the decline in the new admissions to mental hospitals, because that actually rose from 178,000 in 1955 to half a million each year for the 1980s; the admission figures continue to rise yearly.

Rather, the change in the mental hospital resident figures was brought about as a result of the drastic decline in the average length of stay in mental hospitals. In 1955, the average period of hospitalization was six months; by 1975, this had dropped to 26 days (Ray, 1983: 227–274). The decline in the number of patients living in mental hospital facilities at a given time, and the reduction in their average length of stay in these facilities, is due directly to the use of the antipsychotic or phenothiazine drugs, the "major" tranquilizers. Roughly 85 percent of all patients in state, local, and federal mental hospitals receive some form of phenothiazine medication.

One of the phenothiazines, Thorazine (whose chemical name is chlorpromazine), is described as having the following effects on agitated, manic, schizophrenic patients: The drug, one observer wrote, "produces marked quieting of the motor manifestations. Patients cease to be loud and profane, the tendency to hyperbolic association is diminished, and the patient can sit still long enough to eat and take care of normal physiological needs" (Goldman, 1955). The emotional withdrawal, hallucinations, delusions, and other patterns of disturbed thinking, paranoia, belligerence, hostility, and "blunted affect" of patient are significantly reduced (Veterans Administration, 1970: 4).

As a result of the use of the antipsychotics, patients exhibit fewer and less dramatic symptoms of psychosis, become more manageable, and, as a result, have permitted hospitals to discontinue or reduce such ineffective or dangerous practices as hydrotherapy, electroshock therapy, and lobotomies. And, as a result of the administration of these drugs, hospitals have, in the words of one observer, been transformed from "zoo-smelling, dangerous bedlams into places fit for human beings to live and, at times, to recover from psychosis" (Callaway, 1958: 82). By inducing a more "normal" psychological state in patients, it has been possible to release them into the community as outpatients, with only minimal treatment and care in aftercare facilities.

Studies have shown that about three-quarters of all acute schizophrenics demonstrate significant improvement following the administration of phenothiazine drugs, and between 75 percent and 95 percent of all patients relapse if their medication is discontinued (Ray and Ksir, 1987: 237–239). The use of the antipsychotic drugs is regarded as not only effective for most mental patients, but it is also the least expensive of all treatment modalities. However, it should be added that, although these drugs do reduce the most bizarre symptoms of schizophrenia and other mental illnesses, very few mental patients are able to live what is regarded as a completely "normal" existence; one estimate places this at only 15 percent (Veterans Administration, 1970). The phenothiazines do not "cure" mental illness. They calm the agitated, disturbed patients; the symptoms of mental illness are reduced, and patients are no longer as troublesome to others as they once were—they do not manifest their former signs of craziness. Antipsychotics permit the patient to behave in a more socially acceptable fashion; the patient's problems do not surface so painfully or disturbingly.

It is not known just why the antipsychotic drugs have this effect on patients. In any case, psychiatry has not been able to treat mental illness by means of nonchemical means; using the "major" tranquilizers at least keeps patients out of trouble and out of the way of "normals." Some observers cite the use of antipsychotics as a "revolution" in the field of psychiatry (Gove, 1975a: 245). Other observers (Townsend, 1980: 272) are more cautious and see the change not as genuine treatment, but merely as the suppression of troublesome, disruptive behavior.

The phenothiazines are not addictive and very rarely result in lethal overdoses. There are some serious side effects of these drugs, however, including abnormal, involuntary, and sometimes bizarre movements of the tongue, lips, and cheeks; facial tics; tremors; rigidity; and a shuffling gait. These symptoms are treated with a separate type of drug, the anti-Parkinsonian drugs. Patients also complain of feeling "doped up." Their responses are often sluggish, they are less

acute mentally and display less interest in external stimuli, including other people. They tend to be slower in arousal and exhibit a reduced mental acuity and intelligence. Thus, the reduction of the socially and culturally bizarre and unacceptable behavior and thinking of mental patients is bought at a not inconsiderable price.

DEVIANCE AND MENTAL DISORDER: AN OVERVIEW

Mental disorder has both parallels and dissimilarities with other forms of deviant behavior discussed in the earlier chapters, such as drug use, homicide, and homosexuality. (Some forms of deviance are also regarded as "behavioral disorders" such as drug dependence.) On the one hand, both deviance and mental disorder represent a departure from the normative order. Being regarded as mentally "abnormal" by others entails breaking the rules of society and social interaction and behaving in a fashion considered odd, eccentric, bizarre, or troublesome. So to the extent that behavioral manifestations of mental illness result in normative violations, the disruption of smooth social relations, and attracting a socially undesirable label, it represents a type of deviant behavior.

Public attitudes toward the mentally ill are more complicated than they are toward the deviant. Although the mentally disordered may do "immoral" things, this is not necessary to any definition of mental illness. Toward the deviant the dominant emotion is outrage, anger, hostility; the mentally ill attract a feeling more like condescension and pity. The average citizen wishes to have the deviant punished, but wants to keep the mentally ill out of sight and out of mind. The deviant is feared more for the harm we suppose they can do to us or to society as a whole; the insane are feared more for reminding us of what we all could become. Deviants are seen through two contradictory principles: They are sick and act out of compulsive motives, and they are immoral, act out of free will, and are responsible for their actions. The mentally ill person is seen, in contrast, as lacking a free will and, hence, not responsible for his or her actions.

In addition, deviance is nearly always located in specific actions—behavioral or attitudinal spheres. One is not *a* deviant generally; few people even use the term. One is a deviant in specific areas of life—sex, drug use, politics, harming others, and so on. The label of mental illness is almost unique in that it is free-floating, highly generalizable. One is considered mentally ill not because of having done something in a delimited area of life, but because of having done things in many areas that are supposedly manifestations of a psychic disorganization. This is true of practically no other form of deviant behavior.

The major thrust of psychiatric writings published in recent decades has been in the direction of adopting the medical model of mental illness: regarding it on a par with physical illness. This means that the mental patient should be dealt with socially in much the same way as the sufferer of a physical disease should. The social stigma that adhered to the mental patient in the past is regarded in some quarters as an archaic remnant of the past. Being diagnosed as crazy, this view holds, does "not cause others to view the individual as deviant (they already do so) but instead often" will "redefine the deviance in a fairly positive way." Commitment to a mental hospital "tends to shift the person's label from that of being obnoxious and intolerable to that of being mentally ill and in need of help" (Gove, 1975a: 245). Insofar as this is true, then, *mental illness is not a form of deviance.* To the extent that the public sees mental disorder on a par with physical illness, qualitatively no different from, and attracting no more stigma than, contracting cancer, and regards the mentally ill as not responsible for the actions, it is not a form of deviance.

At the same time, it should be recognized that being ill, even physically ill, in our society is actually a form of deviance: It is a significant departure from being self-reliant, taking care of one's obligations; it represents a failure to be healthy, productive, "normal" (Parsons, 1951: 428–479; Freidson, 1970:

205–223). Illness, then, is a violation of a number of strongly held values. To a degree, then, being mentally ill will always be regarded as a form of deviance in the same sense that physical illness is a form of deviance. Falling down on the job, failing to meet one's familial obligations, and disrupting interpersonal relations will always be despised in a society that values performance in these spheres. Being declared mentally ill emphasizes one's performance incapacity. As such, it will always be looked down upon.

ACCOUNT: ENCOUNTER WITH MENTAL ILLNESS

The contributor of this account is a 40-year-old college professor.

One year I was a member of the Graduate Committee of my department. Our job was to review the applications of candidates applying for admission to graduate school in our department. One application caught my eye; let's call him John Spencer. John had excellent grades from a first-rate undergraduate institution, and his Graduate Record Exams were top-notch. The thing was, he attended college off and on. He was in his thirties and had spent 10 years or so of his adult life in mental institutions. In the essay he wrote accompanying his application, he said he didn't want to be stigmatized for having been institutionalized. Reading it, I could only agree; I argued that we should admit him. He will make an excellent student, I said; we shouldn't be guilty of discriminating against him for his past problems. Well, the rest of the committee seemed to be persuaded, and we admitted him. He enrolled in our graduate program the following fall.

John was quiet for a couple of months. And then things started to happen. He took one course with an especially tough professor who handed back a paper he had written with critical comments all over it. John read the comments and flew into a rage right in the classroom. He ripped the paper in half, threw it into the trash, and grabbed the professor by the shoulders, screaming "What right do you have to judge me, you smug, self-righteous bastard?!" The other students in the class were horrified, but they managed to separate John from the professor and escorted him away so that he could cool down.

That clued everyone into the fact that John

was not in complete control. I doubt if very many people in the department knew his psychiatric past before then, but many of them found out about it after. I guess people started becoming a bit leery of him. One of John's problems was that the medication he took for his illness made him stupid if he took too much of it, but if he took too little, he was smart, but crazy. The precise dose at which he was both smart and sane was extremely difficult to find and maintain. Anyway, a few weeks went by. John was in the habit of attaching himself socially to anyone who was the least bit attentive to him or who didn't reject him. Usually they were women. He'd call them incessantly and eventually annoy them and alienate them to the point that they didn't want to have anything to do with him, and then he'd have to search out a new victim.

His latest companion was a fellow graduate student, a woman, and, like him, she was in her thirties. Her name was Katherine. One day, he asked her for a certain article, and she stuck it in his mailbox at school. It had the word "deviant" in the title. He pulled it out of his mailbox and read the title. Perhaps he got it into his head that, somehow, Katherine called him a deviant, who knows? A few minutes later, he was in the hallway talking with a professor. Katherine rounded a corner a few feet away from where John was talking with the professor and began walking toward him. He spotted her, ran over to her, and punched her in the jaw; she slumped to the floor, unconscious. Everyone in the vicinity got very nervous and excited and escorted him away from the area. Matters had suddenly become very serious.

Katherine insisted, for her safety, that John be kept away from the department. All the members of the department had numerous meetings with the campus psychologist and psychiatrist to determine the wisest policy to follow with respect to John's outbursts. The department wished to keep John in the graduate program, but without upsetting any of the other students, who understandably didn't want to be assaulted for some obscure reason. We sent him a memorandum that spelled out the conditions under which he could remain a student in our program. Some of them sound like simple rules for everyday behavior. The memo read approximately along the following lines.

1. You will take courses on a tutorial basis. The course discussions will be confined strictly to academic matters. You will receive individual instruction from each professor teaching your courses; you will meet with them in a room in the library.

2. You are not to come onto the floor where the department is.

3. You are not to go to the computing center, unless you are doing a specific assignment for a course; if so, you must clear it with the individual instructor.

4. You are not to attend meetings or colloquia sponsored by the department.

5. You are not to yell or scream in public places; you are not to curse, harass, or threaten any student or faculty; you are not to hit or strike any student or faculty member.

6. You are to see Dr. McTavish and Dr. Eidelman on a regular basis (as they define this regularity). You are to keep all appointments with them and take any medication they prescribe.

7. Violation of any of these regulations is grounds for dismissal from the program.

At the conclusion of one of our many meetings concerned with the subject of John Spencer, this one with the head of the campus psychological services, a fellow faculty member turned to me—the fellow who was responsible for John being admitted to the program to begin with—and asked, "Nu, Mr. Labeling Theorist?"[4] I shrugged my shoulders and said, "The man's crazy—what can I say?"

Unfortunately, the procedures and rules we laid down didn't work. John was unable to control his behavior, and he eventually admitted himself to a mental hospital a few weeks after this memo was sent to him. He never returned to the program. (From the author's files.)

---

[4]"Nu?" is a Jewish expression that means "So? What do you have to say about this?" Labeling theory is a perspective that holds that nothing is wrong in itself; behavior is wrong only when it is defined as such—and this definition often results in intensifying the behavior in question. The implication of the question was that a labeling theorist would not regard anything John did as wrong in itself, it was only the reactions of the department that made his behavior wrong.

Epilogue

A Turkish film, *Yol,* depicted a prisoner, recently released on a one-week pass, and his wife on a train. They have not been together for over a year. Overcome by their need to be intimate with one another, they slip into a public bathroom and lock in an affectionate embrace. Someone begins pounding on the door and screaming that a man and a woman are inside. A crowd gathers outside the door; the pounding and the screaming intensify. The couple is accused of being pigs, lice, and unspeakable vermin. Fists are clenched in rage. A representative of the train arrives on the scene and ushers the couple through the angry mob, rescuing them from what looks like certain violence. They are seated in his office. Yes, it is true, he says, you are unspeakable vermin, but I don't want any violence on my train. I should probably turn you over to the authorities at the next station, he explains. The woman is hunched over, weeping softly; the man's face is dazed, expressionless. Angry faces outside peer into the windows of the office, seeking punishment for the wicked couple.

Giggling, a man and a woman make their way down the aisle of a 747 flying from New York to Los Angeles. Almost casually, they slip into a bathroom compartment together, close the door, and begin smoking a marijuana cigarette. In those cramped confines, they disrobe and have intercourse standing up. Their faces flushed, their clothes disheveled, the compartment fragrant with the unmistakable odor of marijuana, they emerge just as a man approaches the door. Again, they giggle. The man is momentarily flustered and embarrassed; he returns to his seat and whispers something to his wife. She smiles and whispers something to him. They both laugh. The couple who had sex in the bathroom relax under a blanket, lounging against one another, with dreamy, contented smiles on their faces.

In these two cases, we have an act that could be described as a normative violation. In both Turkey and the United States, a rule exists that states, "thou shalt not fornicate on public transportation." Clearly, the norm is much more strongly held in Turkey, as well as in other Islamic countries, than in the United States, as well as much of the rest of the Western world. (In fact, in some circles in the United States, this rule is probably more honored in the breach than in the observance.) Nonetheless, for these incidents, the first fictional and the second based on an actual event, we may infer that some societies rank high with respect to their members intervening when they observe actions they regard as deviant, while other societies rank low on this scale. What happens when wrongdoing is observed? Do the witnesses intervene, or do they permit the transgressors to go their merry ways?

American society generally, and urban America more specifically, is a low-intervention culture. An act would have to be regarded as more strongly deviant in comparison with elsewhere before witnesses would intervene and halt the progress of the behavior or apprehend the perpetrator. American urban dwellers especially pride themselves on permitting others to "do their own thing," on cultivating a "live and let live" attitude toward life. Yet nonintervention clearly has its limits. Just as not all deviance is necessarily harmful, it is not always harmless, either. What happens to a society that tolerates dangerous forms of behavior? Where does tolerance leave off and chaos begin? When does freedom for some curtail freedom for all? The case of Kitty Genovese, who was raped and then murdered while her neighbors ignored her screams for help, reminds us that not intervening in the actions of others is a most decidedly mixed blessing. Nonintervention in deviant behavior can lead to an episode such as that which occurred in New York City in 1982 that prompted the headlines the next day: "Man

Slain as 30 Persons Watch." A man, sleeping on a rock in Central Park, was attacked by a second man; the assailant began bashing the sleeping man with a wire trash basket, then stabbed him with a sharp stick, and finally tried to sever his head from his body by sawing the victim's throat back and forth with a length of wire. During the entire time the deadly assault took place, no one in a crowd of 30 or 40 people intervened. The alleged assailant, a former mental patient, was arrested and booked without resistance. In this case, intervention would have saved a man's life.

The area around Santa Cruz, California, has been described as something of a paradise on earth. Set in a semirural, gently sloping pastureland that gives way to the Pacific Ocean, flanked at one edge by a redwood forest, its beauty is breathtaking. In the 1960s, Santa Cruz harbored a few writers, painters, and craftspeople; in 1965, the University of California established a campus there. Another attraction of Santa Cruz aside from its astonishing natural beauty was its tolerance for diversity. Travelers on their way to points south discovered the community "would accommodate almost anything in the way of oddball behavior." Santa Cruz became a mecca for the eccentric, the unconventional, for individuals who wished to engage in deviant behavior in peace. It came to be regarded as a "mellow, no-hassle place where the sun always shines and the nightsticks are made of candy." As the number of oddballs grew, the town underwent a not-so-subtle transformation.

One author describes the changes brought about by this tolerance for diversity and unconventionality in Santa Cruz's central district or "mall" in the following words:

Down on the mall a small congregation of street people began to gather.... They dealt a little, stole a little, and spent their days sitting on the sidewalk ... staring with blasted, vacant eyes at the passersby. Very gradually their attitude toward the world that moved around them changed from passive indifference to lurching belligerence, and what was once, depending on your point of view, merely colorful, or distasteful, or weird, or mildly disconcerting, or vibrating with creative energy, became ominous, dangerous. Women passing along the street were increasingly subjected to obscene remarks. A student who ignored a request for spare change was beaten senseless. Muggings and purse snatchings became frequent. A rape here, another there. Merchants began to complain that business was down, thefts were up. All of a sudden (or so it seemed) things were not so savory down there on the mall. The vector of tyranny had reversed itself. The oppressed had become the oppressors (Stegner, 1981: 34).

Commenting on this shift, the author declares, "It has become increasingly uncool over the past decade to be caught in the act of passing judgment on fellow creatures or to expect anything of them in the way of public conduct." Rather than deciding what is good and evil, and acting on that decision, instead, the author argues, we say with a shrug, "Hey, like *whatever*!" We have "lost the capacity to be outraged by almost anything short of Charles Manson."

In the process our sense of helplessness to regulate social conduct has reduced us to passive observers more likely to sit around questioning the validity of our personal reactions to deviant behavior rather than the communal implications of its often savage vulgarity. We founder in the myth of mutual tolerance rather than try to determine the limits of tolerance, and we try to portray ourselves as living in an environment of creative expression rather than a madhouse (Stegner, 1981: 35).

Such an environment, the author concludes, "strikes me as endangered."

Two sociologists argue that the process of tolerating mild, harmless deviance leading to finding serious, dangerous deviance on your doorstep is not inevitable. Where deviants sink roots into the community, widespread deviance seems to be frozen at the mild, harmless stage. Transients have no stake in the future of a town or a city. Residents, however, do, since they must make compromises with and accommodations to other segments of the community with whom they must continue to live.

Sinking roots stabilizes deviants' lives, as it does the lives of conventional citizens. They find less need to act in the erratic ways deviants often behave elsewhere, less need to fulfill the prophecy that because they are deviant in one respect they will be deviant in other, more dangerous ways. . . . The accommodation works in circular fashion. When deviants can live decent lives, they find it possible to behave decently. Furthermore, they acquire the kind of stake they are often denied elsewhere in the present and future structure of the community. That stake constrains them to behave in ways that will not outrage nondeviants, for they do not want to lose what they have. They thus curb their activities according to what they think the community will stand for. The community, in turn, and especially the police, will put up with more than they might otherwise, because they understand nothing else is forthcoming, and because they find that what they are confronted with is not so bad after all. . . . No doubt neither party to such a bargain gets quite what he would like. Straight members of the community presumably would prefer not to have whores walking the downtown streets, would prefer not to have gay bars operating openly. Deviants of all kinds presumably would prefer not to have to make any concessions to straight sensibilities. Each gives up something and gets something, and to that degree the arrangement becomes stable, the stability itself something both prize (Becker and Horowitz, 1970: 16–17).

The authors describe San Francisco's "culture of civility" at the end of the 1960s and the beginning of the 1970s. Few communities are so fortunate to find such a felicitous balance between tolerating acts of unconventionality and intervening in behavior that is truly dangerous. The authors point out that, while the police are much less likely to intervene than elsewhere in the case of prostitution, homosexuality, transvestitism, the public showing of pornographic movies, and marijuana use, they are just as likely to intervene in cases of violence and the sale of truly dangerous drugs. Yet it is not always so easy to distinguish between simple unconventionality and clear-cut acts of victimization.

Public intoxication may become driving while under the influence, which, in turn, can turn readily into vehicular homicide.

Prostitution, once described as a victimless crime, is now recognized as both the common core of a constellation of crimes, including robbery of the customer, as well as an institution that perpetuates the exploitation of women.

Tolerating "nudie movies" was once regarded as a sign of sophistication, one aspect of the "culture of civility" (Becker and Horowitz, 1970: 13). Today, evidence suggests that exposure to pornography may be a factor in precipitating violence against women.

Abortions were once described as a simple crime without a victim (Schur, 1965). Today, it is not a crime and, if the fetus can be regarded as a full human being, as some observers believe, it cannot be seen as a victimless action at all.

Public health officials are not so certain marijuana is as innocuous as was believed a decade or two ago. Moreover, the average age of the initial use of this drug is several years younger today than was true in the past; if tolerating marijuana use among 25-year-olds is one measure of openmindedness, how would we describe ignoring the use of this drug among 12-year-olds?

Acts that harm no one but the actor often entail cost to society; one may harm others by harming oneself. For example, as a result of riding a motorcycle without a helmet, one may be injured. One's injury may result in medical bills that others have to pay; one's death may deprive others of care, nurturance, and financial support.

In short, the distinction between victimless behavior and acts of victimization is extremely fuzzy and often difficult to make. No one would question society's need to punish offenders in behavior where victimization is direct, clear-cut, and extreme. However, where victimization is more indirect, ambiguous, and less extreme, both intervention and tolerance entail dilemmas. To decide in favor of intervention cannot be ascribed to simple prudishness.

Moreover, when the issues of victimization and intervention in deviance are raised, a very narrow focus is adopted. Few observers who debate the limits of the tolerance of deviance consider actions that may be damaging but not deviant—the unethical, dangerous, or illegal practices of the powerful, that is, corporate or white-collar crimes. Some observers wish to redefine these acts so that they are regarded as deviant (Liazos, 1972; Smith, 1973). Moreover, they wish to expand the concept of deviance and crime to include "crimes against the people"—racism, sexism, imperialism, oppression, exploitation. They wish, in other words, to make deviance dependent not on public reaction but on their definition of harm. Aside from the fact that we still have a phenomenon based on public reaction (changing its name does not change the phenomenon itself), it is still necessary to account for the lamentable but nonetheless true fact that public reaction is not based solely on harm or damage to society. While it is a simple matter to attribute this to the injustice of capitalism, nonetheless, it is a reality to be reckoned with. Rather than attempting to drag exploitation and other capitalist ills under the umbrella of deviance, it might be more fruitful to deal with the question of why such acts do not fall under that umbrella at all. It is indeed ironic that many truly dangerous and damaging actions do not generate social intervention, but the sophisticated observer of society must deal with dilemmas such as these.

An adequate understanding of our task as an observer of deviant behavior demands that damaging but respectable (that is, nondeviant) behavior be studied. These disjunctions between public condemnation and objective damage should intrigue us. If we define deviance by public condemnation, we have to find out both the "why" of it—why some behavior attracts a label of immorality—as well as the "why not" of it—why other forms of behavior are not considered immoral. In this way we begin to get at the source of social disapproval. We can never fully understand what is deviant until we get a good look at what isn't. By looking at both, we realize that it is neither "social cost" nor any "objective threat to society" that accounts for behavior being labeled as deviant or legislated as a crime. This should lead us to ask just what it is that does account for them. We couldn't deal with this issue if we concentrated exclusively on deviant or criminal behavior itself.

All of this argues for a view of deviance as a complex phenomenon. Simple, cartoon portrayals of the phenomenon and its practitioners, as well as its detractors and condemners, will not do. To understand deviance, we must get as close to it as we possibly can. To adopt an externalistic view, without an understanding of how or why it is enacted, can only lead to ignorance and error. To attempt to interpret the phenomenon of deviance through the lens of a single, rigid perspective will inevitably distort its essential reality. Deviance is a multifaceted phenomenon, with crucial dimensions that will be ignored or misunderstood by a given, narrow perspective. There are as many varieties of deviance as there are of conventional, law-abiding behavior. To expect a single theory or perspective to account for these varieties is both naive and unrealistic.

Some observers of the social world are impervious to experience; they look at society, deviance included, solely as a means of documenting their previously held views. Facts that do not fit these views are ignored or explained away. Closedminded dogmatists will always be with us (unless it is a hoax or a joke, an organization exists today whose members believe the earth is flat). However, a naturalistic, up-close look at the real world can serve as an antidote to long-held but mistaken views. Get out of your armchair, the sociologist of deviance commands, go forth into the social world and observe firsthand the workings of deviance and respectability—armed, true, with a perspective, insight, information. Yet no perspective should be so inflexible or so strongly held as to be incapable of being falsified; we should always be aware of what manner of evidence will demonstrate its validity, as well as what would show it to be false. Although no society will ever successfully deal with the dilemmas in tolerating and punishing deviance, it is hoped that a study of this fascinating phenomenon will enable us to appreciate these dilemmas.

References

ABEL, ERNEST L., and PHILLIP ZEIDENBERG. 1985. "Age, Alcohol and Violent Death: A Post Mortem Study." *Journal of Studies on Alcohol*, 46 (3): 228–231.

ABEL, GENE G., JUDITH V. BECKER, EDWARD B. BLANCHARD, and ARMEN DJENDERDJIAN. 1978. "Differentiating Sexual Aggressives with Penile Measures." *Criminal Justice and Behavior*, 5 (December): 315–332.

ABEL, GENE G., JUDITH V. BECKER, and LINDA J. SKINNER. 1980. "Aggressive Behavior and Sex." *Psychiatric Clinics of North America*, 3 (April): 133–151.

ABELL, GEORGE O., and BARRY SINGER (eds.). 1983. *Science and the Paranormal: Probing the Existence of the Supernatural*. New York: Scribner's.

ABELSON, HERBERT I., and RONALD ATKINSON. 1975. *Public Experience with Psychoactive Substances*. Princeton, N.J.: Response Analysis Corporation.

ABELSON, HERBERT I., et al. 1973. "Drug Experience, Attitudes, and Related Behavior Among Adolescents and Adults." In National Commission on Marihuana and Drug Abuse, *Drug Use in America: Problem in Perspective*, Vol. 1. Washington, D.C.: U.S. Government Printing Office, pp. 488–861.

ADAM, BARRY D. 1978. *The Survival of Domination: Inferiorization and Everyday Life*. New York: Elsevier.

ADAMS, NATHAN M. 1981. "Portrait of a Pimp." *Reader's Digest* (April): 94–98.

ADLER, FREDA. 1975. *Sisters in Crime*. New York: McGraw-Hill.

ADLER, FREDA. 1979. "The Interaction Between Women's Emancipation and Female Criminality: A Cross-Cultural Perspective." In Freda Adler and Rita James Simon (eds.), *The Criminology of Deviant Women*. Boston: Houghton Mifflin, pp. 407–418.

AGNEW, ROBERT. 1985. "Social Control Theory and Delinquency: A Longitudinal Test." *Criminology*, 23 (February): 47–61.

AGUS, CAROL. 1984. "Unusual Lady, Unlikely Life." *Newsday* (October 24) Part II: 4–6.

AKERS, RONALD L. 1964. "Socio-economic Status and Delinquent Behavior: A Retest." *Journal of*

341

Research in Crime and Delinquency, 1 (January): 38–46.

AKERS, RONALD L. 1968. "Problems in the Sociology of Deviance: Social Definitions and Behavior." *Social Forces*, 46 (June): 455–465.

AKERS, RONALD L. 1977. *Deviant Behavior: A Social Learning Approach* (2nd ed.). Belmont, Calif.: Wadsworth.

AKERS, RONALD L. 1980. "Further Thoughts on Marxist Criminology: Comments on Turk, Toby, and Klockars." In James A. Inciardi (ed.), *Radical Criminology: The Coming Crises*. Beverly Hills, Calif.: Sage, pp. 133–138.

AKERS, RONALD L. 1985. *Deviant Behavior: A Social Learning Approach* (3rd ed.). Belmont, Calif.: Wadsworth.

AMERICAN PSYCHIATRIC ASSOCIATION. 1987. *Diagnostic and Statistical Manual of Mental Disorders* (3rd ed., rev.). Washington, D.C.: American Psychiatric Association.

AMIR, MENACHEM. 1971a. "Forcible Rape." *Sexual Behavior*, 1 (November): 24–36.

AMIR, MENACHEM. 1971b. *Patterns in Forcible Rape*. Chicago: University of Chicago Press.

ANDERSON, ODIN W., and JACOB J. FELDMAN. 1956. *Family Medical Costs and Voluntary Health Insurance: A Nationwide Survey*. New York: McGraw-Hill.

ANONYMOUS. 1976. "Diaper-Clad Man Chased Away: Was It Baby-Face Nelson?" *Winston-Salem Journal* (October 22).

ANONYMOUS. 1985. "AIDS Worry Alters Sex Habits, Study Finds." *The New York Times* (October 13): 41.

APA. See American Psychiatric Association.

ARCHER, DANE, and ROSEMARY GARTNER. 1984. *Violence and Crime in Cross-National Perspective*. New Haven, Conn.: Yale University Press.

ARDREY, ROBERT. 1961. *African Genesis*. New York: Dell.

ARDREY, ROBERT. 1966. *The Territorial Imperative*. New York: Atheneum.

ARMOR, DAVID J., J. MICHAEL POLICH, and HARRIET B. STAMBUL. 1976. *Alcoholism and Treatment*. Santa Monica, Calif.: Rand Corporation.

ASHLEY, RICHARD. 1975. *Cocaine: Its History, Uses and Effects*. New York: St. Martin's Press.

AULETTA, KEN. 1982. *The Underclass*. New York: Random House.

BALKAN, SHEILA, and RONALD J. BERGER. 1979. "The Changing Nature of Female Delinquency." In Claire B. Kopp and Martha Kirkpatrick (eds.), *Becoming Female: Perspectives on Development*. New York: Plenum, pp. 207–227.

BANKOWSKI, ZENON, GEOFF MUNGHAM, and PETER YOUNG. 1977. "Radical Criminology or Radical Criminologist?" *Contemporary Crises*, 1 (1): 37–52.

BARLOW, HUGH D. 1978. *Introduction to Criminology* (2nd ed.). Boston: Little, Brown.

BARLOW, HUGH D. 1987. *Introduction to Criminology* (4th ed.). Boston: Little, Brown.

BARMASH, ISADORE. 1973. "Pilferage Abounds in the Nation's Stores." *The New York Times* (October 28): 9.

BARON, ROBERT A., and PAUL A. BELL. 1977. "Sexual Arousal and Aggression by Males: Effects of Type and Erotic Stimuli and Prior Provocation." *Journal of Personality and Social Psychology*, 35 (2): 79–87.

BARRY, KATHLEEN. 1984. *Female Sexual Slavery*. New York: New York University Press.

BART, PAULINE B. 1975. "Rape Doesn't End with a Kiss." *Viva* (June): 39–42, 100–102.

BART, PAULINE B., and MARGARET JOZSA. 1982. "Dirty Books, Dirty Films, and Dirty Data." In Laura Lederer (ed.), *Take Back the Night: Women and Pornography*. New York: Bantam Books, pp. 201–215.

BART, PAULINE B., and PATRICIA H. O'BRIEN. 1985. *Stopping Rape: Successful Survival Strategies*. New York: Pergamon Press.

BASLER, BARBARA. 1980. "Mugger's Tale: He Prowled Without Fear Through a Fearful City." *The New York Times* (November 17): B1, B4.

BASTONE, WILLIAM. 1986a. "Leona Helmsley Didn't Pay Sales Tax, Why Should You?" *The Village Voice* (November 11): 12.

BASTONE, WILLIAM. 1986b. "The Evaders: The Bulgari Sales Tax Scam." *The Village Voice* (November 25): 12, 22.

BEAUCHAMP, WILLIAM. 1983. "The 2nd AIDS Epidemic." *The New York Times* (August 7): E21.

BECKER, GARY S. 1968. "Crime and Punishment: An Economic Approach." *Journal of Political Economy*, 76 (April): 169–217.

BECKER, HOWARD S. 1955. "Marijuana Use and Social Control." *Social Problems*, 3 (July): 35–44.

BECKER, HOWARD S. 1963. *Outsiders: Studies in the Sociology of Deviance*. New York: Free Press.

BECKER, HOWARD S. (ed.). 1964. *The Other Side: Perspectives on Deviance*. New York: Free Press.

BECKER, HOWARD S. 1967. "Whose Side Are We on?" *Social Problems*, 14 (Winter): 239–247.

BECKER, HOWARD S. 1973. "Labelling Theory Reconsidered." In Howard S. Becker, *Outsiders: Perspectives on Deviance* (2nd ed.). New York: Free Press, pp. 177–212.

BECKER, HOWARD S. 1981. "Review of Walter R. Gove (ed.), *The Labelling of Deviance: Evaluating a Perspective* (2nd ed.)." Beverly Hills, Calif.: Sage, 1981. In *Society*." (May/June 1981): 73–74.

BECKER, HOWARD S., and IRVING LOUIS HOROWITZ. 1970. "The Culture of Civility." *Trans-action*, 7 (April): 12–19.

BECKER, HOWARD S., BLANCHE GEER, EVERETT C. HUGHES, and ANSELM L. STRAUSS. 1961. *Boys in White: Student Culture in Medical School*. Chicago: University of Chicago Press.

BEIRNE, PIERS. 1979. "Empiricism and Critique of Marxism on Law and Crime." *Social Problems*, 26 (April): 373–385.

BELKIN, LISA. 1988. "Texas Judge Eases Sentence For Killer of 2 Homosexuals." *The New York Times* (December 17): 8.

BELL, ALAN P., and MARTIN S. WEINBERG. 1978. *Homosexualities: A Study of Diversity Among Men and Women*. New York: Simon & Schuster.

BELL, ARTHUR. 1976. "The Bath House Gets Respectability." *The Village Voice* (September 27): 19–20.

BELL, DANIEL. 1961. "Crime as an American Way of Life: A Queer Ladder of Social Mobility." In Daniel Bell (ed.), *The End of Ideology: On the Exhaustion of Political Ideas in the Fifties* (rev. ed.). New York: Collier Books, pp. 127–150.

BENEKE, TIMOTHY. 1982. *Men on Rape*. New York: St. Martin's Press.

BENNETT, WILLIAM, and JOEL GURIN. 1982. *The Dieter's Dilemma: Eating Less and Weighing More*. New York: Basic Books.

BEN-YEHUDA, NACHMAN. 1985. *Deviance and Moral Boundaries: Witchcraft, the Occult, Science Fiction, Deviant Sciences and Scientists*. Chicago: University of Chicago Press.

BEN-YEHUDA, NACHMAN. 1986. "The Sociology of Moral Panics: Toward a New Synthesis." *The Sociological Quarterly*, 27 (4): 495–513.

BERGER, PETER L. 1963. *Invitation to Sociology*. Garden City, N.Y.: Doubleday-Anchor.

BERNARD, JESSE. 1983. *The Future of Marriage* (rev. ed.). New Haven, Conn.: Yale University Press.

BERRIDGE, VIRGINIA, and GRIFFITH EDWARDS. 1987. *Opium and the People: Opiate Use in Nineteenth-Century England*. New Haven, Conn.: Yale University Press.

BIDERMAN, ALBERT D., and ALBERT J. REISS, JR.

1967. "On Explaining the 'Dark Figure' of Crime." *Annals of the American Academy of Political and Social Science*, 374 (November): 1–15.

BIEBER, IRVING. 1973. "Homosexuality—An Adaptive Consequence of Disorder in Psychosexual Development." *American Journal of Psychiatry*, 130 (November): 1209–1211.

BIEBER, IRVING, et al. 1962. *Homosexuality: A Psychoanalytic Study of Male Homosexuals*. New York: Basic Books.

BIEBER, IRVING, et al. 1971. "Playboy Panel: Homosexuality." *Playboy* (April): 61ff.

BITTNER, EGON. 1967. "The Police on Skid Row: A Study in Peace-Keeping." *American Sociological Review*, 32 (October): 699–715.

BLACK, DONALD J. and ALBERT J. REISS, JR. 1970. "Police Control of Juveniles." *American Sociological Review*, 35 (February): 63–77.

BLANE, HOWARD T., and KENNETH E. LEONARD (eds.). 1987. *Psychological Theories of Drinking and Alcoholism*. New York: Guilford Press.

BLEUEL, HANS PETER. 1974. *Sex and Society in Nazi Germany*, J. Maxwell Brownjohn (trans.). New York: Bantam Books.

BLUMER, HERBERT. 1969. *Symbolic Interactionism: Perspective and Method*. Englewood Cliffs, N.J.: Prentice-Hall.

BOFFEY, PHILIP M. 1982a. "Showdown Nears in Feud Over Alcohol Studies." *The New York Times* (November 2): C1, C2.

BOFFEY, PHILIP M. 1982b. "Panel Clears 2 Accused of Scientific Fraud in Alcoholism Study." *The New York Times* (November 5): A12.

BOFFEY, PHILIP M. 1983. "Controlled Drinking Gains as a Treatment in Europe." *The New York Times* (November 22): C1, C7.

BOFFEY, PHILIP M. 1984. "Panel Finds No Fraud by Alcohol Researchers." *The New York Times* (September 11): C8.

BOFFEY, PHILIP M. 1988a. "Researchers List Odds of Getting AIDS in Heterosexual Intercourse." *The New York Times* (April 22): A1, A18.

BOFFEY, PHILIP M. 1988b. "Spread of AIDS Abating, But Deaths Will Still Soar." *The New York Times* (February 14): 1, 36.

BOGUE, DONALD J. 1985. *The Population of the United States: Historical Trends and Future Projections*. New York: Free Press.

BOHLEN, CELESTINE. 1988. "Domestic Violence Arrests Quadruple in New York City." *The New York Times* (December 28): B3.

BOHM, ROBERT M. 1982. "Radical Criminology:

An Explication." *Criminology,* 19 (February): 565–589.

BONNIE, RICHARD J., and CHARLES H. WHITEBREAD II. 1970. "The Forbidden Fruit and the Tree of Knowledge: An Inquiry Into the History of American Marihuana Prohibition." *Virginia Law Review,* 56 (October): 971–1203.

BOOKBINDER, BERNIE. 1985. "54% Support Subway Shooting." *Newsday* (January 13): 3.

BORDUA, DAVID J. 1967. "Recent Trends: Deviant Behavior and Social Control." *The Annals of the American Academy of Political and Social Science,* 369: 149–163.

BOWART, WILLIAM H. 1978. *Operation Mind Control: Our Government's War Against Its Own People.* New York: Dell.

BOWKER, LEE H. 1980. "The Institutional Determinants of International Female Crime." Paper delivered at the annual meeting of the Society for the Study of Social Problems, New York, August.

BRACEY, DOROTHY HEID. 1979. *"Baby-Pros": Profiles of Juvenile Prostitutes.* New York: John Jay Press.

BRADEN, WILLIAM. 1970. "LSD and the Press." In Bernard Aaronson and Humphrey Osmond (eds.), *Psychedelics.* Garden City, N.Y.: Doubleday Anchor, pp. 400–418.

BRAITHWAITE, JOHN. 1979. *Inequality, Crime, and Public Policy.* London: Routledge & Kegan Paul.

BRAITHWAITE, JOHN. 1981. "The Myth of Social Class and Criminality Reconsidered." *American Sociological Review,* 46 (February): 36–57.

BRAITHWAITE, JOHN. 1985. "White-Collar Crime." In Ralph Turner (ed.), *Annual Review of Sociology.* Palo Alto, Calif.: Annual Reviews, pp. 1–25.

BRAITHWAITE, JOHN, and VALERIE BRAITHWAITE. 1980. "The Effect of Income Inequality and Social Democracy on Homicide." *British Journal of Criminology,* 20 (January): 45–53.

BRAITHWAITE, JOHN, and GILBERT GEIS. 1982. "On Theory and Action for Corporate Crime Control." *Crime and Delinquency,* 28: 292–314.

BRASHLER, WILLIAM. 1984. "The Big Kill." *Playboy* (November): 93–94, 156–160.

BRASLEY, PATRICK. 1988. "Arrests up in Family Violence." *Newsday* (December 11): Part II, 21.

BRECHER, EDWARD M., et al. 1972. *Licit and Illicit Drugs.* Boston: Little, Brown.

BRIERLY, HARRY. 1979. *Transvestism: A Handbook with Case Studies for Psychologists, Psychiatrists, and Counsellors.* Oxford, Eng.: Pergamon Press.

BRIGGS, KENNETH A. 1984. "Methodists Bar Homosexuals From Ministry." *The New York Times* (May 10): A21.

BRINKLEY, JOEL. 1986. "U.S. Blames New Form of Heroin for Outbreak of Overdose Deaths." *The New York Times* (March 28): A1, B6.

BRODIE, H. KEITH. 1973. "The Effects of Ethyl Alcohol in Man." In National Commission on Marihuana and Drug Abuse, *Drug Use in America: Problem in Perspective,* Vol. 1. Washington, D.C.: U.S. Government Printing Office, pp. 6–59.

BRONSTEIN, SCOTT. 1987. "Study Shows Sharp Rise in Cocaine Use by Suspects in Crimes." *The New York Times* (February 19): B1, B4.

BROOKE, JAMES. 1986. "Drunken Driving Fatalities Declining." *The New York Times* (August 27): B4.

BROWNE, ANGELA. 1987. *When Battered Women Kill.* New York: Free Press.

BROWNMILLER, SUSAN. 1975. *Against Our Will: Men, Women, and Rape.* New York: Simon & Schuster.

BROWNMILLER, SUSAN, et al. 1984. "The Question of Pornography." *Harper's* (November): 31–45.

BUDER, LEONARD. 1977. "Half of 1976 Murder Victims Had Police Records." *The New York Times* (August 28): 1, 34.

BUNKER, JOHN P. 1976. "Risks and Benefits in Surgery." In American College of Surgeons and the American Surgical Association, *Surgery in the United States,* 3.

BURGESS, LOUISE BAILEY. 1973. *Alcohol and Your Health.* Los Angeles: Charles Publishing.

BURGESS, ROBERT L., and RONALD L. AKERS. 1966. "A Differential Association Reinforcement Theory of Criminal Behavior." *Social Problems,* 14 (Fall): 128–147.

BURNHAM, DAVID. 1973a. "Crime Rates in Precincts and Census Data Studied." *The New York Times* (October 16): 45, 51.

BURNHAM, DAVID. 1973b. "Murder Rate for Blacks in City 8 Times That for White Victims." *The New York Times* (August 5): 1, 46.

BURNHAM, DAVID. 1973c. "How Safe Is the City? Statistics Can Mislead." *The New York Times* (October 16): 45, 51.

BURNHAM, DAVID, 1974. "New York Is Found Safest of 13 Cities in Crime Study." *The New York Times* (April 15): 1, 15.

BURROUGH, BRYAN. 1986. "The Embezzler." *The Wall Street Journal* (September 19): 1.

BURSTYN, VARDA (ed.). 1985. *Women Against Censorship.* Manchester, N.H.: Salem House.

BURT, MARTHA. 1980. "Cultural Myths and Supports for Rape." *Journal of Personality and Social Psychology*, 38 (2): 217–230.

BUTTERFIELD, FOX. 1984. "Slaying of Homosexual Man Upsets Confidence of Bangor, Me." *The New York Times* (July 29): 18.

BYCK, ROBERT (ed.). 1974. *Cocaine Papers by Sigmund Freud*. New York: Stonehill.

BYRON, PEG. 1985. "What We Talk About When We Talk About Dildos." *The Village Voice* (March 5): 48–49.

CAHALAN, DON. 1970. *Problem Drinkers*. San Francisco: Jossey-Bass.

CAHALAN, DON, and ROBIN ROOM. 1974. *Problem Drinking Among American Men*. New Brunswick, N.J.: Rutgers Center for Alcohol Studies.

CAHNMAN, WERNER J. 1968. "The Stigma of Obesity." *The Sociological Quarterly*, 9 (Summer): 283–299.

CALLAWAY, ENOCH, III. 1958. "Institutional Use of Ataractic Drugs." *Modern Medicine, 1958 Annual*, Part I (January 1–June 15): 26–29.

CAMERON, MARY OWEN. 1964. *The Booster and the Snitch*. New York: Free Press.

CAPOTE, TRUMAN. 1988. *Answered Prayers: The Unfinished Novel*. Plume.

CASS, VIVIENNE C. 1979. "Homosexual Identity Formation: A Theoretical Model." *Journal of Homosexuality*, 4 (3): 219–235.

CASS, VIVIENNE C. 1984. "Homosexual Identity Formation: Testing a Theoretical Model." *Journal of Sex Research*, 20 (2): 143–167.

CHAMBLISS, WILLIAM J. 1964. "A Sociological Analysis of the Law of Vagrancy." *Social Problems*, 12 (Summer): 67–77.

CHAMBLISS, WILLIAM J. 1967. "Types of Deviance and the Effectiveness of Legal Sanctions." *Wisconsin Law Review* (Summer): 703–719.

CHAMBLISS, WILLIAM J. 1973a. "The Saints and the Roughnecks." *Society*, 11 (December): 24–31.

CHAMBLISS, WILLIAM J. 1973b. "Functional and Conflict Theories of Crime." New York: MSS Modular Publications.

CHAMBLISS, WILLIAM J. 1975. "Toward a Political Economy of Crime." *Theory and Society*, 2 (Summer): 149–170.

CHAMBLISS, WILLIAM J. 1976. "Functional and Conflict Theories in Crime." In William J. Chambliss and Milton Mankoff (eds.), *Whose Law? What Order? A Conflict Approach to Criminology*. New York: John Wiley & Sons, pp. 1–28.

CHAMBLISS, WILLIAM J. 1988. *Exploring Criminology*. New York: Macmillan.

CHAMBLISS, WILLIAM J., and ROBERT B. SEIDMAN. 1971. *Law, Order, and Power*. Reading, Mass.: Addison-Wesley.

CHAMBLISS, WILLIAM J., and ROBERT B. SEIDMAN. 1982. *Law, Order, and Power* (2nd ed.). Reading, Mass.: Addison-Wesley.

CHAPPEL, DUNCAN, and SUSAN SINGER. 1977. "Rape in New York City: A Study of Material in the Police Files and Its Meaning." In Duncan Chappel, Robley Geis, and Gilbert Geis (eds.), *Forcible Rape: The Crime, the Victim, and the Offender*. New York: Columbia University Press, pp. 245–271.

CHASE, NAOMI FEIGELSON. 1975. *A Child Is Being Beaten*. New York: McGraw-Hill.

CHATLOS, CALVIN. 1987. *Crack: What You Should Know About the Cocaine Epidemic*. New York: Perigee Books.

CHURCH, GEORGE J., et al. 1988. "Thinking the Unthinkable." *Time* (May 30): 12–19.

CLARK, MATT, et al. 1985. "AIDS." *Newsday* (August 12): 20–27.

CLARK, JOHN P., and RICHARD C. HOLLINGER. 1983. *Theft by Employees in Work Organizations: Executive Summary*. Washington, D.C.: National Institute of Justice.

CLARKE, GERALD, et al. 1985. "In the Middle of a War." *Time* (August 12): 46.

CLELLAND, DONALD, AND TIMOTHY J. CARTER. 1980. "The New Myth of Class and Crime." *Criminology*, 18 (November): 319–336.

CLINARD, MARSHALL B. 1952. *The Black Market: A Study of White Collar Crime*. New York: Rinehart.

CLINARD, MARSHALL B. 1964. "The Theoretical Implications of Anomie and Deviant Behavior." In Marshall B. Clinard (ed.), *Anomie and Deviant Behavior: A Discussion and Critique*. New York: Free Press, pp. 1–56.

CLINARD, MARSHALL B., and ROBERT F. MEIER. 1985. *Sociology of Deviant Behavior* (6th ed.). New York: Holt, Reinhart & Winston.

CLINARD, MARSHALL B., and RICHARD QUINNEY (eds.). 1967. *Criminal Behavior Systems: A Typology*. New York: Holt, Rinehart & Winston.

CLINARD, MARSHALL B., and PETER C. YEAGER. 1980. *Corporate Crime*. New York: Free Press.

CLOWARD, RICHARD. 1959. "Illegitimate Means, Anomie, and Deviant Behavior." *American Sociological Review*, 24 (April): 164–177.

CLOWARD, RICHARD A., and LLOYD E. OHLIN. 1960. *Delinquency and Opportunity: A Theory of Delinquent Gangs*. New York: Free Press.

COCKERHAM, WILLIAM C. 1981. *Sociology of Mental Disorder*. Englewood Cliffs, N.J.: Prentice-Hall.

COHEN, ALBERT K. 1955. *Delinquent Boys: The Subculture of the Gang*. New York: Free Press.

COHEN, ALBERT K. 1966. *Deviance and Control*. Englewood Cliffs, N.J.: Prentice-Hall.

COHEN, LAWRENCE E., and KENNETH C. LAND. 1987. "Sociological Positivism and the Explanation of Criminology." In Michael R. Gottfredson and Travis Hirschi (eds.), *Positive Criminology*. Beverly Hills, Calif.: Sage, pp. 43–55.

COHEN, LAWRENCE E., and RODNEY STARK. 1974. "Discriminatory Labeling and the Five-Fingered Discount: An Empirical Analysis of Differential Shoplifting Dispositions." *Social Problems,* 11 (January): 25–39.

COHEN, LAWRENCE E., MARCUS FELSON, and KENNETH C. LAND. 1980. "Property Crime Rates in the United States: A Macrodynamic Analysis, 1947–1977, with ex-ante Forecasts for the Mid-1980s." *American Journal of Sociology,* 86 (July): 90–118.

COHEN, STANLEY. 1980. *Folk Devils and Moral Panics*. New York: St. Martin's Press.

COHEN, STANLEY. 1985. *Visions of Social Control*. Cambridge, Eng.: Polity Press.

COHEN, STANLEY. 1988. *Against Criminology*. New Brunswick, N.J.: Transaction Books.

COLEMAN, KATE. 1971. "Carnal Knowledge: A Portrait of Four Hookers." *Ramparts* (December): 17–28.

COLEMAN, JAMES W. 1985. *The Criminal Elite: The Sociology of White-Collar Crime*. New York: St. Martin's Press.

COLLINS, GLENN. 1985. "Impact of AIDS: Patterns of Homosexual Life Changing." *The New York Times* (July 22): B4.

COMBES-ORME, TERRI, JOHN R. TAYLOR, ELLEN BATES SCOTT, and SANDRA HOLMES. 1983. "Violent Death Among Alcoholics: A Descriptive Study." *Journal of Studies on Alcohol,* 44 (6): 938–949.

COMMISSION ON OBSCENITY AND PORNOGRAPHY. 1970. *The Report of the Commission on Obscenity and Pornography*. Washington, D.C.: U.S. Government Printing Office.

CONKLIN, JOHN E. 1972. *Robbery and the Criminal Justice System*. Philadelphia: Lippincott.

CONKLIN, JOHN E. 1981. *Criminology*. New York: Macmillan.

CONNELL, NOREEN, and CASSANDRA WILSON (eds.). 1974. *Rape: The First Source-Book for Women*. New York: New American Library.

CONOVER, PATRICK W. 1976. "A Reassessment of Labeling Theory: A Constructive Response to Criticism." In Lewis A. Coser and Otto Larsen (eds.), *The Uses of Controversy in Sociology*. New York: Free Press, pp. 228–249.

CONRAD, PETER, and JOSEPH W. SCHNEIDER. 1980. *Deviance and Medicalization: From Badness to Sickness*. St. Louis: Mosby.

COOK, PHILIP J., and DANIEL NAGIN. 1979. *Does the Weapon Matter?* Washington, D.C.: Institute for Law and Society.

COOK, SHIRLEY J. 1970. "Social Background of Narcotics Legislation." *Addictions,* 17 (Summer): 14–29.

COSER, LEWIS. 1956. *The Functions of Social Conflict*. New York: Free Press.

CRESSEY, DONALD R. 1953. *Other People's Money*. New York: Free Press.

CRESSEY, DONALD R. 1960. "Epidemiology and Individual Conduct: A Case from Criminology." *Pacific Sociological Review,* 3 (Fall): 47–58.

CULLEN, FRANCIS T., et al. 1982. "The Seriousness of Crime Revisited." *Criminology,* 20 (May): 88–102.

CURRIE, ELLIOTT P. 1968. "Crimes Without Criminals: Witchcraft and Its Renaissance Europe." *Law and Society Review,* 3 (August): 7–32.

CURRIE, ELLIOTT P. 1985. *Confronting Crime: An American Challenge*. New York: Pantheon Books.

CURRIE, ELLIOTT P., and JEROME H. SKOLNICK. 1984. *America's Problems: Social Issues and Public Policy*. Boston: Little, Brown.

CUSKY, WALTER R., LISA H. BERGER, and ARTHUR H. RICHARDSON. 1978. "The Effects of Marijuana Decriminalization on Drug Use Patterns." *Contemporary Drug Problems,* 7 (Winter): 491–532.

DALY, MARTIN, and MARGO WILSON. 1988. *Homicide*. New York: Aldine de Gruyter.

DANK, BARRY M. 1971. "Coming Out in the Gay World." *Psychiatry,* 34 (May): 180–197.

DANK, BARRY M. 1972. "Why Homosexuals Marry Women." *Medical Aspects of Human Sexuality* (August): 14–22.

DAVIES, CHRISTIE. 1983. "Crime, Bureaucracy, and Equality." *Policy Review* (Winter): 89–105.

DAVIS, F. JAMES. 1952. "Crime News in Colorado Newspapers." *American Journal of Sociology,* 57 (January): 325–330.

DAVIS, KINGSLEY. 1937. "The Sociology of Prostitution." *American Sociological Review,* 2 (October): 744–755.

DAVIS, KINGSLEY. 1949. *Human Society*. New York: Macmillan.

DAVIS, KINGSLEY. 1976. "Sexual Behavior." In Robert K. Merton and Robert Nisbet (eds.), *Contemporary Social Problems* (4th ed.). New York: Harcourt Brace Jovanovich, pp. 219–261.

DAVIS, KINGSLEY, and WILBERT E. MOORE. 1945. "Some Principles of Stratification." *American Sociological Review*, 10 (April): 242–249.

DAVIS, NANETTE J. 1971. "The Prostitute: Developing a Deviant Identity." In James M. Henslin (ed.), *Studies in the Sociology of Sex*. New York: Appleton-Century-Crofts, pp. 297–322.

DAVIS, NANETTE J. 1978. "Prostitution: Identity, Career, and Legal-Economic Enterprise." In James M. Henslin and Edward Sagarin (eds.), *The Sociology of Sex: An Introductory Reader* (rev. ed.). New York: Schocken Books, pp. 195–222.

DAVIS, NANETTE J. 1980. *Sociological Constructions of Deviance: Perspectives and Issues in the Field* (2nd ed.). Dubuque, Iowa: William C. Brown.

DAVISON, BILL. 1967. "The Hidden Evils of LSD." *The Saturday Evening Post* (August 12): 19–23.

DAVISON, GERALD C., and JOHN M. NEALE. 1986. *Abnormal Psychology: An Experimental Clinical Approach* (4th ed.). New York: John Wiley & Sons.

DAWN. See Drug Abuse Warning Network.

D'ESPO, D. ANTHONY. 1962. "Hysterectomy When the Uterus is Grossly Normal." *American Journal of Obstetrics and Gynecology*, 83 (January 1): 113–121.

DeFLEUR, MELVIN L., and RICHARD QUINNEY. 1966. "A Reformulation of Sutherland's Differential Association Theory and a Strategy for Empirical Verification." *Journal of Research in Crime and Delinquency*, 3 (January): 1–11.

DeLINDT, JAN, and WOLFGANG SCHMIDT. 1971. "Alcohol Use and Alcoholism." *Addictions*, 18 (Summer): 1–14.

DELPH, EDWARD WILLIAM. 1978. *The Silent Community: Public Homosexual Encounters*. Beverly Hills, Calif.: Sage.

DeLUISE, MARIO, GEORGE L. BLACKBURN, and JEFFREY S. FLIER. 1980. "Reduced Activity of the Red-Cell Sodium-Potassium Pump in Human Obesity." *New England Journal of Medicine*, 303 (October 30): 1017–1022.

DENISOFF, R. SERGE, and CHARLES H. McCAGHY (eds.). 1973. *Deviance, Conflict, and Criminality*. Chicago: Rand McNally.

DIAMOND, IRENE. 1982. "Pornography and Repression: A Reconsideration of 'Who' and 'What.'" In Laura Lederer (ed.), *Take Back the Night: Women on Pornography*. New York: Bantam Books, pp. 183–200.

DIETZ, PARK ELLIOTT, and BARBARA EVANS. 1982. "Pornographic Imagery and Prevalence of Paraphilia." *American Journal of Psychiatry*, 139 (November): 1493–1495.

DiMENTO, JOSEPH. 1986. *Environmental Law and American Business: Dilemmas of Compliance*. New York: Plenum.

DISHOTSKY, NORMAN I., WILLIAM D. LOUGHMAN, ROBERT E. MOGAR, and WENDELL R. LIPSCOMB. 1971. "LSD and Genetic Damage." *Science*, 172 (30 April): 431–440.

DODGE, DAVID L. 1985. "The Over-Negative Conceptualization of Deviance: A Programmatic Exploration." *Deviant Behavior*, 6 (1): 17–37.

DOHERTY, EDMUND G. 1978. "Are Differential Discharge Criteria Used for Men and Women Psychiatric Inpatients?" *Journal of Health and Social Behavior*, 19 (March): 107–116.

DOHRENWEND, BRUCE P., and BARBARA SNELL DOHRENWEND. 1969. *Social Status and Psychological Disorder: A Causal Inquiry*. New York: John Wiley-Interscience.

DOHRENWEND, BRUCE P., and BARBARA SNELL DOHRENWEND. 1974. "Social and Cultural Influences on Psychopathology." *Annual Review of Psychology*, 25: 417–452.

DOHRENWEND, BRUCE P., and BARBARA SNELL DOHRENWEND.1976. "Sex Differences and Psychiatric Disorder." *American Journal of Sociology*, 81 (May): 1447–1454.

DOLL, LYNDA, et al. 1987. "Self-Reported Change in Sexual Behaviors in Gay and Bisexual Men from the San Francisco City Clinic Cohort." Paper presented at the Third International Conference on AIDS, Washington, D.C., June 1–5.

DONNERSTEIN, EDWARD. 1981. "Pornography and Violence Against Women: Experimental Studies." *Annals of the New York Academy of Sciences*, 347 (Part VII): 277–288.

DONNERSTEIN, EDWARD, DANIEL LINZ, and STEVEN PENROD. 1987. *The Question of Pornography: Research Findings and Policy Implications*. New York: Free Press.

DOUGLAS, JACK D. (ed.). 1984. *The Sociology of Deviance*. Boston: Allyn & Bacon.

DOUGLAS, JACK D., and FRANCES CHAPUT WAKSLER. 1982. *The Sociology of Deviance: An Introduction*. Boston: Little, Brown.

DOVER, K. J. 1978. *Greek Homosexuality*. New York: Vintage Books.

DOWD, MAUREEN. 1985. "The Puzzling Death of a Man Bedeviled by His Own Brilliance." *The New York Times* (May 25): 11.

DOWIE, MARK. 1985. "Pinto Madness." In *The Best of Mother Jones*. San Francisco: Foundation for National Progress, pp. 59–69.

DOWIE, MARK, and TRACY JOHNSTON. 1985. "A Case of Corporate Malpractice." In *The Best of Mother Jones*. San Francisco: Foundation for National Progress, pp. 4–17.

DOWNES, DAVID. 1979. "Praxis Makes Perfect: A Critique of Critical Criminology." In David Downes and Paul Rock (eds.), *Deviant Interpretations*. London: Martin Robertson, pp. 1–16.

DOWNES, DAVID, and PAUL ROCK. 1982. *Understanding Deviance: A Guide to the Sociology of Crime and Rule Breaking*. Oxford, England: Clarendon Press.

DRUG ABUSE WARNING NETWORK. 1987. *Annual Data, 1986: Data From the Drug Abuse Warning Network*. Rockville, Md.: National Institute on Drug Abuse.

DUGGAN, LISA. 1988. "Censorship in the Name of Feminism." In Kate Ellis et al. (eds.), *Caught Looking: Feminism, Pornography, and Censorship*. Seattle, Wash.: Real Comet Press, pp. 62–69.

DUGGAN, LISA, and ANN SNITOW. 1984. "Porn Law Is About Images, Not Power." *Newsday* (September 26): 65.

DUGGAN, LISA, NAN HUNTER, and CAROLE S. VANCE. 1988. "False Promises: Feminist Antipornography Legislation." In Kate Ellis et al. (eds.), *Caught Looking: Feminism, Pornography, and Censorship*. Seattle, Wash.: Real Comet Press, pp. 72–85.

DULLEA, GEORGIA. 1988. "Gay Couples' Wish to Adopt Grows, Along With Increasing Resistance." *The New York Times* (February 7): 26.

DUNHAM, H. WARREN. 1965. *Community and Schizophrenia: An Epidemiological Analysis*. Detroit: Wayne State University Press.

DUSTER, TROY. 1970. *The Legislation of Morality*. New York: Free Press.

DUTTON, DONALD G. 1988. *The Domestic Assault of Women: Psychological and Criminal Justice Perspectives*. Boston: Allyn & Bacon.

DWORKIN, ANDREA. 1981. *Pornography: Men Possessing Women*. New York: Perigee.

DWORKIN, ANDREA. 1982a. "Why So-Called Radical Men Love and Need Pornography." In Laura Lederer (ed.), *Take Back the Night: Women on Pornography*. New York: Bantam Books, pp. 141–147.

DWORKIN, ANDREA. 1982b. "For Men, Freedom of Speech; for Women, Silence Please." In Laura Lederer (ed.), *Take Back the Night: Women on Pornography*. New York: Bantam Books, pp. 255–258.

DWORKIN, ANDREA. 1982c. "Pornography and Grief." In Laura Lederer (ed.), *Take Back the Night: Women on Pornography*. New York: Bantam Books, pp. 286–291.

DWORKIN, ANDREA. 1987. *Intercourse*. New York: Free Press.

EASTLAND, JAMES O. (Chairman). 1974. *Marihuana-Hashish Epidemic and Its Impact on United States Security*. Washington, D.C.: U.S. Government Printing Office.

ECKHOLM, ERIK. 1986. "Heterosexuals and AIDS: The Concern Is Growing." *The New York Times* (October 28): A1, C7.

ECKHOLM, ERIC. 1986. "Radon: Threat Is Real, but Scientists Argue Over Its Severity." *The New York Times* (September 2): C1, C7.

ECKHOLM, ERIK. 1988. "Sex Researchers Defend AIDS Book Against Wide Criticism." *The New York Times* (March 8): A14.

EDGERTON, ROBERT B. 1969. "On the Recognition of Mental Illness." In Robert B. Edgerton (ed.), *Perspectives in Mental Illness*. New York: Holt, Rinehart & Winston, pp. 49–72.

EDGERTON, ROBERT B. 1976. *Deviance: A Cross-Cultural Perspective*. Menlo Park, Calif.: Benjamin Cummings.

EDMISTON, SUSAN. 1970. "Murder, New York Style: A Crime of Class." *New York* (August 17): 29–35.

EGAN, TIMOTHY. 1988. "Gay Ex-Soldier Wants to Return to the Army." *The New York Times* (February 12): A18.

EGELAND, JANICE A., et al. 1987. "Bipolar Affective Disorders Linked to DNA Markers on Chromosome 11." *Nature*, 325 (26 February): 783–787.

EISENBERG, LEON. 1972. "The *Human* Nature of Human Nature." *Science*, 176 (April 14): 123–128.

EITZEN, D. STANLEY, and DOUG A. TIMMER. 1985. *Criminology: Crime and Criminal Justice*. New York: John Wiley & Sons.

ELLIOTT, DELBERT S., and SUZANNE S. AGETON. 1980. "Reconciling Race and Class Differences in Self-Reported and Official Estimates of Delinquency." *American Sociological Review*, 45 (February): 95–110.

ELLIOTT, DELBERT S., and DAVID HUIZINGA. 1983. "Social Class and Delinquent Behavior in a

National Youth Panel: 1976–1980." *Criminology*, 21 (May): 149–177.

ELLIS, DESMOND. 1987. *The Wrong Stuff: An Introduction to the Sociological Study of Deviance*. Don Mills, Ontario: Collier Macmillan Canada.

ELLIS, KATE, BARBARA O'DAIR, and ABBY TALLMER. 1988. "Introduction." In Kate Ellis et al. (eds.), *Caught Looking: Feminism, Pornography, and Censorship*. Seattle, Wash.: Real Comet Press, pp. 4–8.

ELLIS, KATE, et al. (eds.). 1988. *Caught Looking: Feminism, Pornography, and Censorship*. Seattle, Wash.: Real Comet Press.

EMPEY, LAMAR T. 1982. *American Delinquency: Its Meaning and Construction* (2nd ed.). Homewood, Ill.: Dorsey Press.

EMPEY, LAMAR T., and MAYNARD L. ERICKSON. 1966. "Hidden Delinquency and Social Status." *Social Problems*, 44 (June): 546–554.

ERIKSON, KAI T. 1962. "Notes on the Sociology of Deviance." *Social Problems*, 9 (Spring): 307–314.

ERIKSON, KAI T. 1964. "Notes on the Sociology of Deviance." In Howard S. Becker (ed.), *The Other Side: Perspectives on Deviance*. New York: Free Press, pp. 9–21.

ERIKSON, KAI T. 1966. *Wayward Puritans: A Study in the Sociology of Deviance*. New York: John Wiley & Sons.

ERMANN, M. DAVID, and RICHARD J. LUNDMAN (eds.). 1978. *Corporate and Governmental Deviance: Problems in Organizational Behavior in Contemporary Society*. New York: Oxford University Press.

ESTRICH, SUSAN. 1987. *Real Rape*. Cambridge, Mass.: Harvard University Press.

EWING, CHARLES PATRICK. 1987. "Prepared Statement." Paper presented to the Select Committee on Children, Youth and Families, U.S. House of Representatives, Washington, D.C., September 16.

FARBER, M. A. 1982. "Researcher Faked Data at Mt. Sinai Medical School." *The New York Times* (December 27): B1, B4.

FARBERMAN, HARVEY A. 1975. "A Criminogenic Market Structure: The Automobile Industry." *Sociological Quarterly*, 16 (Autumn): 438–457.

FARIS, ROBERT E., and H. WARREN DUNHAM. 1939. *Mental Disorders in Urban Areas*. Chicago: University of Chicago Press.

FARRELL, RONALD A., and VICTORIA LYNN SWIGERT (eds.). 1988. *Social Deviance* (3rd ed.). Belmont, Calif.: Wadsworth.

FBI. See Federal Bureau of Investigation.

FEDERAL BUREAU OF INVESTIGATION. 1988. *Crime in the United States, 1987: Uniform Crime Reports*. Washington, D.C.: U.S. Government Printing Office.

FERRACUTI, FRANCO, RENATO LAZAARI, and MARVIN E. WOLFGANG. 1973. "The Subculture of Violence in Sardinia." In Walter C. Reckless, *The Crime Problem* (5th ed.). New York: Appleton-Century-Crofts, pp. 212–215.

FINKELHOR, DAVID. 1979. *Sexually Victimized Children*. New York: Free Press.

FINKELHOR, DAVID, and KERSTI YLLO. 1985. *Licence to Rape: Sexual Abuse of Wives*. New York: Free Press.

FISCHER, ANITA, JANOS MARTON, E. JOEL MILLMAN, and LEO SROLE. 1979. "Long-Range Influences on Adult Mental Health: The Midtown Longitudinal Study, 1954–1974." In Roberta Simmons (ed.), *Research in Community & Mental Health*, Vol. 1. Greenwich, Conn.: Jai Press, pp. 305–333.

FISHBURNE, PATRICIA M., HERBERT I. ABELSON, and IRA CISIN. 1980. *National Survey on Drug Abuse: Main Findings, 1979*. Rockville, Md.: National Institute on Drug Abuse.

FISSE, BRENT, and JOHN BRAITHWAITE. 1983. *The Impact of Publicity on Corporate Offenders*. Albany, N.Y.: State University of New York Press.

FLETCHER, GEORGE P. 1988a. "A Crime of Self-Defense." *Columbia* (November): 16–21.

FLETCHER, GEORGE P. 1988b. *A Crime of Self-Defense*. New York: Free Press.

FLETCHER, MICHAEL A. 1988. "To Legalize or Not, That's the Question." *The Evening Sun* (Baltimore) (August 5): D1, D4.

FORD, CLELLAND S., and FRANK A. BEACH. 1951. *Patterns of Sexual Behavior*. New York: Harper & Row.

FORUM. 1977. "Study Finds Excessive Rate of Medicaid Surgery." *Forum*, 1: 18.

FORWARD, SUSAN, and CRAIG BUCK. 1978. *Betrayal of Innocence: Incest and Its Devastation*. Los Angeles: Tarcher.

FREEDMAN, SAMUEL G. 1986a. "Darkness Beneath the Glitter: Life of Suspect in Park Slaying." *The New York Times* (August 28): A1, B7.

FREEDMAN, SAMUEL G. 1986b. "Death in Park: Difficult Questions for Parents." *The New York Times* (September 11): A1, B10.

FREEDMAN, SAMUEL G. 1986c. "Outcry Raised in Levin Case at Blame-the-Victim Defense." *The New York Times* (December 4): A1, B26.

FREEDMAN, SAMUEL G. 1987. "Evangelicals Fight

Over Both Body and Soul." *The New York Times* (May 31): 30.

FREIDSON, ELIOT. 1970. *Professional Dominance: The Social Structure of Medical Care*. Chicago: Aldine.

FREIDSON, ELIOT. 1970. *Profession of Medicine: A Study of the Sociology of Applied Knowledge*. New York: Dodd, Mead.

FRIEDMAN, MYRA, with MICHAEL DALY. 1985. "My Neighbor Bernie Goetz." *New York* (February 18): 34–41.

FRIEDMAN, WOLFGANG. 1964. *Law in a Changing Society*. Harmondsworth, England: Penguin.

FRIEDRICHS, DAVID O. 1980. "Radical Criminology in the United States." In James A. Inciardi (ed.), *Radical Criminology*. Beverly Hills, Calif.: Sage, pp. 35–60.

GAGNON, JOHN H. 1971. "Physical Strength, Once of Significance." *Impact of Science on Society*, 21 (1): 31–42.

GAGNON, JOHN H., and WILLIAM SIMON (eds.). 1967. *Sexual Deviance*. New York: Harper & Row.

GAGNON, JOHN H., and WILLIAM SIMON. 1973. *Sexual Conduct: The Social Sources of Human Sexuality*. Chicago: Aldine.

GALLAGHER, BERNARD J., III. 1980. *The Sociology of Mental Illness*. Englewood Cliffs, N.J.: Prentice-Hall.

GALLAGHER, WINIFRED. 1986. "The Looming Menace of Designer Drugs." *Discover* (August): 24–35.

GALLUP, GEORGE, JR. 1980. *The Gallup Poll: Public Opinion, 1979*. Wilmington, Del.: Scholarly Resources.

GALLUP, GEORGE, JR. 1986. *The Gallup Poll: Public Opinion, 1985*. Wilmington, Del.: Scholarly Resources.

GALLUP, GEORGE, JR. 1987. *The Gallup Poll: Public Opinion, 1986*. Wilmington, Del.: Scholarly Resources.

GALLUP, GEORGE, JR. 1988. *The Gallup Poll: Public Opinion, 1987*. Wilmington, Del.: Scholarly Resources.

GARFINKEL, HAROLD. 1949. "Research Notes on Inter- and Intra-Racial Homicides." *Social Forces*, 27 (May): 369–381.

GEBHARD, PAUL H. 1969. "Misconceptions About Female Prostitutes." *Medical Aspects of Human Sexuality*, 3 (March): 24–30.

GEBHARD, PAUL H., and JOHN H. GAGNON, WARDELL POMEROY, and CORNELIA V. CHRISTENSON. 1967. *Sex Offenders: An Analysis of Types*. New York: Bantam Books.

GEIS, GILBERT. 1967. "White-Collar Crime: The Heavy Electrical Conspiracy." In Marshall B. Clinard and Richard Quinney (eds.), *Criminal Behavior Systems: A Typology*. New York: Holt, Rinehart and Winston, pp. 139–163.

GEIS, GILBERT. 1981. "Upperworld Crime." In Abraham S. Blumberg (ed.), *Current Perspectives on Criminal Behavior*. (2nd ed.) New York: Alfred Knopf, pp. 179–198.

GEIS, GILBERT. 1984. "White-Collar and Corporate Crime." In Robert F. Meier (ed.), *Major Forms of Crime*. Beverly Hills, Calif.: Sage, pp. 137–166.

GEIS, GILBERT, PAUL JESILOW, HENRY N. PONTELL, and MARY JANE O'BRIEN. 1985a. "Fraud and Abuse of Government Medical Benefit Programs by Psychiatrists." *American Journal of Psychiatry*, 142 (February): 231–234.

GEIS, GILBERT, HENRY N. PONTELL, CONSTANCE KEENAN, STEPHEN M. ROSOFF, MARY JANE O'BRIEN, and PAUL JESILOW. 1985b. "Peculating Psychologists: Fraud and Abuse Against Medicaid." *Professional Psychology: Research and Practice*, 16: 823–832.

GELLES, RICHARD J. 1976. "Abused Wives: Why Do They Stay?" *Journal of Marriage and the Family*, 38 (November): 659–668.

GELLES, RICHARD J. 1979. *Family Violence*. Beverly Hills, Calif.: Sage.

GELLES, RICHARD J. 1987. *Family Violence* (2nd ed.). Beverly Hills, Calif.: Sage.

GELLES, RICHARD J., and MURRAY A. STRAUS. 1988. *Intimate Violence: The Causes and Consequences of Abuse in the American Family*. New York: Simon & Schuster.

GELMAN, DAVID, et al. 1985. "The Social Fallout From an Epidemic." *Newsday* (August 12): 28–29.

GIARRUSSO, ROSEANN, PAULA JOHNSON, JACQUELINE GOODCHILDS, and GAIL ZELLMAN. 1979. "Adolescents' Cues and Signals: Sex and Assault." Paper presented at the Western Psychological Association meeting, San Diego, April.

GIBBONS, DON C. 1977. *Society, Crime, and Criminal Careers: An Introduction* (3rd ed.). Englewood Cliffs, N.J.: Prentice-Hall.

GIBBONS, DON C. 1982. *Society, Crime and Criminal Careers: An Introduction* (4th ed.). Englewood Cliffs, N.J.: Prentice-Hall.

GIBBS, JACK P. 1966. "Conceptions of Deviant Behavior: The Old and the New." *Pacific Sociological Review*, 9 (Spring): 9–14.

GIBBS, JACK P. 1972. "Issues in Defining Deviant

Behavior." In Robert A. Scott and Jack D. Douglas (eds.), *Theoretical Perspectives on Deviance*. New York: Basic Books, pp. 39–68.

GIBBS, JACK P. 1981. "The Sociology of Deviance and Social Control." In Morris Rosenberg and Ralph H. Turner (eds.), *Social Psychology: Sociological Perspectives*. New York: Basic Books, pp. 483–522.

GIBBS, JACK P., and MAYNARD L. ERICKSON. 1975. "Major Developments in the Sociology of Deviance." *Annual Review of Sociology*, 1: 21–42.

GILLESPIE, CYNTHIA K. 1989. *Justifiable Homicide: Battered Women, Self-Defense, and the Law*. Columbus: Ohio State University Press.

GLASER, DANIEL. 1956. "Criminality Theories and Behavioral Images." *American Journal of Sociology*, 61 (March): 433–445.

GLASSER, IRA. 1975. "The Yellow Star and the Pink Triangle." *The New York Times* (September 10): 45.

GLASSNER, BARRY. 1982. "Labeling Theory." In M. Michael Rosenberg, Robert A. Stebbins, and Allan Turowitz (eds.), *The Sociology of Deviance*. New York: St. Martin's Press, pp. 71–89.

GOFFMAN, ERVING. 1959. *The Presentation of Self in Everyday Society*. Garden City, N.Y.: Doubleday-Anchor.

GOFFMAN, ERVING. 1961. *Asylums*. Garden City, N.Y.: Doubleday-Anchor.

GOFFMAN, ERVING. 1963. *Stigma: Notes on the Management of Spoiled Identity*. Englewood Cliffs, N.J.: Prentice-Hall/Spectrum.

GOFFMAN, ERVING. 1971. "The Insanity of Place." In *Relations in Public: Microstudies of the Social Order*. New York: Basic Books, pp. 335–390.

GOLDMAN, DOUGLAS. 1955. "Treatment of Psychotic States with Chlorpromazine." *Journal of the American Medical Association*, 157 (April 9): 1274–1278.

GOLDSTEIN, JEFFREY H. 1986. *Aggression and Crimes of Violence* (2nd ed.). New York: Oxford University Press.

GOLDSTEIN, RICHARD. 1975. "The Menace of Macho." *The Village Voice*, May 12, pp. 5–6.

GOLDSTEIN, MICHAEL J., and HAROLD S. KANT, with JOHN J. HARTMAN. 1973. *Pornography and Sexual Deviance*. Berkeley: University of California Press.

GOLEMAN, DANIEL. 1984. "Violence Against Women in Films Is Found to Alter Attitudes of Men." *The New York Times* (August 28): 19, 20.

GOLEMAN, DANIEL. 1986a. "To Expert Eyes, City Streets Are Open Mental Wards." *The New York Times* (November 4): C1, C3.

GOLEMAN, DANIEL. 1986b. "For Mentally Ill on the Street, a New Approach Shines." *The New York Times* (November 11): C1, C3.

GOLEMAN, DANIEL. 1987. "Brain Defect Tied to Utter Amorality of the Psychopath." *The New York Times* (July 7): C1, C2.

GOLLIN, ALBERT E. 1980. "Comment on Johnson's 'On the Prevalence of Rape in the United States.'" *Signs: Journal of Women in Culture and Society*, 6 (2): 346–349.

GONZALES, LAURENCE. 1985. "Why Drug Enforcement Doesn't Work." *Playboy* (September): 113–114, 148, 194ff.

GOODCHILDS, JACQUELINE D., and GAIL L. ZELLMAN. 1984. "Sexual Signaling and Sexual Aggression in Adolescent Relationships." In Neil M. Malamuth and Edward Donnerstein (eds.), *Pornography and Sexual Aggression*. Orlando, Fla.: Academic Press, pp. 233–243.

GOODCHILDS, JACQUELINE D., GAIL ZELLMAN, PAULA B. JOHNSON, and ROSEANN GIARRUSSO. 1979. "Adolescent Perceptions of Responsibility for Dating Outcomes." Paper presented at the meetings of the Eastern Psychological Association, Philadelphia, April.

GOODE, ERICH. 1969. "Marijuana and the Politics of Reality." *Journal of Health and Social Behavior*, 10 (June): 83–94.

GOODE, ERICH. 1970. *The Marijuana Smokers*. New York: Basic Books.

GOODE, ERICH. 1972. *Drugs in American Society*. New York: Alfred Knopf.

GOODE, ERICH. 1975. "On Behalf of Labeling Theory." *Social Problems*, 22 (June): 570–583.

GOODE, ERICH. 1981a. "Deviance, Norms, and Social Reaction." *Deviant Behavior*, 3 (October–December): 47–53.

GOODE, ERICH. 1981b. "Comments on the Homosexual Role." *Journal of Sex Research*, 17 (February): 54–65.

GOODE, ERICH. 1988. *Sociology* (2nd ed.). Englewood Cliffs, N.J.: Prentice-Hall.

GOODE, ERICH. 1989. *Drugs in American Society* (3rd ed.). New York: Alfred Knopf.

GOODE, ERICH, and LYNN HABER. 1977. "Sexual Correlates of Homosexual Experience: An Exploratory Study of College Women." *Journal of Sex Research*, 13 (February): 12–21.

GOODE, ERICH, and RICHARD R. TROIDEN. 1979. "Heterosexual and Homosexual Activity

Among Gay Males." *Deviant Behavior*, 1 (October–December): 37–55.

GOODE, WILLIAM J. 1973. *Explorations in Social Theory*. New York: Oxford University Press.

GOODMAN, RICHARD A., et al. 1986. "Alcohol Use and Interpersonal Violence: Alcohol Detected in Homicide Victims." *American Journal of Public Health*, 76 (February): 144–149.

GOOTMAN, ROBERTA, and REINA MEKELBURG. 1973. "Silky the Pimp Counts His Money." *Gallery* (September): 32, 108.

GORDON, DAVID M. 1971. "Class and the Economics of Crime." *The Review of Radical Political Economics*, 3 (Summer): 50–75.

GORDON, SUZANNE. 1976. "Is Murder a Just Response to Rape?" *The Village Voice* (February 6): 14–15.

GORER, GEOFFREY. 1966. "Man Has No Killer Instinct." *The New York Times Magazine* (November 27): 47, 82, 92–93ff.

GORER, GEOFFREY. 1967. *Himalayan Village: An Account of the Lepcha of Sikkim* (2nd ed.). New York: Basic Books.

GOTTFREDSON, MICHAEL R., and TRAVIS HIRSCHI (eds.). 1987a. *Positive Criminology*. Beverly Hills, Calif.: Sage.

GOTTFREDSON, MICHAEL R., and TRAVIS HIRSCHI. 1987b. "The Positive Tradition." In Michael R. Gottfredson and Travis Hirschi (eds.), *Positive Criminology*. Beverly Hills, Calif.: Sage, pp. 9–22.

GOULD, LEROY C. 1969. "The Changing Structure of Property Crime in an Affluent Society." *Social Forces*, 48 (1): 50–59.

GOULD, STEPHEN JAY. 1981. *The Mismeasure of Man*. New York: Norton.

GOULD, STEPHEN JAY. 1984. *Hen's Teeth and Horse's Toes: Further Reflections in Natural History*. New York: Norton.

GOULDNER, ALVIN. 1968. "The Sociologist as Partisan: Sociology and the Welfare State." *American Sociologist*, 3 (May): 103–116.

GOULDNER, ALVIN. 1970. *The Coming Crisis of American Sociology*. New York: Basic Books.

GOVE, WALTER R. 1970a. Societal Reactions as an Explanation of Mental ILlness: An Evaluation." *American Sociological Review*, 35 (October): 873–884.

GOVE, WALTER R. 1970b. "Who Is Hospitalized: A Critical Evaluation of Some Sociological Studies of Mental Illness." *Journal of Health and Social Behavior*, 11 (December): 294–303.

GOVE, WALTER R. 1972. "The Relationship Between Sex Roles, Marital Status, and Mental Illness." *Social Forces*, 51 (September): 34–44.

GOVE, WALTER R. 1975a. "The Labelling Theory of Mental Illness: A Reply to Scheff." *American Sociological Review*, 40 (April): 242–248.

GOVE, WALTER R. 1975b. "The Labelling Perspective: An Overview." In Walter R. Gove (ed.), *The Labelling of Deviance*. New York: Wiley-Halstead-Sage, pp. 35–81.

GOVE, WALTER R. 1979a. "The Labelling Versus the Psychiatric Explanation of Mental Illness: A Debate That Has Become Substantially Irrelevant (Reply to Comment by Horwitz)." *Journal of Health and Social Behavior*, 20 (September): 301–304.

GOVE, WALTER R. 1979b. "Sex, Marital Status, and Psychiatric Treatment: A Research Note." *Social Forces*, 58 (September): 89–93.

GOVE, WALTER R. (ed.). 1980a. *The Labelling of Deviance: Evaluating a Perspective*. Beverly Hills, Calif.: Sage.

GOVE, WALTER R. 1980b. "Labelling and Mental Illness: A Critique." In Walter R. Gove (ed.), *The Labelling of Deviance: Evaluating a Perspective*. Beverly Hills, Calif.: Sage, pp. 53–109.

GOVE, WALTER R. 1982a. *Deviance and Mental Illness*. Beverly Hills, Calif.: Sage.

GOVE, WALTER R. 1982b. "Labelling Theory's Explanation of Mental Illness: An Update of Recent Evidence." *Deviant Behavior*, 3 (July–September): 307–327.

GOVE, WALTER R. 1985. "The Effect of Age and Gender on Deviant Behavior: A Biopsychosocial Perspective." In Alice S. Rossi (ed.), *Gender and the Life Course*. New York: Aldine, pp. 115–144.

GOVE, WALTER R., and TERRY FAIN. 1973. "The Stigma of Mental Hospitalization: An Attempt to Evaluate Its Consequences." *Archives of General Psychiatry*, 28 (April): 494–500.

GOVE, WALTER R., and TERRY R. HERB. 1974. "Stress and Mental Illness Among the Young: A Comparison of the Sexes." *Social Forces*, 53 (December): 256–265.

GRANT, BRIDGET F., JOHN NOBLE, and HENRY MALIN. 1986. "Decline in Liver Cirrhosis Mortality and Components of Change." *Alcohol Health and Research World*, 10 (Spring): 66–69.

GRAY, DIANA. 1973. "Turning Out: A Study of Teenage Prostitution." *Urban Life and Culture*, 1 (January): 401–425.

GRAY, SUSAN H. 1982. "Exposure to Pornography and Aggression Toward Women: The Case of the Angry Male." *Social Problems*, 29 (April): 387–398.

GREELEY, ANDREW M., WILLIAM C. MCCREADY, and GARY THEISON. 1980. *Ethnic Drinking Subcultures*. New York: Praeger.

GREEN, EDWARD, and RUSSELL P. WAKEFIELD. 1979. "Patterns of Middle and Upper Class Homicide." *Journal of Criminal Law and Criminology*, 70 (Summer): 172–181.

GREEN, MARK, and JOHN F. BERRY. 1985. "White-Collar Crime Is Big Business." *The Nation* (June 8): 689, 704–705.

GREENBERG, DAVID F. 1976. "On One-Dimensional Marxist Criminology." *Theory and Society*, 3 (Winter): 610–621.

GREENBERG, DAVID F. 1979. "Delinquency and the Age Structure of Society." In Sheldon L. Messenger and Egon Bittner (eds.), *Criminology Review Yearbook*. Beverly Hills, Calif.: Sage, pp. 586–620.

GREENBERG, DAVID F. 1979. "Review of Richard Quinney, *Class, State and Crime: On the Theory and Practice of Criminal Justice*." New York: Longman, 1977. In *Crime and Delinquency*, 25 (January): 110–113.

GREENBERG, DAVID F. (ed.). 1981. *Crime and Capitalism: Readings in Marxist Criminology*. Palo Alto, Calif.: Mayfield.

GREENBERG, DAVID F. 1985. "Age, Crime, and Social Explanation." *American Journal of Sociology*, 91 (July): 1–21.

GREENBERG, DAVID F. 1986. "Marxist Criminology." In Bertell Ollman and Edward Vernoff (eds.), *The Left Academy: Marxist Scholarship on American Campuses*, Vol. 3. New York: Praeger.

GREENBERG, DAVID F. 1988. "The Controversial Age-Crime Relationship." Paper presented to the Conference on Social and Psychological Factors in Juvenile Delinquency, Taipei, Taiwan, August 2–5.

GREENBERG, DAVID F. 1989. *The Construction of Homosexuality*. Chicago: University of Chicago Press.

GREENHOUSE, LINDA. 1986. "High Court, 5–4, Says States Have the Right to Outlaw Private Homosexual Acts: Privacy Law and History." *The New York Times* (July 1): A1, A19.

GREENLY, JAMES R. 1979. "Familial Expectations, Posthospital Adjustment, and the Societal Reaction on Mental Illness." *Journal of Health and Social Behavior*, 20 (September): 217–227.

GREENWALD, HAROLD, and RUTH GREENWALD (eds.). 1973. *The Sex-Life Letters*. Los Angeles: J. P. Tarcher.

GREENWOOD, VICTORIA, and JOCK YOUNG. 1976. *Abortion in Demand*. London: Pluto Press.

GRIFFIN, RICHARD T. 1976. "Grandma Was a Junkie." *Penthouse* (February): 80ff.

GRIFFIN, SUSAN. 1971. "Rape: The All-American Crime." *Ramparts* (September): 26–35.

GRIFFIN, SUSAN. 1981. *Pornography and Silence: Culture's Revenge Against Nature*. New York: Harper Colophon.

GRIFFIN, SUSAN. 1986. *Rape: The Power of Consciousness* (3rd ed.). New York: Harper & Row.

GRINSPOON, LESTER, and JAMES B. BAKALAR. 1976. *Cocaine: A Drug and Its Social Evolution*. New York: Basic Books.

GRINSPOON, LESTER, and JAMES B. BAKALAR. 1979. *Psychedelic Drugs Reconsidered*. New York: Basic Books.

GROSS, LARRY, et al. 1988. *Violence and Discrimination Against Lesbian and Gay People in Philadelphia and the Commonwealth of Pennsylvania*. Philadelphia: Philadelphia Lesbian and Gay Task Force.

GROTH, A. NICHOLAS, with H. JEAN BIRNBAUM. 1979. *Men Who Rape: The Psychology of the Offender*. New York: Plenum Press.

GURLING, HUGH, et al. 1988. "Localization of a Susceptibility Locus for Schizophrenia on Chromosome 5." *Nature*, 336 (November 10): 164–167.

GUSFIELD, JOSEPH R. 1963. *Symbolic Crusade: Status Politics and the American Temperance Movement*. Urbana: University of Illinois Press.

GUSFIELD, JOSEPH R. 1967. "Moral Passage: The Symbolic Process in Public Designations of Deviance." *Social Problems*, 15 (Fall): 175–188.

GUSFIELD, JOSEPH R. 1981. *The Culture of Public Problems: Drinking-Driving and the Symbolic Order*. Chicago: University of Chicago Press.

GUTIS, PHILIP A. 1987. "Homosexual Parents Winning Some Custody Cases." *The New York Times* (January 21): C1, C16.

HABERMAN, PAUL W., and MICHAEL M. BADEN. 1974. "Alcoholism and Violent Death." *Quarterly Journal of Studies on Alcohol*, 33, Part A (March): 221–231.

HAGAN, JOHN, et al. 1980. "The Differential Sentencing of White-Collar Offenders in Ten Federal Court Districts." *American Sociological Review*, 45 (October): 802–820.

HALL, JEROME. 1952. *Theft, Law, and Society* (2nd ed.). Indianapolis, Ind.: Bobbs-Merrill.

HALL, SUSAN. 1972. *Gentlemen of Leisure*. New York: New American Library.

HALL, SUSAN. 1974. *Ladies of the Night*. New York: Pocket Books.

HAMILL, PETE. 1988. "Facing Up to Drugs: Is Legalization the Solution?" *New York* (August 15): 21–27.

HARKEY, JOHN, DAVID L. MILES, and WILLIAM A. RUSHING. 1976. "The Relationship Between Social Class and Functional Status: A New Look at the Drift Hypothesis." *Journal of Health and Social Behavior*, 17 (September): 194–204.

HARLOW, CAROLINE WOLF. 1987. "Robbery Victims." *Bureau of Justice Statistics Special Report* (April): 1–10.

HARRIS, LOUIS, and ASSOCIATES. 1981. *Medical Practice in the 1980's: Physicians Look at Their Changing Profession*. Menlo Park, Calif.: Henry J. Kaiser Foundation.

HARTJEN, CLAYTON A. 1978. *Crime and Criminalization* (2nd ed.). New York: Praeger.

HARTUNG, BETH. 1988. "Between the Lines: Pornography and Feminism." Paper presented at the annual meeting of the Society for the Study of Social Problems, August.

HAWKINS, E. R., and WILLARD WALLER. 1936. "Critical Notes on the Cost of Crime." *Journal of Criminal Law, Criminology, and Police Science*, 26 (January): 679–694.

HAYS, CONSTANCE L. 1988. "Teen-Agers Attack Pair Seen as Gay." *The New York Times* (August 24): B1, B4.

HEALTH, EDUCATION AND WELFARE, DEPARTMENT OF. 1971. *First Special Report to the U.S. Congress on Alcohol and Health From the Secretary of Health, Education, and Welfare*. Washington, D.C.: U.S. Government Printing Office.

HEALTH AND HUMAN SERVICES, DEPARTMENT OF. 1987. *Sixth Special Report to the U.S. Congress on Alcohol and Health From the Secretary of Health and Human Services*. Rockville, Md.: National Institute on Alcohol Abuse and Alcoholism.

HEATHER, NICK, and IAN ROBERTSON. 1981. *Controlled Drinking*. London: Menthuen.

HELLMAN, PETER. 1970. "One in Ten Shoppers Is a Shoplifter." *The New York Times Magazine* (March): 34.

HENDIN, HERBERT. 1975. *The Age of Sensation*. New York: W. W. Norton.

HENRY, JULES. 1941. *Jungle People*. Richmond, Vir.: Augustin.

HEPBURN, JOHN R. 1977. "Social Control and the Legal Order: Legitimated Repression in a Capitalist State." *Contemporary Crises*, 1 (1): 77–90.

HERDT, GILBERT. 1981. *Guardians of the Flutes: Idioms of Masculinity*. New York: McGraw-Hill.

HERDT, GILBERT. 1987. *The Sambia: Ritual and Gender in New Guinea*. New York: Holt, Rinehart & Winston.

HERDT, GILBERT. 1988. "Cross-Cultural Forms of Homosexuality and the Concept 'Gay.'" *Psychiatric Annals*, 18 (1): 37–39.

HERMAN, JUDITH LEWIS, and LISA HIRSCHMAN. 1977. "Father-Daughter Incest: A Feminist Theoretical Perspective." *Signs: Journal of Women in Culture and Society*, 2 (Summer): 735–756.

HERMAN, JUDITH LEWIS, and LISA HIRSCHMAN. 1981. *Father-Daughter Incest*. Cambridge, Mass.: Harvard University Press.

HIATT, HOWARD H. 1975. "Protecting the Medical Commons: Who Is Responsible?" *New England Journal of Medicine*, 293 (July 31): 235–241.

HILLS, STUART L. 1971. *Crime, Power, and Morality: The Criminal-Law Process in the United States*. Scranton, Penn.: Chandler.

HILLS, STUART L. 1980. *Demystifying Social Deviance*. New York, McGraw Hill.

HILSON, ROBERT, JR. 1987a. "An Explosive Mix of Rage, Guns Cause Many Killings." *The Evening Sun* (Baltimore) (December 17): A1, A18.

HILSON, ROBERT, JR. 1987b. "Stories of Anger Illustrate How It Erupts Suddenly." *The Evening Star* (Baltimore) (December 17): A1, A19, A29–30.

HINCH, RONALD. 1983. "Marxist Criminology in the 1970s: Clarifying the Clutter." *Crime and Social Justice*, 13 (Summer): 65–74.

HINCH, RONALD. 1984. *An Analysis of Class, State, and Crime: A Contribution to Critical Criminology*. Hamilton, Ontario: Ph.D. dissertation, Department of Sociology, McMaster University.

HINCH, RONALD. 1987. "Cultural Deviance and Conflict Theories." In Rick Linden (ed.), *Criminology: A Canadian Perspective*. Toronto: Holt, Rinehart & Winston, pp. 177–198.

HINDELANG, MICHAEL J. 1974. "Decisions of Shoplifting Victims to Invoke the Criminal Justice Process." *Social Problems*, 21 (April): 580–593.

HINDELANG, MICHAEL J. 1978. "Race and Involvement in Common Law Personal Crimes." *American Sociological Review*, 43 (January): 93–109.

HINDELANG, MICHAEL J., TRAVIS HIRSCHI, and JOSEPH G. WEIS. 1979. "Correlates of Delinquency: The Illusion of Discrepancy Between Self-Report and Official Measures." *American Sociological Review*, 44 (December): 995–1014.

HINDELANG, MICHAEL J., TRAVIS HIRSCHI, and JOSEPH G. WEIS. 1981. *Measuring Delinquency*. Beverly Hills, Calif.: Sage.

HINES, TERENCE. 1988. *Pseudoscience and the Paranormal: A Critical Examination of the Evidence*. Buffalo, N.Y.: Prometheus Books.

HIRSCHI, TRAVIS. 1969. *Causes of Delinquency*. Berkeley: University of California Press.

HIRSCHI, TRAVIS. 1973. "Procedural Rules and the Study of Deviant Behavior." *Social Problems*, 21 (Fall): 159–173.

HIRSCHI, TRAVIS, and MICHAEL GOTTFREDSON. 1983. "Age and the Explanation of Crime." *American Journal of Sociology*, 89 (November): 552–584.

HIRSCHI, TRAVIS, and MICHAEL GOTTFREDSON. 1985. "Age and Crime, Logic and Scholarship: Comment on Greenberg." *American Journal of Sociology*, 91 (July): 22–27.

HIRSCHI, TRAVIS, MICHAEL J. HINDELANG, and JOSEPH WEIS. 1982. "Reply to 'On the Use of Self-Report Data to Determine the Class Distribution of Criminal and Delinquent Behavior.'" *American Sociological Review*, 47 (June): 433–435.

HIRSCHI, TRAVIS, and HANAN C. SELVIN. 1966. "False Criteria of Causality in Delinquency Research." *Social Problems*, 13 (Winter): 254–268.

HIRSCHI, TRAVIS, and HANAN C. SELVIN. 1967. *Delinquency Research: An Appraisal of Analytic Methods*. New York: Free Press.

HOFFMAN, MARTIN. 1968. *The Gay World*. New York: Basic Books.

HOFFMAN, RICHARD J. 1980. "Some Cultural Aspects of Greek Male Homosexuality." *Journal of Homosexuality*, 5 (Spring): 217–226.

HOLLANDER, XAVIERA. 1972. *The Happy Hooker*. New York: Dell.

HOLLINGSHEAD, AUGUST B., and FREDERICK C. REDLICH. 1958. *Social Class and Mental Illness*. New York: John Wiley & Sons.

HOOKER, EVELYN. 1957. "The Adjustment of the Male Overt Homosexual." *Journal of Projective Techniques*, 21 (March): 18–31.

HOOKER, EVELYN. 1958. "Male Homosexuality in the Rorschach." *Journal of Projective Techniques*, 22 (March): 33–54.

HOOKER, EVELYN. 1965. "An Empirical Study of Some Relationships Between Sexual Patterns and Gender Identity in Male Homosexuals." In John Money (ed.), *Sex Research: New Developments*. New York: Holt, Rinehart & Winston, pp. 24–52.

HOWELLS, KEVIN. 1984. "Coercive Sexual Behavior." In Kevin Howells (ed.), *The Psychology of Sexual Diversity*. Oxford, Eng.: Basil Blackwell, pp. 111–134.

HUDSON, HENRY E. 1986. *Attorney General's Commission on Pornography: Final Report*. Washington, D.C.: U.S. Government Printing Office.

HUMPHREYS, LAUD. 1970. *Tearoom Trade: Impersonal Sex in Public Places*. Chicago: Aldine.

HUMPHREYS, LAUD. 1971. "New Styles in Homosexual Manliness." *Trans-action*, 8 (March–April): 38–46, 64–65.

HUMPHREYS, LAUD. 1972. *Out of the Closets: The Sociology of Homosexual Liberation*. Englewood Cliffs, N.J.: Prentice-Hall/Spectrum.

HUMPHREYS, LAUD. 1975. *Tearoom Trade: Impersonal Sex in Public Places* (enl. ed.). New York: Aldine.

HUMPHREYS, LAUD. 1979. "Being Odd Against All Odds." In Ronald Federico, *Sociology* (2nd ed.), Reading, Mass.: Addison-Wesley, pp. 238–242.

HUMPHRIES, DREW. 1979. "Crime and the State." In Albert J. Szymanski and Ted George Goertzel (eds.), *Sociology: Class Consciousness and Contradictions*. New York: Van Nostrand, pp. 224–241.

HUNT, MORTON M. 1975. *Sexual Behavior in the 1970s*. New York: Dell.

INCIARDI, JAMES A. (ed.). 1980. *Radical Criminology: The Coming Crises*. Beverly Hills, Calif.: Sage.

INCIARDI, JAMES A. 1986. *The War on Drugs: Heroin, Cocaine, Crime, and Public Policy*. Palo Alto, Calif.: Mayfield.

INCIARDI, JAMES A. 1988. "Beyond Cocaine: Basuco, Crack, and Other Coca Products." *Contemporary Drug Problems*, 17 (forthcoming).

JACKMAN, NORMAN R., et al. 1963. "The Self-Image of the Prostitute." *The Sociological Quarterly*, 4 (Spring): 150–161.

JACKSON, BRUCE (ed.). 1974. *In the Life: Versions of the Criminal Experience*. New York: New American Library.

JAMES, JENNIFER, and JANE MEYERDING. 1977. "Early Sexual Experiences and Prostitution." *American Journal of Psychiatry*, 134 (December): 1381–1385.

JANEWAY, ELIZABETH. 1981. "Incest: A Rational Look at the Oldest Taboo." *Ms.* (November): 61–64, 78, 81, 109.

JENSEN, ERIC L., JURG GERBER, and GINNA M. BABCOCK. 1987. "Drugs as Politics: The Construction of a Social Problem." Paper presented at the meetings of the Society for the Study of Social Problems, Chicago, August.

JESILOW, PAUL, HENRY N. PONTELL, and GILBERT GEIS. 1985. "Medical Criminals: Physicians and White-Collar Offenses." *Justice Quarterly*, 2 (June): 149–165.

JOHNSON, ALLAN GRISWOLD. 1980. "On the Prevalence of Rape in the United States." *Signs: Journal of Women in Culture and Society*, 6 (1): 136–146.

JOHNSON, BRUCE D., et al. 1985. *Taking Care of Business: The Economics of Crime by Heroin Abusers.* Lexington, Mass.: Lexington Books.

JOHNSON, DIRK. 1987. "Fear of AIDS Stirs New Attack on Homosexuals." *The New York Times* (April 24): A12.

JOHNSON, KIRK. 1987. "After 2 Years, Goetz Case Still Puzzles," *The New York Times* (March 23): B1, B7.

JOHNSTON, LLOYD D. 1980. "Marijuana Use and the Effects of Decriminalization." Testimony at hearings on the effects of marijuana, Subcommittee on Criminal Justice, Judiciary Committee, U.S. Senate, January 16, Washington, D.C.

JOHNSTON, LLOYD D., PATRICK M. O'MALLEY, and JERALD G. BACHMAN. 1987. *National Trends in Drug Use and Related Factors Among High School Students and Young Adults, 1975–1986.* Rockville, Md.: National Institute on Drug Abuse.

JONES, EDWARD E. 1986. "Interpreting Interpersonal Behavior: The Effects of Expectancies." *Science*, 234 (October 3): 41–46.

JONES, EDWARD E., et al. 1984. *Social Stigma: The Psychology of Marked Relationships.* New York: Freeman.

JONES, HARDIN, and HELEN JONES. 1977. *Sensual Drugs.* Cambridge, Eng.: Cambridge University Press.

JONES, HELEN C., and PAUL W. LOVINGER. 1985. *The Marijuana Question and Science's Search for an Answer.* New York: Dodd, Mead.

JONES, JAMES H. 1981. *Bad Blood.* New York: Free Press.

JUNG, R. T., et al. 1979. "Reduced Thermogenesis in Obesity." *Nature*, 279 (May 24): 322–323.

KALISH, CAROL B. 1988. "International Crime Rates." *Bureau of Justice Statistics Special Report* (May): 1–11.

KALVEN, HARRY, and HANS ZEISEL. 1966. *The American Jury.* Boston: Little, Brown.

KARLEN, ARNO. 1971. *Sexuality and Homosexuality.* New York: W. W. Norton.

KATZ, JACK. 1979. "Legality and Equality: Plea Bargaining in the Prosecution of White-Collar and Common Crimes." *Law and Society Review*, 13 (Winter): 431–459.

KATZ, JACK. 1980. "The Social Movement Against White-Collar Crime." In Egon Bittner and Sheldon L. Messinger (eds.), *Criminology Review Yearbook*, Vol. 2. Beverly Hills, Calif.: Sage, pp. 161–184.

KATZ, JACK. 1988. *Seductions of Crime: Moral and Sensual Attractions of Doing Evil.* New York: Basic Books.

KENDALL, R. E., et al. 1971. "Diagnostic Criteria of American and British Psychiatrists." *Archives of General Psychiatry*, 25 (August): 123–130.

KERR, PETER. 1986a. "Growth in Heroin Use Ending as City Users Turn to Crack." *The New York Times* (September 13): 1, 8.

KERR, PETER. 1986b. "Anatomy of an Issue: Drugs, the Evidence, the Reaction." *The New York Times* (November 17): A1, B6.

KERR, PETER. 1987a. "Crack Addiction: The Tragic Impact on Women and Children." *The New York Times* (February 9): B1, B2.

KERR, PETER. 1987b. "New Breed of Ethnic Gangs Smuggling Heroin." *The New York Times* (March 21): 1, 31.

KERR, PETER. 1987c. "Chinese Now Dominate New York Heroin Trade." *The New York Times* (August 9): 1, 30.

KERR, PETER. 1987d. "Rich vs. Poor: Drug Patterns Are Diverging." *The New York Times* (August 30): 1, 28.

KERR, PETER. 1988. "The Unspeakable Is Debated: Should Drugs Be Legalized?" *The New York Times* (May 15): 1, 24.

KESSLER, RONALD C. 1979. "Stress, Social Status, and Psychological Distress." *Journal of Health and Social Behavior*, 20 (September): 259–272.

KESSLER, RONALD C., and PAUL CLEARY. 1980. "Social Class and Psychological Distress." *American Sociological Review*, 45 (June): 463–478.

KING, CARL F. 1968. "Police Discretion and the Judgment That a Crime Has Been Committed: Rape in Philadelphia." *University of Pennsylvania Law Review*, 117 (December): 227–322.

KING, WAYNE. 1987. "Bakker, Evangelist, Resigns His Ministry Over Sexual Incident." *The New York Times* (March 21): 1, 33.

KINSEY, ALFRED C., WARDELL B. POMEROY, and CLYDE E. MARTIN. 1948. *Sexual Behavior in the Human Male.* Philadelphia: W. B. Saunders.

KINSEY, ALFRED C., WARDELL B. POMEROY, and

CLYDE E. MARTIN, and PAUL H. GEBHARD. 1953. *Sexual Behavior in the Human Female*. Philadelphia: W. B. Saunders.

KITSUSE, JOHN I. 1962. "Societal Reactions to Deviant Behavior: Problems of Theory and Method." *Social Problems*, 9 (Winter): 247–257.

KITSUSE, JOHN I. 1972. "Deviance, Deviant Behavior, and Deviants: Some Conceptual Problems." In William J. Filstead (ed.), *An Introduction to Deviance: Readings in the Process of Making Deviants*. Chicago: Markham, pp. 233–243.

KITSUSE, JOHN I. 1975. "The New Conception of Deviance and Its Critics." In Walter R. Gove (ed.), *The Labelling of Deviance: Evaluating a Perspective*. New York: Wiley/Halstead/Sage, pp. 273–284.

KITSUSE, JOHN I. 1980. "The New Conception of Deviance and Its Critics." In Walter R. Gove (ed.), *The Labelling of Deviance: Evaluating a Perspective* (2nd ed.). Beverly Hills, Calif.: Sage, pp. 381–392.

KLAUS, PATSY A., and MARSHALL DeBERRY. 1985. "The Crime of Rape." *Bureau of Justice Statistics Bulletin* (June): 1–5.

KLAUS, PATSY, and CAROL B. KALISH. 1984. "The Severity of Crime." *Bureau of Justice Statistics Bulletin* (January): 1–5.

KLECK, GARY. 1982. "On the Use of Self-Report Data to Determine the Class Distribution of Criminal and Delinquent Behavior." *American Sociological Review*, 47 (June): 427–433.

KLEIN, JOE. 1985. "The Drug They Call 'Ecstasy.'" *New York* (May 20): 38–43.

KLEIN, JOE. 1989. "Race: The Issue." *New York* (May 29): 32–38.

KLEMESRUD, JUDY. 1973. "Lesbians Who Try to Be Good Mothers." *The New York Times* (January 31).

KLEMMACK, SUSAN H., and DAVID L. KLEMMACK. 1976. "The Social Definition of Rape." In Marcia J. Walker and Stanley L. Brodsky (eds.), *Sexual Assault*. Lexington, Mass.: Heath, pp. 135–147.

KLOCKARS, CARL B. 1980. "The Contemporary Crisis of Marxist Criminology." In James A. Inciardi (ed.), *Radical Criminology: The Coming Crises*. Beverly Hills, Calif.: Sage, pp. 92–123.

KNUPFER, GENEVIEVE, WALTER CLARK, and ROBIN G. W. ROOM. "The Mental Health of the Unmarried." *American Journal of Psychiatry*, 122 (February): 841–851.

KOLATA, GINA. 1989. "Fat-Cell Protein Is Implicated in Obesity." *The New York Times* (January 3): C1, C9.

KOLB, LAURENCE, and A. G. DuMEZ. 1924. "The Prevalence and Trend of Drug Addiction in the United States and Factors Influencing It." *Public Health Reports*, 39 (May 23): 1179–1204.

KOLBERT, ELIZABETH. 1987. "Youths' Buying of Alcohol Fell in '86." *The New York Times* (February 13): B2.

KOLKO, GABRIEL. 1963. *The Triumph of Conservativism*. New York: Free Press.

KOSS, MARY P., and KENNETH E. LEONARD. 1984. "Sexually Aggressive Men: Empirical Findings and Theoretical Implications." In Neil M. Malamuth and Edward Donnerstein (eds.), *Pornography and Sexual Aggression*. Orlando, Fla.: Academic Press, pp. 213–232.

KOSS, MARY P., and CHERYL J. OROS. 1982. "Sexual Experiences Survey: A Research Instrument Investigating Sexual Aggression and Victimization." *Journal of Consulting and Clinical Psychology*, 50 (3): 455–457.

KREISMAN, DOLORES, and VIRGINIA D. JOY. 1974. "Family Response to Mental Illness of a Relative: A Review of the Literature." *Schizophrenia Bulletin*, 10 (Fall): 34–57.

KRESS, JUNE. 1982. "Review of David Downes and Paul Rock (eds.), *Deviant Interpretations*. New York: Barnes & Noble, 1979. In *Contemporary Sociology*, 11 (January): 39–40.

KRIM, SEYMOUR. 1961. "Making It!" In *Views of a Nearsighted Cannoneer*. New York: Excelsior Press, pp. 32–38.

KROHN, MARVIN D., and RONALD L. AKERS. 1977. "An Alternative View of the Labeling Versus Psychiatric Perspectives on Societal Reaction to Mental Illness." *Social Forces*, 56 (December): 341–361.

LaFREE, GARY D. 1989. *Rape and Criminal Justice: The Social Construction of Sexual Assault*. Belmont, Calif.: Wadsworth.

LAING, R. D. 1967. *The Politics of Experience*. New York: Pantheon Books.

LAMBERT, BRUCE. 1988. "AIDS Among Prostitutes Not as Prevalent as Believed, Studies Show." *The New York Times* (September 20): B1, B5.

LANDMAN, JANET T., and ROBYN DAWES. 1982. "Psychotherapy Outcome: Smith and Glass' Conclusions Stand up Under Scrutiny." *Psychological Bulletin*, 37: 504–516.

LANG, JOHN S., with RONALD A. TAYLOR. 1986. "America on Drugs." *U.S. News and World Report* (July 28): 48–49.

LANGAN, PATRICK, and CHRISTOPHER A. INNES. 1986. "Preventing Domestic Violence Against Women." *Bureau of Justice Statistics Special Report* (August): 1–5.

LANGLEY, ROGER, and RICHARD C. LEVY. 1977. *Wife Beating: The Silent Crisis.* New York: Dutton.

LANGONE, JOHN. 1985. "AIDS." *Discover* (December): 28–53.

LANGONE, JOHN. 1988. *AIDS: The Facts.* Boston: Little, Brown.

LANZA-KADUCE, LONN. 1980. "Deviance Among Professionals: The Case of Unnecessary Surgery." *Deviant Behavior,* 1 (April–September): 333–359.

LAUDERDALE, PAT (ed.). *A Political Analysis of Deviance.* Minneapolis: University of Minnesota Press.

LEDERER, LAURA (ed.). 1982. *Take Back the Night: Women on Pornography.* New York: Bantam Books.

LEE, JOHN ALAN. 1978. *Getting Sex.* Don Mills, Ontario: Musson/General Publishing.

LEE, MARTIN A. 1982. "CIA: Carcinogen." *The Nation,* 235 (18): 675.

LEERSEN, CHARLES, with BOB COHN. 1986. "A Gay Conservative Tells His Story." *Newsweek* (August 18): 18.

LEMERT, EDWIN M. 1951. *Social Pathology.* New York: McGraw-Hill.

LEMERT, EDWIN M. 1953. "An Isolation and Closure Theory of Naive Check Forgery." *Journal of Criminal Law, Criminology, and Police Science,* 44 (September–October): 296–307.

LEMERT, EDWIN M. 1958. "The Behavior of the Systematic Check Forger." *Social Problems,* 6 (Fall): 141–149.

LEMERT, EDWIN M. 1972. *Human Deviance, Social Problems, and Social Control* (2nd ed.). Englewood Cliffs, N.J.: Prentice-Hall.

LEMERT, EDWIN M. 1976. "Response to Critics: Feedback and Choice." In Lewis A. Coser and Otto Larsen (eds.), *The Uses of Controversy in Sociology.* New York: Free Press, pp. 244–249.

LENDER, MARK EDWARD, and JAMES KIRBY MARTIN. 1987. *Drinking in America: A History* (rev. ed.). New York: Free Press.

LEONARD, EILEEN B. 1982. *Women, Crime, and Society: A Critique of Theoretical Criminology.* New York: Longman.

LERNER, MELVIN J. 1980. *The Belief in a Just World: A Fundamental Delusion.* New York: Plenum Press.

LESSARD, SUZANNAH. 1987. "The Issue Was Women." *Newsweek* (May 18): 32, 34.

LEVITT, EUGENE E., and ALBERT D. KLASSEN. 1974. "Public Attitudes Toward Homosexuality." *Journal of Homosexuality,* 1 (Fall): 29–43.

LIAZOS, ALEXANDER. 1972. "The Poverty of the Sociology of Deviance: Nuts, Sluts, and Preverts." *Social Problems,* 20 (Summer): 103–120.

LIEBER, ARNOLD L. 1978. *The Lunar Effect: Biological Tides and Human Emotions.* Garden City, N.Y.: Doubleday.

LIEF, HAROLD I. 1977. "Sexual Survey #4: Current Thinking on Homosexuality." *Medical Aspects of Human Sexuality,* 11 (November): 110–111.

LIEM, RAMSAY, and JOAN LIEM. 1978. "Social Class and Mental Illness Reconsidered: The Role of Economic Stress and Social Support." *Journal of Health and Social Behavior,* 19 (June): 139–156.

LINDESMITH, ALFRED R. 1947. *Opiate Addiction.* Bloomington, Ind.: Principia Press.

LINDESMITH, ALFRED R. 1965. *The Addict and the Law.* Bloomington: Indiana University Press.

LINDESMITH, ALFRED R. 1968. *Addiction and Opiates.* Chicago: Aldine.

LINEBAUGH, PETER. 1981. "Karl Marx, the Theft of Wood, and Working Class Composition." In David F. Greenberg (ed.), *Crime and Capitalism: Readings in Marxist Criminology.* Palo Alto, Calif.: Mayfield, pp. 76–97.

LINGEMAN, RICHARD R. 1974. *Drugs From A to Z* (2nd ed.). New York: McGraw-Hill.

LINK, BRUCE G. 1987. "Understanding Labeling Effects in the Area of Mental Disorders: An Assessment of the Effects of Expectations of Rejection." *American Sociological Review,* 52 (February): 96–112.

LINK, BRUCE G., and FRANCIS T. CULLEN. 1989. "The Labeling Theory of Mental Disorder: A Review of the Evidence." In James Greenly (ed.), *Mental Illness in Social Context.* Detroit, Mich.: Wayne State University Press.

LINK, BRUCE G., et al. 1989. "A Modified Labeling Theory Approach to Mental Disorders: An Empirical Assessment." *American Sociological Review,* 54 (June): 400–423.

LINSKY, ARNOLD A., and MURRAY A. STRAUS. 1986. *Social Stress in the United States: Links to Regional Patterns in Crime and Illness.* Dover, Mass.: Auburn House.

LISKA, ALLEN A. 1981. *Perspectives on Deviance.* Englewood Cliffs, N.J.: Prentice-Hall.

LOFLAND, JOHN. 1969. *Deviance and Identity.* Englewood Cliffs, N.J.: Prentice-Hall.

LOFTUS, T. A. 1960. *Meaning and Methods of Diagno-*

sis in Clinical Psychiatry. Philadelphia: Lea & Febinger.

LONGINO, HELEN E. 1982. "Pornography, Oppression and Freedom: A Closer Look." In Laura Lederer (ed.), Take Back the Night: Women on Pornography. New York: Bantam Books, pp. 26–41.

LORD, JESS R. 1971. Marijuana and Personality Change. Lexington, Mass.: Heath Lexington Books.

LORENZ, KONRAD. 1967. On Aggression. Marjorie Kerr Wilson (trans.). New York: Bantam Books.

LUMBY, MALCOM E. 1976. "Homophobia: The Quest for a Valid Scale." Journal of Homosexuality, 2 (Fall): 39–47.

LUNSGAARDE, HENRY P. 1977. Murder in Space City: A Cultural Analysis of Houston Homicide Patterns. New York: Oxford University Press.

LYNN, BARRY W. 1986. Polluting the Censorship Debate: A Summary and Critique of the Final Report of the Attorney General's Commission on Pornography. Washington, D.C.: American Civil Liberties Union.

MAAS, PETER. 1976. King of the Gypsies. New York: Bantam Books.

MACANDREW, CRAIG, and ROBERT B. EDGERTON. 1969. Drunken Comportment. Chicago: Aldine.

MACKINNON, CATHERINE. 1987. Feminism Unmodified: Discourses on Life and Law. Cambridge, Mass.: Harvard University Press.

MAITLAND, LESLIE. 1976. "Rape Study Details the How, the Why, and the Who." The New York Times (July 29): 25, 32.

MALAMUTH, NEIL M. 1981. "Rape Proclivity Among Males." Journal of Social Issues, 37 (4): 138–157.

MALAMUTH, NEIL M., and JAMES V. P. CHECK. 1981. "The Effects of Mass Media Exposure on Acceptance of Violence Against Women: A Field Experiment." Journal of Research in Personality, 15 (December): 436–446.

MALAMUTH, NEIL M., and EDWARD DONNERSTEIN (eds.). 1984. Pornography and Sexual Aggression. Orlando, Fla.: Academic Press.

MALAMUTH, NEIL M., and BARRY SPINNER. 1980. "A Longitudinal Content Analysis of Sexual Violence in the Best-Selling Erotic Magazines." The Journal of Sex Research, 16 (August): 226–237.

MALAMUTH, NEIL M., JAMES V. P. CHECK, and JOHN BRIERE. 1986. "Sexual Arousal in Response to Aggression: Ideological, Aggressive and Sex-

ual Correlates." Journal of Personality and Social Psychology, 50 (2): 330–340.

MALCOM, ANDREW H. 1987. "Nation Is Gaining on Drunken Driving." The New York Times (March 23): A1, A15.

MALTBY, KARIN. 1982. "Review Committee Clears Sobells on Scientific Misconduct Charges." The Journal (Addiction Research Foundation, Toronto) (December 1): 2.

MANDERS, DEAN. 1975. "Labelling Theory and Social Reality: A Marxist Critique." The Insurgent Sociologist, 6 (Fall): 53–66.

MANKOFF, MILTON. 1971. "Societal Reaction and Career Deviance: A Critical Analysis. The Sociological Quarterly, 12 (Spring): 204–218.

MANKOFF, MILTON. 1978. "On the Responsibility of Marxist Criminologists: A Reply to Quinney." Contemporary Crises, 2: 293–301.

MANKOFF, MILTON. 1980. "A Tower of Babel: Marxist Criminologists and Their Critics." In James A. Inciardi (ed.), Radical Criminology: The Coming Crises. Beverly Hills, Calif.: Sage, pp. 139–148.

MANN, PEGGY. 1985. Marijuana Alert. New York: McGraw-Hill.

MANN, PEGGY. 1987. Marijuana: The Myth of Harmlessness Goes Up in Smoke. Indianapolis, Ind.: Medical Education and Research Foundation.

MANNING, PETER K. 1975. "Deviance and Dogma: Some Comments on the Labelling Perspective." The British Journal of Criminology, 15 (January): 1–20.

MARTIN, A. DAMIEN. 1988. "Young, Gay—and Afraid." The New York Times (September 1): A25.

MARTIN, DEL. 1976. Battered Wives. San Francisco: Glide Publications.

MASTERS, WILLIAM H., VIRGINIA E. JOHNSON, and ROBERT C. KOLODNY. 1988a. Crisis: Heterosexual Behavior in the Age of AIDS. New York: Grove Press.

MASTERS, WILLIAM H., VIRGINIA E. JOHNSON, and ROBERT C. KOLODNY. 1988b. "Sex in the Age of AIDS." Newsweek (March 14): 45–52.

MATZA, DAVID. 1969. Becoming Deviant. Englewood Cliffs, N.J.: Prentice-Hall.

MCAULIFFE, WILLIAM E., and ROBERT A. GORDON. 1974. "A Test of Lindesmith's Theory of Addiction: The Frequency of Euphoria Among Long-Term Addicts." American Journal of Sociology, 79 (January): 795–840.

MCAULIFFE, WILLIAM E., and ROBERT A. GORDON. 1980. "Reinforcement and the Combination of Effects: Summary of a Theory of Opiate Addiction." In Dan J. Lettieri et al. (eds.), *Theories on Drug Abuse.* Rockville, Md.: National Institute on Drug Abuse, pp. 137–141.

McCAGHY, CHARLES H. 1967. "Child Molesters: A Study of Their Careers as Deviants." In Marshall B. Clinard and Richard Quinney (eds.), *Criminal Behavior: A Typology.* New York: Holt, Rinehart & Winston, pp. 75–88.

McCAGHY, CHARLES H. 1968. "Drinking and Disavowal: The Case of Child Molesters." *Social Problems*, 16 (Summer): 43–49.

McCAGHY, CHARLES H. 1976. *Deviant Behavior: Crime, Conflict, and Interest Groups.* New York: Macmillan.

McCAGHY, CHARLES H. 1985. *Deviant Behavior: Crime, Conflict, and Interest Groups* (2nd ed.). New York: Macmillan.

McCLEARY, RICHARD, et al. 1981. "Effects of Legal Education and Work Experience on Perceptions of Crime Seriousness." *Social Problems*, 28 (February): 276–289.

McCORMACK, THELMA. 1978. "Machismo in Media Research: A Critical Review of Research on Violence and Pornography." *Social Problems*, 25 (June): 244–255.

McGRATH, PETER. 1985. "New Themes and Old Taboos: Pornographers Test the Outer Limits of Our Morality." *Newsweek* (March 18): 67.

McINTOSH, MARY. 1968. "The Homosexual Role." *Social Problems*, 16 (Fall): 182–192.

MEDAWAR, PETER. 1982. *Pluto's Republic.* New York: Oxford University Press.

MEDEA, ANDREA, and KATHLEEN THOMPSON. 1974. *Against Rape.* New York: Farrar, Straus & Giroux.

MEIER, ROBERT F., and GILBERT GEIS. 1979. "The White-Collar Offender." In Hans Toch (ed.), *The Psychology of Crime and Criminal Justice.* New York: Holt, Rinehart & Winston, pp. 428–445.

MENDELSON, BENIAMIN. 1963. "The Origin of the Doctrine of Victimology." *Excerpta Criminologica*, 3 (May–June): 239–244.

MENDELSON, JACK H., and NANCY MELLO. 1985. *Alcohol Use and Abuse in America.* Boston: Little, Brown.

MERTON, ROBERT K. 1938. "Social Structure and Anomie." *American Sociological Review*, 3 (October): 672–682.

MERTON, ROBERT K. 1948. "The Self-Fulfilling Prophecy." *Antioch Review*, 7 (Summer): 193–210.

MERTON, ROBERT K. 1957. *Social Theory and Social Structure* (rev., ex. ed.). New York: Free Press.

MERTON, ROBERT K. 1968. *Social Theory and Social Structure* (rev., ex. ed.). New York: Free Press.

MERTON, ROBERT K. 1976. "Introduction: The Sociology of Social Problems." In Robert K. Merton and Robert Nisbet (eds.), *Contemporary Social Problems* (4th ed.), New York: Harcourt Brace Jovanovich, pp. 5–43.

MICHALOWSKI, RAYMOND J. 1985. *Order, Law, and Crime: An Introduction to Criminology.* New York: Random House.

MILLER, BRIAN. 1979. "Gay Fathers and Their Children." *The Family Coordinator*, 28 (October): 544–552.

MILLER, BRIAN, and LAUD HUMPHREYS. 1980. "Lifestyles and Violence: Homosexual Victims of Assault and Murder." *Qualitative Sociology*, 3 (Fall): 169–185.

MILLER, JUDITH DROITCOUR, and IRA H. CISIN. 1980. *Highlights from the National Survey on Drug Abuse: 1979.* Rockville, Md.: National Institute on Drug Abuse.

MILLER, JUDITH DROITCOUR, et al. 1983. *National Survey on Drug Abuse: Main Findings 1982.* Rockville, Md.: National Institute on Drug Abuse.

MILLER, WALTER B. 1958. "Lower Class Culture as a Generating Milieu of Gang Delinquency." *Journal of Social Issues*, 14 (3): 5–19.

MILLETT, KATE (ed.). 1973. *The Prostitution Papers.* New York: Avon.

MILLMAN, MARCIA. 1975. "She Did It All for Love: A Feminist View of the Sociology of Deviance." In Marcia Millman and Rosabeth Moss Kanter (eds.), *Another Voice: Feminist Perspectives on Social Life and Social Science.* Garden City, N.Y.: Anchor Press/Doubleday, pp. 251–279.

MILLS, C. WRIGHT. 1943. "The Professional Ideology of Social Pathologists." *American Journal of Sociology*, 49 (September): 165–180.

MILLS, C. WRIGHT. 1962. *The Marxists.* New York: Ballantine.

MILLS, C. WRIGHT. 1963. *Power, Politics and People: The Collected Essays of C. Wright Mills.* New York: Ballantine.

MILLS, JAMES. 1987. *The Underground Empire: Where Crime and Governments Embrace.* New York: Dell.

MOLONY, CAROL. 1988. "The Truth About the Tasaday: Are They a Primitive Tribe—or a Modern Hoax?" *The Sciences* (September/October): 12–20.

MONMANEY, TERENCE. 1988. "The AIDS Threat: Who's at Risk?" *Newsday* (March 14): 42–44.

MORGAN, ROBIN. 1982. "Theory and Practice: Pornography and Rape." In Laura Lederer (ed.), *Take Back the Night: Women on Pornography*. New York: Bantam Books, pp. 125–140.

MORGANTHAU, TOM, et al. 1987. "The Sudden Fall of Gary Hart." *Newsweek* (May 18): 22–28.

MUMFORD, EMILY. 1983. *Medical Sociology: Patients, Providers and Policies*. New York: Random House.

MURPHY, JANE M. 1976. "Psychiatric Labeling in Cross-Cultural Perspective." *Science*, 191 (March): 1019–1028.

MUSTO, DAVID F. 1973. *The American Disease: Origins of Narcotics Control*. New Haven, Conn.: Yale University Press.

MYDANS, SETH. 1988. "20th Century Lawsuit Asserts Stone-Age Identity." *The New York Times* (October 29): 4.

NAFFINE, NGAIRE. 1987. *Female Crime: The Construction of Women in Criminology*. Sydney, Australia: Allen & Unwin.

NANCE, JOHN. 1975. *The Gentle Tasaday*. New York: Harcourt Brace Jovanovich.

NATIONAL INSTITUTE ON DRUG ABUSE (NIDA). 1986. "Highlights of the 1985 National Household Survey on Drug Abuse." Rockville, Md.: National Institute on Drug Abuse.

NELSON, STEVE, and MENACHEM AMIR. 1975. "The Hitchhike Victim of Rape: A Research Report." In Israel Drapkin and Emilio Viano (eds.), *Victimology: A New Focus*. Lexington, Ken.: Lexington Books, pp. 47–65.

NETTLER, GWYNN. 1970. *Explanations*. New York: McGraw-Hill.

NETTLER, GWYNN. 1974. "On Telling Who's Crazy." *American Sociological Review*, 39 (December): 893–894.

NETTLER, GWYNN. 1978. *Explaining Crime* (2nd ed.). New York: McGraw-Hill.

NETTLER, GWYNN. 1984. *Explaining Crime* (3rd ed.). New York: McGraw-Hill.

NEWMAN, GRAEME. 1976. *Comparative Deviance: Perception and Law in Six Cultures*. New York: Elsevier.

NEWTON, ESTHER. 1972. *Mother Camp: Female Impersonators in America*. Englewood Cliffs, N.J.: Prentice-Hall.

NIDA. See National Institute of Drug Abuse.

NIX, CRYSTAL. 1986. "For Police, Domestic Violence Is No Longer Low-Priority." *The New York Times* (December 31): B1, B3.

NORDHEIMER, JON. 1986. "With AIDS About, Heterosexuals Are Rethinking Casual Sex." *The New York Times* (March 22): 7.

NORDHEIMER, JON. 1987. "AIDS Specter for Women: The Bisexual Man." *The New York Times* (April 3): A1, D18.

NORMAN, MICHAEL. 1983. "Homosexuals Struggle Amid Life Style Shifts." *The New York Times* (June 16): A1, B8.

NYE, F. IVAN. 1958. *Family Relationships and Delinquency Behavior*. New York: John Wiley & Sons.

O'BRIEN, JOHN E. 1975. "Violence in Divorce-Prone Families." In Suzanne K. Steinmetz and Murray A. Straus (eds.), *Violence in the Family*. New York: Dodd, Mead, pp. 65–75.

O'BRIEN, ROBERT M. 1985. *Crime and Victimization Data*. Beverly Hills, Calif.: Sage.

O'BRIEN, ROBERT, and SIDNEY COHEN. 1984. *The Encyclopedia of Drug Abuse*. New York: Facts on File.

OMARK, RICHARD C. 1978. "A Comment on the Homosexual Role." *Journal of Sex Research*, 14 (November): 273.

ORCUTT, JAMES D. 1983. *Analyzing Deviance*. Homewood, Ill.: Dorsey Press.

PALYS, T. S. 1986. "Testing the Common Wisdom: The Social Content of Video Pornography." *Canadian Psychology*, 27 (July): 22–35.

PARROT, ANDREA, and STEVEN ALLEN. 1984. "Acquaintance Rape: Seduction or Crime? When Sex Becomes a Crime." Paper presented at the Eastern Regional Society for the Scientific Study of Sex meeting, April 6–8.

PARSONS, TALCOTT. 1951. *The Social System*. New York: Free Press.

PEARLIN, LEONARD I., and JOYCE S. JOHNSON. 1977. "Marital Status, Life-Strains, and Depression." *American Sociological Review*, 42 (October): 704–715.

PECKHAM, MORSE. 1969. *Art and Pornography: An Experiment in Explanation*. New York: Basic Books.

PENDERY, MARY L., IRVING M. MALTZMAN, and L. JOLYON WEST. 1982. "Controlled Drinking by Alcoholics? New Findings and a Reevaluation of a Major Affirmative Study." *Science*, 217 (9 July): 169–175.

PERLMAN, SHIRLEY E. 1986. "Repeat Offender Caught on the Road . . . Again." *Newsday* (December 10): 2, 39.

PETERSEN, ROBERT C. 1979. "Statement on Cocaine." Statement before Select Committee on Narcotics Abuse and Control, House of Representatives, Washington, D.C., July 24.

PETERSEN, ROBERT C. (ed.). 1980. *Marijuana Research Findings: 1980*. Rockville, Md.: National Institute on Drug Abuse.

PETRAS, JOHN W. 1973. *Sexuality in Society*. Boston: Allyn & Bacon.

PFOHL, STEPHEN J. 1985. *Images of Deviance and Social Control: A Sociological History*. New York: McGraw-Hill.

PFUHL, ERDWIN H., Jr. 1986. *The Deviance Process* (2nd ed.). Belmont, Calif.: Wadsworth.

PINES, AYALA M., and MIMI H. SILBERT. 1983. "Early Sexual Exploitation as an Influence in Prostitution." *Social Work*, 28 (July–August): 285–289.

PIVEN, FRANCES FOX. 1981. "Deviant Behavior and the Remaking of the World." *Social Problems*, 28 (June): 489–508.

PLANT, RICHARD. 1986. *The Pink Triangle: The Nazi War Against Homosexuality*. New York: New Republic/Holt.

PLATT, ANTHONY. 1969. *The Child Savers*. Chicago: University of Chicago Press.

PLATT, ANTHONY. 1973. "Interview with Platt." *Issues in Criminology*, 8 (1): 11–22.

PLATT, ANTHONY. 1975. "Prospects for a Radical Criminology in the U.S.A." In Ian Taylor et al. (eds.), *Critical Criminology*. London: Routledge & Kegan Paul, pp. 95–112.

PLATT, ANTHONY. 1978. "'Street' Crime—A View From the Left." *Crime and Social Justice*, 9 (Spring/Summer): 26–34.

PLUMMER, KENNETH. 1975. *Sexual Stigma: An Interactionist Account*. London: Routledge & Kegan Paul.

PLUMMER, KENNETH. 1979. "Misunderstanding Labelling Perspectives." In David Downes and Paul Rock (eds.), *Deviant Interpretations*. London: Martin Robertson, pp. 85–121.

PLUMMER, KENNETH. 1981a. "Building a Sociology of Homosexuality." In Kenneth Plummer (ed.), *The Making of the Modern Homosexual*. Totowa, N.J.: Barnes & Noble, pp. 17–29.

PLUMMER, KENNETH. 1981b. "Homosexual Categories: Some Research Problems in the Labelling Perspective of Homosexuality." In Kenneth Plummer (ed.), *The Making of the Modern Homosexual*. Totowa, N.J.: Barnes & Noble, pp. 53–75.

PLUMMER, KENNETH. 1984. "Sexual Diversity: A Sociological Perspective." In Kevin Howells (ed.) *The Psychology of Sexual Diversity*. Oxford, Eng.: Basil Blackwell, pp. 219–253.

POLICH, J. MICHAEL, DAVID J. ARMOR, and HARRIET

B. BRAIKER. 1980. *The Course of Alcoholism: Four Years After Treatment*. Santa Monica, Calif.: Rand Corporation.

POLIVY, JANET, and C. PETER HERMAN. 1983. *Breaking the Diet Habit*. New York: Basic Books.

POLLNER, MELVIN. 1974. "Sociological and Common-Sense Models of the Labelling Process." In Roy Turner (ed.), *Ethnomethodology: Selected Readings*. Baltimore: Penguin Books, pp. 27–40.

POLSKY, NED. 1969. *Hustlers, Beats, and Others*. Garden City, N.Y.: Doubleday-Anchor.

PONSE, BARBARA. 1978. *Identities in the Lesbian World: The Social Construction of Self*. Westport, Conn.: Greenwood Press.

PONTELL, HENRY N. 1982. "System Capacity and Criminal Justice: Theoretical and Substantive Considerations." In Harold E. Pepinsky (ed.), *Rethinking Criminology*. Beverly Hills, Calif.: Sage, pp. 131–143.

PONTELL, HENRY N. 1984. *A Capacity to Punish: The Ecology of Crime and Punishment*. Bloomington: Indiana University Press.

PONTELL, HENRY N., PAUL JESILOW, and GILBERT GEIS. 1982. "Policing Physicians: Practitioner Fraud and Abuse in a Government Medical Program." *Social Problems*, 30 (October): 117–125.

PONTELL, HENRY N., GILBERT GEIS, and PAUL JESILOW. 1984a. *Practitioner Fraud and Abuse in Government Medical Benefit Programs*. Final report submitted to the National Institute of Justice, U.S. Department of Justice (June).

PONTELL, HENRY N., PAUL JESILOW, and GILBERT GEIS. 1984b. "Practitioner Fraud and Abuse in Medical Benefit Programs: Government Regulation and Professional White-Collar Crime." *Law and Policy*, 6 (October): 405–424.

PONTELL, HENRY N., et al. 1983. "White-Collar Crime Seriousness: Assessments of Police Chiefs and Regulatory Agency Investigators." *American Journal of Police* 3: 1–16.

PONTELL, HENRY N., et al. 1985. "Seriousness of Crimes: A Survey of the Nation's Chiefs of Police." *Journal of Criminal Justice* 13: 1–13.

POPPER, KARL R. 1959. *The Logic of Scientific Discovery*. New York: Basic Books.

PRESS, ARIC, et al. 1985. "The War Against Pornography." *Newsday* (March 18): 58–66.

PROGRESSIVE LABOR PARTY. 1972. "The U.S. Government Is the Biggest Dope Pusher." *PL: Progressive Labor*, 8 (March): 51–74.

PRUS, ROBERT, and STYLLIANOSS IRINI. 1980. *Hook-*

ers, Rounders, and Desk Clerks: The Social Organization of the Hotel Community. Salem, Wisc.: Sheffield.

PURNICK, JOYCE. 1985. "Cartier and 2 Executives Indicted on Taxes." The New York Times (March 20): A1, B5.

QUINNEY, RICHARD. 1963. "Occupational Structure and Criminal Behavior: Prescription Violations by Retail Pharmacists." Social Problems, 11 (Fall): 179–185.

QUINNEY, RICHARD. 1965. "Is Criminal Behaviour Deviant Behaviour? British Journal of Criminology, 5 (April): 132–142.

QUINNEY, RICHARD. 1966. "Structural Characteristics, Population Areas and Crime Rates in the United States." Journal of Criminal Law, Criminology, and Police Science, 55 (June): 45–52.

QUINNEY, RICHARD. 1970. The Social Reality of Crime. Boston: Little, Brown.

QUINNEY, RICHARD. 1972a. "From Repression to Liberation: Social Theory in a Radical Age." In Robert A. Scott and Jack D. Douglas (eds.), Theoretical Perspectives on Deviance. New York: Basic Books, pp. 317–341.

QUINNEY, RICHARD. 1972b. "The Ideology of Law: Notes for a Radical Alternative to Legal Oppression." Issues in Criminology, 7 (Winter): 1–35.

QUINNEY, RICHARD. 1973. "Review of Ian Taylor et al., The New Criminology: For a Social Theory of Deviance." London: Routledge & Kegan Paul. In Sociological Quarterly, 14 (Autumn): 589–594.

QUINNEY, RICHARD. 1974a. Critique of Legal Order. Boston: Little, Brown.

QUINNEY, RICHARD (ed.). 1974b. Criminal Justice in America: A Critical Understanding. Boston: Little, Brown.

QUINNEY, RICHARD. 1975. "Crime Control in Capitalist Society: A Critical Philosophy of Legal Order." In Ian Taylor et al. (eds.), Critical Criminology. London: Routledge & Kegan Paul, pp. 181–201.

QUINNEY, RICHARD. 1979. Criminology: Analysis and Critique (2nd ed.). Boston: Little, Brown.

QUINNEY, RICHARD. 1980a. Class, State, and Crime. New York: Longman.

QUINNEY, RICHARD. 1980b. Providence: The Development of Social and Moral Order. New York: Longman.

QUINNEY, RICHARD. 1982. Social Existence: Metaphysics, Marxism and the Social Sciences. Beverly Hills, Calif.: Sage.

QUINNEY, RICHARD. 1986. "Mystery in the Land: A Journey East." SSSP Newsletter, 17 (Winter): 25–29.

QUINNEY, RICHARD, and JOHN WILDEMAN. 1977. The Problem of Crime: A Critical Introduction to Criminology (2nd ed.). New York: Harper & Row.

RAAB, SELWYN. 1975a. "Plea Bargains Resolve 8 out of 10 Homicide Cases." The New York Times (January 27): 1, 39.

RAAB, SELWYN. 1975b. "Felony Murder Rose 15.7 Here Last Year." The New York Times (March 23): 1, 35.

RAAB, SELWYN. 1976a. "Deliberate Slayings on Increase Here." The New York Times (February 27): 1, 14.

RAAB, SELWYN. 1976b. "33% Slain in New York Don't Know Killer." The New York Times (June 13): 1, 60.

RAAB, SELWYN. 1985. "Man Wrongfully Imprisoned Is to Get $600,000 From City." The New York Times (January 18): B1, B5.

RAND, MICHAEL R. 1988. "Households Touched by Crime, 1987." Bureau of Justice Statistics Bulletin (May): 1–5.

RAVENHOLT, R. T. 1984. "Addiction Mortality in the United States, 1980: Tobacco, Alcohol, and Other Substances." Population and Developmental Review, 10 (December): 697–724.

RAVO, NICK. 1987. "Drinking Age Is Said to Fail for Students." The New York Times (December 21): A1, B15.

RAY, OAKLEY. 1978. Drugs, Society, and Human Behavior (2nd ed.). St. Louis: Mosby.

RAY, OAKLEY. 1983. Drugs, Society, and Human Behavior (3rd ed.). St. Louis: Mosby.

RAY, OAKLEY, and CHARLES KSIR. 1987. Drugs, Society, and Human Behavior (4th ed.). St. Louis: Times Mirror/Mosby.

RECKLESS, WALTER R. 1973. The Crime Problem (5th ed.). New York: Appleton-Century-Crofts.

RECTOR, FRANK. 1981. The Nazi Extermination of Homosexuals. New York: Stein & Day.

REESE, MICHAEL. 1981. "The Growing Terror of 'Gay Bashing.'" Newsweek (March 23): 30.

REID, SUE TITUS. 1982. Crime and Criminology (3rd ed.). New York: Holt, Rinehart & Winston.

REID, SUE TITUS. 1988. Crime and Criminology (5th ed.). New York: Holt, Rinehart & Winston.

REINHOLD, ROBERT. 1988. "Gang Violence Shocks Los Angeles." The New York Times (February 8): A10.

REISS, ALBERT J., JR. 1961. "The Social Integration

of Queers and Peers." *Social Problems*, 9 (Fall): 102–120.

REISS, ELLEN (ed.). 1986. *The Aesthetic Realism of Eli Siegel and the Change From Homosexuality*. New York: Definition Press.

REUBEN, DAVID R. 1969. *Everything You Always Wanted to Know About Sex, But Were Afraid to Ask*. New York: David McKay.

RIMER, SARA. 1985. "Fear of AIDS Grows Among Heterosexuals." *The New York Times* (August 30): A1, B2.

RIMLAND, BERNARD. 1969. "Psychogenesis Versus Biogenesis: The Issues and the Evidence." In Stanley C. Plog and Robert B. Edgerton (eds.), *Changing Perspectives in Mental Health*. New York: Holt, Rinehart & Winston, pp. 702–735.

ROBERTS, MARJORY. 1986. "MDMA: Madness, not Ecstasy." *Psychology Today* (June): 14–15.

ROBINS, LEE N. 1975. "Alcoholism and Labeling Theory." In Walter R. Gove (ed.), *The Labelling of Deviance*. New York: Wiley-Halstead-Sage, pp. 21–33.

ROCK, PAUL. 1973. "Review of Ian Taylor et al., *The New Criminology: For a Sociology of Deviance*." London: Routledge & Kegan Paul, 1973. In *The Sociological Quarterly*, 14 (Autumn): 594–596.

ROCK, PAUL. 1979. "The Sociology of Crime, Symbolic Interactionism and Some Problematic Qualities of Radical Criminology." In David Downes and Paul Rock (eds.), *Deviant Interpretations*. London: Martin Robertson, pp. 52–84.

ROCK, PAUL. 1980. "Has Deviance a Future?" In Hubert M. Blalock, Jr. (ed.)., *Sociological Theory and Research: A Critical Appraisal*. New York: Free Press, pp. 290–303.

ROHTER, LARRY. 1986. "Friend and Foe See Homosexual Defeat." *The New York Times* (July 1): A19.

RORVICK, DAVID. 1980. "Cattle Mutilations: The Truth at Last." *Penthouse* (September): 121–122, 142–143.

ROSENBAUM, MARSHA. 1981. *Women on Heroin*. New Brunswick, N.J.: Rutgers University Press.

ROSENBLUM, KAREN E. 1975. "Female Deviance and the Female Sex Role: A Preliminary Investigation." *British Journal of Sociology*, 26 (June): 169–185.

ROSENHAN, D. L. 1973. "On Being Sane in Insane Places." *Science*, 179 (January 19): 250–258.

ROSS, H. LAURENCE. 1971. "Modes of Adjustment of Married Homosexuals." *Social Problems*, 18 (Winter): 385–393.

ROSS, J. LAURENCE. 1972. "Odd Couples: Homo-sexuals in Heterosexual Marriages." *Sexual Behavior*, 2 (July): 42–49.

ROSSI, PETER, et al. 1974. "The Seriousness of Crimes: Normative Structure and Individual Differences." *American Sociological Review*, 39 (April): 224–237.

ROSSMAN, PARKER. 1976. *Sexual Experience Between Men and Boys: Exploring the Pederast Underground*. New York: Association Press.

ROTENBERG, MORDECHAI. 1974. "Self-Labeling: A Missing Link in the 'Societal Reaction' Theory of Deviance." *The Sociological Review*, 22 (August): 335–354.

ROTHWELL, NANCY J., and MICHAEL J. STOCK. 1979. "A Role for Brown Adipose Tissue in Diet-Induced Thermogenesis." *Nature*, 281 (6 September): 31–35.

RUBIN, GAYLE. 1984. "Thinking Sexuality." In Carole S. Vance (ed.), *Pleasure and Danger: Exploring Female Sexuality*. Boston: Routledge & Kegan Paul, pp. 267–319.

RUBINGTON, EARL, and MARTIN S. WEINBERG (eds.). 1977. *The Study of Social Problems: Five Perspectives* (2nd ed.). New York: Oxford University Press.

RUBINGTON, EARL, and MARTIN S. WEINBERG (eds.). 1987. *Deviance: The Interactionist Perspective* (5th ed). New York: Macmillan.

RUSHING, WILLIAM A. 1978. "Status Resources: Societal Reactions and Type of Mental Hospitalization." *American Sociological Review*, 43 (August): 521–533.

RUSHING, WILLIAM A. 1979a. "The Functional Importance of Sex Roles and Sex-Related Behavior in Societal Reactions to Residual Deviants." *Journal of Health and Social Behavior*, 20 (September): 208–217.

RUSHING, WILLIAM A. 1979b. "Marital Status and Mental Disorder: Evidence in Favor of a Behavioral Model." *Social Forces*, 58 (December): 540–556.

RUSSELL, DIANA E. H. 1975. *The Politics of Rape: The Victim's Perspective*. New York: Stein & Day.

RUSSELL, DIANA E. H. 1982a. "The Prevalence and Incidence of Forcible Rape and Attempted Rape of Females." *Victimology: An International Journal*, 7 (1–4): 81–93.

RUSSELL, DIANA E. H. 1982b. *Rape in Marriage*. New York: Collier Books.

RUSSELL, DIANA E. H. 1982c. "Pornography and Violence: What Does the Research Say?" In Laura Lederer (ed.), *Take Back the Night: Women* on *Pornography*. New York: Bantam Books, pp. 216–236.

RUSSELL, DIANA E. H. 1986. *The Secret Trauma: Incest in the Lives of Girls and Women*. New York: Basic Books.

RUSSELL, DIANA E. H., and NANCY HOWELL. 1983. "The Prevalence of Rape in the United States Revisited." *Signs: Journal of Women in Culture and Society*, 8 (Summer): 688–695.

RYAN, WILLIAM. 1976. *Blaming the Victim* (2nd ed.). New York: Vintage.

SAGARIN, EDWARD. 1973. "The Good Guys, the Bad Guys, and the Gay Guys." *Contemporary Sociology*, 2 (January): 1–11.

SAGARIN, EDWARD. 1975. *Deviants and Deviance: An Introduction to the Study of Disvalued Behavior*. New York: Praeger.

SAGARIN, EDWARD. 1985. "Positive Deviance: An Oxymoron." *Deviant Behavior*, 6 (2): 169–181.

SAGE, WAYNE. 1975. "Inside the Colossal Closet." *Human Behavior*, 4 (August): 16–23.

SAGHIR, MARCEL T., and ELI ROBINS. 1973. *Male and Female Homosexuality*. Baltimore: Williams & Wilkins.

SAMPSON, HAROLD, et al. 1962. "Family Processes and Becoming a Mental Patient." *American Journal of Sociology*, 68 (July): 88–96.

SAPOLSKY, BARRY S. 1984. "Arousal, Affect, and the Aggression-Moderating Effect of Erotica." In Neil M. Malamuth and Edward Donnerstein (eds.), *Pornography and Sexual Aggression*. Orlando, Fla.: Academic Press, pp. 85–113.

SANDERS, ED. 1976. "The Mutilation Mystery." *Oui* (September): 51–52, 92ff.

SANDERS, ED. 1977. "On the Trail of the Night Surgeons." *Oui* (May): 79–80, 121ff.

SANDERS, WILLIAM B. 1980. *Rape and Woman's Identity*. Beverly Hills, Calif.: Sage.

SCHEFF, THOMAS J. 1966. *Being Mentally Ill: A Sociological Approach*. Chicago: Aldine.

SCHEFF, THOMAS J. 1974a. "The Labelling Theory of Mental Illness." *American Sociological Review*, 39 (June): 444–452.

SCHEFF, THOMAS J. 1974b. "Reply to Nettler." *American Sociological Review*, 39 (December): 894–895.

SCHEFF, THOMAS J. 1975. "Reply to Clancey and Gove." *American Sociological Review*, 40 (April): 252–257.

SCHEFF, THOMAS J. 1979. "Reply to Comment by Horwitz." *Journal of Health and Social Behavior*, 20 (September): 305–306.

SCHEFF, THOMAS J. 1984. *Being Mentally Ill: A Sociological Theory* (2nd ed.). New York: Aldine.

SCHMECK, HAROLD M., JR. 1987. "Defective Gene Tied to Form of Manic-Depressive Illness." *The New York Times* (February 26): A1, B7.

SCHMECK, HAROLD M., JR. 1988a. "Theory Explains Slow Emergence of Mental Ills." *The New York Times* (February 2): C3.

SCHMECK, HAROLD M., JR. 1988b. "Region in Brain Is Linked to Obsessive Disorder." *The New York Times* (March 8): C1, C11.

SCHMECK, HAROLD M., JR. 1988c. "Schizophrenia Study Finds Strong Signs of Heredity Cause." *The New York Times* (November 10): A1, B22.

SCHRAGER, LAURA, and JAMES F. SHORT, JR. 1980. "How Serious a Crime?: Perceptions of Organizational and Common Crimes." In Gilbert Geis and Ezra Stotland (eds.), *White-Collar Crime: Theory and Research*. Beverly Hills, Calif.: Sage, pp. 14–31.

SCHUCKIT, MARC A. 1980. "A Theory of Alcohol and Drug Abuse: A Genetic Approach." In Dan J. Lettieri et al. (eds.), *Theories on Drug Abuse*. Rockville, Md.: National Institute on Drug Abuse, pp. 297–302.

SCHUCKIT, MARC A. 1984. *Drug and Alcohol Abuse: A Clinical Guide to Diagnosis and Treatment* (2nd ed.). New York: Plenum Press.

SCHUCKIT, MARC A. 1985. "Overview: Epidemiology of Alcoholism." In Marc A. Schuckit (ed.), *Alcohol Patterns and Problems*. New Brunswick, N.J.: Rutgers University Press, pp. 1–42.

SCHULTE, LUCY. 1986. "The New Dating Game." *New York* (March 3): 92ff.

SCHUR, EDWIN M. 1965. *Crimes Without Victims: Deviant Behavior and Public Policy*. Englewood Cliffs, N.J.: Prentice-Hall/Spectrum.

SCHUR, EDWIN M. 1971. *Labeling Deviant Behavior: Its Sociological Implications*. New York: Harper & Row.

SCHUR, EDWIN M. 1979. *Interpreting Deviance: A Sociological Introduction*. New York: Harper & Row.

SCHUR, EDWIN M. 1980. *The Politics of Deviance: Stigma Contests and the Uses of Power*. Englewood Cliffs, N.J.: Prentice-Hall/Spectrum.

SCHUR, EDWIN M. 1984. "The Labeling Perspective on Deviance: Major Contributions and Acknowledged Limits." Lecture presented at the Department of Sociology, Ohio State University, Columbus, May 9.

SCHUR, EDWIN M. 1984. *Labeling Women Deviant: Gender, Stigma, and Social Control*. New York: Random House.

SCHWENDINGER, HERMAN, and JULIA SCHWEN-DINGER. 1970. "Defenders of Order or Guardians of Human Rights?" *Issues in Criminology*, 5 (Summer): 123–157.

SCHWENDINGER, HERMAN, and JULIA SCHWEN-DINGER. 1974. "Rape Myths in Legal, Theoretical, and Everyday Practice." *Crime and Criminal Justice*, 1 (Spring–Summer): 18–26.

SCHWENDINGER, HERMAN, and JULIA SCHWEN-DINGER. 1975. "Defenders of Order or Guardians of Human Rights? In Ian Taylor et al. (eds.), *Critical Criminology*. London: Routledge & Kegan Paul, pp. 113–146.

SCHWENDINGER, HERMAN, and JULIA SCHWEN-DINGER. 1977. "Social Class and the Definition of Crime." *Crime and Social Justice*, 7 (Spring–Summer): 4–14.

SCHWENDINGER, JULIA, and HERMAN SCHWEN-DINGER. 1983. *Rape and Inequality*. Beverly Hills, Calif.: Sage.

SCOTT, JOSEPH E., and STEVEN J. CUVELIER. 1987a. "Violence in *Playboy* Magazine: A Longitudinal Analysis." *Archives of Sexual Behavior*, 16 (4): 279–288.

SCOTT, JOSEPH E., and STEVEN J. CUVELIER. 1987b. "Sexual Violence in *Playboy* Magazine: A Longitudinal Content Analysis." *The Journal of Sex Research*, 25 (November): 534–539.

SCULL, ANDREW. 1972. "Social Control and the Amplification of Deviance." In Robert A. Scott and Jack D. Douglas (eds.), *Theoretical Perspectives on Deviance*. New York: Basic Books, pp. 282–314.

SCULLY, DIANA, and JOSEPH MAROLLA. 1984. "Convicted Rapists' Vocabulary of Motive: Excuses and Justifications." *Social Problems*, 31 (June): 530–544.

SCULLY, DIANA, and JOSEPH MAROLLA. 1985. "'Riding the Bull at Gilley's': Convicted Rapists Describe the Rewards of Rape." *Social Problems*, 32 (February): 251–263.

SHEEHY, GAIL. 1973. *Hustling: Prostitution in Our Wide-Open Society*. New York: Delacorte Press.

SHEPPARD, NATHANIEL, JR. 1979. "Episcopal Bishops Vote to Reject the Ordination of Homosexuals." *The New York Times* (September 18): A20.

SHERMAN, LAWRENCE W., and RICHARD A. BERK. 1984. "The Specific Deterrent Effect for Domestic Assault. *American Sociological Review*. 49 (April): 261–272.

SHICHOR, DAVID. 1980a. "The New Criminology: Some Critical Issues." *The British Journal of Criminology*, 20 (January): 1–19.

SHICHOR, DAVID. 1980b. "Some Problems of Credibility in Radical Criminology." In James A. Inciardi (ed.), *Radical Criminology: The Coming Crises*. Beverly Hills, Calif.: Sage, pp. 191–212.

SHILTS, RANDY. 1987. *And the Band Played On: Politics, People, and the AIDS Epidemic*. New York: St. Martin's Press.

SHIM, KELLY H., and MARSHALL M. DeBERRY. 1988. "Criminal Victimization, 1987." *Bureau of Justice Statistics Bulletin* (October): 1–6.

SHOEMAKER, DONALD J. 1984. *Theories of Delinquency: An Examination of Explanations of Delinquent Behavior*. New York: Oxford University Press.

SHUPE, LLOYD M. 1954. "Alcohol and Crime." *Journal of Criminal Law, Criminology, and Police Science*, 44 (January–February): 661–664.

SIEGAL, BARRY. 1985. "Murder Case a Corporate Landmark." *Los Angeles Times* (September 15): 1.

SIEGEL, RONALD K. 1984. "Changing Patterns of Cocaine Use: Longitudinal Observations, Consequences, and Treatment." In John Grabowski (ed.), *Cocaine: Pharmacology, Effects, and Treatment of Abuse*. Rockville, Md.: National Institute on Drug Abuse, pp. 92–110.

SIMMONS, JERRY L. 1965. "Public Stereotypes of Deviants." *Social Problems*, 13 (Fall): 223–232.

SIMMONS, JERRY L. 1969. *Deviants*. Santa Barbara, Calif.: Glendessary Press.

SIMON, DAVID R. 1981. "The Political Economy of Crime." In Scott G. McNall (ed.), *Political Economy: A Critique of American Society*. Glenview, Ill.: Scott, Foresman, pp. 347–366.

SIMON, JESSE, and JACK ZUSMAN. 1983. "The Effect of Contextual Factors on Psychiatrists' Perception of Illness: A Case Study." *Journal of Health and Social Behavior*, 24 (2): 186–198.

SIMON, RITA JAMES. 1975a. *Women and Crime*. Lexington, Mass.: D. C. Heath.

SIMON, RITA JAMES. 1975b. *The Contemporary Woman and Crime*. Rockville, Md.: National Institute of Mental Health.

SINGLE, ERIC W. 1981. "The Impact of Marijuana Decriminalization." In Yedy Israel et al. (eds.), *Research Advances in Alcohol and Drug Problems*. New York: Plenum Press, pp. 405–424.

SKOLNICK, JEROME H., and ELLIOTT P. CURRIE (eds.). 1985. *Crisis in American Institutions* (6th ed.). Boston: Little, Brown.

SKOLNICK, JEROME H., et al. 1969. *The Politics of Protest*. New York: Simon & Schuster.

SLOAN, JOHN HENRY, et al. 1988. "Handgun Regulations, Crime, Assaults, and Homicide: A Tale of Two Cities." *The New England Journal of Medicine*, 319 (November 10): 1256–1262.

SLOVIC, PAUL, BARUCH FISCHOFF, and SARAH LICHTENSTEIN. 1980. "Risky Assumptions." *Psychology Today* (June): 44–48.

SMART, CAROL. 1976. *Women, Crime and Criminology*. London: Routledge & Kegan Paul.

SMART, CAROL, and BARRY SMART (eds.). 1978. *Women, Sexuality, and Social Control*. London: Routledge & Kegan Paul.

SMITH, DON D. 1976. "The Social Content of Pornography." *Journal of Communication*, 26 (Winter): 16–24.

SMITH, DUSKEY LEE. 1973. "Symbolic Interactionism: Definitions of the Situation from Becker to Lofland." *Catalyst*, 7 (Winter): 62–75.

SMITH, MARY LEE, GENE GLASS, and THOMAS MILLER. 1980. *The Benefits of Psychotherapy*. Baltimore: Johns Hopkins University Press.

SNITOW, ANN. 1988. "Retrenchment vs. Transformation: The Politics of the Antipornography Movement." In Kate Ellis et al. (eds.), *Caught Looking: Feminism, Pornography, and Censorship*. Seattle, Wash.: Real Comet Press, pp. 10–17.

SNITOW, ANN, CHRISTINE STANSELL, and SHARON THOMPSON (eds.). 1983. *Powers of Desire: The Politics of Sexuality*. New York: Monthly Review Press.

SOBEL, LESTER. 1977. *Corruption in Business*. New York: Facts on File.

SOBELL, MARK B., and LINDA C. SOBELL. 1978. *Behavioral Treatment of Alcohol Problems: Individualized Therapy and Controlled Drinking*. New York: Plenum Press.

SOBELL, MARK B., and LINDA C. SOBELL. 1984. "The Aftermath of Heresy: A Response to Pendery et al.'s Critique of 'Individualized Behavior Therapy for Alcoholics.'" *Behavior Research and Therapy*, 22 (4): 413–440.

SOCARIDES, CHARLES W. 1968. *The Overt Homosexual*. New York: Grune & Stratton.

SOCARIDES, CHARLES W. 1970. "Homosexuality and Medicine." *Journal of the American Medical Association*, 212 (May 18): 1199–1202.

SOCARIDES, CHARLES W. 1972. "Homosexuality—Basic Concepts and Psychodynamics." *International Journal of Psychiatry*, 10 (JMarch): 118–125.

SOCARIDES, CHARLES W. 1973. "Homosexuality: Findings Derived From 15 Years of Clinical Research." *American Journal of Psychiatry*, 130 (November): 1212–1213.

SOCARIDES, CHARLES W. 1975. *Beyond Sexual Freedom*. Chicago: Quadrangle.

SOCARIDES, CHARLES W. 1978. *Homosexuality*. New York: Jason Aronson.

SPARKS, RICHARD F. 1980. "A Critique of Marxist Criminology." In Norval Morris and Michael Tonry (eds.), *Crime and Justice: An Annual Review of Research*, Vol. 2. Chicago: University of Chicago Press, pp. 159–210.

SPENCE, JONATHAN D. 1988. *The Question of Hu*. New York: Alfred Knopf.

SPITZER, STEVEN. 1975. "Toward a Marxian Theory of Deviance." *Social Problems*, 22 (June): 638–651.

SROLE, LEO, et al. 1962. *Mental Health in the Metropolis: The Midtown Manhattan Study*. New York: McGraw-Hill.

SROLE, LEO, et al. 1978. *Mental Health in the Metropolis: The Midtown Manhattan Study* (rev. and enl. ed.). New York: New York University Press.

STARK, RODNEY. 1987. *Sociology* (2nd ed.). Belmont, Calif.: Wadsworth.

STEFFENSMEIER, DARRELL J., and ROBERT M. TERRY. 1973. "Deviance and Respectability: An Observational Study of Reactions to Shoplifting." *Social Forces*, 51 (June): 417–426.

STEGNER, PAGE. 1981. "The Limits of Tolerance." *Esquire* (July): 29–35.

STEIN, S. D. 1980. "The Sociology of Law." *British Journal of Criminology*, 20 (April): 99–122.

STEINEM, GLORIA. 1982. "Erotica and Pornography: A Clear and Present Difference." In Laura Lederer (ed.), *Take Back the Night: Women on Pornography*. New York: Bantam Books, pp. 21–25.

STEINERT, HEINZ. 1978. "Can Socialism Be Advanced by Radical Rhetoric and Sloppy Data? Some Remarks on Richard Quinney's Latest Output." *Contemporary Crises*, 2 (3): 303–313.

STEINFELS, PETER. 1988. "Methodists Vote to Retain Policy Concerning Homosexual Behavior." *The New York Times* (May 3): A22.

STENGEL, RICHARD, et al. 1985. "A Troubled and Troubling Life." *Time* (April 8): 35, 38–39.

STEVENS, WILLIAM K. 1981. "Texas Indictment Puts Focus on Dilemma of Mercy Killers." *The New York Times* (December 10): A1, A18.

STEVENS, WILLIAM K. 1987. "Deaths From Drunken Driving Increase." *The New York Times* (October 29): A18.

STEWART, JAMES R. 1980. "Collective Delusion: A Comparison of Believers and Skepticks." Paper presented at the Midwest Sociological Society, Milwaukee, Wisconsin, April 3.

STOKES, GEOFFREY. 1986. "Bubblehead Slut Dies, Deserves It." *The Village Voice* (September 9): 8.

STOLLER, ROBERT J., and R. H. GEERTSMA. 1963. "The Consistency of Psychiatrists' Clinical Judgments." *Journal of Nervous and Mental Disease*, 137 (January): 58–66.

STONE, MICHAEL. 1986. "East Side Story." *New York* (November 10): 43–53.

STRAUS, MURRAY A., RICHARD J. GELLES, and SUZANNE K. STEINMETZ. 1980. *Behind Closed Doors: Violence in the American Family.* Garden City, N.Y.: Doubleday.

STRAUS, ROBERT. 1976. "Alcoholism and Problem Drinking." In Robert K. Merton and Robert Nisbet (eds.), *Contemporary Social Problems* (4th ed.). New York: Harcourt Brace Jovanovich, pp. 181–217.

SUCHAR, CHARLES S. 1978. *Social Deviance: Perspectives and Prospects.* New York: Holt, Rinehart & Winston.

SULLIVAN, WALTER. 1980. "Violent Pornography Elevates Aggression, Researchers Say." *The New York Times* (September 30): C1, C3.

SUTHERLAND, EDWIN H. 1939. *Principles of Criminology* (3rd ed.). Philadelphia: Lippencott.

SUTHERLAND, EDWIN H. 1949. *White-Collar Crime.* New York: Dryden.

SUTHERLAND, EDWIN H., and DONALD R. CRESSEY. 1978. *Criminology* (10th ed.). Philadelphia: Lippencott.

SUTHERLAND, EDWIN H. 1983. *White-Collar Crime: The Uncut Version.* New Haven, Conn.: Yale University Press.

SUTTER, ALAN G. 1966. "The World of the Righteous Dope Fiend." *Issues in Criminology*, 2 (Fall): 177–222.

SYKES, GRESHAM M., and DAVID MATZA. 1957. "Techniques of Neutralization: A Theory of Delinquency." *American Sociological Review*, 22 (December): 664–670.

SZASZ, THOMAS S. 1960. "The Myth of Mental Illness." *American Psychologist*, 15 (February): 113–118.

SZASZ, THOMAS S. 1961. *The Myth of Mental Illness.* New York: Harper & Row.

TALAMINI, JOHN T. 1982. *Boys Will Be Girls: The Hidden World of the Heterosexual Male Transvestite.* Lundham, Md.: University Press of America.

TANNENBAUM, FRANK. 1938. *Crime and the Community.* New York: Ginn.

TAPPAN, PAUL. 1947. "Who Is the Criminal?" *American Sociological Review*, 12 (February): 96–102.

TAYLOR, IAN. 1981. *Law and Order: Arguments for Socialism..* London: Macmillan.

TAYLOR, IAN, PAUL WALTON, and JOCK YOUNG. 1973. *The New Criminology: For a Sociology of Deviance.* London: Routledge & Kegan Paul.

TAYLOR, IAN, PAUL WALTON, and JOCK YOUNG (eds.). 1975. *Critical Criminology.* London: Routledge & Kegan Paul.

TAYLOR, STUART, Jr. 1986. "High Court, 5–4, Says States Have the Right to Outlaw Private Homosexual Acts: Division is Bitter." *The New York Times* (July 1): A1, A19.

TERRY, CHARLES E., and MILDRED PELLENS. 1928. *The Opium Problem.* New York: Bureau of Social Hygiene.

THIO, ALEX. 1973. "Class Bias in the Sociology of Deviance." *The American Sociologist*, 8 (February): 1–12.

THIO, ALEX. 1988. *Deviant Behavior* (3rd ed.). New York: Harper & Row.

THOITS, PEGGY. 1985. "Self-Labeling Processes in Mental Illness: The Role of Emotional Distance." *American Journal of Sociology*, 91 (September): 221–249.

THOMAS, EVAN. 1985. "The New Untouchables." *Time* (International edition) (September 23): 28–30.

THOMAS, JIM. 1982. "New Directions in Deviance Research." In M. Michael Rosenberg et al. (eds.), *The Sociology of Deviance.* New York: St. Martin's Press, pp. 288–318.

THORNTON, E. M. 1983. *The Freudian Fallacy: An Alternative View of Freudian Theory.* New York: Dial Press.

TITTLE, CHARLES R., and WAYNE J. VILLEMEZ. 1977. "Social Class and Criminality." *Social Forces*, 56 (December): 474–502.

TITTLE, CHARLES R., WAYNE J. VILLEMEZ, and DOUGLAS A. SMITH. 1978. "The Myth of Social Class and Criminality: An Empirical Assessment of the Empirical Evidence." *American Sociological Review*, 43 (October): 643–656.

TITTLE, CHARLES R., WAYNE J. VILLEMEZ, and DOUGLAS A. SMITH. 1982. "One Step Forward, Two Steps Back: More on the Class/Criminality Controversy." *American Sociological Review* 47 (June): 435–438.

TOBY, JACKSON. 1980. "The New Criminology Is the Old Baloney." In James A. Inciardi (ed.),

Radical Criminology: The Coming Crises. Beverly Hills, Calif.: Sage, pp. 124–132.

TOMLINSON, KENNETH Y. 1981. "You'll Be a Hooker—Or Else!" *Reader's Digest* (February): 147–152.

TORREY, E. FULLER. 1988. *Nowhere to Go: The Tragic Odyssey of the Homeless Mentally Ill.* New York: Harper & Row.

TOWNSEND, JOHN MARSHALL. 1978. *Cultural Conceptions of Mental Illness.* Chicago: University of Chicago Press.

TOWNSEND, JOHN MARSHALL. 1980. "Psychiatry Versus Societal Reaction: A Critical Analysis." *Journal of Health and Social Behavior,* 21 (September): 268–278.

TRAUB, STUART H., and CRAIG B. LITTLE (eds.). 1980. *Theories of Deviance* (2nd ed.). Itasca, Ill.: F. E. Peacock.

TRAUB, STUART H., and CRAIG B. LITTLE (eds.). 1985. *Theories of Deviance* (3rd ed.). Itasca, Ill.: F. E. Peacock.

TRIPP, C. A. 1976. *The Homosexual Matrix.* New York: New American Library.

TROIDEN, RICHARD R. 1977. *Becoming Homosexual: Research on Acquiring a Gay Identity.* Ph.D. dissertation, Department of Sociology, State University of New York at Stony Brook.

TROIDEN, RICHARD R. 1979. "Becoming Homosexual: A Model of Gay Identity Acquisition." *Psychiatry,* 42 (February): 362–373.

TROIDEN, RICHARD R. 1988. *Gay and Lesbian Identity: A Sociological Analysis.* Dix Hills, N.Y.: General Hall.

TROUTMAN, PHILIP. 1965. *Velasquez.* London: Spring Books.

TURNBULL, COLIN. 1961. *The Forest People.* New York: Simon & Schuster.

TURNER, CARLTON E. 1980. "Chemistry and Metabolism." In Robert C. Peterson (ed.), *Marijuana Research Findings: 1980.* Rockville, Md.: National Institute on Drug Abuse, pp. 81–97.

TURNER, R. JAY, and JOHN W. GARTRELL. 1978. "Social Factors in Psychiatric Outcome: Toward a Resolution of Interpretive Controversies." *American Sociological Review,* 43 (June): 368–382.

TURNER, WALLACE. 1985. "AIDS Impact Wide in San Francisco." *The New York Times* (May 28): B7.

TURK, AUSTIN T. 1969. *Criminality and the Legal Order.* Chicago: Rand McNally.

TURK, AUSTIN T. 1972. *Legal Sanctioning and Social Control.* Rockville, Md.: National Institute of Mental Health.

TURK, AUSTIN T. 1976. "Law as a Weapon in Social Conflict." *Social Problems,* 23 (February): 276–291.

TURK, AUSTIN T. 1977. "Class, Conflict and Criminalization," *Sociological Focus,* 10 (August): 209–220.

TURK, AUSTIN T. 1980. "Analyzing Official Deviance: For Nonpartisan Conflict Analyses in Criminology." In James A. Inciardi (ed.), *Radical Criminology: The Coming Crises.* Beverly Hills, Calif.: Sage, pp. 78–91.

ULLMAN, LEONARD P., and LEONARD KRASNER. 1969. *A Psychological Approach to Abnormal Behavior.* Englewood Cliffs, N.J.: Prentice-Hall.

UNGERLEIDER, J. THOMAS, GEORGE D. LUNDBERG, IRVING SUNSHINE, and CLIFFORD B. WALBERG. 1980. "The Drug Abuse Warning Network (DAWN) Program." *Archives of General Psychiatry,* 124 (May): 1483–1490.

UNIVERSITY OF MICHIGAN NEWS AND INFORMATION SERVICES. 1988. News release, Ann Arbor, January 12.

VAILLANT, GEORGE E. 1984. "The Disadvantages of DSM-III Outweigh the Advantages." *American Journal of Psychiatry,* 141 (April): 542–545.

VALENTINE, CHARLES A. 1968. *Culture and Poverty: Critique and Counter-Proposals.* Chicago: University of Chicago Press.

VALVERDE, MARIANA. 1987. *Sex, Power and Pleasure.* Philadelphia: New Society Publishers.

VANCE, CAROLE (ed.). 1984. *Pleasure and Danger: Exploring Female Sexuality.* Boston: Routledge & Kegan Paul.

VAN DEN BERGHE, PIERRE L. 1978. *Man in Society: A Biosocial View* (2nd ed.). New York: Elsevier.

VAN DYKE, CRAIG, and ROBERT BYCK. 1982. "Cocaine." *Scientific American* (March): 128–141.

VAN STOLK, MARY. 1972. *The Battered Child in Canada.* Toronto: McClelland & Stewart.

VERHOVEK, SAM HOWE. 1988. "A Week's Killings: A Profile of Violent Death in New York." *The New York Times* (April 8): B1, B4.

VETERANS ADMINISTRATION. 1970. *Drug Treatment in Psychiatry.* Washington, D.C.: U.S. Government Printing Office.

VOLD, GEORGE B. 1958. *Theoretical Criminology.* New York: Oxford University Press.

VOLD, GEORGE B., and THOMAS J. BERNARD. 1979. *Theoretical Criminology* (2nd ed.). New York: Oxford University Press.

VOLD, GEORGE B., and THOMAS J. BERNARD. 1986.

Theoretical Criminology (3rd ed.). New York: Oxford University Press.

VON HENTIG, HANS. 1948. *The Criminal and His Victim.* New Haven, Conn.: Yale University Press.

VOSS, HARWIN L. 1966. "Socioeconomic Status and Reported Delinquent Behavior." *Social Problems,* 13 (Winter): 314–324.

VOSS, HARWIN L., and JOHN R. HEPBURN. 1968. "Patterns in Criminal Homicide in Chicago." *Journal of Criminal Law, Criminology, and Police Science,* 59 (December): 499–508.

WALD, MATTHEW L. 1986. "Battle Against Drunken Driving Should Focus on Alcoholics, Experts Say." *The New York Times* (January 3): 5.

WALKER, LENORE E. 1979. *The Battered Woman.* New York: Harper & Row.

WALLIS, CLAUDIA, et al. 1985. "AIDS: A Growing Threat." *Time* (August 12): 40–47.

WALT, VIVIENNE. 1987. "S. Africa: A Land of Deadly Despair." *Newsday* (November 1): 13.

WANGER, MORTON G., and THOMAS A. BONOMO. 1981. "Crime, the Crisis of Capitalism, and Social Revolution." In David F. Greenberg (ed.), *Crime and Capitalism: Readings in Marxist Criminology.* Palo Alto, Calif.: Mayfield, pp. 420–434.

WARHEIT, GEORGE J., CHARLES E. HOLZER III, ROGER A. BELL, and SANDRA A. AVERY. 1976. "Sex, Marital Status, and Mental Health: A Reappraisal." *Social Forces,* 55 (December): 459–470.

WARREN, CAROL A. B. 1974. *Identity and Community in the Gay World.* New York: John Wiley & Sons.

WARREN, CAROL A. B., and JOHN M. JOHNSON. 1972. "A Critique of Labeling Theory From the Phenomenological Perspective." In Robert A. Scott and Jack D. Douglas (eds.), *Theoretical Perspectives on Deviance.* New York: Basic Books, pp. 69–92.

WARREN, E. J., JR. 1978. "The Economic Approach to Crime." *Canadian Journal of Criminology,* 10: 437–449.

WATSON, RUSSELL, et al. 1987. "Holy War: Heaven Can Wait." *Newsweek* (June 8): 58–65.

WEEKS, JEFFREY, KENNETH PLUMMER, and MARY McINTOSH. 1981. "Postscript: 'The Homosexual Role' Revisited." In Kenneth Plummer (ed.), *The Making of the Modern Homosexual.* Totowa, N.J.: Barnes & Noble, pp. 44–49.

WEINBERG, MARTIN S., and COLIN J. WILLIAMS. 1974. *Male Homosexuals.* New York: Oxford University Press.

WEINER, HERBERT. 1975. "Schizophrenia: Etiology." In Alfred M. Freedman, Harold I. Kaplan, and Benjamin J. Saddock (eds.), *Comprehensive Textbook of Psychiatry,* Vol. 1 (2nd ed.). Baltimore, Williams & Wilkins, pp. 866–890.

WEIS, JOSEPH G. 1987. "Social Class and Crime." In Michael Gottfredson and Travis Hirschi (eds.), *Positive Criminology.* Beverly Hills, Calif.: Sage, pp. 71–90.

WELKOS, ROBERT. 1984. "Doctor Involved in Blindings Is Given a 4-Year Term for Fraud." *Los Angeles Times* (April 27).

WELLS, JOHN WARREN. 1970. *Tricks of the Trade.* New York: New American Library.

WHEELER, STANTON, et al. 1982. "Sentencing the White-Collar Offender: Rhetoric and Reality." *American Sociological Review,* 47 (October): 641–659.

WHITAM, FREDERICK L. 1977. "The Homosexual Role: A Reconsideration." *The Journal of Sex Research,* 13 (February): 1–11.

WHITAM, FREDERICK L. 1983. "Culturally Invariable Properties of Male Homosexuality: Tentative Conclusions From Cross-Cultural Research." *Archives of Sexual Behavior,* 12 (June): 207–226.

WHITAM, FREDERICK L., and ROBIN M. MATHY. 1986. *Male Homosexuality in Four Societies: Brazil, Guatemala, the Philippines, and the United States.* New York: Praeger.

WHITE, BYRON R. 1986. "Excerpts From the Court Opinions on Homosexual Relations: From the Opinion." *The New York Times* (July 1): A18.

WHYTE, WILLIAM F. 1943. *Street-Corner Society: The Social Structure of an Italian Slum.* Chicago: University of Chicago Press.

WIATROWSKI, MICHAEL D., DAVID B. GRISWOLD, and MARY K. ROBERTS. 1981. "Social Control Theory and Delinquency." *American Sociological Review,* 46 (October): 525–541.

WILKERSON, ISABEL. 1987. "Urban Homicide Rates in U.S. up Sharply in 1986." *The New York Times* (January 15): A14.

WILKINS, LESLIE T. 1964. *Social Deviance: Social Policy, Action, and Research.* London: Tavistock.

WILKINSON, GREGG S. 1975. "Patient-Audience Social Status and the Social Construction of Psychiatric Disorders: Toward a Differential Frame of Reference Hypothesis." *Journal of Health and Social Behavior,* 16 (March): 28–38.

WILLIAMS, JOYCE E., and WILLARD A. NIELSEN, JR. 1979. "The Rapist Looks at His Crime." *Free Inquiry Into Creative Sociology,* 7 (November): 128–132.

WILLIS, ELLEN. 1983. "Feminism, Moralism, and

Pornography." In Ann Snitow, et al. (eds.), *Powers of Desire: The Politics of Sexuality*. New York: Monthly Review Press, pp. 460–467.

WILLWERTH, JAMES. 1976. *Jones: Portrait of a Mugger*. New York: Fawcett.

WILSON, EDWARD O. 1975. *Sociobiology: The New Synthesis*. Cambridge, Mass.: Harvard University Press.

WILSON, EDWARD O. 1978. *On Human Nature*. Cambridge, Mass.: Harvard University Press.

WILSON, EDWARD O. 1984. *Biophilia*. Cambridge, Mass.: Harvard University Press.

WILSON, JAMES Q. 1985. *Thinking About Crime* (rev. ed.). New York: Vintage Books.

WILSON, JAMES Q., and RICHARD J. HERRNSTEIN. 1985. *Crime and Human Nature*. New York: Simon & Schuster.

WILSON, WILLIAM JULIUS. 1987. *The Truly Disadvantaged: The Inner City, the Underclass, and Public Policy*. Chicago: University of Chicago Press.

WILT, G. M. 1974. *Toward an Understanding of the Social Realities of Participating in Homicides*. Ph.D. dissertation, Wayne State University, Detroit, Mich.

WINES, MICHAEL. 1988. "Mental Institutions May Be as Empty as They'll Ever Be." *The New York Times* (September 4): 6E.

WISE, DAVID. 1973. *The Politics of Lying*. New York: Vintage.

WOLFE, LINDA. 1987. "The People Versus Robert Chambers: The 'Preppy Killing' Case Comes to Trial." *New York* (October 26): 92–109.

WOLFGANG, MARVIN E. 1958. *Patterns in Criminal Homicide*. Philadelphia: University of Pennsylvania Press.

WOLFGANG, MARVIN E., and FRANCO FERRACUTI. 1967. *The Subculture of Violence*. London: Tavistock.

WOLMAN, BARON. 1973. "A House Is Not a Home in Nevada." *Gallery* (September): 33–34, 105–107, 111–112.

WOODEN, WAYNE S., and JAY PARKER. 1982. *Men Behind Bars: Sexual Exploitation in Prison*. New York: Plenum Press.

WRIGHT, CHARLES. 1984. *Constructions of Deviance in Sociological Theory: The Problem of Commensurability*. Lanham, Md.: University Press of America.

WRIGHT, ERIK OLIN. 1973. *The Politics of Punishment: A Critical Analysis of Prisons in America*. New York: Harper Colophon.

WRIGHT, JAMES D., and PETER H. ROSSI. 1986. *Armed and Considered Dangerous: A Survey of Felons and Their Firearms*. New York: Aldine de Gruyter.

WRIGHT, JAMES D., and PETER H. ROSSI, and KATHLEEN DALY. 1983. *Under the Gun: Weapons, Crime, and Violence in America*. New York: Aldine de Gruyter.

YARROW, MARIAN RADKE, et al. 1955. "The Psychological Meaning of Mental Illness in the Family." *Journal of Social Issues*, 11 (December): 12–24.

YEARWOOD, LENNOX, and THOMAS S. WEINBERG. 1979. "Black Organizations, Gay Organizations, Sociological Parallels." In Martin P. Levin (ed.), *Gay Men*. New York: Harper & Row, pp. 301–316.

YOUNG, JOCK. 1975. "Working-Class Criminology." In Ian Taylor et al. (eds.), *Critical Criminology*. London: Routledge & Kegan Paul, pp. 63–94.

YOUNG, JOCK. 1979. "Left Idealism, Reformism and Beyond: From New Criminology to Marxism." In Bob Fine et al. (eds.), *Capitalism and the Rules of Law: From Deviancy Theory to Marxism*. London: Hutchinson, pp. 11–28.

YOUNG, WAYLAND. 1966. *Eros Denied: Sex in Western Society*. New York: Grove Press.

ZAUSNER, MICHAEL. 1986. *The Streets: A Factual Portrait of Six Prostitutes as Told in Their Own Words*. New York: St. Martin's Press.

ZEITLIN, LAWRENCE R. 1971. "A Little Larceny Can Do a Lot for Employee Morale." *Psychology Today*, 5 (June): 22–26, 64.

ZELLMAN, GAIL L., PAULA B. JOHNSON, ROSEANN GIARRUSO, and JACQUELINE D. GOODCHILDS. 1979. "Adolescent Expectations for Dating Relationships: Consensus and Conflict Between the Sexes." Paper presented at the meetings of the American Psychological Association, New York, September.

ZIMRING, FRANKLIN E., SATYANSHA K. MUKHERJEE, and BARRIK VAN WINKLE. 1983. "Intimate Violence: A Study of Interpersonal Homicide in Chicago." *University of Chicago Law Review*, 50 (Spring): 910–930.

ZINBERG, NORMAN E. 1984. *Drug, Set, and Setting: The Basis for Controlled Intoxicant Use*. New Haven, Conn.: Yale University Press.

Author Index

Subject Index

Person, crimes against the. *See* In-
cest; Murder; Rape; Robbery;
Violence; Wife beating
Peyote, 103
Pharmaceutical industry. *See* Drug
industry
Phenothiazines, 332–33
Pilferage (employee), 270, 287
Playboy (magazine), 153, 154, 158
Pluralistic conflict theory, 71
Police reports, arrest rates, 272–4
Political crime, 306–9
Political reform, 309
Pornography, 11, 142, 143, 151–72
criminalization of, 164–69
effects of, 155–64, 339
themes in advertisements for,
159–62
Positivism:
criticisms of, 53–56
nineteenth-century, 35–36
twentieth-century, 50–53
Poverty. *See* Social class
Power:
conflicts, 75
deviance definition and, 20
governmental abuse of, 306–9
pornography and, 156
rape and, 248, 264, 265
women's lack of, 218
Power of Suggestion, The (Segal),
165n
Prejudice (bias), 11, 42, 44
Professions (the), crime in, 301–6
Prohibition, 75–76, 127, 129–31
Property crime (stealing), 2, 10,
269–88. *See also* Burglary;
Larceny-theft; Motor-vehicle
theft; Robbery; Shoplifting;
White-collar crime
definitions, 269–71, 278
motives for, 276–77, 278, 285
severity for, 273–77
social class and, 277–81
statistics, 272–73, 279, 281, 286
violence in, 273–76
Prostitution, 2, 39, 142–51, 152,
339
*Protestant Ethic and the Spirit of Cap-
italism, The* (Weber), 74
Psychiatry, 303–5, 319, 322–24,
333, 334
Psychoanalytic perspective:
homosexuality, 190–92
mental disorder, 319
Psychopathology, 260–61
Punishment:
of children, 216, 220–22
condemnation and, 15–16, 17,
24–25
effects of, 58–59
for embezzlement, 302

Race:
class, crime, and, 56, 75
cocaine use and, 106–7
criminalization of marijuana
and, 101
drinking and, 135
murder and, 230–31
property crimes and, 284, 286
Rape, 2, 16, 69, 75, 127, 247–68
acquaintance, 249, 265–67
anger, 263–64, 265
arrest rate, 274
defining, 248–54
marital, 259–60
men who, 260–65
murder and, 235, 337
myths, truths, about, 256–59
pornography and, 155, 156, 158,
160, 161, 163, 165, 166
power, 248, 264, 265
sadistic, 262–63, 264, 265
statistics, 257–59
statutory, 248–49
stranger, 267–68
Rationality, free will and, 34–35
Reactive perspective, 15–16, 17–18
Reality:
perception of, and mental disorder, 315
of victimization, 16, 338–39
Rebellion, 42
Reefer Madness, 101
Reflexivity, labeling theory and, 65
Relativity. *See also* Cultural relativity
cliché, 18–19, 20
perspectives on, 14–15
social pathology and, 37
types of, 20–24
Religion, violence and, 235
Repression, 222
Retreatism, 41–42, 46
Rip-offs. *See* Property crime
Ritualism, 41
Robbery, 2, 56, 281–84
arrest rate, 274
defined, 271, 278, 281
severity of, 273–76
social class and, 278–80
statistics, 272, 273, 279, 281–83
Robbins, A. H., Company, 296
Roots (Haley), 270–71
Rules (laws, legal systems):
breaking, 29, 52, 72–76, 306–8,
320. *See also* Crime; Violations
Marxist perspective on, 80–82
social, 10
Rush, B., 129
Rushdie, S., 168

San Francisco, California, 338
Santa Cruz, California, 337–38

Satanic Verses (Rushdie), 168
Schizophrenia, 317, 324, 332–33
Secrecy (secret behavior):
deviance and, 15–16, 17, 63, 64
of homosexuals, 181–82
in political, governmental
crime, 307–8
Sedatives, 94, 97
Self-defense, 227
Self-fulfilling prophecy, 65–66
Self-identity:
homosexual, 187, 196–98,
208–11
rule-breaking and, 303
Self-report surveys, 273
Set and setting, 93
*Sex and Temperament in Three Primi-
tive Societies* (Mead), 214
Sexual behavior. *See also* Bisexuality; Heterosexuality; Homosexuality; Masturbation; Prostitution; Transsexuality
alcohol use and, 125–26, 127
arousal and, 189
double standard, 143, 144
gender preferences in, 188–89
Sexual Behavior in the Human Female
(Kinsey), 187
Sexual Politics (Millett), 147
Shadow criminology, 34
Sheppard, M., 129
Sherman Anti-Trust Act, 298–99
Shoplifting, 270, 281, 284–86,
287–88
Snitch (the), 285–86
Social class. *See also* Middle-class
child abuse and, 222
criminality, race, and, 43–46,
54–56, 75, 284, 286
drinking and, 133–35
mental disorder and, 330–32
murder and, 231–32
property crimes and, 277–81,
284
prostitution and, 148
stratification, 70–71
wife beating and, 217–18
Social disorganization, 37–38
Socialism, 76–77, 78, 81, 86–87
Social pathology, 36–37
Social Pathology (Lemert), 59
Sociobiology, 214
Socioeconomic status (SES). *See*
Social class
Sodomy, 180–81, 182
Special interest groups, 71–75
Status frustration, 43–45
Stealing. *See* Property crime
Steal This Book (Hoffman), 287
Stigma:
AIDS victims, 207
ambivalence, 167–68